THE PREDESTINATION PROBLEM

Third Edition

Published independently by Kindle Self-publishing.

Copyright © Robin J. Giles 2019, 2021, 2024.

Robin Giles has asserted his right under the Copyright, Designs and Patents Acts, 1988, to be identified as Author of this work.

robin@robingiles.co.uk

First published 2019.
Second edition published 2021.
This third edition published 2024.
ISBN:

Unless otherwise indicated, Scripture quotations in English are taken from *The Holy Bible, New International Version (Anglicised Edition)* Copyright ©1979, 1984, 2011 by Biblica (formerly International Bible Society). Used by permission of Hodder & Stoughton Publishers, an Hachette UK company. All rights reserved. 'NIV' is a registered trademark of Biblica (formerly International Bible Society). UK trademark number 1448790.

Unless otherwise indicated, Greek text of the New Testament is taken from The Nestle-Aland 26th Edition *Novum Testamentum Graece,* Copyright © 1963, 1967, 1975, 1983 by United Bible Societies.

Cover graphic by pixabay.com.

Robin J. Giles

THE PREDESTINATION PROBLEM

Third Edition

Did God choose me, or did I choose God?

Searching for a Biblical understanding of Election.

The Church is a field of tulips – flowers of every hue, some pure white, some yellow, some pink or purple, others red, even the deepest red – almost black, and every colour in between. Each one has inherited some of John Calvin's DNA: we are nonetheless one in wonderful diversity.

Dedicated to the memory of my dad, Ralph Giles (1922-2018), who prayed for me, taught me about Jesus and showed me the importance of embracing the whole body of Christ.

CONTENTS

Prefaces x

List of Abbreviations xix

1. **Early Influences** 1
   How I became sensitised to the debate 1
   Some formative influences 7

2. **The Contemporary Divide and its Causes** 10
   Arminius in his Context 14
   Arminius and International Calvinism 22
   Dort *vs* the Remonstrants 23
      a. Canon 1: Predestination, Election and
         Reprobation 25
      b. Canon 2: The Death of Jesus Christ and the
         Redemption of Men thereby. 31
      c. & d. Canons 3 & 4: The Corruption of Man and
         the Method of his Conversion to God . . . 34
      e. Canon 5: The Perseverance of the Saints . . 35
   The Contemporary Legacy Either Side of the Atlantic 40

3. **The Election Terminology** 64
   Foreordination and Foreknowledge 64
   Predestination 65
   Election 66

4. **Perseverance** **70**
    What does 'Apostasy' mean? 73
    I. Howard Marshall's *Kept by the Power of God* . . 79
        a. 2 Timothy 2:12 82
        b. 2 Timothy 1:12 84
        c. Philippians 3:10-11 88
        d. James 5:19-20 91
        e. Jude 22-23 92
        f. 2 Peter 2:20 93
    The Rigorous Passages of Hebrews and 2 Peter . . 100
    My Personal View 115

5. **What is the Proper Human Response to the Grace of God?** **130**
    Free Will: Reality or Illusion? 132
    Pelagianism 139
    Prevenient Grace 143
    Moderate Calvinism and Single Predestinarianism 149
    Saving Grace 154

6. **Divine Sovereignty and Human Responsibility** . . . **161**
    According to Don Carson 161
    Human Freedom 166
    The Nature of Sin 168
    Human Choice 170
    The Sovereignty of God 172
    The Grace of God 179
    Divine Self-Limiting Determinism 182

7. **Who Then is Right – Can Both be Right?** **192**

8. **The Vocabulary of Election** **200**
   a. Election/Elect 201
      i. Eklegomai 202
      ii. Eklogē 204
      iii. Eklektos 208
      iv. Klēroō 213
      v. Hairetidzō 214
      vi. Haireō 215
      vii. Epilegō 217
   b. Predestination 217
   c. Foreknowledge 219
      The Extent of God's Foreknowledge 230
      i. Middle Knowledge or Molinism 232
      ii. Open Theism 237
   d. Calling 238

9. **Christ, the Elect One and Ephesians 1** **248**
   a. What does 'in Christ' mean? 252
   b. Unitary Election 265
   c. Extra-Biblical Sources in Support of a Divine
     Choice of The One 277
      i. The Qumran Literature 277
      ii. The Similitudes of Enoch 278
      iii. The Apostolic Fathers 280

10. **Other Problematical Election Texts** **282**
   a. Mark 13:20: "The elect, whom he has chosen" . . 282
   b. Texts in John's Gospel: 288
      i. Coming to Jesus: John 6:37, 44 & 65 . . . 290
      ii. Chosen by Jesus: John 6:70; 13:18; 15:16 & 19   296
      iii. Given to Jesus by the Father: John 6:39;
         17:6, 9, 24 & 18:9 308

    iv. Belonging to Jesus: John 10:1-18 313
  c. Acts 13:48: "Appointed for eternal life". . . . 315
  d. Acts 18:10: "I have many people in this city" . . 322
  e. Romans 8:29-30: Predestined to be called? . . . 324
  f. Romans 9 to 11: God can do whatever he likes! . 332
  g. 1 Corinthians 1:27-28 and James 2:5:
      People Chosen by God 341
  h. 1 Peter 2:8: Destined for Disobedience?. . . . 342
  i. Revelation 17:8: Names Written in the Book of Life 343

11. Whom Then has God Really Chosen? **352**
  a. Election of People in the Old Testament . . . 352
  b. Election of People in the New Testament . . . 356

12. Conclusion **360**

Epilogue **373**

Appendix 1: Election Vocabulary in the NIV (2011) New Testament **376**

Appendix 2: Relationships between *Beloved*, *Pleasing*, *Chosen* and *Only* **380**

Appendix 3: John Piper's *Five Points*: A Critique . . . **392**
  a. Total Depravity (Chapter 3) 393
  b. Irresistible Grace (Chapter 4) 409
  c. Limited Atonement (Chapter 5) 415
  d. Unconditional Election (Chapter 6) 421
  e. Perseverance of the Saints (Chapter 7) 425
  Conclusion 432

Bibliography	434
Index of Scriptures and Ancient Texts	443
Subject Index	458
People Index	462

Index of Tables

1: *Eklegomai* in the Septuagint (Swete)	204
2: Translations of *barar* in the Septuagint	287
3: Choosing People in the Old Testament	353-4
4: Election Vocabulary in the NIV (2011) New Testament	376-9
5: Gospel Sayings about Jesus as *Beloved*, *Pleasing*, *Chosen* and *Only*	381-2
6: Comparison of the Greek and Hebrew Variants of Matthew 12:18 and Isaiah 42:1	384
7: Verbs of Choosing in Greek Literature	390-1

PREFACE to the First Edition

One of the great conundrums for Christians is the question as to whether God chooses individual people for salvation, or not. Put more personally, we might ask, "Did God choose *you* and *me* to be with him in heaven for eternity, or did we somehow have a personal choice in the matter as the Bible appears to suggest?" Many believers struggle with this puzzle. Indeed, it's a question which troubles many intelligent Bible-believing Christians, and especially, in my experience, young believers. It was certainly true of my own youth. More mature Christians, generally speaking, may have been persuaded one way or the other, or may have found a compromise position. Some may simply have given up looking for a sensible answer, concluding perhaps that if there is an answer then it cannot be known in this life, and relegating the question to mystery – one of those issues they will ask Jesus about when they finally meet him, perhaps. But reflecting on my own youth, something like 50 years ago and more, I clearly remember that it was a perennial topic of hot debate in youth fellowships and Christian Unions – all that stuff about *predestination* over which we seemed to muse endlessly. It's a question which has bothered me for that half century, but I now believe there is a way through which is logical and doesn't do despite to the integrity of human intellect, and, most importantly, is faithful to scripture.

The debate has become polarised between two theological positions; on the one hand, the Reformed or Calvinistic position, and on the other hand, the Arminian or General position, although neither is by any means homogeneous. My conclusion is that neither is wholly biblical, however, and I would suggest that there is a way which avoids the errors of both.

Working through the pros and cons of the debate, I suggest that four main issues are at stake:

1. The first is the purely exegetical question of what the relevant Bible passages really mean.
2. The second is to evaluate the weight of historical interpretation,

which has an obvious bearing on the way scripture has been interpreted over these past 2000 years of Church history and especially since the Reformation.
3. The third is about how we are to understand divine sovereignty. Underlying much of the Reformed approach to Election is a concept of sovereignty which says that I can do nothing, think nothing and say nothing that has not been divinely foreordained. This view has serious implications for any concept of human free will, of course, but logically it also implies that God must be the author of sin, a notion which most Calvinists, as well as other Christians, would emphatically deny.
4. The fourth main issue trumps these three and I think is possibly the key issue. It has to do with the value or legitimacy of the human intellectual faculty. It seems to me that the power of logical argument is often undervalued, possibly in part through a misunderstanding of the Calvinistic dogma of Total Depravity, but also because, taking account of the history of the debate about how Election should be understood, there seems no clear way through to an unambiguous solution. Because of that, we are often asked to believe paradoxes[1] and/or resort to divine ineffability. My contention is that such compromise approaches do a major injustice to scripture and also insult our God-given faculty for clear reasoning.

Much more needs to be said about these four points, of course, and I will attempt to do so in the course of what follows.

I began researching this topic whilst in training for Christian pastoral ministry, but my enquiry has not gone away in the intervening years. It began with an essay written as part of my academic studies and which forms the original basis of this book, but I have tinkered with it and expanded it here and there as I have come across what others have written and where fresh questions have emerged. The result doesn't therefore claim to be a cogent or even completely coherent piece of academic

---

[1] 'Antinomies' might be a better word, i.e., logical contradictions which cannot be resolved, but I will stick with 'paradoxes' because I believe the question of resolution remains open: see Stott (1996), 66.

work – more a kind of patchwork with a bibliography, some of which is now quite dated. The question of how Christians should rightly interpret what the Bible has to say about Election has become like a millstone around my neck. So, I present these thoughts, not so much as a labour of love, but more as a way of shedding a burden which I believe needs to be shared – not so much with academic theologians, who would probably run rings around some of my arguments, but with ordinary believers in the pew[2] for whom certainty is often a distant and elusive prospect.

For instance, I wonder at the kind of confusion which may be caused when believers hear their pastors speak about them being chosen by God, although without any qualification or explanation as to what was meant by 'chosen' nor, indeed, for what purpose they were chosen. The natural assumption, I suggest, would be that the preacher meant a divine choice for salvation, but in almost the next breath he or she may appeal to the congregation for a voluntary response to the gospel. That makes no sense at all to me, and I suspect many would agree. Confusion abounds. I came across an example of this kind of confusion recently. The idea was expressed during a time of intercession in a church I was visiting that God had yet many people in the vicinity of that church.[3] The thought was that, as children from the neighbourhood attended their outreach events, it would become evident which of them were God's chosen ones as they made their respective responses to the gospel – whatever my Reformed friends might have thought was entailed in such responses in terms of whether they were predetermined or not.

The long gestation period of an essay which has now expanded to the proportions of this volume, and which I had hoped might have seen the light of day in 2017, the year we celebrated the Reformation in Europe, does reflect some reluctance to make my view more generally known. There are a number of reasons. I expect some of my Christian friends will be surprised by some of my conclusions – they may even be shocked, but it is not because I am afraid to share what for some will

---

[2] Although a basic familiarity with the biblical languages will be advantageous, though not essential, for some of what follows.
[3] An idea based on Acts 18:10. See Chapter 10d, 309.

be a controversial view, rather it is more because it adds yet another potentially divisive opinion, although by no means new, into the already muddy mix of controversies which besets today's Church. I will be suggesting that many of the theological and doctrinal debates which have afflicted the Church through the centuries haven't so much gone away, but have become dulled and are, at least for some, issues with which they may no longer wish to engage – sterile debates, which generally speaking, folk haven't the heart for any longer because all they seem to do is perpetuate divisions in the Body of Christ.

However, my heart is keen to be part of the answer to our Lord Jesus' prayer the night he was betrayed and subsequently died; firstly, that his people might be one, and secondly and especially, that the evangelistic imperative implicit in his prayer should be realised. Jesus' desire that his people be willingly and visibly one[4] has profound implications for the Church's mission and much of our failure to evangelise the world might on Judgment Day prove to have been due to our neglect of that desire. But this debate also has serious implications for our understanding of the nature of the God we love, worship and serve – not only I, but fellow Christians both sides of the debate. I offer what follows, therefore, not in a divisive spirit nor with any wish to stir up controversy, nor even primarily to correct dear brothers and sisters in Christ whose views may differ from my own, but rather to testify as to why I have come to the more or less settled position I shall be advocating and to offer to my brothers and sisters in the faith what I consider to be a much better view of the God and Father of our Lord Jesus Christ. My desire in breaking up this fallow ground,[5] which has lain more or less undisturbed for centuries because of the ascendancy and general tacit acceptance of Augustine's views on Election, is only to honour God with what understanding of his holy word I have received over this past half-century and more, an understanding to which is being added almost daily.

---

[4] John 17:11, 21.
[5] Jeremiah 4:3; Hosea 10:12.

PREFACE to the Second Edition

"Of making many books there is no end", a wise man once said.[6] And I would say that is especially so even when it's just *one* book! When the first edition of this title was published in 2019, I already knew that I would have to do more work on certain aspects of it – in particular, I needed to beef up the section on the vocabulary of election, notably on the relationship between 'chosen' and 'beloved' and how those concepts relate to 'calling' (Chapter 7);[7] the section on perseverance also needed more work (Chapter 3).

In reviewing the meanings of words, I have included significantly more evidence from the Septuagint (LXX) and corrected a few statistical inaccuracies. Septuagintal studies have taken on greater importance in recent years as Bible students have realised the truth of Karen Jobes' and Moisés Silva's observation that

> The Septuagint, not the Hebrew Bible, was the primary theological and literary context within which the writers of the New Testament and most early Christians worked.[8]

In other words, the Septuagint was effectively the Bible of Jesus and the early Church. Almost certainly, therefore, this Greek translation of the Hebrew Bible should be expected to have had a significant influence on the way the New Testament writers composed their Greek text, particularly with respect to vocabulary, grammar and syntax. It should therefore cast significant light on contemporary translational studies in ways which were not utilised at times when many of the generally accepted interpretations of Scripture were being formulated. It was not that the Septuagint was unavailable to our scholarly forebears, but that its significance was simply not realised to the extent that modern scholarship now accepts.

I realised too that, although I had referred to John Piper in passing, I

---

[6] Ecclesiastes 12:12.
[7] Now Chapter 8d.
[8] Jobes & Silva, 23. This volume is a valuable introduction to the Septuagint and its significance in biblical studies.

was at fault in not having read much of his - the two titles I did possess had remained unread and were gathering dust on my bookshelf. A good friend and brother in Christ shared with me that Piper's *Desiring God* had been one of the most influential books he had ever read, and that it had shaped his Christian life ever since, so, I thought I should read it: which I did with profit, though with certain reservations. But that spurred me on to explore further. I had intended to comment on some of Piper's ideas in this revision, but I realised that a whole new book would be required to do him justice, and, in any case, that would be a critique of the whole TULIP theology which lies beyond the scope of this book even though all five points are referenced here and there. Instead, I have added a second appendix in which I have critiqued his *Five Points*, his exposition of the five points of Calvinism. That appendix may therefore be regarded as a working example of the application of my conclusions to what is a recent sample of Reformed thinking.

In undertaking this review and revision, it has dawned on me with increased force that I have needed to touch on topics which may seem far removed from election or predestination as such, and the indexes will bear that out. Although I recognise that election or the TULIP part of what Reformed Christians believe is but a small portion of the whole of their credo, and that the remainder is held in common (more or less) by many other evangelical believers, the fact that my discussion ranges so widely suggests to me that it is a hugely influential doctrine which affects what is to be believed in a far more radical way than one might have imagined. I suggest that it is so because I am convinced that what one believes about election affects one's understanding of God. I think there is a widely held view that since the differences between Reformed and non-Reformed doctrine are far less than the whole, and therefore some might suggest that the majority of what pretty well all evangelicals believe is the same, I would suggest that if we haven't got a correct view of the character of God, then even that which we say we hold in common will have been nuanced by the way we think of God. To give an obvious example, I suggest that if I were to believe in absolute divine determinism, which I believe is the fundamental basis of Reformed teaching, that will colour everything else I believe – probably without exception. So, I reiterate what I have said already - that it is the reason above all others why I believe getting a right understanding of election is so crucially important.

My thanks to those who have read my first offering and have commented and reported typos. I have not needed to revise many of the conclusions drawn in the first edition, so, with the odd correction and, with the blessing of hindsight and where I have thought it was needed, some expansion and a striving for greater clarity where discussion gets complicated, especially in Chapter 9[9] where I attempt to deal with problem texts which Reformed writers use to make their case, I present this expanded edition with its additional indexes in the hope that it will bring greater clarity to our understanding of our blessed God and Saviour and will be a blessing to all who dip into its pages.

My desire is to extol God, our Lord and Saviour, and to honour his name by presenting a better portrait of him than does either Calvinism or Arminianism.

Robin J. Giles

Cambridge, January 2021.

---

[9] Now Chapter 10.

PREFACE to the Third Edition

In the Preface to the Second Edition of this title, I commented that consideration of the biblical teaching on Election has ramifications throughout the length and breadth of theology. That means, of course, that all kinds of questions arise, which, in turn, means that I find myself struggling to engage with a number of issues in which I am far from expert. Blind spots will inevitably abound therefore. A consequence of that is that, as with the First Edition, I felt that I had left untied even more loose ends, principally, two matters; firstly, Perseverance, or the believer's assurance of salvation, and, secondly, how best to understand Paul's teaching on Adoption and his use of the Greek word *huiothesia*.

Careful examination of the biblical texts relating to these issues leads us to the very heart of the gospel of our salvation – our identity in Christ and our future co-heirship with him in glory. That might seem to be overreaching a notional remit for a book on the subject of Election, but the more I researched, the more persuaded I became that the Bible's teaching on our future state goes hand in hand with an understanding of that to which believers have been predestined. Accordingly, I have created a new Chapter (4) on Perseverance. With regard to Adoption, however, although my first thought was to create an additional appendix, I soon realised that the whole issue of sonship required more than that, and I decided to create a separate title devoted to what is, I believe, the very core of the gospel – our Christian "hope of glory".[10] Furthermore, a somewhat technical section on verbs relating to chosenness has been relegated to an appendix (2) so that readers do not become *too* discouraged whilst reading Chapter 8 on the Election Vocabulary.

My desire to create an account accessible to the average, fairly literate Christian, may have failed to some extent, at least in the opinion of one reviewer (who is probably right). Inevitably, discussions, particularly on the meanings of words (noting the scriptural warnings),[11] call for a degree of technical information (not to say speculation), but I have tried

---

[10] Colossians 1:27. See my forthcoming *Pie in the Sky When You Die?*
[11] 1 Timothy 6:4; 2 Timothy 2:14.

to make such passages more accessible by transliterating Greek and Hebrew words and phrases which occur in the main text, and by expanding scriptural citations by quoting texts reasonably fully. I have also tried to use sources which should be relatively accessible even for readers who do not have ready access to a theological library, although there are some exceptions. This work was never meant to appeal to the popular market for Christian literature, but rather to feed into what I consider to be a needy niche which lies somewhere between superficiality and full-blown academia. The kind of reader I have in mind is the overworked elder or pastor (as I once was, and even in retirement, things do not seem to have eased up appreciably!) who has insufficient time to read much of the wealth of expository literature on offer.

I have sought to clarify certain passages of previous editions, and I have expanded a couple of sections in Chapter 10 on Problematical Texts. As before, I have sought to tidy up a few typos, with thanks to readers who have taken the trouble to notify them to me.

May I then offer this third (and hopefully, last) attempt (the temptation to tinker is almost overwhelming!) to the wider Christian community, with the prayer that God will yet shed more light on his precious word, and thus upon himself, and bring greater blessing to and through his people.

Robin J. Giles.

Cambridge, Eastertide 2024.

List of Abbreviations

BAGD:	W. Bauer, W. F. Arndt, F. W. Gingrich, *A Greek-English Lexicon of the New Testament and other Early Christian Literature* (Chicago & London: University of Chicago Press, 1979).
BDB:	Francis Brown, *The Brown-Driver-Briggs Hebrew and English Lexicon* (Peabody, MA: Hendrickson, 1906).
BECNT:	Baker Exegetical Commentary on the New Testament.
BNTC:	Black's New Testament Commentary.
BST:	The Bible Speaks Today.
CBSC	The Cambridge Bible for Schools and Colleges.
COQG:	Christian Origins and the Question of God.
EBCNIV:	Expositor's Bible Commentary with the New International Version.
ESV:	Holy Bible: *English Standard Version: Anglicized Edition* (London: HarperCollins, 2002).
GNB:	*Good News Bible* (The Bible Societies & HarperCollins, 1994).
HNT:	*Handbuch zum Neuen Testament* (Tübingen).
ICC:	International Critical Commentary.
Institutes:	Calvin, John, *Institutes of the Christian Religion*, Henry Beveridge tr. (Grand Rapids, MI: Eerdmans, One volume edition, 1989).
JB:	*The Jerusalem Bible* (London: Darton, Longman & Todd, 1968).
JSOTSup:	*Journal for the Study of the Old Testament, Supplement Series* (Sheffield Academic Press).
JTS:	Journal of Theological Studies.
KEK:	*Kritisch-Exegetischer Kommentar über das Neue Testament* (Göttingen).
KJV (also AV):	*The Holy Bible Containing the Old and New Testaments* (Cambridge: Cambridge University Press, 1611). Also known as *The King James Version* or *The Authorised Version*.
LXX:	Septuagint.

LXX (Swete):	Henry Barclay Swete, *The Old Testament in Greek According to The Septuagint* (Cambridge: Cambridge University Press, 1909).
MT:	Rudolph Kittel *et al*, *Biblica Hebraica Stuttgartensia* (Stuttgart: Württembergische Bibelanstalt, 1951). Also known as the *Masoretic Text*.
NA26:	Eberhard Nestle & Kurt Aland, *et al*, *Novum Testamentum Graece, The Nestle-Aland 26th Edition* (United Bible Societies, 1983).
NASB:	*Holy Bible: New American Standard* (Nashville, TN: Holman Bible Publishers, 1977).
NEB:	*The New English Bible with the Apocrypha* (Oxford: Oxford University Press & Cambridge: Cambridge University Press, 1970).
NET:	*New English Translation* (Free online version, Bible Studies Press LLC, 2005, 2006, 2017; Hardcopy, Nashville, TN: Thomas Nelson, 2019²).
NETS:	Albert Pietersma & Benjamin G. Wright, eds. *A New English Translation of the Septuagint and Other Greek Translations Traditionally Included Under that Title* (Oxford/New York: Oxford University Press, 2007).
NICNT:	The New International Commentary on the New Testament.
NIDNTT:	Colin Brown ed., *The New International Dictionary of New Testament Theology* (Carlisle: Paternoster, 4 vols., 1986).
NIGTC:	New International Greek Testament Commentary.
NIV:	*The Holy Bible, New International Version (Anglicised Edition)* (Biblica (formerly International Bible Society), 2011). References to earlier editions are indicated by the year of publication.
NRSV:	*The Holy Bible Containing the Old and New Testaments with the Apocryphal/Deuterocanonical Books: New Revised Standard Version: Anglicized Edition* (Oxford: Oxford University Press, 1995).
NTD:	*Das Neue Testament Deutsch* (Göttingen).
OED Compact:	*The Compact Edition of the Oxford English Dictionary* (Oxford: Oxford University Press, 1971).
OED Concise:	*The Concise Oxford English Dictionary* (Oxford: Oxford University Press, 2009).
PHC:	The Pelican History of the Church.

REB:	*The Revised English Bible* (Oxford: Oxford University Press & Cambridge: Cambridge University Press, 1989).
RSV:	*The Holy Bible: Revised Standard Version containing the Old and New Testaments* (London: Oxford University Press, 1963).
RV:	*The Holy Bible: The Revised Version* (Cambridge: Cambridge University Press, 1880 & 1884).
TCGNT	Bruce M. Metzger, *A Textual Commentary on the Greek New Testament: Second Edition* (Stuttgart: Deutsche Biblelgesellschaft, 1994).
TDNT:	Gerhard Kittel & G. Friedrich eds., *Theological Dictionary of the New Testament*, G. W. Bromiley tr. (Grand Rapids, MI: Eerdmans, 1964-76).
TNTC:	Tyndale New Testament Commentaries.
TOTC:	Tyndale Old Testament Commentaries.
TPINTC:	TPI (Trinity Press International) New Testament Commentaries.
WBC:	Word Biblical Commentary.
Works:	Arminius, Jacobus, *The Works of James Arminius DD* in 3 vols.: Vol. I, James Nichols tr. (London: Longman, Hurst, Rees, Orme, Brown & Green, 1825); Vol. II, James Nichols tr. (London: Longman, Rees, Orme, Brown & Green, 1828); Vol. III, William Nichols tr. (London: Thomas Baker, 1875).

Chapter 1

EARLY INFLUENCES

How I became sensitised to the debate

Something like 35 years ago, whilst training for the Baptist Union ministry at Spurgeon's College in London, I was interviewed about my suitability for ministerial accreditation by two senior ministers. We got onto the topic of Election – I don't remember exactly how – perhaps I had mentioned it as one of my theological interests. Their response, however, was to inform me, in no uncertain terms, that it had all been sorted out long ago. That wasn't my experience then, and in three-plus decades of study and pastoral ministry since, what they said has not been borne out in my experience. Furthermore, more recently, I have become aware of a growing debate between Reformed and Arminian authors on the other side of the Atlantic. The debate has not subsided.

Having lived, worked (in secular employment) and worshipped for about 13 years (1969-83) in Edinburgh, the stamping ground of the great Scottish Reformer, John Knox (c. 1514-72), ever before I trained for Christian ministry, I was made acutely aware in the church circles I inhabited that Calvinism was very much the protestant orthodoxy north of the border. I became used to hearing opinions expressed along the lines that some preachers, like the late Billy Graham (1918-2018) no less, were Arminians because they preached that their hearers had a choice to make in response to the gospel. Some would even call them Pelagians, quite wrongly so, of course, although an all-too-common mistake.[1] It is not for me to defend Billy Graham and his like, but I am fairly certain that he also upheld some aspects of Calvinistic doctrine – Perseverance, to name but one. Where his critics thought that might place him theologically, I cannot say – somewhere close to my own position perhaps. What I am saying is that believers who couldn't

---

[1] See Chapter 5, 139, on Pelagius and Pelagianism.

subscribe to full-blown Calvinism were labelled 'Arminian', a pejorative term in what was predominantly a Presbyterian context. However, few, if any, Christians I know personally subscribe to thoroughgoing Arminianism as it is usually understood.[2] Nonetheless, both they and I would have been branded as such.

I was brought up, and remained for most of my time in Scotland, among the Plymouth or Open Brethren. But I found that the dogmas of Reformed theology figured hardly at all among them, even in Edinburgh. That began to change towards the latter period of my association with that particular group of Brethren through the preaching and teaching of a very good friend who had been influenced by the writings of James Packer, especially his *Knowing God*.[3] On the whole, however, the Brethren I knew were more concerned with the equally misleading theorising – 'speculating' might be a better word – surrounding Dispensationalism.[4] However, at one of their New Year's Day conferences, a

---

[2] Also, as it happens, Arminius himself. On the issue of Perseverance, Arminius was ambivalent, although the *Articles of the Remonstrance*, which represented the views of his successors, explicitly denied it; see Chapter 4, 70, 'Perseverance'.

[3] First published by Hodder & Stoughton in 1973. Packer's writings, which became very popular subsequently, express a Reformed bias which seems to have been widely influential in evangelical circles.

[4] Dispensationalism is an interpretation of scripture based on a literal hermeneutic of, in the main, Daniel's seventy-week prophecy (Daniel 9:20ff.) and most of the book of Revelation. There are many variations, but its characteristic ideas include two modes of salvation; for Israel an earthly destiny, and for Christians a heavenly destiny, the Church age being described as a 'parenthesis'; a Secret Rapture when Christ returns and removes his church from the earth, leaving behind the rest of humanity, which will face the Great Tribulation, although it is debated by some as to whether the Church will also pass through that period of suffering before the Rapture. Throughout the Tribulation period the Gospel of the Kingdom will be preached, giving those who missed out on the Rapture a second opportunity to be saved.

Dispensationalism can be traced back to John Nelson Darby (1800-82), an Irish Anglican clergyman and one of the founders of the Brethren movement. His views were popularised in North America through the *Scofield Reference Bible* (C. I. Scofield (Oxford: Oxford University Press, 1909 & 1917)), and have made a comeback this side of the Atlantic especially through Brethren teaching and more recently through the writings, among others, of Hal Lindsay, e.g., *The Late Great Planet Earth* (London: Lakeland, 1970) and Tim LaHaye's *Left Behind* series of novels which depict his view of the events of the second coming in fictional form (see also his apologetic, *Rapture Under Attack* (Sisters, OR: Multnomah Publishers Inc., 1998)). A good, but now somewhat dated, refutation of dispensationalism is Oswald T. Allis' *Prophecy and the Church* (London: James Clarke & Co. Ltd., 1945). See also William E. Cox, *An Examination of Dispensationalism* (Philadelphia, PA: Presbyterian and Reformed

feature of Scottish Brethren ways in those days, we were addressed by an earnest young preacher who, to my amazement, began to churn out Calvinistic jargon – 'Total Depravity', 'Irresistible Grace' and so on. That sensitised me even more to those issues. I recognised where he was coming from theologically, but I didn't have sufficient understanding to be able to satisfy myself as to why I thought he was wrong. Over the intervening years since – this was in the 1970s – I think I have found a way through the dilemma, which I dare to suggest might be the correct way, but it is for my readers to judge whether, in fact, there is such a thing as a correct way and whether, indeed, I have really found it.

It remains a baffling paradox, especially, as it was for me in my own youth, that God apparently invites us to choose him, but that in reality *he* chooses *us*. The inevitable logic of a situation where God chooses some, of course, is that he rejects others, even if that rejection is not deliberate. John Calvin called that paradox "the hidden purpose of God according to which the reprobate are doomed to their own ruin".[5] My aim, however, is to show that, contrary to the view of my Baptist assessors, the debate is still very much alive; that Election is not a paradox at all, and that both Calvinism and, by the same token, Arminianism stand on mistaken exegesis of God's word and faulty logic concerning divine determinism and human free will.

The Calvinist view is that our supposed free will isn't free at all because we are simply unable to make moral choices – at least when it comes to spiritual, as opposed to what we may regard as secular choices. However, a number of New Testament passages apparently say very clearly that we have to make a choice about the offer of eternal life through faith in Jesus.[6] The apostolic preaching throughout the New Testament, and especially in Acts, always called for a response,[7] and in the biblical accounts there were always those who accepted the gift of salvation and those who refused or neglected it. It seems to me then,

---

Publishing Co., 1963); D. M. Beegle, *Prophecy and Prediction* (Ann Arbor: Pryor Pettengill, 1978); Stephen R. Sizer, 'Dispensational approaches to the land' in Johnston & Walker, 142-71.

[5] Calvin, *Commentary* on 2 Peter 3:9.
[6] E.g., John 3:16: "whoever believes"; 2 Peter 3:9: "everyone to come to repentance", etc.
[7] E.g., Acts 2:37; 3:19ff.; 8:14; 10:43; 13:39, etc.

that the big question upon which all of this hangs is simply:

> *What kind of God is it who fabricates the pretence of appearing to offer salvation and sonship to human beings who, in their own perception, have the ability to accept or refuse that offer, but in reality, are unable to choose to do so because their wills are bound in some way?*

It is true that many Reformed preachers do appeal for a response, but in following the example of the New Testament apostles and simply being obedient to the Great Commission,[8] I wonder if they are almost acting out a kind of charade with the expectation that those among their hearers whom God had predestined to eternal life would make their response of faith, perhaps unwittingly making what to them seemed to be a response of the will, but which was really nothing of the sort. That obedience to fulfil the command to preach – "Woe to me if I do not preach the gospel!"[9]–kind of thing, being regarded as the way God had ordained that it should be, and so that is what they do. What they really believe, however, is that the responses to their appeals for repentance and faith, whether embracing or rejecting, are divinely predetermined and have absolutely nothing to do with their hearers' freedom of choice.

I am acutely aware that there are believers who, because of the nature of their faith journey, feel strongly that they had no choice in the matter. I have a friend in mind with whom I have occasionally discussed the matter, but with whom I have never found agreement. I can understand why they may feel that way, especially if they have been saved from lives of deep need or depravity, and as a result have a wonderfully deep appreciation of God's grace and forgiveness and, hence, of their Saviour. On the other hand, others are clear that they had made a deliberate choice. C. S. Lewis, a celebrated case, for example, an author who has made a deep impression on me and has been formative in much of my thinking, described his own conversion to Christ in *Surprised By Joy* not as "The Prodigal Son [who] at least walked home on his own feet", as had the biblical prodigal,[10] but as "a prodigal who is brought in

---

[8] Matthew 28:19f.
[9] 1 Corinthians 9:16.
[10] Luke 15:11-24.

EARLY INFLUENCES

kicking, struggling, resentful, and darting his eyes in every direction for a chance of escape".[11] As is evident from this and others of his writings, even though he often used deeply charged language, Lewis refused to admit the absence of the exercise of free will:

> before God closed in on me, I was in fact offered what now appears a moment of wholly free choice.... I became aware that I was holding something at bay, or shutting something out.... I felt myself being, there and then, given a free choice. I could open the door or keep it shut.... I chose to open ... yet it did not really seem possible to do the opposite.... You could argue that I was not a free agent, but I am more inclined to think that this came nearer to being a perfectly free act than most that I have ever done.[12]

I imagine that Saul of Tarsus might have felt much the same when Jesus arrested him on the Damascus road.[13] Nonetheless, Lewis' intellectual struggle, as he became increasingly aware of the truth of God, was, he says, not so much "man's search for God", as "the mouse's search for the cat".[14] Through it all, and despite the enormous pressure he felt as God *leaned* on him, so to speak, he never denied himself the possibility of rejecting the divine invitation, no matter how pressing he felt it to be.

Did his ego and prodigious intellect prevent him from admitting otherwise? Was it for him a thing of pride? After all, our human instinct is to need to feel that we are in control of our destinies. It's really a question no one can properly answer. My Calvinist friends may insist that the way we see things results from our inability to know the heart and intentions of God adequately, and many, even on the Arminian side of the fence, find refuge in the ultimate ineffability of God, despite feelings which seemed to indicate that they had a choice in the matter. Could it be that, because God's thoughts are higher than ours, even he could not communicate the dynamics of Election to us in a way we

---

[11] C. S. Lewis (*Surprised*), 182f.
[12] Ibid., 179. Roy Clements in P. Lewis *et al*, 105, claims that this account of C. S. Lewis' conversion experience reinforces the Reformed doctrine of Irresistible Grace. My reading of Lewis' account persuades me otherwise.
[13] Acts 9:3-6.
[14] C. S. Lewis (*Surprised*), 182.

could grasp? Is it that we are simply unable to grasp the width, length, height and depth of Christ's love,[15] (even though Paul prays that we might) so that we have to live with a glorious paradox which, hopefully, we shall only really understand the other side of the *parousia*? I find that the predominant response among many Christian friends is that, whereas the gospel calls for a response, we cannot know the mind of God sufficiently well to be sure, so that we must hold both sides of the matter together in tension – and that despite Paul's affirmation that we have the mind of Christ.[16]

One conclusion I draw from this is that any understanding of Election based on personal experience is necessarily unreliable. That is not to deny our innate, God-given intellectual faculties, nor even the internal witness of the Holy Spirit, but personal experience, while providing, on the one hand, the possibility of affirmation of our theological convictions, on the other hand, remains necessarily subjective. The fact that equally sincere and godly people arrive at opposite conclusions, partly, if not largely, I suspect, through their personal experience, tells me that here we are not standing on solid ground.

All that being said, however, it seems to me that we are not dealing with a simple paradox which might be unravelled for us one day; rather we are dealing with the possibility of *deception* on the part of God. Why would God tell us one thing – that we need to choose or reject him – when it would surely be possible for him to find a way to explain the whole deal in a way which wouldn't lead to the kind of confusion and polemic the Church has found itself dealing with for almost twenty centuries? I simply refuse to believe that the God and Father of our Lord Jesus Christ could entertain a deception – any kind of deception, and certainly not a deception which portrays his gospel of grace as an invitation which I could not under any circumstances refuse, nor, for that matter, accept. I believe it would be completely at odds with his nature for that to be so, especially when the relationship between the creature and their Creator resulting from their conversion could not be entered into as a free response of love, even though it might feel just like that.

---

[15] Ephesians 3:18.
[16] 1 Corinthians 2:16.

Yet the Calvinist's God seems to do exactly that – in Reformed teaching God calls us to choose even though we are simply unable freely to do so.

All attempts to solve the riddle based either on experience or logic must therefore be suspect, especially attempts that use complicated terminology or illustrative arguments. I insist then that the only basis on which we may arrive at the right conclusion is by correctly understanding what scripture says.[17] First, I believe, we must try to clear away some of the accumulation of historical debris, the layers of dark varnish from the old master, as it were, and attempt to recover what Paul and the other biblical writers really meant. My contention is that in doing so we shall remove a whole swathe of misunderstandings which have fuelled the Calvinist cause down the centuries.

Some formative influences

In the process of reaching my present view, a number of authors have helped to shape my thinking, all of whom are listed in the bibliography. However, I would draw special attention to *God's Strategy in Human History* by Roger Forster and Paul Marston. What I found particularly helpful was not so much their main text, but their appendix on 'Early teaching on God's and Man's Will' with its extensive footnotes.[18] It provided for me a way into Augustine's theology about Election, original sin, infant baptism, and so on, all of which are contingent, if not foundational, for Calvin's thought and have been for Reformed theology ever since.

I have already mentioned C. S. Lewis, and will be referring in passing to his *The Problem of Pain*. However, a passage from *The* (now quite dated) *Screwtape Letters* has also been a formative influence. For example, in the dialogue between the fictional senior demon, Screwtape, and his understudy, Wormwood, Lewis has Screwtape say,

---

[17] Although we shall discover that there is also a logical issue when we examine the vexed question of divine determinism and human free will. See Chapter 6, 161.

[18] Forster & Marston, 243ff., first published in 1973 by Send the Light and a second 1989 edition by Highland Books. Page numbers are from the 1989 edition.

> One must face the fact that all the talk about His love for men, and His service being perfect freedom, is not (as one would gladly believe) mere propaganda, but an appalling truth. He really *does* want to fill the universe with a lot of loathsome little replicas of Himself – creatures whose life, on its miniature scale, will be qualitatively like His own, not because he has absorbed them but because their wills freely conform to His.[19]

Those familiar with *The Screwtape Letters* will know that Lewis was quite literally playing devil's advocate, so that God and his people are viewed negatively from a supposed demonic point of view, rather than in the positive way Christian apologetic is normally cast. It is important to understand too that when Lewis wrote of the will of a believer conforming to God's will and purpose, he saw it not as a forced obedience, but a free obedience – "because their wills *freely* conform to His", Screwtape says. Those words seem to me to get close to an understanding of God's eternal purposes or 'decrees', if you will. What use, from God's perspective, would be a whole family of *sons*, to use Lewis' and the Bible's word, who love and serve him grudgingly without the freedom *not* to do so? I cannot imagine that God would derive much pleasure at all from such relationships. I don't think I would if my own children feigned love for me out of a sense of duty. Only if the will to obey was given perfectly and genuinely from a position of complete freedom could our Heavenly Father genuinely delight in his people, I would suggest. I was going to write "complete *unobligated* freedom", but none of us can respond to God's grace without some sense of obligation when we realise anything at all of what he in Christ has done for us in setting us free. By a similar token, those who refuse simply cannot have realised anything of God's provision for them, so they simply do not receive a conviction of sin and do not therefore feel the need for repentance and the exercise of faith.

Also, of course, we shall need to examine what kind of freedom we really have as we exercise free will in choosing God, but for now I am going to assume that God is genuine in wanting a conscious, freely given affection from his children rather than the programmed

---

[19] C. S. Lewis (*Screwtape*), 45f. (his italics).

obedience of automata in which Reformed theologians would apparently have us believe.

Chapter 2

THE CONTEMPORARY DIVIDE AND ITS CAUSES

It was not until Augustine's (354-430) life-changing experience of the grace of God in the August of 386[1] that the Church become *sensitised*[2] to the biblical issues surrounding Election and the nature of the human response to the gospel. Before Augustine, it would seem that there was no widely held view, yet the succeeding centuries have seen an ebb and flow of debate about an issue which has turned out to have caused one of the major doctrinal divides in the western Protestant Church. Peter Thuesen says,

> Of all traditional Christian doctrines, few, if any, have caused as much controversy as this question of whether a person's fate in either heaven or hell is sealed from the beginning of time. It is not that Christianity lacks other contentious doctrines. In the earliest centuries of the tradition, Christians were consumed by infighting over the divinity of Jesus and the doctrine of the Trinity. But whereas these questions were more or less settled by the early church councils and the ecumenical creeds they hammered out, there has never been a reigning orthodoxy on predestination. This is evident in the division between eastern and western Christianity, which arose not only over linguistic and political issues but also over predestination, with the East rejecting Augustine's absolutist view that God elects certain persons apart from any foresight of their conduct.[3] Even within the West, strict Augustinianism has

---

[1] Lane, 40.
[2] Erickson, 908.
[3] See Robert Araraki's blog, 'Plucking the TULIP (1) - An Orthodox Critique of the Reformed Doctrine of Predestination', August 12, 2012; <https://blogs.ancientfaith.com/orthodoxbridge/plucking-the-tulip-1-an-orthodox-critique-of-the-reformed-doctrine-of-predestination>. Araraki critiques the Five Points from an Orthodox perspective. He notes that "Aside from a brief encounter in the early seventeenth century, there has been very little interaction between the two traditions". The exception was when Cyril Lucaris, the then Patriarch of Constantinople, came under the influence of Reformed theology. In consequence, he was deposed following the 1672 synod at

always had critics, and this became uniquely apparent in the United States, where doctrinal disagreements routinely gave rise to new factions and denominations. Indeed, ... predestination has been one of the most important but unacknowledged sources of discord in churches across the denominational spectrum.[4]

Since the Reformation in Europe, western Protestantism has flowed in two main theological streams. Each traces its source from or through the sixteenth- and early seventeenth-century Reformation in Europe, and each appears to exist, at least in part, in response to the phenomenon of the Dutch academic and theologian, Jacobus Arminius (1560-1609). Although represented by many different tribes and complexions of belief, so far as the issue of Election or Predestination is concerned, the Reformed or Calvinist tradition is often, perhaps mistakenly, summarised by the popular and convenient standard known as the Five Points of Calvinism, represented by the famous TULIP acronym. The letters of the acronym, which represent the clauses of the *Canons of Dort*, stand for (1) Total Depravity, (2) Unconditional Election, (3) Limited Atonement, (4) Irresistible Grace and (5) the Perseverance of the Saints. However, it is easily overlooked that this popular summary of Calvinism was itself a response by the Calvinistic Counter-Remonstrants to the earlier Five Points of Arminianism which were embodied in *The Remonstrance to the States General*.[5] This document was compiled in 1610, the year following Arminius' death, and was presented eight years later to the Synod of Dort in 1618 in protest against certain strict Calvinistic doctrines which had begun to predominate in the Dutch Reformed Church.

Whether the Five Points of Calvinism and the Five Points of Arminianism adequately represent these two major strands of Protestantism respectively isn't my purpose to debate, but it is worth noting that neither tradition today is by any means uniform.[6] For example, Todd

---

Jerusalem when Calvinism was formally repudiated through *The Confession of Dositheus*: John H. Leith, ed., *Creeds of the Churches* (Atlanta, GA: John Knox Press: 1963), 486-517.
[4] Thuesen, 4.
[5] Bettenson, 268f., and A. W. Harrison, 150f., give the five Articles of *The Remonstrance*.
[6] See Olson (2011), 26ff., a useful chapter on 'Whose Calvinism? Which Reformed Theology'.

Billings, in *Christian Century* magazine (1 December, 2009), writing in reaction to the relatively recent phenomenon of what some have called 'the New Calvinism', a resurgence of Classical Calvinism particularly among younger Christians and often in response to the writings of John Piper, decried its one-sided focus on some of Reformed theology's more exotic doctrines and especially the TULIP scheme. Billings regarded TULIP as peripheral to a tradition which shared many beliefs in common with Arminianism and he criticised the new Calvinists for using it as a "litmus test" of Reformed authenticity. He claimed that "TULIP does not provide an adequate or even accurate distillation of Reformed theology".[7] Likewise, Michael Horton admits that although Election is important in Reformed theology, it should not be regarded as "a central dogma or as a uniquely Calvinistic tenet". "No one", he says, "began with predestination as the heart of Reformed theology; it gained importance to the extent that it was challenged from within".[8] Also, making the point that Calvinism isn't a monolithic system, Roger Olson contrasts the writings of two "renowned" Reformed scholars, Donald McKim and R. C. Sproul, who define and describe it in very different ways. In *Introducing the Reformed Faith*, McKim states that "Reformed" is not a monolithic or closed category, but is an essentially contested concept. He says it is a diverse family which traces its ancestry back to Calvin and further, and he rejects the 'scholasticism' which it became in the hands of Calvin's seventeenth-century successors,[9] saying, "Not all Reformed Christians today subscribe to [the] 'Five Points of Calvinism'".[10] Sproul, on the other hand, in *What Is Reformed Theology?* advocates as strong and absolute a doctrine of God's sovereignty as is possible, and virtually equates Reformed theology with the high Calvinism of TULIP, including Double Predestination.[11] The only ground McKim and Sproul seem to have in common

---

[7] Olson (2011), 21.
[8] Horton, 30. He says, 25, "It is better ... to speak of the Reformed confession of the Christian faith".
[9] Olson (2011), 33f.
[10] Ibid., 35, quoting Donald McKim, *Introducing the Reformed Faith* (Louisville, KY: Westminster John Knox, 2001), 183.
[11] Double Predestination is the doctrine that God predestines both the elect to salvation and the reprobate to eternal destruction, whereas Single Predestination denies the latter. Although he doesn't offer an alternative term, Grudem (2007), 670, 686, says,

is the shared historical lineage of their Reformed heritage, including, although not exclusively determined by Calvin, an emphasis on divine sovereignty, which they mistakenly regard as somehow missing from non-Reformed theologies.[12]

Similar things may be said of Arminianism. Writing from an Arminian point of view, Clark Pinnock says,

> There is a spectrum of Calvinisms all the way from supralapsarian to sublapsarian,[13] and a spectrum of Arminianisms from evangelical to rationalistic. Nor do these spectra represent frozen options – there is a great deal of movement within them.[14]

Although it is true that each broad tradition has many variants, what is also true is that there is a considerable overlap between them. It is very important to hear what Todd Billings and Donald McKim say because the issues of contention between the Reformed tradition and Arminianism occupy but a minor segment of what the vast majority of all Christians believe, the major part of orthodox belief being held in common by both – more or less. That notwithstanding, however, the discussion which follows will focus on what the two traditions teach regarding Election. Thus, when Calvinism and Arminianism are critiqued, it is important to understand that it not the whole span of their doctrines

---

"*double predestination* is not a helpful term because it gives the impression that both election and reprobation are carried out in the same way by God and have no essential differences between them, which is certainly not true.... it blurs the distinctions between them". Election to salvation is a cause of rejoicing and delight – Ephesians 1:3-6; 1 Peter 1:1-3, while reprobation brings sorrow to God's heart – Ezekiel 33:11. "The cause of election lies with God, and the cause of reprobation lies in the sinner." "Another important difference is that the ground of election is God's grace, whereas the ground of reprobation is God's justice."

[12] Olson (2011), 35f., referring to R. C. Sproul, *What Is Reformed Theology? Understanding the Basics* (Grand Rapids, MI: Baker, 1997).

[13] The order of decrees in each of these categories is as follows: **Supralapsarianism**: (1) to save (elect) some and reprobate others, (2) to create both elect and reprobate, (3) to permit the fall of elect and reprobate, (4) to provide salvation for the elect only; **Infralapsarianism**: (1) to create human beings, (2) to permit the fall, (3) to elect some and reprobate others, (4) to provide salvation for the elect only; **Sublapsarianism**: (1) to create human beings, (2) to permit the fall, (3) to provide salvation sufficient for all, (4) to save some and reprobate others; Erickson, 826.

[14] Pinnock, x. Laurence Vance, *The Other Side of Calvinism* (Pensacola, FL: Vance Publications, 1999), cites a large number of differences between Reformed and Arminian belief.

which will be in view, but only their respective views on Election, and in particular their contrasting notions of divine determinism and human freedom. That said, however, although TULIP, or its lack, may not completely characterise one side or the other, I do believe that there is a basic, undergirding mindset in Calvinism which has to do with the nature of God himself and from which flows ideas of divine determinism and the Five Points which flow from it.

Arminius in his Context

In as much as the current division in western Protestantism between Reformed and Arminian theology appears to exist, at least in part, in response to the phenomenon of Jacobus Arminius, his place in the history of the debate is greater than is often recognised. It may therefore be helpful to sketch in some of the salient aspects of his life and work in a little more detail, and outline the issues of the Synod of Dort where much of the historic debate came to an important head.

Arminius lived after the period of primary interest to most Reformation historians, so, relatively little is written about him in English. Holland had no great reformer of its own: there was no one of the stature of the French John Calvin (1509-64), the German Martin Luther (1483-1546) or the Swiss Huldrych Zwingli (1484-1531), and in the nation's struggle to emerge from the domination of Catholic Spain, vast quantities of documentary evidence relating to the period were destroyed. By no means the least reason for the neglect of Arminius, however, is simply that the Dutch language is relatively less well-known than French, German or English, perhaps even than Latin.

Carl Bangs, who has examined Arminius' theology in the context of the dogmatic milieu of his age, has argued that he was not uncharacteristic of his times. In order to understand that conclusion, however, we have to recognise that the Reformation in Holland had no single contributing source. An intermingling of reforming movements from Switzerland, France and the Palatinate[15] certainly contributed, but what happened in

---

[15] Capital Heidelberg, Luther's sphere of influence; became the leading Protestant German state and head of the Protestant Union in 1608.

Holland cannot be seen merely as an extension of events elsewhere.[16] Although the reformers of this indigenous movement were a diverse group, unlike the Reformation elsewhere, it was essentially a lay movement. Some were Catholic priests seeking to reform the Church from within, but all were men independent of the Magisterial Calvinistic Reformers, notably Calvin and Luther, who believed that the Church was, at least to some extent, subject to the secular agencies of government – hence, the term 'magisterial'.[17] Furthermore, in instituting their reforms, the Dutch lay magistrates brought in outside ministers to officiate, many of whom were refugees from the south who held a more precise Calvinism than did the lay church leaders themselves.[18]

Thus, the Dutch Reformation was not a unitary event, and the tendency of some historians to look to the several synods which occurred in the late sixteenth- and early seventeenth centuries as indices of the character of that Reformation is therefore misguided.[19] These were not national synods in the way Dort was to be. On the other hand, however, recognition of this has tempted others to judge affairs prior to Dort by the decisions of Dort. It is important to realise that the purpose of the Synod of Dort was to judge whether the Remonstrant position agreed with the accepted Calvinist confessions,[20] and in their subsequent excommunication of the Remonstrants, the synod did not merely outlaw an heretical or minority party within the Church, but actually excised a genuine and significant sector of the Dutch national reformation which before Arminius had been legitimately part of the Dutch Reformed Church.[21]

The milieu which Arminius entered on his appointments, first as a minister in Amsterdam in the autumn of 1587, "a much loved pastor and preacher",[22] and later as professor of theology at Leiden in June 1603, gradually polarised over the decades leading up to Dort. Interestingly,

---

[16] Carl Bangs in Bratt, 210, 'Arminius as a Reformed Theologian'.
[17] McGrath (2012), 5f.
[18] Bangs in Bratt, 211f.
[19] Ibid.
[20] Dirk Jellema in Douglas (1974), 310.
[21] Bangs in Bratt, 212.
[22] Wilson, 161.

the dispute was not at first about Predestination, as it was to be at the finish, but rather it had to do with the role of the secular magistracy in church order. Arminius always adhered to an Erastian polity, the doctrine that the state had the right to intervene and overrule in church affairs,[23] as had the earlier Magisterial Reformers, in contrast with the Radical Reformers, sometimes known as Anabaptists, who mistrusted secular involvement in church affairs.[24] This confounding of church polity with the quite different issue of Predestination has to be seen against the wider movement within the nation, however. Broadly speaking, the two factions which eventually emerged were, on the one hand, a war party – militaristic, staunchly Calvinistic, anti-Catholic, centralist, politically royalist and ecclesiastically Presbyterian, and, on the other hand, a peace party – trade-minded, theologically tolerant, republican and Erastian. The latter opposed the predestinarian Calvinism of the former, which in turn opposed Arminius. Thus, Predestination, which was to become the "fighting issue",[25] entered the polarisation process almost accidentally as the Erastian views of the indigenous reformers came into conflict with immigrant clergy who held stricter Calvinistic views and the conviction that the magistracy should have no authority in ecclesiastical affairs. It is easy to see that Arminius should have differed theologically from the mainly southern incomers therefore, but the question remains as to whether he was uncharacteristic of the general situation which pertained in Holland prior to Dort.

Bangs argues that Arminius was not a schismatic: he was simply a man of his times.[26] Born and bred a Dutchman, he received the education available to him as a national, and adopted the attitude of other indigenous Dutch reformers towards the stricter Calvinists. His forebears might have been Roman Catholics,[27] but he regarded himself as part of

---

[23] P. Toon in Douglas (1974), 351. Erastianism, possibly incorrectly named after Thomas Erastus (1524-83), a Swiss physician and theologian. Toon points out that the Church of England is sometimes regarded as Erastian because its bishops are appointed by the Crown and major liturgical changes have to be agreed by the British Parliament.
[24] McGrath (2012), 9f.
[25] Bangs, 275.
[26] Bangs in Bratt, 214f., 219.
[27] His parents both died in his early years and he was adopted by Theodorus Aemilius, a priest with sympathies towards Protestantism: <https://en.wikipedia.org/wiki/

the Dutch Reformed Church and contracted to serve it for life. From 1582 he studied at Geneva under Theodore Beza (1519-1605), Calvin's successor at Geneva and the chief spokesman for the Reformed Protestantism of his day, and what is more, he won Beza's commendation. Bangs describes Beza as a "derivative Calvinist", who, in trying to be faithful to Calvin, forced the master's free and creative theology into a strictly coherent system.[28] His rigorously logical "high Calvinism" was to become the essence of Reformed orthodoxy and was to be influential in precipitating the historical Arminian controversy. Beza's Calvinism was not the orthodoxy of the Dutch Reformed Church, however, at least, not until Dort. Despite his extreme supralapsarianism,[29] which denied man any free will, he seems to have had a friendly and tolerant disposition and was able to warmly commend Arminius' intellect and piety,[30] a commendation which led others incorrectly to allege sympathy on Arminius' part to his mentor's views.[31]

Prior to his studies at Geneva, Arminius had adopted the logical methodology of Petrus Ramus (1515-72),[32] a leading figure in the anti-Aristotelian philosophical debate, the humanist[33] reaction to medieval orthodoxy. Ramus lost his life in the St. Bartholemew's Day massacre of August 1572, which claimed the lives of 13,000 Hugenots.[34] He clashed with Beza, not on the ground of Arminius' later dispute with him, since other notable strict Calvinists, like Franciscus Gomarus (1563-1641) and the English William Perkins (1558-1602), with whom Arminius also took issue over Predestination,[35] were also Ramists, but

---

Jacobus_Arminius> (accessed May 2020).
[28] Bangs, 66ff.
[29] Supralapsarianism: an anachronism here since it was not used as a theological term until the Synod of Dort. For definitions of the various lapsarian views, see 13 n13.
[30] Bangs, 73f.
[31] As is reflected in Petrus Bertius' funeral oration for Arminius, *Works* 1.30.
[32] Ramian logic pervades Arminius' writings. The first edition of his *Dissertation on Romans Seven* incorporated a Ramist binary chart, but it was dropped from subsequent editions; *Works* 2.471ff. A letter to his friend Johannes Uitenbogaert (1598) contained a Ramist chart of the doctrine of Predestination; Bangs, 57ff.
[33] See McGrath (2012), 35ff., for an introduction to pre-Renaissance humanism which significantly differs from contemporary humanism.
[34] Wilson, 54.
[35] William Perkins, a leading English Puritan and supporter of Beza's teaching, published the pamphlet: *De praedestinationis modo et ordine* at Cambridge, England in 1598 and

over his opposition to the Aristotelianism which Beza espoused.[36] Naturally, Ramism was opposed by adherents of the old Aristotelian thinking of the humanists, notably Jesuits and the 'Calvinist Aristotelian', Theodore Beza himself.

There is some debate as to whether Arminius had rejected Beza's supralapsarian views before Geneva, but A. W. Harrison tells how he was subsequently forced to examine the issue of Predestination when the church in Amsterdam asked him to refute liberalising views which were being propounded by Dirck Coornhert (1522-90).[37] Ten years previously in 1578, Coornhert had challenged the prevailing supralapsarian view, attracting opposition from two ministers from Delft, Arent Cornelisz and Reynier Donteklok, who held sublapsarian views. They had attacked Beza's views too, and a pamphlet by them was forwarded to Arminius for comment by Martinus Lydius (c. 1539-1601), professor of the new college of Franeker in Friesland. According to Harrison, Arminius at first favoured the Delft position over that of Geneva, so his response never appeared. Further reflection, however, drew him towards Coornhert's position, so that he came to reject both supralapsarian and sublapsarian views as was later reflected in *The Remonstrance*.[38] However, Bangs thinks it more likely that Arminius had

---

an expanded version, *De praedestinationis modo et ordine: et de amplitudine gratiae divinae Christiana & perspicua disceptatio* (*A Christian and Plain Treatise of the Manner and Order of Predestination, and of the Largeness of God's Grace*) the following year at Basel, Switzerland. The precise title of Arminius' response to Perkins was *Dr James Arminius's Modest Examination of a Pamphlet which that very learned divine, Dr William Perkins, published some years ago, on the Mode and Order of Predestination and on the Amplitude of Divine Grace*: Arminius, *Works*, 3.249ff.

[36] Ramus partitioned philosophical arguments into binary dialectics, the characteristic feature being the Ramist (or binary) tree (or epitome), which graphically depicted complex sets of data or arguments on all kinds of subjects based on a thesis-antithesis separation of concepts which were separated left and right. It was a particularly popular device among early Calvinists for the visualisation of theological concepts and gained supporters particularly in Germany and the Netherlands as well as among Puritan and Calvinist theologians in England, Scotland and New England (via the *Mayflower*). See <https://en.wikipedia.org/wiki/Ramism> (accessed May 2020). A Ramist chart, possibly based on one devised by Beza, illustrating God's predestinarian decrees from Perkins' *A Golden Chaine*, 1591, is to be found in Thuesen, 35 (photograph); also (redrawn) in Hinnells, 74f.

[37] A. W. Harrison, 19f., 24f. Spellings of these Dutch names follows Bangs.

[38] Petrus Bertius gives a slightly different account of this tale: Arminius, *Works*, 1.30.

already formed a view contrary to the Geneva orthodoxy before 1582, but that his meek, non-confrontational disposition, consistently in evidence throughout the many challenges to his views in later years, together with Beza's accommodating attitude, allowed him to pursue his studies in Geneva without finding any need to stir up controversy.[39]

Arminius' thought-world was Calvinism. His doctrinal concerns were those of Calvinism, and he often reflected the precise teaching he had received at Geneva.[40] He recognised other positions including Pelagianism and Semi-Pelagianism,[41] consciously distancing himself from them, but underlying all of his writing and teaching was the literature of international Calvinism with its confessions and theologians. Writing to Burgomaster Sebastian Egbertsz in 1607, Arminius commended Calvin's commentaries and interpretation of scripture in the strongest terms: "he stands distinguished above others, above most, indeed, above all."[42]

There is some doubt as to whether Arminius actually signed the Belgic Confession on his induction to the ministry at Amsterdam,[43] but he consistently asserted adherence both to it and to the Heidelberg Catechism.[44] He always portrayed himself as teaching an ancient position

---

[39] Bangs, 75.
[40] Bangs in Bratt, 215.
[41] According to Bangs in Bratt, 219, he "observed wryly that there might be a better fraction which would come closer to the truth".
[42] Bangs, 287.
[43] F. J. Los, *Grepen uit de Geschiedenis van Hervormd* (Amsterdam, 1929), 67, cited by Bangs, 116, raises the question. According to decisions of both the National Synod of Dordrecht (1578) and of Middelburg (1581), ministerial candidates were required to sign the Belgic Confession, but the practice was probably not uniformly observed: Bangs, 110.
[44] The *Belgic Confession* of 1561 and the *Heidelberg Catechism* of 1563 summarised Calvinistic orthodoxy prior to Dort, and together with the *Canons of Dort* comprised the *Three Forms of Unity* adopted at Dort in 1618-19. They remain the official subordinate standards of the Dutch Reformed Church. The chief author of the *Belgic Confession* was the Belgian, Guido de Brès (aka Guy de Bray; c. 1522-67), a man outlawed for preaching Protestantism as the Lowlands neared revolt against Spanish Catholic rule. He was executed for rebellion in 1567. His initial text of 1559, influenced by the *Gallic Confession*, was revised by Franciscus Junius (1545-1602) and was presented to Felipe II of Spain in 1562 in the hope of securing toleration for his Protestant subjects in the Low Countries. In 1566, the text was again revised at a synod at Antwerp and was adopted by national synods held during the last three decades of the sixteenth century.

of the Church held widely among the Reformed pastors in the Low Countries.[45] Because he was never aggressively polemical, preferring a pacific, tolerant disposition, it is hard to find a systematic exposition of his theology in his many writings. However, Bangs identifies his difficult *Examination of Perkins' Pamphlet* (1602) as coming closest to embodying the principal ingredients of his thinking – it contains the "most complete ingredients of Arminius' doctrines of grace" and has become "the basic document of Arminianism".[46] Nonetheless, this pacific and tolerant man could be "a dogged controversialist", particularly as he probed at length Perkins' proposals in what Bangs calls "a battle of proof texts".[47] Curiously, while in earlier years Arminius had been able to conceal himself in his private study so that he could avoid meeting issues head-on, later, when more exposed to public life as a

---

The **Belgic Confession** consists of 37 articles dealing with the doctrines of God, scripture, humanity, sin, Christ, salvation, the Church, and the end times. It became the basis of a counter to the Arminian controversy that arose in the following century, but Arminius opposed the notion that it could be used against his theology. He maintained his affirmation of the *Belgic Confession* until his death in October 1609. The text, again revised at the Synod of Dort in 1618-19, and including in the *Canons of Dort*, was adopted as one of the doctrinal standards to which all office-bearers and members of the Reformed churches of Holland were required to subscribe.

The **Heidelberg Catechism**, sometimes referred to as the *Palatinate Catechism*, was commissioned for his territory by Frederick III, the Prince-Elector of the Electoral Palatinate. Frederick, officially a Lutheran with strong Reformed leanings, wanted to even out the religious situation of his mainly Lutheran territory within what was a predominantly Roman Catholic domain. He aimed to counteract Roman Catholic teachings - the Council of Trent had recently concluded, as well as the views of Anabaptists and others who resisted his reforming influences, particularly on the matter of the eucharist. It was written in 1563 in Heidelberg chiefly by Zacharius Ursinus (1534-83) and Kaspar Olevianus (1536-87). Frederick himself wrote the preface and supervised its composition and publication. He maintained that the catechism was based on scripture rather than Reformed theology. It was divided into fifty-two 'Lord's Days' sections which were designed to be taught successively each Sunday throughout the year, a practice that persists in many Reformed denominations which originate from the Netherlands, and elders and deacons were required to subscribe and adhere to it. A synod in Heidelberg approved the catechism in 1563 and it was adopted at Dort in 1618-19. It proved to be widely influential and became part of the basis for the Westminster *Shorter Catechism* of 1646-47. See Dirk Jellema, Colin Buchannan & Ian Breward in Douglas (1974), 117, 119-201, 153 respectively; <https://en.wikipedia.org/wiki/Heidelberg_Catechism> and <https://en.wikipedia.org/wiki/Belgic_Confession> (each accessed July 2020).

[45] Bangs, 141.
[46] Ibid., 209.
[47] Ibid., 220f., 203.

professor, he would take a more directly combative approach as is exemplified in this instance.

Normally, it seems, Arminius would write only in response to others, and sometimes reluctantly, but he was by no means alone in the views he held. Until Dort there were always those at all levels of church life and academia who agreed with his position. Against heterodox views, he was often seen to be at one with colleagues, although he never hounded so-called heretics as others sometimes did. Indeed, there is no hint that he was unacceptable to the Reformed establishment of Amsterdam, and there was certainly no conflict before 1603.[48] By contrast, he was influential, working harmoniously with moderate Calvinist ministers like Jean Taffin and Franciscus Junius in Amsterdam, and even alongside the extreme Calvinist Petrus Plancius, who in 1617 was to be the chief instigator of accusations levelled against him.

Arminius was only the tenth to be inducted into the ministry of the Dutch Reformed Church at Amsterdam, but he was the first Dutchman. Although opposed by refugee Calvinist clergy from the South, notably his academic colleague, Franciscus Gomarus, a man "fractious in the extreme"[49] who dominated his Leiden years, Arminius was also the first Dutchman to be appointed Professor of Theology at Leiden. His nomination received solid lay support from the curators and burgomasters of the city, and the esteem with which he was held by academic colleagues was further evidenced in his appointment in 1605 as *Rector Magnificus*, the chief officer of the university.[50]

Arminius was therefore very much part of the Church of his day, functioning within its institutions and entering fully into its life and concerns. Whether he may be regarded as moderate in his Calvinism, there can be no doubt that, despite the judgment of F. J. Los that he was no Calvinist when he assumed pastoral office in Amsterdam,[51] by the standard of the Holland of his day, he certainly was.

---

[48] Bangs in Bratt, 149, 159, 166f.
[49] Bangs, 248; Chadwick, 220, attributes to Gomarus "an inflexible mind and a conscientious talent for setting the eternal decrees in their most repellent guise."
[50] Ibid., 265.
[51] Ibid., 78.

Arminius and International Calvinism

It is one thing to demonstrate that Arminius was not atypical of his place and time, but it is quite another to assume that the Calvinism he espoused would find acceptance with other Calvinists further from home. Bangs criticises a modern tendency to assess Arminius' Calvinism by comparing his doctrinal statements with Calvin's.[52] After all, in the Netherlands of the time, John Calvin was not the central point of reference, and in international Calvinism the leading figure at the time was actually Theodore Beza, the "derivative Calvinist". For Arminius, the standard of orthodoxy was always scripture, but the generally accepted tests of doctrine were the Belgic Confession and, to a lesser extent, the Heidelberg Catechism. By what standard of Calvinism should Arminius' particular standpoint then be judged? It is a question which raises the further broader question, of course, as to what extent modern Calvinists may legitimately regard themselves as such. In short, what is a Calvinist? Is there a distinguishing mark, and if so, what is it?

W. S. Reid points out that the term 'Calvinism' came into use largely in the seventeenth century in opposition to the doctrine of Arminius, although it had been used pejoratively by Roman Catholics in the previous century.[53] As a label, it has been used since in a wide variety of ways, and certainly in ways which Calvin himself would not have found acceptable.

Although Calvin repeatedly insisted that his doctrine was that of scripture, others maintain that his characteristic doctrine was a particular interpretation of scripture which did not find universal acceptance. R. W. A. Letham suggests that a major influence upon Calvinistic thinking was a recrudescence of Aristotelian scholasticism through Beza and others, which we have already noted. That led to a greater reliance on reason and it bred a theological climate characterised by "clarity of definition, rigorous deductivism, greater use of causal analysis and liberal employment of syllogism".[54] That certainly feels like modern

---
[52] Bangs in Bratt, 216.
[53] W. S. Reid in Douglas (1974), 179ff.; McGrath (2012), 8f.
[54] R. W. A. Letham in Ferguson & Wright, 571. The *OED Concise*, 1458, defines

Calvinism, for despite a more temperate approach than Arminius encountered in Beza or Gomarus, there is still a characteristic underlying rigorous logic, which I suggest is actually Calvinism's Achilles' heel.[55] For some, this emphasis on rationality drives a wedge between Calvinism and Calvin, and despite his acknowledged "fluid biblicism", we still find an insistence in some modern Calvinistic writings that the Five Points and the post-Dort Reformed confessions adequately summarise the system.[56] Despite Bangs' stricture, it seems not unreasonable therefore to risk the anachronism of comparing Arminius' teaching, as set out by others in *The Remonstrance*, with the findings of Dort. It should not be forgotten that the synod of Dort was not wholly under the influence of Beza's doctrine nor the strict Calvinism of Gomarus which sought to undermine the indigenous reformation in Holland.[57] Although the Remonstrants were on trial at Dort, nonetheless, the synod's inbuilt conservatism does, I suggest, allow us to use its findings with a degree of confidence. So, at the risk of anticipating discussion yet to come, and possibly delving into areas of controversy in more detail than some may find helpful, I propose to briefly summarise the issues which were discussed at Dort in 1618-19.

Dort *vs* the Remonstrants

Although the presenting issue at Dort was at first the role of the magistracy (i.e., the degree to which the secular authorities should exercise authority in church order), the actual issue between the Remonstrants and the strict Calvinism of the day was Predestination. Each of the five points of *The Remonstrance* was intended to soften the increasingly

---

'syllogism' as "a form of reasoning in which a conclusion is drawn from two given or assumed propositions (premises); a common or middle term is present in the two premises but not in the conclusion, which may be invalid". A silly example of a syllogistic fallacy might be, "We keep a stock of garlic because garlic is supposed to keep vampires at bay: we have never seen a vampire, so it must work!"

[55] Modern Calvinists would do well to reflect on the logical inconsistency inherent in, on the one hand, a notion of Total Depravity, which implies among other things that man's rationality is flawed, and on the other hand, an insistence on the coherence of rationality as a structural framework for Calvinism. See Chapter 7, 192.

[56] E.g., W. S. Reid in Douglas (1974), 179ff.

[57] "In so large an assembly... it was impossible to canonise the extreme language of Gomar": Chadwick, 221.

dominant view of Predestination in the Dutch Reformed Church and to salvage something of man's free will.[58] They asked, not for a change in religion, but for revisions of the *Belgic Confession* and the *Heidelberg Catechism*.[59] In summary, then, the issues raised in each of the five points made by the Remonstrants were as follows:

1. They opposed the supralapsarian decree that God had ordained some to eternal life and some to perdition, even though as yet humanity was uncreated and unfallen.

2. They opposed the sublapsarian decree (also in contention in their day) that God considered mankind, not only as created, but as fallen in Adam, and consequently liable to the curse. Furthermore, that God had determined to release some from that fall and destruction, saving them as instances of his mercy, while others, even children of the Covenant, he would leave as examples of his justice, and that without any regard to their belief or unbelief.

3. They objected to the doctrine that Christ died only for the elect, irrespective of whether the supralapsarian decree or the sublapsarian decree might prove to be correct.

4. They opposed Irresistible Grace, the idea that the Spirit of God and Christ caused the elect to believe and be saved by an irresistible force, but that necessary and sufficient grace was withheld from the reprobate.

5. They challenged the doctrine of Perseverance; that saints, those who had received the true faith, could not fall from grace wholly or finally.

The five points of *The Remonstrance*, although not following the exact order of these, are based on them. With the exception of the third and fourth points, concerning what later Reformed doctrine would term Inability or Depravity and Sanctification, which the Synod of Dort accepted as orthodox, the rest were rejected. Dort responded under five headings or canons:

---

[58] R. D. Linder in Douglas (1974), 835.
[59] A. W. Harrison, 149. The Five Points of the Remonstrance are summarised in Harrison, 149f., and Bettenson, 268f.

a. Canon 1: Predestination, Election and Reprobation

Canon 1:7 summarises the synod's response:

> Election is the unchangeable purpose of God, whereby before the foundation of the world he has out of mere grace, according to the sovereign good pleasure of his own will, chosen from the whole human race (which had fallen through their own fault from their primitive state of rectitude into sin and destruction) a certain number of persons to redemption in Christ. From eternity he appointed Christ to be the mediator and head of the elect and the foundation of salvation.[60]

Through all of his writings Arminius was clear that God did not elect individuals, but rather a class of people in Christ. We have noted already how he always claimed adherence to the *Belgic Confession*, often citing it to support his views, but in Article 16 of that confession, irrespectively of the intentions of those who originally framed the wording, he found an ambiguity which he felt could accommodate both his own and the views of his opponents:

> We believe that whereas the whole posterity of Adam is fallen into ruin and damnation through the guilt of the first man, God showed himself to be such as he is, namely, merciful and just: merciful in that he delivers and saves out of this ruination those whom he in his eternal and unchangeable council, through his pure goodness has *elected and chosen in Jesus Christ* our Lord, without any consideration of their good works; and in that he leaves the others in their fall and ruin wherein they themselves have cast themselves.[61]

Thus, two alternative interpretations of this wording were possible:

> (a) that those who are "chosen in Jesus Christ" are believers; in other words, they are constituted 'in Christ' when they become believers, and
>
> (b) that God selects certain people to be believers.

---

[60] Extracts from the Dort Canons are taken from Lane, 136f.
[61] Bangs in Bratt, 218 (my italics): his own translation from the pre-Dort Dutch text of 1562 in J. N. Bakhuizen van den Brink, *De Nederlandsche Belijdenisgeschriften* (Amsterdam, 1940), 89, and incorporating an emendation to his earlier version: Bangs, 223. Cf. the post-Dort text of Article 16 in Cochrane, 199f.

Arminius insisted on the former,[62] rejecting the implicit supralapsarianism of the view which was to be expounded by the Synod of Dort, because, in his view, it made God the author of sin. This imputation of sin to the sum of the divine qualities actually formed the crux of the Calvinist-Arminian debate.[63] Furthermore, the idea that God should elect a "certain number of persons to redemption in Christ" was inimical to Arminius' whole system. He therefore differed sharply from Calvin and the Calvinists of his time on this fundamental and characteristic tenet embodied in the first Canon.

Arminius also differed sharply from his accusers over the divine decrees - a preoccupation of theologians of the time who tried to work out the sequence of decisions God had made with respect to the salvation of humankind. Whereas the first decree, as reflected in the Dort Canons, focuses on mankind, since it treats of God's intention to save some and damn certain other particular persons, Arminius insisted that Predestination must be understood christologically and evangelically. According to him, the object of a first divine decree, as set out in his *Declaration of Sentiments* of 1608,[64] cannot be mankind, whether created or fallen, but Christ. Christ is more than just a means of carrying out some prior non-christological decree; he is the one who obtains the salvation which we had lost, for he is "the foundation of election".[65]

It is worth noting that Arminius states his first decree to be a Single Predestination. This contrasts with the Calvinistic concept of Double Predestination, which, despite a softening of it among many modern Calvinists who teach Single Predestination,[66] is nevertheless the logically rigorous conclusion of Calvin's teaching, as it was with Augustine before him. It is well-known that in the earliest editions of his *Institutes of the Christian Religion*[67] Calvin's doctrine of Predestination was not

---

[62] Ibid.
[63] Sell, 16.
[64] Arminius, *Works*, 1.589f.
[65] Arminius, *Works*, 1.566.
[66] E.g., Peter Lewis *et al.*
[67] For a summary of the successive editions of Calvin's *Institutes*, see McGrath (2012), 247ff.

accorded the importance which later Calvinism gave to it.[68] In the first edition of 1536, he paid it little attention, treating Predestination as an aspect of the doctrine of Providence, but from the 1539 edition onwards, it was treated as a topic of importance in its own right. The final 1559 French edition, in which he devoted four chapters to Predestination, reads like a practical manual for the believer. More systematic than anything Luther ever wrote on the subject, it expounded Predestination as an aspect of the doctrine of Redemption through Christ rather than of Providence.[69] Nonetheless, he clearly, yet apparently reluctantly, accepted its implications of damnation for the non-elect to the extent that he regarded the doctrine of Reprobation, that "Christ died on the cross not for all mankind, but only for the elect", to be a *decretum horribile* - not so much a "horrible decree", as a crude translation might suggest; but an "awe-inspiring" or "terrifying" decree, "something which should induce a sense of awe within us".[70] Calvin admitted that Predestination was "very perplexing" for many, and warned that excessive curiosity about God's secret counsels could be spiritually dangerous: "he who rushes forward securely and confidently instead of satisfying his curiosity will enter an inextricable labyrinth ".[71] He hastened to add that Predestination must nevertheless be preached to the faithful.[72]

In the *Declaration of Sentiments* Arminius had outlined three further decrees. Whereas the first treats of the election of the one in whom others find salvation, the second decrees the election of the Church, the body of those who will repent and believe, and who through perseverance will receive their salvation. Arminius regarded the elect, not so much as an aggregate of individuals, but as a class, the body of those in Christ.[73] His third decree appoints the means of salvation which is to be sufficient and powerful. Concerned as he was to uphold the justice of God, he was adamant that the means of salvation must not be denied

---

[68] Wendel, 263ff.
[69] *Institutes*, 3.21-24: Beveridge, 3:202-58; McGrath (2012), 199.
[70] *Institutes*, 3.23.7: Beveridge, 3:231f.; L. Berkhof, 116; McGrath (2012), 200.
[71] *Institutes*, 3.21.1: Beveridge, 3:204. (Warning duly noted!)
[72] *Institutes*, 3.21.3: Beveridge, 3:205; Thuesen, 30.
[73] Bangs in Bratt, 351.

to the reprobate since, in his estimation, they could not be damned for disobedience to a call which had not been made to them.

Only in his fourth decree does Arminius address the election of individuals: the salvation of some and the damnation of others rests on God's foreknowledge of their merit. "Now why did Arminius have to say *that*?" expostulates Bangs.[74] Why he did not leave it at three absolute decrees of Predestination is difficult to understand. That fourth, *conditional* decree apparently created a weakness in his scheme which was to cause him serious problems, although we shall question if that was really so presently. In any case, arguably, it prevented him from expounding a thoroughly biblical and radical alternative to Calvinism. Although attempting to remain within the limits of biblical language and thought, it seems, nonetheless, that he needlessly transgressed them, and his apparent need to pronounce upon the election of individuals, when he is known to have believed that election was of a class of people, may seem to demonstrate the extent to which he was locked into a Calvinian-Augustinian frame of reference. Perhaps he felt bound to address the issue because he had imbibed the characteristic Calvinistic hermeneutic which blinkered him to the need to question the interpretations of certain New Testament texts which Calvin and his followers interpreted in individualistic terms.[75]

While Calvin asserted that election depended on God's sovereign will and decree: God "foresees the things which are to happen, simply because he has decreed that they are so to happen",[76] the Remonstrants were equally clear that it did not. The Arminian insistence that election depends upon foreknowledge is actually their Achilles' heel, for at face value it drives their doctrine into the circularity of making election dependent upon man's decision, even though it was a decision which God foresaw, in the sense that he knew about it in advance. That being the

---

[74] Bangs, 352 (his italics).
[75] The biblical data will be examined later. Suffice it to comment here that the majority of theological and exegetical texts available today either are written from a Reformed viewpoint or adopt Reformed exegesis. Recognition of this should alert the critical reader to the possibility that certain underlying characteristic presuppositions, especially those regarding semantic issues, are not normally questioned.
[76] *Institutes*, 3.23.6: Beveridge, 3:231.

case, election could not be dependent on divine foreknowledge.

It may nevertheless be possible to tease out of this apparent circularity a sophistication which Arminius' detractors may have missed, and which may account for the apparent illogicalities of his views on Foreknowledge. Arminius' difficulty with Beza's Calvinism was the confounding of knowledge about things in advance and the equation of foreknowledge with predeterminism which had issued in the doctrine of Unconditional Election. In effect, the Calvinist doctrine says we chose God because he first chose us. That is very different from saying, as Arminius seems to have believed, that God placed us in Christ as elect ones when we believed in him. It would be convenient to be able to represent Arminius' doctrine thus, but he does not seem to have forged that final link in his theology which would have enabled him to make the radical departure from Calvinism by postulating Christ as the *only* elect individual. That insight would have to wait until the twentieth century and Karl Barth,[77] although some would say, as would I, that that was precisely what the Apostle Paul meant by our election itself being in Christ.[78]

As Bangs observes, Foreknowledge was not the conceptual problem for Arminius' opponents that it is for moderns[79] for whom it is both a metaphysical and an ontological concept. Indeed, their problem was not with Foreknowledge *per se*, but with the place Arminius afforded to it in his system. He did not help himself in that respect therefore by saying in his *Examination of Gomarus' Theses* (1613 posth.) that foreknowledge was of entities, while knowledge was of possibilities.[80] Logically, at least in modern metaphysics, the opposite must be true:

---

[77] Christ is "the electing God and ... the elected man"; "he is the sole object of this [divine] good-pleasure", "not merely one of the elect but *the* elect of God"; "The election of Jesus Christ may be preached to [the elect] as their own election"; Barth, 103, 104, 106 (his italics), 345.
[78] Ephesians 1:4. See Chapter 9a, 252, 'What does 'in Christ' mean?'.
[79] Bangs, 352.
[80] Arminius, *Works*, 3.535 [NB. Bangs' citation doesn't check out with the edition available]. Arminius objected to Gomarus' proleptic use of "creatures" before creation. They are only "creable", and not salvable until they are created. He asserted that there can be no knowledge of uncreated beings, although there may be foreknowledge of them: foreknowledge is of definite things in the future, while knowledge, in the context of the decree of Predestination, is only of indefinite things!

the possibility of an event can be known, but it cannot be foreknown unless it will actually happen. Consequently, Arminius has been interpreted as implying that foreknowledge has a power link with future events, so most Arminians assert an absolute divine foreknowledge of future contingent events. Thus, although Arminius attempted to adhere to scripture, he seems to have lost coherence in his speculative fourth decree. It is interesting that he was not faulted for it by his contemporaries, however.[81]

It is said that Arminius sought to extricate himself from the inherent illogicality of his four decrees by subordinating the fourth under the christological basis of election, setting it into a soteriological, rather than a metaphysical framework, as in Calvinism. Despite its wording, which links Foreknowledge with salvation and perdition, it seems that Arminius did distinguish the issue of saving faith, on the one hand, from, on the other hand, predestination to conformity with Christ, that is, predestination to "the adoption as sons".[82] He rejected the idea that mankind has no say in conversion, but what he meant by foreknowledge as the basis of salvation was apparently not foreknowledge as the basis of justification and regeneration, but rather the knowledge God had about who would believe, and that being determinative for his decision that they should be conformed to Christ and share his inheritance in glory. Conformity to Christ therefore follows as a consequence upon the exercise of saving faith. Arminius seemed to have differentiated the two issues in a way such that he could affirm what Paul says are the goals of Predestination on the basis of divine foreknowledge, but at the same time deny that a person is saved on the basis of foreknowledge. Arminius' absolute decree held that "believers shall be saved [and] unbelievers shall be damned", but with respect to individuals, the premise of "the foreknowledge of faith and of unbelief [is] not as a law and rule, but as properly precedent".[83] Citing in support John 1:12: "to all who

---

[81] Bangs, 353f.
[82] Romans 8:29; Ephesians 1:5. Adoption is an eschatological event or state, as exegesis of the four or five occurrences of υἱοθεσία should show; Romans 8:15, 23; 9:4; Galatians 4:5; Ephesians 1:5. See *BAGD*, 'υἱοθεσία': "in Paul, only in a transferred sense"; also Chapter 10c, 324, and my forthcoming *Pie in the Sky When You Die?*
[83] Arminius, *Works*, 3.451.

did receive him, to those who believed in his name, he gave the right to become children of God", Arminius claimed that "Ephesians 1 presupposes faith before predestination", for "no one except a believer is predestinated to adoption through Christ".[84]

With this distinction in mind, it may be possible to re-evaluate his apparent illogicality concerning the relationship between foreknowledge and entities. If saving faith is already an established fact, then the divine desire to bring believers to conformity to Christ can be said to be based on foreknowledge; not foreknowledge of the exercise of saving faith, but of the intention of God to bring many sons to glory. We shall again encounter this distinction between the believer and the elect individual with respect to the issue of Perseverance. It may just be the key which, not only solves the riddle of Arminius' apparent inconsistent logic but also unlocks his, and our, whole view of Election. However, it is not a distinction that has been generally understood by Arminians.

b. Canon 2: The Death of Jesus Christ and the Redemption of Men thereby

Canon 2:8 says:

> This was the sovereign counsel and most gracious will and purpose of God the Father: that the quickening and saving efficacy of the most precious death of his Son should extend to all the elect for bestowing upon them alone the gift of justifying faith, thereby to bring them infallibly to salvation. That is, it was the will of God that Christ by the blood of the cross ... should effectually redeem ... all those and those only who were from eternity chosen to salvation.

This second Canon built on the first, which had asserted God's choice of individuals for salvation and, by implication, of individuals for damnation, and directly opposed the second article of *The Remonstrance*:

> Jesus Christ, the Saviour of the world, died for all men and for every man, so that he has obtained for all, by his death on the cross, reconciliation and remission of sins; yet so that no one is a partaker of

---

[84] Arminius, *Works*, 3.453.

this remission except the believers.[85]

Thus, we touch upon the doctrines of Limited Atonement and Irresistible Grace.

Arminius was at one with Calvin over saving grace not being universal. In his *Examination of Perkins' Pamphlet*, he differentiated between a universal election, implied by William Perkins, and the particular election of believers; those whom God predestines to salvation because they are believers. He differed from Calvin, however, appealing to Romans 9:16, to show that those to whom God determined to show mercy were believers.[86] Furthermore, also in response to Perkins, Arminius rejected the Calvinistic distinction between common grace and peculiar grace. He preferred rather to speak of salvation as 'sufficient' or 'applied'.[87] Referring to Hebrews 9:13-14,[88] he distinguished between the offering of a sacrificial victim and the application of the benefits which issued from that sacrifice:

> Between the oblation ... and the application, or sanctification, it is necessary for faith to intervene.... it does not sanctify any but those who believe in Christ.[89]

Arminius therefore allowed that man had both the responsibility and the ability to make a response to the grace of God in order that the benefit of the sacrifice of Christ might be applied to him. In that respect, he was conscious of a fine line drawn between a denial of free will and

---

[85] Bettenson, 268.
[86] Arminius, *Works*, 3.449f.: "In Romans ix. 16, where it is said 'not of him that willeth, nor of him that runneth, but of God that showeth mercy,' the word 'righteousness' is understood. For the discussion in that place is in reference to those, to whom righteousness is properly imputed, not to them that work, but to them that believe, that is, righteousness is obtained not by him that willeth or that runneth, but by him to whom 'God showeth mercy,' namely, to the believer." Although Arminius appears to ignore Paul's context of Israel in Egypt, his exegesis infers that since God showed mercy to Israel and not to Egypt, then the recipients of his mercy were 'believers'.
[87] Bangs, 213.
[88] Hebrews 9:13f.: "The blood of goats and bulls and the ashes of a heifer sprinkled on those who are ceremonially unclean sanctify them so that they are outwardly clean. How much more, then, will the blood of Christ, who through the eternal Spirit offered himself unblemished to God, cleanse our consciences from acts that lead to death, so that we may serve the living God!"
[89] Arminius, *Works*, 3.336.

Pelagianism, both of which he sought to avoid.

In his disputation *On the Free Will of Man and its Powers* (1605)[90] Arminius distinguished five kinds of liberty as applied to the will. Two, which applied to God alone, were freedom from the control of one who commands and freedom from the government of a superior. Two further forms applied to man in his pre-fallen state; freedom from the dominance of sin and from sin's misery, but the liberty which applies to fallen man is the freedom from necessity, which is the essence of the will. He carefully differentiated this from Pelagianism by observing that the will freed from necessity may still not be free from sin. His question then was, Can man will against sin and its dominion? "Yes, he can", Arminius would say, but he does not have the power to do that which is spiritually good except in as much as he is excited by divine grace. Accordingly, he quoted with approval the dictum of Bernard of Clairvaux,

> Take away free will, and nothing will be left to be saved: take away grace, and nothing will be left as the source of salvation ... No one, except God, is able to bestow salvation; and nothing, except free will is capable of receiving it.[91]

So, Arminius consciously distanced himself from Pelagianism by saying that grace only assists man who is weakened by sin. All response to the divine call is the work of grace, so co-operation is not the means to renewal; it is merely its result.[92]

Arminius therefore came close to Calvin in respect of Total Depravity. Indeed, in the same disputation, he strongly affirmed it: "the free will of man towards the true good is ... lost"; it has "no powers whatever except such as are excited by divine grace".[93] Later Arminians would find this agreement with Calvinism hard to swallow, but it must be borne in mind that in saying what he did in that particular disputation, Arminius deliberately avoided aspects of the universal call of the gospel and its effect upon the bound will, which he did not deny. His

---

[90] Arminius, *Works*, 2.189ff.
[91] Arminius, *Works*, 2.196.
[92] Bangs, 340f.
[93] Arminius, *Works*, 2.192.

purpose rather was conciliatory: he had no wish to raise contentious issues even when under attack from Gomarus and his like. In responding to Perkins, however, he did affirm a belief in free will. Although the sinner's free will is "addicted to evil" and "will not be bent to good except by grace", all men have a will flexible to either side of good or evil.[94] He distinguished between the ability to believe, which belongs to nature, and actually believing, which is of grace.[95] The gospel is about the free choice to receive offered grace, but the offered grace itself makes the free choice possible. Arminius, with Calvin, insisted that man does nothing apart from grace. Where he differed from Calvin was in his belief that man can refuse to accept the grace offered: for Arminius and the Remonstrants, "grace is not irresistible; for it is written of many that they resisted the Holy Spirit".[96]

c. & d. Canons 3 & 4: The Corruption of Man and the Method of his Conversion to God

There was no fundamental dispute between the Remonstrants and the Synod over the third and fourth Canons, which were combined, because Arminius was essentially at one with Calvin over Depravity, and he fully agreed with the Calvinistic and biblical doctrine of Sanctification which was all of grace. Thus *Canon* 3/4:3 says:

> All men are conceived in sin and by nature children of wrath, incapable of saving good, prone to evil, dead in sin and in bondage to it. Without the regenerating[97] grace of the Holy Spirit they are neither able nor willing to return to God, to reform the depravity of their nature, nor to dispose themselves to reformation.

And *Canon* 3/4:11:

> When God accomplishes his good pleasure in the elect or works true conversion in them, he does not merely cause the gospel to be preached externally to them and powerfully illuminate their minds by the Holy Spirit ... By the efficacy of the same regenerating Spirit

---

[94] Arminius, *Works*, 3.470.
[95] Arminius, *Works*, 3.482.
[96] Bettenson, 269, quoting Article IV of *The Remonstrance*.
[97] See note on 'regeneration' in Chapter 5, 144.

he pervades the inmost recesses of the man; he opens the closed and softens the hardened heart; he circumcises that which was uncircumcised and infuses new qualities into the will, which though previously dead he quickens; from being evil, disobedient and refractory he renders it good, obedient and pliable; he actuates and strengthens it so that, like a good tree, it may bring forth the fruits of good actions.

e. Canon 5: The Perseverance of the Saints[98]

Thus far, then, we find some areas of agreement and some of disagreement. However, the fifth Canon addresses the issue of Perseverance over which Arminius was ambivalent, although later Arminians would tend to deny it outright. *Canon 5:3* states:

> By reason of the remains of indwelling sin and the temptation of sin and the world, those who are converted could not persevere in a state of grace if left to their own strength. But God is faithful and having conferred grace, mercifully confirms and powerfully preserves them in it even to the end.

The Remonstrants acknowledged a difficulty, however:

> those who are grafted into Christ ... are abundantly endowed with power to strive against Satan ... with the help of the grace of the Holy Spirit.... But for the question whether they are not able ... to forsake the beginning of their life in Christ ... must be the subject of more exact inquiry in the Holy Scriptures, before we can teach it with full confidence of our mind.[99]

Arminius probed the question of Perseverance at length and depth in his response to Perkins, who, with Calvin, asserted eternal security on the basis of their particular view of the nature of Election and the Irresistible Grace of God and its Effectual Call. However, he was not convinced by Perkins' set of proof-texts and concluded that a member of Christ may by sloth and sin become dead and cease to be a member of Christ.[100] Later, in his *Declaration of Sentiments*, Arminius seems to

---

[98] See Chapter 4, 70, 'Perseverance'.
[99] Bettenson, 269.
[100] Bangs, 218f.; Arminius, *Works*, 3.470.

have distanced himself from the question, however, saying that he "never taught that a true believer can either totally or finally fall away from the faith, and perish".[101] He therefore dodged the issue, for he would never say whether he thought a believer could fall away. He recognised passages of scripture which seemed to support the possibility, but he also found passages which taught unconditional perseverance which, he said, were worthy of much consideration.[102] Resolution of this apparent discrepancy lies in Arminius' view that a believer who ceases from trusting in God is no longer a believer. Whereas he affirmed that it is impossible for believers, so long as they remain believers, to decline from salvation, he distinguished between a believer and one of the elect: "believers and the elect are not correctly taken for the same persons".[103] Thus, for Arminius, election to salvation embraced both believing and perseverance in faith.

*****

The Calvinism of Arminius' place and time may not have been so diverse as it is today, but it is fascinating to realise that, when judged by the prevailing standards of the Dutch Church at the turn of the seventeenth century, some modern Calvinists might find Arminius to have been more of a Calvinist even than them, and they may be surprised at the extent to which his writings do not produce the heresies they might have expected to find.[104] As we have seen, J. Matthew Pinson asserts that the context within which Arminius worked out his Reformed theology was very mixed and there was no consensus on the doctrine of Predestination in the Dutch Reformed Church of his time.[105] As a devout Reformed theologian, he was loyal to both the *Heidelberg Catechism* and the *Belgic Confession of Faith*, reaffirming his faithfulness to both on numerous occasions.[106] He also had a high regard for Calvin,

---

[101] Arminius, *Works*, 1.603.
[102] Ibid.
[103] Arminius, *Works*, 2.68, quoting Augustine.
[104] Bangs, 18.
[105] Pinson in Pinnock & Wagner, 155.
[106] Ibid. According to Bangs in Bratt, 216, Arminius affirmed his loyalty to the Catechism and Confession in 1593 before the consistory in Amsterdam and in 1605 responding to the deputies of the Synods of North and South Holland.

both as an exegete and theologian; their only important disagreement being on the particulars of the doctrines of Predestination and the resistibility of divine grace. However, Arminius did not regard Predestination as the essential core of either Reformed theology or of Calvin's theology, and although he differed from Calvin on Predestination, he was, and believed he was, consistently Reformed.[107]

I have already said that I find both the Reformed and Arminian positions to be at fault, and neither is my personal conviction, but on reading for the first time those works of Arminius which were available in English, I confess that I found in him a kindred spirit. Although he was very much a Calvinist of his time, and that, as we have seen, was quite different from the much more rigorous and extreme Calvinism which emerged after the Synod of Dort, and that he claimed to depend entirely on the authority of scripture, nonetheless he was willing to admit to a degree of agnosticism when he found scripture not to be quite so clear as some of his opponents claimed it to be, especially when it came to the issue of the Perseverance of the Saints. I warm to that kind of honesty. I fear, however, that Calvinism, on the other hand, has tended to adopt a characteristically cultic way of thinking, holding that there must be a dogmatic answer to every question which scripture throws up, a tendency borne out by the Reformed complexion of the majority of published systematic theologies where it seems the attempt is made to describe all aspects of the doctrine of God.

For Arminius, the problem with Calvinism was not with the principle of the absolute sovereignty of God as such, upon which that whole doctrinal edifice was built, but that the principle was applied even in the face of contrary scriptural revelation or contrary logic. The post-Dort Calvinists built an edifice of speculative Divine Decrees upon the foundation principle of divine sovereignty,[108] but in so doing they necessarily introduced a degree of selectivity into their biblical reading and interpretation. In other words, where scripture apparently said contradictory things, the post-Dort Calvinists found their answers by resorting to the monolithic logic of the Divine Decrees as deduced by Theodore

---

[107] Ibid., 156f.
[108] See L. Berkhof, 100ff., for a summary of the Divine Decrees.

THE PREDESTINATION PROBLEM

Beza and his like, rather than by wrestling with scripture itself.

Calvin too was sometimes guilty of the same kind of reductionism. For example, in his treatment of passages of scripture which he claimed to affirm or imply faith as the condition governing salvation, Robert Shank, in quite scathing terms, asserts that his "thinking and his treatment of the Scriptures were thoroughly conditioned by the dominance of the concept of faith as a gift of God to man":

> he customarily begins by acknowledging the obvious meaning of the text – which negates his theology, then proceeds to extricate himself, either by burying the point in a mass of theological verbalsmog, blowing up peripheral and tangential considerations as though they were the heart and essence of the matter under consideration in the text, or by candidly asserting the existence of a "hidden purpose of God" supposedly assumed by the Biblical writer – which serves to make the passage merely rhetorical rather than categorical (and often casts the Biblical writer in the role of an exceedingly subtle writer who presumed much on the intuition of his readers). Such accommodation is found again and again in Calvin's treatment of Scripture passages which negate his theology. His ingenious treatment of contrary passages proceeded, we believe, not from insincerity, but from his zeal to find uniformity in the Scriptures and complete substantiation for what he believed to be the teaching of the major definitive passages bearing on the question of election.

Shank continues,

> Calvin's erroneous assumptions so completely conditioned his approach to the Scriptures that he found no place for the candid acceptance of the many affirmations of Scripture positing faith as a factor in man of which God takes account in salvation, and instead labored to accommodate the Scriptures in toto to the affirmations of faith as a gift of God to men. This is reflected in many passages in his works.[109]

Thus, when discussing Limited Atonement, Shank offers this highly critical comment:

> One does not read long from the apologists for Calvinism before

---

[109] Shank (*Elect*), 112ff.

finding them resorting to all manner of ingenious interpretations and applications in an effort to bolster their tottering theology.[110] Rather than seeking exegetical clarity on the texts which Calvin and his disciples found difficult, and in so doing taking the risk that resolution might evade them, the post-Dort Calvinists imposed upon the Bible an interpretative paradigm which lost sight of nuances in scripture which might have saved them from much of the dogmatism and oppressiveness which history has seen in full-blown Calvinism. Rather than trying to resolve the difficulties inherent within the biblical data, they merely reinterpreted inconvenient texts, reinforcing dogma with a confidence apparently borne of intellectual pride. Thus, I would say that in its implicit rejection of even minuscule sections of the divine revelation, the Calvinistic system actually deviates from its own core principle of divine sovereignty and the evangelical dependency on the all-sufficiency of scripture in its entirety.

On the other hand, Arminius rejected certain aspects, not only of some of the extreme forms of the Calvinism of his day, but some of the tenets of Calvinism which have survived to our own day. Why? Because he found them to be unbiblical. Either he was not convinced by them, or he desired to submit them to further study. Those he rejected, he did so because in his view they depended upon a narrowing of the canonical revelation, the tacit rejection of the whole counsel of God in favour of a narrower, though apparently more logical straitjacket. Arminius was not an illogical or ignorant man by any means. Had he been lacking intellectually, his one-time mentor, Theodore Beza, no less, surely could not have commended his intellect so warmly, and it is most unlikely that Beza would have allowed him to be elected to the Chair of Theology at Leiden. Rather, in contrast to his opponents, and despite what they might have claimed, Arminius was a man who placed the divine revelation of scripture on a plane higher than the faculty of human rationality. Paradoxically, however, it is the elevation of rationality which seems to me to be so characteristic of Calvinism. Many, myself included, hold firmly to many of the beliefs held by Calvin and his

---

[110] Ibid., 75.

disciples even in the narrow field of Election. Yet it is not so much in the degree of doctrinal disagreement that we may distinguish Calvinists from others, but in their attitude to the divine revelation of scripture. Arminius was like chalk to the cheese of Calvin's disciples, for, in essence, his outworking of the fundamental presupposition of divine sovereignty, which Calvinists and Arminians claim to hold in common, was quite different from theirs. He held tenaciously – I would suggest honestly, to the biblical revelation despite the intellectual difficulties that clearly created for him.

The Contemporary Legacy Either Side of the Atlantic

That was four centuries ago. What about now? My understanding of today's Church in the West is that a similar polarisation continues to exist between those two positions. However, it isn't an equal balance as if there were a continuum spanning the extremes of Calvinism and Arminianism, and things seems to be different either side of the Atlantic Ocean too. I would suggest that Calvinism, in varying degrees of dogmatism, is the dominant position today, at least on the eastern side of the Atlantic, and I find myself in broad agreement with Peter Lewis:

> It is largely to John Wesley, great man of God though he was, that we must attribute much of the disfavour into which the old 'doctrines of grace' fell among evangelicals of the past 200 years. Yet in the 19th century, notwithstanding, William Carey and the Baptist Missionary Society, the Church Missionary Society and its earliest promoters, C. H. Spurgeon and his outstanding preaching ministry, were all products of (call it what you will) the old Augustinian, Reformed, Calvinistic theology of grace. Now, in the second half of the twentieth century, we are seeing a recovery of the old apostolic doctrines of grace. In Britain this has been outstandingly through the pulpit ministry of the late Dr Martyn Lloyd-Jones and his published sermons on Romans and Ephesians (Banner of Truth). A new generation of evangelicals have rediscovered their roots and uncovered the foundations of their apostolic faith.[111]

Arminianism should not necessarily be regarded as the opposite

---

[111] P. Lewis in P. Lewis *et al*, 63.

position in the wider Church, however. In contrast to modern Calvinism, there seems to be a mixture of a less well focused Arminianism and a whole variety of other positions so far as I can see, at least in Britain. In as much as Calvinism is usually clearly articulated, often aggressively (it must be said), I suggest that it wins the battle for acceptance in the hearts and minds of many, if not most evangelical Christians, who on the whole are not adequately equipped theologically, and for those who don't have a clear view of precisely where the truth lies. The reason, I think, is simply that it is the position they most often and most clearly hear, and so it has become for them the orthodox norm.

That said, however, the predominant version of Reformed teaching is not the rigorous double-predestinatory hyper-Calvinism of Beza and Dort, but rather the single-predestinatory position of the New or Moderate Calvinism described below.[112] Characteristically, the New Calvinism leaves its adherents in an ambivalence regarding some of the certainties of full-blown Calvinism, so that writers like me might be regarded as attempting the impossible in trying to find clarity on a scriptural exposition of Election. That ambivalence is satisfied by the assurance that we cannot know the ultimate mind and purposes of God. I would claim, however, that we can know more than is often assumed.

Thus, evangelical Christians stand either side of the Calvinist-Arminian divide – more or less. Nonetheless, and perhaps surprisingly, as I have already hinted, there seems to be some denial about the importance and relevance of this historical debate in our day. There are many 'tribes' of evangelical churches, but notwithstanding the prevailing unwillingness to engage with the issues, certainly from the non-Reformed side of the fence, the clearest division among Protestants does seem to me to be on this precise issue – Is your doctrine Reformed or not? And with that, generally speaking, one can identify a number of traits which seem to characterise either side of that fence. For example (and I am doing my utmost to be charitable), churches and their leaders on the Reformed side tend to prize their adherence to scripture and their faithfulness to God's truth in the gospel in a way which might suggest that

---

[112] Olson (2011), 13. See below, 53, on the New Calvinism.

they believe their theology to be the only authentically Christian or evangelical one, and that other Christians do not adhere to scripture so faithfully as them. Sadly, that sometimes presents in a prideful way, a trait all too common among the so-called New Calvinists. Sometimes, and it is certainly true of some of the more strongly Reformed churches I know personally, there is also an abhorrence of Roman Catholicism, so they will regard with suspicion, or even avoid ecumenical networks and events in which Roman Catholics are involved. Some of my personal friends are genuine born-again believers, but remain Roman Catholics: we must therefore guard against not "discerning the body",[113] even though some disciples of Jesus have chosen to remain in what many evangelicals might regard as a corrupt system. I also observe that few if any women are numbered among the recognised leaderships of some Reformed churches. On the other hand, non-Calvinistic churches seem to sit lightly – perhaps it would be fairer to say, less dogmatically or less aggressively, on some of the truths of the Christian faith.

In his *Predestination: The American Career of a Contentious Doctrine*, Peter Thuesen traces the influences of the Reformation either side of the Atlantic. Back-tracking something like 80 years before the Synod of Dort, the Reformation in England did not follow the kind of course seen in continental Europe. It is well-known that Henry VIII's dispute with the Vatican and Pope Clement VII over the annulment of his marriage to Catherine of Aragon, and the Pope's eventual decision that his marriage to Anne Boleyn was invalid, created a rift which brought into being the Church of England in November 1534. That left Henry as supreme head of the Church in England with the title, 'Defender of the Faith', which had been bestowed on him by a previous Pope, Leo X. Despite Henry's "lingering sympathies with Catholic doctrine", this set the stage for Thomas Cranmer, the "reform-minded archbishop of Canterbury" to set about moving the Church in a new direction. This became obvious on Henry's death in 1547 with the succession of the nine-year-old Edward VI who through Cranmer's influence and his Protestant education was hailed as the new Josiah, the latter-day

---

[113] 1 Corinthians 11:29.

counterpart to Judah's seventh-century BC reforming boy king.[114]

Two decades prior to Edward's accession, Luther's ideas were being discussed in England, and particularly at Cambridge University and the 'White Horse' group, which included some of the future Reformation leaders in England – Hugh Latimer, Thomas Cranmer, Miles Coverdale and others; possibly also William Tyndale.[115] But it was Henry's personal influence which gave the English movement its impetus through his desire to ensure a smooth transition of power after his death, and particularly through his appointment of Cranmer, who succeeded William Warham as Archbishop of Canterbury on his death in 1532. Henry was not only at odds with the Vatican, but also with the Spanish king, Carlos V, the nephew of Catherine of Aragon, as well as with other Catholic states which were threatening to invade England. Henry raised funding for the preparation of defence measures by the dissolution and plunder of the monasteries, and he formed military alliances with Lutheran states in Europe, notably with Germany. Thus, the stage was set for the adoption in England of Lutheran statements of faith such as the *Ten Articles*. Henry's aims were not primarily religious, but rather political, however. In contrast to the Lutheran Reformation in Germany, the English Reformation was therefore more an "act of state", "political and pragmatic", and it was "in effect, the price paid by Henry … in order to secure and safeguard his personal authority within England".[116]

In the power struggle which ensued in the English court on Henry's death, Edward Seymour, who had strong Protestant inclinations, came to prominence. Through his influence in the Privy Council, Cranmer was enabled to begin a series of reforms, probably the most important of which was the creation and successive revisions of the *Prayer Book* in 1549 and 1552. Cranmer strengthened his position by enlisting the

---

[114] Thuesen, 32; 2 Kings 22f.
[115] McGrath (2012), 227. Evidence for this group's existence is disputed, John Foxe's *Book of Martyrs* being the principal, perhaps only, source. Nonetheless there is a Blue Plaque near the former site of the White Horse Inn, demolished in 1870, at Cambridge, England, which refers to the group as 'Little Germany'. See <https://en.wikipedia.org/wiki/White_Horse_Tavern>, Cambridge (accessed July 2020).
[116] Ibid., 229f.

help of leading Protestant theologians from European universities, among whom were Peter Martyr at Oxford University and Martin Bucer at Cambridge, and, by publishing the *Forty-Two Articles* in 1553, he provided a strong Protestant resource, re-establishing the central place of the Bible in Christian life and thought. However, Edward VI's death was a set-back for the burgeoning movement as the Catholic Mary Tudor ascended the English throne in 1553, and it was not until Elizabeth succeeded her in 1558 that the Protestant conversion of England could resume. Perhaps the most significant document to be formulated in Elizabeth's reign was the *Thirty-Nine Articles of Religion* in 1563, based largely on the *Forty-Two*, and which was to give the Church of England its distinctive theological identity.[117]

Again, it is important to note that all of this took place well before Dort, and historians[118] debate whether there was an informal Calvinist consensus among the late Tudor and early Stuart church leaders, or whether English Protestantism was by then characteristically an "Anglican moderation on contentious doctrinal questions". However, late in Elizabeth's reign, an anti-Calvinist faction emerged at Cambridge University, which, in an attempt to quell the ensuing unrest, prompted the Archbishop of Canterbury, John Whitgift, to issue the *Lambeth Articles* in 1595. Whitgift's *Articles* anticipated Dort's affirmation of Unconditional Election and the Perseverance of the Saints, but to the archbishop's embarrassment, the Queen refused to make them officially binding. In a letter to Whitgift, her privy counsellor noted that she disliked the parading of disputed points of Predestination, "a matter tender and dangerous to weak and ignorant minds",[119] although she was not well-known for toleration, particularly towards emerging nonconformist separatists who refused to adopt her new 1559 *Book of Common Prayer*.[120] It was in this period of cruel oppression, largely engineered

---

[117] Ibid., 231f.
[118] Thuesen, 40, cites Nicholas Tyacke, *Anti-Calvinists: The Rise of English Arminianism, c. 1590-1640*, rev. ed. (Oxford: Clarendon, Oxford University Press, 1990) and Peter White, *Predestination, Policy and Polemic: Conflict and Consensus in the English Church from the Reformation to the Civil War* (Cambridge: Cambridge University Press, 1992).
[119] Ibid. One might wish to add an exclamation mark here!
[120] The original *Book of Common Prayer* was Cranmer's 1549 edition in Edward VI's

by Whitgift,[121] that the Puritan movement came to the fore with the subsequent emigration of the Pilgrim Fathers to North America in 1620 and the founding of the important Massachusetts Bay Puritan colony a decade later.[122]

It was also during the Tudor monarchy and into the reign of James I, that the English Bible had its origins and underwent its most important evolution. In Henry's reign both Miles Coverdale and John Rogers (aka Thomas Matthew) produced versions of the Bible, both based largely on William Tyndale's monumental translation of the New Testament, first published in 1526, together with parts of his Old Testament.[123] Under the aegis of Thomas Cromwell, Coverdale and others were commissioned to produce the Great Bible in 1539 from which sprang two further versions, the Geneva Bible in 1560 and the Bishop's Bible in 1568. The king, James I, disliked the Geneva Bible and at the 1604 Hampton Court Conference commissioned what became known as the Authorised (or King James) Version of 1611. Officially, this was "Newly Translated out of the Originall Tongues",[124] but was actually a revision of the Bishop's Bible and clearly depended on the work of Tyndale and his disciples.[125]

The Geneva Bible, also claiming descent from the Great Bible, was the work of Calvin, John Knox and a host of expert linguists who had been

---

reign. Cranmer revised it with a Reformed emphasis in 1552 and it was reintroduced by Queen Elizabeth with some amendments the year following Queen Mary's death in 1559. The official *Prayer Book* of the Church of England today is the 1662 version which is based on James I's 1604 edition. See <https://en.wikipedia.org/wiki/Book_of_Common_Prayer> (accessed July 2020).

[121] See Stephen Tomkins *passim*; Wilson, 58f. and *passim*.

[122] Thuesen, 8. This is a common generalisation of the reason for the departure of Separatists from England to the New World. On reflection, many of the emigrants saw their departure from England to the Netherlands and subsequent sailing to the New World as an exodus from the slavery of England to the wilderness experience of Holland and eventual departure for the Promised Land. See Tomkins, *The Promised Land*, chapter 29; Wilson, 198ff.

[123] It is not known how much of the Old Testament Tyndale translated into English. His Pentateuch was published in 1530: Moynahan, 188, and it is known that he worked on the historical books from Joshua to 2 Chronicles as well as Ezra, Nehemiah and Esther and probably some or all of the Psalms: Moynahan, 316. It is assumed that much of his original work on the Old Testament was lost.

[124] Title page of the 1611 edition of the KJV.

[125] See Wilson, Chapter 3, 28-40: 'The Genie Out of the Lamp'.

attracted to Geneva through the influence of Calvin. It was a thorough revision of the Great Bible, based on original texts, and was the first English version to be versified. It was published with maps and accompanying interpretative notes which gave the text a clear Calvinistic gloss.[126] It was the first Bible to be mass-produced for the general public and was hugely popular: most households throughout England possessed a copy, and it is known to have been owned by influential figures of the period – Oliver Cromwell, John Bunyan and John Knox, and was quoted by many authors including John Milton and William Shakespeare. And like Luther's Bible in Germany, it had a "formative impact on the language".[127] It may be, as I shall suggest (below, 55), that the conservative instincts of Bible translators have preserved, perhaps unconsciously, a Reformed bias which may have originated in the Geneva Bible and particularly its notes. Its text is not markedly different from the KJV, but the influence of its notes seems to have been transmitted even to modern versions of the Bible and its interpretation.[128]

A decade after the establishment of the New World Massachusetts Bay colony in 1630, and during the period of the English Civil War (1641-51), the English Parliament convened an assembly of divines to address the Puritans' unfulfilled goal of revising the *Thirty-Nine Articles*. Their campaign began with approaches made to James I, and the eventual result was the *Westminster Confession of Faith* of 1647, which remained in force in England until the Restoration of the monarchy in 1660. Across the Atlantic, the New Englanders adopted it as their doctrinal standard, modifying only its Presbyterian model of church government to accommodate the Congregational polity of the colonial churches. Westminster's theology closely resembled Dort's, and included the five points of TULIP, although expressed differently:

---

[126] For example, John 6:37: "God doeth regenerate his elect, & causeth them to obey the Gospel"; Acts 13:48: "None cā beleve, but they whome God doeth appoint before all beginnings to be saved", etc. Notes in similar vein accompany John 17:6; Ephesians 1:1; 1 Peter 1:1f. and 2 Peter 3:9.
[127] Wilson, 38.
[128] E.g., one particular mistranslation, i.e., the use of 'chosen' in Ephesians 1:11 of the Geneva Bible, where the verb is *klēroō*, has survived into the NIV, but Tyndale and the Great Bible, more accurately, have "made heyres" and the KJV has "obtained an inheritance".

Total depravity found expression in the assertion that fallen humans were "dead in sin," having lost "all ability of will to any spiritual good accompanying salvation." Unconditional election appeared in the statement that God elected persons "out of his mere free grace and love, without any foresight of faith or good works ... or any other thing in the creature." Limited atonement emerged in the insistence that Christ saved none "but the elect only." Irresistible grace was implied by the section on "effectual calling," which described how the elect were unfailingly drawn to Christ. Perseverance of the saints was clear in the declaration that the elect could "neither totally, nor finally, fall away from the state of grace.[129]

However, among the American Puritans this "Dort-Westminster consensus" tended to hide some of their internal debates on the finer points of Predestination, debates which to a large extent recapitulated those which had taken place in Europe, and yet remained unresolved. Thuesen comments on two areas of conflict in particular: the supralapsarian-infralapsarian debate and the relationship between Predestination and Covenant.[130]

The "supra-infra" issue focuses on the supposed point in time when God is supposed to have elected individuals – whether "before or after the Fall in the immemorial sequence of God's logic". The issue was really to defend the unconditional nature of Predestination which the New England ministers, imbued with the scholasticism of William Perkins, sought to defend in the face of the Arminian alternative of Conditional Predestination. The conflict underlined the lack of a single Puritan position on Predestination, and most theologians had to concede that both decrees were simultaneously in God's mind, so, in the end, both supra and infra options were accepted as legitimate Reformed positions. The supralapsarians appealed to Thomas Aquinas and the madness of thinking that human merit could possibly cause election, but the infralapsarians on the other hand, also invoked Aquinas "on how Christ's own merit was no cause or condition of God's electing choice".[131]

---

[129] Thuesen, 48.
[130] Ibid.
[131] Ibid., 49-54.

In contrast to the supra-infra debate, which had to do with the inner workings of God's mind, which Thuesen wryly comments, "was a hard thing to probe at best", the debate about the Covenant focused on the "web of complexity about the human side of the predestinarian equation". As Thuesen points out, the question demonstrates that "the Puritans did not ... banish all unconditionality from their thinking about predestination". It was the old question of how to reconcile God's elective sovereignty with the biblical emphasis on the human response.[132] Much of the argument centred on the Mosaic Covenant, and particularly texts like Deuteronomy 30:19: "I have set before you life and death, blessings and curses. Now choose life", but it was plain that for every statement of unconditionality in scripture, there was a statement of conditionality. So far as the rank and file of New Englanders was concerned, therefore, the issues boiled down to questions about how one could know one was elect and whether the words of preachers could be trusted. The significance of all of this for the present lies in the proliferation of anti-Calvinistic views which abound today in America because many more recent Americans saw a fundamental incompatibility between Predestination and human agency.[133] I judge that the same kind of tension pertains this side of the Atlantic, but it takes the form of an inconsistent Calvinism which preaches Single Predestination rather than either Arminianism pure and simple or the more consistent double predestinatory stance.

Thuesen gives an interesting account in a chapter headed, "From Methodists to Mormons",[134] of the ways in which these debates influenced the emergence of factions in the church of America. Indeed, his whole book, subtitled, "The American Career of a Contentious Doctrine", is written to that end. Thuesen claims that Thomas Paine's *Age of Reason* (1794-5), with its "shrewd use of biblical evidence" was influential in stoking discontent against England's George III and the monarchy in general. Thus,

The mixture of republican ideology with the idea that the Bible (if

---

[132] See Chapters 5, 130, and 6, 161.
[133] Thuesen, 54-7.
[134] Ibid., 100-35.

properly interpreted) was a charter of liberties proved a corrosive acid of predestination in the years surrounding the American Revolution and throughout much of the nineteenth century. In this momentous era of nation building, a variety of upstart religious movements burst onto the scene to fill the void left by the disestablishment of the old state churches. What united these disparate groups was opposition to the monarchial God of Calvinism and confidence that a commonsense reading of scripture would bury the old Puritan specters of unconditional election and reprobation.

Thuesen goes on to describe how the "ferment of the republic's first 100 years" would produce "untold numbers of Methodists, both black and white", with their modern Holiness and Pentecostal successors, but also "a raucous din of deists and freethinkers, Universalists, Stone-Campbell 'Christians,' Adventists", including Jehovah's Witnesses and aberrant doctrines such as Open Theism,[135] Christian Scientists, and Mormons – not to mention the fragmentation of the Baptists into a whole array of competing Southern Baptist Conventions.[136] Perhaps some of Thuesen's detail of this complex account can be challenged, but the overall picture cannot. One of the important features of this American evolution for the present day was the emergence of an aggressive adherence to the principle that every Christian had the right to interpret the Bible as he or she saw fit; ironically, the very objection of the Roman hierarchy against the work of the early Bible translators. That development has blighted the Church, particularly in the West, resulting in utter confusion between Old and New Covenants and the rampant proof-texting evident in much popular theological writing, often manifested as a lack of discrimination between the authorial meaning of biblical texts and what people felt God had said to them personally as they read scripture devotionally, a phenomenon which I believe has also contributed to a general lack of discrimination where the Calvinist-Arminian debate is concerned.

Anglicanism, the predominant Reformed tradition in Britain today, although not on the whole strongly Calvinistic, still officially adheres to the *Articles of Religion* (*The Thirty-Nine Articles*) which contains

---

[135] See Chapter 8c(ii), 237, 'Open Theism'.
[136] Thuesen, 172-208: 'Debating the Doctrine: Presbyterians and Baptists'.

among other things, a clear affirmation of an Augustinian understanding of Original Sin (Article 9), Depravity, in other words, the denial of absolute free will (Article 10), and a Calvinistic statement of Predestination and Election (Article 17).[137] Likewise, the more thoroughgoing *Westminster Confession*, which is widely regarded as a systematic exposition of Calvinistic orthodoxy (some would say "scholastic Calvinism"), is the generally accepted basis of Reformed faith for Presbyterian churches of one kind or another. Among many other things, it affirms that the Pope is the Antichrist and that the Roman Catholic mass, specifically with regard to transubstantiation, is a form of idolatry.[138] Together, these two confessions govern the thinking of the majority of Christians in Britain, perhaps throughout the world, at least in theory, although I judge that many ordinary believers including Anglicans, Presbyterians and Roman Catholics, with their own catechisms, happily worship and serve their Saviour in blissful ignorance of the 'small print' of their guiding documents.

Apparently contrary to what I am saying about the prevalence of Calvinism in Britain, however, the Reformed writer, W. R. Godfrey asserts in an article on *Predestination* that the contemporary evangelical Church is "largely Arminian". He says that it is often "as a result of anti-doctrinal bias rather than careful theological reflection".[139] I assume he was writing from an American perspective,[140] but nonetheless I would dispute his claim because it seems to me that he is interpreting the causes of division in the Church through a set of filters different from mine. I suspect that his view is influenced by a widespread recovery of preaching which genuinely calls for a response of faith, a feature of churches which may be labelled 'moderate Calvinist'; in

---

[137] *The Thirty-Nine Articles* as ratified in 1571 can be found in many places including the 1662 edition of *The Book of Common Prayer*. On ordination all Anglican clergy are required to assent to its content: see 'The Declaration of Assents' in *Common Worship* (London: Church House Publishing, 2000), xi. Horton, 29, claims, "divine election is asserted more directly in the *Thirty-Nine Articles* of the Church of England than in the Heidelberg Catechism".

[138] *The Westminster Confession of Faith* 25:6; 29:2, 6. I agree with the latter, but not the former.

[139] Godfrey in Ferguson & Wright, 530.

[140] Godfrey, at the time of his writing, was Professor of Church History at Westminster Theological Seminary, California.

other words, churches and ministers who actually fudge the issues, but nevertheless consciously sit on the Reformed side of the fence even though they teach Single Predestination. What Godfrey regards as an "anti-doctrinal bias" is more likely to be a general unwillingness to enter into the kind of heated debate which some of our Calvinist brethren might welcome, I would suggest. Indeed, it seems to me that thoroughgoing Arminianism is a very rare phenomenon indeed,[141] at least in Britain, and one of my aims is to show that Christians who adhere to a truly biblical stance can be neither Calvinist nor Arminian. Godfrey's observation may possibly identify, not so much an anti-doctrinal bias, but that the majority of Christians today who do not explicitly espouse a Reformed stance are generally *unclear* about Calvinism and Election in particular. However, despite my doubts about the truth of his claim, there may be more than a grain of truth in what he says about believers in non-Reformed traditions in that there may be a general lack of zeal to examine the detail of their own professed theological positions. The uncertainty which results from that contrasts with the attractive certainty with which Calvinism is often expressed. Nonetheless, there seems to be a general bewilderment among evangelicals insofar that they sense that Calvinism *sounds* right, but it would seem that they don't really know why, nor indeed, why not.

I am aware that much of what I have said so far about the contemporary situation has focused on the situation as I see it in Britain, and I may well be influenced by the church situation in my home city of Cambridge which has a number of thriving Reformed churches. The picture the other side of the Atlantic seems to differ from the British scene, however, as its history would indicate, so it will be worth gaining a more up-to-date American perspective.

The late Clark Pinnock was an Arminian writer whose views have probably been largely ignored by those on the Reformed side of the fence because of his espousal of Open Theism (or Open Theology), a view that God's foreknowledge may not be complete: God does not know

---

[141] By which I mean churches which take as their basis of faith the Five Points of Arminianism, from which the Five Points of Calvinism were derived.

the future but reacts as events unfold.[142] That aside, however, he has edited or co-edited a number of books which offer a distinctively Arminian or Wesleyan point of view to the debate. In *The Grace of God, The Will of Man* he asserts the existence of a "Calvinistic hegemony in evangelicalism",[143] a view I believe to be true, especially in view of the perceived dominance of Reformed views in published material. Contrary to what Peter Lewis has said (above, 40), Pinnock writes,

> A theological shift is underway among evangelicals as well as other Christians away from determinism as regards the rule and salvation of God and in the direction of an orientation more favorable to a dynamic personal relationship between God, the world, and God's human creatures. The trend began, I believe, because of a fresh and faithful reading of the Bible in dialogue with modern culture, which places emphasis on autonomy, temporality, and historical change.[144]

Pinnock's perception seems to contradict that of other authors, but that suggests to me that the situation is complex and may trend in opposite directions either side of the Atlantic. He says that

> Augustinian thinking is losing its hold on present-day Christians. All the evangelists seem to herald the universal salvific will of God without hedging. The believing masses appear to take for granted a belief in human free will. It is hard to find a Calvinist theologian willing to defend Reformed theology, including the views of both Calvin and Luther, in all its rigorous particulars now that Gordon Clark is no longer with us and John Gerstner is retired. Few have the stomach to tolerate Calvinian theology in its logical purity. The laity seem to gravitate happily to Arminians like C. S. Lewis for their intellectual understanding. So I do not think I stand alone. The drift away from theological determinism is definitely on.

> At the same time, however, the Calvinists continue to be major players in the evangelical coalition, even though their dominance has lessened. They pretty well control the teaching of theology in the large evangelical seminaries; they own and operate the largest

---

[142] Klein, 296. See Chapter 8c(ii), 237, 'Open Theism'.
[143] Pinnock in Pinnock, 16.
[144] Ibid., 15.

book-publishing houses;[145] and in large part they manage the inerrancy movement. This means they are strong where it counts – in the area of intellectual leadership and property. Thus one comes to expect evangelical systematic theology to be Reformed as it usually is. The key theological articles in the *Evangelical Dictionary of Theology* (1984) are Calvinian, for example. Although there are many Arminian thinkers in apologetics, missiology, and the practice of ministry, there are only a few evangelical theologians ready to go to bat for non-Augustinian opinions. The Reformed impulse continues to carry great weight in the leadership of the evangelical denominations, though less than it did in the 50s.[146]

Writing some 20 years later, however, Roger Olson notes a resurgence of a New Calvinism, especially among younger Christians, but by no means restricted to the young and by no means restricted to North America. He traces the first evidences of this movement to the last couple of decades of the twentieth century. An article in *Time* magazine (12 May 2009) claimed that it was one of the ten great ideas changing the world "right now", and the previous year (2008) a Christian journalist, Collin Hansen, had published *Young, Restless, Reformed: A Journalist's Journey with the New Calvinists*,[147] the first book-length exploration of the phenomenon, which also provided an apt name for the new movement. Olson[148] helpfully outlines the history of the movement from its roots deep in Protestant history beginning with Calvin through Jonathan Edwards (1703-58), "the American Calvin",[149] who famously defended a version of Calvin's theology against what he saw

---

[145] Grudem (2007), 1231, provides a "master list" of systematic theologies indexed at the end of each of his chapters, and categorises them denominationally - Anglican or Episcopalian (2); Arminian - Wesleyan or Methodist (8); Baptist (7); Dispensational (3); Lutheran (2); Reformed or Presbyterian including Grudem's own (12); Renewal or Charismatic/Pentecostal (1) and Roman Catholic (2). Not all are systematic theologies as such, but all are major wide-ranging theological works. The Reformed category includes Calvin and Jonathan Edwards, both of which predate any in other categories, while the earliest Arminian theology is that of Charles Finney in 1847. Although the number of Reformed theologies is slightly greater than those in the Arminian group, they include the oldest, and Reformed publishing houses, notably The Banner of Truth Trust, have a major interest in republishing older Calvinistic works of all kinds.
[146] Pinnock in Pinnock, 26f.
[147] Collin Hansen (Wheaton, IL: Crossway, 2008).
[148] Olson (2011), 16ff.
[149] Thuesen, 16.

as the creeping rationalism of deism in his own day, and on to the contemporary preacher and writer John Piper (b. 1946).[150] Through his numerous widely-read books, which Olson describes as "unusually reader-friendly and scholarly",[151] Piper has attracted a huge following of 'Young, Restless, Reformed' Christians. His genius has been simply to repackage the Calvinist theology of Jonathan Edwards, the reading of which, in the original, can be quite hard going. According to Olson, Hansen interpreted this New Calvinism as a reaction to a general decline of theology and especially an emphasis on God's glory in contemporary American church life; a reaction against the "feel good theology" of many contemporary evangelical churches. From the 1940s to the 80s Calvinism had struggled to hold on to young people, and from the 1970s the popular and mainly non-Calvinistic Jesus Movement and the charismatic Third Wave introduced many Christian teenagers and university students to an exciting faith in God's absolute sovereignty. Christian young people of that generation were about "getting high on Jesus".[152] Thus, "When they hear the message of Calvinism, they latch onto it as their lifeboat from watery, culturally accommodated spirituality". And "Who can blame them?" says Olson.[153]

He suggests that these contemporary 'young, restless, Reformed' believers were largely unaware of Calvinists before John Piper, and he names a number of influential Reformed writers and preachers who had paved the way for the New Calvinism – specifically, Loraine Boettner, James Montgomery Boice, R. C. Sproul, John F. MacArthur and Michael Horton.[154] But undergirding much of this development, credit must be given to the rediscovery in the 1980s, and perhaps earlier, of Jonathan Edwards as "a profound philosopher and theologian as well as an astute observer of nature and amateur naturalist", a "theological mentor" who for John Piper gave the "fullest account of biblical

---

[150] See Appendix 3, 392, on Piper's *Five Points*.
[151] Olson (2011), 16
[152] Ibid., 19.
[153] Ibid., 17.
[154] Michael Horton's *For Calvinism* is a response and complement to Olson's *Against Calvinism*.

Christianity in the modern world".[155]

It is salutary to recognise the extent to which Reformed exegesis dominates the literature of evangelical Christianity today, to the extent that for the majority it is in effect synonymous with biblical orthodoxy. Pinnock asserts it (above, 52f.) and I have already quoted Peter Lewis (above, 40) to similar effect. Vic Reasoner claims that 80 per cent of the commentaries covering Romans 9 advocate Unconditional Election.[156] That is hardly surprising, especially when popular theological reference books contain statements such as, "The historic Augustinian doctrine of predestination remains biblically and theologically compelling".[157] A Calvinist hegemony may not be so easy to demonstrate simply because to do so would require a grasp of the whole vast literature. Perhaps it is a contentious assertion in any case, especially to minds already steeped in Calvinism, but the literature of conservative evangelicalism, on the whole, does seem to me to contain an underlying unquestioned acceptance of John Calvin's and Augustine's understanding of Election. In other words, most evangelical authors and reference texts tacitly, if not explicitly, support the idea that God chooses individuals for salvation, and some writers make much of the idea that one chosen by God must be dearly loved by God. Furthermore, and this is far more serious, I find a Reformed gloss in most versions of the English Bible, mostly, it is to be hoped, an unconscious tendency on the part of their translators.[158]

Although there seems to be a growing Arminian literature in America,[159] evangelical Christians east of the Atlantic who hold views

---

[155] Olson (2011), 20f.
[156] Reasoner in Pinnock & Wagner, 189; citing F. Leroy Forlines, *Classical Arminianism* (Nashville, TN: Randall House, 2011), 97f.
[157] Godfrey in Ferguson & Wright, 530.
[158] See some of the texts considered below, especially where adjectives or nouns in the specialised vocabulary of the election debate are regularly translated as if they were verbs. Also, for example, the tendency of older versions of the NIV to use the phrase, 'sinful nature' when translating *sarx* (σαρξ: 'flesh', e.g., Romans 7:18 and 25), which appears to reflect an acceptance of the doctrine of original sin in its Augustinian form. Admittedly, however, the most recent 2011 edition of the NIV has reverted to 'flesh' in 20 occurrences of *sarx* in Paul's letters (Romans 7:5; 8:3, etc.) and in 2 Peter 2:10, but has retained 'sinful nature' in Romans 7:18, 25.
[159] See references to Clark Pinnock, Roger Olson and William Klein in particular.

contrary to this apparent Calvinist dominance, for whatever reason, not least the accommodation of so-called Moderate Calvinism, seem not to feel the same kind of urgency to write about their convictions, generally speaking. That may give the unfortunate impression that they are either not so concerned about those views, nor indeed, convinced of their truth. I would like to think that, like Arminius, they wish to avoid unnecessary controversy, although, in view of the dominance of a system of theological thought which I, for one, regard as in error, I think it is high time that more did write in order to create a more balanced literature. I have a private theory that those who feel the need to write or preach on specific issues are often those needing to work out for themselves the truth or otherwise of what they seek to assert. I think many preachers do just that, and I am not immune, of course. Indeed, I may be accused of writing for similar reasons, and perhaps with some justification! But why, I ask, is my perception, also noted by Pinnock, that most systematic theologies are written by Reformed authors? Is it because they have a firmer grasp of the truth? In any case, is it ultimately possible to tie up all the loose ends of the doctrine of God and enshrine it between the covers of large tomes? I think not. But that's precisely what I assume systematic theologies aim to achieve.[160]

It seems to me, then, that the Reformed voice dominates in both academic and popular theology on both sides of the Atlantic, and there does seem to be a tacit acceptance among many evangelical Christians that this brand of theology, with its authoritative ring, its commitment to serious biblical understanding, its upholding of the truth (at least, as understood by those committed to it), and sometimes high-sounding and over-complicated terminology, is the biblically orthodox position of the historical Church. Consequently, many are won over, not so much by careful examination of the biblical evidence, but by the rhetoric of its proponents. Indeed, it is salutary to realise just how easily

---

[160] Stott in Edwards & Stott, 37, says, "God did not choose to reveal himself in systematic form, and all systems are exposed to the same temptation, namely to trim God's revelation to fit our system instead of adapting our system to accommodate his revelation. 'Beware of the systematizers of religion!' wrote Charles Simeon of Cambridge." Also, Simeon, Preface to *Horae Homileticae*: "The Author is no friend of systematizers of Theology".

some Christians are swayed simply by majestic rhetoric and high-sounding words and sometimes by lengthy exegetical sermons, rather than by the weight of their content or argument or, indeed, their biblical accuracy. On the other hand, the preaching of those who remain unconvinced by the Reformed position will inevitably at times seem woolly and uncertain when set against the clarity and closely argued positions of Calvinistic preaching with its apparent certainty and comprehensive logic. Those swayed by the appearance of coherence would do well to ponder upon the ultimate ineffability of the God we serve, and, with Arminius, allow themselves space for a margin of agnosticism in some of the things of God.

Most of the pastors I know are not expert theologians (myself included, of course), and it is not unusual to hear worthy expositors of the sacred text asserting, on the one hand, that Christ died for the sins of the whole world, but, on the other hand, also that God chose (by which I think they mean hand-picked) each one of us individually – that is, the Christians who turned up to hear their sermons. I would say that they are claiming two mutually exclusive things. Whilst not wanting to elevate the capacity of human understanding and logic beyond what may be seemly, that does seem to me to be very confusing teaching, a view which must lead some, at least, into a maze full of dead ends, a confusion which gives rise to the familiar questions raised especially among younger Christian people.

Sadly, there are many Christians who avoid the work of exegesis through sheer laziness. Assertions of hair-splitting and the avoidance of argument about the meanings of words[161] may seem worthy reasons for not engaging at close quarters with the relevant texts, but the proper work of exegesis is not well served by such sentiments. As we seek to understand scripture, we handle texts written in no living person's mother tongue, so the importance of word studies should never be underestimated.

Without doubt, the proclamation of the gospel must go on in obedience to the Great Commission. Often, one may be hard put to differentiate

---

[161] 1 Timothy 6:4; 2 Timothy 2:14.

between the content and presentation of evangelistic sermons delivered either by a Reformed preacher or by the adherent of some other theological persuasion. A certain argument runs that the detail of the theology does not materially affect the proclamation and people are brought to faith either way. That may, indeed, be so, and one is thankful that the gospel is preached for whatever reason,[162] but it seems to me that there is a far more important issue at stake. I have already made the point, but it is worth reiterating, that it is ultimately all about the *kind* of God we believe in and proclaim.

If certain scriptures appear to say that Christ died for the whole world,[163] yet, as Calvinists claim, his sacrificial death was effectual only for the Elect, then we are faced with two possible conclusions - either the Bible is unreliable, or we can afford to ignore some scriptures in favour of others which we regard as of greater importance. If, as evangelicals believe, the ultimate author of all scripture is God, then we can hardly avoid the conclusion that the divine author must then be guilty of deception. "Let God be true, and every human being a liar",[164] certainly, but let our handling of scripture be such that God can never be accused of falsehood. One must willingly accept the risk of accusations of hair-splitting as we examine the Scriptures because ultimately, I believe the whole Calvinist debate hinges upon the character and integrity of the God we worship.

We believe in a God of justice, righteousness and fairness, and we also believe he is a God of love, grace and faithfulness. Somehow, we need to keep all of these aspects of the divine in balance and avoid playing them off against each other. This is precisely what is at stake in this debate, however. John Wesley's view of Predestination was fundamentally at odds with that of John Calvin and Martin Luther, and one of the main reasons why he was so opposed to their doctrine of Predestination was that for him it destroyed any meaningful attribution of love and justice to God. Indeed, Wesley thought their doctrine represented "God

---

[162] Cf. Philippians 1:15-18.
[163] E.g., 1 John 2:2.
[164] Romans 3:4.

as worse than the devil; more false, more cruel, and more unjust".[165] But why would he and many others regard God as unjust if he consigned people, apparently without just cause, to an eternal hell? Simply, because he believed that a God of love would not, indeed, could not act in such a way, and that the whole notion of love would be utterly perverted if he could unconditionally damn some and not others, but for no understandable reason:

> Is not such love as makes your blood run cold? ... Can you think, that the loving, the merciful God, ever dealt thus with any soul which he hath made?[166]

In line with Wesley, Clark Pinnock argues that it is obvious why God would make the "risky decision" to create beings like us. Important values such as love and heroism could only exist if he did so, and there were creatures free to practise them. "Finite freedom is required to have love in the full sense", he writes, finding support in C. S. Lewis:

> Why then did God give them free will? Because free will, though it makes evil possible, is also the only thing that makes possible any love or goodness or joy worth having. A world of automata - of creatures that worked like machines - would hardly be worth creating.[167]

In *The Screwtape Letters*, C. S. Lewis writes,

> the Irresistible and the Indisputable are the two weapons which the very nature of His [God's] scheme forbids Him to use. Merely to over-ride a human will ... would be for Him useless. He cannot ravish. He can only woo.[168]

And in *The Great Divorce* he suggests how God will ultimately respect the free choice with which he has endowed his creatures:

> There are only two kinds of people in the end: those who say to God, "Thy will be done," and those to whom God says, in the end, "Thy will be done." All that are in Hell, choose it. Without that

---

[165] John Wesley, *The Works of John Wesley 1872* (Grand Rapids, MI: Baker, 1979), 7:382, quoted by Jerry Walls in Pinnock, 266.
[166] Ibid., 10:229; Walls in Pinnock, 266.
[167] C. S. Lewis (*Mere Christianity*), 49.
[168] C. S. Lewis, (*Screwtape*), 46.

self-choice there could be no Hell.[169]

Pinnock claims that we must be free to enter into the saving relationship with God which he had planned for us. Perhaps "it was risky for God to take the decision to make a world like ours", but we may only conclude that God thought it was "a risk worth taking in view of the benefits which could accrue. Freedom had to be created if the possibility of a personal covenant between God and creatures was to exist. Nothing less would do."

According to scripture, we have rejected God's will for us and turned away from his plan; strong evidence, claims Pinnock, that God made us truly free. Evidently, we are not puppets on a string because we have pitted our wills against God's, and in deviating from his purpose in creating us, we have set ourselves at cross-purposes to him. We act in ways which disrupt God's will and are destructive of the values he holds dear for us. It is surely not possible to believe that God secretly planned our rebellion against him, says Pinnock, and although we may not be able to thwart his ultimate plan for the world, we can certainly ruin his plan for us personally and, like the scribes of Jesus' day, reject his purpose for ourselves.[170]

We could easily stray into the realms of considering whether God's morality was intrinsic to himself or whether he was obliged to act according to some external standard. But to entertain that would be a fairly unfruitful debate, because nothing exists apart from God and his creative activity. Wesley insisted that there was nothing arbitrary in the moral law, but that that law was totally dependent on God's will. Furthermore, he argued that the moral law was perfectly adapted to creation because it was made by the one who was the source of that morality. In other words, something is right because God wills it to be right, and the possibility that God might declare something right which we perceive to be wrong is ruled out because his nature must be the nature with which he created us. And he *is* loving. Our perception of what is right or wrong must therefore, generally speaking, agree with his own

---

[169] C. S. Lewis (*Great Divorce*), 66f.
[170] Clark Pinnock in Basinger & Basinger, 148f.; cf. Luke 7:30.

perception. Thus, it would not be right for God to damn anyone unconditionally, because it would be clear that he would not then be treating that person in a way which fitted his own nature as a loving God. If *we* know that it would not be right for God to treat anyone in that way, we can be sure that he would never do so. This conclusion differs from that of Calvin and Luther, of course. They taught that whatever God does must be right whether or not it seems right to us, because he is the source of morality. While Wesley agreed that God's will was the ultimate source of right and wrong, he nevertheless was adamant that we cannot appeal to the will of God to justify something which is not consistent with what we know of his character as being just and loving.[171]

Traditionally, the Reformed view of Predestination has been associated with a conception of God's nature which emphasises his absolute power and freedom, and consequently the unknowableness of his will by human reason. On the other hand, theories which emphasise God's love assume a greater understanding of his nature by analogy with human nature and consequently lessen the gulf between him and the world he created. If that is correct, the Reformed position yokes together fundamentally alien conceptions of God, the world and morality. So, the issue is not only what God is like, but also, what we can know about God. It is, in other words, an epistemological issue, and that leaves us with the questions as to whether we can know that God is loving as well as just, and whether our intuitive sense of love and justice is sufficiently reliable for us to have some knowledge of the kinds of things God would or would not do. It should not be doubted that God is both loving and just, so the real question must be whether we have a reliable grasp of the nature of love and justice.[172] For John Wesley, it was unthinkable that God should create us in such a way that our strongest moral feelings could not be trusted, and on that basis we could argue that our moral faculties are part of the remaining image of God in us despite our fallenness, and as such they are a basically reliable reflection of God's love and justice. Wesley's conclusion, and I suggest it must be ours too, is that it is not sinful rebellion to insist that a just and loving God

---

[171] Walls in Pinnock, 267ff.
[172] Ibid., 271.

would not unconditionally damn anyone: it is a sound moral insight.[173] Thus, as I have said already, the whole Calvinist debate must hinge upon the character and integrity of the God we worship.

So, where do we go from here?

I hope to go on to show that, despite its apparent orthodoxy, the Calvinistic version of the biblical doctrine of Election is not the only valid interpretation; indeed, I shall attempt to demonstrate that it is based on a misunderstanding of scripture and is therefore deeply flawed. Nonetheless, my primary aim is not simply to disprove anything but rather to demonstrate that a credible theology of Election can be uncovered from scripture when the Reformed overlay – I think it is more impenetrable than simply a veneer – has been stripped away.

Firstly, in Chapters 3 and 4, I will examine the theological issues which the doctrine of Election throws up, then the nature of the human response to the gospel in Chapters 5 and 6. In Chapter 7, I will attempt to describe the Reformed position in more detail, contrasting it with what might be called an Arminian evangelical position. In Chapter 8, I will examine the biblical vocabulary of Election and apply my findings to the exegesis of some key Election passages, then, in Chapter 9, I will examine what I hope will be a thoroughgoing biblical position. Before summarising, Chapter 10 is devoted to a selection of biblical passages which will not have been addressed directly up to that point, but which are either cited on occasion in support of the Reformed view or which often prove problematical for those who are not convinced by it. Chapter 11 is an attempt to tie up some loose ends, considering individuals whom God did choose, and we end with a general Conclusion. There are three appendices: the first lists the Election vocabulary of the New Testament, the second, a more technical section dealing with the relationships within the vocabulary of choosing in the New Testament, and the third a critique of John Piper's *Five Points* of Calvinism.[174]

---

[173] Ibid., 273f.
[174] A further appendix was initially proposed for this edition on the meaning of Paul's word *huiothesia*, a word variously translated 'adoption', 'adoption to sonship',

A fascinating feature of this debate is that both sides claim to hold an equally high view of the authority of scripture. Indeed, sometimes the same texts are cited in support of opposite views, each side holding tenaciously to its own position. It is important therefore to recognise this common high regard for Holy Writ, and care must be taken not to deny the truth of this phenomenon by accusations of ulterior motivation or exegetical sleight of hand.

It has to be acknowledged frankly that it is notoriously difficult to reflect an opponent's view of doctrine both accurately and charitably.[175] Inevitably, elements of caricature and generalisation, if not error, will intrude and I therefore offer my apology to any reader who might feel affronted by any perceived misrepresentation in what I claim their beliefs to be. A proper examination of these issues therefore calls for a high degree of sensitivity, grace and humility as we seek to discover precisely what God has actually said in his written Word.

'sonship', etc., an aspect of our predestination which will be discussed in passing. However, given the scope of its context - the whole issue of sonship, heirship, inheritance and promise, I decided to devote a new title to the subject, *Pie in the Sky When You Die?* which I hope will be published before very long.

[175] An unfortunate example of misrepresentation is Roy Clements' parody of Arminianism, Pelagianism and Roman Catholicism and what he regards as typical evangelistic preaching in P. Lewis *et al*, 103f., 111f.

Chapter 3

THE ELECTION TERMINOLOGY

We have already noted that there is much common ground between Reformed and Arminian doctrine, but where they appear to differ most markedly is in their respective accounts of Election and Predestination. Even here, however, more is often made of supposed differences than actually exists. For example, Arminianism is often, though wrongly, accused of Pelagianism or Semi-Pelagianism, and therefore of being a religion of salvation by works rather than grace and faith.[1] We shall see, however, that both sides espouse a notion of predestination, although we shall also see that both misuse that term when election in the sense of God choosing individuals for salvation is meant. Both Calvinists and many Arminians believe in the divine selection of individuals for salvation, but each explains it differently.

Another issue often regarded as a major difference between Arminians and Calvinists is whether one can forfeit one's salvation: the issue of Perseverance. Although this aspect of the debate is not central to my purpose in writing, for the sake of completeness it is worth saying something about it once I have described the more important differences concerning Election (see Chapter 4, 70).

Four major theological terms – Foreordination, Foreknowledge, Predestination and Election, are encountered in the study of Election. In Reformed writings they are often used interchangeably, although, strictly speaking, each has its own specific meaning and context.

Foreordination and Foreknowledge

According to Millard Erickson, *Foreordination* is the broadest of the three terms and applies to what Reformed thinkers mean by the Decrees

---

[1] For a comprehensive defence of Arminianism see Olson (2006).

of God.[2] Thus, in answer to the question, "What are the decrees of God?" the *Westminster Shorter Catechism* responds,

> The decrees of God are, his eternal purpose according to the counsel of his will, whereby, for his own glory, he hath foreordained whatsoever comes to pass.

However, *Foreordination* and *Foreknowledge* are often equated in Reformed writings simply because all that happens is believed to be divinely foreordained and what is foreordained is, of course, foreknown.[3]

Predestination

Predestination in Reformed thinking, but incorrectly in my view,[4] applies to God's choice of individuals to be eternally saved (the Elect), and also of those to be eternally damned (the Reprobate). This position, known as Double Predestination, was Calvin's own view,[5] and in particular, of those of his disciples who developed the concept of supralapsarianism, the idea that the very first of God's decrees, even before that of Creation or Fall, was to save some and condemn others.[6] A more moderate view, Single Predestination, although less logically rigorous, holds in essence that God chooses some individuals for eternal life, but as Peter Lewis claims, "if a man is lost it is not because God has predestined him to be lost, but because he has rejected the offered love and salvation of God in Jesus Christ".[7] The compelling conclusion to which Calvin and many others were drawn, however, was that divine choice *for* some individuals must predicate divine choice *against* the rest.

---

[2] Erickson, 908.
[3] See Chapter 8c, 219, 'Foreknowledge' with which Foreordination is often equated.
[4] See Chapter 8b, 217, 'Predestination'.
[5] As noted above, 26f., successive revisions of the *Institutes* reveal significant development in Calvin's thinking on Predestination. The first edition of 1536 pays it little attention, while the 1559 edition devotes four chapters to it: *Institutes*, 3.21-24: Beveridge, 202-58; R. Estep, *Renaissance and Reformation* (Grand Rapids, MI: Eerdmans, 1986), 230. Because of its naturally repulsive conclusion, that it implies divine rejection of those not chosen for salvation, Calvin himself called this doctrine of reprobation, "that Christ died on the cross not for all mankind, but only for the elect...": Chadwick, 95, "dreadful" (*decretum horribile*): *Institutes*, 3.23.7: Beveridge, 3:232; L. Berkhof, 116.
[6] Erickson, 918.
[7] Peter Lewis in P. Lewis *et al*, 42f.

Roger Olson quotes Loraine Boettner, who was "impatient, to say the least, with Calvinists who argue for single predestination": "Mild Calvinism' is synonymous with sickly Calvinism, and sickness, if not cured, is the beginning of the end."[8] Although this so-called 'moderate' Calvinism is the more commonly encountered view today, it is the more logically consistent double-predestinarian stance which must represent authentic Calvinism. For reasons which will become apparent, I regard the 'moderate' stance as inconsistent and therefore untenable. Furthermore, with the appearance of the New Calvinism (see above, 53ff.), it is important that the double predestinatory high Calvinism of TULIP should be the stance with which to engage, whether in its infralapsarian or supralapsarian form. In spite of claims of Calvinists to the contrary,[9] Olson says that it does not much matter which form is examined: both will be found to make God morally ambiguous at best and a moral monster at worst. The less *horribile*, but inconsistent, single-predestinatory solution must also be considered in due course, however, because of its predominance on the Reformed scene.

Election

Finally, in Reformed thinking the term *Election* applies to those who are saved, and Reformed thinkers speak of 'the Elect' as those destined for heaven. It is the positive side of Predestination and is often confused with it. Louis Berkhof, for example, representing a strongly Reformed viewpoint, defines Election as

> that eternal act of God whereby He, in His sovereign good pleasure, and on account of no foreseen merit in them, chooses a certain number of men to be recipients of special grace and of eternal salvation.[10]

---

[8] Olson (2011), 44; L. Boettner, *The Reformed Doctrine of Predestination* (Grand Rapids, MI: Eerdmans, 1948), 105.
[9] Ibid., 61.
[10] L. Berkhof, 114, adduces a number of scriptures which will be considered in due course: Matthew 22:14: "many are invited, but few are chosen"; Romans 11:5: "a remnant chosen by grace"; 1 Corinthians 1:27-28: "God chose the foolish things... the weak things... the lowly things of this world..."; Ephesians 1:4: "he chose us in him before the creation of the world to be holy and blameless in his sight"; 1 Thessalonians

Of particular interest is the basis on which God allegedly chooses those who will inherit eternal life. From the divine standpoint, according to Calvinism, we have no choice in the matter – Unconditional Election. Others, however, are equally clear that from both the human and divine perspectives there is a responsible human decision to be made about the gospel. The doctrine of Unconditional Election, the second of the Five Points of Calvinism, rests firmly on a strong conviction of the sovereignty of God. Like the vineyard owner of Jesus' parable,[11] God is not answerable to anyone for his own decisions or actions, and he may dispose of his own property as he chooses – ownership of individuals being implied by creation. Chapter 9 of Romans is claimed to be a key passage for establishing that point.[12] There Paul asserts that God has the right to treat people as he wills:

> Does not the potter have the right to make out of the same lump of clay some pottery for special purposes and some for common use?[13]

This text refers primarily to individuals from the Old Testament, however; people like the Pharaoh of the Exodus, Jacob or indeed the nation of Israel which descended from him; those God chose or rejected in accordance with his own purposes of election in history, but, I would say, with absolutely no hint or consideration of their individual eternal destinies. Calvinists, on the other hand, hold that God's choice of individuals for eternal salvation[14] is entirely consistent with his choice or rejection of those Old Testament persons or groups. Indeed, Reformed writers often seem to assume that God's choice of men and women in the Old Testament was equivalent to the election of believers in Christ,[15] a mistaken view in my opinion. The Calvinist position further asserts that the basis for election is neither the merit of humankind nor

---

1:4: "we know... that he has chosen you"; 1 Peter 1:2: "chosen according to the foreknowledge of God the Father"; 2 Peter 1:10: "make every effort to confirm your calling and election".

[11] Matthew 20:13-15.
[12] See Chapter 10f, 332, for a fuller discussion.
[13] Romans 9:21.
[14] E.g., Ephesians 1:4f.; John 15:16; 6:37, 44, 65; Acts 13:48, etc.
[15] E.g., Roy Clements in P. Lewis *et al.* 113: "the Jews rejected the Christian message, when surely they were God's elect too." Also, I. H. Marshall (1995), 71; H. H. Rowley, *The Biblical Doctrine of Election*, 1950, 166-73.

divine foresight of what will be, because election is the *cause* of faith, not its result. Thus, since election is efficacious, none of the Elect can slip through the net of salvation and find themselves condemned to eternal separation from God. Election is eternal, unconditional and immutable because it was the decree of God before the worlds were formed.

Arminians also believe that God chooses individuals for salvation, although some who follow Arminius more closely will interpret Election as corporate rather than individual.[16] The basis for the understanding that God chooses individuals is God's *foreknowledge* of how a person will respond to him. Hence, since God knows all things, even what will be in the future, he knows who will respond to the invitation of the gospel, and so he chooses them.[17] It has already been observed that a number of New Testament texts are adduced in common by both sides to support opposing points of view, a case in point being 1 Peter 1:1-2, "chosen according to the foreknowledge of God". The point at issue is what is to be understood by divine Foreknowledge. This text is cited in support of opposite conclusions because Foreknowledge is understood differently either side of the debate. For the Arminian, it is simply prior knowledge of what will occur in the future without any determinative element; a literal or common-sense understanding, I would suggest. For the Calvinist, however, Foreknowledge *can* mean precisely that, but since *knowledge* in scripture is sometimes applied in a personal and intimate way, including euphemistically to sexual intercourse, *fore*knowledge must therefore, it is said, also signify the setting of God's affections upon a person in advance of them coming to faith. Thus, Peter Lewis, quoting John Murray, says,

> Many times in Scripture 'know' has a pregnant meaning beyond that of mere recognition. It is used in a sense practically synonymous with 'love', to set regard upon, to know with peculiar interest,

---

[16] Olson (2011), 67. There seems to be a confusion of categories here: Olson affirms predestination on the basis of God's foreknowledge of faith, but that foreknowledge must be of the response of individuals. It is hard to see how he can affirm corporate election on that basis.

[17] Romans 8:29; 1 Peter 1:1f. This, following Origen: Erickson, 911, was also the view of some of the Reformers, e.g., Luther and Bucer: Wendel, 272. The Arminian issues of Molinism or Middle Knowledge and Open Theology and will be considered in Chapter 8c(i), 232, and (ii), 237, respectively.

THE ELECTION TERMINOLOGY

delight, affection and action (see Gen 18:19; Ps 1:6; Amos 3:2; Mt 7:23; 1 Jn 3:1, etc.). 'Whom he foreknew' means 'whom he set regard upon' or 'whom he knew from eternity with distinguishing affection and delight' and is virtually equivalent to 'whom he foreloved'.[18]

Note the leap from the assertion that "many times" the verb to know applies to personal affection, etc., which is perfectly true, to the bland assumption that Romans 8:29 carries that sense automatically. Consequently, Berkhof, rejecting the Arminian view, says,

> it would seem to be impossible to foreknow events which are entirely dependent on the chance decision of an unprincipled will ... Such events can only be foreknown as bare possibilities.[19]

which seems a very strange statement indeed from such a staunch advocate of God's omniscience, but a taste, I suggest, of the confused thinking sometimes encountered in Reformed writings. We will return to the issue of Foreknowledge and the scope of what God can or cannot know when the semantic evidence is examined in more detail.[20]

*****

Thus, the Arminian, armed with scriptures which assert God's will to be that all should be saved[21] opposes the strict Calvinistic view that some are predestined to eternal life and some not. If the scriptures on which these opposing premises are based were not strictly true, then at least in Arminian eyes God could be deemed to be insincere. On the other hand, for the Calvinist the grace of God is irresistible, although for the Arminian, his grace may be resisted. We are thus left with the question as to the real nature of our response to the gospel – to which we will turn in Chapter 5.

---

[18] John Murray, *The Epistle to the Romans*, New International Commentary on the New Testament (Grand Rapids, MI: Eerdmans, 1967), 317, quoted in P. Lewis *et al*, 56.
[19] L. Berkhof, 107.
[20] See Chapter 8c, 219, 'Foreknowledge'.
[21] E.g., 2 Peter 3:9; 1 Timothy 2:3-4; Acts 17:30f.; Ezekiel 33:11; also universal statements like Isaiah 55:1; Matthew 11:28; John 3:16, etc.

Chapter 4

PERSEVERANCE[1]

The Perseverance of the Saints, the fifth point of Calvinism, is probably the most problematical of all, and whether believers can lose their salvation bothers Christians either side of the Calvinist-Arminian divide. For example, Calvinists firmly believe that their election is predetermined, but they may have to live with uncertainty about whether they are truly chosen or not. Sometimes it is said that such concern is itself evidence of personal salvation,[2] and, although it is sad that a believer might doubt their salvation, their concern could not be that of an unbeliever. On the other hand, for Arminians, many of whom also believe that God chooses individuals, the issue is more about whether they will maintain a life commensurate with their election, and their question is, "Will I persevere to the end?" The Reformed conviction that the true believer will persevere and be preserved to the *parousia* can, of course, be logically construed from the foregoing four points of TULIP, and especially from the belief that elect individuals have been divinely selected for salvation. "If God has chosen me, I cannot fail to persevere because God's purposes cannot be thwarted" – although even that isn't without its problems, the main one being the question as to why God would allow temptation to afflict the believer if his purpose was always to preserve. So, asks Howard Marshall, why, if our perseverance is guaranteed, does God not sanctify the converted sinner at the point of conversion, and why does he allow him or her to continue to sin, although, apparently, never to the point of apostasy?[3] On the other hand, the Arminian position, which holds that God's decision to choose some and not others, depending on his foreknowledge of the decision they will freely make, is believed to rely more on the scriptural evidence.

---

[1] In previous editions of this book Perseverance was included in the chapter on Election Terminology. However, because the topic is a matter of major contention between Calvinism and Arminianism it deserves separate and more extensive treatment.
[2] P. Lewis *et al*, 153.
[3] I. H. Marshall (1995), 262.

However, in Marshall's opinion, both schools of thought have tended to play down the significance of the Bible's teaching on which the other has built its case, and as a result, contemporary evangelicalism has tended to underemphasise final perseverance.[4] Our concern therefore is that justice be done to both aspects of the matter, and it is primarily on the scriptural evidence that this discussion must focus.

Thus, the Reformed stance on Perseverance is fairly cut and dried,[5] enshrined as it is in the TULIP formula, but there is considerable variation within the other camp. It was one of the questions which Arminius himself was never able to resolve to his own satisfaction and on which he apparently remained ambivalent. Despite that ambivalence, however, the *Articles of the Remonstrance*, which represented both his own and the views of his successors, explicitly denied that a Christian could be certain about being 'once saved, always saved', believing that total apostasy was always a possibility, a position that most contemporary Arminians have adopted. According to Olson, Arminius' strongest statement was,

> I should not readily dare to say that true and saving faith may finally and totally fall away.[6]

We have already noted that Bangs finds the fundamental ingredients of Arminius' thinking in his 1602 *Examination of Dr. Perkins' Pamphlet*,[7] a work he regards as the most difficult of all Arminius' output. With regard to eternal security, Arminius' position, as set out in his response to William Perkins, was that believers may fall from true grace and that it was "a possibility that Perkins had not disproved".[8] Based on Matthew 16:18: "I tell you that you are Peter, and on this rock I will build my church, and the gates of Hades will not overcome it", Perkins had

---

[4] Ibid., 15f., an opinion first set forth in 1969 in the first edition of *Kept by the Power of God*, but not my personal experience, brought up as I was among conservative evangelicals of a dispensationalist caste.
[5] See Chapter 2e, 35, and Chapter 4, 70.
[6] Olson (2006), 187; quoting Arminius' 'Examination of Dr. Perkins' Pamphlet': *Works*, 3.454. Olson (2011), 52, citing Arminius, *Works*, 1.667, says that Arminius "declared that he was unable to decide about this doctrine and left it for further study."
[7] Arminius, *Works*, 3.249ff.
[8] Bangs, 221.

said that faith was the 'rock' over which 'hell'[9] would not prevail, and the promise of eternal security was to all who were built on that rock. However, Arminius claimed that Perkins' use of the word 'faith' was equivocal, saying that it was one thing for hell not to prevail against the rock, but it was entirely another for people to fall away from that rock. Perkins also claimed support from three verses in Matthew's Gospel: "And lead us not into temptation, but deliver us from the evil one" (6:13); "Whoever acknowledges me before others, I will also acknowledge before my Father in heaven" (10:32) and "For false messiahs and false prophets will appear and perform great signs and wonders to deceive, if possible, even the elect" (24:24). Arminius retorted that not all believers may ask for protection from temptation, and being deceived was not the same thing as deliberately departing from Christ.

Perkins had objected to the notion that believers could be lost, citing Romans 11:23: "And if they do not persist in unbelief, they will be grafted in, for God is able to graft them in again." Ignoring the context, which is not about unbelieving Christians, but about unbelieving Israel and the possibility of their turning to Christ, Arminius responded that, according to Hebrews 6 and 10, it was possible for believers to be lost, and also for them not to be restored through repentance. Nonetheless, those defecting from Christ would not require a second ingrafting or a second baptism because "baptism, once applied to an individual, is to him a perpetual pledge of grace and salvation, as often as he returns to Christ". Arminius' arguments are difficult to follow, partly because they depend on a number of controversial issues including how the so-called *rigorous* passages from Hebrews[10] should be viewed and how baptism is to be understood.

The point Arminius found the most convincing of all Perkins' claims, however, was that based on 1 John 3:9: "No one who is born of God will continue to sin, because God's seed[11] remains in them; they cannot

---

[9] Older English versions regularly but incorrectly translate 'Hades' as 'hell'. See my forthcoming *Pie in the Sky When You Die?* on the intermediate state between death and resurrection.
[10] Hebrews 6:4-8 and 10:26-31. See below, 100ff.
[11] There is discussion about the precise meaning of *sperma* (σπέρμα), 'seed' in this context. Stott (1964), 129f., provides a useful summary of the various ways in which it

go on sinning, because they have been born of God." While admitting that this was Perkins' most persuasive argument, he said that the strength of it depended on the divine seed remaining in the one born of God. He suggested that the possibility remained that that seed might be lost nonetheless, concluding that a member of Christ can become dead through sloth and sin and thereby cease to be a member of Christ.[12]

What does 'Apostasy' mean?

It is crucially important for this discussion that the term 'apostasy' be understood - whether it implies total loss of eternal life, or whether the one apostatising may finally be saved despite having abandoned their faith in Christ. Howard Marshall describes the pattern of the Christian life as "a continual relationship to God in which His gracious gifts are received by faith". The believer receives the once-for-all free gift of eternal life from God at the moment of conversion, but is "continually faced by temptations which jeopardize his faith". Therefore, he claims, the Christian lives in "a state of tension", growing towards the goal of sinlessness, the process known as sanctification, but facing the "danger of succumbing to temptation through failure to trust in God", a failure which may result in "complete abandonment of faith and surrender to temptation", apostasy, when "the divine life would cease to exist in the man".[13]

In the New Testament, a failure to persist in faith is expressed by words which mean 'falling away', 'drifting' and 'stumbling',[14] and the word

---

was understood from Augustine on, and suggests various meanings, summarising thus: "We shall probably never know for certain precisely what John intended, or his readers understood by *sperma autou*. But whether the implanted and abiding seed is the word of the gospel, or the Holy Spirit, or the divine nature thus imparted (cf. 2 Pet. i. 4), John's meaning is the same, namely that it is the Christian's supernatural birth from God which keeps him from sinning". Another view, offered by Robert Yarbrough, 195, relates to *sperma* meaning 'offspring' or 'progeny', and makes essentially the same point. See also Chapter 9, 267-9, on Galatians 3:16-20, where Wright's (2013) view is considered; also my forthcoming *Pie in the Sky When You Die?* on *huiothesia*.

[12] Bangs, 217ff.
[13] I. H. Marshall (1995), 22.
[14] Marshall cites *piptō* (πίπτω: 'to fall'), e.g., Romans 11:11, 22; 14:4; 1 Corinthians 10:12; 13:8; Hebrews 4:11; Revelation 2:5; *parapiptō* (παραπίπτω: 'to fall away', 'transgress'): Hebrews 6:6; and *parareō* (παραρρέω: 'to drift away'): Hebrews 2:1.

'apostasy', although not found in many English language Bibles as applying to believers,[15] tends to be understood as meaning a clear denial and rejection of Jesus Christ, and hence a total repudiation of the gift of life which he bestows. The word *apostasia* (ἀποστασία) only occurs twice in the New Testament, but does not relate to Christians at all,[16] while the related noun, *apostasion* (ἀποστάσιον) occurs in the three Gospel passages where Jesus mentions a "certificate of divorce", the *apo-* prefix signifying separation.[17] It also occurs four times in the Septuagint with the same meaning.[18]

Although the actual vocabulary of apostasy is not very common, Marshall claims that the ideas themselves are more frequent than might be supposed, nonetheless.[19] What remains unclear, however, is whether apostasy implies the total loss of eternal life for the erstwhile true believer, the reversal of their rebirth and the cessation of the divine life within them, or whether, the gift of eternal life remains the possession of even the most ardent apostate. In other words, does the loss which scripture forecasts for those who may turn away from Christ simply result in a temporal result of their decision; the seed of eternal life, although suppressed, remaining in the erstwhile Christian who is saved ultimately "as through fire"?[20] Apostasy is the action of the one rejecting faith, but the question remains as to whether that necessarily determines God's response.

The root *skandal-* (σκανδαλ-: 'to stumble', 'offend'), is also important.

[15] NET translates *parapiptō* in Hebrews 6:6 as 'apostasy'.

[16] Acts 21:21 is a turning away from Moses and the Mosaic law; 2 Thessalonians 2:3 refers to the rebellion when the man of lawlessness is revealed. In papyrus documents, *apostasia* is used politically of rebels. *Apostasia* occurs four times in LXX: Joshua 22:22 – "rebellion" (NETS) (against God); 2 Chronicles 29:29; Jeremiah 2:19 and 1 Maccabees 2:19 where NETS translates *apostasia* as "apostasy".

[17] Matthew 5:31; 19:7; Mark 10:4. See Thayer, 57f.

[18] LXX Deuteronomy 24:1, 3; Isaiah 50:1; Jeremiah 3:8.

[19] I. H. Marshall (1995), 23. Although the word 'apostasy' does not occur in most English translations, the verb *aphistēmi* (ἀφίστημι) is used of giving up the faith in Luke 8:13: "they fall away"; 1 Timothy 4:1: "abandon the faith" and Hebrews 3:12: "turns away from the living God", and is used of departure from God in the LXX. Marshall distinguishes between the possibilities of a general increase of wickedness and godlessness in the unbelieving world, i.e., 'the final apostasy' in dependence on 2 Thessalonians 2:3 and 1 Timothy 4:1, and the denial of the faith by erstwhile believers.

[20] 1 Corinthians 3:14f.

Anthony Badger suggests that apostasy means merely the loss of one's *inheritance* of or in the kingdom. For many interpreters there is little or no difference between these alternatives, but Badger, in a rather literalistic way, and reading scripture through dispensationalist spectacles, interprets some of the relevant texts in relation to what he calls the 'Bema Seat' judgment of Christ when rewards are dispensed for faithful service in this life.[21] "It is", he says, "an issue of rewards or loss of them which is conditioned upon perseverance, obedience, and continuation in the body of Christian truth".[22] In my view, he mistakenly regards the Christian's heirship and inheritance of the kingdom[23] as those rewards which will be lost when the "carnal" Christian fails to build his or her life on the foundation of Christ.[24] Although there certainly are texts which relate to the loss of rewards, this, I suggest, is a distortion of the Bible's teaching on the meaning of 'sonship' and our 'inheritance' in Christ, which is of far greater importance soteriologically than Badger seems to realise.[25] There is a real difference between the two: on the one hand, our inheritance of the kingdom is really equivalent to our obtaining eternal life - the terminology of inheriting does not imply benefits added to our eternal salvation, but it does enrich the understanding of our hope and carries the promise of attaining the full rights of sonship. On the other hand, the gain or loss of rewards without forfeiture of eternal life is actually the expectation of every believer as our discipleship is assessed by Christ when we "stand before God's judgment seat".[26]

The overriding consideration for me is the recognition that to fall away or apostatise, whether that be the result of severe temptation or deprivation or not, nonetheless describes the action of the erstwhile believer

---

[21] Anthony Badger, 320f. 'Bema Seat', a term often found in dispensational writings, and probably unfamiliar to many. The Greek *bēma* (βῆμα: 'step' or 'tribunal') is found 12 times in the New Testament, and usually means a legal seat of judgment or tribunal, e.g., particularly in this context: Romans 14:10 and 2 Corinthians 5:10. See also my comments on Dispensationalism, 2 n4.
[22] Ibid., 322.
[23] Ibid., and 168, citing 1 Corinthians 6:9; Galatians 5:21; Ephesians 5:5 and James 2:5.
[24] 1 Corinthians 3:10-15.
[25] See Chapter 10e, 324, on Adoption and my forthcoming *Pie in the Sky When You Die?*
[26] Romans 14:10; 2 Corinthians 5:10.

– it is the *human* rejection of the grace of God. Scripture repeatedly warns of the possibility, but, on the other hand, it seems to say very little about how God will respond to our wilful abandonment of faith in Jesus. My own reservations, of course, do not conclusively resolve the question of the meaning or implications of apostasy, given that it is not really a biblical word (at least, not in this context), but I would question whether we can assume that the divine seed of 1 John 3:9 can ever die, even though it may never germinate or grow, let alone produce fruit.

A number of authors have written to support either side of the question, of course. Among them, Robert Shank's *Life in the Son* is a sustained argument against the doctrine of Perseverance. His case really opens with Chapter 4: 'Can Eternal Life be Forfeited?'[27] where he discusses four of Jesus' discourses. The first is Jesus' interpretation of the parable of the Sower in Luke 8:11-15, where Shank questions whether the verb 'believe' (*pisteuō*) refers to saving faith. The wording, "believe and be saved" (verse 12) seems to indicate that it does, so that those who "believe for a while" (verse 13) would appear to have been individuals who had committed their lives to Christ, but had abandoned faith in some way.[28] Marshall supports this conclusion, saying that the first appearance of this verb is the aorist participle, indicting the initial act of faith, while the second is in the present continuous tense, indicating a continuing attitude.[29] Likewise, the word 'retain' or 'keep' (*katechō*) the word of God (verse 15) also suggests the need to persevere in faith for salvation to be guaranteed.

Shank's second passage is the parable of the Unprepared Servant in Luke 12:42-46, where Jesus teaches about the need for watchfulness in

---

[27] Shank (*Life*), 31-48. Although William W. Adams' *Introduction*, xi-xix, makes great claims for the book, it is not an easy-read, partly because Shank's exposition ranges over scriptures and aspects of the subject which do not immediately appear obviously related, and some of his argumentation relies on somewhat dogmatic repetition veering towards *verbalsmog* – a word he coins in his *Elect in the Son*, 113, with respect to Calvin's writings. His case is further confused by a statement towards the end of the book, 312 n2, where he offers the comment that he uses the term 'apostasy' as a "comprehensive term embracing any departure from God and saving grace, whether deliberate or casual." He would therefore apparently categorise the commission of serious sin as apostasy.
[28] Shank (*Life*), 32f.
[29] I. H. Marshall (1978), 325.

the face of the master's delayed return – clearly an eschatological scenario. Shank reasonably interprets the scene as one of service in the Kingdom, and whether that service is faithful or not.[30] Although the punishment of dismembering the unfaithful and unwatchful servant (verse 46) – "He will cut him to pieces", might seem extremely harsh, he is nevertheless assigned "a place with the unbelievers", a punishment which, again, suggests a loss of salvation.

The third of Jesus' discourses is the parable of the Unmerciful Servant in Matthew 18:21-35, his response to Peter's question about the number of times he should forgive another who had sinned against him (verse 21). Shank maintains that God's forgiveness is conditional, the teaching being that God will forgive us if we "forgive our brother or sister from the heart" (verse 35).[31] In this case, however, it seems more difficult to relate the punishment of the unmerciful servant – the impossible situation of imprisonment and torture until he had paid back all he owed - to the foregoing example where the subject of the parable was assigned a place among unbelievers. There is an obvious link with the Lord's Prayer, however, and specifically Jesus' words following the prayer itself:

> For if you forgive other people when they sin against you, your heavenly Father will also forgive you. But if you do not forgive others their sins, your Father will not forgive your sins.[32]

Morris comments, "to fail to forgive others is to demonstrate that one has not felt the saving touch of God",[33] while Carson relates God's unwillingness to forgive as relating to the effectiveness of one's prayers.[34] Neither seems to consider it to be indicative of a loss of salvation, however, and, more generally, there seems to be some reluctance among commentators to make the equation and spell out the consequences in salvation terms.

The fourth of Shanks' examples is the True Vine discourse of John

---

[30] Shank (*Life*), 34f.
[31] Ibid., 39.
[32] Matthew 6:14f.
[33] Morris, 149.
[34] Carson (1995), 175.

15:1-6. His opening comment on this passage asserts that it contains "some of the most solemn and intimate words ever uttered by our Saviour concerning the nature of the relation between Himself and all who would be His.... These words ... contain a cardinal axiom of the Christian life – indeed, the foundation principle governing the relation of Christ and the individual".[35] Whereas Jesus was concerned about his disciples bearing fruit, their fruitfulness depending on the degree to which they abided in him, Shank interprets the casting away of unfruitful branches as the divine response to apostasy, and, on his reckoning, their loss of salvation. He attacks what he regards as a typical Reformed response, that those whom Jesus would throw away to be burned were not truly his to the extent that we might engage new-birth terminology. However, he quotes Alexander MacLaren as saying that "separation is withering"; "withering means destruction", and "If we would avoid the fire, let us see to it that we are in the Vine."[36]

This section of John's Gospel is fraught with difficulties. There seem to be two main interpretative options: firstly, that Jesus as the vine represents the true or renewed Israel. This option is reinforced by its clear allusion to imagery from Ezekiel 15:1-8. Carson suggests, however, that, although that thought may have been in John's mind, his primary thought would have been that the fruitless branches represented apostate Christians. The major difficulty with this latter option is that John had affirmed already in his Gospel that true disciples are preserved to the end, and that there is no way that those incorporated in the vine could be other than genuine disciples.[37] I would suggest (contra Shank) that the best way to interpret Jesus' warning, would be to take it as just that – a warning, using his characteristic hyperbole, rather than a prediction of a loss of salvation.

---

[35] Shank (*Life*), 40f.
[36] Alexander MacLaren, *Expositions of Holy Scripture: St. John*, Vol 2 (New York: George H. Doran Company, 1910), 15-17; Shank (*Life*), 44-7.
[37] Carson (1991), 511-5, citing John 6:37-40 and 10:28: see my comments on these texts, 290ff.

Howard Marshall's Kept by the Power of God

Another author who has made a case against Perseverance is the late Howard Marshall.[38] His *Kept by the Power of God* is a survey through each of the categories and authorial groupings of the Bible, especially of the New Testament, in an attempt to discover how their various writers understood the nature of Election; whether the Elect could be assured of heaven come what may, or whether a measure of uncertainty might be attached to it all.

He begins by examining the meaning of *eklektoi*, 'the elect',[39] claiming that in the Old Testament the word indicates those chosen by God for salvation and those regarded as God's servants. "It is one of the many titles applied to the people of God and indicates that their existence as His people, their reception of His salvation, and their enrollment in His service all rest upon His prior choice of them."[40] I would seriously question the idea that Old Testament *eklektoi* were chosen for salvation, however, and certainly not in the sense normally conveyed in the New Testament with eschatological implications.[41] Israel, as a nation (although not individual Israelites), was chosen by God, not so much for eternal salvation, but rather for 'salvation' in a broad *temporal* sense (i.e., for preservation and prosperity, and as a witness to the nations) as they took possession and occupied the Land promised to Abraham and his 'seed', an aspect which is clearly spelled out throughout the book of Deuteronomy,[42] and which, admittedly, may justifiably be interpreted as a territorial type of eternal glory.[43] That blessedness in the Land was wholly dependent on the people's fealty to the Covenant, however, so that their eventual failure resulted in temporary expulsion and exile. A remnant did nevertheless return to Palestine so that the

---

[38] It was a serious oversight that in previous editions of this book I failed to take account of Marshall's *Kept by the Power of God*, an important biblical survey with regard to the Perseverance of the Saints.
[39] See Chapter 8a(iii), 208, on *eklektos*.
[40] I. H. Marshall (1995), 71.
[41] See Chapter 11, 352, 'Whom Then has God Really Chosen?'.
[42] E.g., Deuteronomy 4:40; 5:16, 33, etc.
[43] For Brendan Byrne's tracing of the development of 'the promise' concept through Jewish writings, see my forthcoming *Pie in the Sky When You Die?*

promise to Abraham, that the Land would be his and the possession of his 'seed' in perpetuity, might be fulfilled.[44]

It must be stressed that divine choosing was never of individuals except where the choice was to appoint to some specific task, and that without any sense of preferment for salvation in eschatological terms. There are, of course, many individuals of true faith in the pages of the Hebrew Scriptures, saints whose eternal salvation can be assumed with a high degree of certainty irrespectively of the provisions of the Law of Moses and the Covenant, but because their faith in Yahweh was relational and real, and not simply a matter of ritual observance.[45] I would suggest that they were men and women who enjoyed a personal relationship with Yahweh, despite not having the continual indwelling of the Holy Spirit which is the experience of latter-day saints under the New Covenant. Therein is somewhat of an enigma, but I would suggest that those Old Testament saints may be exemplified by those Jewish contemporaries of Jesus who readily espoused the faith of the gospel and who were said in John's Gospel to already belong to God - those given to Jesus by the Father.[46] Nonetheless, Marshall does qualify that divine election by saying that God's choice was "not independent of the willingness of the individual to receive it, nor is its nature such that a man cannot renounce it", with which I agree, but he then incorrectly, in my view, extended the principle to the Church – "After a detailed study H. H. Rowley concludes that for the Church, as the heir of Israel's election, her election is conditional upon her desire to retain it."[47] I find that conclusion an unwarranted inference, but Marshall seems to run with it and apparently allows it to influence his decision as to the conditionality or otherwise of election throughout the New Testament.

Marshall notes that *eklektoi*, as a title for the people of God, underwent

---

[44] Genesis 12:7; 13:15; 15:18-20. Note the promise was to Abraham and his "seed": see Chapter 9b, 267-9, for discussion on Galatians 3:16-20.

[45] Cf. the many expressions of personal devotion especially in the Psalms. I was struck recently by the comparison between the kings Saul and David found in 1 Chronicles 13:3 - words of David: "Let us bring the ark of our God back to us, for we did not enquire of it (or 'him') during the reign of Saul."

[46] John 6:39; 17:6, 9, 24; 18:9. See Chapter 10b(iii), 308.

[47] H. H. Rowley, *The Biblical Doctrine of Election* (London: Lutterworth Press, 1950), 166-73.

some development in the intertestamental period, especially as seen in 1 Enoch and the Dead Sea Scrolls and especially in sectarian and apocalyptic circles. That, he suggests, may have been the route by which it entered the Gospels where, chronologically, it is first encountered as referring to believers in Mark's Gospel and in the parallel passages in Matthew.[48] Nonetheless, he feels that the Gospels do not really help us understand the implications of what it is to be chosen.[49] Furthermore, there may even be a sense in Luke 18:7-8 of the elect succumbing in the face of persecution:

> And will not God bring about justice for his chosen ones, who cry out to him day and night? Will he keep putting them off? I tell you, he will see that they get justice, and quickly. However, when the Son of Man comes, will he find faith on the earth?

Will any of the Elect remain at the *parousia*? So, concludes Marshall, "It is not, therefore, the faithfulness of God in answering prayer which is doubtful but the perseverance of disciples in continuing to pray". Consequently, these verses may indicate the possibility of apostasy by the Elect,[50] and if that be so, then the possibility of apostasy may also be found in Mark 13:22:

> For false messiahs and false prophets will appear and perform signs and wonders to deceive, *if possible*, even the elect.

Whether that is the case will depend on the meaning assigned to "deceive" or "lead astray" (RSV) in this verse. According to Marshall, this Greek construction[51] in the New Testament indicates purpose or a contemplated result, and nowhere is it used to indicate an actual result.[52] Thus, it is the result *intended* by the false christs and prophets, but we are not told whether they would succeed in their deceptive purpose.[53] However, the phrase "if possible" might be taken either as expressing

---

[48] Mark 13:20, 22, 27; Matthew 24:22, 24, 31; also Matthew 22:14; Luke 18:7.
[49] I. H. Marshall (1995), 71.
[50] Ibid., 72; G. Schrenk in *TDNT*, IV, 188.
[51] I.e., *Pros* followed by the articular infinitive: *pros to apoplanan* (πρὸς τὸ ἀποπλανᾶν).
[52] Except perhaps Matthew 5:28: "anyone who looks at a woman lustfully" translates πᾶς ὁ βλέπων γυναῖκα πρὸς τὸ ἐπιθυμῆσαι αὐτήν, where πρὸς τὸ ἐπιθυμῆσαι means "with a view to desire": Alfred Marshall, 16.
[53] Ibid., although the parallel in Matthew 24:24 has *hōste planēsai* (ὥστε πλανῆσαι) which expresses no more than an expected result.

the thought in the mind of the deceivers: "Let us lead them astray if we can", or possibly Jesus' own thought: "They will try to lead the elect astray, if such a thing is possible". Marshall suggests that the words are most naturally taken as an unfulfilled condition, so the possibility of apostasy is not then implied. Nonetheless, as he surveys the New Testament writings, he comes to the conclusion that apostasy of the Elect cannot be ruled out, even though the form of expression in these Gospel texts suggests it to be at least a remote possibility.[54] Notwithstanding that, he notes the significance of the saying immediately following: "So be on your guard",[55] which does suggest that the elect have some responsibility for resisting their falling away.

When he comes to Paul, Marshall identifies three texts which he suggests might cast doubt on absolute certainty where the believer's perseverance is concerned. They are 2 Timothy 2:12, 1:12 and Philippians 3:10-11.

a. 2 Timothy 2:12

2 Timothy 2:12 is often quoted as an assurance of our perseverance:

> If we died with him, we will also live with him;
> if we endure, we will also reign with him.
> If we disown him, he will also disown us;
> if we are faithless, he remains faithful,
> for he cannot disown himself.[56]

This forms part of one of five so-called 'faithful sayings' found in the Pastoral Epistles.[57] It may have been a well-known verse or part of a hymn current in the first-century Ephesian church. In the preceding verses, where Paul had been writing about the power of the gospel and his sufferings for its sake, saying that he endured them for the sake of the Elect so that "they too may obtain the salvation that is in Christ Jesus, with eternal glory",[58] it seems that the mention of 'endurance' in

---

[54] Thus Matthew 24:24 adds *kai*: "*even* the elect".
[55] I. H. Marshall (1995), 72f.; Mark 13:23.
[56] 2 Timothy 2:11b-13.
[57] The other four sayings are 1 Timothy 1:15; 3:1; 4:9f. and Titus 3:5-8a.
[58] This verse is often construed as referring to "those who are elect but do not yet believe;

2:10 led him to include the saying of verse 12 to encourage Timothy to emulate his own endurance.

The first two lines, which are synonymously parallel, speak of our death to sin at conversion and baptism, the two of which coincide in New Testament conversion accounts. They also speak of the continual need to endure if we are to share in Christ's heavenly glory. The third line then presents an antithesis echoing the warning of Jesus to his disciples about the danger of denying him presumably under persecution,[59] for he will 'deny' those who 'deny' him. The fourth line contrasts with that, because, even if we lack faith, as opposed to disbelieving,[60] he nevertheless remains faithful both to himself and to us, suggesting, among other things that we can turn back to him and discover his unchanging attitude to us. The saying might therefore be said to be a word of "consolation for a frightened conscience":

> the faithfulness of Christ does not preclude the possibility of His disciples being faithless, but it simultaneously indicates His readiness to help those whose faith is weak. The possibility of denial of Christ is admitted, but it is emphasized that Christ continues to care for His disciples and is ready to welcome them back to fellowship if they will respond to His call.[61]

Whereas all five 'faithful sayings' are encouragements about aspects of salvation, this one seems to add the caveat that salvation requires perseverance, and so, although it is a call to endurance, and apparently suggests the possibility of a falling away, it nevertheless allows for temporary unfaithfulness. [62] The possibility of *disowning* Christ is

---

e.g., Guthrie (1957), 144, but Paul is more probably referring to the quality of salvation – "with eternal glory", which believers will one day "experience": Mounce, 514.

[59] Matthew 10:33 and Luke 12:9 use the same verb, *arneomai* (ἀρνέομαι: 'to deny'). The meaning of *arneomai* is flexible, and may not therefore signify a total dissociation or abandonment of the subject of the verb. Of the 33 New Testament occurrences, most (14) refer to contradiction of things spoken, and others (18) concern the disowning of persons or beliefs. One instance, Luke 9:23, refers to denial of oneself!

[60] Marshall claims that although *apisteō* (ἀπιστέω) usually means 'to disbelieve' or 'to refuse to believe', here it means 'to be faithless', 'to be unfaithful' or 'to lack faith'. *BAGD* supports this; cf. Romans 3:3.

[61] I. H. Marshall (1995), 132f., quoting J. Jeremias, *Die Pastoralbriefe*, NTD (Göttingen, 1953⁶), 48f. The view of some that God's faithfulness makes it impossible for him to acknowledge those who deny him seems unlikely.

[62] Mounce, 48f.

interpreted by William Mounce as apostasy, while he regards *faithlessness* as a position short of that, rather like Peter's denial of Jesus, a position from which he did recover.[63] The passage therefore seems to differentiate between outright rejection of Christ, on the one hand, and what we might regard as wounds of conflict, which have driven the believer to a loss of faith or even to agnosticism.

Taken at face value, then, it is a difficult saying, but it probably seems best to regard it as an encouragement for the believer to persevere and endure, and to trust in the utter faithfulness of God, a faithfulness bound up in his essential being against which he cannot act in opposition. The prospect of eternal loss in the face of apostasy therefore seems real, but we can rely on God's faithfulness to sustain us through the ups and downs of our lives, and in that sense, the threat remains remote for those who seek to endure.

b. 2 Timothy 1:12

Marshall's second text which might cast doubt on absolute certainty where perseverance is concerned is 2 Timothy 1:12:

> That is why I am suffering as I am. Yet this is no cause for shame, because I know whom I have believed, and am convinced that he is able to guard what I have entrusted to him until that day.

He suggests that the probable point here, where, in effect, Paul says he is not ashamed of the gospel and will not deny his apostolic calling, is that God knows those who are truly his, and although they have not been predestined to a salvation from which they cannot fall away, they nevertheless are assured of God's gracious care of them as they put their trust in him.

However, this NIV reading represents the tendency of previous generations of scholarship to understand *parathēkē* (παραθήκη: 'deposit') in terms of what may be deposited with God,[64] and many see it as the promise of God's faithfulness in his ability to bring the believer through

---

[63] Ibid., 519; Matthew 26:69-75; John 21:15-19.
[64] I. H. Marshall (1995), 134.

to glory. In other words, Paul knows the one in whom he has placed his trust and is convinced that he is able to preserve his "deposit" until the day of judgement,[65] a demonstration of his unshakeable confidence in God's faithfulness. However, the phrase, "what I have entrusted to him" is ambiguous. It translates *tēn parathēkēn mou* (τὴν παραθήκην μου), which means "my deposit". *Parathēkē* occurs twice elsewhere in the Timothy letters (although nowhere else in the New Testament) where Timothy is urged to "guard what has been entrusted to [his] care" and to "Guard the good deposit that was entrusted to [him]".[66] Contrary to the NIV, but in line with its usage elsewhere, Mounce says that the 'deposit' is usually understood as something entrusted *by* God, and which he can safeguard - Paul's apostolic ministry or the Christian message, perhaps.[67] The view that Paul's 'deposit' was something he entrusted to God – his faith for salvation, perhaps too his life, his apostolic ministry, or his converts, etc., would make the verse a contender for supporting Perseverance. But the point is moot, and evangelical scholars take sides on the issue, although, for what it is worth, my view is that Mounce is probably correct. In line with the way *parathēkē* is used elsewhere, and significantly in 1:14, the 'deposit' Paul had in mind was probably the gospel commission and message, the same divine 'deposit' vouchsafed to Timothy - which he also should guard:

> Guard the good deposit that was entrusted to you—guard it with the help of the Holy Spirit who lives in us.[68]

Whichever rendering should prove to be correct, however, these verses do express Paul's great confidence in God to preserve both the gospel and its preachers, but the uncertainty over the interpretation of *paratheke* tends to neutralise them as heart-warming assurances of salvation.

What also can be said, though, is that even Paul himself was not exempt from the need to strive to persevere. Elsewhere, he describes his

---

[65] Ibid.; cf. Psalms 31:5; Luke 23:46; Acts 7:59 and 1 Peter 4:19.
[66] 1 Timothy 6:20; 2 Timothy 1:14. In all three cases, it is the *parathēkē* that is to be guarded.
[67] Mounce, 487f.
[68] 2 Timothy 1:14.

Christian experience as a good fight and a race to be run, aspects of the ways he preserved his allegiance to God so that he could look forward with confidence to receiving his "crown of righteousness", the fulness of being in glory with Christ. He therefore enjoins similar efforts upon Timothy,[69] and in similar vein in 1 Corinthians 9:24-27:

> Do you not know that in a race all the runners run, but only one gets the prize? Run in such a way as to get the prize. Everyone who competes in the games goes into strict training. They do it to get a crown that will not last; but we do it to get a crown that will last for ever. Therefore I do not run like someone running aimlessly; I do not fight like a boxer beating the air. No, I strike a blow to my body and make it my slave so that after I have preached to others, I myself will not be disqualified for the prize.

Here, Paul likens his apostolic and evangelistic work to running a race, saying in effect that, if God's servants wish to please their master, they must run with determination to get the prize. It is not enough simply to enter the race: if they are to win the victor's wreath, an athlete must also submit to a strict training regime and complete the course. Similarly, all who enter for the Christian 'race' must be self-disciplined so that they might win, not a biodegradable wreath which was awarded to athletes in the Greek games, but an incorruptible, lasting crown. And Paul expands the simile – he writes of running for the mark, boxing in order to hit his opponent, keeping his body fit by pummelling it; and in it all his goal is to avoid failing to pass the test and so be disqualified after having preached to others.

Unlike the crown for which Paul was striving in the verses previously noted, the crown here does seem to be a reward for faithful service.[70] Nonetheless, the meaning of being "disqualified" is not so clear.[71] If it is about failing to win the crown for faithful service, the question of loss of salvation does not arise, of course, and we can therefore link the

---

[69] I. H. Marshall (1995), 135; 2 Timothy 4:7f.: "the crown of righteousness" is "eternal life" as opposed to any kind of reward, because it will be awarded to *all* who have longed for Christ's appearing; 1 Timothy 4:10; 6:12, 19.

[70] 1 Thessalonians 2:19; Philippians 4:1; 1 Peter 5:4. In 2 Timothy 4:8; James 1:12; Revelation 2:10; 3:11 the crown is salvation.

[71] I. H. Marshall (1995), 120.

idea with the passage referred to above about the so-called 'Bema' judgments of Christ where we shall enter heaven having had our works tested by the fire of judgment, with or without any reward.[72] Some, in theory at least, will enter heaven 'by the skin of their teeth', while others will bear rich rewards. On the other hand, it might refer to a fear, which Paul himself might have had, that he should be disqualified from salvation even though he had been the instrument of bringing the news of salvation to others. Marshall points out that in 1 Corinthians 9:25 the thought of the race and its prize begins to give way to the general concept of the Christian's self-discipline, a shift which then links with the following section in chapter 10 where Paul goes on to discuss the fate of those who fail to keep their bodily passions under control and who sin in the same way as the Israelites who perished in the wilderness after having escaped from Egypt.[73] Nonetheless, there is the promise that God will not permit temptation to overcome the believer - another powerful evidence of God's faithfulness in seeking to preserve his children, a provision for endurance and perseverance which must nonetheless be actively grasped and pursued by the one being tempted.[74]

Marshall suggests therefore that in 1 Corinthians 9:27, Paul raises the possibility of his own rejection on the day of judgement owing to his failure to pass the test. That failure would not be due to poor Christian service, but to not resisting the temptations of the body. It seems that Paul felt no such temptation,[75] however, and it would seem that his overwhelming feeling was not so much of confidence in his own salvation,[76] but was rather to do with the perseverance of some of his converts at Corinth, a concern he expresses in 2 Corinthians 13:5-7:

> Examine yourselves to see whether you are in the faith; test yourselves. Do you not realise that Christ Jesus is in you—unless, of course, you fail the test? And I trust that you will discover that we have not failed the test. Now we pray to God that you will not do anything wrong—not so that people will see that we have stood the

---

[72] 1 Corinthians 3:10-17.
[73] I. H. Marshall (1995), 121; 1 Corinthians 10:1-10.
[74] 1 Corinthians 10:13.
[75] Marshall cites 1 Corinthians 7:7, where Paul had discussed sexual temptations.
[76] Ibid.

test but so that you will do what is right even though we may seem to have failed.

The phrase "unless ... you fail the test" (13:5) is telling because it might suggest that, if that be the case, then Christ was not in them. Although Paul was defending his own standing in Christ in the Corinthian correspondence, his concern here was that the believers there should not depend on his standing (whatever they might think of him), but rather on their own willingness to seek to persevere. It was therefore *their* Christian lives which were under examination, so, was Paul challenging them to examine themselves about the reality of their own Christian faith?[77] That doesn't seem to be the precise situation that Paul envisaged, however, and it seems certain that he was writing to people whom he did regard as being in Christ, but who had fallen into sin and had yet to repent; believers whom he would discipline when he had opportunity to visit them.[78]

So, concludes Marshall, Paul did not regard grace as a mechanism for carrying believers to perfection without any effort on their part. And, while he anticipated the final perseverance of the vast majority of his converts, he never regarded that perseverance as predetermined or inevitable. His care of all the churches involved him in constant prayer and labour lest any should fall away, an outcome that would be the cause of him having run his course in vain, perhaps. At the same time, writes Marshall, "the believer who commits himself to the grace of God must rightly beware lest he fall away", although "he can at the same time rest assured that nothing can separate him from the love of God and can rejoice in the hope of final salvation".[79]

c. Philippians 3:10-11

A third Pauline text which Marshall considers as possibly suggesting a failure to persevere and which might lead to loss of salvation is Philippians 3:10-11:

---

[77] Ibid., 121f.
[78] Ibid., 122; 2 Corinthians 12:19.
[79] Ibid., 125.

I want to know Christ—yes, to know the power of his resurrection and participation in his sufferings, becoming like him in his death, and so, *somehow*, attaining to the resurrection from the dead.[80]

It is the word "somehow" or "if possible" (RSV) in verse 11 that gives rise to the idea that the believer's participation in the resurrection to life[81] might depend on their success in persevering. Marshall claims that the construction used (*ei pōs* with the subjunctive) might cast doubt on the attainment of the desired result, and it must be acknowledged that the context of the section, Philippians 3:7-11, does have a provisional feel about it. Paul seems to be saying that in order to "gain Christ and be found in him" (3:8f.), he should have counted as loss all the things he previously had regarded as gains, but the tone of these verses might suggest some doubt as to how successful he had been in doing so. Elsewhere, however, he does look forward with confidence to believers attaining precisely that end, and earlier in the same letter[82] he had expressed complete certainty about his own union with Christ after death.

Marshall doubts the suggestion of E. Lohmeyer that Philippians was an exhortation to martyrdom by one who himself was standing on the brink of martyrdom, and that therefore martyrdom was the interpretative key to the letter. He says that, in any case, Paul could not have been absolutely certain of attaining martyrdom, and so could not be sure that he would attain the special resurrection which was the supposed prerogative of the martyr,[83] but he does suggest that the real key to understanding Philippians 3:11 is the expression, to "be found in him [Christ]" (3:9), an expression, which he says, "is surely eschatological", and words which must agree in meaning with those which follow in verses 10 and 11. He suggests that Paul could not have known how his earthly life would end when he wrote Philippians, and, in any case, he

---

[80] Philippians 3:10f.: Greek: τοῦ γνῶναι αὐτὸν καὶ τὴν δύναμιν τῆς ἀναστάσεως αὐτοῦ καὶ [τὴν] κοινωνίαν [τῶν] παθημάτων αὐτοῦ, συμμορφιζόμενος τῷ θανάτῳ αὐτοῦ, εἴ πως καταντήσω εἰς τὴν ἐξανάστασιν τὴν ἐκ νεκρῶν.
[81] Acts 24:15; Romans 6:5; 1 Corinthians 6:14; 15 passim; Revelation 20:5f.
[82] Philippians 1:23.
[83] I. H. Marshall (1995), 119; E. Lohmeyer, *Die Briefe an die Philipper, Kolosser und an Philemon*, KEK (Göttingen, 1959), 141.

would not have regarded his martyrdom as inevitable.[84] Furthermore, so far as we know, he did not die soon after writing Philippians. If he had doubts, they were not about his destiny but rather about his route to it. Marshall therefore concludes that since Paul was certain about his own perseverance, the passage cannot express doubts about it.[85]

In addition to these three texts, Marshall draws attention to other New Testament verses from Paul and others which have a bearing on Perseverance. For example, when discussing the process implied by the *Golden Chain* of Romans 8:29-30:[86]

> For those God foreknew he also predestined to be conformed to the image of his Son, that he might be the firstborn among many brothers and sisters. And those he predestined, he also called; those he called, he also justified; those he justified, he also glorified.

he argues that continuation of that process requires a human response. "Justification in Paul", he says, "is always by faith, so that the completion of the whole chain of blessings is dependent upon faith", and future glorification[87] depends on the believer's readiness to suffer. Quoting John Wesley, he writes,

> St. Paul ... does not deny that a believer may fall away and be cut off between his special calling and his glorification, Romans 11:22. Neither does he deny that many are called who are never justified. He only affirms that this is the method whereby God leads us step by step towards Heaven.[88]

Perhaps unsurprisingly, most of Marshall's evidence derives from Paul's letters, but he also draws attention to verses from elsewhere, particularly from the so-called Catholic Epistles:

---

[84] Philippians 1:24f.; 2:24. That clarity would come later when writing 2 Timothy 4:6.
[85] I. H. Marshall (1995), 120.
[86] See Chapter 8d, 238, 'Calling'.
[87] Romans 8:17.
[88] I. H. Marshall (1995), 103, quoting John Wesley, *Explanatory Notes on the New Testament*, 1754. Romans 11:22: "Consider therefore the kindness and sternness of God: sternness to those who fell, but kindness to you, provided that you continue in his kindness. Otherwise, you also will be cut off."

d. James 5:19-20

> My brothers and sisters, if one of you should wander from the truth and someone should bring that person back, remember this: whoever turns a sinner from the error of their way will save them from death and cover over a multitude of sins.

James was clearly addressing Christian believers whom he calls "brothers".[89] If one of their number falls into error, he or she may be restored through the ministry of others, but James says that restoration saves them from death. Marshall suggests on that showing, that the backslider would be in danger, not merely of the penalty of physical death, but of eternal condemnation.[90] Furthermore, he asserts, "If a backslider does not confess his sin and repent, he becomes a witting sinner and is in danger of loss of salvation".[91] However, in view of the fate of Ananias and Sapphira in Acts 5, and mention of those who had "fallen asleep" through abuse of the communion meal in 1 Corinthians 11:30, I suggest that we cannot be certain of what kind of 'death' is meant by James and other writers. However, recalling Paul's criticism of the Corinthian church in 1 Corinthians 11, we may note what he says about judgment there:

> For those who eat and drink without discerning the body of Christ eat and drink judgment on themselves. That is why many among you are weak and ill, and a number of you have fallen asleep. But if we were more discerning with regard to ourselves, we would not come under such judgment. Nevertheless, when we are judged in this way by the Lord, we are being disciplined so that we will not be finally condemned with the world.[92]

Apparently, Paul regarded even the judgment of 'falling asleep' as a form of discipline – harsh, nonetheless. Although chastisement was always meant to be both educational and remedial, the stated aim of the discipline in both James and Paul was to avoid the condemnation that

---

[89] Tasker, 142: a 'brother' is obviously a "converted Christian".
[90] Douglas Moo, 195, says that in James, death refers to eschatological punishment. He cites 1:21 for comparison, but the relevance of that verse is not clear.
[91] I. H. Marshall (1995), 160.
[92] 1 Corinthians 11:29-32.

the world would receive, suggesting that those chastised and who rejected the remedy of repentance would, with non-believers, also suffer the loss of eternal life.

e. Jude 22-23

> Be merciful to those who doubt; save others by snatching them from the fire; to others show mercy, mixed with fear—hating even the clothing stained by corrupted flesh.[93]

There are at least three different Greek readings of Jude 22,[94] which possibly sprang from different understandings of *diakrinomenous* (διακρίνομένους), "those who doubt".[95] According to *BAGD*, the verb *diakrivō* (διακρίνω) in its active forms has the basic meaning of 'to separate' or 'arrange', hence, 'to differentiate' or 'judge', while in the middle voice, 'to take issue', hence, 'to doubt'. While *BAGD* assigns this latter meaning to *diakrinomenous* here, others translate the participle as "those who are under judgment". The verb also occurs in Jude 9, to which *BAGD* assigns the meaning 'to dispute' - the archangel Michael disputing with the Devil about the body of Moses. Marshall, with J. N. Birdsall, however, favours the 'judgment' option, understanding the fire from which they may be snatched to be the fire of the final judgment. In support of this, 'fire' also occurs in Jude 7b:

> In a similar way, Sodom and Gomorrah and the surrounding towns gave themselves up to sexual immorality and perversion. They serve as an example of those who suffer the punishment of eternal fire.

where, clearly, the 'fire' is the final judgment. Thus, Marshall favours Jude 22-23 as evidence that apostasy leading to eternal loss is part of Jude's theological understanding.

---

[93] Jude 22f.
[94] I. H. Marshall (1995), 164f., summarises the three basic variations.
[95] Ibid., 165, citing J. N. Birdsall, 'The Text of Jude in P72', JTS, n.s. XIV, 1963, 394-9. See also Green, 187, who, contra Birdsall's evidence from P[72], argues for the longer tripartite expression as reflected in the RV and RSV.

f. 2 Peter 2:20

There is a clear relationship between 2 Peter and Jude,[96] not least in that both letters deal with false teachers and their ultimate destinies, men who had insinuated themselves into their respective church fellowships.[97] Marshall observes that the similarity of the way they are described in each letter suggests that Peter was dealing with the same kind of heretics, although his description of them is not quite so precise as Jude's. Jude's wording may suggest that they were not believers in Jesus, but Peter, possibly writing about a different group of false teachers, says that they had denied "the sovereign Lord who bought them", that their denial had brought "swift destruction on themselves" and that they had "left the straight way and wandered off to follow the way of Balaam", all forms of expression which suggest that they were lapsed believers.[98] Peter makes their connection with the truth even more explicit:

> If they have escaped the corruption of the world by knowing our Lord and Saviour Jesus Christ and are again entangled in it and are overcome, they are worse off at the end than they were at the beginning.[99]

If they were lapsed believers, then, clearly, they were subject to judgment, which is described in various ways: "destruction", "they ... will perish" and "blackest darkness is reserved for them".[100] So, Michael Green observes, "There can be little doubt that the false teachers had once been orthodox Christians".[101]

Marshall makes a concluding observation on 2 Peter:

> For Peter a Christian is one who has been called and elected by God; he has been redeemed by Christ, obtained faith, and been granted

---

[96] Fifteen of the 25 verses of Jude also appear in whole or part in 2 Peter, and they share many ideas, words and phrases in common.
[97] Jude 4.
[98] I. H. Marshall (1995), 168f.; 2 Peter 2:1, 15. The mention of Balaam raises the interesting question of his precise relationship with Yahweh. He is said to address God by name and to have received divine visitations: Numbers 22-24; especially 22:8f., etc.
[99] 2 Peter 2:20.
[100] 2 Peter 2:2, 12, 17.
[101] Green, 118.

the power and the promises of God so that he may live a righteous life characterized by the Christian virtues (2 Peter 1:1-11; 2:1). Thus he grows in the knowledge and grace of Christ, and looks forward to being found unspotted at the *parousia* (2 Peter 3:14, 18). Through divine grace the Christian progresses in holiness.

But this progress is not automatic. The believer must make his calling and election sure so that he may at last enter into the eternal kingdom of Christ (2 Peter 1:10f.). Election does not offer absolute assurance of salvation, for perseverance is also necessary: 'a glorious entry into the eternal kingdom is granted only to Christians who have successfully exerted themselves to live a faultless life.'[102] Lack of perseverance cannot be interpreted to mean that a man was never truly converted, since the description in 2 Peter 1:1-11 is plainly of Christians; nor can it be alleged that Peter teaches salvation by works, since the works are in fact the evidence of divine grace. Through such perseverance a Christian will never stumble, i.e. 'fall into deadly sin.' Yet such stumbling is not impossible, and there is much point in Peter's final warning against being led astray (2 Peter 3:17).[103]

*****

This is the basic conclusion Marshall reaches throughout his examination of the New Testament witness, including the *rigorous* passages of Hebrews,[104] where he expresses a view which also represents his general conclusions:

> The view which has commended itself to us is the so-called 'saved and lost' theory. On this view a Christian may be saved and then lost through deliberate apostasy.[105]

Furthermore, he says:

> the New Testament refers in an admittedly small number of cases to Christians falling into apostasy. There are passages which speak prophetically of the love of many growing cold and of men departing from the faith, and there are other passages where men who once believed are said to have fallen into sin and apostasy.... we have

---

[102] H. Windisch & H. Preisker, *Die katholischen Briefe*, HNT (Tübingen, 1951³), 87.
[103] I. H. Marshall (1995), 170f.
[104] Ibid., 137-57. See below, 100ff.
[105] Ibid., 145.

seen that the possibility of genuine Christians falling into apostasy is not to be explained away.[106]

While there is naturally some uncertainty about the interpretation of some of these passages, at the very least they show that the possibility that the apostasy of genuine Christians is predicted and described cannot be ignored or dismissed.[107] Nevertheless, he fails to find an unequivocal biblical statement to that effect. What is more, throughout his whole exegesis of the relevant texts, many of his conclusions seem to have a provisional quality about them, and typically he pursues his argument by asking the question, "If the conclusion reached ... is a sound one", and the like.[108]

So far as I can recall, I have always believed in the Perseverance of the Saints, although I would have called the doctrine 'assurance of salvation'. Perhaps the Reformed hegemony I allege has predisposed me to do so, and that reinforced by songs such as Daniel W. Whittle's (1840-1901) *I know not why God's wondrous grace*, with its refrain based on a common interpretation of 2 Timothy 1:12, which we have just considered:

> But I know whom I have believèd;
> And am persuaded that He is able
> To keep that which I've committed
> Unto Him against that day.

But, as I review the scriptural evidence once again, I confess that I am unwilling to draw quite the same conclusions as Marshall, and find myself aligned, not so much with traditional Arminianism, but more or less with Arminius himself and his uncertainty, which seems to me to spring from his honesty in interpreting scripture and his refusal to be forced into a dogmatic conclusion when scripture seems to be unclear. I likewise have to admit to a certain degree of agnosticism over the matter

---

[106] Ibid., 198, 257 n8. Marshall cites as the most important of these passages Matthew 24:10-12; Mark 13:22; Luke 8:13; 12:10; Acts 20:29f.; 1 Corinthians 5:3-5; 11:30-32; Galatians 5:4; 6:13 [*sic*, 6:8 perhaps]; Philippians 3:18f.; 1 Timothy 1:19f.; 4:1; 6:10; 2 Timothy 2:26; 4:10; 2 Peter 2:18ff.; 1 John 5:16; Jude 22f.; Revelation 3:2, some of which were discussed above.
[107] Ibid., 257 n8.
[108] E.g., Ibid., 53, 82, etc.

therefore.

That said, however, some New Testament texts do appear to assure me that I am safe once I have trusted Christ for salvation – favourites being, for example, John 10:14:

> I am the good shepherd; I know my sheep and my sheep know me...

and the verses following:

> My sheep listen to my voice; I know them, and they follow me. I give them eternal life, and they shall never perish; no one will snatch them out of my hand. My Father, who has given them to me, is greater than all; no one can snatch them out of my Father's hand. I and the Father are one.[109]

Likewise, the opening verses of Colossians 3:

> Since, then, you have been raised with Christ, set your hearts on things above, where Christ is, seated at the right hand of God. Set your minds on things above, not on earthly things. For you died, and your life is now hidden with Christ in God. When Christ, who is your life, appears, then you also will appear with him in glory.[110]

Although immediately following these words, I am exhorted to put to death the things which belong to my earthly nature.[111] I am impressed by the feeling of apparent irreversibility of that of which Paul wrote, and I would link this text with the end of Romans 8, where he asks, "Who shall separate us from the love of Christ?", answering his own question with the strong affirmation that, in effect, *nothing* "will be able to separate us from the love of God that is in Christ Jesus our Lord."[112]

Furthermore, I find comfort in the logic of the presumed irreversibility of the concept of new birth: can one born from above be unborn?[113] Robert Shank challenges this idea, however. He says that although

---

[109] John 10:27-30.
[110] Colossians 3:1-4.
[111] Colossians 3:5.
[112] Romans 8:35-9.
[113] John 3:3, 7; 1 Peter 1:23. John uses the expression *gennēthē anōthen* (γεννηθῇ ἄνωθεν), while Peter uses *anagegennēmenoi* (ἀναγεγεννημένοι). Other references to spiritual rebirth are John 1:13; 3:5, 6, 8; James 1:18; 1 Peter 1:3; 1 John 2:29; 3:9 (twice); 4:7; 5:1, 4, 18 (twice).

there is an analogy between physical and spiritual birth, it is "a popular and serious error" to assume an equation between the two. His argument may be summarised as follows. Firstly, he claims that physical birth marks the beginning of life "*in toto*", whereas spiritual birth only marks the transfer from "one mode of life to another". He seems to ignore the fact that "*in toto*" doesn't include the beginning of our spiritual regeneration, however. Secondly, we have no prior knowledge of, and can give no consent to our physical birth, whereas, he says, we must have prior knowledge in order to consent to our rebirth. He then points out that biological birth produces life which is independent of an individual's parents, while spiritual birth confers dependent life: we begin to participate in the life of Christ, "who is our life".[114] Undoubtedly, there are significant differences, but that is the nature of life from above. There cannot be an exact comparison, but I am strongly drawn, nonetheless, to the irreversibility of both kinds of birth.

In similar vein, to cross over from death to life and to receive the seal of the Holy Spirit – God's mark of ownership, would seem to be irreversible features of what it is to become a child of God.[115] But all this does leave the question of where those now stand who sadly have turned away from the faith, some of whom may be beloved friends. I *might* be persuaded that they were never truly born again and were never regenerate in the first place; that they were never really indwelt by the Holy Spirit even though to all appearances they were, and we believed them to be regenerate by the fruit they once bore.[116] That thought inevitably gives rise to all sorts of emotions, but thankfully, I am not called upon to judge them because "the Lord knows those who are his",[117] and if they are to be won back, I can only pray for them, live consistently as a persevering believer and bear witness to them.

A typical Reformed view is that God works concurrently with us. As Greg Haslam puts it,

> The Scriptures demonstrate that God's work runs concurrently with

---

[114] Shank (*Life*), 89-91, citing Colossians 3:4.
[115] John 5:24; Ephesians 1:13.
[116] Matthew 7:16, 20.
[117] 2 Timothy 2:19.

ours. They do not give any credit to us, but show that the grace of God elicits some activity from us and in us, as he preserves and keeps us. Put at its simplest, he preserves and we persevere. We persevere because he preserves.[118]

Haslam is careful to point out that this apparent synergy is not equal as though we do half the work and God does the rest:

> God does it all; when we get to glory it will be one hundred percent due to God. We persevere only because he preserves us, but that is why it is also one hundred percent us. The decisions we make, the resistance we offer to temptation, the way we walk with God – our perseverance rests one hundred percent on those, as they rest one hundred percent on him.[119]

We may pile up scripture references which would seem to indicate an apparent irreversibility of regeneration and eternal security of those who have sincerely trusted in Christ, but in addition to some of those we have considered above, we must also take account of texts, admittedly fewer in number, which seem to indicate some conditionality to that security. For example, from Paul:

> Consider therefore the kindness and sternness of God: sternness to those who fell, but kindness to you, *provided that* you continue in his kindness. *Otherwise*, you also will be cut off.[120]

> By this gospel you are saved, *if* you hold firmly to the word I preached to you. *Otherwise*, you have believed in vain.[121]

> But now he has reconciled you by Christ's physical body through death to present you holy in his sight, without blemish and free from accusation—*if* you continue in your faith, established and firm, and

---

[118] In P. Lewis *et al*, 135, citing Jude 21, 24; Revelation 3:10; Philippians 2:12.

[119] Ibid., 136, citing Philippians 1:6; 1 Corinthians 1:8; 1 Thessalonians 5:23f.; Hebrews 13:5. A somewhat strange logic: I suggest 'synergy' might be a better form of expression.

[120] Romans 11:22. The verses immediately following were taken by William Perkins to demonstrate the eternal security of believers (above, 72) – illustrating the folly of ignoring context. The context, of course, is Paul's concern for ethnic Israel, and the possibility that, although unbelieving, Jews may yet be regrafted into their own olive stock: those who "do not persist in unbelief" are therefore Jews, not backsliding Christians.

[121] 1 Corinthians 15:2.

do not move from the hope held out in the gospel.[122]

if we endure, we will also reign with him. *If* we disown him, he will also disown us.[123]

Jesus taught in similar vein:

> Whoever acknowledges me before others, I will also acknowledge before my Father in heaven. But whoever disowns me before others, I will disown before my Father in heaven.[124]

And the parallel, but extended, passage in Luke's Gospel:

> I tell you, whoever publicly acknowledges me before others, the Son of Man will also acknowledge before the angels of God. But whoever disowns me before others will be disowned before the angels of God. And everyone who speaks a word against the Son of Man will be forgiven, but anyone who blasphemes against the Holy Spirit will not be forgiven.[125]

It is not at all easy, indeed, it may not be possible to reconcile all the texts we have considered so far in trying to resolve the apparent contradiction that scripture seems to witness both for and against Perseverance. On the face of it, these quotations seem to say that my security in Christ is conditional upon me holding firmly to the word, continuing in my faith and not disowning Christ. The most commonly encountered explanations of such apparent denials of Perseverance present at least two alternatives. One suggests that the idea of losing one's salvation is nothing more than a warning against half-heartedness or a lukewarm commitment and service. Thus, John Stott commenting on Romans 11:22, says,

> Not that those who truly belong to him will ever be rejected, but that continuance or perseverance is the hallmark of God's authentic children.[126]

Likewise, Revelation's letters to the seven churches of Asia,[127] for

---

[122] Colossians 1:22f.
[123] 2 Timothy 2:12. See also above, 82-4.
[124] Matthew 10:32f.
[125] Luke 12:8-10.
[126] Stott (1994), 301, also citing Hebrews 3:14; 1 John 2:19.
[127] Revelation 2 and 3.

example, do not threaten forfeiture of salvation, but they do urge those churches to persevere and receive rewards for so doing – as, indeed, does the whole of the book of Revelation. So, the message is not so much that of dire consequences following a cooling of spiritual ardour, but the loss of rewards.

The second approach differentiates between that kind of backsliding, on the one hand, and apostasy, on the other. In other words, one's faith and commitment may wane for any number of reasons – the cares of this world, opposition, persecution, the feeling that prayer has not been answered, the inability to find answers to intellectual objections to faith, and so on, as in the Parable of the Sower perhaps,[128] but apostasy, is the deliberate, conscious turning away and deliberate denial of one's former trust and commitment to Christ. Many would recognise within themselves a need which answers to the human desire for self-determination, and just as we may feel the need to be permitted to exercise free will in receiving Christ, there might also be an argument for the possibility of rejecting him further down the line. In other words, does our release into freedom in Christ remove our ability to reconsider and then deny our commitment to him?[129] That is the sort of dilemma which certain passages from Hebrews apparently throw up, and so Hebrews becomes the battleground of debate over the issue.

The Rigorous Passages of Hebrews and 2 Peter

Three New Testament passages in particular create exegetical problems for those who deny the possibility of apostasy: two from Hebrews and one from 2 Peter:

> It is impossible for those who have once been enlightened, who have tasted the heavenly gift, who have shared in the Holy Spirit, who have tasted the goodness of the word of God and the powers of the coming age and who have fallen away, to be brought back to repentance. To their loss they are crucifying the Son of God all over again and subjecting him to public disgrace. Land that drinks in the

---

[128] Matthew 13:3-8, 18-23 and parallels.
[129] Traditional demonology suggests a similar expression of free will in Lucifer's fall and rebellion.

rain often falling on it and that produces a crop useful to those for whom it is farmed receives the blessing of God. But land that produces thorns and thistles is worthless and is in danger of being cursed. In the end it will be burned.[130]

If we deliberately keep on sinning after we have received the knowledge of the truth, no sacrifice for sins is left, but only a fearful expectation of judgment and of raging fire that will consume the enemies of God. Anyone who rejected the law of Moses died without mercy on the testimony of two or three witnesses. How much more severely do you think someone deserves to be punished who has trampled the Son of God underfoot, who has treated as an unholy thing the blood of the covenant that sanctified them, and who has insulted the Spirit of grace? For we know him who said, 'It is mine to avenge; I will repay,' and again, 'The Lord will judge his people.' It is a dreadful thing to fall into the hands of the living God.[131]

If they have escaped the corruption of the world by knowing our Lord and Saviour Jesus Christ and are again entangled in it and are overcome, they are worse off at the end than they were at the beginning. It would have been better for them not to have known the way of righteousness, than to have known it and then to turn their backs on the sacred command that was passed on to them. Of them the proverbs are true: 'A dog returns to its vomit,' and, 'A sow that is washed returns to her wallowing in the mud.'[132]

Taken at face value, these texts appear to teach the possibility of apostasy, a deliberate falling away of those who have truly placed their faith in Jesus; those who have known the indwelling of the Holy Spirit and have experienced the blessings of the Kingdom. As already noted, many expositors and preachers attempt to explain this by saying that those in view were never truly born again, and that is the standard Reformed stance. Admittedly, there are a number of scriptures which appear to support such a view; Jesus' Sermon on the Mount teaching about false disciples or the 'sheep and goats' passage of Matthew 25,[133] for example. I have no doubt, however, that Hebrews was written to

---

[130] Hebrews 6:4-8.
[131] Hebrews 10:26-31.
[132] 2 Peter 2:20-2.
[133] Matthew 7:21-3; 25:31-46.

THE PREDESTINATION PROBLEM

genuine Christian believers, and it is of crucial importance to determine whether that is indeed so, because whether or not the possibility of apostasy and eternal loss can be inferred from the letter hangs on that issue. The recipients of Hebrews were addressed as "holy brothers", sharers in the "heavenly calling"[134] and sharers in Christ; they formed part of the household of God, although Hebrews adds the caveat, "if indeed we hold firmly to our confidence and the hope in which we glory", suggesting that their continuing membership of God's household was conditional upon their perseverance.[135]

Marshall asserts that the vast majority of scholars accept that they were true believers, but writers of what he calls "the Calvinistic school", such as John Owen (1616-83),[136] hold that they were not. That is, as I have said, the standard Reformed response: since those to whom Hebrews was written had fallen, or could fall away, clearly, they were not of the Elect, since God had predetermined the eternal security of true believers. However, Marshall claims that careful study of the descriptions provided in Hebrews 6:4-6a (quoted above), the very verses upon which Owen based his assessment of the spiritual state of the recipients of the letter, as it happens, conclusively supports the view that genuine Christian experience is what was being described in Hebrews. Incidentally, Marshall describes the recipients of the letter as "lapsed", but in context they seem not to have reached the point of falling away, even though they may have seriously considered doing so (see below).

There is a fair amount of commentary on the verses from Hebrews 6, reflecting a variety of interpretations. Westcott, for example, discusses the correlation of the four participles - "enlightened" (*phōtisthentas*: φωτισθέντας) and "tasted" (*geusamenous*: γευσαμένους) (6:4); "becoming" (*genēthentas*: γενηθέντας) (i.e., "becoming sharers"), and the

---

[134] See Chapter 8d, 238, on 'Calling'.
[135] Hebrews 3:1, 6, 14.
[136] Marshall focuses on John Owen as an exemplar of the Reformed view: John Owen, *The Nature and Causes of Apostasy from the Gospel*, in William H. Goold, ed., *The Works of John Owen D. D*, Vol. 7 (New York: Carter & Bros., 1852), 2-261, which is really a critique of the Roman Catholic Church of the 16th century. See also David N. Samuel, *Apostasy*, <https://cofec.org/resources/essays-and-articles/apostasy-from-the-writings-of-john-owen/> (accessed August 2021), a blog of the Church of England (Continuing) which summarises Owen's work on apostasy.

repeated "tasted" (6:5), saying that the relationships between them are not clear. He also observes that the conjunctions in the Greek are not decisive, offering the view that "The choice between the three constructions [which he had already discussed] will be decided by individual feeling as to the symmetry of expression and thought". He suggests that there are two basic statements: firstly, with regard to divine action: the Christian has been illuminated by "consciousness of the reception of the gift of life" and by "participation in the power of a wider life", and secondly, with regard to individual experience; the believer has tasted the "beauty ... of revelation" and "the spiritual powers of the new order".[137]

Engaging directly with Owen, Marshall makes four points on these participles. Firstly (a), he says, the 'lapsed' had "once been enlightened" (6:4). The verb, *phōtidzō* (φωτίζω) must refer to the light of the gospel received in Christian instruction,[138] but it can also be used to describe the experience of conversion and was later used of baptism in fact. However, the use of "once" (*hapax*: ἅπαξ), would be strange if the reference were merely to the reception of a course of instruction, and it seems more probable that the actual acceptance of such teaching is what was meant.[139]

Secondly (b), Marshall observes that the 'lapsed' had also "tasted the heavenly gift" (6:4). The verb 'to taste', *geuomai* (γεύομαι) sometimes has the nuance of savouring a small sample of food or drink, as in ordinary English usage,[140] and is so understood here by Calvin and Owen.

---

[137] Westcott (1889), 147. Guthrie (1983), 141, on the other hand, suggests, "The last three [participles] are apparently intended to make clear the sense in which the first [i.e., "enlightened"] is used".
[138] As in Hebrews 10:32; John 1:9; Ephesians 1:18, etc.
[139] I. H. Marshall (1995), 142. *Phōtidzō* also occurs in Hebrews 10:32: "Remember those earlier days after you had received the light", referring to those knew that they "had better and lasting possessions" (Hebrews 10:34). Marshall and Owen point out that 'enlightened' was later used of baptism; see Bruce (1990), 145 n39, and Ellingworth, 320, who observe that the Syriac Peshitta uses *phōtidzō* as a reference to baptism both here and in Hebrews 10:32; also Justin Martyr, *First Apology* 61:12f.; 65:1, uses the verb and its related noun, *phōtismos*, to describe baptism, and in such a way as to show that it was in current usage among his Christian acquaintances. Westcott (1889), 146, translates, "those who were once *for all* enlightened" (my italics).
[140] And as in Matthew 27:34.

However, it is an Old Testament usage,[141] and Marshall claims that recent scholars agree that the idea is that of experiencing the flavour of what is eaten, the amount consumed not being at issue.[142] Thus, when Christ is said to have tasted death,[143] there is no suggestion that he experienced anything less than its full bitterness and actually died.[144] Hebrew's point therefore is that those to whom he was writing had genuinely experienced conversion and were regenerate. Exactly what is meant by "the heavenly gift" is uncertain, however, but in view of the reference immediately following to the Holy Spirit, Marshall thinks it unlikely that it is only the Holy Spirit,[145] and that it most probably means "the whole gift of salvation" including the reception of the indwelling Holy Spirit.[146]

Furthermore (c), it is said of the 'lapsed' that they "have shared in the Holy Spirit" (6:4). Marshall points out that nowhere in the New Testament is an experience of the Spirit, such as is described here, attributed to anyone who was not a Christian. With respect to 'sharers' or 'partakers' (RSV) (*metochoi*: μέτοχοι), Guthrie argues that the same sense must be meant as in Hebrews 3:1, where those "who share in the heavenly calling" are powerfully and remarkably addressed in a way that clearly affirms their regenerate state, and especially so when one considers the way the concept of God's call is applied throughout the New Testament.[147] He says that "The idea of sharing the Holy Spirit is remarkable" and that it "at once distinguishes the person from one who has no more than a nodding acquaintance with Christianity".[148] Some have argued that the absence of the definite article[149] suggests that the

---

[141] Guthrie (1983), 141, e.g., Psalms 34:8: "Taste and see that the LORD is good", also 1 Peter 2:3.
[142] E.g., J. Behm in *TDNT*, I, 675-7.
[143] Hebrews 2:9, also Matthew 16:28; 9:1; Luke 9:27; John 8:52, etc.
[144] Although David Samuel, op. cit., generally agrees with Owen, on this point he agrees with Marshall.
[145] Although Ellingworth, 320, thinks otherwise.
[146] Guthrie (1983), 142; I. H. Marshall (1995), 142. Hewitt, 107, suggests that Christ himself is meant; the one who came down from heaven; cf. John 3:13, 31f.; 4:32, 35.
[147] Hebrews 3:1: "holy brothers and sisters, who share in the heavenly calling": Greek: ἀδελφοὶ ἅγιοι, κλήσεως ἐπουρανίου μέτοχοι. See Chapter 8d, 238, on 'Calling'.
[148] Guthrie (1983), 142.
[149] Greek: μετόχους γενηθέντας πνεύματος ἁγίου.

personal Holy Spirit is not meant, but Bruce says that that is not sufficient to indicate whether it is the giver or his gifts that are in view.[150] On the other hand, Bruce refers to Simon Magus from Acts 8, who apparently understood the Christian message, was baptised and had hands laid upon him, but, according to Peter, remained "full of bitterness and captive to sin".[151] In later patristic writers, there is evidence, the accuracy of which, it has to be said, is far from certain, that some decades later Simon Magus, the magician and possible Gnostic, became a determined opponent of Christianity,[152] and Bruce asks in what sense "a man like that could have partaken of the Holy Spirit". Nonetheless, it can be said of the Simon of Acts 8 that he had "tasted the goodness of the word of God and the powers of the coming age" through observing the miracles of Philip,[153] if in no other way. So far as John Owen's account of Hebrews 6:4 is concerned, all that he could conclude was that "the Holy Ghost is present with many as unto powerful operations with whom he is not present as to gracious habitations; or, many are made partakers of him in his spiritual gifts who are never made partakers of him in his saving graces, Matthew 7:22, 23".[154] David Samuel, in support of Owen says, "since the Holy Spirit pervades Gospel ordinances, to that degree they have been partakers of the Holy Spirit, but not in the full sense".[155] Although this Reformed view seems less to be based on exegesis of the passage, and more on the logic of TULIP, it does not seem that the arguments either way can be conclusive, and it cannot be ruled out that those who prophesied and cast out demons in Jesus' name in Matthew 7 may have done so by the power of deceiving demons, and not by the genuine power of the Holy Spirit.

Finally (d), Marshall points out that the 'lapsed' had "tasted the goodness of the word of God and the powers of the coming age" (6:5). Here the direct object of the verb 'to taste' is in the accusative case, although

---

[150] Bruce (1990), 146.
[151] Ibid., 147; Acts 8:23.
[152] See, for example, <https://en.wikipedia.org/wiki/Simon_Magus> (accessed August 2021).
[153] Bruce (1990), 147; Acts 8:13.
[154] John Owen, op. cit. (above, 102 n136), 26.
[155] David Samuel, op. cit.

in the preceding verse it was followed by a genitive direct object.[156] Although admitting that Greek grammar is not always strictly adhered to in the New Testament, C. F. D. Moule holds that that accusative direct object of the verb is "virtually a substantival clause" giving the meaning "tasted that the Word of God is good".[157] In other words, the word of God is the gospel of salvation, and to taste that it is good means to have had a personal experience of its goodness through receiving its benefits.[158] Furthermore, Marshall thinks that the "powers of the coming age" are unlikely to be miracles but are rather the blessings of future salvation which are already partially realised.[159]

Moreover, the so-called 'lapse' of these believers is indicated by the verb *parapiptō* (παραπίπτω) (6:6) which here must mean 'to fall away from the faith'. Although the corresponding noun *paraptōma* (παράπτωμα) means a single lapse or act of sin,[160] and although the passage was later understood in that way by Montanists and Novatians, it seems very unlikely that a single act of transgression is meant. Ellingworth says that the context "virtually requires a reference to apostasy",[161] meaning a total renunciation of Christianity, although what kind of action might have been involved is left vague, perhaps intentionally,[162] and perhaps for no other reason than that it had yet to occur.

The problem with these passages from Hebrews and 2 Peter is that the way the potential or actual apostates are described explicitly seems to indicate genuine conversion and regeneration - a being born again and being translated from darkness into light. Indeed, I suggest, that it would be hard to find more explicit language in scripture to describe real Christians. To suggest then that "those who have once been

---

[156] Compare *geusamenous te tēs dōreas* (γευσαμένους τε τῆς δωρεᾶς: genitive) with *kalon geusamenous theou rhēma* (καλὸν γευσαμένους θεοῦ ῥῆμα: accusative).

[157] C. F. D. Moule, (1959), 36: i.e., *kalon theou rhēma* (καλὸν θεοῦ ῥῆμα) is equivalent to *kalon einai theou rhēma* (καλὸν εἶναι θεοῦ ῥῆμα).

[158] Cf. 1 Peter 2:3.

[159] I. H. Marshall (1995), 143. Cf. Hebrews 9:11.

[160] *Parapiptō* occurs only here, and *paraptōma* 19 times in the New Testament. In the LXX *paraptōma* means 'transgression,' and *parapiptō* means 'to transgress' (translating *'asham* in Ezekiel 22:4) and 'to act faithlessly' or 'be treacherous' (translating *mā'al* in Ezekiel 14:13; 15:8; 18:24; 20:27). Cf. Wisdom 6:9; 12:2.

[161] Ellingworth, 322.

[162] I. H. Marshall (1995), 142-4.

enlightened, who have tasted the heavenly gift, who have shared in the Holy Spirit, who have tasted the goodness of the word of God and the powers of the coming age", those who have "escaped the corruption of the world by knowing our Lord and Saviour Jesus Christ" and "have known the way of righteousness" – to suggest that they were not genuine Christians who had been "born again, ... through the living and enduring word of God", as Peter describes his readers early in his first letter,[163] may make one wonder how Hebrews or Peter could possibly adequately describe otherwise those who were genuine fellow brothers and sisters in Christ.

In addition to these considerations, George Turner provides a summary list of supplementary evidence throughout Hebrews which supports the genuineness of the faith of those being warned:[164]

- They were partakers of the heavenly calling (3:1),
- Unbelievers would not have been exhorted to "hold firmly" or "unswervingly" (3:6; 4:14; 10:23),
- Unbelievers would not have been exhorted to "love and good deeds" (10:24),
- Unbelievers could not have endured with joy the spoiling of their possessions (10:32-36),
- They are referred to as "sons" (12:5-8),
- They are exhorted to brotherly love (13:1-6; cf. Galatians 5:22f.; 1 John 3:14; 4:7f.),
- They are urged to offer spiritual sacrifices (13:15f.) and
- Would the writer have asked for prayer support from unregenerate readers (13:18)?

Furthermore, he lists the potential dangers in which they stood:[165]

- Forsaking the gospel (2:1-4),
- Losing their Christian profession (3:6, 14; 4:14; 10:23),
- Lapsing into disobedience (3:12; 4:11; 6:4-6),
- Falling into mortal sin (10:26-31),
- Losing heart (12:3),
- Despising the Lord's discipline (12:5-10),

---

[163] 1 Peter 1:23.
[164] Turner, 104f., based on an unpublished essay by E. C. Smith.
[165] Ibid., 105.

- Forfeiting their blessings like Esau (12:14-17; Genesis 25:29-34),
- Refusing to hear God (12:25f.) and
- Being perverted by heresy (13:9).

Hewitt, in line with the RSV of Hebrews 6:6: "if they then commit apostasy", suggests that the writer was putting forth a merely hypothetical scenario: in other words, an imaginary, and without any correspondence to a real-life or even potential, situation, because no one had yet fallen away,[166] but that does not fit the context of the letter. There is, a sense in which the case was hypothetical of course, because he was describing what would happen if his readers ever reached the fatal decisive stage of apostasy, albeit a stage they had not yet reached. But if the situation was purely hypothetical, one would need to ask why the writer would issue such dire warnings. Turner says, "Only a forced exegesis can interpret Hebrews 6:1-8 as referring to a hypothetical case of unregenerate Jews, a situation which cannot be duplicated today.... The warning of this passage was a real warning against a real danger."[167]

On the face of the evidence so far, I have to conclude that these passages do indeed describe genuine Christians who may apostatise, and that leaves the seemingly inevitable conclusion that scripture does teach the possibility that I can be saved and yet lose my salvation. What is more, the possibility seems to exist that a believer may turn so far from Christ that it becomes impossible for them to repent and return:

> It is impossible for those who have once been enlightened ... and who have fallen away, to be brought back to repentance.[168]

But is that impossibility an unwillingness on God's part to countenance mercy, or is it more to do with the apostasy being so serious that the apostate's heart has become hardened and so is simply incapable of or unwilling to seek restoration?[169] Marshall points out that it is not said at what point the line is crossed when the apostate can no longer find opportunity for repentance. It is simply sufficient to know that there is

---

[166] Hewitt, 108.
[167] Turner, 104.
[168] Hebrews 6:4-6.
[169] Turner, 107.

a line which may be crossed, and the only way to avoid crossing that line is by pressing onwards instead of falling back.[170]

But there is another way of looking at these *rigorous* passages. A major impediment to accurate biblical exegesis is failing to take account of what are usually called the introductory issues of any biblical text. For example, it is said, both of Arminius and Perkins, that they took scripture as literally as possible irrespective of context, and much argumentation often encountered more widely today does tend to be of that proof-text variety, where context or the distinctive character of the particular book of the Bible from which texts are lifted are not sufficiently taken into account.

I am greatly influenced by Barnabas Lindars' *Theology of the Letter to the Hebrews*. He argues that, contrary to certain other expositors, Hebrews "is not a theological treatise, but an urgent address to the original readers, who are on the brink of taking action which their leaders regard as nothing short of apostasy".[171] The general context of Hebrews has been viewed traditionally as a situation where a group of Jewish-heritage believers were in danger of reverting to their former Judaism.[172] This supposed background differed from the kind of situation which Paul and other New Testament writers commonly encountered, however, and, particularly in Paul's case, spent considerable efforts attempting to counteract. Paul's battle was with those of a mentality often called 'Judaising'[173] – Jewish-background Christians who continued to adhere to their Jewish heritage with all the legal and ritual provisions of the Mosaic economy, and who were zealously convinced that fellow Jews who believed in Jesus should continue to conform, but, more seriously for Paul, that gentile believers too should adopt Jewish ways and be circumcised. Lindars builds a persuasive case for a slightly different scenario, however, where, perhaps because of a perceived delay of the *parousia*, a group of believers in a certain

---

[170] I. H. Marshall (1995), 151.
[171] Lindars, xi.
[172] Ibid., 4.
[173] N. T. Wright (2013), 853 n225, points out the inappropriate, though common usage, of the term 'Judaiser', which properly refers to Gentiles who were trying to become Jewish. However, I retain the term here because it is commonly understood thusly.

community, known to the writer, though not to us, were "not wilfully and defiantly disobedient, but deeply troubled in conscience"[174] because they had lost faith in the efficacy of Christianity to deal with their post-baptismal sin. He suggests that their situation may have been similar to that of believers at Thessalonica who seemed to have been seriously disconcerted by the fact that some of their number had died, even though the *parousia* had yet to occur,[175] a situation distinctly different from the influences of itinerant Judaisers who created havoc in the largely gentile churches with which Paul corresponded:

> the whole point at issue is a felt need on the part of the readers to resort to Jewish customs in order to come to terms with their sense of sin against God and need for atonement. Thus the central argument of the letter is precisely a compelling case for the complete and abiding efficacy of Jesus' death as an atoning sacrifice.[176]

Lindars suggests that Hebrews' readers had received the gospel and were genuine believers in Jesus, but they had not fully appreciated that his sacrifice had dealt fully with every aspect of their sin. They might have understood that Christ's death covered past sins, but, in view of the delayed *parousia*, to their way of thinking, and with a consciousness of sins they had committed since their conversion and baptism, they felt the need for ongoing forgiveness and thus a reversion to the Old Covenant sacrificial system where atonement for sin and forgiveness was a regular annual, if not more frequent, preoccupation. The writer's response was therefore to carefully craft an urgent letter to meet that pressing situation, the main thrust of which was to demonstrate the total efficacy of Christ's redemptive work as the "once for all"[177] sacrifice for sins. The thrust of Lindars' argument, then, is that an understanding of the *rhetoric* of Hebrews is essential for a correct understanding of the writer's purpose. Thus,

Hebrews is notable for its highly skilled composition and powerful

---

[174] Lindars, 43, 59, citing Hebrews 9:9, 14; 10:2. "Conscience" or "consciousness", *suneidēsis* (συνείδησις) is a key concept in the argument of Hebrews, and 9:14 is perhaps a key verse.
[175] Ibid., 13; 1 Thessalonians 4:13-5:11.
[176] Ibid., 10.
[177] Hebrews 10:27; 9:12, 26; 10:2, 10.

rhetorical effect. We have seen that recognition of the rhetorical character of Hebrews is fundamental for a true understanding of the letter. It has been carefully composed to persuade the readers to abandon their wish to return to the Jewish community in order to heal their troubled consciences, and to renew their confidence that healing is to be found in the gospel and its expression in Christian life.[178]

As we have seen, a commonly asked question is whether the recipients of the letter were truly born-again, regenerate, Spirit-filled Christians, and the descriptions given of them in Hebrews 6:4-5 and 10:26 (see above) leaves me in no doubt that they were. Nonetheless, there are those who, believing that apostasy is impossible for the true believer, are forced to the conclusion that this description of them was merely a nominal outward show of conformity with the gospel. On the contrary, I would suggest. This kind of literature and its species of argument are somewhat foreign to our accustomed Greek-thought-based literary culture. So, the writer, not doubting that his readers had not yet apostatised, and believing that they would be persuaded not to – so apostasy had not and would not happen – appeals to them in extreme hyperbolic terms, bordering at times on sarcasm perhaps, which on a surface reading may give the modern reader the impression that he believed they could (perhaps, would) lose their salvation. Thus, again quoting Lindars with reference to Hebrews 6:

> First he shows the dire consequences of apostasy (4-6), adding an agricultural metaphor to suggest the divine judgment (7-8). Then he changes his tune and assures the readers that he knows that they have not actually committed apostasy, urging them to recall their first zeal and to maintain it to the end (9-12). These two contradictory suggestions enhance the impression that the danger of apostasy is real and that Hebrews is trying to pull them back from the brink.

Unfortunately, for the purposes of this discussion: (i.e., whether Perseverance is a valid biblical concept) Hebrews does not make clear what he actually believed, although his language does give a strong impression that apostasy is a possibility even for true believers in Jesus. We are simply left with the impression that he thinks his protégés could

---

[178] Lindars, 26.

sacrifice their faith in Christ and be eternally lost, an impression nonetheless reinforced by his reference to Esau's renunciation of his birthright:[179]

> It leaves 'no chance to repent' (12.17), because the reconciliation, which is a permanent effect of the establishing of the covenant through the sacrifice of Christ, has been thrown away.[180]

Lindars does offer a personal opinion about the writer's imagined true feelings, however:

> He is speaking to readers who, he fears, are about to take an irrevocable step. What he would say to them if they did take it and then subsequently sought reconciliation we cannot say. But I suspect that, in spite of what he says here, he would welcome them with open arms![181] It is unsound to assume that in a work of such marked rhetorical character the writer should never allow himself some element of exaggeration.[182]

And I suggest that is precisely the point. With this brilliantly argued and most cogent of all the New Testament correspondence, we encounter a piece of literature which might seem quite foreign to us in a number of respects, not least in the kind of exaggerated rhetoric which appears to be used purely for effect. Again, Lindars writes,

> recognition of the rhetorical devices which Hebrews uses has been shown to be essential to a correct assessment of his writing, and many passages have been wrongly interpreted through failure to realise this. Hebrews should always be read with an eye to the intended effect on the readers. This means that special attention should be paid to the emotional impact of what Hebrews has to say.[183]

A similar conclusion might also be drawn with respect to 2 Peter 2:20-22 (also quoted above, 101). Unlike the recipients of Hebrews, however, the objects of Peter's criticism were not bewildered believers who

---

[179] Genesis 25:29-34.
[180] Lindars 69f., quoting the RSV.
[181] Particularly if Lindars is right, since their anticipated move away from the gospel had been triggered by a basic error rather than an attitude of defiance.
[182] Ibid., 70.
[183] Ibid., 136.

did not know what to do about their post-baptismal sins (assuming Lindars to be correct): they were what Peter calls "false prophets":

> But there were also false prophets among the people, just as there will be false teachers among you. They will secretly introduce destructive heresies, even denying the sovereign Lord who bought them—bringing swift destruction on themselves.[184]

Peter describes them as once having escaped the "defilements of the world through the knowledge of our Lord and Saviour Jesus Christ". And, comparing the wording of 2 Peter 1:3-4 with 2:20,

> His divine power has given us everything we need for a godly life *through our knowledge* of him who called us by his own glory and goodness. Through these he has given us his very great and precious promises, so that through them you may participate in the divine nature, having *escaped the corruption in the world* caused by evil desires.

> If they have *escaped the corruption of the world by knowing* our Lord and Saviour Jesus Christ.

Peter uses identical terminology of the believers to whom he addressed his letter and the false prophets in their midst. Peter Davids makes what I think is a sound case for the genuineness of the original conversion of those false prophets, thus removing any sense that their salvation was ever in doubt when they first professed to believe.[185] So, as with Hebrews, a case cannot be made that the conversion of either group referred to was illusory, but that apostasy was nevertheless a reality, either in prospect or actuality. The conclusion that cannot be drawn with any certainty, however, is whether that apostasy would result in the loss of their eternal salvation. I confess that I still have difficulty in deciding whether apostasy means eternal loss, and I wonder whether the two issues, apostasy and eternal loss, may have been linked more in the Medieval mind than in the thoughts of the writers of scripture or, more to the point, in the mind of God.

It is worth noting that these passages under discussion emanate from a

---

[184] 2 Peter 2:1.
[185] Davids, 248, with reference to 2 Peter 2:20 (NRSV).

Jewish worldview, as, of course, do the sayings of Jesus which we have already noted. It is also true that Jesus himself on occasion used exaggerated language saying, for example, that anyone who would aspire to follow him must *hate* their closest kin and even their own lives, or that his followers should eat his flesh and drink his blood.[186] No one would seriously suggest that Jesus' commands should be taken literally, but, as with the Hebrews and 2 Peter passages, that exaggeration underlines the crucial importance and heightens the impact of what is being said, and must therefore be understood in terms of their emotional effect.

My conclusion then, is that, although the authors do appear to believe that apostasy is a possibility, these so-called *rigorous* passages from Hebrews 6 and 10, together with the 2 Peter passage, prove nothing either way with respect to Perseverance, and while we should take the prospect of apostasy extremely seriously, we could be left in the same limbo in which Arminius seems to have found himself. Although I am convinced that Hebrews recognises the genuineness of his readers' conversions, I am not convinced that his extreme rhetoric necessarily brings their eternal security into doubt. Rather, that their imminent turning back to their Jewish roots was for him an unthinkable resort which caused him to use all of his literary powers to deflect them from a disastrous outcome – not the disaster of hell, perhaps, but of lives not lived in the freedom into which Christ had purchased for them, a return to the "slavery" of Judaism.[187]

When thinking of that Jewish world view, it is worth reflecting that one frequently encounters proof-texting from Old Testament sources. In that context, Ezekiel 33 comes to mind, for example:

> If I tell a righteous person that they will surely live, but then they trust in their righteousness and do evil, none of the righteous things that person has done will be remembered; they will die for the evil they have done. And if I say to a wicked person, "You will surely die," but they then turn away from their sin and do what is just and right ... that person will surely live; they will not die.... If a

---

[186] E.g., Luke 14:26; John 12:25. In both cases the Greek verb translated "hate" is *miseō* (μισέω). John 6:53-6.
[187] Galatians 5:1.

righteous person turns from their righteousness and does evil, they will die for it. And if a wicked person turns away from their wickedness and does what is just and right, they will live by doing so.[188]

Great caution needs to be exercised when applying the principles of Old Testament texts in a New Testament evangelistic context, however. I say *principles* because expositors of the Word need to do their homework when it comes to juggling texts from different contexts – especially those from either side of the covenantal divide. Elsewhere, however, Ezekiel clearly points forward to a new covenant context, especially when he writes,

> I will give them an undivided heart and put a new spirit in them; I will remove from them their heart of stone and give them a heart of flesh. Then they will follow my decrees and be careful to keep my laws. They will be my people, and I will be their God.[189]

remarkable words from his context of a covenant of Law, an aspect that Ezekiel underlines when referring to the people keeping God's laws. But the context is Old Covenant, and it falls therefore under the blessings and curses of Deuteronomy 27 and 28. If that is indeed the case, then the 'living' and 'dying' of the above passages must be regarded in that light and not necessarily in an eternal light.

My Personal View

We seem now to have reached somewhat of an impasse in our consideration of the 'P' of TULIP. I want therefore to set down some personal conclusions, which I hope will clarify my own position and hopefully rescue any of an Arminian frame of mind from uncertainty about the permanency of their salvation, and any Calvinistic friends who may lack assurance that they are indeed elect.

I have alluded (above, 72) to 1 John 3:9, William Perkins' proof-text which Arminius found most persuasive, and which for me too creates an anchor for my own sense of eternal security:

---

[188] Ezekiel 33:13-19.
[189] Ezekiel 11:19f. Cf. Jeremiah 31:31-34.

> No one who is born of God will continue to sin, because God's seed remains in them; they cannot go on sinning, because they have been born of God.

Here again is the new birth, a concept that to my mind absolutely defies any sense that it might be reversible. But consider the idea of 'God's seed' remaining in a person. Westcott commenting on this verse, says,

> the principle of life which He has given continues to be the ruling principle of the believer's growth. God gives, as it were, of Himself to the Christian. He does not only work upon him and leave him. The germ of the new life is that out of which the mature man will in due time be developed.[190]

The miracle of the new birth is that God gives us his own nature, a reincarnation and radical transformation that I suggest cannot be reversed or annulled. Peter describes that *remaining* seed as 'imperishable':[191] it cannot die; it is indestructible: all it can do is grow, although its growth may be slow or stunted by our unresponsiveness to the work of the Holy Spirit. Combine that thought with Paul's words:

> Therefore, if anyone is in Christ, *the new creation has come*: the old has gone, the new is here![192]

The short phrase, "the new creation" (*kainē ktisis*: καινὴ κτίσις) suffers from a variety of translations, however, e.g.,

- 'he is a new creation': NIV (1984), ESV, NET;
- 'he is a new creature': Tyndale, KJV, RV;
- 'there is a new creation': RV margin, REB;
- 'Anyone who is joined to Christ is a new being': GNB,
- '*let him be* a new creature': Geneva Bible,

A literal rendering might be, 'If anyone is in Christ, new creation', but whether Paul's intention was to say that the believer in Christ becomes a new being or whether he or she is simply part of a whole new created order is probably moot, although Barrett translates the phrase, "there is

---

[190] Westcott (1892), 107.
[191] 1 Peter 1:23.
[192] 2 Corinthians 5:17: Greek: ὥστε εἴ τις ἐν Χριστῷ, καινὴ κτίσις· τὰ ἀρχαῖα παρῆλθεν, ἰδοὺ γέγονεν καινά.

a new act of creation".[193] Without getting embroiled in Barrett's discussion of possible rabbinical links, it seems clear that he believes Paul to be enunciating a completely new sphere of being in parallel with the "new covenant" of 2 Corinthians 3:6;[194] a renewed universe to replace the old - as is spelled out in the parallel second part of the verse: "the old has gone, the new is here!"[195] We are therefore part of that creative activity – everything changes when we trust in Jesus and we are translated into that new order, the kingdom of the Son. It is hard to see then how that process could be reversed if a person, having once been genuinely saved, decides to rescind their faith or apostatise. Nonetheless, Shank claims that the process can be reversed since the words "if anyone is in Christ" create a condition to the renewing transformation of the new birth. He says,

> In Christ, the believer is indeed "a new creation" – God's "workmanship, created in Christ Jesus" (Eph. 2:10). But he is only such *in Christ*, from whom it is possible to be severed (John 15:1-6), and he is therefore not a spiritual "creation" incapable of destruction ...[196]

For me, the apparent irreversibility of it all would gainsay such a view, particularly since we are not considering anyone who is not in Christ.

A major problem for many Christians, especially for Arminians, I suppose, is a residual sense that we need to obey the law, or however that might be expressed – please the Lord and so on - in order to maintain our saved standing and our assurance of salvation. What that error overlooks, however, is that whenever we sin, our transgressions have already been atoned for, because Christ has died for us, and we have received by faith the benefits of his sacrifice. We therefore live in the benefit of having the Holy Spirit, God's own *seed*, within us. We are not what we were in our former unregenerate days, and although the

---

[193] Barrett (1973), 162.
[194] Ibid., 173; 2 Corinthians 3:6a: "He has made us competent as ministers of a new covenant".
[195] On the question as to whether the new heavens and new earth are creations *de novo* or cleansed renewals of the original creation of heaven and earth, see my forthcoming *Pie in the Sky When You Die?*
[196] Shank (*Life*), 367. See above, 77f., on Shank's interpretation of Jesus' True Vine discourse.

transformation will not be complete until we meet Jesus face to face, we are nevertheless citizens of a new creation – "the old has gone". Our identity is no longer in Adam, but in Christ: we are children of God, born anew into a *living* hope.[197]

Jesus' words in John 10 also add to the growing catalogue of my assurance texts:

> My sheep listen to my voice; I know them, and they follow me. I give them eternal life, and they shall never perish; no one will snatch them out of my hand. My Father, who has given them to me, is greater than all; no one can snatch them out of my Father's hand. I and the Father are one.[198]

a kind of double assurance – safe in Jesus' hand, and safe in the Father's hand too. Paul says something similar:

> For you died, and your life is now hidden *with Christ in God*. When Christ, who is your life, appears, then you also will appear with him in glory.[199]

Thus, Paul appears to claim that our new life - the becoming part of God's new creation, is safeguarded in the strongbox of heaven – the safest place possible - in God himself. This is powerful language, which I believe serves to show, as Paul states elsewhere, that absolutely nothing can separate believers from "the love of God in Christ Jesus".[200] This is not an isolated thought confined to this verse in Paul's Colossian letter though. In the previous chapter, where he discusses the efficacy of baptism – the acted-out picture of our death, burial and resurrection with Christ as we make our confession (*sacramentum*) of faith, he says, "God made you alive with Christ",[201] a phrase which translates the Greek verb *sudzōopoieō* (συζωοποιέω), which means to 'make alive *with*',[202] the *su*- prefix (short for *sun*) reinforcing the 'together with' aspect of the verb. Thus, the clear implication is that our

---

[197] 1 Peter 1:3.
[198] John 10:27-30.
[199] Colossians 3:3f.
[200] Romans 8:38f.
[201] Colossians 2:13.
[202] See also Ephesians 2:5.

new life is so intimately bound up with Christ's resurrection life that it should be impossible to reverse the process – to be unborn-again, so to speak, and the bond is so strong that it is certain that we will appear with him in glory.

A further aspect of that unalterable relationship with God which Christians enjoy may be found in the concept of the *firstborn*. For example, Hebrews, when contrasting the old covenant of law, and its terrifying judgments, with the new, describes the new as

> Mount Zion, the city of the living God, the heavenly Jerusalem.... thousands upon thousands of angels in joyful assembly ... the church of the *firstborn*, whose names are written in heaven.[203]

The plural word 'firstborn' (*prōtotokōn*: πρωτοτόκων), being, not Christ himself, although elsewhere he is described as the firstborn,[204] but the 'firstborn ones' whose names are written in heaven.[205] The idea of the firstborn is probably a somewhat neglected, although nonetheless important, strand of Old Testament typology. Although the concept was integral to the way of life of the ancients, the idea emerged significantly for Israel when the firstborn of Egypt were slain in the final catastrophic plague as Israel was delivered from slavery.[206] God then commanded Moses to consecrate every firstborn male of Israel,[207] and once the Law had been given at Sinai, they were then counted and individually paired with the Levites:

> The LORD said to Moses, 'Count all the firstborn Israelite males who are a month old or more and make a list of their names. Take the Levites for me in place of all the firstborn of the Israelites, and the livestock of the Levites in place of all the firstborn of the livestock of the Israelites. I am the LORD.'[208]

On the face of it, that might seem rather an odd thing to do. The following verses of Numbers 3[209] recount how Moses counted and listed

---

[203] Hebrews 12:22f.
[204] Luke 2:7; Romans 8:29; Colossians 1:15, 18; Hebrews 1:6; Revelation 1:5.
[205] See Chapter 10i, 343, on Revelation 17:8.
[206] Exodus 12:29f.
[207] Exodus 13:1f.
[208] Numbers 3:40
[209] Numbers 3:42-51.

the firstborn males a month old and more, determining that their number, 22,273, exceeded the number of Levites by 273.[210] These surplus firstborn ones then had to be 'redeemed' by a levy of five shekels per head and the money handed over to the priests. The significant point of all this was that Yahweh was substituting the Levites for all the firstborn male individuals of the other tribes, so, Levi was identified as special in the sense that the whole tribe would be set apart to serve Yahweh in the Israelite cult in place of the firstborn males of all the other tribes.

There is some speculation by both Christian and Jewish authors about why the tribe of Levi was selected to serve the priestly functions. But a possible solution of that somewhat puzzling substitution may be seen in the religious or cultic significance of firstborn males in Israelite society before the Law was given. Many believe that in ancient near-eastern (and many other) cultures the firstborn son had a special priestly status in his family setting, a custom that presumably Israel naturally and automatically adopted. Certain responsibilities and privileges sat upon his shoulders, but he would inherit a 'double portion' of his father's estate so that he could assume executive leadership of the family on his father's death. This became consolidated following the slaying of the Egyptian firstborn when God commanded Moses to consecrate to him every firstborn male of Israel, whether human or animal.[211] Why the firstborn of Egypt should have been sentenced to death is not absolutely clear, but one might assume that it was God's judgment on those who held the reins of power and authority in Egyptian society. That authority was therefore affirmed in Israel. Had Israel's subsequent history taken a different course, the transference of that authority and duty to Levi might perhaps not have happened, but the incident of the Golden Calf created the situation where Levi came to significant prominence as they sided with Moses against the other tribes in defence of faith in Yahweh and rejection of idolatry, in which Aaron, of course, was a primary guilty party.[212] The significant upshot was the

---

[210] The very round total number of Levites (22,000) presents a problem of the way census figures are reported in the Old Testament, but that is not a topic for now.
[211] Exodus 13:2; also, Exodus 22:29b-30; Numbers 3:13; 8:17.
[212] Exodus 32:26-9.

pronouncement by Moses upon Levi, "You have been set apart to the LORD today, for you were against your own sons and brothers, and he has blessed you this day." A cynic will not fail to note that Levi was the tribe to which Moses himself belonged, and that Aaron was his blood brother, but scripture clearly wants us to see in these events a zeal for God and the honour of his name, which may well have entailed an element of family loyalty. The violent propensity seen in the incident, where the tribe of Levi was responsible for the deaths of about 3,000 Israelites, was also evident in the earlier savage reprisals carried out by Levi, partnered by his full-brother Simeon, against the inhabitants of Shechem for the defilement of their sister Dinah.[213] That caused their father, Jacob, to 'bless' them in somewhat negative terms:

> Simeon and Levi are brothers -
> their swords are weapons of violence....
> I will scatter them in Jacob and disperse them in Israel.[214]

And that 'blessing' was realised as the tribe which descended from Simeon was eventually absorbed into Judah, and Levi was allotted no territory of its own except for 48 cities, six of them cities of refuge, scattered throughout the territories of the other tribes.

Whereas all Israel had been designated "a kingdom of priests and a holy nation"[215] prior to the giving of the Law and the Golden Calf incident, God rewarded the tribe of Levi by conferring upon them the priestly honours and responsibilities of the firstborn of Israel's other tribes, who presumably retained their other family and civil rights and responsibilities. Thus, emerged a new class of Israelites identified as 'firstborn ones' who enjoyed a special relationship with God through the cult, and who would be Israel's teachers, vicars and leaders in the theocracy that Israel would become.[216]

---

[213] Genesis 34.
[214] Genesis 49:5, 7b.
[215] Exodus 19:6.
[216] *The Book of Jubilees*, a Jewish pseudepigraphal work, probably from around the turn of the first century BC, offers three reasons for the choosing of the Levites as Israel's priesthood: (1) 30:18f.: to reward Levi and Simeon's zeal in punishing the inhabitants of Shechem after the defilement of their sister Dinah (Genesis 34): "he was zealous to execute righteousness and judgment and vengeance against all who arose against

Having identified the concept of the firstborn in its Old Testament context, its significance for Christians is the way the New Testament applies it first to Christ and then includes believers in him. Although the firstborn in Old Testament contexts was literally the first male to 'open' the womb of his mother, as the tribe of Levi adopted the role of the firstborn in Israel, that aspect gave way to the status of pre-eminence, importance and authority of what it was to be a firstborn son with all its significance for heirship. We see that in the New Testament's descriptions of Christ – "the firstborn among many brothers and sisters"; "the firstborn over all creation"; "the firstborn from among the dead", and "the ruler of the kings of the earth".[217] But when we encounter Hebrews 12:23, we find the most amazing statement of sonship as firstborn status is conferred upon believers in Jesus – "the church of the firstborn, whose names are written in heaven". I wonder how many Christians really appreciate what God has conferred upon us as we have been incorporated into Christ by faith, and how all of this appeals to me as being absolutely certain but also irreversible.

We might still wish to hold on to something of Arminius' doubts when considering Perkins' exposition of 1 John 3:9 – that the divine seed in us might be lost. We may also be swayed by some of the texts we have considered which seem to suggest that our eternal security is not absolutely certain, but I am persuaded otherwise. The believer who walks with the Lord and knows the witness in his or her spirit that they are

---

Israel"; (2) 31:12-17: Jacob, having fled from Laban, and accompanied by Judah and Levi, is said to have visited his parents whilst visiting Bethel when the elderly Isaac bestowed his blessings on his two sons. This fits into the narrative of Genesis 35:1-15: "May the LORD give you and your seed very great honour. May he draw you and your seed near to him from all flesh to serve in his sanctuary as the angels of the presence and the holy ones.... And they will tell my ways to Jacob and My paths to Israel."; (3) 32:1-9: Whilst at Bethel, Levi dreamed that God had ordained him as priest. Years before at Bethel Jacob had dreamed of the stairway to heaven and had promised God that he would tithe everything God gave him if he returned safely (Genesis 28:20-2). Jacob makes good his promise to tithe, but Levi, according to Charles (1913), 61, as the tenth son, is part of the tithe and so is also dedicated to Yahweh. Charles seems to have mistakenly interpreted the mention of Levi's other ten brothers (Benjamin had yet to be born), as meaning that Levi was the tenth son: he was actually the third son of Jacob. Translations of *Jubilees* by O. S. Wintermute in Charlesworth (1983), 2:113-7.

[217] Romans 8:29; Colossians 1:15, 18; Revelation 1:5.

God's child (son) should never doubt their eternal security in Christ. Paul makes that crystal-clear:

> The Spirit you received does not make you slaves, so that you live in fear again; rather, the Spirit you received brought about your adoption to sonship. And by him we cry, '*Abba*, Father.' The Spirit himself testifies with our spirit that we are God's children. Now if we are children, then we are heirs—heirs of God and co-heirs with Christ, if indeed we share in his sufferings in order that we may also share in his glory.[218]

> Because you are his sons, God sent the Spirit of his Son into our hearts, the Spirit who calls out, '*Abba*, Father.' So you are no longer a slave, but God's child; and since you are his child, God has made you also an heir.[219]

And as a final thrust in this discussion of the validity or otherwise of a doctrine of Perseverance, I would suggest that Romans 11:29 is worthy of consideration:

> for God's gifts and his call are irrevocable.

As will become plain when I discuss the meaning of God's calling in Chapter 8, a case can be made for the idea of calling being another way of describing our election, a sense which Paul often employs.[220] We may be accustomed to interpreting this verse along the lines of God's appeal to humanity to embrace Jesus as Saviour and Lord, in other words, the proclamation of the gospel, a perfectly valid use of the term, of course, although the context is of the placing of God's call on his ancient people, Israel and their patriarchs in order to fulfil their role as his ambassadors for his elective purposes in history. However, elsewhere Paul seems to link those who are the called with the Elect.[221] That being the case, to be assured that God's calling is "irrevocable" must surely affirm the permanency and security that a believer has in

---

[218] Romans 8:15-17.
[219] Galatians 4:6f. The word is "son" (*huios*: υἱός), although Romans 8:16 has "child" (*teknon*: τέκνον). See my comments on 'sonship' in Chapter 9b, 265, and my forthcoming *Pie in the Sky When You Die?* on *huiothesia*.
[220] See Chapter 8d, 238, on 'Calling'.
[221] Romans 1:6f., 8:28; 1 Corinthians 1:2, 24; Hebrews 9:15; Revelation 17:14; etc.

Christ.[222]

In conclusion then, although I cannot find an unequivocal statement of Perseverance in scripture, I firmly believe that scripture does teach our eternal security in Christ, and confirms the validity of such a doctrine. The crucial issue is not whether it is true, however, but whether I am *assured* of its truth. It seems to me that there is sufficient scripture to assure me of my eternal security, and at least one New Testament document, 1 John, was written with the express intention of assuring believers of just that.[223] I may be accused of some special pleading, but my faith clings especially to the verses from John 10 (quoted above 96).[224] What might happen if I were to turn my back on Jesus, I cannot say for certain. Hebrews only hints at the outcome – "It is a dreadful thing to fall into the hands of the living God",[225] but if we do fall short, I believe we can and must cast ourselves onto God's boundless compassion as he seeks prodigals who have strayed, no matter how determinedly.[226]

It is a matter of how we see scripture and its purpose for our sanctification. We could take an almost Pharisaic stance, as Shank seems to do, and claim that it must be clearly stated in scripture if we are to stake our faith on it, but I don't believe that God wants us to find our assurance in just the printed page; rather, our *certain hope* is to be found in the experience of our relationship with him as it is mediated by the Holy Spirit. I would not wish to be understood as claiming that because the Bible may be ambiguous on the subject, that therefore my assurance can never be sure, but I do want to underline the purpose for which I believe scripture has been given, namely, to encourage us towards a life

---

[222] It should be noted that Shank (*Life*), 358, singles out Romans 11:29 as a text which has been misunderstood by advocates of Unconditional Security. He claims that the assumption that God cannot withdraw is gift of justification and salvation is incorrect, and that the correct context of the text concerns the corporate election of Israel, and that, despite Israel's present unfaithfulness, God's promises to them will ultimately be fulfilled. He is correct, of course, but I take the saying to be a general principle of God's providence which applies to Israel just as much as it applies to his calling in the lives of his redeemed in Christ.
[223] 1 John 5:13.
[224] John 10:14, 27-30.
[225] Hebrews 10:31.
[226] Luke 15:3-7, 11-32.

of faith where, by the very experience of knowing God better each day, our certainty of perseverance is also deepened. Just as the love of friendship or marriage is affirmed and deepened through ongoing commitment and intercourse (in the wider sense of the word), so is our certainty of the reality of our relationship with God.

It is good that Christians today are scripture-literate, relatively speaking, and we certainly have the huge advantage, even over our brothers and sisters of the first century, let alone in times before the Bible was translated into our mother tongues, of owning our own copies of scripture and studying them whenever we might choose. But I wonder sometimes whether we have been tempted to replace the Holy Spirit with scripture. Is there, even among evangelical Christians, a tendency to honour a trinity of Father, Son and Holy Scriptures? I recall a visit I once made to a Jewish synagogue and the reverence that was accorded to the Torah scroll as it was paraded through the congregation: no eye was turned away from it, and no back towards it. That seemed to me like a species of idolatry. But what scripture does enjoin upon us is to live by the Spirit, not by the Word, although affirming that the Spirit will never countermand or contradict the Word. And it is by that Spirit-affirming way of life that we can be completely assured of our salvation.

As already mentioned, John's first letter was written expressly to assure his readers that their salvation was certain:

> I write these things to you who believe in the name of the Son of God so that you may know that you have eternal life.[227]

I began this section with reference to 1 John 3:9, but the verses which follow provide a kind of four-fold checklist of what it is to walk with the Lord and thus be assured of our salvation:

- The one who does right, although expressed negatively: "anyone who does not do what is right is not God's child."
- "We know that we have passed from death to life, because we love each other.... as he commanded us.... The one who keeps God's

---

[227] 1 John 5:13; cf. John 20:31.

commands lives in him, and he in them. And this is how we know that he lives in us".
- We do what pleases him – the role of conscience: "This is how we know that we belong to the truth ... if our hearts do not condemn us, we have confidence before God".
- "We know it by the Spirit he gave us.".[228]

Although we must admit that loving one another is not always the easiest thing, and it is that aspect of our discipleship that John particularly emphasises, what is perhaps more problematical is the fourth item in this list – the awareness and experience of the Holy Spirit. We live in days when many Christians seem to have lost the certainty we see so clearly in the New Testament, and particularly in the Acts of the Apostles. All I can suggest is that recovery of that vital experience can come only through a willingness and determination to cultivate our personal experience of God through our private devotional life, our public church fellowship, including a welcome acceptance of Spirit-guided prayer ministry, and through finding out what pleases the Lord and following through on that conviction.

Problems will inevitably arise if our walk with Jesus falters or becomes less committed. If we backslide or pass through severe trials – the 'Dark Night of the Soul'[229] or some other experience where God seems far distant or even non-existent,[230] our only recourse is to persevere. If our walk with the Lord falters, we are bound to doubt, even though the truth of scripture will never change, but in reality, I am absolutely persuaded that our salvation is never imperilled. But if we walk with the Lord, and persevere in difficult times, the witness of the Holy Spirit, as scripture affirms, will continually assure us of our hope in Christ - in the words of an old, but much-loved song:

> He lives! He Lives! Christ Jesus lives today!
> He walks with me and talks with me
> Along life's narrow way.
> He lives! He lives, salvation to impart!

---

[228] 1 John 3:10-24.
[229] St. John of the Cross, *Dark Night of the Soul*, available in many editions.
[230] Many years ago, during a period of backsliding the Holy Spirit never failed to remind me that I was God's child – an almost schizophrenic experience!

> You ask me how I know he lives –
> He lives within my heart![231]

If we turn from Christ and decide that the Christian faith is a delusion, however, I am not convinced that the Bible reveals what our final end might be. There are texts that seem to affirm our perseverance, and others which warn of total loss. I must therefore find my assurance, not in the balance of probabilities when juggling texts, but rather in committing all my ways to the one who has predestined that the church should finally be glorified. In Chapter 9 we will see that our election is never of individuals,[232] but of the *body* of those who trust Jesus as Saviour and Lord. But, just as I joined the Elect through choosing Christ, might the possibility so too exist that I may reject Christ and forfeit the destiny that true believers will inherit? That would pierce God's heart of love, but is he not the kind of God who honours the decisions we may make?

Although Howard Marshall arrives at a conclusion different from mine so far as whether a falling away can result in the loss of one's salvation, and that is because I am not convinced that apostasy ever means that the divine seed dies within us, we do agree on the saving strategy that scripture consistently enjoins. His main conclusion, and mine, then is that "the way to persevere is simply - by persevering".

> The believer is not told that he is one of the elect and therefore cannot fall away, nor is there any particular aspect of his faith or character which indicates that he is the kind of person who cannot fall away. He is simply told to continue in obedience and faith and to trust in the God who will keep him from falling. He perseveres by persevering. Perseverance is not some particular quality of faith or something to be added to faith, but the fact that faith continues. To speak of the need to develop endurance, as the New Testament does, is the same thing as saying that one must continue to believe despite every temptation to disbelieve.[233]

Although God enables us to resist temptation, we are not protected from

---

[231] The chorus of Alfred H. Ackley's (1887-1960) hymn; *I serve a risen Savior*, written in 1933.
[232] Chapter 9, 248.
[233] I. H. Marshall (1995), 208.

its reality, nor the need to resist it. Thus, when an Arminian friend asks, "Can I be sure I will persevere?" there can be no straightforward 'Yes' or 'No' response; simply the kind of response Jesus gave when he was asked, "Lord, are only a few people going to be saved?" His response was, "Make every effort to enter through the narrow door ... Strive to enter in".[234] Furthermore, that response seems not dissimilar from his answer to Peter's enquiry about the fate of John: "what is that to you? *You* [thou] must follow me".[235] Our response has to be intensely personal, and our determination to persevere has to be without reference to what others may be doing or saying. God will, of course test our faith, but the growing body of experience of his faithfulness will surely defend our ability, with God's help, to resist the temptation to apostatise even when pushed to extremes. The New Testament discourages us from speculating; rather it encourages us to continue to grow in grace and discover that the process of maturation in Christ will itself bring the confidence which lifts us above the fear of falling away. "It is ... in this idea of growth and development in faith that the key to the problem is to be found."[236] "Such a paradox arises because the New Testament knows neither the rigid logic of Calvinism nor the 'casualness' of Arminianism but teaches us to put our trust in God."[237]

Marshall sums up his final conclusion in *Kept by the Power of God* as follows:

> Our answer, therefore, to the theological problem which gave rise to this study, is a refusal to press the New Testament to give a logically rigid solution. The New Testament is content to hold together the facts of perseverance and apostasy in paradox, and to rest the confidence of the believer not on a logical argument but on the faithfulness of the God in whom he must continually trust. As he thus trusts, he finds that God is indeed faithful and that only his own wilfulness and failure to trust can cause him to fall; as he grows in trust, he is able to proclaim with the voice of faith that nothing can separate him from the love of God. Not even the last enemy, death, and the physical and mental weakness which may precede it can

---

[234] Luke 13:23f. (KJV).
[235] John 21:21f.
[236] I. H. Marshall (1995), 209.
[237] Ibid., 211.

break the 'relationship with God enjoyed by His people during their earthly lives; He remains faithful, so that they are kept by the power of God?[238]

This conclusion that scripture doesn't provide a definitive answer strikes me as the possible reason why Arminius couldn't reach a dogmatic solution to the puzzle of Perseverance. What scripture does teach, however, answers not only to the injunction that each individual Christian live by faith and not by sight,[239] but also to Arminius' honest personal integrity and scholarship.

The book of Revelation is all about the perseverance of the Church, and we must cling to the very last words of the New Testament: Christ's words to us, in effect, are, "Hang on in for I am coming soon". Our response is not to muse about whether or not we can 'hang on' or whether we are truly chosen: our response is to emulate the wise servants, the prospect of whose master's coming energises and motivates our whole being, and whose coming glory eclipses all other thoughts so that our response can only be, "Amen. Come, Lord Jesus".[240]

And finally, to give the Apostle Paul the last word, let me share 1 Timothy 4:8:

> godliness has value for all things, *holding promise* for both the present life and the life to come.

The issue is less about whether our salvation is secure, therefore, and much more often about whether we are sure about it.

---

[238] Ibid.
[239] 2 Corinthians 5:7.
[240] Matthew 24:45, etc.; Revelation 22:20.

Chapter 5

WHAT IS THE PROPER HUMAN RESPONSE TO THE GRACE OF GOD?[1]

Christians, on the whole, believe that in the pre-Fall creation order God imparted the ability to make free moral choices when he bestowed his image upon our first parents.[2] That is clear from the story of Adam and Eve[3] who lived in the idyllic environment of the Garden of Eden where they were charged with exercising daily choices about their diet, the work they should do, the naming of the fauna in the garden, and presumably the flora too,[4] and so on. It seems that they were afforded complete freedom of choice; the only prohibition laid upon them being that they were not to eat the fruit from the Tree of the Knowledge of Good and Evil. Implicitly, however, they *were* encouraged to partake of the other tree specifically mentioned, the Tree of Life in the centre of Eden, the symbol of their innocent relationship with their Creator, the source of all life.[5] That relationship is strongly suggested by their habitual companionship with God as daily they would walk with him in the garden, an assumption based on God's search for the couple following their disobedience.[6] However, exercising their freedom in disobeying God's singular prohibition, they brought about the Fall, which

---

[1] See also Chapter 6, 161.
[2] Genesis 1:26.
[3] Many Christian anthropologists accept evolutionary theory, and some accord to Adam and Eve the role of custodians of a kind of proto-temple, symbolised as the Garden of Eden, where God could be encountered and was represented symbolically by the Tree of Life at the centre of the garden. See, among others, John Walton (2015), who describes Adam and Eve as 'archetypes' rather than biological progenitors. That view has serious implications for notions of Original Sin, of course, because, if true, not all human beings who lived before the Flood could be said to have originated biologically in Adam and Eve. Presumably, that would then make Noah the 'one man' of Acts 17:26, and together with his wife, sons and daughters-in-law the common biological ancestors of all subsequent humanity: Genesis 10:32.
[4] Proving that the oldest profession is not what is normally assumed, but is that of the taxonomist!
[5] Genesis 2:16f.
[6] Genesis 3:8.

entailed the distortion of God's image in them and, most importantly, their loss of access to the Tree of Life – a catastrophic event symbolic of the severing of their relationship with God and their consequent loss of spiritual life – their deaths.[7]

This is what Calvinists call 'Total Depravity', the first of the Five Points of Calvinism. It is an unfortunate term because the 'total' element always requires some explanation, and specifically what it does not mean. Louis Berkhof, for example, points out that Total Depravity in Reformed understanding is "inherited pollution", but before elaborating on what he means by that he first points out how the doctrine can easily be misunderstood. It does not imply, he says,

> (1) that every man is as thoroughly depraved as he can possibly become; (2) that the sinner has no innate knowledge of the will of God, nor a conscience that discriminates between good and evil; (3) that sinful man does not often admire virtuous character and actions in others, or is incapable of disinterested affections and actions in his relations with his fellow-men; nor (4) that every unregenerate man will, in virtue of his inherent sinfulness, indulge in every form of sin ... Positively, it does indicate: (1) that the inherent corruption extends to every part of man's nature ... and (2) that there is no spiritual good ... in relation to God, ... but only perversion.[8]

Thus, Total Depravity does not assert that humankind became absolutely corrupt in every conceivable way, even though that could reasonably be inferred from the cast of the terminology. It would seem that the fact that goodness can be found even in unregenerate people exposes that notion as false, although even the good they may do is regarded by some – they would say by God, as sinful nonetheless.[9] Rather, what is meant is that *every aspect* of what it is to bear God's image was degraded. We cannot therefore *perfectly* display any aspect of godlikeness, and in consequence, according to Calvinism, we are totally

---

[7] Genesis 3:24.
[8] L. Berkhof, 246f., cites John 5:42; Romans 7:18, 23; 8:7; Ephesians 4:18; 2 Timothy 3:2-4; Titus 1:15; Hebrews 3:12. It should be noted that, although these texts affirm the sinfulness of the human condition, none of them even suggests that this 'pollution' is passed on through the generations in any way.
[9] Piper (2013), 17ff., cites Romans 14:23, "Everything that does not come from faith is sin". See Appendix 3a, 393, on Piper's *Five Points* and 'Total Depravity'.

unable to make correct moral choices without divine aid. We can choose among less than perfect options, but to choose to obey God is beyond our capability. For Martin Luther, for example, free will operated in the natural sphere, but in the spiritual sphere it was for him the "Devil's greatest whore"[10] who should be rejected and stigmatised out of hand and "ought to be drowned in baptism",[11] the act whereby we are saved, according to Lutheranism. The Reformed understanding of Total Depravity then is to be unrighteous, to be dead in transgressions and so objects of wrath; it is blindness to the light of the gospel, and the inability to come to God unless drawn by him.[12]

Free Will: Reality or Illusion?

At this point, it is worth reflecting briefly on the long-standing philosophical debate that continues to rage, but without resolution, so far as I can see, about the reality or otherwise of the notion of free will. The assumption that free will is an illusion is a dogmatic position, and most often springs from disbelief in the supernatural and reliance on a mechanistic physical realm. The question that raises, of course, is whether my belief in free will is determined solely by a belief in God and in what the Bible teaches about the supernatural.

Some atheistic scientists appear to arrogate to themselves the right to make decisions about the non-material realm which Christians believe in, and draw conclusions from their mind experiments, but why should that be so when the scope of their disciplines must be confined to the physical workings of creation? That seems ultimately arrogant, if not irresponsible. That is not to say, of course, that Christian believers always get things right. But there does seem to be a search among some non-believing scientists for something they can call 'god'. I particularly have in mind Professor Brian Cox' *Universe* TV documentary series, in which he relentlessly pursues the possibility of life elsewhere in the universe.[13] His suggestion that the sun must be the closest thing to

---

[10] George, 74.
[11] Martin Luther, *Works*, Erlangen Edition, 5:16, 142-8.
[12] Romans 3:1-23; Ephesians 2:1-3; 2 Corinthians 4:3f.; John 6:44.
[13] Brian E. Cox, *Universe*, 'The Sun: God Star', BBC2 October/November 2021; "The

what might be called 'god', yet in the face of disbelief in the truth as Bible-believers see it, seems to betray a yearning for something supernatural. I'm not sure where that places him among the vast numbers of sun-worshippers, ancient and modern.

A recent article in *The Guardian* newspaper by Oliver Burkeman (27 April 2021) and correspondence following[14] underlined for me the quandary that results from that kind of disbelief. Burkeman rehearses the usual aspects of deterministic thinking that spring from the belief that the physical universe of cause and effect is all that there is, although he does recognise the findings of quantum physics which indicate that at the level of atoms and electrons some events appear to be genuinely random, and therefore cannot be predicted in advance. He also considers the notion of compatibility,[15] but concludes that the solution must be either-or, and not both-and – otherwise known as 'illusionism'. However, he concludes his article with this thought,

> I personally can't claim to find the case against free will ultimately persuasive; it's just at odds with too much else that seems obviously true about life.

As Christian believers, we can only trust the senses and intellect that God has bequeathed to humanity, and which, although damaged through the Fall, nonetheless remain as our witnesses to the reality he created and that which to us is "obviously true". Furthermore, our God-given sentience brings with it an ability to conceive original thoughts and to be creative, just like the one in whose image we are made. Inevitably, however, to some extent our thoughts and actions are responses to external, as well as internal, stimuli which are beyond our control, and which we often barely understand – "consciousness and its relationship to the quantum realm in which randomness (i.e.,

---

modern story of the stars as told by science … places them firmly in the realm of the gods."

[14] See <https://www.theguardian.com/news/2021/apr/27/the-clockwork-universe-is-free-will-an-illusion?CMP=Share_iOSApp_Other>; <https://www.theguardian.com/world/2021/apr/29/the-battle-for-free-will-in-the-face-of-determinism?CMP= Share_iOSApp_Other> and <https://www.theguardian.com/world/2021/may/02/free-will-debate-rages-on-or-is-it-all-an-illusion?CMP=Share_iOSApp_Other> (accessed December 2022).

[15] See Chapter 6, especially 165 n11, and 166 n15.

indeterminism) has been proven to be real", for example, according to one respondent. He continues, "Given our lack of understanding about consciousness, any argument against free will is at best incomplete and at worst requires a quasi-religious leap of faith around something we do not understand enough to make such bold claims". Furthermore, in the words of another respondent, "If we are always deterministically fated to be led down a wired neural pathway towards a conclusion that we cannot escape, we have no real basis for assuming that it bears any relation to the actual nature of things." There has to be a degree of cause and effect in our lives – responses to stimuli, but over and above all of that, whether or not we are able to put into effect the things we desire or need, we must nevertheless trust in our ability to make objective decisions. Our wills may, indeed, be bound, although perhaps not to the extent advocated by Martin Luther in his *On the Bondage of the Will*, but I believe there is no limit to what we may imagine or dream of.

Mention of Martin Luther in this context permits a brief aside on his book, *On the Bondage of the Will* (*De Servo Arbitrio*), published in 1525 in response to Desiderius Erasmus' *On Free Will* (*De libero arbitrio diatribe sive collation*), which was published the previous year as a public attack on Luther's teachings. *On the Bondage of the Will* is often regarded as the definitive statement of the Reformed position which, in its strongest form denies free will to mankind.[16] Luther's basic position was an inflexible belief in total divine foreknowledge and foreordination,

> For if we believe it to be true, that God fore-knows and fore-ordains all things; that He can be neither deceived nor hindered in His Prescience and Predestination; and that nothing can take place but according to His Will, (which reason herself is compelled to confess;) then, even according to the testimony of reason herself, there can be no "Free-will" - in man, - in angel, - or in any creature![17]

---

[16] Clark H. Pinnock in Basinger & Basinger, 157 n26: "Luther constructed this rigorous connection [between divine sovereignty and human free will] in *Bondage of the Will*."
[17] Luther (*Cole*), Conclusion, Section 167. Section numbering follows Henry Coles' 1823 translation of Melancthon's edition of Luther's text.

He writes at great length attempting to show that the notion of human free will is logically and theologically unwarranted. However, some care must be exercised here because we cannot assume that what Luther and Erasmus understood by 'free will' was what we might understand by it. Luther says that '"Free-will" is a downright lie',[18] but it is quite clear that what he was arguing against was the exercise of free will as a means of obtaining grace for salvation, which for him was tantamount to the addition of works to faith. He frequently refers to Pelagianism,[19] clearly his main fear, and he comes close to accusing Erasmus of that very error. It does seem, however, that he believed free will to operate in the natural sphere, and that mankind was permitted

> "Free-will," not in respect of those which are above him, but in respect only of those things which are below him: that is, he may be allowed to know, that he has, as to his goods and possessions the right of using, acting, and omitting, according to his "Free-will;" although, at the same time, that same "Free-will" is overruled by the Free-will of God alone, just as He pleases: but that, God-ward, or in things which pertain unto salvation or damnation, he has no " Free-will," but is a captive, slave, and servant, either to the will of God, or to the will of Satan.[20]

However, Luther's usage of the term 'free will' departs from mine in that he regarded it as an active thing, an ability to pursue grace. I and many Arminians would believe in a God-given ability to make decisions with respect to good or ill, for or against grace, and that in varying degrees our pursuit of grace would have to be assisted by the Holy Spirit.[21] On the other hand, the refusal of divine grace and the pursuit of godlessness would presumably be energised by the Devil. It is crucially important to make that distinction: the difference between deciding and pursuing. Luther, erroneously in my view, regarding the *ability* to pursue as the exercise of free will. He writes much about our inability to follow rules, notably the divine commandments, but does not appear to consider what might motivate one to try to follow those rules

---

[18] Luther (*Cole*), Introduction.
[19] See below, 139, 'Pelagianism'.
[20] Luther (*Cole*), Preface, Section 26.
[21] Although I believe we are freer than that: see below, 143, 'Prevenient Grace'.

or, indeed, to take a different path. No matter how impossible it might be for one to pursue the path of obedience, there must remain some kind of freedom with which to decide to take one course or another. That was not a consideration for Luther, however, since he believed that God's determinative will controls everything without exception, including whether we take the path of grace or the road to destruction. Erasmus seemed to take a similar view with regard to the efficacy of free will, although he did permit the ability in mankind to pursue grace, as can be seen from Luther's hints about Pelagianism and when he reflected back to Erasmus his own definition of free will: he quotes Erasmus:

> Moreover I consider Free-will in this light: that it is a power in the human will, by which, a man may apply himself to those things which lead unto eternal salvation, or turn away from the same.[22]

It might therefore be said that Luther missed the point!

So far as making choices about mundane issues as opposed to divine issues is concerned, Alister McGrath, writing about the supposed conflict between science and faith, writes, "many natural philosophers [i.e., scientists] of the sixteenth and seventeenth centuries became increasingly suspicious of the reliability of unaided human reason as a way of arriving at truths about nature, using the kind of deductive processes familiar from Greek philosophy".[23] He goes on to attribute this scientific rejection of reason to its reliance on the limitations of human rationality "traditionally expressed by the Christian doctrine of original sin". Thus, experimentation rather than pure reason became the basis for reliable knowledge. Clearly, those early empiricists were mistaken because even the design and interpretation of their experiments would require considerable powers of disciplined intellect. Likewise, the discipline of mathematics, upon which the whole of the scientific enterprise ultimately depends, is fundamentally and purely logical.

To bring an allusion to McGrath's work on the relationship between science and religion into a discussion about Election simply underlines

---

[22] Luther (*Cole*), Discussion, Section 41.
[23] McGrath (2015), 34.

the enormous, and I would say deleterious, influence of ideas about Total Depravity - not so much "original sin", as McGrath puts it, which abounded following the Counter-Reformation. Happily, modern science seems to have recovered a better equilibrium, but I draw attention to McGrath's observation because it seems to me that Reformed thinking, both ironically and inexplicably, is shot through with a deep ambivalence about the value and efficacy of human intellect. On the one hand, much of the way in which Reformed doctrine has developed and is expressed depends on a highly developed system of logical argument, but on the other hand, Reformed theological considerations cause the ability of the human mind to be denigrated. It is simply not possible to have it both ways.

Many non-Reformed believers, on the other hand, although not in any way denying the fallenness of humankind, or our need of salvation and the restoration of God's image in us, assert that we may freely respond to the gospel, and accept or reject it unaided. That said, however, there are variations of opinion as to whether our acceptance of the gospel can be entirely without divine assistance. Arminians do not deny that our freedom of choice might be thwarted by other factors, especially if they have been brought about by sinful choices or practices – Paul, for example, writes of those whose consciences have become seared.[24] What Arminians do reject, however, is the dogma that we do not have the ability to choose to obey the gospel.

There is considerable debate surrounding the issues of divine determinism and free will. One significant theory as to how this enigma might be resolved, however, entails the notion of *compatibility*, sometimes called 'contra-causal freedom'.

A helpful volume on the Predestination-Free Will debate is that edited by the Basinger brothers where four authors, representing different perspectives state their positions and each in turn critiques the others. John Feinberg, a self-confessed determinist, sets out his belief that God ordains all things, and in doing so, provides a helpful (although sometimes confusing) taxonomy of the range of views on determinism and

---

[24] 1 Timothy 4:2.

indeterminism. Although as a determinist, he regards indeterminism (the notion that human free will is valid) as false,[25] he notes a number of misconceptions about indeterminism. First, he notes that while indeterminism claims that a person's act is free if it is not causally determined, there are indeed influences of the will prior to choosing that may incline the will in one direction or another at the point of decision making. None of them is sufficiently strong to cause the agent to choose one thing over another, however. A second misconception about indeterminism is that it assumes that free choice is random because it is claimed to be without a point or reason. Choices are always made for a reason, but no causal explanation can be given as to why the chooser would act according to one particular reason or another. Nonetheless, on the assumption of indeterminism, people do cause their own actions: "Indeterminists merely deny that there is anything which *causes the person* to do the act." Thus, irrespective of the direction that the chooser decides to pursue, he or she can still choose contrary to those causes, since they do not decisively incline them in one direction or another.[26]

It is worth observing that there is a significant difference between the kind of determinism which relates to the physical sciences (see above, 133f.) as opposed to theological determinism, however. Whereas in science, cause and effect can be seen or inferred reasonably decisively, at least in theory, the things which affect personal choices are far more complex, and will usually, if not always, defy identification.[27]

Although a determinist, Feinberg does regard himself as a *compatibilist*, however: that is, one who regards his actions as free, even if causally determined so long as the causes are not constraining. This is the view often referred as *soft determinism* or *compatibilism*. Feinberg regards genuinely free human action as *compatible* with non-constraining

---

[25] Bruce Reichenbach in Basinger & Basinger, 54, points out that Feinberger regards indeterminism as false because a believer could still apostatise if they could do whatever they willed. Reichenbach cites Hebrews 6:4-6; 10:26-9; Luke 8:6f., 13; John 15; Romans 11:22; Revelation 3 and Acts 5:1-11 as scripture passages which "teach that apostasy is possible and must be guarded against: see Chapter 4,70, on 'Perseverance'.
[26] John Feinberg in Basinger & Basinger, 20f.
[27] Ibid., 23.

sufficient conditions which incline the will decisively in one way or another. Thus, he claims that an action can be regarded as free, and cites an illustrative scenario of compatibilism, where a person, not having intended to take a particular course of action, does so when faced with some of the consequences or advantages of taking that action. His ultimate action was causally determined, yet it was done freely (compatibilistically), since he was not constrained to act against his desires.[28]

Pelagianism

The historic conflict between Augustine and Pelagius often clouds this issue. Thuesen observes that it is sometimes forgotten that Augustine's first thoughts on Predestination, which were based on Romans 8:29: "For those God foreknew he also predestined to be conformed to the image of his Son", insisted that "God only predestined those whom he knew would believe and follow the call". That view, expressed in an unfinished pair of commentaries published in 394 and 395, sounds intriguingly similar to the teaching of Arminius. However, barely two years later, he reached the radically different conclusion that God did not choose Jacob (or anyone else) in view of foreseen faith: he admitted that at first, he had "really worked for the free choice of the human will, but the grace of God won out." On the basis of that conclusion, he was to write his most famous work, the *Confessions* (387-400), the work which helped to spark off the whole Pelagian Controversy, and in which he recounted how he believed God had chosen him despite his earlier life of sexual immorality and religious scepticism.[29]

Pelagius (c. 355-c. 420),[30] a well-educated layman – some say he was a monk; fluent in Greek and Latin, and a learned theologian, was well-known in Rome towards the end of the fourth century, where he had

---

[28] Ibid., 24-6. Feinberg, 29 & 31, claims that compatibility makes sense of Ephesians 1:11, and other texts, which he claims to be the clearest expression of God's sovereignty. It will be clear that I do not agree with his position: see also Chapter 8a(iv), 213, on *klēroō*.

[29] Thuesen, 19.

[30] Mark W. Elliott, "Pelagianism", in Ian A. McFarland, David A. S. Fergusson, Karen Kilby & Iain R. Torrance, eds., *The Cambridge Dictionary of Christian Theology* (Cambridge: Cambridge University Press, 2011), 377.

lived since 380 as a harsh practising ascetic and persuasive speaker. Contemporaries, including Augustine, said he was British and a "saintly man", although Jerome thought he was Irish, and on account of his portly, but tall stature, suggested he was "stuffed with Irish porridge".[31] Despite being regarded as an arch-heretic by many even to the present day, his teachings are sometimes now taken more seriously, and it is well-worth bearing in mind that many of those who crossed-swords with the better-known and respected figures of historical theology were often men who took scripture seriously and thought deeply as they wrestled with some of the Church's doctrines, even though they arrived at conclusions which history has evaluated as heterodoxy. Indeed, as David Edwards observes, they should probably be regarded as "pioneers in the theological task which must be ours".[32] It is salutary that much of what we know of Pelagius comes from Augustine's own writings and from the way he influenced Augustine's thinking. All that has survived of his written output are a commentary on Romans and his expositions of Paul's thirteen epistles.

The issue which seems to have sparked off the controversy between Augustine and Pelagius was a public reading from the *Confessions* by a Roman bishop, and in particular Augustine's prayer in Book 10 which expressed the powerlessness of humans to obey God and bring about their own election: "Give what you command, and command what you will".[33] To Pelagius' indignation, and being critical of Augustine's earlier position in *On Free Choice of the Will*, he saw those words as reducing humans to mere puppets, insulting not only their own integrity but also the goodness of their Creator. Furthermore, attributing the moral laxity of Roman society to Augustine's theology of divine grace, he began to teach a very strict and rigid moralism which emphasised a natural, innate human ability to attain salvation. "So", says Thuesen,

> began more than a decade of bitter debate in which Pelagius, set

---

[31] *Scotorum pultibus praegravatus*; <https://en.wikipedia.org/wiki/Pelagius> (accessed July 2020).
[32] Edwards in Edwards & Stott, 109.
[33] Augustine, *Confessions* 10.29.40. This account is thought by some to be apocryphal, but Augustine refers to the occasion in *De Dono Perseverantiae* (On the Gift of Perseverance) 20.53.

opposite the influential Augustine, became the whipping boy of Western theology after his positions were condemned by a succession of councils, emperors, and popes.... Yet the real weight of the Pelagian controversy was in the volume of polemical literature produced, including some of Augustine's most unqualified and influential defenses of predestination.[34]

Pelagius apparently[35] believed that we are born in a neutral state so far as sinfulness is concerned, but, according to Theodore Beza, Augustine's definition of Original Sin entailed the belief that all sinned in Adam, the *federal* head of the human race, so he held that all are born sinners.[36] Augustine reasoned that since, in a sense, all were in Adam's loins, which, of course, is true in biological terms if the DNA of all humanity is derived from Adam and Eve's, everyone since Adam shared in his act of disobedience and all must therefore share his condemnation. Pelagius differed sharply from Augustine, holding, in theory at least, that we are able to live sinless and morally pleasing lives before God, while for Augustine, often referred to as "the doctor of grace",[37] only an experience of divine grace can restore a person's ability to please God.

For long periods after Augustine a compromise position known as Semi-Pelagianism held sway, however. Augustine's basic insight on the primacy of God's electing grace was destined to become more or less the official line in the western Church. However, a contemporary, John Cassian, a monk from Gaul, expressed concern about the difficulty in reconciling strict Predestination with the biblical assurance that God

---

[34] Thuesen, 19f.
[35] 'Apparently', because few of Pelagius' writings have survived and most of what is known of his teachings has been drawn from Augustine's polemic against him and from the way he influenced Augustine's later thinking.
[36] Federalism or Covenantalism is a notion refined by Beza, based on Calvin's work and enshrined in the *Westminster Confession* (1646). Adam is recognised not merely as the biological head of the human race, but also as its *federal* representative. Thus, all are born corrupt because they are representatively implicated in his sin and guilt. This representative incorporation is the root of each person's inherent disposition to sin. It is a relationship which all confirm by their own sinful acts: thus, according to Augustine, a person is not a sinner because he or she sins; rather, they sin because they are sinners: J. E. Colwell in Ferguson & Wright, 642.
[37] *Doctor gratiae*; McGrath (2012), 66.

"desires everyone to be saved".[38] His solution, later misleadingly to be called Semi-Pelagianism, did not deny Original Sin, as had Pelagius, but did allow for a measure of human cooperation with God. Cassian believed that the human capacity to choose the good was not obliterated by Adam's sin but was merely injured. Humans retain enough God-given natural ability to take the initial step toward Christ, although additional grace is needed to bring the process of salvation to completion. Therefore, those who fail to exercise their wills in taking that initial step are entirely culpable for their own damnation and are, in fact, acting against God's own will for all to be saved.[39] Thus, Augustine's critics insisted, "it cannot be doubted that there are by nature some seeds of goodness in every soul implanted by the kindness of the Creator".[40]

On this view, God and the individual accomplish synergistically what is needed for salvation. Whereas Pelagianism teaches that we do not need God's grace to enable us to respond to the gospel or to continue to please God, Semi-Pelagianism says that because the Fall weakened our moral nature, we do require strengthening grace. The initial act of responding to God is due to free will, so the first step towards conversion is "ordinarily taken by the human will and that grace only supervened later",[41] that grace assisting the believer in a life of faith and good works. These views were condemned by several popes and church councils; Pelagianism at Carthage in 418 and Ephesus in 431, and Semi-Pelagianism at the Council of Orange in 529, which declared that grace was necessary at the beginning as well as throughout the Christian life.[42] Confusion easily arises if the Arminian view is not distinguished from either of these two positions because Arminianism is not primarily about whether a person may freely respond to God or not. Nonetheless, from time-to-time Arminians have been unjustly accused of Semi- if not full-blown Pelagianism. Arminius certainly held neither view, and he took pains to make that clear. He did not believe that

---

[38] 1 Timothy 2:4.
[39] Thuesen, 21f.
[40] Pelikan, 323f.
[41] Frank L. Cross & Elizabeth A. Livingstone, eds., *The Oxford Dictionary of the Christian Church* (Oxford: Oxford University Press, 2005), 1491.
[42] Horton, 31.

man's free will was not bound, but he did believe that only by the grace of God could a person respond to the gospel.[43]

That Arminians have also recognised that people have a problem responding to God's grace is evident in their doctrine of Prevenient Grace. This is the grace given indiscriminately to all which enables them to believe – the salvation-bringing grace, that, according to Thiessen, has appeared to all.[44]

Prevenient Grace

It may be worth briefly considering the meaning and validity of the notion of Prevenient Grace at this point. The term is often linked with John Wesley (1703-91), but it was a concept espoused by Arminius, if not by some of his predecessors, and it is central and crucial to standard Arminian theology.[45] Arminius ascribed all of salvation to the grace of God and, despite what later Calvinists may have claimed, fervently denied that he attributed any part of the work of salvation to human effort.[46] Both Calvinism and Arminianism have as the basis of their respective doctrines of grace the conviction that humankind is utterly unable to offer anything towards their salvation, so, as has already been argued, it is unwarranted to accuse Arminianism of Pelagianism or even Semi-Pelagianism. Both Calvinism and Arminianism affirm our need for divine grace in order to elicit our response of faith. Thus, classical Arminian theology, such as that of John Wesley, affirms Total Depravity and our utter helplessness even to exercise good will towards God apart from his assisting grace. It attributes the sinner's ability to respond to the gospel with repentance and faith to Prevenient Grace – the illuminating, convicting, calling, and enabling power of the Holy Spirit working on the sinner's soul which frees them to choose or reject saving grace. Arminius strongly believed in Prevenient Grace as being regenerative. For him, it was

---

[43] E.g., Arminius, *Works*, 2.192, 482.
[44] Titus 2:11; H. C. Thiessen, *Introductory Lectures in Systematic Theology* (Grand Rapids, MI: Eerdmans, 1949), 344ff., cited by Erickson, 920.
[45] Olson (2011), 67.
[46] Ibid.

not only persuasive; it also renews the person in the image of God and liberates the will so that the person can for the first time exercise a good will toward God in repentance and faith. It even communicates the gifts of repentance and faith to the person, who must only accept and not resist them.[47]

This is the Arminian interpretation of the "drawings" of God in John 6:44, etc.[48] God does not draw irresistibly but persuasively, leaving us able to say 'no' as well as 'yes'. Thus, Prevenient Grace is enabling but resistible.[49] Quoting Baptist theologian Robert E. Picirilli, Olson writes,

> What Arminius meant by "prevenient grace" was that grace that precedes actual regeneration and which, except when finally resisted, inevitably leads on to regeneration. He was quick to observe that this "assistance of the Holy Spirit" is of such sufficiency "as to keep at the greatest possible distance from Pelagianism."[50]

It should be apparent from these quotations from Olson and Picirilli that the term 'regeneration' is used in different ways by different writers.[51] Reformed writers tend to attribute regeneration, which they also equate with the new birth, to the effects of *effectual* or *Prevenient grace* which precede conversion and enable faith to be exercised. Regeneration is therefore the initial part of the precise sequence of events which constitutes the process from rebirth to glorification based on the *Golden Chain* of Romans 8:29-30.[52] Given that they believe an individual has been divinely chosen, the next part of the process is the divine unconditional gift of *regeneration* which awakens the individual to respond to this *effectual* or *prevenient* grace. Thus, Augustine, who envisaged grace under several aspects, taught that the first was "prevenient grace", by which God initiates in our souls whatever good we think or aspire

---

[47] Olson (2006), 163.
[48] See Chapter 10b(i), 290, 'Coming to Jesus'.
[49] Olson (2011), 169.
[50] Ibid., quoting Robert E. Picirilli, *Grace, Faith, Free Will* (Nashville, TN: Randall House, 2002), 153.
[51] See Appendix 3a(i), 399-401, on the way John Piper and other Reformed writers use the terms 'conversion', 'salvation' and 'regeneration'.
[52] A phrase derived from William Perkins' *A Golden Chaine* of 1591. See Chapter 8d, 238, on 'Calling' and Chapter 10c, 324, on Romans 8:29-30.

to or will.[53] John Piper says,

> We will not repent and believe unless God does His work to overcome our hard and rebellious hearts. This divine work is called *regeneration*. Our work is called *conversion*.
>
> We must first experience the regenerating work of the Holy Spirit. The Scriptures promised long ago that God would devote Himself to this work in order to create for Himself a faithful people.
>
> John teaches most clearly that regeneration precedes and enables faith. Everyone who believes that Jesus is the Christ *has been* born of God. (1 John 5:1)[54]

On the other hand, I have always understood regeneration to be the enlivening of the human spirit, the being-born-again event, which is the *result* of the exercise of saving faith rather than the *enabling* of saving faith. Rather than being an external donation of grace which triggers the process of repentance and faith, regeneration is a process more or less synonymous with sanctification, the internal process by which God makes us morally righteous like himself.

This, of course, causes us to recognise yet another distinction, that between what Martin Bucer in the 1530s called "justification of the ungodly" (*iustificatio impii*), which consists of God's gracious forgiveness of human sin, and "justification of the godly" (*iustificatio pii*), which consists of the obedient human response to the moral demands of the gospel as modelled for us by Christ. Later Protestant theology refers to the first justification simply as 'justification' and the second as 'regeneration' or 'sanctification'. McGrath describes Bucer's 'double justification' thus:

> First, the believer's union with Christ leads directly to his or her *justification*. Through Christ, the believer is declared to be righteous in the sight of God. Second, on account of the believer's union

---

[53] Augustine, *Enchiridion*, 32; *De natura et gratia* (On Nature and Grace), 35, cited by Kelly, 367. Marcus Dods ed., *The Works of Aurelius Augustine Bishop of Hippo*, Vol IX, *The Enchiridion*, 32, 199, quotes, "We read in Holy Scriptures, both that God's mercy 'shall prevent me,' [Psalms 59:10: note that 'prevent' means 'to go before'] and that His mercy 'shall follow me' [Psalms 23:6]. It 'prevents' the unwilling to make him willing; it follows the willing to make his will effectual."

[54] Piper (2011), 64-6 (his italics).

with Christ—and *not* on account of his or her justification—the believer begins the process of becoming like Christ through regeneration. Where Bucer argued that justification causes regeneration, Calvin asserts that both justification and regeneration are the results of the believer's union with Christ through faith.[55]

For Reformed thinkers, this view of regeneration poses no problem because God's grace for them is irresistible in any case, so the regeneration which brings about faith in Christ also automatically brings about the new birth.[56] However, in today's milieu, these two definitions of 'regeneration' are not often distinguished except in Reformed writings such as John Piper's *Desiring God*. The non-Reformed mind is likely therefore to misunderstand the rubric of *The Book of Common Prayer* for the baptism of infants: "Seeing now, dearly beloved brethren, that *this Child is* regenerate, and grafted into the body of Christ's Church ...", a sticking point for those who practise believer's baptism and who understand 'regeneration' to refer to the process of the new birth taking hold and developing the image of our Creator within us.

To return to our discussion of Prevenient Grace, it is clear that, since both Calvinists and Arminians believe in human inability – that we are unable to offer anything at all towards our salvation, and that our response of faith requires divine aid, there is in both systems the need for a divine grant of grace in order for the sinner to place his or her trust in Christ. In the Calvinistic system that grace is usually termed Effectual Grace, and in Arminianism, Prevenient Grace. However, the bestowal of such grace cannot be demonstrated in a practical sense, and some writers claim that there is no biblical warrant for either in any case. Vic Reasoner says that "the dogmatic category which cannot be substantiated biblically is what Calvinists term 'effectual grace'."[57] Indeed, citing Erickson, writing specifically about Prevenient Grace, he claims,

> The problem is that there is no clear and adequate basis in Scripture for this concept of a universal enablement. The theory, appealing though it is in many ways, simply is not taught explicitly in the

---

[55] McGrath (2012), 131 (his talics).
[56] See Klein, 299f., for a brief discussion of regeneration.
[57] Reasoner in Pinnock & Wagner, 187.

Bible.[58]

If it is true that the biblical basis for such a belief is entirely lacking, we are driven back to examine the basis for that belief and the validity of that inability, and that in turn will force us to examine the nature of free will. The requirement for an extra grace, whether effectual or prevenient, is demanded by the abhorrence of any sense that we can contribute to our salvation, so we need also to examine the nature of saving faith and whether it is, as many allege, God's gift.

Since effectual and prevenient grace are apparently constructs demanded by theological preconception rather than by exegetical conclusion, I find myself unable to subscribe to either notion; the idea of effectual grace because I do not believe God chooses individuals, and the notion of prevenient grace because it can be affirmed neither from scripture nor from practical experience. It seems to me that here there is a problem in that, if divine grace were to be dispensed either indiscriminately to all or specifically to those divinely chosen, how would we know whether an individual was so blessed, and, in making our own response of faith, how would we know that it was either divinely motivated or an entirely human response? That objection applies specifically to the Arminian position of prevenient grace because it seems to me that there can be no difference between, on the one hand, that kind of grace and the inbuilt human ability to respond or not, and, on the other hand, the gift of conscience bequeathed through our creation in God's image. If such a denial of a gift of grace can be upheld, we could easily be moved back into Pelagian or Semi-Pelagian territory, so it becomes important that we find a solution to the questions concerning the nature of saving faith and free will. We need to find a line between the conviction that salvation is all of grace and that free will is a reality, but that it does not confer the ability to contribute meritoriously to the response of faith beyond the ability to simply make that response. These issues will be examined in due course.

It seems to me then, that, since Prevenient Grace is claimed to be bestowed on all people, thus allowing them the freedom to respond to the

---

[58] Ibid., quoting Erickson, 925.

gospel, I would prefer to think that it is none other than part of the divine image which the Fall has not obliterated. All can respond to the gospel therefore, not by a *prevenient* grace, but by the grace of *freedom of choice* which was bestowed upon all in Creation.

*****

Arminians therefore believe that the decision for eternal life or death resides in the gift of choice of the individual, even though it may only be exercised with divine assistance which is conferred indiscriminately upon all. Since God through the gospel appeals for a human response, they insist that we must have the capacity to make an appropriate response. On this particular point Calvinistic writings can become very confusing, if not contradictory, and it seems to me that many of those contradictions arise from inadequate definitions of free will.[59] For example, I suggest that Loraine Boettner lapses into absurdity when attempting to illustrate the proposed paradox that sin does not remove man's freedom of choice, but merely its proper use. He illustrates his point with the assertion that a bird with a broken wing is free to fly, but is unable to do so; likewise, "the natural man is free to come to God but [is] not able".[60] That strikes me as a very strange notion of freedom. Many similar attempts to illustrate this seeming paradox abound. Likewise, Louis Berkhof claims that Election is not inconsistent with free will:

> the Bible certainly does not proceed on the assumption that the divine decree is inconsistent with the free agency of man.[61]

because man can exercise free will in other areas such as the attainment of knowledge, etc.[62] That we cannot exercise free will in the crucial area of responding to the gospel does not appear to Berkhof and others to invalidate their argument. Another example is Erickson's suggestion that the way to reconcile what the Bible appears to say about free choice and God's irresistible grace is that "God makes his offer so appealing

---

[59] Carson (2002), 206f.
[60] Boettner, 'Predestination' in E. F. Harrison, ed., *Baker's Dictionary of Theology* (Grand Rapids, MI: Baker, 1960), 65, cited by Erickson, 917.
[61] L. Berkhof, 106.
[62] Ibid., 248.

that they *will* respond affirmatively".[63]

Moderate Calvinism and Single Predestinarianism

A range of more moderate positions, which lessen the impact of strict Calvinism, specifically the logic of divine rejection of those not chosen, have come to prominence more recently. I would suggest that these more palatable moderate views, which promote Single Predestination, are, as often as not, symptoms of an inability to fully assimilate the unpalatable logic of the so-called *dreadful decrees* – Total Depravity and Unconditional Election. If such positions are indeed based upon the core concepts of Calvinism, as claimed, then they cannot be regarded as logically rigorous and really ought to be excluded from serious consideration. However, in as much as they have become common, if not predominant, in contemporary Reformed proclamation and writing, due consideration must be given to them. I note that Michael Horton in his recent defence of Calvinism, *For Calvinism*, adopts a single-predestinatory stance, but denies that Double Predestination has any place in Reformed teaching. He says that

> Often, when the term "Calvinism" is mentioned, people think of an arbitrary God who drags some people into heaven kicking and screaming, while telling others who want to be saved that they're simply not on the list. Sometimes this caricature is actually given life by hyper-Calvinists. However, it has never had any place in the Calvinist system.[64]

Such over-the-top special pleading seems to me to be a flat denial of the classical Reformed view, and certainly a distancing from the New Calvinism.[65] A number of the examples I have chosen to illustrate these moderate views are drawn from Peter Lewis, Roy Clements and Greg Haslam's *Chosen for Good*, a popular exposition of modern Reformed doctrine by a number of contemporary writers. The book teaches Single Predestination and, although not stated, its chapter order

---

[63] Erickson, 927 (his italics).
[64] Horton, 57.
[65] See Chapter 2, 40, 'The Contemporary Legacy'.

is organised on the pattern of TULIP, the Five Points of Calvinism.

The essential issue over which much modern Reformed teaching departs from classical Calvinism is the question of whether God, in choosing some for salvation, condemns others to eternal loss, i.e., Double *versus* Single Unconditional Election. For example, Peter Lewis says,

> Scripture commits us to the doctrine of unconditional predestination to eternal life, but not to that of unconditional predestination unto eternal damnation.... as though God simply decided that he would create some for heaven and some for hell. That is more than Scripture tells us and is, in my opinion, a quite monstrous idea.... If a man is saved it is because he has been elected in the love of God to this salvation, and if a man is lost it is not because God has predestined him to be lost, but because he has rejected the offered love and salvation of God in Jesus Christ.... Salvation is all of God, damnation is all of man.[66]

Lewis continues in a footnote:

> in regard to the decree of reprobation, we read in the *Confession* [i.e., *The Westminster Confession of Faith*]: 'The rest of mankind, God was pleased, according to the unsearchable counsel of his Own will ... to pass by and to ordain them to dishonour and wrath *for their sin*, to the praise of his glorious justice.' The phrase 'for their sin' is crucial. The 'passing by' is the rejection *of fallen* beings, men and women considered (albeit long before the event) as having rejected God. They are rebels before they are rejected.[67]

I would say that Lewis thus requires us to suspend rationality. The logic that God chooses certain men and women to salvation but does not choose the rest to eternal loss makes no sense, and no amount of saying that these things "do not contradict each other in God's wisdom" but "only in our limited minds ... for the Creator is incomprehensible to his creatures",[68] casts any light on the conundrum. The rational view, which I believe is the biblical view, is that no one deserves salvation; indeed, all have sinned and have fallen short. But if God then chooses to select some sinners but leaves aside others who are no more nor less

---

[66] In P. Lewis *et al*, 42f.
[67] Ibid., 43 n1 (his italics).
[68] Ibid., 44.

deserving of being chosen, then he must consciously have rejected those whom he had not chosen. Furthermore, if Lewis asks us to believe only those things that scripture affirms, then some important generally accepted theological conclusions might also be called into question.[69] I have quoted more than I might otherwise have done from Lewis because, in his zeal to find a rationale, he apparently crosses the line between Calvinism and Arminianism in claiming in effect that God's rejection of the Reprobate is based on foreknowledge of their rebellion – "They are rebels before they are rejected" – and thus he appears to draw a conclusion that is inconsistent with his basic Reformed position.

In my view, Lewis gets himself into a muddle of contradictions. For example, he asserts that the doctrine of Predestination is established in the life and passion of Christ – the doctrine "shows us the greatest, freest person in the world being predestined to do his work".[70] "Was Jesus a robot?" he asks. Of course, he wasn't, but in deviating in his argument from the issue of election for eternal salvation to the divine foreordination of the work Jesus came into the world to do, he makes a serious mistake: he equates in essence the foreordination of Christ's redemptive work with the foreordination of sinners to eternal life. The former has nothing to do with my response to the gospel, except, of course, in terms of making provision for eternal salvation, but the latter has everything to do with my eternal destiny. Furthermore, whereas Lewis had previously claimed that God's rejection of the reprobate was based on foreknowledge of their rebellion, he says, "In the light of Acts 2:23 and 4:27-28 *foreknowledge is clearly on the basis of foreordination*".[71] He fails to mention that, although scripture clearly teaches that Jesus' suffering was foreordained, as the two Acts references make abundantly clear, God's predestining will in that instance had nothing to do with the Reformed view that sinners are predestined to eternal life.[72] As it happens, he also confuses the distinction between

---

[69] Perhaps the most important being the doctrine of the Trinity, let alone the speculative Calvinistic teachings about the Divine Decrees, etc.
[70] In P. Lewis *et al*, 47.
[71] Ibid., 56 (his italics).
[72] See Chapter 8c, 219, 'Foreknowledge'.

Foreordination and Predestination by failing to use the word 'predestined' in the way that scripture does.[73]

He compounds his error by quoting with approval what he says is "a serious warning against misusing this word 'foreknowledge'" from Donald McLeod:

> The very meaning of election to salvation is that our obedience is the result (and therefore cannot be the cause) of the divine choice. Our first movements towards God are due to His grace: 'Except a man be born again he cannot see the kingdom of heaven' ... 'unto you it is given to believe on him' ... Election based on faith and repentance is nothing other than love earned by faith and repentance. And then grace is no more grace.[74]

Classical Calvinism denies that reprobation is on the basis of God's foreknowledge, but it does become confused about the basis upon which he rejects or passes over people, invoking terminology such as *preterition* (literally, 'a passing by'), a term favoured by infralapsarians, in order to avoid any hint that the sinner might have deserved his or her reprobation and thereby making God the author of their sin. Berkhof says preterition is

> a sovereign act of God ... in which the demerits of man do not come into consideration.... The reason for preterition is not known by man. It cannot be sin, for all men are sinners.[75]

Although I find the Reformed doctrine of Election and Reprobation unacceptable, I do find Berkhof's account of it consistent. He is clear that "the doctrine of reprobation naturally follows from the logic of the situation"; that is, if God chooses some, then the rest are automatically excluded.[76] So far as Lewis' claims are concerned, however, it seems to me that in departing from strict Calvinism, he and his like only create more difficulties for themselves.

The confusion continues. In a chapter on Irresistible Grace, Roy

---

[73] See Chapter 8b, 217, on 'Predestination'.
[74] In P. Lewis *et al*, 57, quoting Donald McLeod, *Banner of Truth* magazine, April 1969.
[75] L. Berkhof, 115f. *The OED Concise*, 1137, defines 'preterition' as "the rhetorical technique of referring to something by professing to omit it".
[76] Ibid., 117.

Clements continues in similar vein with respect to the human response to the gospel, and propounds a view where he seeks to differentiate between human responsibility and capability:

> The Bible's doctrine of salvation hinges on the fact that man is responsible to God, but that he does not have the ability to please God and will be justly punished for that failure.[77]

We have already seen very similar views from Loraine Boettner and Louis Berkhof, above. The integrity of statements like these must seriously be questioned because they represent God as being just while demanding something impossible for us to accomplish. That is transparently wrong, but the formal Reformed response to that criticism would be that our inability to please God is self-imposed because of our "perverted choice made in Adam".[78]

It is worth noting that this view exposes a Calvinistic tendency to present a legalistic gospel. In other words, their emphasis is upon transgression of God's laws. The New Testament, on the other hand, although teaching that we all deserve punishment for our sins – indeed, we already stand under condemnation,[79] also teaches that Christ, in substituting himself for us, has died bearing the sins of the whole world, and therefore removes that judgment from us all. The decisive sin which keeps an individual out of heaven is not therefore that of failing to please God nor of transgressing his laws, but is the wilful rejection of Christ, the sin-bearer,[80] an action which, incidentally, I suggest

---

[77] In P. Lewis *et al*, 121.
[78] L. Berkhof, 250. The scope of this book does not permit more than very brief discussion of Original Sin, an issue fundamental to the Reformed understanding of man's culpability. Any formulation of the doctrine is fraught with difficulties, not least in that following man's expulsion from the protective environment of Eden with its immediate access to God, his consequent unprotected exposure to demonic forces and concomitant engagement in spiritual warfare is invariably overlooked. Any doctrine of sin which fails to take into account the powers of darkness is unbiblical and consequently inadequate, but Reformed writings often portray humankind as independent agents, as if there were no Devil, despite us not having complete free will, and the effects of demonic influences on our decision-making faculties and our response to temptation are often ignored. See, for example, John Colwell's article on *Sin* in Ferguson & Wright, 641ff.; also above, 141 n36, on Federalism.
[79] Romans 3:23; 5:12; John 3:18.
[80] John 3:19, 36.

requires the ability to choose.

Saving Grace

Another important aspect of the Reformed view with respect to man's inability to please God is the assertion that faith cannot be generated as an unaided response to the gospel. This is implicit in what has already been said about the need for a prevenient grace, the Arminian view, or an effectual grace, the Reformed view. The nature of saving faith needs to be explored in more detail therefore because it is claimed that Paul asserts that faith itself is the gift of God and cannot be generated by an unregenerate person. It is often said that "Arminians affirm *synergism* ... while Calvinists affirm *monergism*".[81] Monergism means 'one-working', or God's grace being the sole effectual source of election, redemption, faith and perseverance; in other words, the affirmation that we have no executive role in the process of our new birth and that it is all of God. On the other hand, *synergism* is 'working-together', a co-operation between God's grace and human will and activity. This definition is often the leverage used to accuse Arminianism of Pelagianism or Semi-Pelagianism, although that would be emphatically denied by most Arminians. The issue usually comes down to the way saving faith is understood and whether on an Arminian understanding that would qualify as a meritorious *work*, thus denying that our salvation is all of God and "not by works".

Paul says in Ephesians 2:8-9,[82]

> For it is by grace you have been saved, through faith – and this not from yourselves, it is the gift of God – not by works, so that no-one can boast.

---

[81] E.g., Horton, 16.
[82] I accept the traditional ascription of Ephesians to the Apostle Paul, which is deemed not to have been disproved by critical scholarship. See Tom Wright's (2013), 56ff., robust critique of scholarly fashion in his defence of possible Pauline authorship of Ephesians, Colossians and 2 Thessalonians in particular, although he doesn't come completely clean in affirming Ephesians as genuinely Pauline: "Ephesians and 2 Thessalonians are highly likely to be Pauline": Wright (2013), 61, although in Wright (2003), 236, he admits that he can see no real difference between, on the one hand Ephesians and Colossians, and, on the other hand, the rest of Paul's letters.

But Peter Lewis says,

> It is something of a red herring to protest that 'the gift of God', which is said to be not 'from yourselves', may in the Greek (as in the English!) refer not to 'faith' but 'salvation', for it should surely be clear from our study that we cannot look for saving faith from the unregenerate sinner. Faith – that is, true and saving faith – implies a cleared [sic] understanding (however small) of the things that come from God, a true desire for God in his holy love and lordship, and a heart which is out of love with sin, sorrowing for a godless life. Man by nature is now incapable of such a self-transformation. He cannot rise above himself.[83]

Lewis thus pays lip-service to the debate centring on the question of whether it is faith or salvation or both which Paul claims to be God's gift, and to be not from ourselves, but he seems to dismiss the matter as of lesser importance than the debate surely merits. He allows his prior theological assumptions – "we cannot look for saving faith from the unregenerate sinner" – to take precedence over the grammar of the verse. However, Peter O'Brien, discussing the response of faith as the means by which God's grace is appropriated, concludes by saying,

> the response of faith does not come from any human source but is God's gift. This interpretation is grammatically possible, assuming that the term denotes 'faith' and not Christ's 'faithfulness', and it is consistent with Pauline teaching elsewhere (cf. Phil. 1:29). However, the context demands that *this* be understood of salvation by grace as a whole, including the faith (or faithfulness) through which it is received.[84]

Other authors agree; the consensus being that Paul is referring to the whole package of salvation-by-grace-through-faith as being not of ourselves, but of God. That being the case, logically the essential part of that package must be 'salvation', a salvation qualified by the grace in

---

[83] P. Lewis in P. Lewis *et al*, 35f.
[84] O'Brien, 175 (his italics), with many others. Stott (1979), 83, to name but one, points out that the pronoun 'this', an adverbial accusative, is neuter, while 'faith' or 'faithfulness' is feminine. O'Brien cites J. A. Robinson, *St. Paul's Epistle to the Ephesians* (London: Macmillan, 1904), 157, who agrees that "the difference of gender is not fatal to such a view" but concludes on contextual grounds that the wider reference to 'salvation by grace' is demanded.

which it is offered and the faith by which it is received. The point Paul makes is that this salvation cannot be earned, but it is still obtained through faith. The Reformed conclusion is that faith would be a meritorious work if it were not God's gift to us. What is more, faith must also at least be part of God's gift because it cannot constitute part of what a lost soul must do to be saved. Clearly, if it is the whole salvation-by-grace-through-faith package which is God's gift, faith cannot be a meritorious act whereby the sinner coming to Jesus makes some contribution, no matter how small, towards the purchase of his or her salvation. Much is often made of this point in Reformed writings. I would suggest, however, that that is to make more of faith than is required. Peter Lewis, for instance, sees faith as a response impossible for the "unregenerate sinner" to make. He says that saving faith requires some understanding of the things of God and a "true desire for God in his holy love and lordship, and a heart which is out of love with sin, sorrowing for a godless life",[85] a view which seems to agree with Hebrews 11:6:

> without faith it is impossible to please God, because anyone who comes to him must believe that he exists and that he rewards those who earnestly seek him.

I wouldn't wish to engage in an exercise of categorising different kinds of faith, but clearly, Lewis' insistence on faith being a conscious response to what is known of God and of a need for repentance is far beyond what can be expected of the sinner coming to the foot of the Cross. I suggest that he is guilty of bolstering a preconception by exaggerated rhetoric. His view also betrays a tendency among Reformed expositors to regard faith as a cerebral activity. Clearly, it is that as we work out the contours of what we believe on our journey towards maturity in Christ, but I do not believe it could be true of a spiritual infant or as one yet to be born; one who has not come to faith through reasoned apologetic, having weighed up the pros and cons of the gospel, and especially not of one who desperately cries out to God for salvation in ignorance of whether he really exists or not. It can certainly never be true of the one who cries out, "God, if you are there, please save me!"

---

[85] P. Lewis in P. Lewis *et al*, 36.

WHAT IS THE PROPER HUMAN RESPONSE TO THE GRACE OF GOD?

We are all aware of such testimonies.

A similar kind of exaggeration or parody is seen elsewhere in the same volume where Roy Clements, writing about Irresistible Grace, refers to an anecdote from the well-known Reformed writer, James Packer.[86] The story relates an occasion when in student days Packer fell overboard into the River Thames (the Isis) at Oxford. He imagined that his friends might have encouraged him to get out of the water by his own efforts had he so wished. Alternatively, they could have refused to help because it would have interfered with his free will to help himself. Clements equates these two responses with Pelagianism and Arminianism respectively, wrongly so in my view. With respect to the former, he says that Pelagianism is akin to the White Queen's advice to Alice: "You can believe if only you practise a bit more". Alice's response, of course, was to retort, "It's no use trying. I can't believe impossible things."[87] Surely, however, the true nature of saving faith, in essence, has little or nothing to do with believing about things: rather it is to grasp the hand of the one reaching out to save the drowning man, *trusting*, or perhaps only *hoping*, that the saviour's hand can effect a rescue.

That response is far from cerebral, requiring not even a superficial knowledge, let alone a deep knowledge of whom it is that offers to save him, there being no necessary nor real understanding of his plight beyond the need for salvation. Indeed, none of the criteria Lewis lists (above, 155) is needed for the response of saving faith. It is the only response a person in conscious need of salvation can make – mustard seed faith or *trust*.[88] It may be, of course, that the drowning man, given a calmer situation, far less fraught with imminent danger, would not have chosen that means of rescue. Perhaps C. S. Lewis' conversion story (above, 4f.) might fit such a scenario, but I would suggest that at the point of his response of faith, even he recognised the urgency, the desperation perhaps, of his situation as an unbeliever; hence his resistance to the inevitable. Saving faith must often, I suggest, be

---

[86] Ibid., 102f.
[87] Lewis Caroll, *Through the Looking Glass*. Caroll's text has "one *can't* believe impossible things".
[88] Matthew 17:20; Luke 17:6.

exercised in the face of doubt, and often the sinner grasping the hand of Jesus can have very little or no real appreciation of what they are really getting themselves into. The other alternative, of course, sees the drowning man refusing the offer of help or looking for some better offer, the outcome of which would be sadly obvious, but it would remain his choice to refuse the offer of salvation.

'Faith' is a difficult word, and the concept of faith can be confusing. I think Peter Lewis confuses *belief*, in the sense of the body of understanding which is accepted by faith and which develops and enlarges as the Christian matures, on the one hand, with the *response of faith*, on the other. A far better translation of *pistis* (πίστις) in many biblical texts would therefore be 'trust'. Commenting on Luke 18:16-17, where Jesus, having called children to himself, says, "the kingdom of God belongs to such as these", Howard Marshall says,

> the basic thought is that of the sheer receptivity of children, especially infants, who cannot do anything to merit entry into the kingdom.[89]

The parallel passage in Matthew 18:2ff. draws attention to a child's humility, but even a child, characteristically biddable and trusting, must respond to being bidden. Likewise, Jesus taught in the Beatitudes that the kingdom of heaven belongs to the "poor in spirit",[90] which I take to mean, perhaps among other things, those who would never dare to think that their faith amounted to anything much.

Texts like these from the Gospels may illustrate the nature of the faith response, but they still do not adequately answer the Reformed claim that even a child-like response cannot be generated by the unaided will of the sinner. It seems to me that Peter Lewis and many like him, elevate saving faith to something far more than it really is: they attribute to *trust* a whole weight of meaning which would make it obvious that no one could generate it in and of themselves, and that it could only be given to them by divine grace. This seems to be a symptom of a Reformed tendency to develop themes to their logical conclusion – to

---

[89] I. H. Marshall (1978), 682f.
[90] Matthew 5:3.

absurd lengths, far beyond what is reasonable or sensible and then shoot them down – what some might call 'straw men' or 'Aunt Sallys'. Common sense suggests that there is a basic fallacy in doing that, although it is an argumentation technique which is very hard to counter.

Roy Clements' reference to Alice's struggle in believing is worth returning to because, in order to arrive at the point where faith must be exercised, a considerable mental tussle may first have had to take place. Where I believe he is mistaken, however, is in the view that the tussle *constitutes* the exercise of faith. Faith, or as I would prefer, *trust* is simply the surrender – the struggle to make sense of things is past and that struggle may not even have been completely resolved intellectually. The only resort of the sinner is simply to give in to God. That isn't by any stretch of the imagination an intellectual exercise: it is simply the drowning man submitting himself to being grasped by his rescuer.

The issue that needs to be resolved then is that of Inability, a corollary of Total Depravity, and we therefore return to the question: Is there anything within us which can respond to the grace of God unaided? My answer is, "Yes, there is". God invites, indeed commands[91] us to repent and place our trust in Christ, and since he issues that edict, our God-given faculty of rationality and logic demands that we must have some ability to respond and for which we take absolute responsibility as free agents. Some may say that by invoking *synergism* I am placing myself within the Pelagian or Semi-Pelagian camp. Perhaps 'synergism' isn't the best word to use because it does suggest that each party contributes some *work* to the relationship even though Arminians would argue that the human contribution does not amount to works in any degree. And I would agree, because the nature of saving trust is purely a reaction borne of the realisation that to refuse the offer of rescue can only bring disaster. Reformed writers will disagree, but it is an issue I want to explore more deeply in the context of the early work of a distinguished biblical scholar, namely Don Carson, whose work on *Divine Sovereignty and Human Responsibility* we will consider in the next chapter.

---

[91] Acts 6:7; 17:30; Romans 1:5; 2 Corinthians 7:15; 2 Thessalonians 1:8; 1 Peter 4:17.

As I hope to show, much of the debate hinges upon the issue of human free will as set against the nature of divine sovereignty.

Chapter 6

DIVINE SOVEREIGNTY AND HUMAN RESPONSIBILITY

I open this discussion of the relationship, or tension, between divine sovereignty and human responsibility with reference to Don Carson's treatise, *Divine Sovereignty and Human Responsibility: Biblical Perspectives in Tension.* It is a masterly and thorough exploration of the biblical perspectives such as I am not aware has been undertaken elsewhere to quite the same depth. However, before launching into a partial critique of what is actually the published digest of his PhD thesis, which was submitted to Cambridge University in 1975, I would first say that Carson is rightly regarded with the highest esteem among evangelical biblical scholars and laypersons alike, including myself. His exegetical and communication skills are abundantly evident from his prodigious published output, and many academics and church leaders owe him a debt of gratitude for help and insights gained from his labours. It is therefore with not a little trepidation that I venture to engage with some of what he asserts.

According to Don Carson

Divine Sovereignty and Human Responsibility deals with the complete scriptural landscape of the subject. While my present concerns lie specifically within the sphere of Election, nonetheless, it cannot be divorced from a broader theological context. In pursuance and defence of my own thesis, however, the main point I wish to make has to do specifically with what is understood by divine sovereignty and how that understanding impinges upon how we are to understand human freedom of choice.

Twice Carson throws down the gauntlet to those who would disagree with his conclusions. He asserts that there are no easy answers to questions about how the incarnation bears upon the relationship between

God's sovereignty and man's responsibility, or how we might understand how or when "does an absolutely sovereign God *begin* to reign, or *promise* to reign?"[1] He says,

> I frankly doubt that finite human beings can cut the Gordian knot.... The sovereignty-responsibility tension is not a problem to be solved; rather, it is a framework to be explored. To recognise this is already a major advance, for it rejects those easy 'solutions' which impose alien philosophical constructions upon the biblical data, or which dismiss those elements of the biblical data not conducive to the investigator's system. To explore this tension is to explore the nature of God and his ways with men.
>
> Yet although we must not too readily adopt simplistic 'solutions', neither must we too easily succumb to the viewpoint that the tension is intrinsically illogical. To admit we do not possess enough pieces of the puzzle to complete the picture is a far cry from saying that the pieces belong to quite different puzzles and therefore could not be related to each other even if we were given the rest of them. In other words, part of the purpose in exploring the sovereignty-responsibility tension theologically and exegetically lies in the value of a mature reflection on the problem, a reflection which deals fairly with the data and is simultaneously resistant to charges of irrationality and incoherence.[2]

And my response to that is that I couldn't agree more, although I do believe we can move on a little further than he seems willing to go in probing the essence of divine sovereignty. Furthermore, towards the end of his book, he makes explicit what had been an implicit challenge:

> I have argued at length that a fair treatment of the biblical data leaves the sovereignty-responsibility tension restless in our hands. If a person disagrees with this conclusion and seeks final solutions to the problem, we will enjoy little common ground in the debate.

And further,

> It is no answer to me to tell me that my presentation of the sovereignty-responsibility tension still embraces certain unresolved tensions. Of course, it does. But to correct me you must not claim to

---

[1] Carson (2002), 1 (his italics).
[2] Ibid., 2. Note the importance Carson places on human rationality.

resolve all the tensions, for such delusion is easily exposed. Rather, if you wish to convince me that your theology in this matter is more essentially Christian than my own, you must show me how your shaping of the tension better conforms to the biblical data than mine does.[3]

Well, here goes then! Carson is correct in saying that trying to "resolve all the tensions", which would involve unpicking the Reformed position point by point, is probably a fatuous exercise, although what I believe is needed is indeed a radical overhaul of the whole metanarrative of Calvinism. However, the challenge he issues, coming as it does from a scholar of his stature, albeit with the relative youth of a postgraduate student,[4] ought to be enough to frighten off even the most competent exegete. However, as he begins to outline his approach to the problem, and in so doing provides definitions of Predestination and Election, immediately a discordant note is sounded. He defines *Election* as referring to "soteriological predestination"[5] and says it is the sense in which he uses the term throughout his book. It must also be true therefore that it is how he understands Election generally. His definition makes the cardinal mistake, commonly found in Reformed writings, of confusing Election with Predestination. That definition is not in agreement with my own understanding as I shall go on to explore in Chapter 8, but inevitably it colours his understanding of Election as he surveys the biblical material.

Carson's strategy is first to survey the Old Testament's teaching on the topic as he explores the scope of what he says is the "remarkable tension between divine sovereignty and human responsibility"[6] as acted out in the pages of the Hebrew Scriptures. The scope is enormous, so he resorts to sampling representative passages. Limiting the scope of the biblical material thus, presents no problem because the tension is plainly found wherever one looks in scripture and he cannot be accused of selectivity in order to support a particular viewpoint. He concludes his survey of the Old Testament with the following passage, which is

---

[3] Ibid., 220f.
[4] Carson was born in 1946 and his doctoral thesis was submitted in 1975.
[5] Ibid., 2.
[6] Ibid., 16.

of particular importance because in it he offers a number of possible interpretations of divine sovereignty which are pertinent to this discussion:

> The idea that God really is the sovereign disposer of all is consistently woven into the fabric of the Old Testament, even if there is relatively infrequent explicit reflection on the sovereignty-responsibility tension. Taken as a whole, the all-embracing activity of the sovereign God in the Old Testament must be distinguished from *deism*, which cuts the world off from him; from *cosmic dualism*, which divides the control of the world between God and other(s); from *determinism*, which posits such a direct and rigid control, or such an impersonal one, that human responsibility is destroyed; from *indeterminism and chance*, which deny either the existence or the rationality of a sovereign God; and from *pantheism*, which virtually identifies God with the world. Yet the sovereignty of God in the Old Testament is not permitted to devour human responsibility.[7]

He then follows a similar line of enquiry through the intertestamental and other Jewish literature, including the Septuagint, apocryphal and pseudepigraphal works, the Dead Sea Scrolls, the Targums and rabbinic literature, and the writings of Josephus. Although he detects the rise of a distinct tendency towards legalism and merit theology throughout the period in which these works originate, he concludes that *"none of this literature resolves or evades the question of divine sovereignty and human responsibility"*.[8]

Coming to the New Testament, Carson nominates John's Gospel, on which he has become expert, for investigation. Again, this selection has no apparent ulterior motive, and he comes to very similar conclusions, although they are underlined and highlighted in the ministry and sacrificial death of Christ:

> It is in the life and death of Jesus Christ that the problem of free will and predestination finds its most poignant expression, and here, too, if anywhere, it must find its solution. The predetermined one freely chooses his appointed destiny: 'not what I will, but what thou wilt' (Mark 14.36). In Christ, the elect of God, perfect freedom and

---

[7] Ibid., 35 (my italics).
[8] Ibid., 120 (his italics).

absolute determination intersect; human freedom and divine omnipotence meet and are one. The problem of free will and determination can be solved only in the new humanity of Jesus Christ.[9]

I am not sure that I can accept this view simply because, as we have seen before,[10] it seems to confuse soteriological issues with the unique election and free will of Christ in relation to his ministry and redeeming work. It is one thing to establish divine determinism in relation to many aspects of the story of redemption, but to assume that it applies automatically to the issue of the salvation of individuals is quite another. His conclusion also begs the question as to whether fallen humanity can exercise the same kind of freedom of choice as Jesus did. Inasmuch as the relationship Jesus enjoyed with the Father in his incarnation might be regarded as similar to that of Adam prior to the Fall (although that might be questioned), can a direct analogy with the kind of freedom we enjoy be assumed?

That apart, however, in John's Gospel Carson comes to the ultimate impasse. He clearly sees God's sovereignty everywhere but, against that and creating an equal tension,[11] also the truth that men and woman have the responsibility to respond to the gospel:

> Each of the factors that go into the Old Testament's picture of human responsibility has re-surfaced in the fourth Gospel. Emphases may be a little different – e.g., men are not so much described as seeking the Lord, as exhorted to do so; and God's pleas for repentance now find their most eloquent expression in the incarnation and

---

[9] Ibid., 158, quoting Alan Richardson, *An Introduction to the Theology of the New Testament* (London: SCM, 1958), 197f., although Carson draws exception to his use of 'solution' and 'solved': Carson (2002), 246 n122.

[10] See my criticism of Peter Lewis above, 151.

[11] In later writings, Carson uses the term 'compatibilism', e.g., *How Long, O Lord?: Reflections on Suffering and Evil* (Grand Rapids, MI: Baker Academic, 2006²), 190, but he runs into problems with other disciplines where the term is used differently. See T. H. McCall, *An Invitation to Analytic Christian Theology* (Downers Grove, IL: IVP, 2015), 61; "Compatibilism is generally taken to be the view that *determinism* and freedom – not *divine sovereignty* and freedom – are compatible" (his italics), and 71: "We are a long way from the conclusion that compatibilism is demanded by biblical theology, and we only get the impression that it is by way of using the same terms differently and talking past one another across disciplines". See also John Feinberg on Compatibilism above, 138f.

death/exaltation – but the same ingredients are there.

In addition, several facts have repeatedly come to light: (1) Unlike much intertestamental literature, John does not tie human responsibility to freedom (in the sense of absolute power to contrary). Freedom, for John, is freedom from sin, i.e. the performing of God's will. (2) Human responsibility for John is not incompatible with inability, provided it is moral inability. (3) There is no unambiguous evidence for merit theology in the fourth Gospel.[12]

Human Freedom

At the risk of fragmenting the argument, and in the light of this statement about the nature of freedom in John's Gospel, it is important at this point to make an important distinction. Whereas one of my primary concerns here is to understand the meaning of human freedom of choice, Carson in the above quotation has identified a note in John's Gospel which moves us on to a different kind of freedom, the freedom we have in Christ as sons of God and the first fruits of his new creation.[13] This distinction is often not recognised so that discussions of human freedom can become very confusing. For example, Berkouwer writes,

> For when theologians discussed human freedom, they were not concerned with the freedom of a self-sufficient "being" but rather with the freedom of the man of God.[14]

My concern, however, is with the freedom of choice of what Berkouwer calls a "self-sufficient being", in other words our 'libertarian freedom', "not from the power of sin or depravity, but from necessity",[15] while

---

[12] Ibid., 175.
[13] 2 Corinthians 5:17; James 1:18; Galatians 5:1, etc.
[14] Berkouwer, 313.
[15] J. Matthew Pinson in Pinnock & Wagner, 160. In a footnote Pinson qualifies the term 'libertarian freedom' as follows: "The reason for the redundancy of the phrase "libertarian freedom" is probably to distinguish it from the soft-deterministic notion called "compatibilism." Compatibilism holds that divine determinism and human freedom are compatible. Yet, libertarians insist, the only way compatibilists can make divine determinism and human freedom compatible is to redefine free will to mean, not *the ability to have chosen otherwise*, but rather *the ability to do what one wants to do*. In other words, Arminians believe that freedom is, by definition, the ability to have done something other than what one did in fact do. Compatibilists do not believe individuals

his main concern, of course, was with a broader concept of freedom, as opposed to just freedom of choice. It is more or less universally acknowledged that our freedom of choice, whether or not we are yet free in Christ, is inevitably limited by external constraints, what Berkouwer calls "'unfreedom' caused by tyrannies – political, personal, physical, psychological, etc.",[16] and that the freedom of the will enjoyed by Adam in the Garden of Eden was lost or somehow limited through his disobedience and fall. There is much speculation about the dynamics of all this – whether Adam's freedom of choice was qualitatively different from the freedom of choice a post-Fall person might enjoy, whether believer or not. It is hard to find concrete biblical testimony either way, so conclusions tend to be drawn based on philosophical rather than biblical criteria. For Calvin, as for Augustine before him, the "great powers of free will" with which man was created were lost through sin, and as fallen man his will was enslaved, so he is unable to leave his path of "alienation and rebellion" through his own powers.[17] But Berkouwer goes on to assert that

> divine grace forgives this perversion of freedom, this rebellion, and annihilates its effects, and so renders man once again truly free.[18]

I hope you can see the point I am trying to make here. It seems to me that Berkouwer is in danger of confusing freedom of choice with man's newfound freedom in Christ, at least in the minds of his readers, although he does point out that he is actually referring to the freedom of sonship, which is "actualized precisely" in submission to God's will, not the "freedom" of arbitrary choice; quoting Schlier,

> man attains control over himself only by letting himself be controlled.[19]

---

have such freedom. So they have to redefine freedom as the quality of not being coerced (or at least, the Arminian would respond, *not feeling as though* one has been coerced) – the ability to do what one wants to do. So compatibilists simply believe that God, through regeneration prior to faith, determines that the will of the elect will *want to* desire God." (his italics).

[16] Berkouwer, 311.
[17] Ibid., 318f.
[18] Ibid., 321.
[19] Ibid., 326, quoting H. Schlier in Gerhard Kittel, *Theologisches Wörterbuch*, 492.

That fulness of freedom, "the freedom and glory of the children of God",[20] will only be fully realised at our resurrection, but we have the present to contend with where our freedom in both senses is limited. We have yet to enter fully into the complete experience of what it is to be sons of God, even though that is our true identity as believers in Jesus even now: our freedom of choice is not unbound, and we have not yet been rendered "truly free", as Berkouwer puts it. Nonetheless, although what we may wish for will often be unattainable, there can be no limit to what we may desire or dream of. Our desires for holiness may be real indeed, but we can only achieve any degree of sanctification through the empowering of the Spirit of God as we permit him to be at work within us, and even then, we will usually experience frustration because of the ever-present unredeemed nature of Adam with its rebellious desires within us. Likewise, our desires in other directions will often be thwarted through the residual sinfulness of our old nature with which our new nature is constantly at war.[21]

It seems to me then to be pointless to compare our present state with that of Adam in his pre-Fall innocence. To do so would, in my opinion, violate Paul's dictum of not going beyond what is written.[22] But clearly, Adam was susceptible to the same external pressures and temptations as are we. That same *serpent* is ever present today as then, and although we know in measure the difference between good and evil, we have retained Adam's freedom of choosing between obedience and disobedience, even though our ability to obey in practice may be limited by all kinds of factors.

The Nature of Sin

Incidentally, we often read of *sin* and *fall*, and find ourselves in consequence thinking of those categories in a way which is weighted towards evil deeds. In other words, we think of sin as wrongdoing. Sin *is* wrong, of course, but I suggest that its true nature will elude us unless

---

[20] Romans 8:21.
[21] Romans 7:21ff.
[22] 1 Corinthians 4:6.

we think in terms of obedience and disobedience. Sin is really that which displeases God and is contrary to his nature, and therefore mars our relationship with him.

It is worth digressing briefly to consider this point further because there seems to be considerable confusion in the literature between the usage and meanings of the nouns 'sin' and 'sins', singular and plural, on the one hand, and 'to sin' or 'sinning', the verbal or participle forms, on the other. The biblical authors may mean slightly different things by 'sin' (*hamartia*: ἁμαρτία - singular), especially Paul. Charles Talbert notes that 'sin' normally means actions that violate some social norm, usually associated with a church body's view,[23] but, according to L. T. Johnson, Paul views it in a different light:

> Sin is not a moral category but a religious one. The distinction is of fundamental importance. He [Paul] does not suggest that every pagan was lost in vice or that every Jew is incapable of virtue. But Jews and Greeks can be virtuous — they can do good deeds. Immorality may be a result and sign of sin, but it is not itself sin.
>
> Sin has to do with the human relationship with God — or, better, with the breaking of the human relationship with God. In this sense, the opposite of sin is not virtue but faith. Sin and faith are, for Paul, the two basic options available to human freedom vis-à-vis the power and presence of God. Paul makes the disjunction explicit in [Romans] 14:23 — "Whatever is not out of faith (*ek pisteos*) is sin (*hamartia*)" — but it is presumed throughout. Paul uses the singular *hamartia* for the same reason. It is a matter not of "sinful acts" but of a fundamental disposition of human freedom, a basic rebellion of the will against God.[24]

Thus, Paul also speaks of 'sins' in moral terms when dealing with matters concerning "sensuality, social justice, and personal evil. But ... such sins are ultimately sins against God", and therefore according to Richard Longenecker, "Such an understanding of 'sin' and 'sins' needs to be in the forefront of our Christian consciousness and

---

[23] Charles H. Talbert, *Romans* (Macon: Smyth & Helwys, 2002), 102.
[24] L. T. Johnson, *Reading Romans: A Literary and Theological Commentary* (Macon, GA: Smyth & Helwys, 2001), 47f., cited by Longenecker (2016), 373f.

understanding".[25]

Human Choice

Returning to Carson's analysis of human responsibility, he concludes that "John holds men responsible for their plight"[26] and the choices we may make are real choices. Quoting C. K. Barrett, he says, when people come or see or believe,

> the seeing is real seeing, the coming real coming, and the believing real believing, man's seeing, man's coming, man's believing.[27]

On the other hand, God's sovereignty is not impugned:

> Theoretically, belonging to Jesus could describe the believer's position after coming to faith. However, as with the idea of being given to Jesus, John more commonly speaks of a *prior* belonging that is unequivocally predestinatory. This idea is expressed in several passages in the fourth Gospel, but nowhere more forcefully than in John 10.[28]

> It is not clear how Jesus' choice of some men out of the 'world' (15.19), and the Father's gift of these men out of the 'world' (17.6) fit together; but in any case, the soteriological predestination is uncompromising.[29]

It seems to me that Carson arrives at a position not unlike the commonly encountered paradox where apparently conflicting truths must be held together in tension, a solution which I find unacceptable on logical grounds and unnecessary on exegetical grounds.[30] Furthermore, I find myself at odds with his opinions on some specific passages, most of which will be considered in Chapter 10: *Other Problematical Election Texts*. For example, when critiquing Karl Barth's views on Election, he says,

> both Paul and John (and other New Testament writers for that

---

[25] Longenecker (2016), 374.
[26] Carson (2002), 163.
[27] Ibid., 168; C. K. Barrett, *New Testament Essays* (London: SPCK, 1972), 64.
[28] Ibid., 188 (his italics). See Chapter 10b(iv), 313.
[29] Ibid., 192. See Chapter 10b(i), 290, and 10b(iii), 308.
[30] See Chapter 7, 192.

matter) speak of *individuals* being elected to salvation (e.g., John 17.9; Acts 13.48; Rom. 9; Col. 1.26f.). That such election is 'in Christ' (Eph. 1.4) does not affect its individuality.[31]

The key passages in Carson's book, so far as my own interests are concerned, are those which consider the *nature* of the human response on the one hand, and the *nature* of God's sovereignty on the other, and seek to find definitions for each. It is common in Reformed literature to encounter doubts or even denials of human freedom of choice in the matter of responding to the gospel, or debates about what exactly is meant by freedom, but Carson does make what I consider to be a cast-iron case for our response needing to be genuine and for the plight of the lost being their own responsibility; what he calls "absolute power to contrary";[32] in other words, the ability to do otherwise than one actually does or to choose between options or opposites, i.e., the libertarian sense of free will. Absolute power to contrary is an idea rejected by almost every Calvinist writer[33] because it is regarded as making God's will contingent upon human decision.

---

[31] Ibid., 216 (his italics). It will be clear that I do not agree with this claim that individuals are elected to salvation. Furthermore, other than the Colossians 1:26f. reference, which I do not consider relates to election as such, the other four texts will be considered in more detail below – see Chapter 10, 308, 315, 332, and Chapter 9a, 252.

[32] Ibid., 175, 208, etc. Nowhere (so far as I can see) does Carson define what he means by "absolute power to contrary". Following the definition of A. A. Hodge, *Evangelical Theology* (London: Banner of Truth, 1890), 157, which he considers to be in better agreement with the scriptural evidence he has reviewed, he concludes, 207, that 'absolute power to contrary' is not the position he prefers, finding it less satisfactory than a 'free agency' position. See also R. A. Shenk, *The Wonder of the Cross: The God Who Uses Evil and Suffering to Destroy Evil and Suffering* (Eugene, OR: Pickwick Publications, 2013), 178: "Real freedom is freedom to obey God without restraint or reserve. It is not absolute power to contrary; it is wanting to please God at every moment" (another example of confusing freedom of choice with freedom in Christ). In *How Long, O Lord*, 190, Carson says, "Human freedom cannot involve absolute power to contrary; that is, it cannot include such liberal power that God becomes contingent … some of the best treatments of the will have argued that freedom (sometimes called "free agency") should be related not to absolute power to contrary, but to voluntarism: that is we do what we want to do, and that is why we are held accountable for what we do". If God were made contingent, "the cross becomes an afterthought in the mind of God". For a comprehensive consideration of human freedom see G. C. Berkouwer's chapter on 'Human Freedom', 310ff.

[33] Pinnock, 100.

The Sovereignty of God

What is far more important in this context, however, is to consider what is implied when scripture asserts the absolute sovereignty of God.[34] I said in my original Preface (above, xi) that this issue must trump all the other issues I had identified; namely, (a) how we should interpret the relevant scriptures; (b) how we should interpret the history of biblical exegesis, and consequently how that affects our understanding of those texts today, and (c) how we should evaluate the legitimacy of the human intellectual faculty. All of these are contingent upon how we understand God's sovereignty and how he determines or permits what we may think or say or do. If we conclude that all of this is totally out of our control and is predetermined, it removes any efficacy from our logical and therefore volitional processes. There can then be nothing to be gained by even considering the value of human rationality, let alone how that rationality might be put to use in analysing what the Bible has to say about – well, anything. It has profound implications for epistemology too – how we can possibly know what we think we know about anything. It must therefore be the key issue in determining whether Calvinism is correct in its understanding of Election.

Having scoured what admittedly is a limited number of Reformed authors (a comprehensive survey would be a lifetime's work), there seems to me to be some slight reluctance, at least among contemporary writers, to express clearly and unequivocally the belief that we have no say in anything we may think or say or do, and thus to draw out the wider implications of such belief, one of those implications being, of course, the conclusion that God thereby becomes the author of evil. An exception is Carson's apparently approving quote from James Packer:

> God's control is absolute in the sense that men do only that which he has ordained that they should do.[35]

This is one of the most explicit statements I have seen of a concept that undergirds much of Calvinistic thought. Taken at face value, and

---

[34] Although, see Carson's discussion on *The boundaries of 'free will'*, (2002), 206ff.

[35] Ibid., 207, quoting J. I. Packer, 'Providence' in J. D. Douglas ed., *New Bible Dictionary* (Leicester: IVP, 1962). See Packer, 29, 102, for similar quotations.

despite the Reformed objection that divine sovereignty does not remove human culpability, in claiming God's *absolute* control, it implies that every thought, word and deed I may make is already predetermined by God. Although it may appear to me that I chose to think those thoughts, speak those words and act as I did, the truth of the matter is entirely different because I had absolutely no freedom of choice. Although Reformed authors may not often or readily express that view explicitly, it clearly undergirds their understanding of Total Depravity and Inability and seems to me to be ultimately foundational for the Reformed understanding of Election.

Likewise, in his treatment of Providence, Louis Berkhof[36] seems to assume that the definition of divine sovereignty implies, among many other things, the foreordination of all human choices. So far as I can see, however, he isn't prepared to come clean with a clear unequivocal statement to that effect. The best I could find in his *Systematic Theology* was,

> The Bible teaches that even the minutest details of life are of divine ordering.[37]

I am drawn to the conclusion that to lay out and expand on that particular assertion would invite all sorts of objections and complications, so, he and other Reformed writers I have seen then add all sorts of caveats and complications. For example,

> So God also enables and prompts His rational creatures, as *second causes*, to function, and that not merely by endowing them with energy in a general way, but by energizing them to certain specific acts. He worketh all things in all, I Cor. 12:6, and worketh all things, also in this respect, according to the counsel of His will, Eph. 1:11.[38]

Berkhof's mention of second causes is noteworthy because it is an idea frequently put forth in Reformed writings to absolve God from the accusation of being the creator and instigator of evil. Horton says that Calvin himself, like Aquinas, employed Aristotelian categories of

---

[36] L. Berkhof, 165-79.
[37] Ibid., 169.
[38] Ibid., 173 (my italics).

primary and secondary causality to teach that God does not directly cause or bring about sin. Calvin regarded the idea that God could be the author of evil as blasphemous, of course.[39] I would say, not only blasphemous but entirely ridiculous. Many of these discussions seem to have lost sight of the essential nature of evil and sin (see above, 168-70). To even contemplate that God might instigate evil would be to suggest that he had invented some kind of self-harming strategy. We must get away from the idea that sin and evil are entities with a life of their own: they are in essence assaults against the person and character of God himself. Thus, to suggest that God is the author of evil would be analogous to the idea of him 'cutting off his nose to spite his face'. I do not believe that even God could create the means to harm himself, although the Cross may be an important exception.[40] That aside, however, invoking secondary causes is also a baffling idea. In essence, it begins with the indisputable assertion that God is the primary cause who determines all outcomes, but within that divine providence are secondary causes which knowingly, or more likely unknowingly, influence the decisions we may make because of other decisions and actions. Thus, by taking a step backwards from human self-determination, God, it is claimed, cannot be accused of determining our sinful actions: he merely permits them.

As with other attempts to circumvent some of the logical conclusions of classical Calvinism, there is no consensus even among Reformed writers. Jonathan Edwards, for example, taught the strongest possible doctrine of God's rule, claiming that he does not work through secondary causes; he is not only the all-determining reality, but everything without exception is directly and immediately caused by him, including evil. Edwards insisted that all things, including sin and evil, follow from "an infallible previous fixedness of the futurity of the event" (meaning all events), such that everything happens according to a "universal, determining providence" that imposes "some kind of necessity

---

[39] Horton, 48; Calvin, *Institutes*, 3.23.4f.: Beveridge, 3:228-30.
[40] Especially if Jesus had chosen not to submit to God's will in Gethsemane: Matthew 26:39, etc.

of all events."[41]

> God does decisively, in his providence, order all the volitions of moral agents, either by positive influence or permission: and it being allowed on all hands, that what God does in the affair of man's virtuous volitions, whether it be more or less, is by some positive influence, and not by mere permission, as in the affair of a sinful volition.[42]

Olson points out that by "permission" Edwards means that God does not make people sin, but he does render it certain, although he rightly queries why Edwards and other Calvinists feel the need to use permissive language when their overall explanation of God's providence requires something more direct and active.[43] Indeed, we have already noted that classical Calvinism maintains a consistency which the various single-predestinatory versions of it do not. Accordingly, Cottrell, from an Arminian perspective, claims that true Calvinism "is a true determinism and has no place for genuinely free will":

> Efforts to make a place for free will by redefining it and by introducing the concepts of second causes and permission are not successful, because they break down when examined in the light of the Calvinistic *sine qua non*, the unconditional decree. The only way to arrive at a real alternative to determinism is to abandon the notion of unconditionality as essential to the definition of divine sovereignty.[44]

Likewise, Berkhof, dealing with perceived objections from Pelagians, Semi-Pelagians and Arminians, says,

> They maintain that a *previous* concurrence, which is not merely general *but predetermines man to specific actions*, makes God the responsible author of sin. Reformed theologians are well aware of the difficulty that presents itself here, but do not feel free to circumvent it by denying God's absolute control over the free actions of

---

[41] Olson (2011), 74; quoting Jonathan Edwards in C. A. Holbrook ed., *The Great Christian Doctrine of Original Sin* (New Haven, CT: Yale University Press, 1970), 402, and 'Freedom of the Will' in *The Works of Jonathan Edwards* (New Haven, CT: Yale University Press, 1957), 1:431.
[42] Jonathan Edwards, *The Works of Jonathan Edwards*, 1:434.
[43] Olson (2011), 74.
[44] Cottrell in Pinnock, 106.

His Moral creatures, since this is clearly taught in Scripture, Gen. 45:5; 50:19, 20; Ex. 10:1, 20; II Sam. 16:10, 11: Isa. 10:5-7; Acts 2:23; 4:27, 28.[45]

Incidentally, I do not agree that the texts Berkhof cites here or in the previous quotation can be applied in the specific way he applies them. I have already commented on this tendency to generalise from specific contexts, but he does seem to have an unfortunate tendency to apply what are undeniable references to God's more general purposes in a way which denies individual responsibility. For instance, he cites the prompting of Joseph's brothers to sell him into slavery, the hardening of Pharaoh's heart, the divine prompting of Shimei to curse David and the Assyrian attack on Israel – none of these examples of divine action can possibly be evidence of curtailment of the moral choices of individuals;[46] they simply express God's purposes, but say nothing about how those purposes were or will be worked out in specific detail.

Berkhof's admission that his doctrine *might* impute sin and evil to God is, of course, a very serious consequence of God's total divine ordering of everything and is a notion that most Calvinists, as well as Christians generally, would emphatically wish to deny. But clearly, if those Berkhof considers to be in error see in Reformed doctrine an insistence that God claims "absolute control over the free actions of His moral creatures", then I have to conclude that no amount of complicated counter-argument on his part can effectively deny that position, and he is forced to hide behind the admission that "the problem of God's relation to sin remains a mystery".[47]

It should also be noted that Calvinists do not limit the sphere of God's determinism to the realm of his sentient creatures, but to the whole of the created order. For example, Paul Helm in his *The Providence of God*, which is widely considered to be a contemporary classic of Calvinist thought, says,

> Not only is every atom and molecule, every thought and desire, kept

---

[45] L. Berkhof, 174 (his italics).
[46] I have already commented on the Acts references: see above, 151, and will comment further on Ephesians 1:11 in Chapter 8a(iv), 213, *klēroō*, etc.
[47] L. Berkhof, 175.

in being by God, but every twist and turn of each of these is under the direct control of God.... the providence of God is 'fine-grained'; it extends to the occurrence of individual actions and to each aspect of each action.[48]

Likewise, a similar comprehensive statement of absolute divine sovereignty is found in R. C. Sproul:

> If there is one single molecule in this universe running around loose, totally free of God's sovereignty, then we have no guarantee that a single promise of God will ever be fulfilled.... Maybe that one molecule will be the thing that prevents Christ from returning.[49]

A valid response to that kind of extreme determinism must engage with a concept of God in creation setting up the whole gamut of physical law such that every particle, whether sub- or supra-atomic, must behave according to those laws. The question then remains as to whether or not the Creator maintains overall control even of the mass of randomness which constitutes the workings of the universe and yet manages it from running out of control as it gradually moves towards its destiny of total entropy;[50] in other words, is God truly omnipotent? Clark Pinnock responds to that question saying, "The power to create a world with free agents in it is surely omnipotent power!" Quoting Søren Kierkegaard, Pinnock asserts that "only an omnipotent being would have the kind of power needed in such a project. The power of tyranny can make people [and things] obey on command, but it calls for a higher kind of power to create and work with the delicate flower of human freedom."[51] It is my conviction that God is certainly able to do all of that, but without having to micromanage the whole thing. And I dare to suggest that that says far more of his divine majesty and omnipotence, and magnifies his glory beyond any speculation about his alleged minute control of

---

[48] P. Helm, *The Providence of God* (Downers Grove, IL: IVP, 1994), 22 and 104, quoted by Olson (2011), 81.
[49] Olson (2011), 57, quoting R. C. Sproul, *Chosen by God* (Wheaton, IL: Tyndale, 1988), 27.
[50] Entropy does seem to be the ultimate end of the created order according to our current understanding of cosmology, but see my comments on the new created order in my forthcoming *Pie in the Sky When You Die?*
[51] Clark Pinnock in Basinger & Basinger, 153, citing Søren Kierkegaard, *Journals* (New York: Harper and Row, 1958), 113.

everything.

Returning from subatomic physics and cosmology to the realms of human and divine activity, we noted in one of the passages quoted above (164) that it is clear that Carson distinguishes what the Bible teaches about the nature of God's interaction with humankind from deism, cosmic dualism, determinism, indeterminism and chance, and pantheism, and I would add *panentheism* to the list. Panentheism is the belief that God and the world are interdependent realities, an idea considered by most orthodox Christians to be heretical. But Olson suggests that Jonathan Edwards' strong doctrine of sovereignty – divine determinism, though not deliberate, more an inconsistency, "is a slippery slope that leads logically down into panentheism" because he seemed to be moving towards the conclusion that God is in some way dependent on creation.[52] Nonetheless, it seems to me that Carson steers very close to a determinism "which posits such a direct and rigid control, or such an impersonal one, that human responsibility is destroyed".[53] He appears to be saying that any freedom of choice exercised by humankind, especially with respect to our response to the gospel, would be in direct contradiction to the divine foreordination "with certainty"[54] of all we think or do or say. Herein, I think, lies the problem and hence the challenge he issues to those who think they know better than him, or who believe they have solved the problem (see above, 162f.).

This discussion could become very confusing.[55] There are many views, many of which, as we have seen, resort to philosophical categories or nuanced definitions of terms in relation to divine sovereignty. Carson seems to say that there is no real consensus; a view which takes into account all the biblical data he has surveyed, including the ultimate ineffability of God, but which also affords due worth to the power of human rationality. Clearly it is most unsatisfactory to resort to paying one's money and taking one's choice, as the old adage puts it, so I have

---

[52] Ibid., 76.
[53] Carson (2002), 35
[54] Ibid., 206.
[55] See, for example, Carson's somewhat inconclusive discussions on *The nature of divine 'ultimacy'*, *The 'will(s)' of God*, etc.: (2002), 210ff.

to question the value of any one of the many contradictory conclusions drawn by scholars who, admittedly, are probably far more able than me – theologically, exegetically, philosophically, logically, and so on.

But why, I ask, does a claim on God's behalf that he is sovereign mean that every thought, word or action that I may make is preordained? I am very willing to accept, indeed, for me, it is a given that God *knows* all of these things, including what will be in the future, not only in the bundle of human life, but even in the breadth of the physical world too, from the subatomic to the cosmic[56] – that is all encompassed in my understanding of his omniscience and foreknowledge, but not predestination. I suggest that somehow, we need to differentiate between what it means for God to know everything in advance, and for that *not* to mean that he has decreed all events throughout all time and on into the future: in other words, separating Foreknowledge from Predestination, two terms which we have already noted are commonly equated in Reformed writings.

The Grace of God

Calvinism is very strong in its assertion that salvation is by grace and grace alone – a truly biblical concept which all should gladly affirm. Indeed, many Reformed churches these days, especially Calvinistic Baptist churches, prefer to call themselves 'Grace' churches, so avoiding the older, more forbidding-sounding labels of 'Strict' and/or 'Particular'. It seems to me, however, that a concept of grace which insists that God has preordained everything, especially everything I think I have chosen to do, loses the loving warmth of a Creator's heart and can become very cold and impersonal indeed.

Grace surely inheres in the character of God himself. It is the characteristic of his very being from which expressions of his love flow. Indeed, Tom Wright, in the context of Romans 5:21, says, "'Grace' here is obviously a shorthand for 'the true God, acting freely and

---

[56] See Chapter 8c, 219, 'Foreknowledge' and 230, 'The Extent of God's Foreknowledge. On other theories of God's omniscience, see 232, 'Molinism' and 237, 'Open Theism'.

generously'".[57] Thus, although 'grace' is often used in scripture as a kind of shorthand for the effects or outworkings of divine grace,[58] it is not a rigid kind of tool or mechanism with which God dispenses favour and salvation to his Elect, the way Calvin himself and, indeed, many Reformed writers, seem to have understood it.[59] Nor is grace a quantifiable thing which Calvin at times seemed to have regarded as being in danger of being so diluted as to be incapable of embracing all of humanity. For example, Shank refers to Calvin's reflection that he had received more than a hundred times as much grace as some others.[60]

According to McGrath,[61] grace as a quantifiable resource or substance seems to have been a legacy of late medieval theologians as they developed their views about Mary, the mother of Jesus. This rested on the Vulgate translation of Luke 1:28, Gabriel's words to Mary: "the one who is full of grace", which suggested to them the image of "a reservoir full of a liquid (grace)". Although Erasmus of Rotterdam (1466-1536) and Lorenzo Valla (1407-57)[62] before him pointed out that the Greek meant "favoured one", grace as a kind of substance nevertheless seemed to have lingered on in Calvin's thinking, even though, as McGrath claims, the idea was abandoned at the time of the Reformation.

Grace, rather than being a thing or a quantifiable instrument, is therefore God's very nature which causes him to express favour and love to all of Adam's fallen race. To my mind, that must imply a divine detachment from the kind of determinism upon which Calvinism necessarily seems to insist therefore.[63] Frequently, in Reformed writings,

---

[57] N. T. Wright (2003), 250; Barclay, xviii: "Grace ... is not an idea or a thing but a radical, divine dynamic"; 143: "grace is not a 'thing' but Christ himself".
[58] E.g., Romans 1:5; 12:3; 15:15; 1 Corinthians 3:10; Galatians 2:9, etc.
[59] See Shank (*Elect*), 106f.
[60] Shank (*Elect*), 107; Calvin, *Concerning the Eternal Predestination of God*, 11.
[61] McGrath (2012), 50.
[62] Valla made extensive notes on the Greek text of the New Testament which, when discovered by Erasmus in 1505, became influential in the preparation of his Greek text of the New Testament. See McGrath (2012), 48.
[63] Apparently, Calvin was ambivalent about whether God's will was determinative or indeterminative. When considering whether God's call to salvation was an authentic unconditional Particular Election and Reprobation, he posits determinism most of the time, but when faced with the possibility that God could be accused of responsibility

God is credited with all good and is distanced from evil, but if grace truly is grace, and so we can avoid any suggestion of determinism, God can be blamed neither for all evil nor, by the same token, be praised for every good deed.[64] Grace must allow us to make free choices – to have absolute power to contrary perhaps, and that even within the sphere of our freedom in Christ as is evidenced by New Testament references to saints continuing to sin.[65]

The Reformed stance often asserts that by refusing to allow God to predetermine our every whim we thereby limit or minimise him. But why should we in our wisdom think that we can so limit God that he cannot be gracious to the extent that he freely permits us to make free choices in all aspects of life, sacred and secular, irrespectively of whether those choices result in salvation or eternal loss, or whether they bring material or emotional loss or joy and blessing?

> we do not deal with two subjects that are on the same level, but with a Subject who in sovereign love makes room for other subjects and allows his actions to be determined and limited by them, yet without thereby losing anything of the sovereignty of his own subjectivity.[66]

This quotation from Hendrikus Berkhof suggests to me that Reformed doctrine may have made a cardinal error in some of its assumptions about the implications of divine sovereignty. It is worth challenging those assumptions therefore, so I will enlist the considerations of a number of self-confessed Arminians to help shed some light on the question.[67]

---

for sin he reverts to indeterminism. See Shank (*Elect*), 138-40, who cites a number of representative quotations from Calvin, *Concerning the Eternal Predestination of God*: indeterminism: 4; 8:5; 10:14; determinism: 8:4; 10:11, 12, and *Institutes*, 3.23.8.

[64] God's permissive will must apply both to good and evil. If we wish to deny that God has any part in evil, I suggest that we must also allow that he does not *necessarily* instigate all the good that people, especially unbelievers, do.

[65] E.g., 1 John 1:8, etc.

[66] Hendrikus Berkhof, 217. Incidentally, I suggest that this might be a good way to understand *kenoō* (κενόω) – "he emptied himself" in Philippians 2:7 (literal translation).

[67] See, in particular, Pinnock, Olson (2011 & 2006); Klein, and Pinnock & Wagner of which one reviewer says, "I cannot think of a more dangerous unbiblical teaching than Calvinism! I recommend this book highly. The reader should buy one for himself/herself and buy one for each Presbyterian/Reformed minister in town and give it to him/her as a gift!."

Divine Self-Limiting Determinism

Consistent Calvinism has a deterministic view of sovereignty which says that the unconditioned will or decree of God is the only true cause of every event in the universe without exception. A corollary of that is that the human will is not truly free no matter how hard our Reformed brothers and sisters may claim otherwise. Jack Cottrell says that to say that God has an eternal plan that includes "whatsoever comes to pass" is not in itself objectionable, but what makes it objectionable and unbiblical is the claim that God's plan is both efficacious and unconditional. In other words, the decree is said to be efficacious because whatever happens, happens by virtue of the fact that it was included in the decree and is therefore deterministic.[68] Many Calvinists attempt to deny this conclusion, however, trying to get round what seems to be its unassailable logic by looking for alternative definitions of free will.[69]

Cottrell staunchly maintains that "Calvinism is still a theology of determinism as long as it declares that nothing God does can be conditioned by man or can be a reaction to something in the world" because "this idea of unconditionality completely rules out any meaningful notion of human freedom".[70] He begins to make his case by arguing that the Calvinistic view of sovereignty was formulated in an intuitive manner, certain assumptions being made about what *must* be the case if God were sovereign – i.e., omnicausality and unconditionality.[71] In other words, philosophical categories have intruded upon and shaped theological considerations.

Calvinism says that if the decree is conditional in any way God cannot be sovereign, but Cottrell does not agree. Such an idea is an *a priori* assumption and is not well thought out, an assumption to which John Frame refers as one of those premature "intuitions" that, upon reflection, turn out to be incorrect.[72] We can probably agree that God's

---

[68] J. Cottrell in Pinnock, 99ff.
[69] See comments on Free Will and Compatibilism, above 132-9; Feinberg in Basinger & Basinger, 20-22; Chapter 8c, 219-32, 'Foreknowledge'.
[70] J. Cottrell in Pinnock, 102ff.
[71] Ibid., 106.
[72] Ibid., 107, referring to Frame in Carson & Woodbridge, 224.

original and primary purpose for creation was unconditional, although we may not be able to say precisely what that purpose was, but we do not have to agree that the eternal decree included a specific purpose for every specific moment in the existence of every specific particle of creation. Frame says that, rather than claiming that sovereignty has no limitations, we must use sound theological thinking to work out what kinds of limitations are inappropriate to divine sovereignty, and, indeed, what sorts of 'limitations' would be limitations in reality.[73] Thus,

> By not intervening in their decisions *unless* his special purposes require it, God respects both the integrity of the freedom he gave to human beings and the integrity of his own sovereign choice to make free creatures in the first place.[74]

By way of illustration, Cottrell cites the specific example of the occurrence of sin. In the face of sin, he says, "God's love was bound to express itself in *grace,* involving a plan of redemption centered around his own incarnation and the offer of forgiveness for all who would accept it." His love could not do otherwise because his nature would require it. At the same time, however, "God's holiness was bound to express itself in *wrath,* determining the very nature of the required redemption and ultimately requiring the eternal punishment of hell for unrepentant sinners."[75] This observation is interesting and important: we may gladly accept that God's love flows from his nature of grace, but we do not always follow the argument through to the conclusion that those who spurn his love will become objects of his wrath. Cottrell is surely correct in concluding that limitations such as these do not contradict God's sovereignty because they are *self*-limitations. They are a *part* of the sovereign decree (should there be such a thing), not a violation of it:

> If they were limitations imposed on God from outside God, then his sovereignty would indeed be compromised. But they are *God's own choice,* and as such are not the negation of sovereignty but the

---

[73] Ibid., 108
[74] Ibid., Cottrell quoting from his own *What the Bible Says About God the Ruler* (Joplin, MO: College Press, 1984), 187ff. (his italics).
[75] Ibid., 109.

very expression of it.[76]

God's sovereignty is God's absolute freedom to do whatever He ordains to do ... God created man in His own image, and in His sovereign and absolute freedom He ordained that man was to have a limited amount of freedom; and that was God's sovereign decree; that man should have some freedom. So, *when man exercises his freedom, he is fulfilling the sovereignty of God*, not cancelling it out.[77]

God is free to do as he pleases, and that must include the freedom to limit himself and to permit men and women to carry out their own plans even when their actions fly in the face of his will and purposes.[78] Cottrell argues therefore that such total control as God exercises over all he has made does not require a predetermination or causation of all things. "God's sovereignty is *greater* than that!" Quoting Miner Raymond, he maintains that,

God is competent to govern an infinite number of morally responsible beings, persons who have power within limits of determining what they will do; and we insist upon it that this concept of a divine government is incomparably superior to that of our opponents.[79]

It is important to examine further why the history of theology has taken this particular course towards determinism and why therefore we find ourselves today in the midst of a Reformed hegemony. In a chapter on 'God as Personal', John E. Sanders examines what he calls the *control beliefs* we bring to scripture.[80] These are beliefs like John Frame's *premature intuitions*, but which have deeper historical roots. They have shaped our understanding of scripture, and, in the case of Reformed theology, he claims them to have been the result of a synthesis of Greek and biblical thought. Sanders maintains that as guidelines were developed for interpreting biblical metaphors they began to function like

---

[76] Ibid., 110 (his italics).
[77] Klein, 298, quoting A. W. Tozer, *The Sovereignty of God*, audio tape (Christian Publications, 1997), in Samuel Fisk, *Election and Predestination* (Eugene, OR: Wipf & Stock, 2002), 170 (my italics).
[78] J. Cottrell in Pinnock, 110, citing 1 Corinthians 16:7; Hebrews 6:3; James 4:15.
[79] Ibid., quoting Miner Raymond, *Systematic Theology* (Cincinnati, OH: Walden & Stowe, 1877), 1:505f.
[80] J. E. Sanders in Pinnock, 167ff.

axioms in geometry, taking on incontestable certitude. They were formulated under the belief that the Greek philosophical way of speaking of God as impassible, immutable, timeless, etc., was superior to the anthropomorphic way as father, changeable, suffering, etc. The Church has followed this path for so long now that we take that way of thinking for granted and now find it difficult to critically examine those control beliefs about the nature of God.[81]

W. G. MacDonald observes that "the classical doctrine of election" makes "little reference to history". But, he says, we are committed "to know no more than the Bible divulges". Thus, rather than approaching "God's decisions from eternity as if we had footing there as his prepositive equal, and *on our own* were able to intuit the equivalent of the data of revelation", he says that we "must begin with *historical* (inclusive of verbal) revelation". He suggests that "to attempt to begin with eternity, the realm so dear to philosophical constructions, we would have no foundation outside ourselves against which to see and interpret the inspired words about what went on in the divine strategy of selection 'before creation'." To begin with biblical history, on the other hand, "leads us to Christ Jesus, in and through whom we find the full revelation of what God is like." MacDonald insists that the "Bible must not be pressed through a philosophical sieve", as many theologians would attempt, squeezing the doctrine "to fit the shape of an inscrutable mystery". To do so "blocks out revelation and makes their pronouncements on the subject dubious". Our task, therefore, is to "focus spiritual eyes on God's revelation, not to fill a void presumed to be otherwise inscrutable".[82]

If we wish to be faithful to the Bible, we must therefore make the effort, however difficult or painful, to examine the absolutistic lenses of our Bible-reading spectacles to discover whether the image of God we see through them is actually the same as the biblical portrait.[83] Can this 'classical theism', with its synthesis of Greek philosophic natural

---

[81] For example, *The Westminster Confession of Faith*, 2:1: God is "without body, parts, or passions, immutable", is often regarded as a statement of orthodoxy.
[82] W. G. MacDonald in Pinnock, 207f. (his italics).
[83] Sanders in Pinnock, 169; see also, Keith Ward, 24-64, 'The Aristotelian Legacy'.

theology and biblical theology, be synonymous with biblical theism? asks Sanders.[84]

If our understanding of Election were to be based on any sort of human activity, that would presumably imply conditionality and mutability in God. It follows therefore that where these implications are unacceptable, which is the position of most Bible-believing Christians, God has to be the sole cause of salvation and damnation, indeed the sole cause of everything if he is not conditioned by anything external to himself. Otherwise, Calvinism would have to conclude that God would cease to be God because he is not the cause of all events. As we have seen already, grace was often conceived of as a material force acting irresistibly on the objects of God's benevolence. Thus, if grace can be resisted, God's will can also be resisted, implying conditionality in God.[85]

Sanders says that, despite its logical consistency and the renown of many of those who have taught it, the Reformed perspective has many fatal flaws, the three most important, in his view, he then enumerates. The first and foremost difficulty with the absolutistic conception of God (because the other difficulties derive from it), is that logically it entails monism or theopanism - that the universe emanates from, or is a projection of God. In other words, God is the only actor in the drama and humans are but characters in the novel of existence. The second major flaw is determinism: if the characters do only what the novelist determines, then the novelist is responsible for all that happens. Both Augustine and Calvin acknowledged this to be the case, and both attempted to argue for a form of soft-determinism or compatibilism, in other words, that human freedom and divine determinism are not contradictory, by distinguishing between remote and proximate causes. The third major problem is that absolutism robs the biblical language about God of genuine meaning by denigrating it to the status of *mere* anthropomorphism:

How can a timelessly immutable Being plan, anticipate, remember,

---

[84] Ibid., 172.
[85] Sanders in Pinnock, 171f.

respond, punish, warn, or forgive, since all such acts involve temporality and mutability. A timelessly immutable God cannot "answer" prayer, as this would imply that God "responds" to our prayer.[86]

Sanders concludes that those who prefer to speak of God in Greek philosophic terms fail to realise that those terms are just as anthropomorphic as the metaphors in the Bible.[87] He maintains that one of the key control beliefs for a truly biblical view of God is that the biblical metaphors about God themselves are the best sources to discover who God *really* is and that as such they portray him as personal. Even as Trinity, the Godhead is the model of loving interpersonal relationships,[88] and as our Creator he freely enters into dynamic interpersonal relations with us. Thomas Fretheim summarises this clearly:

> The world is not only affected by God; God is affected by the world in both positive and negative ways. God is sovereign over the world, yet not unqualifiedly so, as considerable power and freedom have been given to the creatures. God is the transcendent Lord; but God is transcendent not in isolation from the world, but in relationship to the world. God knows all there is to know about the world, yet there is a future which does not yet exist to be known even by God.[89] God is Lord of time and history, yet God has chosen to be bound up in the time and history of the world and to be limited thereby. God is unchangeable with respect to the steadfastness of his love and his salvific will for all creatures, yet God does change in the light of what happens in the interaction between God and the world.[90]

Sanders claims that the interpersonal relational metaphors which convey the 'personalistic' nature of God, such as marriage, childrearing and adoption, tend to predominate in scripture. In raising children, God's aim is to preserve and increase the value in their lives: nonetheless he encourages them to participate in their own development, but in doing so, he does not do everything for them nor does he protect them

---

[86] Ibid., 172.
[87] Ibid., 173.
[88] A common construal of the Trinity, but see Ward, 108.
[89] Note here the influence of Open Theism, a notion I reject. See Chapter 8c(ii), 237.
[90] Sanders in Pinnock, 174, quoting T. Fretheim, *The Suffering of God* (Philadelphia, PA: Fortress, 1984), 35.

from all suffering and failure.[91] He chooses to be related to humanity in such a way that we become a factor in his life. Our love and obedience give him joy, while our faithlessness grieves him. Although he established the rules by which the 'game of life' operates, he nevertheless saw fit to bind himself to those rules, especially in the incarnation, and thereby would be vulnerable even to the point of being crucified.[92]

Again, Sanders lists five important advantages of viewing the relationship between God and us as personal rather than absolutistically:

> First, the relationship is a genuine dialogue, not a monologue, so monism is avoided. Second, because Yahweh's will is not always accomplished, he is not the cause of all that happens. This means that Yahweh is not responsible for human sin. We are solely responsible, and this is good news since sin is forgivable but causation is not. Third, our biblical views of prayer are indeed meaningful. Yahweh is not a coercive parent manipulating us into making a request. We are free to ask and possibly change Yahweh's plans should he consider it prudent. Fourth, not only are human beings free but *Yahweh is free* to respond to prayer, to love in changing ways, and to experience joy and pain because he is not bound by inexorable knowledge or an immutable will. Finally, the prima facie meanings of the biblical text are allowed to stand without having to measure up to Greek philosophic standards.[93]

In a chapter entitled 'The Universality of God's Love',[94] Fritz Guy develops this theme. He says,

> One of *the* most serious ways in which the course of Christian theology has been misled by its classical and medieval heritage has been the assumption that the primary fact about God is omnipotent sovereignty and that the evidence of this sovereignty is the exercise of power to control events, including the actions of all of humanity. This assumption has kept a large part of the Christian tradition, both Catholic and Protestant, from hearing the gospel with clarity,

---

[91] Ibid.
[92] Ibid., 175f. Even taking the risk that Jesus might decide not to take the path of obedience to the Cross, presumably!
[93] Ibid., 178 (his italics).
[94] F. Guy in Pinnock, 31ff.

because it has misunderstood the character of God.[95]

Guy says that a great but seldomly recognised irony is that some Christians who hold a high christology have nonetheless failed to let it guide their understanding of God. Jesus' commandment and demonstration of self-giving service was not simply a useful strategy for successful human relationships but was actually *the* revelation of the nature of the divine governance (sovereignty) of the world, and in washing his disciples' feet he clearly demonstrated the nature of that governance.[96]

Thus, loving is not simply one of a number of divine activities, along with creating, sustaining, and judging, but is what all of the activities of God accomplish. There is no doctrine of God's love alongside the doctrines of creation, humanity, salvation, church, and ultimate destiny because it is the inner content of all the doctrines of Christianity: it "is what they are all *about*".[97] As such God's love makes possible a radically different understanding of both him and created reality. For instance, his will becomes attractive rather than coercive, a delighting rather than a deciding, and even as "the desire of the lover for the beloved".[98] God's will does not necessarily mean his *specific* intention in any given situation, and that what he decides has to actually happen. Rather, it may mean God's *general* intention and the values with which he is pleased. Thus, apart from a predestinarian presupposition, it becomes apparent that God's will should always be understood in terms of intention and desire:

> The will of God now becomes, not the orders of a superior directing what a subordinate must *do*, but the longing of a lover for what the beloved *is*.[99]

The grandest and final imagery the Bible uses for God's love is precisely that of lover and beloved, bridegroom and bride. The marriage of Christ and the Church is the last act of the long love affair between

---

[95] Ibid., 33 (his italics).
[96] Ibid., 34, citing John 13:1-20. Guy prefers the term 'governance' rather than 'sovereignty' because the latter often carries the connotation of theistic determinism.
[97] Ibid., 35 (his italics).
[98] Ibid., quoting Robert Farrer Capon, *Hunting the Divine Fox* (Minneapolis, MN: Winston/Seabury, 1985), 38.
[99] Ibid., quoting Capon, 39 (my italics).

God and creation.[100] But it is important to note that God's relationship with the world as the divine lover is a non-competitive relationship, not unlike the relationship between husband and wife, at least when the ideal pre-Fall creation order is realised,[101] or the nurturing relationship of parent and child. Guy again comments,

> It is surely a failure to recognize the noncompetitive relationship between God and creation that has enabled predestinarians beginning with Augustine to argue for unconditional election on the ground that to suppose that salvation requires some sort of human acceptance would be to detract from the divine honor.[102]

The good news is the fact that the whole world of humanity is the object of God's love.[103] And just as it is the divine love which intends and wills and works for the salvation of as much of humanity as possible, so it is the divine love which respects human freedom of choice, even to the extent of allowing humanity to reject the love which has created, sustained and redeemed it. If that rejection should happen, it is nonetheless recognised and respected by the very love which is rejected:

> For this love loves so extravagantly that it is willing to risk eternal anguish rather than turn its beloved humanity into an object to be controlled by the will of another, even a divine Other.[104]

Taking all of this is into account – that the concept of divine sovereignty or governance needs to be re-evaluated in line with the predominant biblical paradigm of God's love for all he has made, I suggest that Carson's claim that there is no solution to the tension he finds in scripture between human responsibility and divine sovereignty is seriously challenged.[105] His cardinal error, indeed, the error which underlies the

---

[100] Ibid.
[101] Eve was created from Adam's side and in their complementary togetherness they constituted humanity: Genesis 2:22f.; 1:27.
[102] Guy in Pinnock, 48 n18, cites Boice, 517, as a contemporary exponent of this idea: "If we have a part in salvation, then our love for God is diminished by just that amount."
[103] Ibid., 37f., citing in order John 3:16; 1 John 4:14; Philippians 2:10f.; Ephesians 1:9f.; 1 Timothy 2:4; 4:10; 2 Peter 3:9; Colossians 1:20; Hebrews 2:9; Isaiah 53:6; John 1:29; 1 John 2:2; Romans 5:18; 2 Corinthians 5:14f.; 1 Timothy 2:6; Matthew 20:28; Isaiah 55:1, 7; Matthew 11:28.
[104] Ibid., 45.
[105] See above, 162f.

whole Reformed metanarrative, is the apparently unconscious reliance on the classical categories of biblical interpretation which Pinnock, Sanders, Guy and others have drawn to our attention. The fact that the solution I am advocating militates against the brainwashing we have all undergone since Augustine and the resultant confusion in our theology of Election doesn't make it inherently unlikely or impossible: rather it speaks of the glory of our God who has a higher regard for the intellectual faculty he has bequeathed on us than often we have afforded it. Our sovereign God has decreed that I can choose him or reject him - with all the provisos we will encounter in scripture, especially in some passages in John's Gospel,[106] a choice he nevertheless lovingly invites each of us to make in the certain knowledge that our choices are not illusory but are indeed really real.

I give the last word of this chapter to Terry Miethe whom I suggest delivers the *coup de grace* to the Reformed understanding of divine determinism, and whose words, if we had considered them first, might have made the writing of this chapter unnecessary:

> In essence determinism [philosophical or theological] is one of those theories which ... "are so preposterously silly that only very learned men could have thought of them." Whether or not we are in fact free is a question only for those who wish to play games with concepts. Once we see what the question is we see that the very possibility of considering it *as a question to which true or false answers may be given* presupposes the fact of freedom.[107]

---

[106] See Chapter 10b, 288ff.
[107] Terry Miethe in Pinnock, 84f., quoting Samuel M. Thompson, *A Modern Philosophy of Religion* (Chicago, IL: Regnery, 1955), 179 (his italics and square brackets), who in turn quotes a 'Professor Broad' without citation.

Chapter 7

WHO THEN IS RIGHT – CAN BOTH BE RIGHT?

On the face of it, the Arminian position seems to have more in its favour than Calvinism, but both have profound defects. The principal defect they share is the belief that God chooses individuals for salvation[1] – but more of that later. Even the range of views in the moderate single-predestinatory middle ground on the Reformed side of the fence, which I have briefly touched upon, fails to provide a solution because I believe those positions sacrifice intellectual integrity.

For instance, a commonly encountered way of attempting to reconcile election with human freedom visualises the two opposing positions as the opposite faces of a coin or the two sides of a door or doorway, neither of which can be seen simultaneously. Taking the latter illustration, we are asked to visualise a door bearing on one side God's revelation of election and his invitation to us to respond to the gospel. The other side of the door, which we can see only once we have accepted the invitation and passed through the doorway, reveals our obligation to believe because unknowingly we have been the objects of God's elective choice. In other words, the two positions, although apparently irreconcilable, are made out not to conflict at all because the door or coin is an indivisible unit, each side representing the truth from God's and man's perspectives respectively, but the truth is nonetheless one, allegedly. C. H. Spurgeon's appeal, for example,

> Brethren, be willing to see both sides of the shield of truth. Rise above the babyhood which cannot believe two doctrines until it sees the connecting link.[2]

---

[1] Although Olson (2011), 67, claims that Arminians who follow Arminius believe election to be corporate.
[2] C. H. Spurgeon's sermon, 'Faith and Regeneration' of 1871: *The Metropolitan Tabernacle Pulpit*, Vol. 18 (Pilgrim, Pasadena, 1971), 137, quoted by Fisk (title page).

insists that we must hold apparently conflicting doctrines in unresolved tension. This is certainly the position of many believers today, both lay and ordained. In another sermon Spurgeon likens "the purpose of God and the free agency of man" to "two facts that run side by side, like parallel lines". The space between, he says, is the "place to kneel in, adoring and worshipping him whom you cannot understand".[3]

Recently, I came across a similar illustration from Nicky Gumbel, the well-known and respected Anglican pastor and author of the *Alpha Course* and many other publications which have emanated from that popular introduction to the Christian faith. Commenting on Matthew 11:25-30, which he claims teaches both a Reformed understanding of Predestination and human free will, he says,

> I find it difficult to get my mind around this paradox. However, I have found the following illustration helpful. Imagine a room with an arched doorway. The outside of the arch is inscribed with the words, 'Come to me, all you...' (v.28). In other words everyone is invited into the room. When you get into the room, on the inside of the same arch is written, 'No one knows the Father except the Son and those to whom the Son chooses to reveal him' (v.27b).
>
> In other words, free will is a doctrine for everyone. No one can say, 'I am not going to become a Christian because I have not been chosen.' The invitation is to all. On the other hand, predestination is a doctrine of assurance for those who *are* Christians. Once you have accepted the invitation and entered, you can know that God has chosen you and therefore he will not let you go.[4]

Fisk's use of this quotation is actually out of context and could be misleading. Thereby he implies that Spurgeon was making a case for the view against which I am presently arguing. However, Spurgeon was not addressing anything remotely related to election, but rather the inability of certain people to accept both "the work of Christ for us" and "the operation of the Holy Spirit in us", the issue being their inability to accept that saving faith is "at the same time the duty of man and the gift of God" (quotations from the same sermon). Nevertheless, Fisk's use of the quotation probably does aptly summarise Spurgeon's view (see Fisk, 63) as well as a particular approach to the alleged paradox of God's choice of individuals and their choice of him.

[3] In P. Lewis *et al*, 33, quoting from *The Metropolitan Tabernacle Pulpit*, vol. 39, 169.

[4] Nicky Gumbel, *Bible in One Year*, 14 January 2017: www.bibleinoneyear.org/bioy/commentary/2417/en (his italics). A more recent comment of 23 April 2017 (www.bibleinoneyear.org/bioy/commentary/2517/en) claims that the actions of Judas in betraying Jesus, Peter's denial and Jesus' 'going' in Luke 22:22 and 34 illustrate the principle

It seems evident that even great men of God like C. H. Spurgeon (1834-92) or Charles Simeon (1759-1836), both of whom stood on the Augustinian side of the debate and both being great evangelists, struggled with the tension between divine determinism and human responsibility and consequently displayed a degree of ambivalence about their Reformed standing. William Estep, for example, reports Spurgeon as famously saying, "I fear I am not a very good Calvinist because I pray that the Lord will save all of the elect and then elect some more."[5] And at a Thursday evening service at the Metropolitan Tabernacle, Spurgeon "dared to go far beyond his creed, and in his passion for the souls of men cried, 'Lord, hasten to bring in all Thine elect—and then elect some more.'"[6] Likewise, Handley Moule reports Simeon, who, during his youth and early adulthood had experienced first-hand the Calvinist-Arminian debate in Cambridge, England in the latter part of the eighteenth and into the nineteenth century, wrote to a friend in 1825, "The truth is not in the middle, and not in one extreme, but in both extremes." Intensely conscious of the controversy of his day and of the limits of the human point of view, Simeon also wrote, "I am like a man swimming in the Atlantic, and I have no fear of striking one hand against Europe and the other against America."[7] Nonetheless, he sought to find common ground in a characteristically eirenic spirit, and even in his oft-reported exchange with John Wesley, then 56 years his senior, which occurred soon after his ordination to the ministry, probably in 1784, he completely sidestepped the issues which really divided the two men.[8] Both Spurgeon and Simeon seemed to struggle with the logical

---

of divine Predestination and human responsibility. This is a misleading claim because the context of Luke 22 is not soteriological.

[5] William R. Estep, 'The Making of a Prophet: An Introduction to Charles Haddon Spurgeon', *Baptist History and Heritage* 4, October 1984, 6.

[6] W. Y. Fullerton, *C. H. Spurgeon: A Biography* (London & Edinburgh: W. Williams & Norgate, 1920), Chapter 8: 'An Intimate Interlude'.

[7] Simeon, writing in the third person, "is persuaded that neither Calvinists nor Arminians are in exclusive possession of that system" (i.e., the system of the Holy Scriptures): Preface to *Horae Homileticae*.

[8] Simeon, Preface; Handley C. G. Moule, 77-80. Simeon's questioning of Wesley, often construed as demonstrating Wesley's inconsistent Arminianism, touched only on Depravity, the sinner's total dependency on the grace of God for salvation, the denial of any possibility of salvation being earned through good works and dependency on the grace of God to preserve the believer to God's heavenly kingdom. Wesley and Simeon

conclusions of their Augustinianism, denying, with many others before and after them, the possibility of consistency in their positions.

It is true that certain aspects of theology cannot readily be explained in terms which satisfy our innate need for logical resolution and comprehension – for example, the issue which Spurgeon actually addressed in the sermons cited above (192f.), the paradox of faith needing to be exercised, apparently out of our freedom to choose, but it also, allegedly, being God's sovereign gift to us. The ultimate example of biblical revelation which defies logical analysis is probably the concept of the Trinity, of course. However, I suggest that the nature of that kind of incomprehensibility is significantly and qualitatively different from that of Election. The Trinity is the best summary we have of the biblical data about the Godhead, even though the Bible never elaborates a complete synthesis and never uses the word 'Trinity', and indeed, sometimes leaves unresolved loose ends.[9] To completely understand the Trinity would surely make God finite because it would bring him into the realm of our imperfect capacity to understand. That we cannot adequately explain it does not invalidate it, however, but merely underlines the limitations of our human capacity and demonstrates God's ultimate ineffability.

But Election is of an entirely different order, I would suggest. I cannot accept that there is any *a priori* reason why the issue should not be comprehensible even within the finite bounds of the human mind because we are not dealing with a notion akin to the nature of the Godhead, which we cannot know in an ultimate sense: we are simply trying to understand "his ways with men",[10] a strategy, albeit divine, which has been revealed for the salvation of the world. We cannot fully know the mind of God or fathom his ultimate purposes, but it appeals strongly to me that, if God truly loves us and really wishes to communicate his way of salvation to our *depraved* race, it seems inherently unlikely that

---

were at one on all these points, but the contentious issues of Unconditional Election and Limited Atonement did not feature in the exchange. Thus, Simeon was able to claim agreement and seek unity between them "in those things wherein we agree".

[9] E.g., Paul's teaching in 1 Corinthians 15:28 about Christ ultimately being subject to God, and the identity of the one occupying the throne in Revelation 4:2; 5:6.

[10] Carson (2002), 2.

he would do so in terms inaccessible to us since we are the very ones who need to hear and heed the message of the gospel, and then make a rational decision about it.

If we attempt to hold together both sides of the Election debate, as suggested by Spurgeon, Gumbel and others of a Reformed ilk, we will enmesh ourselves in a tangle of irreconcilably contradictory ideas, and ultimately, we will commit intellectual suicide. However, strongly affirming that God is not a God of confusion,[11] and that humankind was made in his image as rational beings, I believe we should not only seek, but expect to find a solution which does due justice not only to all the biblical data but also to the integrity of human rationality, no matter how limited that might be. We do indeed admit that our mental faculties have been impaired by the Fall, but that is very different from saying that human rationality is fundamentally flawed. Two plus two will always make four. Setting aside the ambivalence we have already noted in some of the Reformers' thinking about the appropriate spheres in which we may exercise freedom of choice, it is abundantly clear that humankind has made huge steps of progress technologically, especially in more recent decades, through applying our God-given curiosity and intellect to harness to an amazing degree the forces of the natural world about which we are gaining knowledge almost daily. I don't think a Calvinist could possibly dissent from that proposition – indeed, Calvin certainly didn't: he "waxed eloquent about the 'natural gifts' of fallen people, who are able by the help of God's Spirit through common grace to achieve great things in the arts and sciences."[12] However, a rigorist, like Martin Luther, would differentiate between our ability to comprehend the world of nature, on the one hand, and the things of God, on the other. I suggest that the logical result of that kind of dualism removes God far beyond our reach, leaving us in a limbo of ignorance where we could never know for certain whether what we believed even about divine things, let alone the down-to-earth aspects of daily life, was true or not.

Let me try to explain what I mean by that. If it were true that only

---

[11] 1 Corinthians 14:33 (KJV).
[12] Olson (2011), 43; Calvin, *Institutes*, 2.2.13f.: Beveridge, 2:234-6.

regenerate individuals could know and understand the things of God, at least in part, we would be driven to ask how we could ever know for sure that we were regenerate; that is, in the sense of having been born again. A Calvinist would say that each of us begins our natural life in a state of unregeneracy and therefore *depravity* and *inability*.[13] The rigorous application of the notion of Total Depravity therefore leads us into an intellectual oblivion which C. S. Lewis called "a form of devil-worship".[14] There is here a crucial epistemological question, and we must take very seriously indeed the logic that if it were not possible to have a reliable inkling of God's character or purposes *prior* to our conversion, then we could have absolutely no confidence in what we knew either before or after conversion. If that were not the case, Christianity could be nothing but a pathetic illusion. The reality, however, is that what we discover in experience through and *after* conversion does not appear to conflict fundamentally with what was known beforehand. Some aspects of our understanding will inevitably have changed, and we may have had to unlearn certain things, but our conversion did not bring a radically altered understanding; instead, it brought the beginnings of a clarity and divine illumination, a filling-out of what we knew beforehand, but not a fundamental change in what we already knew. For example, most of us will have come to a deeper understanding of our own lostness and need of a Saviour through the process of conversion.

Since Calvinists apparently fail to draw this conclusion, I would say that their system is demonstrably bankrupt. When we touched on the issues of ability and responsibility above, we saw the kind of logical contradictions which Calvinism can throw up. We must therefore challenge dogma which calls into question our innate ability to be rational. The fact that a believer in Jesus does indeed discover an unbroken continuity between the mindset and understanding of their unregenerate and regenerate days, respectively, does, I believe, call into question any alleged qualitative fallibility of the power of human reason and knowledge in the sphere of responding to God, a fallibility which Total

---

[13] See L. Berkhof, 247f., for a definition of 'inability'.

[14] C. S. Lewis (*Problem of Pain*), 25.

Depravity, as taught by Calvinism, asserts.

That sincere, godly, Bible-believing people throughout the age of the Church have failed to solve the problem of Election certainly suggests there is no easy solution. Paradoxically, but not, I think, contrary to what I am claiming, I would suggest that one of the most common cardinal errors of Calvinism appears to be an over-reliance on rationality when trying to make sense of scripture. Indeed, Reformed writers and teachers seem to glory in their capacity to comprehend the intricacies of their own system of logic and terminology. In support of that, I observe that the leadership of many Reformed churches in the UK largely comprise bodies of relatively young, academically qualified, though not necessarily theologically qualified, men (women tend not to be involved in their leadership: at least, they are not often formally recognised as such). That suggests to me that those churches select people for leadership who have the intellectual capacity for juggling the complexities of Reformed terminology, which, in turn, suggests that such churches are less confident in their reliance on potential leaders who have not benefitted from further education or beyond, despite their spiritual maturity or wisdom. Modern Calvinism, it seems, relies heavily on bright, intellectually active minds to support its theology. An unfortunate consequence of an over-reliance on intellect, of course, may be a down-playing of teaching on and the practice of spiritual gifts. Thus, we find the paradox where, on the one hand, there is a denial of the efficacy of human rationality in grasping the complexities of Election – a feature of so-called moderate Calvinism which leads, among other things, to the compromise positions I have commented on, but on the other hand, we also see in Calvinism a strong reliance on the intellectual capacities of those charged with teaching its dogmas.

I am not suggesting, of course, that we do not need academically qualified minds in leadership in our churches, and I do believe we can use rationality with a high degree of confidence, but to place it on a plane higher than the revelation God has given, and yet deny its competency in the area of theological thinking, will sooner or later lead us astray. To say that will seem to contradict what I have just asserted but bear with me as we look in more detail at the biblical evidence.

It will probably not be easy to find a solution to the conundrum of Predestination, if indeed a solution is to be found. It seems to me that answers must be sought in the text of scripture, and there alone. Trying to observe the human condition dispassionately, we have already observed that we cannot say for certain that our God-given rationality will carry the day. Neither can we be wholly reliant on personal feelings about our own part in our experience of God. Some will wonder at the grace and ineffability of God to the extent that they will feel they had no choice in their response to the gospel. Others, like C. S. Lewis, for example (see above, 4f.), most definitely feel the choice was all theirs, even though they may have felt God's heavy hand upon them as he pursued them to the foot of the Cross. I also wonder at the reliance of some on the scholarship of the Reformers and their predecessors with their highly developed and complex web of nigh-impenetrable theological method and terminology. The saintliness of most of the Reformers was undoubtedly profound, their reforming achievements hugely significant and their academic acumen, without doubt, prodigious, but I think we are on shaky ground if we place too much reliance on any of those things.

Present-day scholarship has opened up for all – for academic and laypeople alike, a wealth of understanding of the original biblical languages through highly efficient electronic research tools and a better understanding of historical contexts and the languages related to biblical Hebrew, Greek and Aramaic. We have therefore unprecedented opportunity today for more accurate and cogent exegesis than was ever possible for Calvin or Arminius in the sixteenth and early seventeenth centuries, let alone Augustine in the fourth. I strongly suggest then that, if it proves possible to deduce a coherent doctrine of Election, and one which most importantly does not discredit scripture in any way, it will only be discovered by careful exegesis of the biblical data. And to that we now must turn.

Chapter 8

THE VOCABULARY OF ELECTION[1]

Word studies are fraught with pitfalls. A not uncommon mistake when trying to establish the exact meaning of any particular word in any language, whether ancient or modern, let alone in any of the three languages of the Bible – Hebrew, Aramaic and Koinē Greek, all of which are dead languages,[2] is to assume that any aspect of that word's meaning may apply in any context wherever it may be found, an error known as *illegitimate totality transfer*.[3] This is one of the problems with the family of translations which attempt to consistently match the same English words with particular Greek or Hebrew words – the KJV-ESV family, for example. The situation is exacerbated with translations like *The Amplified Bible*,[4] where the reader is faced with a number of possible meanings and is left to choose which is thought to fit best. To the undiscriminating reader, the unfortunate inference may be that any one of the renderings on offer will do, but such is very much not the case because language does not work that way:

> Modern linguistic theory teaches that the meaning of a given word is not located primarily in the word itself but is determined by the relationship the word has to other words in the context of a given occurrence (syntagmatic) and by the contrast it forms with other

---

[1] Some of the following is quite technical so I have represented the relevant Hebrew and Greek words both literally and in English transliteration at their first mention except when quoting phrases in the original languages. See also Appendix 1, 376, 'Election Vocabulary in the NIV (2011) New Testament', which lists every occurrence of statements concerning choosing in the NIV.

[2] Biblical Hebrew was probably not a commonly spoken language even in the time of Jesus; Aramaic, in tandem with Koinē Greek, being the *lingua francas* of first century Jews in Palestine. Modern Hebrew is a nineteenth-century reinvention of Biblical Hebrew with simplified grammar and many loanwords. Modern Greek has evolved from ancient dialects but is sufficiently different as to make Koinē Greek difficult for contemporary Greek speakers to understand. Derivatives of Aramaic are still spoken today among various people groups of West Asia, notably the Assyrians.

[3] An expression coined by James Barr, 218. This is Don Carson's 13th exegetical fallacy – see Carson (1984), 62.

[4] Zondervan, 1987.

words which share its semantic domain (paradigmatic).[5]

Thus, the *precise* meaning of a word can only be deduced from its context, and, especially where the word has a wide semantic range, great care must be taken to understand that context. This will become clear with some of the examples examined in this and Chapter 10.

We have already seen that the main English words of the Election vocabulary are *Election, Predestination* and *Foreknowledge*.[6] I will examine each in turn before looking at some of the key New Testament passages where they occur. For good measure, I will also examine the idea of *Calling* which appears to be related. The aim of this section is simply to try to discover the meanings of these words and how they are used in their biblical contexts so that we can then go on to apply those findings to the key texts and see how they function theologically.

It should be recognised that none of the words under consideration is common in the New Testament, and some are quite rare, so we don't have the luxury of examining a wide range of contexts as would be the case with more common words. Consequently, it is sometimes hard to generalise about meaning since the frequency of any particular word is limited and may be used in contexts which are quite restricted in scope. Furthermore, meaning cannot be prescribed *precisely* by usage in other Greek texts, especially texts from other eras, geographical regions or even other dialects of ancient Greek, nor necessarily even by the way a particular word is used by other biblical writers. Consequently, as I say, the *contexts* of these words must be examined with care.

a. Election/Elect

The three main elements in the Election word group are the verb *eklegomai* (ἐκλέγομαι), the noun *eklogē* (ἐκλογή) and the adjective or participle *eklektos* (ἐκλεκτός). The vocabulary of Election is particularly problematical because not all are verbs. I hope to show the importance of this point because in some key texts many modern translations treat

---

[5] Karen H. Jobes, 'Distinguishing the Meaning of Greek Verbs in the Semantic Domain for Worship', in Silva, 202. See also Barr, 107-60, 263-82.

[6] See Chapter 3, 64; Foreordination is not dealt with here specifically.

them all as though they were verbs, suggesting meanings which lend unwarranted support to a Reformed interpretation.

Louis Berkhof's claim that the verb *eklegomai* and the noun *eklogē*, together with their Old Testament Hebrew equivalent *bachar*

> stress the element of choice or selection in the decree of God respecting the eternal destiny of sinners ... that God selects a certain number of the human race and places them in special relationship to Himself.[7]

is an unwarranted overstatement. No doubt, the New Testament vocabulary of Election sometimes carries specialised theological meaning, perhaps even often, but whether it is so in "the great majority of cases", as *The New International Dictionary of New Testament Theology*[8] asserts, surely must be determined from the contexts of these words.

i. Eklegomai

The verb *eklegomai* (ἐκλέγομαι) occurs only 22 times in the New Testament[9] and 122 times in the canonical books of the Septuagint.[10] It means 'to choose' and has a semantic range very similar to the English verb as well as its Hebrew equivalent, *bachar* (בָּחַר). Since in the New Testament it always occurs in the middle voice,[11] James Packer[12] and others suggest that it has reflexive overtones, thus meaning to "choose

---

[7] L. Berkhof, 112. Among his citations for *eklegomai* and *eklogē*, Berkhof includes 2 Thessalonians 2:13 where the verb is actually *haireō*. See below, 215f., for discussion of this verse.
[8] Gerhard Nordholt in *NIDNTT*, 1.533.
[9] Of the twelve disciples: Luke 6:13; John 6:70; 13:18; 15:16 (twice), 19; Acts 1:2; of Matthias: Acts 1:24; of Stephen: Acts 6:5; of "our fathers": Acts 13:17; of Paul: Acts 15:7; of emissaries: Acts 15:22 (twice), 25; of the elect: Mark 13:20; Ephesians 1:4; of the foolish, weak and lowly things of the world (three times): 1 Corinthians 1:27-28; of the poor: James 2:5; of Christ: Luke 9:35 (several variants of this verse exist, but the more difficult reading adopted by the NA26 is the rare perfect passive participle, *eklelegmenos* (ἐκλελεγμένος). See I. H. Marshall (1978), 388); of Mary's choice of "what is better": Luke 10:42; of places of honour at a feast: Luke 14:7 (KJV).
[10] See Table 1 below, 204. Word counts in the Septuagint are based on Swete's "diplomatic" (i.e., more or less exact reproduction) edition of the Codex Vaticanus (also known as Codex B). See Appendix 2, 380, for a comparison of *eklegomai*, *hairetidzō* and *haireō* in the New Testament, Septuagint and Greek literature in general.
[11] Lothar Coenen in *NIDNTT*, 1.539.
[12] In Douglas (1980), 435; see also Hawthorne & Martin, 226.

out for oneself". Not every occurrence convincingly supports that view, however, as a number of examples in non-soteriological contexts, in Acts, for instance,[13] demonstrate. Furthermore, although *eklegomai* in the New Testament usually refers to choices of people (e.g., the twelve disciples and other individuals), Christians in various states, the Elect, the foolish, the weak and lowly things of the world, the poor and Christ himself, twice the verb also refers to abstract objects, notably, Mary's choice of "what is better" and of places of honour at a feast.

Some of these texts will be discussed in more detail below, but in summary, apart from inanimate objects and named individuals, which clearly had been chosen to fulfil some particular role (i.e., Matthias, Stephen and Paul), and apart from instances where Christ himself is said to have been chosen, all other occurrences refer to the choice of groups or categories of people rather than individuals. An important point I shall be making more fully is that *eklegomai* is *never* used where an individual is said to be chosen for salvation, although possible exceptions to this conclusion may be Jesus' choice of the twelve apostles in John 6:70 and 15:16, etc., where the question is raised as to whether or not he chose them for eternal life as some Reformed writers would assert. That issue will be considered in Chapter 10, as will the reference in Mark 13:20 where the Elect are explicitly said to be chosen.[14]

In contrast to the usage of *eklegomai* in the New Testament, Table 1 (below) summarises its usage in the canonical books of the Septuagint where almost all occurrences translate the Hebrew *bachar*. Occasionally in the Septuagint some of these verbs are found interchangeably: Judges 5:8 has *eklegomai* in Codex Vaticanus (B) while Alexandrinus (A) has *hairetidzō*; and Joshua 24:15 has *eklegomai* in A, but *heireō* in B, for instance.

An interesting feature of the distribution of the verb throughout Greek literature in general is that *eklegomai* appears relatively rarely. Generally speaking, *haireō* predominates, and only in Judeo-Christian literature – the Septuagint, the New Testament and the Apostolic Fathers, is

---

[13] E.g., Acts 6:5; 15:7, 22, 25.
[14] Chapter 10a, 282, and 10b(ii), 296.

eklegomai more frequent than *haireō*; indeed it seems to replace *haireō* as the verb of choosing in these texts (see Table 7 below, 390f.).

Table 1: *Eklegomai* in the Septuagint (Swete):

Hebrew MT		Frequency	Usage
bachar	בָּחַר	116[15]	Choice of options (19), person(s) – kings, priests, etc. (24), peoples – mostly Israel (19), places – mostly Jerusalem (43), also wives, gods/idols, stones, wood, fasts.
barar	בָּרַר	2	Set apart, purify, consecrate: 1 Chronicles 16:41, Daniel 11:35.
laqach	לָקַח	1	Acquire/receive learning: Proverbs 24:47.
qabal	קָבַל	1	Choose an option: 1 Chronicles 21:11.
qabats	קָבַץ	1	Assemble, bring together: Joel 2:16.
toor	תּוּר	1	Seek out, explore: Deuteronomy 1:33.

ii. Eklogē

Although common in secular Greek, the abstract noun *eklogē* (ἐκλογή) is found only seven times in the New Testament,[16] although never in the Septuagint. It may be translated 'a choosing' or 'an election'. The usual claim is that it always represents objects of God's choice and never refers to inanimate objects like a seat or a personal preference. However, twice the NIV translates *eklogē* as if it were a verb. The first occurrence is Romans 11:5: "at the present time there is a remnant *chosen* by grace", and the second is 1 Thessalonians 1:4: "we know, brothers and sisters loved by God, that he has *chosen* you". I will examine these two texts in more detail, because, although it may not be possible to say categorically that the NIV translations are incorrect, I think the evidence casts some doubt on those readings.

Firstly, in Romans 11:5 a more neutral possible translation of the phrase, "a remnant *chosen* by grace",[17] which affords *eklogē* its proper

---

[15] The *barah* (בָּרָה: to eat, consume) of 1 Samuel 17:8 is clearly a misspelling of *bachar*. See the critical apparatus of Kittel's *Biblia Hebraica*.
[16] Acts 9:15: "my chosen instrument"; Romans 9:11: "God's purpose in election"; Romans 11:5 "a remnant chosen by grace"; Romans 11:7: "the elect"; Romans 11:28: "election"; 1 Thessalonians 1:4: "that he has chosen you", i.e., the church at Thessalonica; 2 Peter 1:10: "election".
[17] Greek: λεῖμμα κατ' ἐκλογὴν χάριτος γέγονεν.

function in speech as a noun, although admittedly clumsier, may be "a remnant according to a choice (or an election) through grace". In the next verse (11:6) "grace" (*chariti*: χάριτι), which is clearly instrumental (i.e., "by grace"), enabling the act of choosing, stands in apposition to "an election of grace" (*eklogēn charitos*: ἐκλογὴν χάριτος) in verse 5, and in contrast to "by works" (*ex ergōn*: ἐξ ἔργων) in verse 6. Thus the "grace" of Romans 11:5 is the basis upon which the choice is made, that is, "an election (or choice) based on grace" – i.e., God's grace, as opposed to human works.

A Reformed understanding of Romans 11:5 would then be that God had predestined the *individuals* comprising this remnant group to be elect through his grace. A couple of features should be noted about the phrase which suggests otherwise, however. Firstly, individuals are not directly in view. The context of Romans 11 is Paul's argument that, despite the inauguration of the New Covenant, God had not rejected Israel. Just as in Elijah's day he had preserved 7,000 prophets who had remained faithful to him and had not bowed the knee to Baal,[18] so in the early days of the gospel proclamation God had set apart, or perhaps planned, that a 'remnant' from Israel should exist which would ultimately be incorporated into Christ by faith and become part of the Church – the founding membership of the Church, indeed. Whether Paul had in mind a remnant in principle which had yet to fully emerge or, more likely, that he was thinking of all the Jews who had already bowed the knee to Christ, is hard to say. Either way, God certainly knew their individual identities, but it was the *group* that was elect, so it is not correct to postulate a choosing of individuals.

Furthermore, and contrary to the normal presupposition, the phrase "an election/choice of grace" does not make explicit the identity of the one making the choice. Could it be then that the choice was not God's, as is usually assumed, and is evident by the way the NIV has translated the verse, but instead be a human choice? Owing to the Reformed control belief paradigm or hegemony which I have alleged, election is usually assumed to be about God's choice of others, whether humans,

---

[18] Romans 11:4; 1 Kings 19:18.

angels, or whomever, but I suggest that need not always be the case. The Greek text does not specifically nominate the one who chose the believing remnant, so grammatically their election stands in abstraction. Thus, considering again my suggested rewording – "a remnant according to an election (or choice) through grace", the question might be asked, could this have been a choice made by the individuals who belonged to that remnant, just as the 7,000 prophets had chosen not to bow the knee to Baal and thereby chose to serve God? Could it be that the 'grace' in my phrase, "an election through *grace*", was the divine *accommodation* which permitted individuals of the remnant to exercise their personal free choice?[19] A somewhat speculative solution perhaps, but either way I think *ekloge* makes better sense translated as a noun rather than as a verb. Indeed, I would prefer that *ekloge* always be translated as the noun it is because otherwise scripture would appear to say that God actively selects individuals, thus creating convenient but nonetheless misleading texts in support of the Reformed position.

Furthermore, *ekloge* need not refer to a chosen object or person, but may simply mean their state of *chosenness*. This distinction may not be easy to grasp because, understandably, it could be argued that individuals included in the elect group presumably had been chosen individually. However, that need not be the case because incorporation into a select group may come about in a variety of different ways. So, this distinction is, I believe, significant.

The second occurrence where the NIV treats *ekloge* as a verb is 1 Thessalonians 1:4: "we know, brothers and sisters loved by God, that he has *chosen* you".[20] Again, I suggest it would be better to translate the verse as, "knowing, brothers loved by God, *your election*", which once again affords *ekloge* its proper place in speech as a noun. In other words, rather than Paul acknowledging that the Christians at Thessalonica had been chosen by God, he actually recognises their place within the elect community of God's people, presumably because he knows of their confession of Christ and has seen evidence of spiritual fruit manifested

---

[19] Cf. Acts 18:27: "those who by grace had believed": Greek: τοῖς πεπιστευκόσιν διὰ τῆς χάριτος.
[20] Greek: εἰδότες, ἀδελφοὶ ἠγαπημένοι ὑπὸ [τοῦ] θεοῦ, τὴν ἐκλογὴν ὑμῶν.

in their lives resulting from their elect status, as he goes on to enumerate in the following verses (1:5ff.). Again, it could be argued that this might mean exactly the same thing – if they are part of the Elect, then they must have been chosen, the assumption to which I have just alluded – but we shall see that that is not necessarily so. In any case, by correcting the verbal use of the noun, the questionable relationship between 'God' and the pronoun 'you' (i.e., "*God... has chosen you*"), which the NIV and some other translations introduce for the sake of clarity, is thereby broken.

That would then open the possibility of a reading similar to the alternative I have suggested for Romans 11:5. By making a slight alteration to my suggested translation – "knowing, brothers loved by God, your *choice*", we arrive at another possibility. Again, the identity of the one making the choice is ambiguous because *ekloge* is a noun, not a verb, and therefore without either subject or object, so the possibility exists that Paul may be referring here too to a human choice which had been permitted and facilitated through God's grace. Whether this was Paul's intended meaning either in Romans 11:5 or the Thessalonians text remains moot, but the point I wish to underline is that translators must take care not to import assumed meaning or interpretation where the text is ambiguous, and meaning should not be sacrificed for the ease of flow of the language.

These two examples illustrate where I find many modern versions of the Bible problematical in that preference is afforded to the tradition of Reformed thinking which I think has dominated biblical exegesis and translation at least since the Reformation and the Geneva Bible. And I have to admit that, whenever these passages are read in public, my own convictions are challenged, albeit temporarily. Nonetheless, it is important to recognise that *ekloge* is a noun because, if it is accorded the force of a verb when associated with objects chosen by God, the Reformed view, that God actively selects individuals for salvation, is artificially strengthened in a way which is not immediately apparent from the Greek text and, indeed in my opinion, was probably not the original writer's intention.

iii. Eklektos

The third and more common component of the vocabulary of Election, is the participle *eklektos* (ἐκλεκτός) which occurs 22 or 23 times in the New Testament[21] and is normally taken to mean 'chosen' or 'chosen one(s)', 'elect' or 'elect one(s)' - plural. In other words, it usually refers to an individual or group of individuals who have been chosen or favoured by God, or, as I would prefer to put it, are found to be in a state or position of chosenness or favour.

In 18 of the 22 instances, *eklektos* is translated in the NIV simply as an adjective, sometimes as a noun, and, except when referring to individuals – Christ (i.e., "the Chosen One" or "cornerstone"), or Rufus (possibly) - is to be construed collectively, a group of chosen ones, "the Elect", "God's Elect", etc. The word does not therefore need to confer the force of being actively selected because in most cases individuals are not in view, except in the sense of belonging to that special group or class which comprises those who have been *added* to it, the Elect. The two places in 2 John which refer respectively to the "the lady chosen by God" and "your sister, who is chosen by God",[22] are apparent exceptions, but for a number of reasons, it is generally accepted that they refer to congregations rather than to particular women.[23]

---

[21] (a) Singular: "the Chosen One": Luke 23:35; "the living Stone... chosen by God": 1 Peter 2:4; "a chosen... cornerstone": 2:6; "Rufus, chosen in the Lord": Romans 16:13; the elect lady/sister: 2 John 1, 13; a chosen race: 1 Peter 2:9; also "chosen together with you" (*suneklektos*: συνεκλεκτός): 1 Peter 5:13; (b) plural collective: "many are invited, but few are chosen": Matthew 20:16 (KJV); 22:14; "the/his elect": 24:22, 24, 31; Mark 13:20, 22, 27; "his chosen ones": Luke 18:7; "those whom God has chosen": Romans 8:33; "God's chosen people": Colossians 3:12; "the elect angels": 1 Timothy 5:21; "the elect": 2 Timothy 2:10; "God's elect": Titus 1:1; 1 Peter 1:1/2; "chosen ... followers": Revelation 17:14.

[22] 2 John 1 and 13.

[23] Klein, 108, lists six reasons: (1) New Testament writers refer to the church in figurative terms ('bride': Ephesians 5:24-32; Revelation 21:9f.; Galatians 4:26; 'elect [woman]': 1 Peter 5:13); (2) John probably wrote to a single local congregation under his care, and the 'children' (2 John 1 and 13: Greek *tekna*) are probably its members; (3) the lack of personal references points to a congregation more than to an individual; (4) John's exhortations to love better fit a church than an individual (5-6); (5) the letter's opening speaks to a community more than to an individual (1-3); and (6) the interchange of singular and plural terminology points to a community.

However, like *eklogē*, *eklektos* is also sometimes translated as if it were a verb in the NIV.[24] By thus depriving the word of its natural substantive force, and making it appear to mean an active choosing of individuals for salvation, translators have again provided the Reformed mind with further misleading proof texts. Thus, with Balz & Schneider, I suggest that

> A predestinarian misunderstanding of the belief in election is thus rejected ... the elect are those who have followed the invitation into the kingdom of God through Jesus Christ and have realized their call in a life of faith.[25]

It is important to note, however, that *eklektos* can also have a more general and non-soteriological meaning. For instance, where the NIV of Romans 16:13 says that Rufus is "chosen in the Lord", other versions, the RSV, for example, translate *eklektos* as "eminent". F. F. Bruce also suggests 'choice' or 'outstanding' as possible suitable alternatives.[26] That is not to say that Rufus and others named in Romans 16 were not among the Elect in a theological sense, but in that this single reference of what is a relatively unusual word departs from the otherwise general sense of being individually chosen by God, either for salvation or for some other purpose, it is evident that *eklektos* can have a broader meaning than to be selected. An important referent for the adjective *eklektos*, which clearly does not signify a divine choice of fallen men and women for salvation, is Christ himself, which I will consider presently.[27]

Thus, I have established, at least to my own satisfaction, that the words just considered, *eklektos* and *eklogē*, when applied to the election of God's people, should not be treated as though they were verbs. In other words, except when their objects are singular, whether individuals or things, they never actually describe *acts* of divine selection, but rather indicate the *status* which the body of believers shares with Christ into whom individuals have been incorporated through faith. When the

---

[24] Matthew 22:14; Romans 8:33; 16:13 (possibly); 1 Peter 2:4; 5:13, also 1 Peter 1:2 where the verb is absent from the Greek text, but is interpolated into the NIV text; also, Matthew 20:16 (KJV).
[25] Balz & Schneider, I, 417.
[26] Bruce (1963), 274.
[27] See Chapter 9, 248.

Election vocabulary is applied to believers, the words are always plural or collectively singular.[28] Thus, even though they may be construed as indicating God's deliberate choice, they do not actually indicate his choice of individuals. Nonetheless, it must always be insisted upon that the response people may make to the appeal of the gospel can only be as *individuals*. No one is saved merely by association with the believing community or by birthright – only by the exercise of individual and personal faith in Christ.

On a more speculative note, it may be asked if it were possible that a phrase incorporating one of these nouns or adjectives was simply an idiomatic way of expressing a verb in New Testament Greek – some sort of Hebraism, perhaps. Although that in effect is the way Bible translators sometimes treat these words, it is essentially a linguistic and idiomatic question and stands apart from conclusions which may be drawn on the usual straightforward grammatical grounds. It may be well and good to have established on the grounds of the best available scholarship that it is never legitimate to treat *eklektos* or *eklogē* as if they were verbs, but if it could be demonstrated that they could have meanings equivalent to *eklegomai*, the translations I have been criticising could be legitimate. A supplementary question, of course, is that if that were the case, why would the biblical writers not simply have used a verb available to them to express what they had meant to say? I suspect that speculative questions like this can only lead into grammatical cul-de-sacs, however, and the only other possible example of which I am aware is the way the noun *huiothesia* is sometimes understood as meaning 'to adopt'[29] (i.e., as if it were a verb). That notwithstanding, however, David Daniell, in his Introduction to the British Library's facsimile edition of Tyndale's 1526 New Testament,[30] points out that a

---

[28] Collective nouns, which grammatically have traditionally been regarded as singular are today widely treated as plural. Thus, "The government *have* decided...", etc. My preference is to resist that tendency.

[29] Although the NIV does not always translate *huiothesia* as a verb, except in Romans 8:15; Ephesians 1:5 and possibly Galatians 4:5, it is often understood in popular exegesis in terms of Christians having been adopted into God's family. See my forthcoming *Pie in the Sky When You Die?*

[30] David Daniell ed., *The New Testament: A Facsimile of the 1526 Edition Translated by William Tyndale* (Peabody, MA: Hendrickson, London: The British Library, 2008).

THE VOCABULARY OF ELECTION

characteristic of Greek, as compared with Latin, is its preference for verbs over nouns. He gives as an example Mark 1:9 where Tyndale has "Jesus came from Nazareth", whereas the Latin uses a noun - "the arrival of Jesus", etc.[31] That suggests to me that, when New Testament Greek uses a noun, generally speaking, it should be translated as such.

In line with the exceptional use of *eklektos* in Romans 16:13 of Rufus, another possibility may exist, and I stress *possibility* because I am not aware of a comparable example of what I am about to suggest anywhere else in scripture, including the Septuagint. When Matthew cites Isaiah 42:1, he does not follow the Hebrew exactly – Matthew 12:18 has,

> Here is my servant whom I have chosen,
> *the one I love*, in whom I delight.

whereas Isaiah, when translated from the Hebrew text, has "*my chosen one* in whom I delight". Matthew uses *agapētos* (ἀγαπητός, 'beloved') while the Septuagint agrees with the Hebrew, translating *bachiri* (בְּחִירִי, 'elect') with *eklektos* (ἐκλεκτός, 'chosen'). Howard Marshall suggests that Matthew's unexpected use of *agapētos* may be due to an assimilation of the baptismal saying of Mark 1:11; "You are my Son, whom I love".[32] That may, indeed, be possible because *eklektos* and *agapētos* seem to be interchangeable in those contexts, both words carrying implications of belovedness and uniqueness. A similar interchangeability is found in the parallel accounts of the Transfiguration where Luke uses the participle *eklelegmenos* (ἐκλελεγμένος, related to *eklektos*), while both Matthew, Mark and also Peter use *agapētos*.[33] I shall explore the relationships between these words in more detail below.[34]

Eklektos can also imply specialness or even uniqueness in certain contexts. In the Septuagint its meaning is sometimes clearly to do with value, worth or even purity, and it sometimes occurs in contexts where the word has nothing at all to do with selection, but rather with

---

[31] Daniell, ii.
[32] I. H. Marshall (1990), 127.
[33] Luke 9:35: "This is my Son, whom I have chosen"; Matthew 17:5, Mark 9:7 and 2 Peter 1:17: "This is my Son, whom I love".
[34] Appendix 2, 380.

211

desirability,[35] though, admittedly, a desirable object would more likely be selected.[36] There are also 17 cases where the Hebrew passive participle (i.e., verbal adjective) of *bachar* isn't represented in the Septuagint by *epilegō* or any other verb, but with an adjective, usually to do with military prowess.[37] Marshall also shows that the meaning of *agapētos* in the Septuagint can be ambiguous because it can be translated either as 'beloved' or 'only', although wherever a son or daughter is the grammatical object the meaning is always about uniqueness – 'only'.[38]

It may then be worth considering whether Paul's reference to Rufus is so exceptional. It is usually regarded as the exception, but, along with these septuagintal examples, it may provide evidence for a more general sense applicable in other instances so that *eklektos* may sometimes mean 'choice' (an adjective) or 'favoured', or in some way 'special', rather than *eklektos* being a choosing for salvation.

Apart from the three Greek words just considered, there are four other New Testament words which are often translated 'chosen' or 'elect': *klēroō, hairetidzō, haireō* and *epilegō*, two of which are *hapax legomena*.[39] Furthermore, on the strength of Hebrews 5:1 - "Every high priest is *selected* from among the people", Louw & Nida include *lambanō* (λαμβάνω) in their 'To choose' category along with *eklegomai* and *haireomai*.[40] *Lambanō* is a very common word[41] with the general sense of 'to take', 'to acquire', 'to obtain', but not to do with choosing as such, so I shall exclude it from further consideration.

---

[35] Forster & Marston, 130, perhaps not unlike Paul's reference to Rufus in Romans 16:13. See above, 208, *eklektos*.
[36] L. Coenen in *NIDNTT*, 1.537; e.g., Proverbs 8:19; Song of Songs 6:10, where the LXX uses *eklektos* in a free rendering of *bara* (בָּרָה) which means 'pure' or 'clear'; Jeremiah 3:19; Haggai 2:7, etc.
[37] See Table 3, 353f. and n11, where in the LXX soldiers or warriors are said to be 'select', 'able', 'mighty' or 'young', etc., rather than actively 'chosen' or 'selected'.
[38] I. H. Marshall (1990), 127.
[39] I.e., found only once in the New Testament.
[40] Louw & Nida, 30.86; 57.55.
[41] *Lambanō* occurs 258 times in 243 verses in the New Testament, and 1271 times in 1191 verses in the Septuagint (Swete - all books).

iv. Klēroō

The NIV of Ephesians 1:11 reads, "In him we were also *chosen*", but the verb is actually *klēroō* (κληρόω) which appears only once in the New Testament. *Klēroō* does not actually mean 'chosen' but has to do with being appointed or being obtained by lot, hence being made a heritage or personal possession.[42] The NIV and some other versions are therefore misleading since evidently Paul is saying nothing about election as such. Earlier in the same context in verse 4 he had already said that we were chosen in Christ, so it would seem unnecessarily repetitive to say that we were *also* chosen, unless, of course, he was contrasting the election first of Israel or the apostles, the 'us' of verse 4 - "he chose us in him", with the addition of the Gentiles, possibly implied by the 'we' of verse 11 where he may be referring to himself or Jewish-heritage believers. However, careful analysis of the personal pronouns of the first few verses of this opening passage of Ephesians shows that not to be the case.

The personal pronouns do need special attention, however, because analysis of them will reinforce the idea of *klēroō* being about part of God's inheritance rather than there being a sense of chosenness. There is no antecedent to the 'us' of verse 4, certainly not a Jewish identity, so we cannot infer an exclusively Jewish referent, and we can safely assume that Paul was including all believers from whatever cultural or faith background. However, the later 'we' of verse 12 – "*we*, who were the first to hope in Christ", does mark a distinction between Jewish believers and his gentile readership, and in verse 13 he says that gentile believers had been brought into the blessings he had been enumerating – "And *you* also were included". Moreover, the broader context of verses 11 to 14 is of "those who are God's possession" and their inheritance (1:14), so Paul is saying that the status of Israel as God's

---

[42] *BAGD*, 435 suggests "in whom our lot is cast", although it could mean to be destined or chosen. In Classical Greek *klēroō* means 'to be chosen by lot'. The related verb *klēronomeō* (κληρονομέω) also has to do with inheriting or coming into the possession of something. O'Brien, 115, suggests that the wording, "we are claimed by God as his portion" makes better sense of the passive voice. See also J. A. Robinson, *St Paul's Epistle to the Ephesians* (London: Macmillan, 1904), 146: "we have been chosen as God's portion", quoted by O'Brien, 115 n111.

inheritance under the Old Covenant is now conferred upon the whole of God's Elect,[43] Jews as well as Gentiles, and that Gentiles also share in the spiritual blessings which he had enumerated in the preceding verses. Further on in Ephesians 2:11ff., also addressing his gentile audience, Paul says a similar thing; that they had been brought near and made fellow citizens with the 'saints', the 'saints' being Jewish-heritage believers. Thus, the Old Testament language of Israel being God's treasured possession now also applies to gentile believers:

> For the LORD's portion is his people,
> Jacob his allotted inheritance.[44]

Thus, although *klēroō* does *imply* chosenness and incorporation into the Elect, though certainly not by lot, as would be the meaning in Classical Greek, that is not the point Paul is making.

v. Hairetidzō

The second rare word, *hairetidzō* (αἱρετίζω) is found in the New Testament only in Matthew 12:18; "Here is my servant whom I have chosen", an inexact quotation or paraphrase of Isaiah 42:1, and 21 times in 20 verses in the canonical books of the Septuagint. However, whereas Matthew uses *hairetidzō* to translate the Hebrew *bachir* (בָּחִיר), as the translators of the Septuagint regularly did for many other occurrences of the same Hebrew word, they did not use *hairetidzō* in that particular verse in Isaiah nor in many other places where the object of God's choosing was in view. In the Septuagint the participle *eklektos* (ἐκλεκτός) – "my chosen one", was used instead. It would therefore be difficult to differentiate the meaning of *hairetidzō* from *eklegomai*[45] and, since in Matthew's context the implied object of the verb is Christ, I accept that in that case God's servant had been divinely chosen.

---

[43] Cf. Deuteronomy 32:9; Exodus 19:5, etc. See Stott (1979), 45f.
[44] Deuteronomy 32:9.
[45] See Appendix 2, 380, for discussion on 'Relationships between 'Beloved', 'Pleasing', 'Chosen' and 'Only''.

vi. Haireō

The third rare word, *haireō* (αἱρέω) is closely related to *hairetidzō* (αἱρετίζω). It occurs just three times in the New Testament: (a) Philippians 1:22: "what shall I choose?"; (b) Hebrews 11:25: "he chose to be ill-treated", and (c) 2 Thessalonians 2:13: "God chose you *as firstfruits*", although older editions of the NIV have, "God chose you *to be saved*". *Haireō* also occurs only seven times in the canonical books of the Septuagint, but it is nevertheless by far the most common verb of choosing in the breadth of ancient Greek literature (see Table 7, 390f.).

The difference between the renderings of the Thessalonians text depends, not on translator's choice, but on a preference for one or other of two well-known textual variants.[46] If the most recent edition of the NIV is correct – "firstfruits", then another Reformed proof text is neutralised or at least cast into doubt. I would argue for the "firstfruits" variant in any case, since to be chosen to be saved would be theologically unlikely on my thesis. Despite F. F. Bruce's and Wanamaker's reservations,[47] I suggest that Paul's identification of the believers at

---

[46] Whether 'firstfruits' or 'to be saved' is what Paul intended hangs on a textual variant of 2 Thessalonians 2:13, i.e., whether his amanuensis or later copyist wrote *aparchēn* (ἀπαρχὴν) or *ap archēs* (ἀπ' ἀρχῆς), respectively, bearing in mind that the original might have been in capital letters with no accents and no word spacings: ΑΠΑΡΧΗΝ and ΑΠΑΡΧΗΣ, respectively. The most recent version of the NIV opts for 'firstfruits', but the balance of probability seems to be fairly even. Bruce (1982, *Thessalonians*), 190, favours 'firstfruits', although he says he has difficulty with the sense with which Paul might have used that word. It is worth reflecting upon whether Paul would have used *haireō* (αἱρέω) had he meant to say, "God chose you to be saved". The alternative 'firstfruits' option therefore seems to fit more comfortably with the admittedly rare New Testament usage of the verb. Interestingly, according to *BAGD*, 24, *haireō* in its active form, although not found in the New Testament, appears in the Epistle to Diognetus with the meaning to *pick* a fruit. In English, 'pick' and 'choose' are very close in meaning. It may therefore be reasonable to ask whether the Greek might be rendered, "God picked (or 'harvested') you as firstfruits", a sense that accords with the harvest of people for the Kingdom and an offering to God: Revelation 14:4.

[47] Bruce (1982, *Thessalonians*), 190; Wanamaker, 266. Although Wanamaker prefers the 'from the beginning' option, he also argues that from the context 'firstfruits' makes sense, not as a temporal term, but as an indication of the belovedness and value of the Thessalonian Christians to God. He feels that Paul would "hardly suggest that his readers had a greater "qualitative significance" over other converts", but that need not rule out the sense that they were nevertheless valued as a firstfruits offering for God;

Thessalonica as being among the first to turn to Christ in the region could make sense historically and geographically although, of course, his first contact in Macedonia was at Philippi – Lydia and the Philippian gaoler – whence he travelled on to Thessalonica.[48] Perhaps it was at Thessalonica that the first identifiable church was established in Macedonia, which of course, is included in the region we know today as Europe, so it was an important strategic church plant. It is also possible that Paul's emphasis was not so much on their temporal priority, but upon their preciousness and value as his offering to God.

Haireō is found in the canonical books of the Septuagint just eight times in eight verses, and translates three different Hebrew verbs:[49]

- *'amar* (אָמַר): to say, speak, utter (x2).[50]
- *bachar* (בָּחַר) to choose, elect, decide for (x4).[51]
- *haphets* (חָפֵץ): to take delight in, be pleased with (x1).[52]

The eighth occurrence, Isaiah 38:17a, has no corresponding Hebrew text and NETS translates it as, "For you have *chosen* my soul".

The ubiquity of *haireō* in the wider Greek corpus seems to indicate that it was the general word of choosing in the ancient Greek world, but in those texts, it seems to carry the nuance of making a decision about a situation, as opposed to the choosing of a person, which the middle voice of *eklegomai* (ἐκλέγομαι) does carry. That fits the contexts of the Philippians and Hebrews texts too, so 2 Thessalonians 2:13 might therefore legitimately be rendered, "God *decided* that you should be firstfruits".

---

see Exodus 23:16-19; 34:22-26; Leviticus 2:12; 23:17; Numbers 18:12, etc.

[48] Acts 16:6-17:9.

[49] Also in compound form in Deuteronomy 7:6f. and 10:15 where it translates *bachar*, the usual Hebrew word for choosing.

[50] Deuteronomy 26:17f.: "You have *declared* this day that the Lord is your God" and "the Lord has *declared* this day that you are his people".

[51] Joshua 24:15 (Codex A: Codex B has *eklegomai*): "Choose for yourselves this day whom you will serve"; 2 Samuel 15:15: "Your servants are ready to do whatever our lord the king *chooses*"; Job 34:4: "Let us *discern* for ourselves what is right"; Jeremiah 8:3: "the survivors of this evil nation will *prefer* death to life".

[52] 1 Samuel 19:1: "Jonathan had *taken a great liking* to David".

vii. Epilegō

The fourth unusual word is the verb *epilegō* (ἐπιλέγω) which occurs twice in the New Testament and 22 times in the Septuagint (all books). In Acts 15:40, "Paul *chose* Silas", the verb in the middle voice speaking of Silas being selected by Paul, in this instance, to accompany him on his proposed journey through Syria and Cilicia. The second occurrence in John 5:2 refers to "a pool, which in Aramaic is *called* Bethesda". There, the verb, which is passive, is about naming,[53] a usage which in English sometimes comes close to choosing – for example, where the members of a sports team are *named*, meaning to be selected.

*****

In summary then, all the words in the New Testament which are claimed to indicate the activity of choosing *can* carry both theologically technical and soteriological as well as mundane meaning, a point always to be borne in mind when extravagant linguistic claims are made, particularly from the Reformed side of the debate.[54] I don't deny that these Election words can carry soteriological meaning, only that they cannot automatically be assumed to do so wherever they occur. Their contexts must be carefully examined before their precise meanings can be determined.

b. Predestination

Prooridzō (προορίζω), the second main word of the Election vocabulary, occurs only six times in the New Testament.[55] It is usually translated 'predestine' or 'predestinate', and always means 'to determine beforehand' or 'to ordain'. It usually refers to future events or the future state or status of the Elect; that is, as I hope to demonstrate, the eschatological destiny of suffering and glorification of the those who are already elect.[56] The six occurrences are: (1) Romans 8:29: "those God

---

[53] *BAGD*, 295.
[54] That equates with Don Carson's eighth semantic fallacy: Carson (1984), 45ff.
[55] Acts 4:28; Romans 8:29f.; 1 Corinthians 2:7; Ephesians 1:5, 11.
[56] Balz & Schneider, III, 159.

foreknew he also *predestined* to be conformed to the image of his Son"; (2) 8:30: "And those he *predestined*, he also called"; (3) Ephesians 1:11-12: "in him we were also chosen,[57] having been *predestined* ... [to] be for the praise of his glory" and (4) Ephesians 1:5: "he *predestined* us for adoption to sonship". The remaining two instances of *prooridzō* have nothing to do with the future status of the Elect, although 1 Corinthians 2:7 does speak of (5) "God's wisdom ... that has been hidden and that God *destined* for our glory", which I understand to mean that God has revealed his plan for the salvation and glorification of those who will trust Christ for salvation. The last instance (6) is Acts 4:28: "They did what your power and will had *decided beforehand* should happen", on which I shall comment presently,[58] and which simply means what it says, having no reference to the salvation of believers, but rather to the actions of those who were instrumental in bringing about the crucifixion of Christ.

The actual meaning of *prooridzō* is not in contention, but rather the *goal* to which predestination points. Contrary to Reformed teaching, the goal of predestination in the New Testament is *never* the eternal destiny of the Elect *per se*, although it does constitute the essence of their eternal being, so it is quite incorrect to speak of people being predestined to *salvation* either "before the creation of the world" (Ephesians 1:5) or at any other time. In Romans 8 and Ephesians 1, the purpose of God's predestination is, firstly, that believers should be wholly like their Saviour, Jesus, and, secondly, that they should in some way demonstrate God's glory so that they, and possibly others too, will respond in praise to God for what he has done in saving them. Arguably therefore, predestination may have both eternal and temporal aspects – the process of conformity to Christ begins at the point of new birth and continues throughout the earthly pilgrimage of a believer in Christ, and therefore forms a crucial part of their witness to the world. That notwithstanding, however, Ephesians 1:12 may imply nothing for our earthly life; rather that the witness of our Christ-likeness may be for the enhancement of Christ's splendour in glory as he is honoured – as F. F. Bruce puts it,

---

[57] See above, 213, *klēroō*.
[58] See below, 221.

"in the presence of human beings and angelic powers when men and women, redeemed from sin, live in accordance with his will and display the family likeness which stamps them as his children".[59] The third goal of predestination is about believers receiving adoption as sons, which I understand to be the transformation of the believer into complete Christ-likeness and fitness to share Christ's inheritance in glory through resurrection.[60]

When these contexts are properly understood, the commonly encountered confusion in Reformed writings between Election and Predestination is clearly exposed. The basic problem for Reformed readers with the interpretation of these verses seems to be that they have simply failed to assimilate the biblical sentences beyond the word 'predestined' and so have misidentified its stated goal. If it is assumed that divine predestination is always for salvation, it is no wonder that the impression is gained that God's purpose is to foreordain the salvation of some and not others, and that might explain how the error of equating Election and Foreordination has come about. My contention, however, is that in all of these cases, and elsewhere, the goal to which believers are predestined is a wholly different thing from their obtaining salvation, although that goal is, of course, consequent and dependent upon their new birth. Thus, the attainment of the predested goal can only be realised once salvation has already been received – faith in Christ is therefore the prerequisite of predestination, not its result.

c. Foreknowledge

The third main component of the Election vocabulary is the verb *proginōskō* (προγινώσκω: 'foreknow') with its corresponding noun *prognōsis* (πρόγνωσις: 'foreknowledge'). These occur five times and twice respectively in the New Testament.[61] They are probably the most

---

[59] F. F. Bruce, *The Epistle to the Ephesians* (London: Pickering & Inglis, 1961), 264, quoted by O'Brien, 118.
[60] See Chapter 10e, 325-8, on Adoption, and my forthcoming *Pie in the Sky When You Die?*
[61] *Proginōskō*: Acts 26:5: "they have known me for a long time"; Romans 8:29: "those God foreknew he also predestined"; 11:2: "God did not reject his people, whom he foreknew"; 1 Peter 1:20: "he was *chosen* before the creation of the world"; 2 Peter

contentious words in the whole debate, and have given rise to an extensive literature.

The Greek verb *ginōskō* (γινώσκω), obviously related to *proginōskō*, and the Hebrew *yāda'* (ידע) have very similar semantic ranges, both with each other and also, as it happens, with the English verb 'to know'. As well as intellectual cognisance and familiarity, they also include the ideas of personal affection and can mean sexual intimacy, which the Oxford English Dictionary[62] claims originally to have been a Hebraism probably introduced into the English language through the Bible. However, Reformed thinkers tend to assume that this intimate aspect of *ginōskō* was *necessarily* also incorporated by the biblical writers into their intended meaning of the compound *proginōskō*. So, Louis Berkhof writes,

> The meaning of the words *proginoskein and prognosis* in the New Testament is not determined by their usage in the classics, but by the special meaning of *yada'*. They do not denote simple intellectual foresight or prescience, the mere taking knowledge of something beforehand, but rather a selective knowledge which regards one with favor and makes one an object of love, and thus approaches the idea of foreordination.

He cites four scripture verses, saying of them,

> These passages simply lose their meaning, if the words be taken in the sense of simply taking knowledge of one in advance, for God foreknows all men in that sense.[63]

Berkhof's claim that the meanings of "*proginoskein and prognosis*" in the New Testament are not determined by their usage in the classics affirms that outside the New Testament *proginōskō* always means 'to know beforehand', as is confirmed by Rudolph Bultmann, who, claiming God's foreknowledge was an election or foreordination of his people, opted for a special New Testament sense of 'election' not found

---

3:17: "since you have been forewarned"; *prognōsis*: Acts 2:23: "by God's deliberate plan and foreknowledge"; 1 Peter 1:2: "chosen according to the foreknowledge of God".
[62] *OED Compact*, I-K, 745.
[63] L. Berkhof, 112; citing Acts 2:23 (cf. 4:28); Romans 8:29; 11:2 and 1 Peter 1:2.

elsewhere.[64] On the other hand, H. A. W. Meyer claimed precisely the opposite; that despite Romans 11:2 and 1 Peter 1:20, *proginōskein* never means anything else than to know beforehand in the New Testament.[65] Klein also comments, "if there is a use of foreknowledge that means *elect,* it is found only in the NT."[66]

Despite this caveat, however, we cannot simply dismiss those who insist on a special New Testament meaning for the Foreknowledge vocabulary, and we still need to examine the evidence. Starting with the texts to which Berkhof refers we can see that not all of them support his assertion. For example, in Acts 2:23, Peter addressing the Pentecost crowds in Jerusalem, says, "This man was handed over to you by God's deliberate plan and *foreknowledge*", with which Berkhof links Acts 4:28: "They did what your power and will had decided beforehand should happen". This is not even a case of God foreknowing a person, here Jesus, and certainly not in the sense that he had placed his affection upon him. Rather it is about God knowing in advance what would happen to him, because, one assumes, he had foreordained that it should be. I would suggest therefore that Berkhof is wide of the mark with regard to these two references in Acts. However, his three remaining texts do fit his argument and will be considered in more detail below.[67] They are Romans 8:29: "For those God *foreknew* he also predestined to be conformed to the image of his Son"; Romans 11:2: "God did not reject his people, whom he *foreknew*",[68] which gets closer to what Berkhof asserts, and 1 Peter 1:2: "chosen according to the *foreknowledge* of God the Father".

Walter Elwell notes that some interpreters regard the verbs, *prooridzō* (προορίζω: predestine) and *proginōskō* (προγινώσκω: foreknow) as virtual synonyms.[69] Thus, where Paul speaks of a person being known by

---

[64] Rudolph Bultmann, *TDNT*, 1.715f., cited by Klein, 133 n5.
[65] H. A. W. Meyer, *Critical and Exegetical Commentary on the New Testament: Epistle to the Romans*, 2 vols. (Edinburgh: T. & T. Clark, 1873, 1874), 2:93, cited by Klein, Ibid.
[66] Klein, 133 n6.
[67] Romans 8:29: 223f.; Romans 11:2: 224-6; 1 Peter 1:2: 226-9.
[68] See also Chapter 10e, 324, and 10f, 332.
[69] Elwell in Hawthorne & Martin, 228.

God, Berkhof appeals to the use of the verb *ginōskō* as coming very close to the idea of predestination.[70] We have noted his claim that what he calls "the special meaning of *yāda*'", by which he means a sense of relationship or favour, determines the meaning of the Greek verb *proginōskō*, but examination of its use in the Old Testament simply fails to support that assertion. For example, *yāda*' is used both of intellectual and intimate sexual knowledge just one chapter apart in Genesis 3 and 4.[71] Moreover, William Klein points out that 'to know' does not by itself imply election, although it can mark the intimate and special relationship God has with certain people, and it may have elective significance when combined with other elements. For example, Jeremiah 1:5: "Before I formed you in the womb I *knew* you, before you were born I *set you apart*; I *appointed you* as a prophet to the nations", is full of elective significance for *yāda*' linked as it is with the setting apart and appointment of Jeremiah as a prophet. Although the idea of choosing is not intrinsic to knowing, the context may incorporate the idea in certain instances, and here God's knowledge of Jeremiah or, indeed, of a people, e.g., in Amos 3:2, may well indicate his special choice of them.[72] Even so, that election is not concerned with eternal salvation, but with terrestrial roles or destinies.

Again, the respective contexts in which words are found must be determinative in deducing their precise meaning, and their interpretation cannot be demanded on linguistic or semantic grounds alone. Furthermore, I find it difficult to see how the related compound words with the prefix *pro-* (προ-) can be translated naturally as meaning to place love or favour upon beforehand. It seems simpler and more natural to interpret all seven occurrences of *proginōskō* more straightforwardly, although perhaps in a prophetic sense, as meaning to know about beforehand.[73] God's omniscience rules out any problem with such a

---

[70] L. Berkhof, 112; 1 Corinthians 8:3; Galatians 4:9; 2 Timothy 2:19.
[71] Genesis 3:5: "For God *knows* that when you eat ... *knowing* good and evil"; 4:1: "Adam *made love* to his wife Eve".
[72] Klein, 8. The NIV of Amos 3:2: "You only have I chosen of all the families of the earth", translates *yāda*' as 'chosen'.
[73] *TDNT*, 1.716.

concept.[74] Thus, I consider that most of the passages in which 'foreknowledge' appears should be interpreted naturally in that way. Not every case is straightforward, however, as consideration of the three remaining texts cited by Louis Berkhof will show.

Firstly, Romans 8:29 has been an important text since the Reformation:

> those God foreknew he also predestined (*proōrisen*: προώρισεν) to be conformed to the image of his Son, that he might be the firstborn among many brothers and sisters.

The Reformers debated whether election was on the basis of God's foreknowledge or not. Calvin concluded that it was not; rather that election was based on God's sovereign decree.[75] Quite apart from that, however, and logically, God must know who will be elect irrespectively of what might cause them to be so. Unfortunately, the historical arguments have prevented many interpreters from grasping Paul's more probable point that God's eternal purpose[76] for those whom he knew would be saved, or perhaps those he had got to know[77] (my preferred choice of meaning), was that ultimately they should be like his Son. I suggest therefore that predestination, at least in this text, is not about election at all, but is about the sanctification of the Elect and their gradual conformity to Christ, a transformation that will be completed at the *parousia*.

However, foreknowledge in this text is not simply an aspect of divine omniscience. I suggest that it is best taken in the sense of those God had got to know in the church at Rome by the point in time that Paul (actually Tertius)[78] penned the letter, and probably from the perspective of the fulfilment of the 'hope' in which they were saved – the hope which is promised in verse 29 – conformity to the image of Christ.[79] Paul is writing to believers, those whom God knew in the sense that a

---

[74] Assuming that those who advocate Open Theism or Molinism, respectively, have got it wrong; notably C. H. Pinnock in Horton, 200 n8, and Kenneth Keathley in Pinnock & Wagner, 161 n50. See below, 230, 'The Extent of God's Foreknowledge'.
[75] *Institutes*, 3.21.5: Beveridge, 3:206-8.
[76] Romans 8:28.
[77] See also Chapter 10c, 324, for discussion of Romans 8:29f.
[78] Romans 16:22.
[79] Romans 8:24.

relationship had been established between himself and them. He was therefore writing to people God already knew and with whom he had formed a relationship at some point in the past, although not necessarily in the distant past – most probably, the point in time when each one had placed their trust in Jesus. Take, for example, individuals who had become Christians only a year previously (say): it could still be said of them that God had known them for a while, so from the temporal standpoint of the writing of the letter, and certainly from the standpoint of their eventual resurrection, they were foreknown by God. I suggest therefore that Paul was simply referring to those in the church whom God already knew in relational terms, and not to a relationship which had been divinely decreed before the foundation of the world, or at any other time.

Berkhof's second text is Romans 11:2:

God did not reject his people, whom he foreknew.

This is a more difficult text, even if the Reformed interpretation can be shown to be wanting, because it must be asked in what sense God foreknew Israel. Unlike Romans 8:29, where Paul was writing of Christian believers, whom, I suggest God had got to know, here he is writing of his native people, the nation of Israel, a people who did enjoy God's choosing of them through the covenant with Abraham. Nonetheless, something of the sense I suggested for Romans 8:29 may also apply here because of that covenant relationship.

It may not be possible to arrive at a firm conclusion, but it should be borne in mind that this statement appears towards the end of a long passage, chapters 9 to 11 of Romans, in which Paul considers the place of Israel in the purposes of God. A major presupposition of the Reformed hermeneutic is that the choice of the people of Israel, and also of individuals like Abraham, Pharaoh and Jacob, is typical of the election of believers in Christ. No doubt, these are instructive parallels and types, but I suggest that it is incorrect to assume that the eternal destiny of those characters was ever under consideration in their Old Testament settings. The purpose of their choice by God, including his choice of Jacob, was limited to the framework of terrestrial history and had nothing to do, not directly anyway, with their respective eternal destinies.[80]

The importance of this conclusion should not be minimised, and an important passage in this context is the whole of the ninth chapter of Romans where Paul appears to be saying that God is perfectly free to choose whomever he will whether for destruction or glory. What is easily overlooked, however, is that this is what might be called a 'What if?' passage.[81] In other words, Paul was speculatively posing a scenario which we might assume to be hypothetical. He was arguing against believing Jews who objected to the inclusion of non-Judaising Gentiles into the Church, and who believed that God would be acting unfairly in receiving them in view of the Jews' own longstanding heritage in Abraham. All Paul was saying, I suggest, is that God *could* consign to wherever whomever he liked if that was his will, and who are we to argue with that? The question as to whether that is the way God *would* act, however, is not considered. Because he is gracious, he does not behave capriciously like the deities of some other cultures, and surely it would be going too far to suggest that Paul believed God could or would behave in such an arbitrary way. However, in the process of his argument, he does cite some biblical examples of individuals whose salvation or reprobation seemed possible – Jacob and Esau, being prime examples.[82] What must not be overlooked, however, is that Paul's whole thesis, and what he has cogently set forth in the earlier chapters of Romans, is that no one, whether Jew nor Gentile, can be saved except through faith in Christ, a principle that applies retrospectively even to characters who lived before the Cross. In my view, therefore, to use Romans 9:22-23 as a proof text for the idea that God has chosen in advance those who would be saved, would negate Paul's whole teaching that salvation is through faith alone.

That is not to say, of course, that Pharaoh and Jacob and others had no

---

[80] Although, see my comments on Israel's election and adoption in Chapter 10e, 324.
[81] Romans 9:22f.: "*What if* God, although choosing to show his wrath and make his power known, bore with great patience the objects of his wrath—prepared for destruction? *What if* he did this to make the riches of his glory known to the objects of his mercy, whom he prepared in advance for glory".
[82] Romans 9:13.

influence in salvation history.[83] In the immediate context of Romans 11:2 there is no precise grammatical antecedent to the objects of God's foreknowledge, but the whole of Paul's discussion had focused upon Israel with whom God was in covenant relationship: he also knew about them, he foresaw their destiny and was therefore able to foretell their salvation.[84] A perhaps less plausible alternative understanding of this passage, proposed by Forster and Marston, may be that God, clearly seeing the character of Israel beforehand, and understanding their thinking and reactions – in other words *knowing* what they were like, could regard the nation as ultimately elect because of the promises he had made to them.[85] My own conclusion is that Paul had in mind the covenant relationship God had with Israel: he was not about to break his covenant promises even though Israel broke its side of the covenant. A few verses further on (11:7), Paul distinguishes between the elect component of Israel and others who were hardened, however. It seems unlikely, then, that he had in mind that the elect ones had been foreordained to salvation, but rather that they were those who were disposed to covenant faithfulness, and hence would have been receptive to the gospel when they heard it, while those who were not elect were so because of "their transgressions" (11:11).

The third of Berkhof's texts which feature the idea of foreknowledge, is 1 Peter 1:2: "chosen according to the foreknowledge of God the Father". He claims that this and the other two texts he cites make no sense, if taken "in the sense of simply taking knowledge of one in advance". But that view cannot be upheld simply because there is nothing in their contexts that would indicate a meaning other than that God's foreknowledge was knowing about what would transpire in the course of time and that, more or less in agreement with Berkhof, they were in relationship with God, though only from the inception of the respective covenants and their incorporation into them.

However, a difficulty does remain because, according to the NIV of 1

---

[83] See Chapter 10f, 332.
[84] Romans 11:26.
[85] Thayer, 538; Forster & Marston, 194 (page numbers from the 1989 Highland edition).

THE VOCABULARY OF ELECTION

Peter 1:2,[86] it is the chosenness of Peter's readers that was foreknown by God. The Greek is far from straightforward: the NIV of verses 1 and 2 has,

> Peter, an apostle of Jesus Christ, to God's elect, exiles, scattered throughout the provinces of Pontus, Galatia, Cappadocia, Asia and Bithynia, who have been chosen according to the foreknowledge of God the Father, through the sanctifying work of the Spirit, to be obedient to Jesus Christ and sprinkling with his blood.

A literal translation, closely following the Greek word order, of what is actually a trinitarian formula, might run,

> Peter, an apostle of Jesus Christ to [the] chosen[,][87] sojourners of [the] dispersion ... according to [the] foreknowledge of God Father, in sanctification of [the] Spirit, to obedience and sprinkling of [the] blood of Jesus Christ.[88]

There is no verb anywhere in the Greek text of these opening words of 1 Peter, and "chosen" in verse 2 has been supplied in the NIV presumably to sustain the idea of verse 1 of the chosenness of Peter's target readership. Other translations do much the same, but the absence of a verb creates both a difficulty and a number of possibilities. Thus, recognising that the principal Greek texts contain no punctuation, the sentence reduced to its essence may be read in a number of different ways; "chosen [ones] ... to obedience", or perhaps "foreknown ... to obedience", or even "foreknown ... to be sojourners" or "foreknown ... to be chosen" – there are a number of credible possibilities, the verb being implied, but its identity at best being obscure.

There seem to be two likely possibilities. First, if the imported verb

---

[86] The difficulty is compounded by the RSV's "chosen and *destined* by God the Father" or the NEB's "chosen *of old*", etc.
[87] Grudem (1988), 50ff., regards the adjective 'chosen' (ἐκλεκτοῖς) as qualifying 'sojourners', hence the possible lack of a comma. He admits that this would be a unique combination in ancient Jewish and Christian literature, and most other commentators regard the adjective as a general title meaning "chosen ones who are ...", etc. My preference would be "elect, sojourners".
[88] 1 Peter 1:1f.: Greek: Πέτρος ἀπόστολος Ἰησοῦ Χριστοῦ ἐκλεκτοῖς παρεπιδήμοις διασπορᾶς Πόντου, Γαλατίας, Καππαδοκίας, Ἀσίας καὶ Βιθυνίας, κατὰ πρόγνωσιν θεοῦ πατρὸς ἐν ἁγιασμῷ πνεύματος εἰς ὑπακοὴν καὶ ῥαντισμὸν αἵματος Ἰησοῦ Χριστοῦ, χάρις ὑμῖν καὶ εἰρήνη πληθυνθείη.

were to be removed, it could be interpreted simply along the lines of God knowing in advance about the dispersion and eventual sanctification of those elect people – a word of comfort, in the sense that nothing happens to God's people without his knowledge and consent, rather than the tautology – if God be God, then he is bound to know everything that will be. But an alternative, which keeps the idea of chosenness in place, but reiterates it as an adjective rather than a verb, is also possible. The problem with acceptance of the verbal form is removed if the Reformed idea that their chosenness had to be accomplished in what Grudem and others call "eternity past" is abandoned. Even from his Reformed standpoint, Grudem recognises the difficulty created by focusing too narrowly on the adjective "chosen", which he points out in the Greek text is some distance – nine words away from the phrase "according to the foreknowledge of God the Father":

> The NIV and NASB, having focused too narrowly on the adjective 'chosen' as the reference point for 'according to the foreknowledge of God the Father', now must continue the same pattern, giving the puzzling result, 'chosen ... by the sanctifying work of the Spirit'. This makes little if any sense, for (1) it is hard to imagine how an activity (sanctifying work) could perform a personal action (choosing), and (2) God's choosing, according to Scripture, is in eternity past, whereas the Spirit's sanctifying work, according to the rest of Scripture, is something present: but how can something in eternity past (God's choosing) be done 'by' something that begins only in the present (the Spirit's sanctifying work)? (Kelly, p. 43,[89] has to import an entirely new idea into the text: 'This predestining choice ... has been made operative by the sanctifying ... action of the Spirit.')
>
> It is much easier, again, to see the phrase 'in sanctification of the Spirit' as referring to the entire present status of Peter's readers.[90]

I tend to agree, although the distance between the adjective and the phrases it is supposed to govern may still argue against that particular solution. However, if one's understanding of the election of Peter's

---

[89] I.e., J. N. D. Kelly, *A Commentary on the Epistles of Peter and Jude*, Black's New Testament Commentaries (London: Black, 1969), 43.
[90] Grudem (1988), 51.

readers is their incorporation into Christ, rather than the divine purpose for them decreed before the creation of the world, the whole sentence would make a great deal of sense as it stands in the NIV and other versions, if the adjective 'elect', in other words, *belonging* to the Elect, rather than 'elected', is substituted for the phrase "who have been chosen", because it describes how the three-fold work of Father, Spirit and Son is involved in the dynamic of their incorporation into Christ: it describes the process of regeneration when, in my view, believers are added to the body of the Elect.[91]

There is one further occurrence of foreknowledge in 1 Peter which is often overlooked – the NIV of 1 Peter 1:20 has:

He [Christ] was *chosen* before the creation of the world, but was revealed in these last times for your sake.

Comparing this with the Greek[92] and translating it literally, we see that the NIV translators have substituted 'chosen' for 'foreknown':

He having been *foreknown* on one hand from [the] foundation of [the] world, manifested on the other hand in [the] last of the times because of you.

Clearly, 'chosen' is an interpretative interpolation which doesn't accurately reflect the Greek; the verb being *proginōskō*, not *eklegomai*. The translators of the NIV seem to have been influenced by the Reformed hegemony which I believe has biased their translation elsewhere. I suggest then that the verse should be understood in terms of the Christ, of whom it was known beforehand would come, having now come – in other words, foreknown by God although only now "made manifest" to humanity.[93] Incidentally, there is no need to postulate any idea of favour or the bestowal of love upon the one foreknown, even though it is Christ himself who is the object of that divine foreknowledge. There is no need either to infer Christ's pre-existence from this verse: that doctrine can safely be established on the grounds of other scriptures.

---

[91] See Chapter 9, 248.
[92] 1 Peter 1:20: Greek: προεγνωσμένου μὲν πρὸ καταβολῆς κόσμου φανερωθέντος δὲ ἐπ᾽ ἐσχάτου τῶν χρόνων δἰ ὑμᾶς.
[93] Thayer, 538.

In summary, then, I suggest that divine foreknowledge does not need to be forced into the mould suggested by Berkhof and other Reformed exegetes – the idea that it usually carries the idea of chosenness in the sense of favoured or loved. Often it will carry the sense of knowledge about an event or a person in advance, perhaps with a prophetic edge, and sometimes it will have a relational nuance as I suggest for Romans 8:29 and 11:2, but even then, not in the sense that those who are in relationship with God are so by divine decree, but only as they enter into that relationship through covenant – Israel through the Abrahamic covenant, and Christians through their incorporation into Christ.

The Extent of God's Foreknowledge

Divine Foreknowledge is perhaps the key issue in the whole Calivinst-Arminian debate. The relationship between what God knows, or can know, and the basis on which he may decree events in the world or in individual lives, and how that relates to the notion of human self-determination, is the big question.

Christians have always affirmed the truth of the premise that God knows everything, including the whole future of the universe. That is my conviction too: there can be no limits to what God knows, and I would suggest that to conceive otherwise would lead us into perilous terrain, perhaps teetering towards blasphemy. Indeed, even to question what we think God may or may not do, or think, or know or intend, might cause us to run the risk of divine censure not unlike that against Job and his so-called comforters as they attempted to second-guess his purposes:

> Who is this that obscures my plans
> with words without knowledge?[94]

Although the Reformed notion that God's foreknowledge is determinative of what will happen, whether in the lives of individuals and even physical matter itself, it has nevertheless created questions about how, if true, human freedom might then operate – whether it is illusory or

---

[94] Job 38:2.

real. And so, we encounter views along the lines that divine election of individuals must be on the basis of God's foreknowledge of whatever decisions we might make. That, of course presupposes a degree of human self-determination, and theologians, even from the Reformed side of the fence, have struggled to explain the dynamics of how we might hold together both divine and human determinism.[95]

The kind of muddle in which we may find ourselves might spring from a belief that because God knows what I will do and decide, then what I did and decided must have been predetermined by God. In other words, free will is an illusion. On the other hand, however, others, Arminian friends in particular, would say that just because God knows the future doesn't mean that what I decide was all the while predetermined by him.

Bruce Reichenbach has this to say: if it is true that God knows all truths, he must know our decisions and actions ever before they occur. Thus, what will happen cannot differ from what eventually transpires, otherwise God's 'belief' would be false; an obvious impossibility. However, if it is true that we cannot do anything which God does not know, then it must follow that we are not free, or so it is assumed. But, says Reichenbach, that would be to confuse "the order of causes (what brings something about) with the order of knowledge (the basis on which we know something)". His argument goes along the lines that since what God knows is the event itself, he will know it only if it actually happens, and it is because it eventually occurs that God knows it will happen. It cannot then be true that the event depends on God's foreknowledge because his foreknowledge depends on the event occurring. It is true that the event happens with God's foreknowledge of it, but that does not cause it to happen. "One must be careful not to confuse the conditions which provide the basis for our knowledge of what happens with the conditions which cause the event to happen. Knowing something to be true does not make the event occur."[96]

---

[95] See Chapter 3, 66-9, 'Election'; also Chapter 6, 161, 'Divine Sovereignty and Human Responsibility'.
[96] Bruce Reichenbach in Basinger & Basinger, 110. Unfortunately, Reichenbach, 175f., cites a number of examples of how we might foreknow certain events, but in every

That is all to do with discrete events, but what about the whole gamut of human and natural events? Relatively recently, under the "devastating influence of process theology", it has been suggested that God may, indeed, not know all future events with absolute certainty. In the words of one process theologian, that would mean that "God is watching with bated breath."[97] Thus, before moving on from consideration of the biblical teaching about divine Foreknowledge, we should note a couple of views which, in effect, limit the scope of what God can know. There are two main contenders.

i. Middle Knowledge or Molinism

In a chapter entitled *Middle Knowledge: A Calvinist-Arminian Rapprochement?*, William Craig advocates a means of reconciling Calvinism's divine sovereignty and the Arminian conviction of genuine human freedom, a view known as Middle Knowledge or Molinism.[98] Middle knowledge is knowledge of counterfactuals; that is, knowledge of what would have happened if something else had occurred. Advocates claim that if God knows the future via middle knowledge, then we can still have indeterministic freedom because he does not actually know what *will* happen. God could still be omniscient in the sense of knowing everything that could happen and knowing what would happen if other things occurred, however,[99] but he still only knows what is.

Luis de Molina (1535-1600), a Spanish Jesuit priest and a firm advocate of human freedom, sought to reconcile the conflict he saw between Predestination and freedom, the issue which, from his Catholic perspective, he mistakenly regarded as the main point of the Protestant

---

case, we cannot know with absolute certainty, as God can: we may only know with a degree of probability. A solar eclipse, for example, can be predicted with near certainty, but we cannot know whether some other catastrophic astronomical phenomenon might prevent it from happening. Likewise, we may be able to 'know' where we might eat breakfast tomorrow, and even what we will eat, but any number of other factors may prevent such a 'foreknown' event.

[97] Norman Geisler in Basinger & Basinger, 71, quoting Bernard Loomer, "A Response to David Griffin", *Encounter* 36, no. 4 (Autumn 1975), 365.

[98] W. L. Craig in Pinnock, 141ff., a view also advocated by Kenneth Keathley; see Pinson in Pinnock & Wagner, 161 n50.

[99] John Feinberg in Basinger & Basinger, 33.

Reformation. In 1588, he published *The Compatibility of Free Choice with the Gifts of Grace, Divine Foreknowledge, Providence, Predestination and Reprobation*, better known by its Latin short title, *Concordia*. It was "perhaps the most sophisticated attempt, at least since the Reformation, to theorise how God could unfailingly foreknow the contingent acts of his free creatures".[100] It challenged the seeming determinism of stricter Thomism and suggested that predestination was subsequent to divine foreknowledge of human merits. But it was a foreknowledge of a special kind, *scientia media* or 'middle knowledge'.[101]

Determined to preserve the notion of genuine human freedom while still upholding divine omniscience, Molina recognised two alternative aspects of God's knowledge which equated respectively with two of Thomas Aquinas' three aspects of omniscience; 'natural knowledge' (*scientia simplices intelligentiae*) - God knows all the *possibilities*, and 'free knowledge' (*scientia visionis*) - God knows what *actually exists* at any time in the actual world.[102] But between these two aspects of divine knowledge, Molina suggested that there must be an interposition of the divine will, a 'middle knowledge'. By *natural knowledge*, 'natural' because he regarded it as essential to God's nature, he postulated that God knew every contingent state of affairs that could possibly obtain. That included every possible permutation of every possible outcome governed by the free choices of individual human beings as well as the 'chance' events of nature. On the other hand, *free knowledge* logically followed both from *natural knowledge* and from God's decision of which of an infinite number of possibilities would actually be, and which, of course, wouldn't. Thus, if for example, God had chosen to create a different world, the content of his *free knowledge* would be different, so what he knew would depend on the kind of world he chose to create.

Thus, according to Molina, *middle knowledge* stands between *natural*

---

[100] Thuesen, 224.
[101] Ibid., 140.
[102] Molina regarded the third of Aquinas' aspects of divine knowledge, *scientia approbationis*, simply as the divine decision as to which individual order of being God chose to exist, and not therefore as a kind of knowledge as such.

and *free knowledge*. It is the aspect of God's omniscience prior to any decision as to which contingent events should occur under any hypothetical set of circumstances. William Craig offers the following illustration:

> by his natural knowledge God knows that ... Peter when placed under a certain set of circumstances *could* either deny Christ or not deny Christ,[103] being free to do either under identical circumstances, by his middle knowledge God knows what Peter *would* do if placed under those circumstances.[104]

Middle knowledge cannot then be reduced to either natural or free knowledge but shares features of both. Because natural knowledge is prior to any free decree of God's will, and the content of his middle knowledge does not lie within the scope of his power, he cannot therefore control what he knows through such knowledge. Thus, using Craig's 'Peter' example, God could not have known in the sphere of his *middle knowledge* what Peter would have done in the particular circumstances in which he was placed, and, on that basis, would then not know what Peter would have done in other sets of circumstances. Instead, the opposite is true: prior to God's decision to create a set of circumstances, he knew what Peter would do within any possible order of circumstances; then, given the decision of his will to bring about a particular set of circumstances, he would then know what Peter would do. Furthermore, since middle knowledge is prior to the divine will, its content lies outside the scope of God's omnipotence. Because the content of divine middle knowledge depends upon what the creatures themselves would choose to do, God cannot control what he knows by his middle knowledge. Middle knowledge, then, is like natural knowledge in that it is prior to the decision of the divine will, but it is also like free knowledge in that such knowledge depends on a decision of free will - not God's, but the free will of his creatures. It is therefore God's middle knowledge which supplies the basis for his foreknowledge of contingent events in the actual world. And by knowing what every possible creature would do under any possible circumstances, God knows what

---

[103] Matthew 26:69-75; Mark 14:66ff.; Luke 22:54ff.; John 18:15-18, 25-27.
[104] William Craig in Pinnock, 147 (his italics).

will in fact take place in the world.

Applied to Election, middle knowledge was thus the means whereby God knew who would unfailingly, yet freely, have faith. The full logic of Molina's position, especially as it was developed by the Jesuit Francisco Suarez (1548-1617) and others, was complex and (obviously) difficult to understand, but because Molina maintained that God still determined the particular circumstances of each individual, some naturally wondered if middle knowledge left any more room for free choice than did the traditional Thomist position. Other critics found it simply nonsensical to speak of contingent choices that humans *definitely* might make because God could know only what they *might* do in a genuinely contingent situation, and even Molina had to admit that divine foreknowledge of free human choices was "inscrutable". Like Arminius, however, he was motivated by the belief that God gave all people enough assistance to enable them to freely choose whether to accept or reject Christ, so God's *middle knowledge* ultimately *depended* on human free will.[105]

Prior to Augustine, predestination was typically regarded as being based on divine foreknowledge: God predestined those to be saved whom he foreknew would freely place their faith in Christ. With the advent of Pelagianism, however, Augustine advocated the need of a prevenient grace if anyone was to come to faith, because people could never come to Christ on their own initiative.[106] Predestination thus became the arbitrary gift of God, unrelated to his foreknowledge. Hence, without a doctrine of middle knowledge, it is supposed that one has to hold either that predestination is based on the divine foreknowledge of human decisions (Arminianism) or that there is no consideration of human free decision (Calvinism).

This was the dilemma which Molina sought to resolve,[107] and, if he was correct, he had devised "a remarkably ingenious basis for God's knowledge of the future", says Craig. By knowing what every possible

---

[105] Thuesen, 140f.
[106] See Chapter 5, 143, 'Prevenient Grace'.
[107] Craig in Pinnock, 155.

free creature would do in any possible situation, God could, in bringing about a particular situation, know what the creature would freely do. That situation will, of course, depend on previous contingent causes, so God would have to know what earlier circumstances he should have to bring about in order to get precisely the situation he desired, and that resultant situation would then constitute part of the circumstances for still further free decisions which God would foreknow. These sets of circumstances thus combine to form an infinite number of possible world orders from which God, by willing his own free actions, including the decision to create, selects one to bring into actuality. Thus, he foreknows with certainty everything that happens in the world.

To work through even some of the possible permutations of all this would prove quite baffling, but in summary we may see that this theory of middle knowledge, if correct, supplies not only the basis for divine foreknowledge but also the means of reconciling that foreknowledge with creaturely freedom and contingency.[108]

It is interesting that while Arminius was aware of Molina's views, he did not incorporate them into his doctrine of Foreknowledge. Although he insisted that prevenient grace gives humans genuine freedom, his typically scholastic explanation of the nature of divine foreknowledge of human choices and his occasional references in his writings to "middle knowledge" did lead some interpreters to conclude that he accepted Molina's ideas.[109] However, nowhere does he suggest that God, knowing what everyone would do in any given circumstances, selected the possible world, from among all possible worlds, in which exactly what he desired to occur would occur, while at the same time permitting human beings to retain their freedom. Instead, he argued that God knew the future infallibly and certainly. Thus, God knew anyway what everyone was freely going to do in the actual world, including their union with Christ through faith or their rejection of him through impenitence and unbelief.[110]

---

[108] Ibid., 146ff.
[109] Thuesen, 39.
[110] Pinson in Pinnock & Wagner, 161.

THE VOCABULARY OF ELECTION

Molina's theory of middle knowledge may well have some attraction for a contemporary mindset which might think in terms of a multi-universe, but I suggest it suffers from a complexity and cleverness not dissimilar from some classical Calvinistic theorising, and so falls short of what can be known from the pages of scripture. It also depends on a type of Greek philosophical categorisation similar to what we saw in Chapter 6 when considering the sovereignty of God. We may not easily be able to reconcile divine foreknowledge with human responsibility, but this, I suggest, is not the way to do it.

Scripture portrays a God who knows the beginning from the end, and we may assume every stage between.[111] We may have to agree with the Teacher that "no one can fathom what God has done from beginning to end",[112] so we are forced back onto mystery. What we can know, however, is that there is none like him who can "make known the end from the beginning", one who will do all that he pleases[113], the one who describes himself as "the Alpha and the Omega, the First and the Last, the Beginning and the End".[114]

ii. Open Theism

Brief mention has already been made of Open Theism. It is a relatively recent movement in evangelical Arminian Seventh-day Adventist circles which came about as a reaction to the view that divine foreknowledge in both Reformed and Arminian theology predicates a kind of determinism. Richard Rice's *The Openness of God* controversially proposed that God's knowledge of future contingents was in some sense limited.[115] This development, which advocated that God does not

---

[111] Scripture often implies inclusivity (merism) when using expressions such as "Dan to Beersheba", e.g., Judges 20:1, etc., "a proverbial expression for the whole land": Cundall & Morris, 199, or "Alpha and Omega", e.g., Revelation 22:13, etc.
[112] Ecclesiastes 3:11.
[113] Isaiah 46:10.
[114] Revelation 21:6; 22:13.
[115] Thuesen, 124. Richard Rice, *The Openness of God: The Relationship of Divine Foreknowledge and Human Free Will* (Nashville, TN: Review and Herald, 1980). Also, the subsequent key text, Clark H. Pinnock, Richard Rice, John Sanders, William Hasker, and David Basinger, *The Openness of God: A Biblical Challenge to the Traditional Understanding of God* (Downers Grove, IL: InterVarsity, 1994).

have exhaustive foreknowledge of the acts performed by free creatures, moves beyond the standard Arminian view toward a socinian position.[116] In other words, God's omniscience is limited to what would *definitely* happen in the future, but not to what *might* happen. If God were to know every possible future, Open Theists believe that human free will would not be possible and so they rejected a *hard* and deterministic view of omniscience. Citing Clark Pinnock and William Hasker, Horton says that these writers, although claiming to affirm the omniscience of God, do not explain how "all knowledge" can exist when God is "ignorant of the vast majority of future actions (namely, those brought about by human decision)".[117] That would mean that God does not know the future, but simply reacts as events unfold.[118]

Clark Pinnock, for example, argues that it is not possible to reconcile God's omniscience with "conditional elements" in some Old Testament prophetic words which seem to imply a divine ignorance of the outcomes of his people's decisions – where, for example, the LORD says to Jeremiah that he had hoped Judah, having witnessed his judgment on the northern kingdom, would have repented, or his instruction to Ezekiel to pack his belongings for exile in sight of the Judahite exiles: "Perhaps they will understand".[119] Matthew Pinson points out that Arminius would have disagreed: "The reason he would have opposed this notion is that he did not believe, like both open theists and classical Calvinists, that God's foreknowledge of future free contingencies causes them or makes them necessary."[120]

d. Calling

In addition to the three basic word categories which relate to Election; *Election* itself, *Predestination* and *Foreknowledge*, I would add *Calling*. I suggest that the New Testament meaning of the call of God has

---

[116] Horton, 59.
[117] Ibid., 200 n8. Klein, 296 n47, adds David Basinger, Gregory Boyd and John Sanders to Horton's list of advocates of Open Theism.
[118] Klein, 296, quoting Stephen Yuille, "How Pastoral Is Open Theism?", *Themelios* 32/2, 2007, 47.
[119] Jeremiah 3:6-8; Ezekiel 12:3: Pinnock in Pinnock, 25f.
[120] Pinson in Pinnock & Wagner, 161.

not been given the consideration it deserves in the literature because of the way we customarily think of God's call – either through the gospel, an invitation to which we may respond, or in terms of his calling to some kind of service or vocation, or, indeed, the way we may think of our own calling or crying out to God in prayer for salvation or in time of need. All of these aspects are valid, of course, but there is a growing body of opinion which sees divine calling as having a *formal* definition which more or less identifies our calling with our election, and which some would say is the predominant sense in which Paul, in particular of the New Testament writers, writes of the divine call.[121]

A number of related words in the Greek text are translated "call", but that rendering can be fluid, and sometimes different words are used synonymously and at times distinctly. The basic verb, *kaleō* (καλέω) is found 148 times in the New Testament, most frequently in the Synoptic Gospels and Acts, although only twice in John. It usually relates to the naming or labelling of people, places or things,[122] but it can also mean 'to call together',[123] 'to call out from',[124] 'to invite'[125] or, most significantly perhaps, 'to call' in the sense of 'to invite to follow'.[126] However, as we shall see (below), Paul seems to equate our calling with our election. In other words, we, the body of Christ, are 'the Called', and others who have refused the invitation of the gospel are not among 'the Called', despite the possibility that they may have heard and rejected a preacher's evangelistic call of invitation.

A second Greek verb is *epikaleō* (ἐπικαλέω), which occurs 30 times,

---

[121] Klein, 254; Barclay, 43 n11.
[122] E.g., Matthew 2:23: "he would be called a Nazarene"; Mark 11:17: "My house will be called a house of prayer"; Luke 1:32: "He ... will be called the Son of the Most High"; John 1:42: "You will be called Cephas"; Acts 1:12: "the hill called the Mount of Olives", etc.
[123] E.g., Matthew 2:7: "Herod called the Magi secretly"; Luke 19:13: "he called ten of his servants", etc.; cf. usage of *proskaleomai* to mean 'to summon' in the Synoptics and Acts and once in James 5:14.
[124] Matthew 2:15: "Out of Egypt I called my son".
[125] E.g., Matthew 22:3: "those who had been invited to the banquet"; John 2:2: "Jesus ... had also been invited to the wedding", etc.
[126] E.g., Matthew 4:21||Mark 1:20: "Jesus called them" (James and John); Luke 5:32: "I have not come to call the righteous"; Matthew 22:3: "to call those who had been invited", etc.

mainly in Acts, and as with some occurrences of *kaleō*, usually means 'to name'.[127] However, there are three other senses in which the verb is used, the most common being to 'call on God' or 'call on the name'.[128] That sense is extended, particularly in Luke's account of Paul's trial before Porcius Festus in Acts 25, where Paul "appeals" to Caesar, also when Stephen "prayed" (literally, 'called out and said') as he was being stoned to death, and where the emissaries from Cornelius "called out" to ask where Peter was staying in Joppa.[129] Two further occurrences of *epikaleō* relate to a quotation by James, both in Acts and in his own letter, from Amos 9:12: "all the nations that bear my name", literally, the name of God being *called upon* the nations.[130] This naming sense reflects "the common Old Testament practice of naming the name of God over a man, who is in that way God's possession because God has revealed and made Himself known to him".[131] Klein claims that, although no choosing sense is implied here, this text affirms that God's people, especially now even the Gentiles, bear the name of God. "God is not choosing persons out, but applying to them the status 'Christian'"[132] or elect.

A third verb is *proskaleomai* (προσκαλέομαι) which occurs 29 times, and is found only in the Synoptics and Acts, and in James 5:14 where sick people are exhorted to call on the elders of the church. The sense in the majority of cases is about summoning to oneself or gathering people together, a meaning we have also seen for *kaleō*.[133] There are three exceptions, however. Two relate to God's call on Barnabas and Saul to the work to which he had called them, and to preach in Macedonia, respectively,[134] but the third is found in Peter's Pentecost

---

[127] E.g., Matthew 10:25 (the only Gospel occurrence): "If the head of the house has been called Beelzebul"; Acts 1:23: "Joseph called Barsabbas", etc.
[128] E.g., Acts 2:21; Romans 10:13: "Everyone who calls of the name of the Lord"; 1 Corinthians 1:2; "who call on the name", etc.
[129] Acts 25:11; 28:19; 7:59; 10:18.
[130] Acts 15:17: the NRSV has "the Gentiles over whom my name has been called"; James 2:7.
[131] Karl Schmidt, *TDNT*, 3.498; quoted by Klein, 81. E.g., Numbers 6:27.
[132] Ibid.
[133] E.g., Matthew 10:1: "Jesus called his twelve disciples to him"; Mark 15:44: "Pilate ... Summoning the centurion", etc.
[134] Acts 13:2; 16:10.

sermon:

> Peter replied, 'Repent and be baptised, every one of you, in the name of Jesus Christ for the forgiveness of your sins. And you will receive the gift of the Holy Spirit. The promise is for you and your children and for all who are far off—for all whom the Lord our God will *call*.'[135]

Here Peter identifies the recipients of salvation as "all whom the Lord our God will call." The verb could be taken in its usual sense of invitation, - "all whom the Lord our God will call" *to himself*, as in 26 of the 29 instances of the verb, but here *proskaleomai* appears to have a salvific sense, the sense preferred by Paul, according to Klein, because no exceptions are made: all who are called are saved. It would be difficult to make a case for the root of the verb (*kaleō*) to *normally* have a salvific component (i.e., God's call to salvation), but, suggests Klein, in "calling" here, God isn't so much inviting, but rather applying salvation and granting people the status of "Christian" – "salvation comes only to those God calls". Thus, he claims, the second chapter of Acts helps us to understand God's calling. Earlier, Peter had made very clear that people must *call* upon the Lord to be saved. His quotation of Joel 2:32 in Acts 2:21: "everyone who calls on the name of the Lord will be saved", in combination with the statement of God's call in Acts 2:39, shows not only that he viewed the appeal and opportunity for salvation to be universal and unrestricted, but that salvation seems to require two necessary calls: people must call on God, and God must call people, and the scope of that salvation is universal – Jews and all those far off – Gentiles too.[136]

Incidentally, it may be noted that Luke is particularly fond of using the *kaleō* word group and, probably owing to greater linguistic proficiency in a more cultured kind of Greek than other New Testament writers used, he is the only New Testament writer to use compounds of the verb which occur in superior Koinē, e.g., *eiskaleō*, 'invite'; *metakaleomai*, 'have brought to oneself', etc.[137]

---

[135] Acts 2:38f.
[136] Klein, 80.
[137] L. Coenen, *NIDNTT*, 1.273. Coenen's article on 'Call', Ibid., 273-6, although clearly

For the sake of completeness, there are two other members of this word group; the noun *klēsis* (κλῆσις) which is found 11 times, mainly in Paul, although once each in Hebrews and 2 Peter but not at all in the Gospels or Acts, and the adjective *klētos* (κλητός) with 10 occurrences, again, mainly in Paul and once each in Matthew, Jude and Revelation. These two words then, with the addition of *kaleō*, are essentially Pauline and he puts them to specifically theological uses.

Paul uses *kaleō* 29 times, *klēsis* eight times and *klētos* seven times, and according to Coenen, almost always with the sense of divine calling,[138] a usage also taken over by Hebrews, and 1 and 2 Peter. Writing from a distinctly Reformed point of view, Coenen sees this calling as preparatory and anticipatory of a commitment of faith; in his words, "the process by which God calls those, whom he has already elected and appointed, out of their bondage to this world, so that he may justify and sanctify them (Rom. 8:29f.), and bring them into his service". He says that "Paul's language stresses this divine initiative and Romans 4:17 shows that God's call means a new existence, equivalent to a new creation".[139] This seems to be in agreement with Matthew 22:14 where those who are "called" are invited but not necessarily "chosen", by which I take Matthew to mean "saved". However, Klein claims that for Luke and Paul the "called" *are* the saved; they have already appropriated the promise and they bear God's name.[140] Furthermore, he suggests that this naming sense is critical because he believes it provides the key to Paul's understanding of calling such that to be a Christian is to be called a child of God and to bear his name.[141]

When reading the relevant passages in Paul's letters, one cannot avoid the distinct impression that he regards those whom he addresses, who are members of the body of Christ, as 'the called', and I would suggest, if that be the case, then 'called' comes close in meaning to 'elect',

---

Reformed in flavour, will repay careful study.

[138] Ibid., 275. The five exceptions are all for *kaleō*: 1 Corinthians 10:27: "If an unbeliever invites you to a meal"; 15:9, where Paul says, "I ... do not deserve to be called an apostle", and his three quotations from the Septuagint; Romans 9:7, 25 and 26.
[139] Ibid.
[140] Klein, 94; Acts 2:39; 15:17.
[141] Ibid.; cf. Matthew 5:9.

THE VOCABULARY OF ELECTION

although Coenen suggests otherwise. For example, Paul addresses church members as 'called ones' (*klētoi*),[142] and he writes to those "called to be his [God's] holy people" – literally those "called saints" (*klētoi hagioi*).[143] Furthermore, he exhorts the Corinthian believers to consider their calling so that they would realise the contrast between what they once were before they believed in Christ and what they had become in Christ, although their social status may not necessarily have changed. Indeed, Paul even refers to the pre-Christian situations they had occupied at the time they were called as their callings,[144] suggesting that each person's condition in life was that to which God had called them to occupy. Furthermore, there is a distinct sense that "*when* he/you/they were called" indicates the specific point in time when individual Corinthian Christians became believers,[145] rather than that it was an irresistible call through the gospel based on a prior election. This perspective, I suggest, makes sense of Romans 8:29-30 where Paul lays out the order of the steps or *chain* of salvation:[146]

> For those God foreknew he also predestined to be conformed to the image of his Son, that he might be the firstborn among many brothers and sisters. And those he predestined, he also called; those he called, he also justified; those he justified, he also glorified.

The understandable conclusion that may be drawn by our Reformed brothers and sisters is that, since our calling follows God's foreknowledge and predestining of us, the divine choice of who will be saved anticipates the call of the gospel to which we will respond in faith. However, as Paul assures the Roman Christians of these definitive salvific events, the divine *calling* (*kaleō*) does not precede, but rather follows the pretemporal actions of foreknowing and predestining. Thus, *calling* carries forward the designation of believers as "the

---

[142] Romans 1:6f.; 8:28; 1 Corinthians 1:2, 24.
[143] Romans 1:7; 1 Corinthians 1:2.
[144] 1 Corinthians 7:20, where the word is *klēsis*.
[145] 1 Corinthians 7:18-24 contains seven such cases (the NIV's "called to faith" in 7:22 is a translator's gloss: the Greek is ὁ γὰρ ἐν κυρίῳ κληθεὶς δοῦλος ἀπελεύθερος κυρίου ἐστίν); also 1 Corinthians 1:26; Acts 2:39; Romans 8:28, 30; 9:24; Ephesians 4:4; Hebrews 9:15; Jude 1, etc. Romans 11:29 and 2 Peter 1:10 link calling with election, and Revelation 17:14 links calling with chosenness.
[146] See Chapter 10e, 324, on Romans 8:29f.

Called" (8:28), and marks the point of reception or application of salvation for those who are included in those two prior actions.[147] It is also worth pointing out that Romans 8:28 describes those who have been called as "those who love him" and "have been called according to his purpose", not something that might be said of unbelievers – a point that for me clinches the argument that Paul views "the called" not just as everyone who hears the message of the gospel, effectually or otherwise, but rather everyone who has *received* the message and has been born from above. C. K. Barrett says, "Calling brings God's purpose into time", and "In human terms, calling is conversion".[148] James Dunn agrees that this calling is in fact our conversion – the verb "called" here "denotes divinely accomplished conversion", not the appeal of the preacher.[149] Thus, those who are (the) Called are then justified and will be glorified. Paul, in the context of Romans 8 is therefore emphasising assurance and the security of believers who are experiencing opposition and oppression, and the final verses of the chapter confirm that God will complete the salvation of those who are *called* in spite of all obstacles and opposition.[150]

Thus, God not only chose the Church to be his own people, but he also achieved that act of ownership through his *call*. Although there are several nontechnical uses of the concept of call in the New Testament, as we have seen, the technical or salvific sense thus makes clear that the "called ones" are those "called to be Christians" or perhaps better "called Christians" – the saints, the faithful, the believers, the Church.[151] All the foreknown and predestined ones are "the called" and those who love God are the called ones.[152]

As already mentioned, a Reformed response to all of this will inevitably be that what we are discussing is really God's Effectual Call. In other

---

[147] Klein, 181.
[148] C. K. Barrett, *The Epistle to the Romans*, Black's New Testament Commentaries (London: Continuum, 1991), 160, cited by Klein, 181.
[149] James D. G. Dunn, *Romans*, WBC (Dallas, TX: Word, 1998), 485, cited by Klein, 181.
[150] See Chapter 10e, 324, on Romans 8:29f.
[151] Romans 1:6 (literally, "called of Jesus Christ": κλητοὶ Ἰησοῦ Χριστοῦ); 1 Corinthians 1:24; Jude 1; Revelation 17:14.
[152] Romans 8:28ff.

words, only those God calls through the gospel will be saved in any case: he does not call those whom he has not predestined to be his sons, so it is no surprise that the called are those whom he has chosen. My response can only be to appeal to the argument already set out to the effect that, because the appeal of the gospel is to whomsoever, the Reformed view that the Elect comprise only those divinely identified and brought through to salvation through his Irresistible Grace is incorrect. This has been the theme throughout this book. I firmly believe that the gospel presents us with a choice, a choice for life or death, and a choice which God honours. If that is true, then to describe his saints as "called, chosen and faithful"[153] must mean something different from simply those who have responded to the irresistible call of God into an inheritance which he had already determined they should receive.

As has already been said, Klein suggests that the sense of "to assign a name" best captures the nuance of this technical or formal sense of *call*. By the divine act of calling, those who were formerly not God's people have become the people of God,[154] and herein lies the connection between Election and Calling. Those who are "the Called" are the Elect, and by God's call they become members of the elect people of God. As Brian Abasciano puts it,

> For Paul, calling and election are closely related. Calling is the application and appellation of election, the act of designating a group as God's elect people.[155]

Indeed, Revelation 17:14 equates the 'called' with God's 'chosen and faithful followers',[156] which again suggests that both Election and Calling apply to those who have already believed in Jesus. Thus, "to name" better grasps the performative function of the action of calling than does the translation "to invite" to become a member of the people of God, although at times the two senses are difficult to separate. As already noted, these two senses will, of course, merge in Reformed thinking

---

[153] Revelation 17:14.
[154] Klein, 254; Romans 9:24-26; 1 Peter 2:9.
[155] Brian J. Abasciano, *Paul's Use of the Old Testament in Romans 9:1-9: An Intertextual and Theological Exegesis* (London & New York: T. & T. Clark, 2005), 201, cited by Klein, 254.
[156] "Followers" is another NIV gloss: the Greek is κλητοὶ καὶ ἐκλεκτοὶ καὶ πιστοί.

because there the invitation of the gospel is regarded as effectual for those foreordained to salvation, in the sense that God's invitation causes people to belong to him. On the contrary, however, God's calling in the sense we have been considering is his response to their faith: it does not create faith.[157]

Despite the fact that people respond individually to the gospel in becoming Christians, the evidence of the New Testament suggests that Calling, like Election, is primarily corporate in its orientation. The "call of God" brings into existence a people who have an obligation to exhibit God's character in their actions. Alan Richardson agrees,

> Broadly speaking there is no emphasis at all in the NT upon the individual's call, and certainly no suggestion that he ought to hear voices or undergo emotional experiences. The fact is that *klēsis* is a social conception and it is significant that except in the special case of Paul in Rom 1:1 and 1 Cor 1:1 the word *klētos* is never found in the singular. Christians are corporately "the called" and corporately "the elect" and they are these things because they are one body in Christ, the Elect One.[158]

Nonetheless, in 1 Corinthians 7:17-24, Paul does ask each individual in the Corinthian congregation to recall the situation in life when God "called" him or her. God applies salvation to people individually and each person has a "call" as a part of the body of Christ and has a responsibility to be holy. Nevertheless, the New Testament writers do stress the corporate call, and corporate language dominates the theology of "calling". Thus, the elect body of Christ is also the body which God called into fellowship with his Son Jesus Christ our Lord, but we do also have a calling in the world.[159]

As a footnote to this section on Calling, it may be worth noting the possible etymological connection between the Greek word normally used for 'church', *ekklēsia* (ἐκκλησία), and *kaleō*, *ekklēsia* being a compound noun comprising *ek*, 'out of' and *kaleō*, 'to call'. Etymology

---

[157] Klein, 254 n61.
[158] Alan Richardson, *An Introduction to the Theology of the New Testament* (London: SCM, 1958), 274, cited by Klein, 255.
[159] Klein, 256; 1 Corinthians 1:9. See Chapter 9, 248.

THE VOCABULARY OF ELECTION

does not necessarily prescribe meaning, and the word generally applies to all kinds of gatherings in Greek literature.[160] Barr observes that the Old Testament uses two words to describe Israel as the congregation of God, namely *'edah* and *qahal*, and both are translated in the Septuagint in different places by *sunagōgē* and *ekklēsia*, although in the later parts of the scriptures, *qahal* translated by *ekklēsia* is more usual. Furthermore, *qahal* is based on the same root as *qol*, the Hebrew word for 'voice', suggesting that "the OT *qahal* was the community summoned by the Divine Voice, by the Word of God". It therefore seems possible that a similar link between the *kaleō* word group and *ekklēsia* might have existed in the mind of Paul, if not elsewhere.[161] It may be that an over-familiarity with the word 'church' and its basis in Greek has obscured this connection, however, especially, as I have been trying to make a case for Paul's particular understanding of *kaleō* and its word group.

The distribution of the word *ekklēsia* in the New Testament is interesting.[162] Just over half of its occurrences are found in Paul's writings - 62 of 114 occurrences, although not at all in Romans apart from five occurrences in the last chapter. This statistic may suggest that it was a favourite word of Paul to describe the gatherings of Christian believers, although he must have had good reason not to use it in Romans.[163] Clearly, believers are 'called-out ones', but given the range of possible meanings embodied in the *kaleō* word group, could *ekklēsia* in Paul's mind also have signified the body of *called ones*?

---

[160] F. F. Bruce (1972), 196.
[161] Barr, 119.
[162] Coenen, *NIDNTT*, 1.296ff.
[163] Chapter 10f, 332, on Romans 9 to 11 comments on the organisation of the early Roman church and 334 n153, on the absence of *ekklēsia* from all but the last chapter of Romans.

Chapter 9

CHRIST, THE ELECT ONE AND EPHESIANS 1

Having established the principle that in the New Testament chosenness to salvation is never about individuals, but that nonetheless the Elect ones, the body of believers in Jesus, are said to be chosen, or at least in some sense special, it remains to ask in what sense we may be said to be chosen if God does not choose us individually.

It may be apparent by now that I have deliberately avoided explicit reference to the first chapter of Ephesians. This is because I believe it contains an important element which might provide a key with which to unlock a workable and reliable biblical understanding of Election, even though it has been a key passage for both sides in the historical debate. Indeed, G. C. Berkouwer, a prominent Calvinist theologian, referring to Ephesians 1:4 and 9 and 2 Timothy 1:9, has written,

> The history of the doctrine of election may be interpreted as an effort to understand the meaning of these words.[1]

I have tried to show that the Reformed position has serious defects, not least in that many biblical texts, which should, or at least, *could* be construed as theologically neutral, are interpreted by Calvinists with specific theological nuance and with a bias towards their doctrines of Irresistible Grace and Unconditional Election. The Arminian view, although, in my opinion, more faithful to scripture, has its problems too; a major shortcoming being its inability to adequately answer the Calvinist dogma of the divine decree of Predestination. Whereas Calvinism in its classical form is at least logically rigorous on the issue of Foreknowledge, despite its dependence upon what I would regard as unacceptable definitions, the fatal flaw of Arminianism is its logical

---

[1] G. C. Berkouwer, *Divine Election* (Grand Rapids, MI: Eerdmans, 1960), 135, quoted by Shank (*Elect*), 27.

circularity – the assertion that God's choice of individuals is based on his foreknowledge of their response to the gospel. Ultimately that is self-contradictory: if election depends upon an individual's free choice, then it cannot also be said to be God's choice unless one is willing to adhere to the impossible logical gymnastics of the two-sides-of-the-coin or doorway kind of theory, which we considered earlier.[2]

We should note that some important theologians, who have recognised the difficulties inherent in these two opposing positions, have made their own attempts to solve the dilemma.

The first deserving mention is Calvin himself, of course. He evidently saw problems in the scriptures, but in searching for solutions, not only tried to explain away certain passages which didn't suit his convictions, but in so doing devised a huge labyrinth of complex terminology, which was then elaborated by his followers, such that only those with the will and intellectual competency to make the attempt could make sense of it – take, for example, the terminology of the divine decrees: supralapsarianism, infralapsarianism, sublapsarianism, etc.[3] I have always felt that theology which requires such complex terminology is probably suspect, and in any case, it will always be incomplete. I suggest that if Calvin had not seen problems with the conclusions he drew, he would not have written in such complex terms in order to find a way around his dilemma. Furthermore, his disciples would not have needed to develop ever more complex terminology, and that much of the angst of succeeding Church history might in consequence have been avoided.

Historically too, Arminius, although himself a Calvinist,[4] at least in terms of the prevailing theological complexion of his time and place, recognised the inadequacy of the strict Calvinism which prevailed in The Netherlands at the turn of the seventeenth century. He adamantly opposed the supralapsarian decree of Calvinism, which in effect relegated Christ to no more than just a means of accomplishing the redemption of the Elect, whom, according to Calvin and his followers, God had

---

[2] Chapter 7, 192.
[3] See above, 13 n13.
[4] Bangs, 18. See Chapter 2, 10.

made the objects of his first decree. What is more, he actually came tantalisingly close to the position to which I am heading, that of seeing Christ as the one elect individual, and the Elect being a class of people who would receive salvation and share Christ's elect status through their incorporation into him. Thus, working within the accepted terminology of the divine decrees which prevailed at the time, Arminius did regard Christ himself as the sole object of God's first decree, and that those who would be delivered from their fallen state and obtain eternal salvation would do so through that elect one.[5] However, we have already noted the probability that, because he was locked into the Calvinistic-Augustinian frame of reference of his day, in framing his fourth decree, which addressed the election of individuals to either salvation or damnation, he effectively prevented himself from drawing the conclusion that God does not choose individuals.[6]

A major contributor to the debate in the twentieth century was Karl Barth. Although standing in the Reformed tradition, he accused Calvinism of misreading the Bible through its metaphysical belief that God's relation with the world was static, in other words, a kind of deism. He therefore developed the idea of God having a dynamic relationship with the world; what he called a "holy mutability". Although he understood Election in terms of God's choice of individuals, his view, in complete contrast to Calvin's, was that by divine design Election encompassed all. Everyone is elect in Christ unless he chooses to become

> one who is isolated over against God by his own choice, and who in and with this isolation must be rejected by God.[7]

Barth's perception therefore was that God was apparently predisposed to choose *for*, rather than reject. Thus, he asserted that the one who deliberately isolates himself against God by his own choice is overruled by God – "the choice of the godless man is void".[8] That thinking eventually led him into a kind of universalism, a conclusion which

---

[5] Arminius, *Works*, 1.566.
[6] See Chapter 2, 10.
[7] Barth, 316, quoted by Shank (*Elect*), 105f.
[8] Ibid., 306.

nonetheless he apparently rejected.[9] However, in seeing Christ as central to everything it seems to me that he came very close to the solution towards which I am heading:

> Christ is 'not merely one of the elect but *the* elect of God'; Christ is 'the electing God and ... elected man'; he is 'the sole object of this [divine] good-pleasure'.[10]

Although Barth developed this line of thought at great length, he seemed to stop short of the crucial step towards the resolution of saying that the Elect are so because of their inclusion in Christ. Instead, he treated Christ's election typologically, making it a pattern for those who would believe, and his eventual conclusion was that "the election of Jesus Christ may be preached to [the Elect] as their own election".[11]

More recently, Robert Shank, building on Barth's idea of Christ as both elect, and elector in unity with the Father, an idea he traces back to Calvin,[12] develops the idea of Christ "the Election".[13] So concerned is he to maintain a christocentric doctrine, however, that he appears to fall short of taking the crucial step of permitting humankind to accept or refuse the grace of God.

Hendrikus Berkhof also tried to resolve the debate but in a different way. He argued that the issue of Election cannot be separated from a covenant context, the context of "God's fellowship with us" in our responsibilities, guilt, conversion and obedience. To do so "causes accidents", he claimed. Election is but the divine side of the covenant made between its unequal partners, while the human side of the covenant is faith.[14] That resolution seems to me to be more illusory than real, and not very different from Spurgeon's 'shield of truth' argument.[15]

An important ingredient has been missing from the discussion thus far. Bearing in mind something of the thinking of Barth and Arminius, we

---

[9] Shank (*Elect*), 106.
[10] Barth, 106 (his italics); 103f.
[11] Ibid., 345.
[12] Shank (*Elect*), 37.
[13] Ibid., 44f.
[14] H. Berkhof, 479f.
[15] See Chapter 7, 192.

now turn to Ephesians where I believe all should become much clearer. Although, having said that, we will encounter some complexities there which we first need to clarify.

a. What does 'in Christ' mean?

The first problem we encounter as the opening words of Ephesians are considered is what Paul meant when he used the phrase, 'in Christ'.[16] This little phrase and its equivalents; 'in him' or 'in whom', occur eleven times within the space of the twelve verses which comprise his opening *berekah*, or paean of praise, to God for all the blessings he had bestowed upon his people. To list them, Paul says we are blessed with every spiritual blessing (1:3), we are chosen in order to be holy and blameless in God's sight (1:4), we are predestined to the adoption of God's sons (1:5), we have redemption through the blood of Christ and the forgiveness of sins (1:7), we are made God's heirs or perhaps his inheritance (1:11)[17] and we are sealed with the promised Holy Spirit (1:13). All of these spiritual blessings are said to be 'in (or possibly, 'through') Christ'. It is especially important to note that our election is also 'in Christ' (1:4).

In that Calvinism affirms individual election – God's choice of individuals both to salvation and to reprobation, I can only conclude that there is a significant difference between the way the Calvinist Fathers understood the phrase 'in Christ' and the way others understand it. Calvin's thinking can be traced back at least as far as the early fifth century to

---

[16] Greek: ἐν Χριστῷ. I assume Pauline authorship of Ephesians. See, among many other commentators, O'Brien, 4ff. N. T. Wright (2013), 56ff., 1514f., suggests that if Paul did not write Ephesians, then, in line with many other commentators, it must have been written by "someone close to him, consciously developing and imitating him, drawing deeply on several aspects of his other writing to produce a general, overall summary of his teaching". If that be the case, I see no reason not to include Ephesians within the accepted Pauline corpus. The differences that clearly exist between Ephesians and what others regard as genuinely Pauline writings may be accounted for in terms of the differences in purpose and occasion of writing. The geographical location of the recipient church is not mentioned in the best Greek texts, so, unlike his other letters, Ephesians is likely to be a kind of encyclical, addressed not only to the church at Ephesus, but also to other Christian communities including Laodicea. Indeed, Marcion identifies a letter to Laodicea as Ephesians: O'Brien, 4; cf. Colossians 4:16.

[17] See Chapter 8a(iv), 213, *klēroō*.

CHRIST, THE ELECT ONE AND EPHESIANS 1

Augustine who taught that those who should repent were chosen of God:

> Therefore God elected believers; but He chose them that they might be so, not because they were already so.[18]

However, moving forward a millennium and delving into the writings of the founding fathers of Calvinism, one encounters statements which clearly affirm our election 'in Christ', or at least the recognition that it was taught in the New Testament. For example, Calvin's own words,

> Paul testifies indeed that we were chosen before the foundation of the world; but he adds, in Christ (Eph. 1:4).[19]

> [Christ] is the beloved Son, in whom the love of the Father dwells, and from whom it afterwards extends to us. Thus Paul says, "In whom he hath made us accepted in the Beloved (Eph. i. 6)."[20]

The Canons of Dort,[21] the official Calvinist rebuttal of the Arminian *Remonstrance*, also affirms that election is in Christ. *Canon* 1:7 summarises the synod's response to Arminius' view of Election:

> Election is the unchangeable purpose of God, whereby before the foundation of the world he has out of mere grace, according to the sovereign good pleasure of his own will, chosen from the whole human race (which had fallen through their own fault from their primitive state of rectitude into sin and destruction) a certain number of persons to redemption *in Christ*. From eternity he appointed Christ to be the mediator and head of the elect and the foundation of salvation.[22]

The Belgic Confession and the Heidelberg Catechism contain similar

---

[18] Augustine, *The Predestination of the Saints*, 34, quoted by Forster & Marston, 131 n49. It is worth working through their detailed critique of Augustine's thought and some of the difficulties in which he found himself – see 149 n3 and their Appendix, 243ff: *Early Teaching on God's and Man's Will*.

[19] Calvin, *Concerning the Eternal Predestination of God* (Cambridge: James Clarke & Co., Ltd., 1961), 8:6, quoted by Shank (*Elect*), 31.

[20] *Institutes*, 3:2:32: Beveridge, 3:498.

[21] Also known as the *Canons of Dordrecht*, and formally entitled *The Decision of the Synod of Dort on the Five Main Points of Doctrine in Dispute in the Netherlands*, is the verdict of the Synod of Dort, held in 1618-19, against the Arminian *Remonstrance*. See Chapter 2, 23, 'Dort vs. the Remonstrants'.

[22] This extract from the Dort Canons is taken from Lane, 136f. (my italics).

phraseology, wording which Arminius found sufficiently ambiguous to permit the accommodation of both his own views and those of his opponents:

> We believe that whereas the whole posterity of Adam is fallen into ruin and damnation through the guilt of the first man, God showed himself to be such as he is, namely, merciful and just: merciful in that he delivers and saves out of this ruination those whom he in his eternal and unchangeable council, through his pure goodness has elected and chosen *in Jesus Christ* our Lord, without any consideration of their good works; and in that he leaves the others in their fall and ruin wherein they themselves have cast themselves.[23]

Similar affirmations of this key phrase, "chosen in Jesus Christ our Lord", are also to be found in more recent Reformed writers including, for example, G. C. Berkouwer:

> God's election is election in Christ.[24]

In the modern era, there has been considerable debate about what a number of scholars see as this "puzzling"[25] *in Christ* phraseology. Paul, more frequently than any other New Testament writer, uses the Greek preposition *en* linked with some designation of Jesus Christ.[26] A. Deissmann, however, felt it was unintelligible Greek to link *en* with a personal name,[27] and suggested that Paul must have thought of Christ as a kind of impersonal *continuum*, like the gaseous atmosphere in which we live and which, reciprocally, is also within us like the air within our lungs.[28] C. F. D. Moule, on the other hand, considering

---

[23] *The Belgic Confession*, Article 16: Carl Bangs' own translation in Bratt, 218, from the pre-Dort Dutch text of 1562: J. N. Bakhuizen van den Brink, *De Nederlandsche Belijdenisgeschriften* (Amsterdam, 1940), 89, incorporating an emendation to his earlier version: Bangs, 1971, 223 (my italics). Cf. the post-Dort text of Article 16: A. C. Cochrane, *Reformed Confessions of the Sixteenth Century* (London: SCM, 1966), 199f.
[24] G. C. Berkouwer, *Divine Election* (Grand Rapids, MI: Eerdmans, 1960), 149, 162, quoted by Shank (*Elect*), 28.
[25] C. F. D. Moule (1977), 51, names a number of contemporary theologians who express 'puzzlement', and adds, "I am among the puzzled myself."
[26] Ibid., 54.
[27] But see below, 258 n43.
[28] A. Deissmann, *Die neutestamentliche Formel 'in Christo Jesu'*, 1892, quoted by C. F. D. Moule (1977), 60 (Deissmann's italics), but a view no longer held by many at the time of Moule's writing in 1977.

Paul's use of *en*, says,

> all allowances made for the wide range of this preposition and the looseness of some of its uses and the curiosities of its distribution in the Pauline writings,[29] there remains a residue of occurrences where it is difficult to escape the impression that Paul is using *en* with a name for Christ in a genuinely (though metaphorically) locative sense.
>
> In at least a few passages, Christ (or the Lord) seems to be the 'place', the *locus*, where believers are found.[30]

Moule also quotes C. H. Dodd with approval, who, when writing on John's Gospel, says,

> [Christ] was the true self of the human race, standing in that perfect union with God to which others can only attain as they are incorporate in Him.[31]

He also surveys a number of suggestions about the meaning of Paul's 'in Christ' phrase made by relatively recent New Testament scholars. For example, he speculates about how intimate friends may be involved 'in' each other, or that 'in Christ' might signify a sphere of influence, that it might be about living in an atmosphere informed by the love of Christ, that it might be a consciousness of Christ, or mean in a Christ-conditioned way, and so on. He concludes that, although more work is needed on the definition and distribution of "this strange usage", he cannot escape the feeling that Paul identifies his location in Christ almost as a kind of "geographical identity".[32]

When it comes to Ephesians, however, which incidentally Moule, in company with many others, does not consider to be Pauline, he denies

---

[29] Moule excludes Ephesians from the Pauline corpus here.
[30] C. F. D. Moule (1977), 55f., cites as examples Romans 8:1; 16:7; 1 Corinthians 15:22; 2 Corinthians 5:17; Philippians 3:8f., and in relation to whole congregations, Galatians 1:22; Philippians 1:1; 1 Thessalonians 1:1; 2:14; 2 Thessalonians 1:1. See also Cranfield (1975), 833ff., especially with regard to Romans 6:11 and 8:1.
[31] Ibid., 50f., citing C. H. Dodd, *The Interpretation of the Fourth Gospel* (Cambridge: Cambridge University Press, 1953) who reasons that Dodd's idea is transferable from John to Paul.
[32] Ibid., 62, referring to W. D. Davies, *The Gospel and the Land* (Berkeley, CA: University of California Press, 1974), 164ff. See also Chapter 9, 'The Promise to Abraham Fulfilled', in my forthcoming *Pie in the Sky When You Die?*

'in Christ' an incorporative meaning no matter where the phrase may occur.[33] Thus, Ephesians, which begins with a glorious series of 'in Christ' or 'in him' phrases, including being 'chosen in Christ', cannot, in his view, be used to support a thesis of our divine election because of our incorporation into Christ. Apparently, we need to rely on what he regards as the more reliably Pauline corpus to establish the truth that the believer individually, as well as corporately, is incorporated into Christ.

To bring the whole issue of the meaning of incorporation up to date, we need to take into account Tom Wright's major work – *Paul, and the Faithfulness of God* in his *Christian Origins and the Question of God* series.[34] He too seems to sit on the fence with respect to the authorship of Ephesians, incidentally,[35] but he asserts,

> In passage after passage in Paul the point being made is that *Jesus, as Messiah, has drawn together the identity and vocation of Israel upon himself.*[36]

In a previous chapter he had expounded his understanding of Jesus' messiahship in Paul's writings. He admits that, like messiahship, the issue of corporate christology remains controversial among biblical commentators, it having "been a puzzle for many years, and even those who have made it central have not given accounts of it which have carried conviction among other researchers".[37] But Wright concludes:

> the two 'unknowns' are mutually explanatory: the 'unknown' solution to the question of *en Christō* goes with the normally 'unknown' Pauline feature of Jesus' Messiahship. To put it plainly: the 'incorporative' thought and language which so pervades Paul is best explained in terms of his belief that Jesus was Israel's Messiah.[38]

---

[33] Ibid., 63, referring to J. A. Allen, 'The "in Christ" Formula in Ephesians', *New Testament Studies* 5.1 (Oct. 1958), 54ff., who claims that the reference is to God's electing will operating through Christ.

[34] See also Longenecker (2016), 686-94: 'Excursus: Paul's Use of "in Christ Jesus" and Its Cognates'.

[35] Although, see Chapter 5, 154 n82.

[36] N. T. Wright (2013), 825 (his italics).

[37] Ibid., among whom he includes Albert Schweitzer and E. P. Sanders, and mentions that Moule's work suffered a similar response.

[38] Ibid. N. T. Wright's discussion needs to be carefully considered: all I can do here is to

He goes on to suggest that

> Paul ... exploited the notion of 'Messiahship' in such a way as to say two things in particular. First, the vocation and destiny of ancient Israel, the people of Abraham, had been brought to its fulfilment in the Messiah, particularly in his death and resurrection. Second, those who believed the gospel, whether Jew or Greek, were likewise to be seen as incorporated into him and thus defined by him, specifically again by his death and resurrection. The full range of Paul's 'incorporative' language can be thoroughly and satisfactorily explained on this hypothesis: that he regarded the people of God and the Messiah of God as so bound up together that what was true of the one was true of the other.[39]

Wright envisages Paul reflecting on what to him would have been familiar scriptures, but in the light of his new-found knowledge of the death and particularly the resurrection of Jesus, re-reading them with new understanding. For Paul, the resurrection of Jesus would have carried particular significance. As an educated scholar of Torah and a Pharisee, Paul understood the promise of God to raise the nation of Israel from the dead, a promise reflected in Martha's response when Jesus promised that her brother Lazarus would rise again – "I know he will rise again in the resurrection at the last day".[40] The significance for Paul of Jesus' resurrection was that he had gone ahead of the general resurrection at the last day, "the firstborn from among the dead", "the firstfruits of those who have fallen asleep",[41] and, as he reflected on the promise of a general resurrection, it dawned on him that Jesus' resurrection as an individual embraced the resurrections of each and every one of his faithful people. He *was* the renewed Israel - the body of Christ in his resurrection, and it demonstrated his messiahship. So, the ancient understanding of 'corporate personality',[42] to which Wright draws attention, a social concept generally held by ancient peoples

---

try to summarise briefly the salient points.
[39] N. T. Wright (2013), 826.
[40] John 11:23f. Also Ezekiel's Dry Bones prophecy: Ezekiel 37.
[41] Colossians 1:18; 1 Corinthians 15:20; also Colossians 1:15; Romans 8:29, 1 Corinthians 15:23, and non-Pauline references to Christ as the 'firstborn', Hebrews 1:6; Revelation 1:5.
[42] See below, b, 265, 'Unitary Election'.

including Israel, informs for Paul incorporation phrases such as 'in Adam', 'in you' (referring to Abraham) or 'in Isaac'.[43] It is supposed that Paul, with the hindsight of Christ's passion, then linked that understanding with his developing theology of the believer's incorporation into Christ and proved to himself that Jesus was indeed the Messiah. Wright thinks it unlikely that Paul would already have seen such passages of scripture as laying a foundation for a theology of incorporation: simply, that, as he re-examined them in the light of the resurrection, he would have made new connections. He began to see that "the vocation and/or destiny of people could be bundled up within the vocation and/or destiny of that one person ... and that he then transferred that notion to the Messiah".

Another important example from the Hebrew Scriptures is the notion that the people of Israel were somehow incorporated in their king, so that when David slew Goliath, for example, he represented the nation in doing so; thus, in standing where king Saul should have stood as Israel's champion, he qualified himself to take up the throne of Israel:[44]

> To be 'in the king', or now, for Paul, 'in the anointed one', the Messiah, is to be part of the people over which he rules, but also part of the people who are defined by him, by what has happened to him, by what the one God has promised him. That is how Paul uses the incorporative language of *en Christō* and similar phrases.[45]

Wright briefly examines three "obvious" texts[46] which demonstrate his point. (1) The first is Romans 3:1-26, where he points out that it is not universal sin that concerns Paul, but Israel's unfaithfulness (3:2f.), which is dramatically resolved by the revealing of God's righteousness (3:21) through the "redemption which is in Messiah Jesus".[47] Thus,

---

[43] Adam: 1 Corinthians 15:22 – *en tō Adam* (ἐν τῷ Ἀδάμ); Abraham: Genesis 12:3 - "through you"; LXX *en soi* (ἐν σοί); Genesis 18:18 - "through him"; LXX *en autō* (ἐν αὐτῷ); Isaac: Genesis 21:12 - "through Isaac"; LXX *en Isaak* (ἐν Ἰσαάκ). In each Old Testament reference, the Hebrew name or pronoun is prefixed by ב, which is regularly translated 'in': hence the Greek *en*.
[44] 2 Samuel 19:44; 20:1; 1 Kings 12:16; 1 Samuel 17.
[45] N. T. Wright (2013), 830.
[46] Ibid., 830-2.
[47] Romans 3:24: *dia tēs apolutrōseōs tēs en Christō Iēsou* (διὰ τῆς ἀπολυτρώσεως τῆς ἐν Χριστῷ Ἰησοῦ), which the NIV translates "through the redemption that came by Christ

through the redeeming action of Christ's faithfulness to the divine "Israel-purpose", those who believe are declared to be "in the right". (2) The second passage is Galatians 2:15-4:11 where Paul's argument turns on the distinction between the promises made to Abraham, which have been fulfilled in Christ, and the giving of the Law, which has "done its God-given job", and so is no longer relevant for defining the identity of God's people. Thus, the single family promised to Abraham[48] can be identified with Christ (3:16 and 26-29), "the 'son of God' who shares that sonship with all who ... can call God 'father' (4:6-7)". Thus, the whole point of the summary of Galatians 2:19-20:

> For through the law I died to the law so that I might live for God. I have been crucified with Christ and I no longer live, but Christ lives in me. The life I now live in the body, I live by faith in the Son of God, who loved me and gave himself for me.

is to demonstrate Paul's belief that Israel as a whole is "summed up and redefined in and by *Christos*". (3) Wright's third passage is Philippians 3:2-11 where Paul discovers that Christ himself, who has already been vindicated by God, is "the one and only place where [his] security is to be found". This new-found conviction contrasts with the things he previously had thought were to his profit, but now considers as loss (3:7), things he had previously "sought for through his intense observance of Israel's Torah" and which would be vindicated on the last day. His circumcision is no longer to be found in old-covenant Israel - "If you want to know where Israel is ... look to Israel's Messiah. If you want to see 'the circumcision', look to those who belong to Israel's Messiah." Wright underlines these three passages, as follows:

> We miss the force of the passage unless we see that here, just as in Romans 3 or Galatians 3, the Messiah is the *place* where, and the means by which, Israel's destiny is realized and membership in Israel, in the 'circumcision' is assured.[49]

He then goes on to show, contrary to the judgment of many commentators, how Paul uses his many incorporative phrases with exactness

---

Jesus".
[48] See below, 267-9, on Galatians 3:16-20.
[49] N. T. Wright (2013), 831f. (my italics).

and precision, never saying, for example, *eis Christon* ('into the Messiah') when he means *en Christō* ('in the Messiah').[50] Thus, at a stroke, Wright brushes aside much learned debate about the way Paul allegedly uses such messianic or christological phrases which are prefixed by *en*, *eis* or *sun*, and so on:

> Once we grasp the meaning of Messiahship in his writings, there is no need to flatten out his very precise language, or chop it or stretch it on the Procrustean bed of our own de-messianized (and often de-Judaized) theological understandings.[51]

So, he summarises,

> The principal argument in favour of this entire hypothesis is the way in which the elements of Pauline soteriology, normally regarded as disparate and to be played off against one another, come together in a fresh, and remarkably coherent, way when viewed from this angle.[52]

I suggest then, that incorporative terminology has been reasonably well established in Paul's writings. That being the case, I also suggest that the nuance of them cannot be denied when other 'in Christ' occurrences are encountered in Ephesians.

Returning specifically to the first chapter of Ephesians then, where I suggested that we may find the key to resolving the uniqueness of Christ's election, the decisive point for me is that the writer of Ephesians (whoever he may have been) ends his string of 'in Christ'-dependent phrases with a statement about how believers, in context Gentiles, in contrast to those from a Jewish background, became incorporated into Christ:

> And you also were *included* in Christ when you heard the message of truth, the gospel of your salvation. When you believed, you were

---

[50] Ibid., 833f. See, for example, 2 Corinthians 1:21, where most translations have with the NIV, "Now it is God who makes both us and you stand firm *in Christ*.", but where the Greek text has *eis Christon*. "Paul's point here is precisely that the fissures that have opened up between him and the Corinthian community need repair, and that it is God who will do this, bringing them together 'into the Messiah', that is, into the unity which they properly possess 'in him' but which is now seen as the goal of a journey."
[51] Ibid., 832.
[52] Ibid., 830.

marked in him with a seal, the promised Holy Spirit.[53] However, resolution is still a step or two away because readers of the Greek text will note that Ephesians 1:13 does not explicitly mention incorporation at all; indeed, it is the sealing of the Holy Spirit which is the divine action consequent upon the readers' hearing and believing the gospel, not their inclusion in Christ. The two halves of the verse begin simply with the words "in whom" (*en hō*: ἐν ᾧ), but the NIV and NEB,[54] among others, have chosen to use the language of incorporation, even though at first sight the Greek does not require it. Nonetheless, some translators have recognised that the writer appears to have the idea of incorporation in mind, a sense carried over from the preceding verses where we have already recognised that there is no consensus according to Moule and others about whether or not 'in Christ' is meant in a locative sense. It could be, of course, that "included in Christ" simply implies becoming part of the community of Christ, the Church, which, of course, it does according to Wright because it is primarily incorporation into Christ in whom is the Church.[55] There is clearly a difficulty with respect to the ellipsis in this verse where a verb, absent from the Greek, is required to make sense of the wording in English translation. Various versions work round it in different ways. The RSV-group opts for a more literal rendering and word order, although the KJV supplies the verb 'trusted' – "In whom ye also *trusted* after that ye heard".[56]

There can be no reasonable doubt that on the basis of texts other than Ephesians, Moule and Wright make a good case for a Pauline concept of incorporation into an inclusive Christ.[57] Whether the concept can

---

[53] Ephesians 1:13: Greek: Ἐν ᾧ καὶ ὑμεῖς ἀκούσαντες τὸν λόγον τῆς ἀληθείας, τὸ εὐαγγέλιον τῆς σωτηρίας ὑμῶν, ἐν ᾧ καὶ πιστεύσαντες ἐσφραγίσθητε τῷ πνεύματι τῆς ἐπαγγελίας τῷ ἁγίῳ.

[54] The RSV, its more recent revisions, and the ESV avoid incorporative language, opting for more literal translations.

[55] N. T. Wright (2013), 834: "*Christos* denotes 'the Messiah and his people', or perhaps better 'the Messiah as the representative of his people', the one *in whom* that people are summed up and drawn together, with the main point being the *unity* of that company, and in particular their unity across traditional boundary-lines."

[56] 'Trusted' is italicised in the KJV indicating that the word was supplied to make good sense.

[57] C. F. D. Moule's chapter, 'The corporate Christ', (1977), 47-89, where he surveys a

legitimately be found in Ephesians 1 remains a moot point with some, given that there is uncertainty in certain circles about the authorship of the letter, and that in any particular occurrence of the phrase 'in Christ' there will be debate as to its exact meaning, whether locative, instrumental or other. However, given that Paul's authorship of Ephesians has not been decisively disproved, and that, in any case, the idea of a corporate Christ is not exclusive to Ephesians, I am not convinced that it would be wrong to read these verses in Ephesians 1 in an incorporative sense.

My conclusion then is that we are elect *because* we are now in Christ in a *locative* sense, and we were "included in Christ when [we] heard the word of truth, the gospel" and believed it (1:13), a conclusion with which O'Brien agrees:

> It is in Christ, that is, because of our incorporation in him, that God has blessed us. It is in him that Jewish believers ... and Gentile Christians ... now belong to the redeemed humanity.[58]

> God's election of believers to be his sons and daughters[59] is intimately related to their being in Christ the Chosen One ... and that the bounty which he lavishes on them 'consists in their being caught up into the love which subsists between the Father and the Son'.[60]

Furthermore, commenting on the phrase 'in him'[61] at the end of Ephesians 1:10, O'Brien says,

> Although this expression might be understood as instrumental, suggesting that the *Messiah* is the means (or instrument) through whom God sums up the universe, it is better to take the phrase as referring

---

wide range of the biblical terminology, including the body of Christ, etc., as well as the use of the preposition *en*, will reward the reader, not only with the force of his argument, but with the wealth of ancillary information and opinion for which he was justly held in high esteem. *The Origin of Christology* was first published in 1977 reflecting research on the use and meaning of 'in Christ' when there were clearly differences of opinion between eminent New Testament scholars.

[58] O'Brien, 91f.

[59] I would add the caveat that adoption is about sonship as opposed to slavery in Paul and would suggest therefore that gender-inclusive language in translation obscures the significance of sonship and is therefore inappropriate.

[60] O'Brien, 105. His quotation is from G. B. Caird, 'The Descent of the Spirit in Ephesians 4:7-11', *Studia Evangelica* 2, 1964, 36.

[61] "to unite all things *in him*" (ESV): the NIV has "under Christ": the Greek is ἐν αὐτῷ.

to him as the sphere in line with the earlier instances of this phrase within the paragraph (vv. 3-7, 9). Christ is the one *in whom* God chooses to sum up the cosmos, the one in whom he restores harmony to the universe. He is the focal point, not simply the means, the instrument or the functionary through whom all this occurs. The previous examples of 'in Christ' and its equivalents within the *berakah* focussed on the Son as God's chosen one in whom believers have been blessed. Now in vv. 9 and 10 the stress is placed on the one in whom God's overarching purposes for the *whole* of the created order are included.[62]

I suggest then, that the NIV is correct to use its interpretative gloss in Ephesians 1:13. The Greek says that gentile believers had entered by faith into "every spiritual blessing in Christ", which Paul had already claimed for Jewish believers or perhaps the apostles - "we, who were the first to put our hope in Christ", blessings which he goes on to enumerate in verses 3 to 12. In other words, in contrast to the way the Calvinist Fathers apparently understood the phrase 'in Christ', no one is chosen *outside* of Christ, but at the point of repentance the believer is incorporated into Christ, in a *locative* sense almost certainly, and receives the Holy Spirit, who is God's mark of ownership.

This conclusion is supported by Grant Osborne. Writing on Ephesians 1:3-12, he says,

> Next to Romans 9-11, this is the most important passage for the Pauline doctrine of predestination. Here we are told that "before the foundation of the world" God "chose us in him," "destined us in love to be his sons," and "appointed [us] to live for the praise of his glory." ... The phrase "before the foundation of the world" is a Hebraism for "from eternity" and refers to God's eternal decree of redemption. That decree is eternal and immutable. Yet there are striking similarities to Rom 8:29-30. In both passages Paul is speaking to believers, and the "we-you" terminology in both is paralleled by the election itself, which is not to eternal life but to "holy and blameless" lives (v. 4), to sonship (v. 5, note the parallel to "conformed to the image of his son," Rom 8:29), and to living "for the praise of his glory" (v. 12). While redemption and forgiveness are a central part of this passage (v. 7), the election itself looks at

---

[62] O'Brien, 111f. (his italics).

believers only and does not consider election out of unbelief, i.e., election here looks at the benefits of the salvation act, not at the act itself.[63]

Osborne also finds support in Arminius who argued that in Ephesians 1, faith is presupposed as the basis of predestination.[64]

If it can be shown that this first occurrence of the 'in Christ' phrase in the opening section of the letter we are considering should be construed in a locative sense, then it would seem logical that the other occurrences which immediately follow should be construed similarly. I suggest that the conclusion I have drawn about the 'in him' references in verse 13 reinforces the case for a locative sense for the first occurrence of 'in Christ' in verse 3, and I would reiterate the concept that context is a more reliable indicator of meaning than grammatical considerations alone. I would suggest therefore, in summary, that this Ephesians passage should be read as a reliable text from Paul which teaches that the blessings we have received, including our election, are *because* we are in Christ, contrary to the opposing view that one may be elect, either singly or collectively, outside of Christ.

Klein writes,

> In summary, Paul argues that election is the corporate choice of the church "in Christ." Before the foundation of the world God made his choice: those in Christ would be his people. To trust in Christ *activates* one's participation in the elect body of Christ. Paul posits the goal of this election: in Christ the chosen ones would become

---

[63] Grant R. Osborne in Pinnock & Wagner, 214f.
[64] Ibid.; Arminius, *Works*, 3.490. Klein, 154f., cites other writers, both Reformed and Arminian, who concur with this view; e.g., J. Armitage Robinson, *St. Paul's Epistle to the Ephesians* (London: Macmillan, 1904), 23-7; B. F. Westcott, *Epistle to the Ephesians* (London: Macmillan, 1906), 8; K. Snodgrass, *Ephesians*, New International Version Application Commentary (Grand Rapids, MI: Zondervan, 1996), 49; F. F. Bruce, *The Epistles to the Colossians, to Philemon, and to the Ephesians*, New International Commentary on the New Testament (Grand Rapids, MI: Eerdmans, 1984), 254; J. K. S. Reid, "The Office of Christ in Predestination", *Scottish Journal of Theology* 1, 1949, 5-19, 180; K. Stendhal, "The Called and the Chosen. An Essay on Election", in A. Fridrichsen ed., *The Root of the Vine* (London: Dacre, 1953), 68; H. Ridderbos, *Paul: An Outline of His Theology* (Grand Rapids, MI: Eerdmans, 1975), 347; C. L. Mitton, *Ephesians*, New Century Bible (London: Oliphants, 1976), 46; and Marcus Barth, *Ephesians*, Anchor Bible, 2 vols. (Garden City, NY: Doubleday, 1974), 108.

holy and blameless. God elects people not for privilege, but so that he may produce a holy people. This reminds us of God's purposes in choosing Israel to be his people.[65]

In conclusion therefore, I would suggest that the determinative factor in all of this is what the author of Ephesians meant when he wrote,

> Praise be to the God and Father of our Lord Jesus Christ, who has blessed us in the heavenly realms with every spiritual blessing *in Christ* (1:3).

Furthermore, if God's choice of "us in him before the creation of the world",[66] does not mean that Christ was the Elect One, and that we as individuals partake in his election (not our own) as we enter by faith into what is Christ's, then it is very difficult to see why Paul did not omit the 'in him' phrase altogether and simply say, "He chose us before the creation of the world". It seems that on a Calvinistic understanding the crucial expression 'in him' might then be entirely redundant.

b. Unitary Election

In Ephesians, indeed in the New Testament as a whole, references to the Elect are always to the Church collectively and in its entirety and without respect to dispensation. Ephesians was written to a body (perhaps bodies) of believers and the personal pronouns are plural, but there are a number of explicit references elsewhere in the New Testament to individuals being chosen, including five (possibly six) references to Christ alone as the Elect One of God. The christological references are:

> (a) Matthew 12:18, "Here is my servant *whom I have chosen*",[67] where the evangelist paraphrases Isaiah 42:1 to demonstrate that Jesus is the one foretold in scripture. Clearly, his aim was to show that Jesus was the Messiah, God's Chosen One.
>
> (b) Luke 9:35, "This is my Son, *whom I have chosen*",[68] the words

---

[65] Klein, 155 (his italics).
[66] Ephesians 1:4.
[67] Greek: ἰδοὺ ὁ παῖς μου ὃν ᾑρέτισα. See Chapter 8a(v), 214, *hairetidzō*.
[68] Greek: οὗτος ἐστιν ὁ υἱός μου ὁ ἐκλελεγμένος. There are at least four variants of this phrase: see Table 5, 381f.

of God the Father at the Transfiguration.

(c) Luke 23:35, "let him save himself if he is God's Messiah, *the Chosen One*".[69] This is an interesting and possibly significant text because the words are the taunt of the hostile Jewish religious leaders who witnessed the crucifixion of Jesus. If these words were what was actually said, they provide important attestation to an aspect of contemporary messianic expectation among those who were presumably well versed in the Hebrew Scriptures to the effect that the expected Messiah was also known as God's Chosen One.

(d) 1 Peter 2:4, "the Living Stone ... *chosen by God* and precious to him".[70]

(e) 1 Peter 2:6, "I lay a stone in Zion, a *chosen and precious* cornerstone",[71] quoting Isaiah 28:16.

(f) Although the majority text of John 1:34 has, "I have seen and I testify that this is the Son of God", as is reflected in the 1984 edition of the NIV, the 2011 edition has "I have seen and I testify that this is God's Chosen One".[72]

We have already noted evidence of the possible interchangeability or overlap in the respective meanings of *eklektos* (ἐκλεκτός) and *agapētos* (ἀγαπητός) when applied to Jesus in the contexts of his baptism and transfiguration.[73] This observation might permit us to draw into consideration other possible points of evidence from the New Testament. For instance, Howard Marshall draws attention to the textual variant of John 1:34 just noted, where he claims "the more probable reading" has *eklektos* in place of *agapētos*.[74] He says that in this context *eklektos* would be the highest title applied to Jesus, pointing unmistakably to Isaiah 42:1. Furthermore, we can also consider the word *monogenēs* (μονογενής: 'unique' or 'one and only')[75] which is another minority

---

[69] Greek: σωσάτω ἑαυτόν, εἰ οὗτος ἐστιν ὁ χριστὸς τοῦ θεοῦ ὁ ἐκλεκτός.
[70] Greek: λίθον ζῶντα ... παρὰ δὲ θεῷ ἐκλεκτὸν ἔντιμον.
[71] Greek: τίθημι ἐν Σιὼν λίθον ἀκρογωνιαῖον ἐκλεκτὸν ἔντιμον.
[72] NA26 has ὁ υἱὸς τοῦ θεοῦ. Other variants include ὁ ἐκλεκτός τοῦ θεοῦ, ὁ ἐκλεκτὸς υἱός τοῦ θεοῦ and ὁ μονογενὴς υἱός τοῦ θεοῦ.
[73] Matthew 12:18 and Luke 9:35. See Chapters 8a(iii), 211, *eklektos*; 10a, 284, 'Mark 13:20', and Appendix 2, 380, for fuller discussions.
[74] I. H. Marshall (1990), 122f. Marshall's preference for the *eklektos* variant in John 1:34 is also supported by Barrett (1978), 178. See also NET, 1996, note A.
[75] Luke 7:12; 8:42; 9:38 (twice); John 1:14, 18; 3:16, 18; Hebrews 11:17; 1 John 4:9.

reading of John 1:34 and also occurs soon afterwards in the same context in John 3:16. There is, then, a small cluster of New Testament words which, as well as carrying the underlying idea of chosenness, also suggest uniqueness, value and belovedness, a notion reinforced by the various translations of Hebrew words meaning 'only son/child' or 'beloved' by *agapētos* in the Septuagint.[76]

The case for the uniqueness of Christ's election may also be supported by considering two further areas of New Testament evidence; firstly, the terminology of sonship and, secondly, Paul's 'one seed' analogy in Galatians 3:16-20. Firstly, with regard to sonship, generally speaking, the New Testament applies the plural forms of the two nouns *huios* (υἱός: 'son') and *teknon* (τέκνον: 'child') to Christians collectively. There are two exceptions, however; firstly, the singular is used where the respective writers are particularising in otherwise plural contexts,[77] and, secondly, where the context is not theological. In other places the singular forms of these nouns invariably refer to Christ. Sons or daughters[78] of God are not therefore envisaged individually and may only be regarded individually as standing 'in Christ', *the* Son.

Furthermore, we shall see that Paul's interesting exegesis of Galatians 3:16-20 will prove germane. As Tom Wright points out,

As far as Paul was concerned, the reason the creator God called Abraham in the first place was to undo the sin of Adam and its

---

[76] *Agapētos* occurs 18 times in 17 verses in the canonical books of the Septuagint, six of which translate *yachid* (יָחִיד - occurs 12 times in MT), 'only son/child': Genesis 22:2, 12, 16; Jeremiah 6:26; Amos 8:10; Zechariah 12:10, and six translate *yadid* (יָדִיד - occurs 8 times in 7 verses in MT), 'beloved': Psalms 45 title [MT 44:1]; 60:5 [59:7]; 84:1 [83:2]; 108:6 [107:7]; 127:2 [126:2]; Isaiah 5:1.

[77] Galatians 4:7: "So you are no longer a slave, but God's child; and since you are his child, God has made you also an heir" (however, this rendering of *huios* as 'child' misses a theologically important point about sonship, because Paul is contrasting sonship with slavery and therefore includes daughters into the category of sons); and Hebrews 12:7 (NIV 1984): "For what son is not disciplined by his father", although the 2011 edition of the NIV avoids gender specific language: "For what children are not disciplined by their father".

[78] The one New Testament reference to daughters of God: 2 Corinthians 6:18: "and you will be my sons and daughters", occurs in a quotation of 2 Samuel 7:14: "I will be his father, and he shall be my son", which Paul seems to conflate with Isaiah 43:6: "Bring my sons from afar and my daughters from the ends of the earth"; D. J. A. Clines in Howley *et al*, 1475.

effects. Paul's basic contention, in the area of election, was that, through the Messiah and the spirit, this God had done what he promised Abraham he would do.[79]

Thus, in this 'one seed' passage Paul showed that the promises God made to Abraham in Genesis envisaged a singular seed, usually (apparently) construed as an individual, arising among Abraham's progeny whom Paul identifies as the Christ (3:16). The promises which include Abraham's seed[80] are set in terms of a covenant relationship in which the Promised Land is pledged in perpetuity to Abraham's progeny and of which circumcision is the covenant sign.[81] So, when Christ becomes the covenant partner it is assumed that the framework for the fulfilment of the promise to Abraham is transposed, since Paul clearly envisages an inheritance far wider than the earthbound scope of the Abrahamic covenant. My point is not to debate the transposition from the temporal and territorial, the Promised Land to eternity and the cosmos,[82] but to note that the focus of election in the New Testament is always upon Christ. This transcends the scope of proof texts since I believe it shows that the election of the Son of God is a key underlying paradigm of scripture.

It is unfortunate that this Galatians passage has often been regarded as odd; "an example of Paul's extraordinary (and, some have said, 'rabbinic') methods of exegesis", says Tom Wright in a long chapter entitled "The People of God, Freshly Reworked". "Paul has not forgotten, as many exegetes have, the *incorporative meaning* of the honorific[83] *Christos*."[84] In the passages from Genesis, where God promises to

---

[79] N. T. Wright (2013), 784 (his italics).
[80] Genesis 12:7; 13:15f.; 15:5, 18; 17:7-10; 22:17f.
[81] Genesis 17:7-10.
[82] But note Byrne, 68ff., who traces this trend through intertestamental Jewish writings.
[83] N. T. Wright (2013), 824: "*Christos* is in fact neither a proper name (with denotation but no necessary connotation) nor a 'title' as such (with connotation but flexible denotation, as when 'the King of Spain' goes on meaning the same thing when one king dies and another succeeds him). It is rather, an *honorific*, which shares some features of a 'title' but works differently." See M. Novenson, *Christ among the Messiahs: Christ Language in Paul and Messiah Language in Ancient Judaism* (New York: Oxford University Press, 2012).
[84] Ibid., 869 (his italics). "Indeed, the passage has become something of a favourite with people who want to be able to say, 'Look how strangely the early Christians – and particularly Paul – read the Bible!'"

Abram/Abraham's *seed* an everlasting possession of the land of Canaan, the Hebrew word *zerà* (זֶרַע: 'seed'), which appears no less than 13 times in these texts, is a collective noun, as 'seed' also can be in English. However, the insistence of most Bible translations in rendering the word 'offspring' or 'descendants', as in the NIV, for example, has given the impression that Paul is forcing this collective noun, contrary to its sense in its Hebrew Genesis context, into what to us would be a strange interpretative nuance, in other words, treating it as a singularity and focusing its meaning on the *person* of Christ as an individual. Wright points out that the "tricky" word *sperma* (σπέρμα: 'seed') also regularly functions in Greek as a collective noun and means 'family', as does its Hebrew counterpart, *zerà*, although it too is often misleadingly translated 'descendants'.[85]

Thus, the point Paul makes is simply that God promised Abraham a *family* - just *one* family, not two, but that the context in which these verses are found in Galatians, the conflict between law and promise, threatens to create two distinct families. This for Paul was the issue implicit in the dispute between himself and Peter in the previous chapter of Galatians[86] where Peter withdrew from table fellowship with uncircumcised gentile believers in deference to Jewish-heritage believers. Paul's point was that the law cannot be allowed to overthrow the intention of the original promise made to Abraham. God intended to give Abraham just one family, the singular seed, and the point he goes on to make in Galatians 3:27-29 is that this is precisely what God did in the Messiah – not the individual personage of the Messiah, but the family of Messiah, according the honorific, 'Messiah' or 'Christ', its incorporative meaning. Rather than being a strange piece of 'rabbinic' exegesis, then, Paul's 'one seed' illustration becomes a key to both his and our understanding of Election.

Thus far I have been driving at the point that the only really chosen one is Christ himself, but on the basis of Galatians 3 it becomes clear that he is the culmination of an elective process which began with Abraham,

---

[85] Ibid., 868.
[86] Galatians 2:11ff.

the one chosen to be the father of faith for all who would believe and through whom the whole world would enter into the saving purposes of God. Through Abraham's one family would come the Messiah, the one who would bring the whole process of salvation history to its climax, as he would realise in his own death the promise hinted at in God's call to Abraham to sacrifice his only son Isaac. Immediately following that demonstration of Abraham's faith, and in line with his earlier prophetic reply to Isaac's enquiry about the provision of a sacrificial animal – "God himself will provide the lamb for the burnt offering",[87] God reiterated the promise of blessing for the whole world, the divinely appointed remedy for the sin of the world, and the means of bringing about universal reconciliation:

> The angel of the LORD called to Abraham from heaven a second time and said, 'I swear by myself, declares the LORD, that because you have done this and have not withheld your son, your only son, I will surely bless you and make your descendants as numerous as the stars in the sky and as the sand on the seashore. Your descendants will take possession of the cities of their enemies, and through your offspring all nations on earth will be blessed, because you have obeyed me.'[88]

> The argument of Galatians is that the divine purpose in election has found its goal (and hence its redefinition) in the Messiah, so that one cannot go back to Torah in order to confirm or solidify one's membership in the family.... It is only when that context is forgotten (in the rush to have Paul speak about the difference between law-piety and faith-piety, between different sixteenth-century models of justification and assurance) that the focus of what he is actually saying is ignored.[89]

A similar pattern, although extending only as far back as Jacob, may also be traced through the gradual unfolding of the role and identity of the LORD's Servant, *Ebed Yahweh*, in the book of Isaiah.[90] We have already encountered Isaiah 42:1, Matthew's proof text for the

---

[87] Genesis 22:8.
[88] Genesis 22:15-18. The NIV's 'descendants' and 'offspring' translate the three occurrences of *zerà*.
[89] N. T. Wright (2013), 869, 871.
[90] Ibid., 879, makes a similar point when considering 2 Corinthians 5:11-6:2.

identification of Christ with Isaiah's Chosen Servant figure, and clearly both Matthew and Luke saw a significant connection between Jesus and Isaiah's Chosen One too. The first occurrence in this sequence is Isaiah 41:8f. where the nation, Israel and Jacob in synonymous parallelism, is identified with the Chosen Servant:

> But you, O Israel, my servant,
> Jacob, whom I have chosen.

Furthermore, chapter 41, together with Isaiah 42:19, where the servant is accused of being blind and deaf:

> Who is blind but my servant,
> and deaf like the messenger I send?
> Who is blind like the one committed to me,
> blind like the servant of the LORD?

creates a literary *inclusio* which encompasses a passage dealing with the ideal Servant of Yahweh, the personal judge of the nations (42:1-17).[91] This has the structural effect of setting an agenda for the exposition of the Servant theme which follows. Thus, through the succeeding six chapters of Isaiah (43 to 48), the Servant, always grammatically singular, is identified with Jacob-Israel. There is an exception, which is not part of the sequence, where the plural use of the noun refers to God's servants, the prophets (44:26). However, when we arrive at chapter 49, a clearly unitary Servant figure emerges out of Jacob-Israel. He is one who will be formed in the womb to restore Jacob and gather Israel (49:5f.). In sharp contrast to the foregoing corporate identity of the blind servant of 42:19, he is a wise and righteous servant, a person who will be the sacrifice whereby many will be justified.

There seems then to be a kind of typological paradigm running through this section of Isaiah which traces the election of Israel through to the emergence of God's Elect One, whom with hindsight Christians clearly recognise to be the Christ. Thus far, the paradigm is incomplete, however, for from chapter 54 on, the singular Servant is replaced by a community of Servants of Yahweh, e.g., Isaiah 54:17:

---

[91] For a technical analysis of the literary structure of this section of Isaiah, see O'Connell, 151ff.

> No weapon forged against you will prevail,
> and you will refute every tongue that accuses you.
> This is the heritage of the *servants of the* LORD,
> and this is their vindication from me.

I suggest then, that this whole series of 'servant' references maps out a framework which pre-echoes, and in which we may therefore understand, the New Testament concept of Election. God's 'purpose in election' can be traced in these latter chapters of Isaiah first from the identification of the Servant with Jacob and his *seed* or *family* to the ultimate focus which is the perfect, righteous Servant, the Messiah. After he has made atonement, those whose sins he bore, his offspring (53:10: *zerà*), then constitutes a new family of servants whose election is effected in and through the ideal Servant. They are never envisaged as being chosen individually: rather their chosenness is conferred on them by their association with the Suffering Servant.[92]

It seems then, that the key concept of the New Testament doctrine of Election is that one individual, and only one, is chosen by God. That principle applies at every stage of the unfolding redemption drama. Therefore, apart from those who are chosen to fulfil particular roles or tasks – kings, priests, artists, apostles, etc., individuals may be regarded as elect in a soteriological sense only in as much as they are incorporated into the Elect One, whether the Elect One be Jacob-Israel or Christ. It is through and in Christ therefore that individuals enter into and share the sphere of his election by their exercise of faith in him.

William Klein's *The New Chosen People* is a recent comprehensive study in which he argues for corporate rather than individual election. Asking, "How might we grasp the significance of this portrayal of election as a corporate action?",[93] a concept we noted in passing when considering Wright's work on the corporate Christ (above, 256ff.), he quotes Otto Eissfeldt who argued for a concept which he called

---

[92] The Servant passages in Isaiah are: (a) corporate Israel (singular): 43:10; 44:1f., 21; 45:4; 48:20; (b) the ideal Servant (singular): 49:3-7; 50:10; 52:13; 53:11; (c) redeemed Israel (plural): 54:17; 56:6; 63:17; 65:8-15 (65:15 differentiates between 'chosen ones' who are cursed, and 'servants' who are blessed; cf. national Israel and renewed Israel in Romans 9-11); 66:14.

[93] Klein, 12.

"corporate solidarity" or "corporate identity", particularly of blood-communities who owe their being and destiny to a particular ancestor:

> To Israelite thought, which in this connection is quite in harmony with Semitic thought in general and also has parallels outside the Semitic world, unity is prior to diversity, the community prior to the individual; the real entity is the community, and the individuals belonging to it have their origin therein.[94]

From his survey of the New Testament evidence concerning Election, Klein concludes,

> the NT writers viewed Jesus as God's "elect one," an individual chosen by God for his role or task (see Luke 9:35; 1 Peter 2:4-6).... I conclude that Christ's status as the "elect one" answers the question of how the church secures its elect status. The church acquires its election from the fact of Christ's election—by being "in Christ." A. Richardson puts it this way: "If Christians are 'the elect,' it is because they are 'in Christ,' because they are baptized into the person of him who alone may with complete propriety be called the Elect of God."[95]

The whole concept of "corporate solidarity" may be somewhat foreign to contemporary western thinking, dominated as it is by an individualism, which, in turn, would be foreign to the writers of the New Testament. Indeed, McGrath cites in particular the nineteenth-century Swiss historian, Jacob Burckhardt, who argued that the Renaissance of the fourteenth and fifteenth centuries gave birth to the modern era as people first began to think of themselves as individuals as the communal consciousness of the medieval period gave way to individual consciousness.[96] Citing Bruce Malina, Klein argues that instead of being

---

[94] O. Eissfeldt, 'The *Ebed-Jahwe* in Isaiah xl.-lv. In the Light of the Israelite Conceptions of the Community and the Individual, the Ideal and the Real.' *Expository Times* 44, 1933, 264.

[95] Klein, 240; A. Richardson, *An Introduction to the Theology of the New Testament* (London: SCM, 1958), 279.

[96] McGrath (2012), 36, citing Jacob Burckhardt, *The Civilization of the Renaissance in Italy* (London: Penguin Books, 1990). This fact may, of course, raise questions about the ways in which pre-Reformation theologians viewed individualism, and in particular, how that might influence our understanding of Augustine, many centuries before the Renaissance, with respect to original sin and our being in Adam, and so on. There might be a case for arguing that Calvin and his like cast Augustine's ideas into a wholly

individualistic, New Testament people, as well as those of many non-western cultures today, were *dyadic*. That is, they conceived of themselves not as separate entities, but in relation to others, whether in terms of the qualities of their families, villages, cities or nations.[97] This might shed light for us on Paul's presentation of the Church as incorporated into Christ and should help to explain the numerous corporate metaphors employed by New Testament writers to describe the Church – body of Christ, house (temple), bride, people of God, and not least, "in Christ." First century Christians, and believers who lived before the Renaissance, found their identity as members of this inclusive organism, so that when they approached the basic theological issues they did so in a corporate frame of reference. Thus, says Tom Wright,

> To be ... 'in the anointed one', the Messiah, is to be part of the people over which he rules, but also part of the people who are defined by him, by what has happened to him, by what the one God has promised him. This is how Paul uses the incorporative language of *en Christo* and similar phrases.[98]

Indeed, Wright makes the point that in Paul's writings the idea of Election is not so much to do with democratic choices or with "the technical sense of 'election' in the elaborate technical schemes of the sixteenth and seventeenth centuries", but with the sense which most writers on first-century Judaism and Christianity today understand it as referring to God's choice of Israel and that with the connotation of his divine choice being "for a particular purpose".[99] He argues therefore that Paul's understanding of election of people has to be seen in this corporate sense: God chose Abraham first, and through him Israel, for the

---

new and more rigorous light through seeing them through individualistic rather than communal eyes. That observation might account for the greater logical rigor with which Calvin developed the doctrine of grace compared with Augustine; McGrath (2012), 198. It might therefore be worth re-evaluating Augustine's theology in the light of a pre-Renaissance sense of corporate solidarity, but that is well beyond the scope of this book.

[97] Ibid., B. J. Malina, *The New Testament World: Insights from Cultural Anthropology* (Louisville, KY: Westminster John Knox Press, 2001), 58ff. See also Walton & Walton, 179ff., '*Ḥerem* Against Communities Focuses on Destroying Identity, Not Killing People of Certain Ethnicities'.

[98] N. T. Wright (2013), 830, quoted by Klein, 241.

[99] Ibid., 774f.

salvation of the world, but that goal was achieved through the chosenness of the Messiah.[100] Our election is therefore as incorporated into Christ as a body.

Thus, Paul clearly sees a solid continuity of electness from Abraham right through to Christ and his Church – "If you belong to Christ, then you are Abraham's seed, and heirs according to the promise".[101] There is therefore no room for notions of Replacement Theology or Supersessionism. Israel has not been abandoned and there is no disjunction or discontinuity between God's dealings with Israel and the Church no matter how much one may regard Israel as being unworthy of God's continued covenant faithfulness toward them. As Wright has so cogently argued, God's elective purposes do not fracture with the advent of the Christ; rather he becomes the key focus in scripture creating continuity between the Abrahamic and New Covenants. For the Israel of faith, Abraham is father, and Christ is the means by which God accomplishes his purposes promised to Abraham. Thus, for faithful Israel, the gospel provides the means for their continuity in covenant relationship with Yahweh – continuance in their cultivated olive stock, to use Paul's analogy from Romans 11, while for believing Gentiles, the new birth engrafts them as wild olive branches into the rootstock of Israel's covenant relationship with their Creator.[102]

Thus, back to Klein:

> The central salvific actions that Christ accomplished for his people accrue to them because of their solidarity with him.[103]

For Klein, Romans 5:12-21 is the classic text where Paul sees people in corporate terms. Thus, when Paul asserts in Romans 5:12 that "all sinned" he cannot mean that all people individually committed an act of sin *at the time* that Adam disobeyed, although no one doubts that all individually have sinned in life. And while some say that Paul claims that all have inherited a sinful nature as a result of Adam's act, he

---

[100] Ibid., 815ff.
[101] Galatians 3:29.
[102] See Romans 11:17-24.
[103] Klein, 241.

actually makes no causal connection to a "sinful nature" or so-called "original sin" in these verses. Rather, Paul views the human race corporately: what Adam did, we all did, and do.[104] For western Christians in particular, this may be an extremely difficult concept to either express or grasp. On the analogy with the 'in Christ' discussion above, we need to grasp that to be 'in Adam' entails none of the theoretical conclusions drawn through Augustinianism and concepts of Original Sin which place us in Adam such that we did what he did *when he did it*, but rather that we do what he did because we share the same nature, just as 'in Christ' we share his sonship and will one day share his inheritance in eternal glory.

Thus, the Church is God's elect body and Christians are "elect ones" because of their incorporation into Christ. Certainly, individuals are said to be chosen to perform tasks or ministries, but when election to salvation is the focus, the New Testament evidence declares not that God has chosen individuals, but rather a community, the Church. So, the question which I posed at the beginning of this chapter – How can there be an elect body where none of its members is chosen individually? – simply betrays a modern take on New Testament (not to say oriental) categories which would be quite alien to the thinking of the biblical authors.

This understanding of corporate election obviates many of the debates surrounding Election, of course. If God's choice is of a body or category of people and not of individuals, all the arguments over the basis of his choices, whether for or against, and the whole concept of divine decrees and their ordering, simply disappear and render worthless whole libraries of tomes which argue the toss over the basis on which God chose you and me. Just as under the Old Covenant, a person entered into the solidarity of Israel by birth, so in the New, we enter the "renewed Israel",[105] God's Elect, by the new birth, a spiritual birth from

---

[104] Ibid., 241f.
[105] N. T. Wright (2013), 826 n154, draws exception to the phrase 'new Israel' used by A. E. J. Rawlinson, 'Corpus Christi' in G. K. A. Bell & D. A. Deissmann eds., *Mysterium Christi: Christological Studies by British and German Theologians* (London: Longmans, Green & Co., 1930), 232: "The phrase 'new Israel' is ... going too far; at most, Paul might have said 'renewed Israel'."

above through faith placed in the Messiah, the one promised in the Old, the One and only Chosen of God.[106]

c. Extra-Biblical Sources in Support of a Divine Choice of The One

Thus far, our consideration of the Messiah as God's Chosen One has been based entirely on the evidence of canonical scripture, but there are a number of extra-biblical sources which may have been available to the New Testament writers and which may therefore have contributed to their thought world. Some of these sources seem to reinforce this understanding of the divine choice of the One and demonstrate the concept of Christ's election which I am trying to establish. Thus, in bringing this chapter to a close, I will refer briefly to three important literary sources; the Qumran literature known as *The Dead Sea Scrolls* from the period immediately before Christ, *The Similitudes of Enoch*, part of a composite work possibly emanating from periods both before and after the time of Jesus, and the late first- and early second-century body of correspondence known as *The Apostolic Fathers*.

i. The Qumran Literature

Evidence from the intertestamental period, and from the Qumran literature in particular, is tantalising. It is sometimes claimed that God's Chosen One, or God's Elect One, is a title found in this literature.[107] If so, it may have formed part of the first-century Jewish messianic expectation. However, it is not known to what extent the Qumran community may have influenced Judaism generally since it seems to have been an isolated Jewish sect. Nonetheless, the title or honorific might have formed part of the basic fabric of New Testament thought and, if so, may be evidence to support the concept of the unique chosenness of the Messiah. We have already noted that the concept was embedded in the words Luke placed on the lips of the Jewish leaders at Calvary.

---

[106] Klein, 243ff.
[107] 4QMessAr; Vermes, 306f. or 4Q534 *4QNoah ar*; F. G. Martinez & E. J. C. Tigchelaar, *The Dead Sea Scrolls* (Grand Rapids, MI: Eerdmans, 1997-98), 2:1071.

However, the focus is upon a poorly preserved and difficult to decipher Aramaic fragment in which the title "elect of God" is found. It is thought by some to be a horoscope of the Messiah; others think it more likely to have been part of an account of the legend of Noah's miraculous birth which is found elsewhere in the Qumran literature.[108] In support of this latter alternative, Joseph Fitzmyer argues that it points to someone, Noah perhaps, chosen by God for a specific task or role, but not a salvific role, at least not in the sense I am debating:[109] Noah's role could, of course, be regarded as salvific in that his obedience provided salvation from the Flood. Though tantalising, this reference proves to be an unlikely support for my thesis, therefore.

ii. The Similitudes of Enoch

The Similitudes of Enoch[110] or *The Book of the Parables of Enoch*, comprises chapters 37 to 71 of *The Book of Enoch*, often also known as *1 Enoch* to distinguish it from *The Secrets of Enoch* and *The Book of the Palaces*, which were later apocalypses, also known as *2* and *3 Enoch* respectively.[111] *1 Enoch* is a composite Jewish pseudepigraphal work which many believe to have emanated largely from the last two centuries before Christ.[112] *The Similitudes* refers to a figure who is portrayed as having messianic characteristics and who is repeatedly called 'The Elect One' (*ho eklektos*: ὁ ἐκλεκτός), one also known as 'The Son of Man' and 'The Righteous One',[113] clear messianic references. God chose this messianic Son of Man to fulfil a task (46:3; 48:6), which was to "choose the righteous and holy from among them ... that they should

---

[108] 1QapGen II; Vermes, 305, 252f.; Barrett (1978), 178.
[109] Klein, 32 n39; J. A. Fitzmyer, 'The Aramaic 'Elect of God' Text from Qumran Cave 4', *Catholic Biblical Quarterly* 27, 1965, 348-72.
[110] Charles (1917), 56-95; Charlesworth (1983), 1.13-89.
[111] W. O. E. Oesterley in Charles (1917), xiii.
[112] B. M. Metzger in Gæbelein, 171; Charles (1917), xiv. See also Gabriele Boccaccini ed., *Enoch and Qumran Origins: New Light on a Forgotten Connection* (Grand Rapids, MI: Eerdmans, 2005).
[113] Rowland, 95, lists occurrences of these titles in 1 Enoch as follows: (a) Son of Man: 46:1ff.; 48:2ff.; 62:5ff.; 69:26ff.; 71:17; (b) Elect One: 39:6f.; 40:5; 45:3ff.; 49:2ff.; 51:3; 52:6ff.; 53:6; 55:4; 61:5ff.; 62:1ff. Klein, 20, also lists references to the Righteous One at 38:2 and 43:6.

be saved" (51:2).[114] Thus there are parallels to what we find in the Old Testament where Election language is used to designate individuals chosen by God to accomplish appointed missions.[115] This may therefore point to an element in Jewish messianic expectation such as is reflected in Luke 23:35, the abuse directed towards the crucified Jesus.

The majority of *1 Enoch* is widely accepted among specialists in the field of Jewish pseudepigraphy to be pre-Christian, many agreeing that the work probably predated AD 70 and may even have predated Jesus.[116] But there is no absolute certainty about the date of the *Similitudes* which contains the material of interest in this context, so there is uncertainty as to whether it was extant in the New Testament period and whether it could constitute testimony to the possibility of the identification of the Elect One with a messianic figure, and therefore be sufficiently early to have influenced the popular expectation of Messiah and be formative for the New Testament interpretation of Jesus as the Messiah. That being the case, however, the possibility cannot be ruled out that the ideas contained in the *Similitudes* were in currency much earlier. Many now believe the work as we know it to be late, certainly post-AD 70,[117] and many see in it clear Christian influences. Telling evidence against an earlier date is its complete absence from the Qumran literature, despite the presence of Aramaic fragments from other parts of *1 Enoch*,[118] and also from the Greek translation.[119] The value of this evidence hangs on its date, of course, but it seems increasingly likely that the *Similitudes of Enoch* can no longer with confidence provide grounds in the New Testament period for a popular expectation of a Messiah who was known as The Elect or Chosen One. The fact remains, however, that those elements remain within the text even though its final form

---

[114] Klein, 20. Choosing the righteous in this context is not about election in the sense in which I am writing, but is about the advent of the Elect One who comes to separate the righteous from the unrighteous; cf. Hebrews 9:28; Matthew 25:32f.

[115] See Chapter 11a, 352.

[116] J. H. Charlesworth, *Jesus Within Judaism* (London: SPCK, 1988), 17.

[117] David W. Suter in Gabriele Boccaccini ed., *Enoch and the Messiah Son of Man: Revisiting the Book of Parables* (Grand Rapids, MI: Eerdmans, 2007), 415ff., suggests that *The Similitudes* may date from between 50 BC and AD 117.

[118] J. T. Milik ed., *The Books of Enoch: Aramaic Fragments of Quran, Cave 4* (Oxford: Clarendon, 1976).

[119] Suter in Boccaccini, 417.

may have been redacted by Christian writers. That in itself, of course, provides evidence of the currency of an 'Elect One' terminology from around the general period of interest and almost certainly from the sub-apostolic period.

iii. The Apostolic Fathers

We are on safer ground in the sub-apostolic period because *The Apostolic Fathers*, a body of correspondence from between AD 70 and 135,[120] provides post-New Testament evidence in support of the thesis of the election of Christ alone. If, indeed, the idea can be found in this corpus, it seems reasonable to assume that it would be similar, if not identical, to that hinted at in the New Testament itself. Perhaps the best example is 1 Clement 64:

> God ... who chose out the Lord Jesus Christ, and us through [*dia*: διά] him for 'a peculiar people'.[121]

Clement, the putative late first-century correspondent of the church at Rome,[122] writes of the divine election of individuals "through" as well as "in" Christ. In that their election is channelled through the election of Christ, the Elect One, these two expressions are probably similar in meaning. Several references to Christians having been chosen by God in a collective sense are found elsewhere in 1 Clement,[123] and in the prologue of Ignatius' Ephesian letter:

> to the ... church at Ephesus ... marked out since the beginning of time for glory unfading and unchanging; and owing its unity and its election to the true and undoubted Passion.[124]

Thus, apart from Paul's assertion, sometimes overlooked or understood

---

[120] Holmes, 1.
[121] Kirsopp Lake, *The Apostolic Fathers* (London/Cambridge, MS: Heinemann/Harvard University Press, 1912), 118f.; see also Holmes, 64.
[122] Holmes, 24f.
[123] E.g., 1 Clement 29:1: ἐκλογης μερος; 30:1: ἁγιου ουν μερις ὑπαρχοντες ποιησωμεν τα του ἁγιασμου παντα, and several textual variants; 32:4: ἐν Χριστῳ Ἰησου κληθεντες; 46:4: ἐκλεκτοι του θεου, suggests a corporate sense of election; 46:6: μια κλησις ἐν Χριστῳ; 50:7: ἐκλελεγμενους ... διά Ἰησου Χριστου; 64: ἐκλεξαμενος τον κυριον Ἰησου Χριστον και ἡμας δι᾽ αὐτου; 65:2: κεκλημενων ὑπο του θεου και δι᾽ αὐτου.
[124] Staniforth & Louth, 61; Homes, 86.

differently, and not always clearly reflected in translation, that our election is in Christ (NT Ephesians 1:4), Clement seems to provide clearer statements even than any of the New Testament writers, of the unitary election of Christ and of our election in him. It is also significant that Ignatius regarded the election of the Ephesian church, not to any preordained divine decree, but to the events of the passion, Christ's sufferings and sacrificial death, whereby saving faith becomes the basis of the Christian gospel.[125]

---

[125] It has to be conceded, however, that, although Staniforth & Louth attribute the election of the Ephesian believers to the passion of Christ, Holmes, 86, attributes their election to "genuine suffering", presumably their own. The Greek phrase is: ἐν πάθει ἀληθινῷ.

Chapter 10

OTHER PROBLEMATICAL ELECTION TEXTS[1]

A number of New Testament passages, which do not necessarily employ any of the specific Election vocabulary considered in Chapter 8, are also relevant because they may be used to support a Reformed point of view. I shall deal with them in canonical, rather than any logical order, and ironically, we begin with a text which poses a particular problem, but for which resolution is not immediately apparent!

a. Mark 13:20: "The elect, whom he has chosen"

> If the Lord had not cut short those days, no one would survive. But for the sake of the elect, *whom he has chosen*, he has shortened them.

In view of what has gone before, this verse presents a particular problem because Mark says that the Elect have been chosen,[2] and a reasonable inference would be that the Elect of Mark 13:20 had been individually chosen for salvation. That may seem obvious, and to some to argue otherwise will seem perverse. However, my contention is that individuals may be called elect in a soteriological sense only insofar as they have been included into Christ, *the* Elect One.[3] Thus, neither the individual nor the elect group has been chosen or nominated as such, but their chosenness has been conferred upon them by their incorporation into Christ.

Mark's qualification of the term 'elect' (*eklektous*: ἐκλεκτοὺς) by the

---

[1] See also Fisk, 93-148, 'Scriptures Calling for Special Attention', where he reviews several of the texts discussed below and in addition Matthew 20:16; 22:14; John 10:26; 12:39; Acts 2:23; 16:14; Romans 3:11; Ephesians 1:4f., 11; 2 Thessalonians 2:13; 1 Peter 1f.; Revelation 13:8, most of which I comment on elsewhere.
[2] Mark 13:20b: Greek: ἀλλὰ διὰ τοὺς ἐκλεκτοὺς οὓς ἐξελέξατο ἐκολόβωσεν τὰς ἡμέρας.
[3] See Chapter 9, 248.

phrase, "whom he has chosen" (*exelexato*: ἐξελέξατο) is an interesting tautology because, had he meant that elect individuals had been divinely selected for salvation, then, perhaps surprisingly, it is the only text in the whole of the New Testament which says, or appears to say so, explicitly. Here *eklektos* (ἐκλεκτός) appears in its plural accusative form (*tous eklektous*) and is correctly translated as the noun it is - 'chosen ones'. Why then Mark should qualify it by adding "whom he has chosen" is puzzling, especially since such wording does not appear in the parallel passage in Matthew 24:22.[4] It would seem to be an unnecessary tautology especially since there is no evidence of any irregularities or variants in the Greek text. Cranfield regards it as a "characteristically Semitic redundancy", a pleonasm (i.e., an unnecessary repetition) perhaps, as noted by Bruce Metzger "in accord with Mark's style", but neither offers any explanation of its possible significance.[5] Apart from Cranfield's rather dismissive comment, other commentators do not seem to find it an oddity, at least, not in the way I do. I therefore have to assume that for most it doesn't create the problem it causes me.

However, Mark does not say for what purpose the Elect had been chosen, whether their choosing was for salvation - the usual assumption, or whether some other subject, purpose or situation was in mind as he penned those words. Conceivably, he may have had in mind that the Elect had been chosen to pass through the time of tribulation which Jesus was predicting in the immediate context, or perhaps in addition they had been chosen to be protected from harm during that time.

Grant Osborne, in a chapter entitled, 'Exegetical Notes on Calvinist Texts',[6] points out that the Olivet Discourse is the only place in the Gospels where "elect" is used of Jesus' followers, so, he says, it is important to understand Jesus' use of the title in these contexts. He says

---

[4] Assuming Marcan priority, it would seem that Matthew deliberately omitted this phrase.

[5] Cranfield (1977), 21, 404, draws attention to the unmistakable 'Semitic flavour' of Mark's Greek throughout his Gospel. He also contrasts this Election phrase with the tautology of the previous verse (Mark 13:19): "the beginning of creation *which God created*" (RSV, but disguised in the NIV), which is also omitted from its parallel in Matthew 24:19.; Metzger (*TCGNT*), 93, note on Mark 12:23; Maclear, 20, cites as examples, Mark 1:13, 45; 3:26; 4:8, 33f.; 5:23; 6:25; 7:21; 8:15; 14:68.

[6] Grant R. Osborne in Pinnock & Wagner, 199. See also Mark 13:22, 27; Luke 18:7; Matthew 24:22, 24, 31.

that in the Old Testament the title is used to designate the people of God[7] and that many scholars have noted that in both testaments election "is conditional upon (one's) desire to retain it".[8] In other words, God does not choose individuals against their wills and the designation "elect" or "chosen one" does not guarantee that that person will never deny God's gift of salvation. I think it would be easier to accept such an understanding when election in the Old Testament is viewed as a divine choice for service of some sort or other, rather than for salvation.[9] However, Osborne claims that this seems to be indicated in the parallel passage in Matthew 24:24, where Jesus warns that the deception of the Antichrist will be so severe that "if possible, even the elect" will be deceived and as a result apostatise. I would say that, if true, that understanding of "elect" differs from New Testament usage elsewhere, notably Paul's. Admittedly, Osborne comes from a decidedly Arminian standpoint, but, if his view is valid, the designation, "elect, whom he has chosen" might then be construed as a way of saying 'those who are really saved'; i.e., those who in other contexts might still apostatise, but who have reached a place where apostasy is no longer a possibility.[10]

When the basic Election vocabulary was under consideration in Chapter 8, I speculated about the meaning of *eklektos* and its links and possible interchangeability with *agapētos* in certain contexts.[11] Thus, if the meaning of the noun *eklektos* can include a sense of belovedness as well as chosenness or even uniqueness, is it possible that the related verb *eklegomai* may sometimes, at least, have a similar range of meaning? Applying that possibility to this text may therefore provide a solution which resolves the tautology along the lines of "for the sake of the elect, *who are beloved*" or "special" in some way, rather than "*chosen*". Thus, when our English versions speak of the elect being chosen, might Mark have had in mind that they were beloved or choice rather than selected? That would certainly provide a reason why they might

---

[7] Ibid., Psalms 105:6, 43; Isaiah 65:9f.
[8] Ibid., quoting I. H. Marshall (1975), 52. See also Chapter 4, 70, 'Perseverance'.
[9] See Chapter 11a, 352.
[10] See Chapter 4, 70, 'Perseverance'.
[11] See Chapter 8a(iii), 211, and Appendix 2, 380.

be preserved through the perilous times ahead of which Jesus spoke. I tentatively suggest therefore that Mark envisages the Elect as the body of believers who will be called to live through tribulation but will nonetheless enjoy divine protection because they are *beloved*. Unfortunately, however, apart from the instances discussed in Chapter 8, I am not aware of any convincing evidence of similar usage in the New Testament, and none of the 32 occurrences of *exelexato* (ἐξελέξατο: aorist indicative 3rd person of *eklegō*) in the Septuagint, including four in apocryphal books, seem to carry a meaning beyond that of being chosen.

However, returning to Cranfield's comments about the Semitic flavour of Mark, another possibility presents itself, namely a semiticism such as is not uncommonly found in the New Testament where the infinitive absolute of a Hebrew verb is sometimes closely associated with another form of the same verb, or a cognate noun, and expresses emphasis. Although the idiom is paralleled in classical Greek, New Testament occurrences seem to be derived from the Septuagint, especially in Luke and Acts.[12] According to Jobes and Silva, the New Testament authors only use this peculiar combination of a finite verb with a participle of the same (or similar) verb in imitation of the Hebrew infinitive absolute construction when quoting the Old Testament directly,[13] and again, whether Mark can be shown to be quoting from the Hebrew remains debatable. However, there are two places where *eklektou* and *eklektos* occur in a similar kind of construction in the Septuagint. The Old

---

[12] David A. Black, "New Testament Semitisms" in *The Bible Translator* 39/2: April 1988, 215-23, cited by Michael D. Marlowe, 'The Semitic Style of the New Testament', <http://www.bible-researcher.com/hebraisms.html>, 2004 (accessed December 2022). Black offers a number of examples: in the Old Testament, Genesis 2:17: "you will surely die", renders the literal "dying you will die", and New Testament examples include Luke 22:15, where the expression "I have eagerly desired" translates *epithumia epethumēsa* (ἐπιθυμίᾳ ἐπεθύμησα) – literally, "with desire I have desired", and Mark 4:41, where *ephobēthēsan phobon megan* (ἐφοβήθησαν φόβον μέγαν) is translated, "they were terrified" – literally, "they feared a great fear".

[13] Jobes & Silva, 187 and n7: "The Hebrew construction is often rendered in the LXX with a finite verb preceded by a cognate noun in the dative case (e.g., περιτομῇ περιτμηθήσεται": "circumcised with circumcision" (NETS), "Genesis 17:13"). This approach would have seemed less strange to a Greek reader ... and is used in the NT, especially by Luke." See also Jobes & Silva, 270f.

Testament passages comprise firstly, a psalm of praise in 2 Samuel 22:26f.:

> To the faithful you show yourself faithful,
> to the blameless you show yourself blameless,
> to the *pure* you show yourself *pure*
> but to the devious you show yourself shrewd.[14]

This, with minor differences is repeated as Psalms 18:25f. [LXX 17:26f.].[15] The difference between these and Mark 13:20 is that each has a future verb (*eklektos esē*: ἐκλεκτὸς ἔσῃ) while Mark's verb is aorist (*exelexato*: ἐξελέξατο). Furthermore, NETS and the NIV translate the Septuagint *eklektos* as 'select' and 'pure' respectively. Thus, it may be debatable whether our *eklektous hous exelexato* is a case of this Semitic idiom or something like it.

The operative Hebrew word here is *barar* (בָּרַר) which occurs 18 times in 16 verses[16] with a variety of renderings in the Septuagint represented by nine different Greek words (see Table 2 below). Only twice in the Septuagint is the Hebrew *barar* translated with a clear sense of something being chosen or selected – both in 1 Chronicles. Whether Mark was aware of this range of senses in which *barar* was translated in the Septuagint, we cannot know: neither can we know whether he thought that *eklektos* and *eklegomai* in the Greek of his day always meant chosen in the sense of being selected. Given that we have already seen evidence that *eklektos* can mean 'choice' or 'select' (adjectives) or in some other way 'special',[17] I suggest then that we allow some of that

---

[14] LXX (Swete): μετὰ ὁσίου ὁσιωθήσῃ, καὶ μετὰ ἀνδρὸς τελείου τελειωθήσῃ καὶ μετὰ ἐκλεκτοῦ ἐκλεκτὸς ἔσῃ, καὶ μετὰ στρεβλοῦ στρεβλωθήσῃ, although verse 26 has τελείου τελειωθήσῃ ('perfect', 'complete'). NETS translates: "With the devout you will be deemed devout, and with the *perfect* man you will be deemed *perfect*, and with the *select* [possibly "excellent"] you will be *select*, and with the *crooked* you will be deemed *crooked*." (my emphases). The MT of verse 27 has עִם־נָבָר תִּתָּבָר (*im navar titavar*).

[15] LXX (Swete): μετὰ ὁσίου ὁσιωθήσῃ, καὶ μετὰ ἀνδρὸς ἀθῴου ἀθῷος ἔσῃ καὶ μετὰ ἐκλεκτοῦ ἐκλεκτὸς ἔσῃ, καὶ μετὰ στρεβλοῦ διαστρέψεις, although verse 26 has ἀθῴου ἀθῷος ('unpunished', 'faultless'). NETS translates: "With the devout you will be deemed devout, and with the *innocent* man you will be *innocent*, and with the *select* you will be *select*, and with the *crooked* you will *pervert*." (my emphases).

[16] See *BDB*, 140f.

[17] See Appendix 2, 380.

OTHER PROBLEMATICAL ELECTION TEXTS

latitude to this problematical verse. If the suggestion be correct that Mark was replicating a Hebrew idiom, whether consciously or not, the problem yet remains as to how it should be translated. I can only suggest that, if the redundancy produced by the idiom is merely to emphasise the chosenness of the Elect, the translation "for the sake of the elect" without qualification would be entirely adequate and appropriate.

Table 2: Translations of *barar* in the Septuagint:[18]

LXX Greek	Occurrences in LXX	References LXX [MT]	Translations NIV	NETS
aphoridzō (ἀφορίζω)	85 in 64 vs.	Isaiah 52:11	pure	separated
diakrivō (διακρίνω)	28 in 28 vs.	Ecclesiastes 3:18	test	discern
eklegomai (ἐκλέγομαι)	137 in 133 vs.	1 Chronicles 16:41	chosen	chosen
		Daniel 11:35 (Old Greek)	purified	purified
		Daniel 12:10 (Theodoton)	purified	choose
eklektos (ἐκλεκτός)	106 in 101 vs.	1 Chronicles 7:40	choice	select
		1 Chronicles 9:22	chosen	selected
		Esdras B 15:18 [Nehemiah 5:18]	choice	choice
		2 Samuel 22:27 (x2)	pure	select
		Psalms 17:27 [18:26] (x2)	pure	pure, select
elendzō (ἐλέγξω)	64 in 63 vs.	Ezekiel 20:38	purge	select
katharos (καθαρός)	151 in 141 vs.	Job 33:3	upright	pure
		Jeremiah 4:11	cleanse	clean
metastephō (μεταστρέφω)	24 in 24 vs.	Zephaniah 3:9	purify	change
odzus (ὀξύς)	20 in 20 vs.	Isaiah 49:2	polished	sharp
paraskeuadzo (παρασκευάζω)	15 in 15 vs.	Jeremiah 28:11 [51:11]	sharpen	equip

---

[18] Definitions for the Greek throughout the LXX may be found in Taylor.

Again, making the point that readers of the New Testament can be swayed by the predisposition of translators and commentators to attribute technical or soteriological meaning to vocabulary which can also be used in ordinary everyday ways, I suggest that the precise meaning of Mark 13:20 remains at best ambiguous, but that it *need* not refer to the chosenness of the elect for salvation. In any case, I do not believe that Mark would deliberately teach the election of individuals because that would contradict other strands of scripture. Accordingly, I suggest that translators should find ways of interpreting the text in agreement with the general teaching of the New Testament, which I maintain does not teach Particular Election.

b. Texts in John's Gospel

In Chapter 6, I critiqued Don Carson's *Divine Sovereignty and Human Responsibility: Biblical Perspectives in Tension*, where he deals with some of the passages from John's Gospel which follow in this section. An important conclusion he draws from his survey of John, indeed from scripture as a whole, is that both the sovereignty of God and human responsibility are clearly portrayed everywhere, hence the 'tension' of his title. He therefore refuses to accept any minimisation of the need and importance for people to freely respond to the grace of God, although he does add a caveat to what he understands by human freedom.[19] However, my contention is that he cannot accept human responsibility to entail 'absolute power to contrary' because his understanding of God's sovereignty is at fault. Unless the twin concepts – God's sovereignty and man's freedom of choice, are meant to stand in tension in scripture – a notion I find difficult to accept, then one or other (if not both) of Carson's concepts is certainly wanting, and in what follows I shall try to explain why I think that is so.

In John there are apparently a number of aspects of Election theology which I will list following some of Carson's own categories. They are

---

[19] Carson (2002), 209: "On biblical grounds ... I do not think that notions of human freedom which entail absolute power to contrary can be maintained. As a result, until better formulations come along, I prefer to adopt a view of 'free will' along the lines of 'free agency'".

passages which speak of (i) coming to Jesus, (ii) being chosen by Jesus, (iii) being given to Jesus by the Father and (iv) belonging to Jesus. Some of the conclusions I shall draw may be somewhat speculative, but, even though inconclusive, I nevertheless offer them as serious alternatives to the Reformed contention. Much of what follows and the conclusions I shall draw also relate to similar or parallel passages in the other Gospels, notably Matthew 11:25-30[20] and Luke 10:21-22, although there are no exact parallels in the Synoptics of any of the Johannine verses under consideration.

A number of the verses in the next three sections are from the Bread of Life Discourse in chapter 6 of John's Gospel.[21] Before looking at them, it will be helpful to make some general comments about the nature of that section of the Gospel, parts of which have given rise to a number of controversies which have created historical divisions in the wider Church.

Jesus' teaching on the Bread of Life contains language which is purposely meant to challenge the thinking of his hearers, specifically Pharisees, whom, it must always be borne in mind, would have been observant Jews in the main, and can therefore be regarded as believers from the Old Covenant dispensation.[22] Sadly, this aspect of Jesus teaching has not always been grasped by some gospel preachers who have lifted it out of context as though it applied directly to an unbelieving gentile audience. Nonetheless, the whole passage is about how one obtains eternal life, so it can be regarded as the gospel framed for the Jews of John's time. Furthermore, Jesus often used extreme language, including hyperbole. This is particularly evident when he spoke of eating his flesh and drinking his blood,[23] notions which would have been totally repugnant to his audience, as is made evident by their scandalised reaction. Divisions have also arisen in the Church which hinge upon how those particular words relate to holy communion or the mass.

---

[20] See Nicky Gumbel's comments, 193.
[21] John 6:25-59.
[22] My use of "dispensation" is not an admission of subscription to Dispensationalism: see above, 2 n4: some of its concepts are valid nonetheless.
[23] John 6:51-6.

However, three verses which contain similar phraseology provide a way forward in exegeting these puzzling sayings, I suggest, verses which contain the words, "I will raise them up at the last day".[24] Comparison of 6:40 and 54 shows clearly that they convey the same message:

> For my Father's will is that everyone who looks to the Son and believes in him shall have eternal life, and I will raise them up at the last day. (6:40)
>
> Whoever eats my flesh and drinks my blood has eternal life, and I will raise them up at the last day. (6:54)

I suggest then that a particular sacramentalist view, which takes the words of verse 54 absolutely literally, must be called into question. That aspect of doctrine isn't our primary concern, of course, but I simply want to draw attention to the fact that this section of John's Gospel contains a number of pitfalls which should alert us to the possibility of deliberately shocking language emanating from the lips of Jesus, as well as other difficulties which, without careful examination, might lead the unwary exegete astray.

i. Coming to Jesus: John 6:37, 44 & 65

In three places Jesus speaks of those who will come to him:

> All those the Father gives me will come to me, and whoever comes to me I will never drive away. (6:37)
>
> No one can come to me unless the Father who sent me draws them, and I will raise them up at the last day. (6:44)
>
> He went on to say, 'This is why I told you that no one can come to me unless the Father has enabled them.' (6:65)

At first sight John 6:37 might be thought to refer to *individuals* coming to Jesus. However, the NIV rendering of the first part of the verse; "*All those* the Father gives to me", disguises a Greek neuter collective, and therefore singular, expression, *pan ho* (πᾶν ὅ: 'all those' or 'all which') with its expected singular verb *hēxei* (ἥξει: 'will come'). According to

---

[24] John 6:39, 40, 54.

Barrett, this neuter singular expression, which is used where the plural masculine *pantes hous* (πάντες οὕς) would be expected if John was referring to individuals, strongly emphasises the *collective* aspect of the Father's gift of believers to Jesus.[25] In other words, because individuals are simply not under consideration, the expression cannot be interpreted to support the Calvinistic doctrine of Irresistible Grace, according to which *individuals* are irresistibly drawn to Christ. Rather, it is a *body* of people which is given to Christ. This is the case with most occurrences of the collective use of the participle *eklektos* incidentally. Notwithstanding that, however, in the latter part of verse 37, "whoever comes to me"; the masculine singular substantive participle *ton erchomenon* (τὸν ἐρχόμενον), literally, "*the one* coming to me", does have individuals in view.[26] And that could raise the question as to why Jesus might drive away those who had been irresistibly drawn to him.

The individual is also in view in John 6:44, "No one can come to me unless the Father who sent me draws them". This might appear to support the notions of Arminian prevenient or Calvinistic effectual grace that we need from God in order to respond to the invitation of the gospel. That prevenient grace should be available to all indiscriminately without reference to any supposed elect status is denied by Carson,[27] however, because when verse 6:44 is linked with 6:37a, and despite what I have pointed out with respect to the collective singular noun in 37a, he sees this drawing of the Father as being selective of individuals, and a grace dispensed to all, he says, would negate the negative note, i.e., the 'no one' and 'unless', of verse 44.

Discussions in the literature about the drawing of the Father encompass views both Reformed and of those who do not see soteriological predestination in John. Some draw attention to the use of the verb, *helkuō* (ἑλκύω: 'draw') which also occurs in John 12:32: "And I, when I am lifted up from the earth, will *draw* all people to myself". Klein points out that *helkuō* in its eight occurrences in the New Testament can be used either literally or figuratively. On the one hand, for example, a

---

[25] Barrett (1978), 294.
[26] See below, b(iii), 308.
[27] Carson (1991), 293.

fishing net or a person can literally be forcibly dragged against their will: on the other hand, a person can be drawn or attracted, usually voluntarily, to a place or an outlook by the force of reason or argument.[28] Carson says that here the drawing is selective,[29] the former sense, but he denies that the verb alone can be determinative of meaning; rather that the respective contexts of each passage must be taken into account. Klein argues from the context for the latter sense, however, saying that a divine "effectual drawing" is alien to the text:

> If any "selection" is going on here, the Jews themselves are doing it. By persisting in unbelief, they disqualify themselves from participation in eternal life. Nothing suggests that their unbelief is due to God's failure to "draw" (elect) them.
>
> Nothing here indicates that all whom God draws do in fact come to Jesus. It is one thing to say, "No one can come to Jesus apart from God's pull," but quite another to say, "God only pulls certain people, and all those he pulls do in fact come to Jesus." *John asserts only the former.*[30]

In the previous chapter, John 5, Jesus had criticised the teachers of Israel for their unbelief:

> You study the Scriptures diligently because you think that in them you have eternal life. These are the very Scriptures that testify about me, yet you refuse to come to me to have life.[31]

The onus is therefore upon each individual as to whether they allow the teaching of the Father to draw them or not. I suggest then that the context of John 6 is non-elective. The drawing is much like the reeling in of a fish on an angler's line, but there being no consideration as to how the fish became hooked in the first place – even fish can make choices.

I believe it is true that we can *do* nothing of ourselves before coming to Christ because we are spiritually dead. But the dynamic of it, I suggest, is not to resort to a prevenient or effectual enabling, nor a predestinarian understanding, but to the dynamic that, when we cease from resisting

---

[28] Klein, 114.
[29] Ibid., 115 n68; Carson (2002), 185.
[30] Ibid., 115 (his italics).
[31] John 5:39f.

the grace of God offered in the gospel and are willing to say 'yes', then the Holy Spirit becomes active within us because it is at that point that we become regenerate[32] – the new-birthing process has begun and the drawing of the Father is activated and becomes inevitable. The life-giving energising work of the Father through the Holy Spirit is therefore required in the process of our coming, as opposed to the initial triggering of the process or in the decision to come to Christ for salvation.[33] The drawing of the Father is through his teaching, his word, however. Whether John consciously had in mind the *logos* of his prologue here cannot be assumed with certainty. But if it was so, then we could infer that he meant us to understand that Jesus' own teaching was the Father's teaching and was the lure or bait, to use my angling analogy, which when heard, and by implication listened to and internalised, has drawing power, as Jesus went on to explain in the next verse (6:45): "Everyone who has heard the Father and learned from him comes to me". Thus, it is the one who hears and *responds* to God's word who comes to Jesus; both hearing and responding being acts of the will, of course. The one drawn must engage with the evidence and make a positive response – learning from God. John consistently identifies this response with having faith or believing. Klein thus finds himself in agreement with Rudolf Bultmann:

> It is now perfectly clear what is meant when it is said that the Father "draws" men to him. The *pas*[34] already indicates that it does not refer to the selection of a chosen few, but that any man is free to be among those drawn by the Father ... This 'drawing' occurs when man abandons his own judgment and 'hears' and 'learns' from the Father, when he allows God to speak to him.[35]

The third and final text in this section about 'Coming to Jesus' is John 6:65: "No one can come to me unless the Father has enabled them".

---

[32] Note that I use terminology such as 'regeneration', 'conversion', 'new birth', etc., differently from some Reformed writers. See Chapter 5, 144-6; also Appendix 3a(i), 400f., for the way John Piper and others use these terms.

[33] See the note in Chapter 7, 192f. n2, on Spurgeon's quotations regarding the holding of apparently irreconcilable doctrines.

[34] I.e., the 'everyone' of John 6:45.

[35] Klein, 115 n70; Rudolph Bultmann, *The Gospel of John: A Commentary* (Oxford: Blackwell, 1971), 231f.

Really, it says no more than that the Father is involved in the *process* of conversion, as one would expect. Jesus says that he had already told his disciples this, presumably referring back to his words in verse 44. However, Klein also draws attention to the verse immediately prior to 6:65 because it raises the question about Jesus' knowledge of who would believe and whether that might shed any light on 6:65. John 6:64 reads,

> 'Yet there are some of you who do not believe.' For Jesus had known *from the beginning* which of them did not believe and who would betray him.

The question it raises is whether the phrase "from the beginning" (*ex archēs*: ἐξ ἀρχῆς) implies that Jesus had pretemporal foreknowledge and therefore knew who would reject him, and whether that could imply that he had already decided to accept some and reject others. The phrase *ex archēs* is rare, occurring in the New Testament in only two places: here and in John 16:4, but the more frequently used construction translated "from the beginning" is *ap' archēs* (ἀπ' ἀρχῆς)[36] which usually means "from the beginning of time" or something similar when the context demands it. However, in John 16:4 and 6:44, "*ex archēs* plainly refers to the beginning of Jesus' association with the disciples and not to some eternal beginning".[37]

As already suggested, the Father's enabling operates from the moment a person ceases from resisting his overtures of grace. God then enables the new believer to progress further on what is actually a journey of faith which begins the moment he or she turns towards their Saviour, or desists from facing away, a journey which continues throughout the whole of their life. The process begins by looking to the Son[38] when a conscious commitment to Christ is made, and the journey continues on

---

[36] Matthew 19:8; 24:21; Mark 13:19; Luke 1:2; John 15:27 (has *ap' arches*, but clearly refers to the beginning of Jesus' ministry: "And you also must testify, for you have been with me from the beginning."); Acts 26:4; 1 John 1:1; 2:13; 3:8; 2 John 5 (twice); omitting 2 Thessalonians 2:13. See also John 8:25.
[37] Klein, 120.
[38] John 6:40. Cf. John 3:14f., where the 'lifting up' of the Son of Man is typified by the healing elevation of the snake in the wilderness. In the Old Testament context, Numbers 21:9 says that anyone bitten by one of the venomous snakes and who *looks* at the bronze snake will not succumb to the venom but will live.

as the believer is progressively drawn and is gradually transformed into the image of their Creator.

My conclusion therefore is that the wider context of these verses is not that of Irresistible Grace at all, but is actually about Perseverance. "Whoever comes to me I will never drive away" or "cast out" (6:37) is really about the preservation of those who have been received by Christ: *ekballō* (ἐκβάλλω), "wherever it is used in John, implies the 'casting out' of something or someone already 'in'" according to Carson.[39] Thus the context of John 6 emphasises the believer's choice when responding to the word of God in the obedience of faith. It is about the Lord enabling and preserving the believer onwards to the point of resurrection, and is not therefore an overseeing and enabling of the whole process governed by a prior divine predestining choice.

A number of other expressions should also be noted in the immediate context of these verses, each of which arguably implies an exercise of will on the part of a believer:

> "They will all be taught by God" (6:45a) – no one can be taught unless they are willing to receive the teaching;
>
> "Everyone who has heard the Father and learned from him" (6:45b) – likewise, hearing is a voluntary action;
>
> "Whoever eats of this bread" (6:51) – eating is also a voluntary action, and as we have seen, is equivalent to looking to the Son and believing: "My Father's will is that everyone who looks to the Son and believes in him shall have eternal life." (6:40)

Thus, the whole passage is set in a context in which individuals exercise choices about listening or eating, which are metaphors for spiritual responses they might make. It is important to recognise, nonetheless, that although the decision to be drawn lies entirely with the individual, only the Father can actually draw a person to Christ. However, the precedence of verse 6:35 should not be overlooked: "Whoever comes to me ... and whoever believes in me" strongly suggests that volition is involved in the coming and being drawn. The enabling is from God

---

[39] Carson (2002), 184.

(6:65) through the power of his word, but whether one comes to Jesus or not depends ultimately upon that person's willingness to listen and be drawn. It should also be noted, incidentally, that contrary to the Calvinistic doctrine of a Limited Atonement, the offer of new life is to all:

> This bread is my flesh, which I give for the life of the world. (6:51)

Therefore, in flat contradiction to the Reformed error of a Particular Atonement, the context of these sayings of Jesus in John 6 must be seen to be about the offering of himself to whomever, and the drawing and enabling terminology in the context should be interpreted in that light.

ii. Chosen by Jesus: John 6:70; 13:18; 15:16 & 19

Four verses in John refer to Jesus choosing his apostles:

> Have I not chosen you, the Twelve? Yet one of you is a devil! (6:70)
>
> I know those I have chosen. (13:18)
>
> You did not choose me, but I chose you and appointed you so that you might go and bear fruit—fruit that will last. (15:16)
>
> you do not belong to the world, but I have chosen you out of the world. (15:19)

Before reflecting on these important verses, it is worth considering what would have been the usual process of a rabbi acquiring his disciples (*talmidim*)[40] in first-century Judaism.[41] We cannot be absolutely certain about any of this because, apart from the New Testament, most of our information about Judaism at the time of Jesus comes from the *Mishnah*, an early third-century compendium of Jewish oral traditions from the time of Jesus and beyond. However, there is evidence that in first-century Judaism, promising young boys who had completed their bar mitzvah studies would have been encouraged to continue their

---

[40] Singular, *talmid* (תַּלְמִיד): occurs only in 1 Chronicles 25:8.
[41] Sources for this background information are articles by Doug Greenwold, 'Follow Me: A Contextual Reflection on Jesus' Call', 2008, at <www.preservingbibletimes.org>, and David N. Bivin, 'Jesus' Education', 2016, at <www.jerusalemperspective.com/articles/>.

religious education through the study of *The Yoke of Torah*. If still showing promise, they may then have become attached to a rabbi with whom they would spend a number of years, typically from the age of 17 to 20, honing their ability to relate what they had learned from Torah to the practicalities of everyday life. There is evidence too that the initial contact with a rabbi would not normally have been initiated by the rabbi himself, but by the student, presumably in consultation with his parents, although there would then be a rigorous selection process to undergo after which the chosen rabbi would issue the invitation to "Follow me". Doug Greenwold points out that the implication of that invitation would have been, "Come and be with me as my disciple **and submit** to my authoritative teaching".[42]

We can only speculate about the educational attainments of Jesus and his chosen disciples, but, according to David Bivin, it seems likely that they all would have had access to a fair standard of Torah education. Despite comments reflected by the Gospel writers which seem to point the other way,[43] Galilee, being a less rural region and more exposed to the outside world, offered better educational opportunities even than Judea in the first century. The lives of most of the disciples, however, would have been devoted to trades – fishing, tax collecting, etc., and the raising of families, rather than to the advancement of their education. Nonetheless, it seems probable that in company with most young Jews they still would have undergone a pre-bar mitzvah memorisation of the Hebrew Scriptures and would have acquired at least a working knowledge of the Hebrew language. It is therefore unfortunate and probably quite wrong to assume that they were unlearned and ignorant of the scriptures.[44] Indeed, had they progressed to the normal rabbinical apprenticeship, it would be assumed that they already knew the

---

[42] Greenwold: his italics and emphases.
[43] E.g., John 1:46; Acts 2:7.
[44] Bivin quotes from the text of a 1985 lecture given by Professor Shmuel Safrai (1919-2003) from the Hebrew University, a scholar in the fields of Jewish history, Talmud and Bible. Safrai quotes Jerome (342-420), who learned Hebrew from local Jewish residents in Bethlehem, as saying, "There doesn't exist any Jewish child who doesn't know by heart the history from Adam to Zerubbabel". Safrai admits that Jerome was prone to exaggeration, but adds, "In most cases his [Jerome's] reports have proved reliable."

scriptures and their further education would have been more about the testing of their understanding of God's word rather than their knowledge of it. Likewise, our knowledge of Jesus' religious education is very limited, but we do know that at the age of twelve he was found by his parents in the temple courts both asking and answering questions to the amazement of the rabbis.[45] We have no evidence that he was a *talmid*, however.

The point of this background speculation, if true, is that Jesus as a rabbi reversed the accepted protocol of his day. Greenwold says, "In that first-century Semitic culture, rabbis did not take the initiative to approach young men with the invitation to 'follow me'. But Jesus did." So, when those early disciples heard the young rabbi say that they had not chosen him, but he them (15:16), they may well have wondered what kind of rabbi he really was, because most probably they would not have gained the level of education which other potential *talmidim* might have achieved. That then raises the obvious question as to why Jesus said, "I chose you". Could it have been simply to underline his reversal of the conventional norm?

Back to the texts themselves, however. On first appearances, these sayings seem to apply first and foremost to Jesus' choice and calling of the Twelve to bear 'fruit' and that through their prayer lives that fruit should proliferate in terms of their apostolic and missional ministry. How that ministry was defined and worked out can be traced throughout the New Testament and early church period as the Church, first founded at Jerusalem, sent out its missionaries throughout the known world. However, it is not uncommon for these four sayings of Jesus, especially John 15:16, to be understood to apply also to the calling to *faith* of the disciples, and by extension to men and women generally. Thus, many writers take them to apply primarily, if not exclusively, to election to salvation and with universal scope for all believers throughout all time.

Before commenting on that aspect of interpretation, it is notable that the first two quotations, John 6:70 and 13:18, belong together in that

---

[45] Luke 2:46f.

both, within their respective contexts, refer to the betrayal of Jesus by Judas Iscariot. The former implies that Judas was indeed one of those chosen by Jesus, although 13:18, if removed from that general context, might imply the opposite - that Judas wasn't a chosen one, and that his inclusion among the Twelve would serve to underscore his eventual destiny as the betrayer. If the whole of verse 18 is considered,

> I am not referring to all of you; I know those I have chosen. But this is to fulfil the scripture: 'He who shares my bread has lifted up his heel against me.'

the opening words might suggest that Judas wasn't a chosen one, whether for apostleship or salvation, but that he would be the exception who would serve as a foil to the roles and destinies of the remaining eleven apostles, if not the whole of the believing community. However, with Carson, I would suggest the opposite, that Judas was indeed one of the chosen: "Have I not chosen you, *the Twelve?*" (6:70).[46] Klein points out that Judas must have shared the election status of the other eleven because after his suicide the apostles felt compelled to replace him with another whom the Lord had also chosen.[47] The exception to which Jesus refers follows from the previous verses where he had washed his disciples' feet, indicating that Judas was not clean (13:10) and that he would refuse to "do these things" (13:17); i.e., be unwilling to serve rather than be served, presumably. Thus, when Jesus says that he knows those he has chosen, he does include Judas, but being aware that his teaching did not apply to him, he singles him out as an exception because he knows them all in the sense that he understands their hearts and motives. Although these verses are some distance from chapter 15, John 13:18 certainly belongs within the same general context of Jesus' upper-room discourse contained in chapters 13 to 17, and in my view that reinforces the argument that his choosing of the Twelve was not about their ultimate salvation.

Carson, however, assumes without question that Jesus' choosing of the Twelve in 15:16 and 19 was to salvation.[48] There seems to be nothing

---

[46] Carson (1991), 470.
[47] Klein, 250; Acts 1:21-26.
[48] Carson (2002), 191.

specific in the contexts of these verses to indicate that that was the case, however, so to extrapolate their meaning in that sense is, I believe, an exegetical fallacy rather akin to the kind of interpretation where promises given under the Old Covenant are applied uncritically under the New[49] – the basic mistake of prosperity teaching, for example. Unless one is predisposed to read this whole context in salvific terms, therefore, it seems to me that there is nothing that would indicate other than a purely local meaning which applied to the specific situation of the disciples whom Jesus addressed, and it would seem unnecessary to apply these texts more widely than to the calling of the Twelve to their apostolic roles, a conclusion which I suggest is affirmed by Jesus' words to them in the same discourse – "And you also must testify, for you have been with me from the beginning."[50]

However, some further thought does need to be given to John's intentions as he recorded these words of Jesus. There is always the danger of reading the Gospels as though they were a kind of diary of sequential events; simply describing the words and deeds of Jesus as they happened and leaving nothing out. It is important to take into account that, in the activity of creating the Gospels, the sayings of Jesus are invested with deeper significance than a simple diarising of them would bear. In the form in which we find them in the canonical Gospels, in as much as they were deliberately selected for inclusion by the evangelists, they became, in effect, the words of the Gospel writers themselves. I am not suggesting that they invented Jesus' sayings, but what cannot be denied is that they selectively chose to report or emphasise some sayings and deeds and not others. John virtually admits as much himself when he comments that "the whole world would not have room for the books that would be written" to contain accounts of all the things Jesus did and presumably all that he said too,[51] and we know of at least one saying of Jesus which does not appear in the Gospels.[52] The volume of dominical sayings must have been vast, and no doubt Jesus would have

---

[49] See below, b(iii), 308.
[50] John 15:27.
[51] John 21:25.
[52] Acts 20:35. There may, of course, be other sayings which the New Testament writers did not specifically attribute to Jesus.

repeated much of his material as he moved from place to place, perhaps introducing variations to suit different audiences and situations. Such repetition would have increased the memorability of his teaching in a culture which was largely dependent on oral transmission and memory rather than on written records, of course.[53] The point I am making is that the selection exercised by the Gospel writers from what must have been a vast wealth of material must therefore have related to each of their respective purposes in writing. Undeniably, those purposes would contain a high degree of simply reporting, but inevitably also with theological emphasis in mind as they pursued their objectives. That must have been especially true of John who is widely regarded as the most theologically reflective of the four Gospel writers.

The precise purposes with which the different evangelists wrote can only be guessed at ultimately, but in the case of John, there is a much clearer sense of an evangelistic purpose than with the Synoptic Gospels. I agree with Carson that John's Gospel is in essence a kind of evangelistic appeal to fellow Jews,[54] and in accordance with that, particularly striking is his interplay of singular and plural pronouns in the dialogue between Jesus and Nicodemus in John 3 and in the reflection that follows that exchange. Of particular note is the plural 'you' of 3:7 – "*You* [*humas*, ὑμᾶς] must be born again",[55] which clearly points beyond the person of Nicodemus to the nation, or perhaps to the ruling class of Jews that he represented, reinforcing the idea that John was writing to persuade fellow Jews, perhaps including proselytes and God-fearers, of the truth of Jesus as their promised Messiah.

That said, however, the question remains as to whether John could have had a wider purpose as he reported those words of Jesus about the

---

[53] See Walton & Sandy.
[54] Carson (1991), 90ff. Stephen Neill, 338, reports that the distinguished Jewish Rabbinics scholar, Israel Abrahams, once significantly claimed that John was "the most Jewish of the four". Smalley, 140ff.; 59ff., summarises views on John's audience and possible Jewish influences: a number of earlier scholars regarded John as being written for Jews, whether unbelieving, Diaspora or believing, but more recent scholarship tends to cite a more Hellenistic audience or the 'Johannine church', presumably in Ephesus. Carson (1991), 91, says that the view that John's Gospel was aimed at evangelising Jews and proselytes "has not been popular, but is gradually gaining influence".
[55] Also, John 3:11, which I take not to be Jesus' words, but John's.

Twelve being chosen for their future apostolic roles, as distinct from the majority of his followers to whom those particular roles were not assigned. First of all, since the emphasis is about Jesus' choice of them for fruit-bearing of a particular kind, rather than for salvation, it seems likely that John would have wanted to underline the importance of the apostolic function of those men, an importance which should not be minimised seeing that they would carry the primary responsibility for the custodianship and dissemination of the facts about Jesus, both for the Church and for the unevangelised world, until such time as that role would be superseded by their Gospels and letters, the canonical writings of the New Testament. That writing process would only come to completion towards the end of the lives of those of the apostles who would survive to write or supervise the writings which would go under their names; John being, by general agreement, the last to do so. Furthermore, the idea of a group of people being chosen by one whom John clearly had described in his prologue as being none other than God incarnate, would, I suggest, resonate with the people of Israel, the chosen people of God. It strongly appeals to me that the calling of the Twelve to bear fruit echoes the purpose of God's election of Israel – that the whole world would be blessed through Abraham's seed.[56]

The other question which remains, apart from the possibility of a Reformed soteriological understanding of them, of course, is whether John intended these reported words of Jesus to bear universal scope for all disciples into the future. Without doubt, all believers in Jesus are called to 'bear fruit', especially in the terms implicit in Jesus' words – 'fruit' in their preaching and teaching ministries and in the efficacy of their prayers, but more importantly, the 'fruit' of regeneration demonstrated through righteousness in both their own and other lives saved through their ministry.[57] This is especially clear in the immediately preceding context where Jesus teaches about the fruitfulness of those who abide in him,[58] the true vine, and John, it seems, links the fruit of regeneration there with the fruit to which Jesus called the Twelve to bear in 15:16.[59]

---

[56] Genesis 12:3; Galatians 3:8, 14. See Chapter 9b, 267ff..
[57] Carson (1991), 523f.
[58] John 15:1-8.
[59] K. Smith, 46, identifies John 15:1-17 as a chiastic unit.

However, whereas fruit-bearing for those who abide in Christ is assured, according to the NIV, the Twelve are said only to be appointed that they *might* bear fruit. Just as history showed that Israel did not always bear the fruit intended in God's covenant with Abraham, there was no certainty that the apostles would succeed in doing so either, their fruitfulness being dependent on their faithfulness in prayer in Jesus' name.[60] John 15:16 might therefore be seen to embody or imply an *invitation* to become regenerate rather than the *fait accompli* of the Reformed interpretation.

The fact that Judas Iscariot was numbered among the chosen apostles strongly suggests a limitation on the context I am advocating;[61] indeed, I would say that his inclusion proves the case against the Reformed view. Who, in any case, would readily admit to the possibility of being a 'devil' (*diabolos*: διάβολος), as Jesus refers to Judas in 6:70? But the possibility that John was addressing, albeit obliquely, the Israel of his day, and perhaps also believers in general in the future, suggests to me that salvation was not his purpose here. If anything, it should have been received by John's (assumed) Jewish audience as a challenge to respond to Jesus' choice of any of them to bear fruit. In other words, Jesus' choice of the Twelve in John's mind as he wrote was possibly more about the fulfilment of Israel's mandate to fill the earth with "the knowledge of the LORD as the waters cover the sea", and thus bring blessing to the nations,[62] rather than being about the salvation of some of Jesus' disciples. This, it seems to me, accords with one of John's preoccupations, i.e., that of demonstrating the supersession of the old wine of the Old Covenant by the New.[63]

Ultimately, the question of John's purpose in reflecting particular words of Jesus can only be a matter of informed speculation. However, I think expositors and preachers of the Word would do well to consider

---

[60] Carson (1991), 524.
[61] Shank (*Elect*), 40, however, regards John 6:70 as belonging to a context different from 15:19, which he asserts does refer to election "to salvation rather than to the Apostolate". It is worth bearing in mind that Jesus addressed Peter personally (the verb is singular) as 'Satan' in Matthew 16:23||Mark 8:33.
[62] Isaiah 11:9; Habakkuk 2:14; Genesis 12:3.
[63] Also John 1:16: see below, b(iii), 308.

more carefully, than is sometimes the case, the ultimate purpose of the biblical writers, especially those who reported the very words of Jesus, even though the purposes of some of his words may not always be crystal clear.

Comment also needs to be made on John 15:19, however: "You do not belong to the world, but I have chosen you out of the world", because the idea of being chosen out of the world has also occasioned a number of conflicting views. For example, contrary to the view I am advocating, and claiming that "here the election is to salvation rather than to the Apostolate", Robert Shank quotes Frédéric Godet:

> *Exelexamēn, I have chosen*, indicates here the call to faith, not the apostleship; by this word *to choose* Jesus would designate the act by which He has drawn them to Himself and detached them from the world.[64]

And later in his book, Shank adds that by its very nature Christian discipleship invites the enmity of the world. Thus, he says,

> the choice to the Apostolate, as well as the call to salvation, imposed the circumstance of ethical separation from the world, and this is the import of Christ's words rather than fiat reprobation of most of the world for whom He was about to die'.[65]

Thus, setting aside the question of whether Jesus' calling of the Twelve was to salvation, which we have already considered, there are a number of issues combined in these two statements which may betray some rather confused thinking about the ultimate end of the world. In its opposition to God's purposes, the world certainly is destined for destruction, but, as hinted at by Shank, some Reformed exegetes apparently suggest that since the disciples were saved by being chosen out of the world, the world must therefore lie in reprobation.[66] What is meant by that requires some examination, and careful elucidation of the meaning of 'the world' in its Johannine contexts is therefore called for.

---

[64] Shank (*Elect*), 40; quoting F. L. Godet, *Commentary on the Gospel of John* (Grand Rapids, MI: Zondervan, 1879-80), II, 302 (his italics).
[65] Ibid., 180.
[66] Although he makes no citations so far as I can see.

OTHER PROBLEMATICAL ELECTION TEXTS

In John's Gospel 'world' (*kosmos*: κόσμος) is a very common and important word and concept.[67] In general it does not signify the totality of creation[68] as we would understand the universal concept of *cosmos* today, but rather the world of people and their affairs on earth, especially as they stand in opposition to God's purposes. For example, even in John 1:10 the world, which came into being through the Word, is personalised and is capable both of knowing *and* not knowing its Maker. Sometimes the expression is '*this* world',[69] being not simply equivalent to the rabbinic 'this age', in contrast to a future world, but rather standing in contrast to another world, a world which already exists. In other words, 'this world' is a lower world corresponding to the world *above*,[70] a relationship which some have described as a 'vertical' concept. John deliberately combines these two ideas, so he presents Jesus both as the means by which an eschatological future is anticipated, as in the Synoptic Gospels, but also as an envoy from the other heavenly world. Because 'this world' contrasts with that heavenly realm, it hates Jesus and his disciples, yet the world below into which he comes is also the scene and object of his saving mission,[71] a mission which is grounded in God's love for that world.[72]

It is noteworthy that in John 3:16 the *kosmos* is divided between those who believe and those who do not, at least potentially so, and it is that division which accounts for the apparently contradictory things which are said about the relationship between Christ and the world. On the one hand, he is the Saviour of the world,[73] and it is emphatically repeated that he did not come to judge the world,[74] but on the other hand, other texts say that he did come to judge the world[75] and he overcame

---

[67] The summary of *kosmos* which follows is largely based on Barrett (1978), 161f. The use of *kosmos* in John's other writings - 1 and 2 John and Revelation, is entirely consistent with his usage in the Gospel.
[68] E.g., John 11:9, "this world's light"; 17:5, "before the world began", 17:24, "before the creation of the world" and 21:25, "the whole world would not have room".
[69] John 8:23; 9:39; 11:9; 12:25, 31; 13:1; 16:11; 18:36.
[70] See especially John 8:23; 18:36.
[71] John 1:9f.; 3:17, 19; 6:14; 8:26; 10:36; 12:46; 16:28; 17:13, 18; 18:20, 37.
[72] John 3:16.
[73] John 4:42; cf. 1:29; 3:17; 6:35, 51; 8:12; 9:5.
[74] John 3:17; 12:47.
[75] John 9:39; 12:31; cf. 3:18; 5:30; 8:16, 26; 12:48.

it.[76] Furthermore, the enemy who is overthrown is the "the prince of this world"[77] and those who choose to remain under his power are destined to be judged and condemned along with him.[78] Thus it can be said both that an outcome of Jesus' ministry was that the world would not recognise him, the Son, the Father or the Holy Spirit,[79] but at the same time his aim that the world should know and believe[80] would be fulfilled at least in part. In contrast to all of this, however, in two places *ho kosmos* does in fact mean 'everyone'.[81]

Some care must therefore be exercised when assertions are made about the reprobation or not of the world. Clearly, the context is important, but, just as with the Elect, and in contrast to the Elect, the world in the main simply represents a category of humanity comprising individuals out of harmony with, or even in opposition to God's purposes. In that sense, the world does lie in reprobation, although individuals belonging to the world still have a choice to make whereby they may transfer their citizenship from 'this world' below to the heavenly sphere by being born from above.

A difficulty arises, of course, when Jesus' words in John 15:19 about the apostles being chosen out of the world are considered, especially if my assertion is correct that Jesus' choice of them was not for salvation, but specifically for apostleship and fruit-bearing. One might have to draw the conclusion that, if salvation is not the issue here, and if Jesus was not calling them to salvation and that the world represents those opposed to God, then they would still be part of that reprobate world. That cannot be a correct assumption because Jesus had told them in almost the same breath that they no longer belonged to the world. I think the answer lies elsewhere,[82] but clearly, in light of the summary given above, some careful distinctions need to be made about the meanings of *kosmos* in its different contexts in John's Gospel.

---

[76] John 16:33.
[77] John 12:31; 14:30; 16:11.
[78] John 3:18; Revelation 20:10, 15.
[79] John 1:10; 14:17; 17:25.
[80] John 17:21, 23.
[81] John 12:19; 18:20.
[82] See below, b(iii), 308.

Thus, when Jesus tells the Twelve that he had chosen them out of the world, I believe he simply means that the role for which he had chosen them stands in contradiction to the general purposes and disposition of the rest of humankind, and for that reason they no longer belong to the world and would therefore be hated by it. There can be no doubt that any true believer who commits to the cause of Christ, will encounter opposition, simply because by so committing themselves they offer opposition to the 'prince of this world' as well as to those who, in the main, unwittingly align themselves with his evil purposes. Carson, however, goes so far as to say that the *purpose* of these verses, John 15:18 and 19, is to "eliminate the surprise factor when persecution does break out", and that because John was writing "primarily in theological categories ... these verses are relevant in any historical situation where the church faces the fires of persecution".[83] He is correct, of course, in saying that anyone who chooses Christ will place themselves at enmity with the world, but I doubt that that was the reason why Jesus spoke those words: I suggest they were for encouragement, rather than to warn the Twelve.

In summary then, whereas Carson and others see these passages about Jesus' choosing in a predestinatory light, about election to eternal life, as well as having significance for the immediate circumstances of the Twelve, I am not persuaded that these words of Jesus have that wider significance for election to salvation. I find the inclusion of Judas Iscariot among the chosen to be a major stumbling block to accepting that here we are dealing with soteriological matters. That is not to say, of course, that Judas could not have repented and made a commitment of faith before or even during his suicide, although I judge the testimony of scripture suggests otherwise.[84] I believe that these words of Jesus should be taken simply at face value – that he chose the Twelve out of their former work-life situations to flourish in their newfound tutelage under him, and that they do not necessarily imply anything for any other disciples except in the sense that all true disciples of Jesus will

---

[83] Carson (1991), 524f.
[84] See John 17:12; Acts 1:25: the early church evidently believed that Judas was not saved at the end: "this apostolic ministry, which Judas left to go where he belongs", although, admittedly, that is ambiguous.

encounter similar kinds of experiences. In particular, what Jesus says about them not choosing him has nothing to do with the choice they and we each must make when responding to the gospel. Rather, it would be parallel to a Christian responding to the call of God to a particular sphere of service or ministry. Many who have responded to such a call would testify that although persuaded of the reality of a divine call on their lives it would not necessarily have been their choice to have taken that particular course of service had they not been called.

iii. Given to Jesus by the Father: John 6:39; 17:6, 9, 24 & 18:9

There are five references to the Father giving people to Jesus in John's Gospel:

> that I shall lose none of all those he has given me. (6:39, cf. 6:37)

> I have revealed you to those whom you gave me out of the world. They were yours; you gave them to me and they have obeyed your word. (17:6)

> I pray for them. I am not praying for the world, but for those you have given me, for they are yours. (17:9)

> Father, I want those you have given me to be with me where I am. (17:24)

> I have not lost one of those you gave me. (18:9)

Of the three verses from John 17, Carson says, "it is clear that the giving by the Father of certain men to the Son *precedes* their reception of eternal life and governs the purpose of the Son's mission" so "the priority of God's election is thus vigorously affirmed".[85] He also says elsewhere that because God gave the disciples to Jesus (17:6), they must have "belonged to God antecedently to Jesus' ministry".[86] Thus, throughout John's Gospel, Carson assumes without question, rather than by demonstration (it must be said), that this kind of language is to be understood in terms of election to eternal salvation.

---

[85] Carson (2002), 187.
[86] Carson (1991), 558.

However, I would propose a different approach to interpreting these passages which resorts neither to Calvinism nor to Arminianism. Neither does it force the biblical data onto the Procrustean bed which many moderate Calvinists adopt; that which exhorts us to hold conflicting ideas in dynamic tension, the prevailing Reformed mindset from which I feel even Carson has not been able to free himself. There is a far simpler, and I suggest, more obvious approach, which takes into account the salvation-historical context of Jesus' sayings, and which should provide explanation sufficient to avoid having to juggle with theological and philosophical conundrums.

The way I suggest these passages may be squared with the thesis that God does not predestine men or women to salvation is to observe that the circumstance of these sayings lies at the historical and spiritual intersection of the times or dispensations of the Old and New Covenants. Carson, giving advice to would-be preachers says, "it is essential to locate the Gospels in their proper place in the stream of redemptive history".[87] I totally concur, and will attempt to do just that. An example might be the way John reflects on the disciples' failure to understand some of Jesus' words and actions only to grasp their meaning later on.[88] It is important to appreciate that when Jesus uttered these sayings recorded by John it could be said that they were not yet fully into the New Covenant dispensation, although John, writing something like a half century after the death and resurrection of Christ, certainly postdating all of Paul's letters and probably all of the other New Testament writings too, definitely stood in the era of the New Covenant. But the disciples in the context of the Gospel belonged to the Old in the sense that, even before they were called to follow Jesus, they were believers under the dispensation of the Law of Moses. I therefore agree with Carson that before they were given to Jesus, they already belonged to God. It would seem perverse for Jesus to choose men to join his band of pupils who were not observant Jews, and even Judas Iscariot and Simon the Zealot must have shown some sort of promise, at least that of being willing to accept Jesus' invitation to follow him at the start of his

---

[87] Ibid., 101.
[88] E.g., John 8:27; 10:6; 12:16; 13:7; 20:9.

ministry. We don't know how Simon fared ultimately, but clearly Judas didn't go the distance and, like many Jews both then and since, he failed to make good his 'adoption', becoming instead, in Jesus' words, a 'son of perdition'.[89]

My point is that it is not necessary, and should not be done in any case, to read back into the text a later theological development concerning Election which applied primarily to the dispensation which was dawning at the point in time when Jesus was 'glorified'.[90] I suggest therefore that what qualified these men, so that it could be said of them that they belonged to the Father, was the same which could be said of all other Old Testament saints or any Jew for whom faith was of the heart rather than, but not without, external observance of the Mosaic Law and Jewish traditions. I suggest that the significance of this observation is reinforced when the likely purpose of the writing of the Gospel, on which I have already commented, is borne in mind. It is true that all things and people belong to God by dint of their common standing as created beings, but I think it goes deeper than that, and we can say that these Jews were God's possession because they were faithful believers in him under the economy of Moses. It is also worth pointing out that we cannot write off people in terms of Election simply because they belong to a period prior to Christ's 'glory'. To do that on a Calvinistic understanding would consign them, without exception, to reprobation without the possibility of conversion.[91]

It seems an obvious question to ask, that although John wrote theologically as he looked back over that half-century to those three years he had shared with Jesus, why he should not have recognised that he was bridging two distinct dispensations of grace, the very phenomenon which apparently he does recognise in the prologue of his gospel. John 1:16 in the NIV 2011 edition correctly reads,

Out of his fullness we have all received grace *in place of* grace

---

[89] The KJV of John 17:12 has the Hebraism, "son of perdition" while the NIV has "the one doomed to destruction": *huios tēs apōleias* (υἱὸς τῆς ἀπωλείας), rather than *huiothesia* (υἱοθεσία): Romans 9:4.
[90] John 12:16, etc.
[91] See above, b(ii), 296.

already given.

whereas the 1984 edition has,

> From the fulness of his grace we have all received *one blessing after another*.

Unfortunately, earlier editions of the NIV, following the majority of translations before it, failed to recognise that "one blessing *after* another", possibly implying the succession of a number of blessings, ought to read "one blessing *instead of* another",[92] the first 'blessing' (better, 'grace') being the Old Covenant, and the second being the New, as verse 16, paralleled antithetically by 17, amply demonstrates:

> For the law was given through Moses;
> grace and truth came through Jesus Christ.

John does therefore seem to be fully aware of the location of the events he is recording in historical or dispensational terms, "their proper place in the stream of redemptive history" as Carson puts it, so our first resort should be to recognise the fact and understand what he wrote in the light of it.

It is worth underlining this point because John 1:16 and 17 form an important part of the prologue of the Gospel where John introduces the themes of his core message which he will go on to elaborate throughout the succeeding chapters. Indeed, the theme of transition from the Old to the New Covenant dominates the second part of the prologue (1:14-18) and finds possible early expression in the Gospel's first 'sign' of water changed to wine at the marriage at Cana.[93] The fact that interpreters have, on the whole, failed to recognise the true meaning of the Greek *anti* in verse 16 suggests to me that this aspect of John's message, may not have been fully recognised by exegetes generally – that,

---

[92] Greek: χάριν ἀντὶ χάριτος (*charin anti charitos*), where *anti* means 'instead of'. This does not suggest a succession or a piling up of many graces and certainly not 'in opposition to', as *anti* might be construed in English, but the replacement of one grace by a better grace. The most recent edition of the NIV recognises this error and has "grace in place of grace already given". Carson (1991), 132, says, "the most convincing view takes *anti* in one of its most common uses (and by far the most common in the LXX) to mean 'instead of'."

[93] John 2:1-11. See also above, b(ii), 296, on John 15:16.

although John regarded the Law as God's gift of grace to Israel, in Christ a better and more perfect grace had been given to them through the gospel in the advent of the *logos*.[94] This is especially significant in view of the probable purpose for which the Gospel was written, that is, as I have already suggested, as a kind of evangelistic appeal to fellow Jews.

This emphasis for the Gospel as a whole comes into yet sharper focus when the chiastic structure of the prologue is examined. Quoting from the most recent edition of the NIV and setting out the passage as arranged by Kym Smith, note the correspondences and contrasts between verses 14b to 15c and 15d to 17 respectively:

> full of *grace and truth*.
> (*John* testified concerning him.
> He cried out, saying, 'This is the one I spoke about when I said, "He who *comes after me*
> has *surpassed me*
> because he was *before me*"'.)
> Out of his fulness we have all received grace *in place of* grace already given.
> For the law was given through *Moses*;
> *grace and truth* came through Jesus Christ.[95]

---

[94] Cf. 2 Corinthians 3:7-9; 1 Timothy 1:8, etc.
[95] John 1:14b-17. The Greek text laid out in the same way is:

> πλήρης χάριτος καὶ ἀληθείας.
> Ἰωάννης μαρτυρεῖ περὶ αὐτοῦ
> καὶ κέκραγεν λέγων·οὗτος ἦν ὃν εἶπον ὁ ὀπίσω μου ἐρχόμενος
> ἔμπροσθέν μου γέγονεν,
> ὅτι πρῶτός μου ἦν.
> ὅτι ἐκ τοῦ πληρώματος αὐτοῦ ἡμεῖς πάντες ἐλάβομεν καὶ χάριν ἀντὶ χάριτος
> ὅτι ὁ νόμος διὰ Μωϋσέως ἐδόθη,
> ἡ χάρις καὶ ἡ ἀλήθεια διὰ Ἰησοῦ Χριστοῦ ἐγένετο.

Italics are intended to clarify the correspondences and contrasts between the respective tiers of the chiasm. See Kym Smith, 19, 198. Smith's whole thesis is that John's Gospel is based on 70 chiasms. Although some of his conclusions may seem fanciful, his account is worthy of consideration. See George Mlakuzhyil's scathing critique in *Christocentric Literary-Dramatic Structure of John's Gospel* (Rome: Gregorian & Biblical Press, 2011), 141ff. The presence of a huge amount of chiastic material throughout the Gospel is self-evident, and on Smith's analysis, John's prologue comprises the first two chiasms of the Gospel (1:1-13 and 14-18). This seems to hold water

This kind of chiastic analysis has become a focus of scholarly debate, especially when it comes to delimiting the bounds of literary units in the biblical text. Today, few would deny their presence throughout much of scripture in both poetry as well as in many prose passages, but different authors might use slightly different criteria for delimiting and describing the chiasms they find. Although such criteria are descriptive and should only be used prescriptively with care, what cannot be denied is that these structures clearly exist in the text.

Thus, in answering Jesus' call to follow him, the disciples began a journey of adventure through the intersection or overlap of the two covenants during which they would emerge into the dawn of the New Covenant through a faith which would continue to develop as they underwent the discipling of Jesus and as they responded to the challenges of his ministry as they shared their lives with him, but above all of that, their reception of the gift of the Holy Spirit at Pentecost. That journey would bring them through issues which would bedevil the New Testament Church – issues to do with their Old Covenant heritage in Judaism such as circumcision, food laws, sabbaths and festivals, and so on, with which most of them would struggle. Thus, to say that they already belonged to the Father need not imply anything of a New Covenant understanding of Predestination or Election, nor even of trusting Jesus for salvation – simply that they were believers under the 'grace' made available to them through Moses, pre-echoed in Abraham's faith, and most of them would become believers under the new 'grace' in Jesus, of course. The donation of them to Jesus by the Father is therefore simply an expression of divine providence.

iv. Belonging to Jesus: John 10:1-18

The Good Shepherd passage of John 10 also needs to be considered in

---

even on a cursory examination. See also R. A. Whitaker, *John*, The IVP New Testament Commentary Series (Leicester: IVP, 1999), 45, who recognises the claims of P. F. Ellis, *The Genius of John: A Composition-Critical Commentary on the Fourth Gospel* (Norwich: Liturgical Press, 1984) and B. Barnhart, *The Good Wine: Reading John from the Center* (Chicago, IL: Paulist, 1993) that the Gospel of John is based on "an intricate series of chiasms".

view of the following comment by Carson:

> Those who are given to Jesus must in some sense peculiarly belong to him. The connection is made for us in 17.9f.: those the Father gives to Jesus are God's, and all that belongs to Jesus belongs to God and vice-versa. Theoretically, belonging to Jesus could describe the believer's position *after* coming to faith. However, as with the idea of being given to Jesus, John more commonly speaks of a *prior* belonging that is unequivocally predestinatory. This idea is expressed in several different passages in the fourth Gospel, but nowhere more forcefully than in John 10.[96]

Some aspects of this claim have been addressed already, particularly in the context of John 6, but chapter 10 must also be considered if for no other reason that Carson goes on to say that "no chapter in John (except perhaps John 6) has been the subject of such wide-ranging debate".[97]

When Jesus says, "I am the good shepherd; I know my sheep and my sheep know me" (10:14), I would understand those sheep to be those who by faith had become elect, so the context is soteriological. In view of the Reformed tendency to equate Foreknowledge with divine choosing, it is worth pointing out that this verse says both that Jesus *knows* his sheep and that his sheep *know* him. The same verb (*ginōskō*) is used in both cases, as in verse 15 following: "just as the Father *knows* me and I *know* the Father". In this context *ginōskō* cannot therefore equate with the choosing of Jesus' sheep because we would then have to say that his sheep chose him; not that I would find that problematical, but we would have to understand that Jesus and the Father chose each other too.[98]

The relationship described, especially the voice recognition criterion: "his sheep follow him because they know his voice" (10:4), is clearly one of familiarity, security and of belonging in the most profound of ways – and this as distinct from those who are robbers, hirelings or wolves (10:8 and 12). Exegetes debate the identity of the other sheepfold (10:16), but light is shed on the passage if it is understood that three

---

[96] Carson (2002), 188 (his italics).
[97] Ibid.
[98] Klein, 128. See Chapter 8c, 219, 'Foreknowledge'.

sheepfolds are envisaged. The first represents Judaism, overseen by false shepherds and gatekeepers - the contemporary Jewish religious leaders, notably the Pharisees, to whom the discourse was addressed, and who had cast out the blind man of chapter 9 from the synagogue. From that first sheepfold, Jesus calls Jews and God-fearers, who will hear his voice, into the safety of his own sheepfold (10:7). Many accepted Jesus as their Messiah, not because they were divinely predestined to salvation, but because they were already disposed to accept the new revelation founded upon what they already believed about Messiah. Their inclusion in Jesus' sheepfold, was for them a matter of personal choice, even though for most it would also have been in continuity with the religious culture in which they had been nurtured from birth. If that supposition is correct, they, in Judaism, lay the earlier side of the dispensational line from the New Covenant. With respect to the identity of the third sheepfold, my preference, with Carson, is to Gentiles who will respond to the Christian message as proclaimed by the apostles.[99] The Good Shepherd discourse is therefore a sharp criticism of those who kept Israel in thrall through insistence on observance of the minutiae of the Law, both Moses' and their own:[100] yet another evidence of John's evangelistic thrust.

Whereas many commentators see predestination to salvation everywhere in this passage, I would once again suggest that there is nothing of the sort here necessarily. The main emphasis in any case is upon the character and role of the shepherd, not the sheep. Beyond the call of Jesus, how the shepherd will acquire his sheep is not the important question addressed in this context. For that we must look elsewhere in scripture.

---

[99] Carson (1991), 390: "The category presupposed by 'other sheep' is *Gentiles*, even if *in practice* the Gentiles most open to evangelism were God-fearers and others profoundly sympathetic to the Jewish heritage of monotheistic revealed religion. They are amongst those John is seeking to evangelize." This view is reinforced if the sheepfold of John 10:1-6 is regarded as Judaism, while that of 10:7-10 represents Jesus' own domain.

[100] Matthew 23:13-15, etc.

c. Acts 13:48: "Appointed for eternal life"

> all who were *appointed* for eternal life believed.

For many of a Reformed frame of mind, this text clearly indicates that certain gentile people from Pisidian Antioch, on hearing the preaching of Paul and Barnabas, believed in Jesus because they were foreordained to receive eternal life. However, the word translated 'appointed' is the relatively uncommon word, *tetagmenoi* (τεταγμένοι), the perfect passive participle[101] of *tassō* (τάσσω), which, according to the *BAGD*, when used with an abstract noun means "to belong to" or "to be classed among those possessing".[102] It is noteworthy that the *BAGD* does not list 'preordained' or 'foreordained' among its possible meanings.[103] The *NIDNTT* gives the word the possible meanings of 'arrange' or 'appoint' and says that *tassō* is common in classical Greek where its meaning was primarily military, meaning to draw up troops or ships in battle array, and so to post or station them. Consequently, the verb came to mean "to direct or appoint someone to a task, and to arrange, set up and put in order things or plans which would otherwise be indefinite and uncertain".[104] Care must be taken not to afford undue emphasis to etymology in determining the meaning of *tassō*, but some authors do suggest that in the New Testament it is nuanced by the sense of military arrangement which is found in its classical usage.

F. F. Bruce, a self-confessed Calvinist,[105] prefers the sense of 'enrolled' or 'inscribed', a meaning also found in some Greek papyri.[106] To belong to or be classed among those possessing eternal life certainly suggests an association with the Elect even before the gospel had been heard and responded to, and Bruce links that association with the enrolment of the names of believers in the Book of Life,[107] implying that

---

[101] Traditionally understood as a 'divine passive': W. G. MacDonald in Pinnock, 227.
[102] *BAGD*, 806.
[103] Neither does H. G. Liddell & R. Scott's classical dictionary according to L. S. Keyser; quoted by Fisk, 111.
[104] *NIDNTT*, 1.476.
[105] See his Foreword to Forster and Marston.
[106] Bruce (1952), 275.
[107] Bruce (1972), 110; e.g., Luke 10:20; Philippians 4:3; Revelation 13:8, etc. See section i. below, 343, on Revelation 17:8.

their salvation was predetermined. Other authorities disagree, however. Dean Henry Alford, following a reading (presumably the KJV) which translates *tetagmenoi* as 'ordained', says that it is not the usual term given that meaning, and he prefers 'disposed to' as fitting the context better. Similarly, Alexander Maclaren says that 'adapted' or 'fitted' would be more relevant and accordant with the context, so that the reference then would be to the "frame of mind of the heathen, and not to the decrees of God".[108]

Another solution advocated by L. S. Keyser, and, according to Fisk, confirmed by Vine, is that due weight should be given to the Greek word order where, "It is said of those who, having believed the Gospel, 'were ordained to eternal life'."[109] In other words, the ordination or appointment to eternal life of those Gentiles was the *consequence* of their believing, a view which would certainly agree with my way of thinking. However, I have found no Bible version, even amongst the oldest English versions, which follows the Greek word order in that way: all interpret Luke's words in the sense that belief was consequent upon and followed 'appointment'. That doesn't mean Vine and others are incorrect, of course, even though the weight of scholarship seems to be against them, but it does militate against what could be a simple decisive denial of the Reformed interpretation.

It seems possible, if not probable, that the Latin Vulgate's rendering of Acts 13:48 skewed Augustine's own understanding of this text – not only Augustine but the majority of the early Latin-speaking western Church, for which, on the whole, Greek was not a first language. Hence, the KJV and translations following it, as well as the Church in later times, and particularly those more disposed to an Augustinian view of things, have adopted that understanding even despite the likelihood that they would have rejected the authority of the Vulgate which translates *tetagmenoi* as *praeordinati* ('preordained').[110] On the other hand, according to Fisk and Shank, the Eastern Greek Fathers, who had

---

[108] Alford and Maclaren are cited by Fisk, 109ff.
[109] Fisk, 111; Vine, 1:68; Greek: καὶ ἐπίστευσαν ὅσοι ἦσαν τεταγμένοι εἰς ζωὴν αἰώνιον.
[110] The Vulgate of Acts 13:48b runs: *et crediderunt quotquot erant praeordinati ad vitam aeternam.*

a superior grasp of the language in which Paul wrote, and who habitually used the Greek text of the New Testament, as did the Palestinian church, did not interpret Acts 13:48 to be about the selection of individuals by God for salvation.[111] Nonetheless, it has become the standard Reformed interpretation and therefore the prevailing understanding in the contemporary western Church.

In view of the range of opinions suggested for the meaning of *tassō*, it is probably worth summarising its usage in the New Testament. It occurs only eight times, five of which are in Luke's writings.[112] The NIV adopts a range of meanings – 'appointed', 'being set' or 'placed', 'assigned', 'arranged', 'established' and 'devoted'. The related verb *prostassō* (προστάσσω), which occurs seven times in Matthew, Mark and Acts, always carries the sense of commanding, instructing or ordering, as does the more common *diatassō* (διατάσσω), the latter probably having a more directive or authoritarian sense.[113]

Acts 13:48 is the only place in the New Testament where *tassō* has been construed as meaning anything like divine foreordination, so we are left with the question as to why Luke chose not to use a more precise theological turn of phrase, perhaps using a word selected from the vocabulary of Election already reviewed, if that was what he had meant to say.

It is hard to identify a single English verb or phrase which would adequately translate *tassō* in every case, but so far as Acts 13:48 is

---

[111] Fisk, 111f.; Shank (*Elect*), 183f; a view they attribute to Henry Alford, *The Greek Testament*, 153f., who, in turn quotes from Christopher Wordsworth, *The New Testament in the Original Greek, with Introduction and Notes* (Oxford & Cambridge: Rivingtons, 1877), 108.

[112] Matthew 28:16: the mountain where Jesus had *told them* to go; Luke 7:8: the centurion being a man under authority ('*being set*' implied, but not in the parallel Matthew 8:9 which has *eimi* (to be) in place of *tassomenos*); Acts 13:48: Gentiles having been *appointed* to eternal life; 15:2: Paul and Barnabas *appointed* to go up to Jerusalem; 22:10: Paul being told all that he would be *assigned* to do; 28:23: Jews in Rome *arranged* to meet Paul on a certain day; Romans 13:1: the authorities *established* by God, and 1 Corinthians 16:15: the household of Stephanas which *devoted* itself to the service of the saints.

[113] Other cognates also occur, e.g., *tagma* (τάγμα): a 'class', 'division', 'military rank' (*hapax legomenon*); *hupotassō* (ὑποτάσσω): 'to be subject to', 'to subordinate' (38x), and *taxis* (τάξις): 'an order', e.g., a priestly order (9x), all of which have military connotations.

OTHER PROBLEMATICAL ELECTION TEXTS

concerned, something like the rather tautologous expression, "all who were *going to believe* for eternal life believed", might fit the bill, or, to quote F. B. Meyer, who seemed to home in on the military ordering nuance from classical Greek, "they discovered that they were in line with an eternal purpose"[114] – but certainly not an Election-laden phrase which many Bible versions imply, whether intentionally or not.

Howard Marshall writes,

> It could be taken in the sense that God had predestined certain of them to believe (cf. 16:14; 18:10). But it could also refer to those who had already put their trust in God in accordance with the Old Testament revelation of his grace and were enrolled in his people, or perhaps it means that the Gentiles believed in virtue of the fact that God's plan of salvation included them. Whatever be the precise nuance of the words, there is no suggestion that they received eternal life independently of their own act of conscious faith.[115]

Marshall's words simply demonstrate the fact that what Luke had in mind when he wrote will probably always evade definitive interpretation. While there are evidently a number of possible credible explanations of Luke's phrase, there is no consensus on the exact meaning of the verb in question.

Despite all this, however, it should be noted that Luke is referring to Gentiles, although not God-fearers, whom we assume would have associated with the synagogue-attending Jews. Those *appointed* for eternal life should by rights have been Jews, of course; ordained to eternal life in a sense similar to the way Paul describes Israel in Romans 9:4: "Theirs is the adoption to sonship; theirs the divine glory", etc. That was God's foreordained purpose for Israel, his Chosen People. In other words, it was always God's purpose that his ancient people should embrace their Messiah and enter into his predestined purposes along with gentile believers who would be 'grafted in' to the rootstock of the true Israel.[116] It was the Jews of Pisidian Antioch who ought therefore to

---

[114] F. B. Meyer, *Through the Bible Day by Day* (American Sunday-School Union, 1914), Vol. 6.
[115] I. H. Marshall (1980), 231.
[116] Romans 11:17.

have responded naturally and positively to the gospel proclaimed by Paul and Barnabas because they had been conditioned by their own scriptures, as well as their cult and culture, to eagerly welcome the news of their long-awaited Messiah. Once again, context comes to the rescue as Klein underlines the fact that "The Jews' failure to gain eternal life is ascribed to their rejection of the Word of God, not to God's previous decision to keep their names from the book of those predestined to believe." He draws attention to the irony of Paul and Barnabas' words to their fellow Jews in Acts 13:46:

> We had to speak the word of God to you first. Since you reject it and do not consider yourselves worthy of eternal life, we now turn to the Gentiles.

"So," continues Klein, "the Jews disqualified themselves; it was not God's failure to elect them." It is important to note the implication of this statement that the Jews' disqualification was a matter of their own choice. W. G. MacDonald observes that this episode is preceded by Paul's warning to the Jews whom he had addressed the previous Sabbath day: "Take care that what the prophets have said does not happen to you", followed by Habakkuk 1:5:

> Look, you scoffers, wonder and perish,
> for I am going to do something in your days
> that you would never believe, even if someone told you.[117]

"There is no hint of determinism in such an admonition", he says, and "The passage that follows points up their recalcitrant unbelief".[118] By the same token therefore, and in contrast to the Jews' choice to refuse the gospel, the Gentiles who were saved that day had accepted the message and the gift of eternal life, not because of some divine selection, but by their own choice. This all fits the larger context of Acts, of course. Luke's pattern for salvation was that people made the decision to call upon Jesus or reject him; those accepting the word qualifying themselves, and those rejecting the word disqualifying themselves from eternal life. Thus, citing Peter's Pentecost sermon, Klein shows that by

---

[117] Acts 13:40f.; Habakkuk 1:5.
[118] W. G. MacDonald in Pinnock, 227.

using the middle form of the verb *epikaleō* when quoting Joel 2:32: "everyone who *calls* on the name of the Lord" (Acts 2:21), Peter emphasised that *all* those who *call on* the name of Jesus *for themselves* will be saved.[119] On the other hand, some, although by no means all, of the city's Gentiles, responding to the gospel they heard from the lips of the Jewish evangelists, and realising that the message was for them as well as for the Jews, adopted the right of appointment and were *disposed to* receive eternal life in place of the unbelieving Jews, and so they enthusiastically believed the gospel. In any case, Luke's use of *hosoi* (ὅσοι: "all who" or "as many as") cannot refer to a specific number who were appointed but indicates those Gentiles who responded as distinct from those who did not.[120] Furthermore, I am certain that Luke did not believe that individuals were foreordained to receive eternal life, as some would read this text, for no better reason than his reporting of Paul's words to representatives of the Ephesian church later on in Acts 20:

> Therefore, I declare to you today that I am innocent of the blood of any of you. For I have not hesitated to proclaim to you the whole will of God.[121]

Clearly, Luke and Paul alike understood that the eternal destiny of men and women was contingent upon their hearing and obeying the gospel. From what he said to the Ephesian church, Paul's belief, perhaps with Ezekiel 33:7-9 in mind, was evidently that, had he withheld the gospel invitation from them, he would have been in grave danger of being guiltily responsible for the final demise of those who never accepted the gospel invitation – eternal separation from their Creator; nothing at all to do with whether or not they had been chosen in the sense our Reformed brethren would claim. In Paul's view, people had to hear the gospel and respond to it. If they never heard it, they would risk eternal loss.[122]

Thus, it seems that Luke deliberately contrasts the opposite reactions of

---

[119] Klein, 83 (his italics).
[120] Ibid., 82; citing Gerard Delling, 'τάσσω', *TDNT*, 8.28.
[121] Acts 20:26f.
[122] Cf. Acts 18:6; 1 Corinthians 9:22, etc.

the Gentiles and Jews of Antioch that day. Both groups made deliberate choices, for and against, respectively, and Luke chose his vocabulary accordingly to rhetorically reinforce that ironic contrast. Again, I would strongly suggest that we need to sweep away the Reformed mindset, which may have been reinforced, among other things, by the Vulgate reading of the text and which I believe has almost brainwashed many of us, and allow whatever the true meaning really is to conform with the overall New Testament line I am advocating.

d. Acts 18:10: "I have many people in this city"

because I have many people in this city.

Earlier I referred to this text as an example where I once had heard a well-intentioned children's worker speak about children and young people attending evangelistic events at her church. Clearly, with a Reformed understanding, she said that in the course of time it would be expected that some of them would come to faith, and it would then become apparent which of them were among those whom the Lord had chosen from the locality.

In view of the stage Paul had reached in his evangelisation of Corinth, it seems unlikely that these "many people" were yet believers in Jesus. But that cannot rule out the possibility that they were devout Jews with a heart-faith in God, and who, known by God, would respond positively to the gospel, much as we saw in connection with passages in John's Gospel which refer to those given to Jesus by the Father.[123] Accordingly, Howard Marshall and others understand this text to refer to an as yet unconverted group of people (*laos*: λαός) in the city of Corinth whom God knew would respond to the gospel preached by Paul and his associates.[124] If that is so, then the issue is about foreknowledge rather than foreordination. Here again, the noun, *laos* is a singular collective noun with a singular verb, *esti* (ἐστί) – 'a people', rather than individual persons. But it would not make sense in English to translate the expression as 'a much people' or 'a many people'. In whatever way that

---

[123] See section b(iii), 308, above.
[124] I. H. Marshall (1980), 296.

OTHER PROBLEMATICAL ELECTION TEXTS

semantic puzzle may best be resolved, however, it remains that Christ's words to Paul did not envisage many *individuals* as such, but rather a *body* of people regarded by the Lord as being in some way his. Accordingly, pointing out that *laos* "is the regular word for the chosen people, Israel (almost without exception)", and that in Corinth there was "a new community, taking the place of the Jewish population", Alfred Marshall suggests that the phrase should be translated "I have a great people".[125]

The context of the verse is the Lord Jesus encouraging Paul in a vision not to neglect the proclamation of the gospel in Corinth because, despite fierce opposition, there would yet be those who would respond and place their faith in Christ. Although the emphasis isn't upon the dynamics of their coming to faith – whether they would be irresistibly drawn or not, the question does remain as to whether Luke had that in mind as he wrote. Clearly, God knew who would become his by their exercise of faith: the question is whether they had a choice in the matter. Robert Shank has this to say about their identity:

> they were people who, not having heard and believed the Gospel as yet, already were positively disposed toward God – people in whom the Gospel would find ready acceptance. Peter's words in the house of Cornelius are pertinent at this point: "Truly I perceive that God shows no partiality, but in every nation any one who fears him and does what is right is acceptable to him" (Acts 10:34f. RSV). The point is not that such people do not need the Gospel, but rather that such people are disposed to believe the Gospel even before they hear it because they are positively disposed toward God, a fact of which God takes account, as the scriptures imply.[126]

In support of the possibility of that kind of phenomenon, Shank goes on to reflect on stories from mission fields where people have eagerly anticipated the arrival of missionaries because their hearts were already hungry for the knowledge of God.

I confess I am drawn to Shank's view that Luke uses a somewhat unusual turn of phrase in a non-Reformed way. The meaning hinges on the

---

[125] Alfred Marshall, xvi, 549.
[126] Shank (*Elect*), 196.

verb 'have' – "I *have* many people in this city" – whether it means to be possessed as objects owned by God, or whether the sense is looser, something akin to "I have so many people on my side" (JB), for example. What can be said with certainty is that this text cannot support a Reformed view because individuals are simply not in view. God chooses neither individuals nor particular groups of people for himself unless it is to perform specific roles or tasks here on earth.

e. Romans 8:29-30: Predestined to be called?

> For those God foreknew he also predestined to be conformed to the image of his Son ... And those he predestined, he also called; those he called, he also justified; those he justified, he also glorified.

These verses embody the *Golden Chain*, a phrase coined by William Perkins in his book, *A Golden Chaine*, which first appeared in 1591 - "the unbreakable sequence of salvation spelled out by the apostle Paul".[127] According to Thuesen,

> the entire chain of events - election, vocation (calling), faith, adoption, justification, sanctification, and glorification - was like a series of "inseparable companions" that "goe hand in hand." If a person could be assured that she had experienced one of them, then the rest would unfailingly follow.[128]

Similarly, to experience any one of the links in the chain could be taken as reliable evidence that a person was already the beneficiary of the first link - election - the assurance of salvation.

We have already seen that it is not necessary to interpret divine foreknowledge in a Reformed way.[129] These verses may therefore be reworded thus:

> For those God had already got to know he ordained that they should become like his Son ... so he called them and justified them and glorified them.

The crucial issue or contention here, it seems to me, is the idea that our

---

[127] Thuesen, 34f.
[128] Ibid., 66, quoting William Perkins, *A Golden Chaine*, 1591.
[129] See Chapter 8c, 219, 'Foreknowledge'.

calling from God is claimed in Reformed teaching to be *consequent* upon our being foreknown and predestined, as could be argued from Romans 8:30. In other words, the Reformed view is that only those who have been predestined to salvation are called by God, that is in the sense that they receive the gospel invitation effectively. I hope I have already shown from our earlier examination of the Predestination and Foreknowledge vocabulary [130] that, although divine Foreknowledge certainly does encompass our salvation, Predestination does not. Paul deliberately uses two different verbs for those two terms which have quite different meanings, so, our predestination relates to aspects of our regeneration which are not yet completed, and which result from our incorporation into Christ and the body of the Elect. Verse 30 therefore simply describes the processes we go through until we arrive at our completion – the final state in glory. If we are truly born again, we have been predestined to be conformed to Christ's image. As we saw in Chapter 8, we have to be called in order that we may respond to that calling and so enter into God's eternal salvific purposes, but God also assigns to us the status of 'called', which, as I have suggested, is very similar, if not identical, to our status of being elect.[131] But that transformative process of sanctification – conformity to Christ's image or the image of our Creator,[132] must continue until Christ appears again in glory – as verse 30 continues: "those he called, he also justified; those he justified, he also glorified", a string of aorist verbs with mantic force, i.e., speaking predictively of the future.

It is worth considering the broader context of these verses in Romans 8, however. The latter half of the eighth chapter of Romans contains some very interesting material which has given rise to a fair amount of controversy. For example, Paul mentions the struggle and tendency to decay that "the whole creation" is going through whilst awaiting the revelation of "the sons of God" (8:19). In this context he also uses the word 'adoption' (8:23) and writes about the 'good' promised to those who love God and are called according to his purpose (8:28).

---

[130] See Chapter 8, 200ff.
[131] See Chapter 8d, 238, 'Calling'.
[132] Romans 8:29; 1 Corinthians 15:49; 2 Corinthians 3:18; Colossians 3:10.

In popular hermeneutics, and therefore in common Christian parlance, both our adoption and 'the good', are frequently seen as promises we have already received, or in the case of the latter may receive imminently. Thus, for example, we may hear believers equating their rebirth with their adoption – "God has adopted me/us into his family", having in mind, perhaps, a concept of the adoption of orphaned or abandoned children into the care of new adopting parents. They interpret Paul's use of the idea of adoption anachronistically, whereas the Roman practice of Paul's day was to do with the adoption of adults, adoptees who would inherit the estate of their adopted father. There has been debate over which model of adoption Paul may have had in mind; whether a Hebrew or Roman-Greek model. It might be surprising if Paul had chosen the latter, even though in Israel adoption was never practised in the legal form familiar in the gentile world,[133] the exception perhaps being the case of levirate marriage where a posthumous son would perpetuate the name and inheritance of his mother's dead husband.[134] In any case, the adoption Paul writes about appears to be about part of the *future* 'hope' in which we were saved (8:24) and the inheritance rights of the adopted son, not about our induction into God's family.

It is probably worth elaborating on this point because the noun *huiothesia* (υἱοθεσία) is treated as if it were a verb in the NIV of Ephesians 1:5, similar to the way *eklektos* and *eklogē* are translated in some modern versions.[135] When read in context, however, it becomes apparent that adoption is linked to conformity to the likeness of Christ, and, as I have suggested, the issue is often clouded by the assumption that it is just another way of describing the new-birth and our entry into the kingdom.[136] However, careful exegesis of the five contexts in which *huiothesia* occurs[137] suggests that the adoption to which saints are predestined is a present status which, like many other aspects of our Christian

---

[133] Both Brendan Byrne and James Scott make strong cases for a Jewish basis for Paul's concepts of adoption and sonship. See my forthcoming *Pie in the Sky When You Die?* in which I argue for a Roman model more familiar to his readership.

[134] Cranfield (1975), 379f.; Bruce (1982, *Galatians*), 197.

[135] See Chapter 8a(ii), 204, and 8a(iii), 208.

[136] See W. A. Elwell in Hawthorne & Martin, 227.

[137] Romans 8:15, 23; 9:4; Galatians 4:5; Ephesians 1:5, but never in the Septuagint.

journey and glorification, awaits completion at the *parousia*, and has far-reaching eschatological implications. This is most clearly seen in Romans 8:23 where, in the context of our future hope, the apostle writes of believers eagerly awaiting their adoption as sons, a transformation which he equates with "the redemption of our bodies", which I take to mean our resurrection and the completion of our conformity to Christ.

Romans 9:4, where Paul enumerates the advantages his own people, the people of Israel, possess is important in this connection: "Theirs is the adoption to sonship". Indeed, I suggest that this may be the key for our understanding of what Paul means by *huiothesia* because it links with the discussion of Romans 9 (section f. below, 332) where the continuity of relationship between the Abrahamic and New Covenants is advocated. In Paul's mind, the possession of 'the adoption' is a feature of what it was for Israel to be in covenant relationship with God under the Mosaic economy. Thus, rather than our adoption as Christians being something new and divorced from Israel, it should best be understood as in continuity with Israel's adoption. Both our entry into the status of the Elect and of adoption come through faith in Christ, and neither, I suggest, is used as a synonym for *becoming* a Christian. Equally, adoption and election belong first and foremost to faithful Israel, and those who are Gentiles may enter into both states of being in continuity with those saints who have gone before from Abraham and beyond.[138] It is probably not incorrect therefore to speak of our adoption as our *becoming* sons of God because the Spirit of adoption is conferred upon us as we respond to the gospel and receive our new birth.[139] However, Paul's usage of the word seems to depend more upon its etymology which is presumed to be a compound of *huios* (υἱός: 'son') and the verb *tithēmi* (τίθημι: 'to put', 'place' or 'lay') or perhaps the noun *thesis* (θεσίς: 'a placing').[140] The emphasis therefore is more upon our *status* of

---

[138] See also Chapter 8a(iv), 213, *klēroō*.
[139] Romans 8:15. Vine, 1:32, says, "God does not adopt believers as children; they are begotten as such by His Holy Spirit through faith".
[140] Vine, 1:31; *thesis* does not occur in the New Testament. Vine, 1:68, adds 'to appoint' or 'to ordain' among the wide semantic range of *tithēmi*, and cites John 15:16: "I chose you and *appointed* you so that you might go and bear fruit" (ἐγὼ ἐξελεξάμην ὑμᾶς καὶ ἔθηκα ὑμᾶς ἵνα ὑμεῖς ὑπάγητε καὶ καρπὸν φέρητε). Note that reliance upon etymology can often be misleading because the meanings of words often evolve away from their

sonship, in other words, those who will inherit, a status which will be fully realised in the eschaton, rather than our entry into sonship in the here and now. Furthermore, to emphasise the latter – *becoming* will only obscure the more important emphasis in Paul's usage on our *being* sons of God.

The second issue, the 'good' of verse 28, is also commonly understood to be experienced during our ongoing earthly Christian pilgrimage, at least in part. In other words, the thought is that we will find ourselves in a better place some day before we die, and we will be able to look back on the bad times we are currently experiencing with joy when we receive the fulfilment of the promise. I suspect that this way of thinking may be influenced, at least to some extent, by the ying-yang of eastern religions or the folk-religion idea that "what goes round comes round". That kind of dynamic, the experience of good times balancing out former bad times, is, of course, not unknown in the life of a believer, although I would doubt that the bad ever quite eclipses the good, but I don't believe that is what Paul meant and it certainly has not been promised to us unless, that is, we plunder promises made to Israel under the Old Covenant.[141] We can experience great joy in the Lord on occasion, but how, to use an extreme example, could the promise be realised if the bad we experienced was what brought our earthly life to an end, as is the experience of many contemporary martyrs of the Church each passing day? If there is good to be experienced it has to be in the next life, and that is exactly what I believe Paul meant. What is more, that good will more than compensate for the bad times experienced before our resurrection.

Again, context is determinative, and it is important to see that the meaning of the whole passage of Romans 8:18 to the end of the chapter is governed by what precedes it in verse 17:

> Now if we are children, then we are heirs—heirs of God and co-heirs with Christ, if indeed *we share in his sufferings* in order that we may also share in his glory.

---

original coinage and usage.
[141] Psalms 91 being a prime example.

OTHER PROBLEMATICAL ELECTION TEXTS

Paul introduces this governing concept of suffering in verse 17 as a consequence of our being brought into the status of sonship and heirship.[142] From verse 18 on, he brings into focus the experience of suffering, which is the expectation of all true believers. That was the very obvious lot of many Christians in Paul's day and as it has been throughout the world to the present day as the Church experiences apparently unprecedented oppression under fundamentalist Islamic and other religious or politically motivated antagonistic regimes. Therefore, what he says about creation being freed from its bondage to decay, about our adoption, and about the good which results from being called of God is all projected into the future – it is yet to be. This is especially clear in verses 23 and 24 where Paul equates our adoption with "the redemption of our bodies", saying that it is the *hope* in which we were saved. In other words, none of it is fully within our present experience, and our resurrection and conformity to the image of Christ (8:29) to which God has predestined us, are fundamentally part of our future being.

That being the case, it is worth revisiting our understanding of Foreknowledge in this context.[143] The NIV of Romans 8:29 says,

> those God foreknew he also predestined to be conformed to the image of his Son.

Nothing is said here about God's foreknowledge of those predestined as being before the foundation of the world or similar, as in 1 Peter 1:20 where the reference is to divine foreknowledge of Christ in any case.[144] The Reformed take on this verse is just that, however; that God's foreknowledge of us is from what some would term "eternity past". It seems to me, however, that the verb, "foreknew", is best construed as being about a relationship with God, but that this foreknowledge of his people is from the perspective of that future hope of Romans 8, a future that may best be seen in the sense of those he already knew or was in relationship with. Thus, I would suggest as a better translation,

> those God knew already [or 'had got to know'] he ordained that they

---

[142] E.g., Mark 10:30; Acts 14:22; John 16:33; Hebrews 12:7ff.; Psalms 116:15, etc.

[143] See Chapter 8c, 219, 'Foreknowledge'.

[144] Note, the verb in 1 Peter 1:20 is "foreknown" rather than "chosen" as in the NIV; see Chapter 8c, 219, 'Foreknowledge'.

should become like his Son.

The verses that follow from 8:31 to the end of the chapter only really make sense if they are seen as the joyful anticipation of what will transpire at the *parousia* in the face of all the opposition and evil that the world and the Devil can muster against the Church of God. Our present experience, according to Paul, is to "face death all day long" (8:36), and even though there will be joyful reprises and respites along the way, it will only be when Christ finally appears, and when the true sons of God are finally revealed, that these future promises will be fully realised. The whole passage therefore points up the antithesis between sufferings and glory (8:17), and any Election concepts that fall into the passage, especially the foreordained conformity to Christ's image, must be interpreted as coming to ultimate fulfilment in the future rather than in the present, and certainly not in the past.

That being the case, we need then to consider what we are to make of the next part of the text – verse 30:

> And those he predestined, he also called; those he called, he also justified; those he justified, he also glorified.

I have already alluded to Perkins' *Golden Chain* which sees the elements of this list of predestined outcomes as a series in strict order of their eventual fulfilment. There seems to be in Calvinism a preoccupation, if not an obsession, with ordering events in the divine dispensation such that the sequence of the divine decrees takes on an importance which many may wonder at, and which has generated a whole baffling vocabulary of its own. Wayne Grudem in his *Systematic Theology*, provides a list of the *ordo salutis* or Order of Salvation, the sequence of events which is accepted by many Reformed writers:

1. Election (God's choice of people to be saved),
2. The gospel call (proclaiming the message of the gospel),
3. Regeneration (being born again),
4. Conversion (faith and repentance),
5. Justification (right legal standing),
6. Adoption (membership in God's family),
7. Sanctification (right conduct of life),

8. Perseverance (remaining a Christian),
9. Death (going to be with the Lord),
10. Glorification (receiving a resurrection body).[145]

This is basically the *Golden Chain* amplified with stages added by some Reformed interpreters.[146] We have seen already that some of the terminology involved in this list is used differently by Calvinists compared with many other evangelicals.[147] For example, I would say that election (1), or, as I would prefer, the inclusion into the Elect, follows the gospel call (2); that regeneration and justification (3 and 5) happen at the point of our response of faith, conversion (4) being a term which describes that whole spiritual transaction; that sanctification, perseverance and continuing regeneration (7, 8 and 3) form integral parts of the Christian's pilgrimage, and adoption and glorification (6 and 10) describe the ultimate goal of the whole process. On the other hand, Grudem says that the sequence begins with election (1); stages 2 to 6 and part of 7 are involved in becoming a Christian; 7 and 8 work themselves out in this life; 9 occurs at the end of this life and 10 occurs when Christ returns. I am not even sure that my own ordering of these events can be quite so precise, but some of the differences between my own and Grudem's ordering demonstrate a disparity based, not only on the Reformed usage of soteriological vocabulary and a theology based on assumed divine decrees, but on a mindset that seeks to categorise and pigeon-hole every aspect of the doctrine.

However, referring back to Romans 8:30, and in summary, I would reiterate that predestination is not to salvation, but to the ultimate goal of glorification, and the 'links' in the *Golden Chain* may or may not form a sequence in order of their occurrence as Paul writes them down. There are three elements in particular, the order and significance of which I think need to be clarified – calling, justification and glorification. I have made a case for calling in this context being not so much the call of the gospel, neither general nor effectual, but the placing of the divine name of ownership upon the person who comes in faith to

---

[145] Grudem (2007), 670.
[146] Thuesen, 222.
[147] See Chapter 5, 144-6, and Appendix 3a(i), 400f., on the nature of saving faith.

Christ.[148] That and justification simultaneously place us in relationship with God as his sons and, whereas our whole Christian experience has been a gradual process of sanctification (hopefully), the end result is our glorification as we share what it is to enter into the inheritance of Christ – again an element in Paul's list that must instantly happen as we receive our resurrected bodies. We *are* thus predestined to be called, as I have subtitled this section of the chapter, an expression which I take to mean to truly, finally and fully become God's beloved sons – adoption complete.

f. Romans 9 to 11: God can do whatever he likes!

Chapters 9 to 11 of Romans are often regarded in Reformed thinking as the key biblical passage which demonstrates the sovereignty of God in the election of individual believers. The inference is that individuals can have no choice in the matter (9:19ff.). But not all interpreters agree that Paul makes any reference at all to divine Predestination here. W. G. Kümmel, for example, maintains that these chapters are entirely about the ultimate fate of Israel:

> An exposition that pays close attention to the context [Romans 9-11] ... shows that these statements in their entirety do not at all intend to speak of the problem of divine predestination, of the election or reprobation of men.[149]

In earlier chapters of Romans, Paul had laid down the foundation of individual justification on the basis of individual faith in Christ. What he addresses in these three chapters is what for him was the vexed issue of God's dealings with his own and Christ's natural kin, the privileged people of Israel (9:4f.), and, in particular, whether God had rejected them since the dispensation of grace had been inaugurated.

There is increasing recognition among scholars that Romans is indeed a real letter written into a specific historical situation, the situation at Rome, and out of Paul's own circumstances. Thus, as we saw when we

---

[148] See Chapter 8d, 238, 'Calling'.
[149] Kümmel, 232.

considered the rigorous passages of Hebrews,[150] there is much more interest in the *Sitz im Leben* of the New Testament correspondence today, and commentators increasingly apply historical-critical methods to their exegesis. Commentators on Romans debate many things,[151] but among them two issues in particular which have a bearing upon how chapters 9 to 11 should be construed. Firstly, whether the letter was written to Jewish or gentile Christians, or both, and, secondly, whether these three chapters form merely a digression from Paul's main theme, or whether they are actually the heart of his letter towards which he had been working progressively throughout the preceding chapters. David Pawson argues convincingly, I would say, for the latter; that these chapters do indeed form the heart of Romans and that they directly address the specific issue and context into which Paul was writing.[152]

When the church at Rome was founded it was undoubtedly Jewish in constitution, probably comprising a mixture of Jews, proselytes and God-fearers, that is Gentiles who had espoused the Jewish faith. We know nothing of how the church came into being, although it seems probable that some of its founding members had been among Jews from Rome who had heard Peter's preaching in Jerusalem at the Feast of Pentecost following Jesus' death and resurrection.[153] It is presumed that as they returned to Rome those new believers formed the nucleus of a new church, which may well have been based around the many

---

[150] See Chapter 4, 70, 'Perseverance'.

[151] See Longenecker (2011), 55-166, who discusses the two most contentious questions in contemporary debate on Romans: to whom the letter was addressed and its purpose.

[152] Pawson, 1021f. Pawson doesn't make citations, but his main source seems to be Wolfgang Wiefel, 'The Jewish Community in Ancient Rome and the Origins of Roman Christianity' in Donfried, 85-101. Wiefel's original work was published in German in 1970 and was translated into English for the first edition of Donfried's symposium in 1977. His ideas, which include a detailed description of the dozen or so Jewish synagogues in Rome at the time of Paul's writing, did not seem to have surfaced elsewhere, nor had been widely commented on until Richard Longenecker adopted Wiefel's and P. S. Minear's ideas - 'The Obedience of Faith: The Purposes of Paul in the Epistle to the Romans', *Studies in Biblical Theology* 2/19 (London: SCM, 1971) in his *Introducing Romans* and subsequent commentary, *The Epistle to the Romans*, 2016. Donfried, lxx, describes Wiefel's original work as a "pathbreaking essay" and says, 104, it is of "fundamental importance for a possible reconstruction of the historical background of Romans". Although not having seen Wiefel's paper, Minear arrived at a similar conclusion independently: Donfried, 106.

[153] Acts 2:10 specifically mentions visitors from Rome.

synagogues of Rome at the time.[154] As well as, one supposes, new converts from Rome itself, to these would have been added many Christians, both Jews and Gentiles, who travelled for a variety of reasons to the metropolis. In consequence of that presumed origin, it seems that the first Roman Christians looked eastwards towards Jerusalem as their mother church and their complexion of religion would have been distinctively Jewish.[155] However, some time before AD 54, probably in the year 49, the Emperor Claudius, who was antagonistic towards Jews, placed a ban on their free association and expelled some or all of their entire population, possibly about 40,000, from the city. Apparently, he did not discriminate between practising Jews and Jewish-background Christians, so among them were Priscilla and Aquila, believers who subsequently encountered Paul at Corinth.[156]

Thus, Pawson speculates that when Claudius died in AD 54 and Jews began to return to Rome, encouraged to do so by the new emperor, Nero, they found *their* church still in existence, but its leadership having been taken over by gentile believers, who perhaps didn't welcome back their Jewish brethren with wide open arms, especially if they were intent on regaining their former influence and leadership.[157] Many commentators on Romans recognise that relations between Jewish-heritage believers and gentile Christians were difficult when Paul wrote Romans, but few, if any, go to the extent which Pawson postulates. He claims that "this background helps to unlock the letter to the Romans"

---

[154] Wiefel in Donfried, 91f. Some see the absence of the word *ekklēsia* from all but the 16th chapter of Romans as evidence of a loose, non-centralised Christian community, but see Günter Klein in Donfried, 41f.

[155] Longenecker (2011), 83, citing Raymond E. Brown, in R. E. Brown & J. P. Meier eds., *Antioch and Rome: New Testament Cradles of Catholic Christianity* (New York: Paulist, 1983), 103f., and Joseph A. Fitzmyer, *Romans: A New Translation With Introduction and Commentary*, Anchor Bible, (New York: Doubleday, 1993), 33.

[156] Acts 18:1f. The expulsion of Jews from Rome is attested by Suetonius (69-130), *Life of Claudius* (c. AD 120), 25:4, and seems to have been precipitated by civil disorder sparked off by disputes between Jews and Christian believers over Christ, presumably the issue of the messiahship of Jesus of Nazareth: Suetonius writes 'Chrestos', which is most likely a careless spelling of 'Christus'. Claudius would not have differentiated between Jews and Christians, so all (or many) who were associated with the synagogues in Rome were expelled. See Wiefel in Donfried, 92ff.

[157] Donfried, 48, suggests too that changes in theology and internal structures may have precipitated a crisis.

and that "we find that almost every part of it is dealing with this situation". I agree that when Romans is read in that light, Pawson's theory can be very persuasive, and, if true, it would indeed make chapters 9 to 11 the heart of Paul's greatest epistle.

The crucial question which dominates that section of Romans, if not the whole letter then, is "Did God reject his people?" (11:1). It was a key issue which troubled Paul and both confronted and bedevilled the whole of the first century Church in a gentile world, a Church with a founding membership of Jews and God-fearers but made cosmopolitan by the conversion of Gentiles. Thus, amidst all the vexed questions about the relevance or otherwise of the Law of Moses, this more profound question concerning God's purposes in history, and specifically the history of Israel, demanded Paul's attention.[158]

If the whole epistle is correctly to be construed in this way, it does seem logical and obvious that Paul should first wish to lay a foundation of justification by faith in order to shift the argument of Israel's destiny away from a basis of covenant and the Law of Moses to that of faith, the true basis of God's justification for all mankind, both Jew and Gentile. This is the point Paul reaches at the end of chapter 11. Just as there is no difference between Jew and Gentile in that all had sinned (3:22f.), still there is no difference, for "God has bound everyone over to disobedience so that he may have mercy on them all" (11:32).

In order to reach that conclusion, Paul posits two distinct Israels or 'families', to allude to his earlier 'one seed' analogy from Galatians 3:16-20.[159] On the one hand, his own people, his biological kin (9:3), ethnic Israel, the natural offspring of Abraham through Isaac, had on the whole rejected the gospel, while, on the other hand, there were the non-biological spiritual offspring of promise, those who have been justified by faith (9:6-8). Paul shows that some of the former, ethnic Israel, were chosen, while some were rejected for God's "purpose in election"

---

[158] Some may see here the beginnings of Replacement Theology (Supersessionism). This view asserts that God no longer regards Israel as his chosen people and had no further purposes for them to be worked out in history. This passage actually provides the antidote to that misguided theory.

[159] See Chapter 9b, 265.

(9:11), an expression I take to mean as something like 'salvation history'; in other words, the historical process which culminated in the appearance of the Messiah and his redemptive work. Balz & Schneider concur, maintaining that *eklogē* (ἐκλογή) in the expression "in order that God's purpose in *election* might stand", reflects not on Jacob's nor Isaac's personal salvation but on their God-given roles in playing their parts in the divine strategy of Israel's history.[160] Thus, in first laying the foundation of justification by the exercise of personal faith, Paul, in a general way, had shown that Israel had failed to gain righteousness because they did not pursue it by faith (9:32). By contrast, however, the Gentiles, some at least, had succeeded in gaining righteousness through faith (9:30).

Justifying faith can never operate at the collective level, however. With Paul it was always individual and personal. Since, then, the idea of God's "purpose in election" cannot contradict what he has already established on the level of the individual, *eklogē* here cannot refer to the election of individuals to salvation. Our individual ultimate, post-terrestrial destiny is not here in view. Rather, God's "purpose in election" is all about the creation of an elect people, Israel, his inheritance here on earth.[161] And through the shaping of that people's history and the moulding of individual lives within that history (9:14-21), his purpose was to bring into the world his unique Chosen One, the Christ, so that through faith exercised in him by individuals the world would begin to see the emergence of a new people of God, a spiritual second, or renewed Israel. Paul is not concerned therefore with individuals in this context but with people *en masse* (9:22-29). He is concerned with the formation and differentiation of two mutually exclusive categories; on the one hand, the Elect, spiritual Israel, those having a righteousness based on faith (9:30), and, on the other hand, the Reprobate (not Paul's word), who in failing to exercise faith failed to gain righteousness, and including, as it happens, some of ethnic Israel, who had hoped for, but failed to gain righteousness by their observance of the Law (9:31-32).

By the time Paul reaches chapter 10, however, he is clearly no longer

---

[160] Balz & Schneider, I, 419.
[161] E.g., Exodus 19:5; Deuteronomy 32:9, etc. Cf. Ephesians 1:11.

referring to the Israel of faith of chapter 9, but once again to ethnic Israel (cf. 11:1). Despite their failure to obtain salvation when Christ came (10:1) due to their stubborn refusal to believe the gospel (10:16, 21), they are nonetheless not rejected by God *as a people* (11:1). The fact that some, albeit a minority of Israelites, had trusted in Christ for salvation proved precisely that to Paul's mind, but until the partial hardening which God had placed upon ethnic Israel would be lifted, they would not be saved as a nation (11:25-26). Paul explains that this hardening was like the hardening of the heart of the Pharaoh of the Exodus (cf. 9:17-18) which the account in the book of Exodus attributes in the first place to Pharaoh's own will.[162] It is not until the fifth of the ten Egyptian plagues were completed that God himself was said to have hardened Pharaoh's heart.[163] Thus the salvation of national Israel will come about when God's hardening of them is lifted (11:26). Then they will be included in the Elect on the same basis as Gentiles and other Jews who have preceded them; that is through faith in Christ on the basis of individual choice.[164]

I would suggest, then, that to interpret Romans 9 to 11 as a sort of digression about the mechanics of God's decree of Election for individual men and women, is to completely miss Paul's point, and possibly miss the point of the epistle as a whole. Having chosen a privileged nation, which he called his own, in order to bring forth the Saviour of the world, God did not discard them once their purpose in salvation had been accomplished through their Messiah. Rather, in line with his promise to Abraham,[165] he ordained that they with the Gentiles should be united in the true Israel, the children of promise (9:8).

That said, however, there remain a number of issues, especially in this ninth chapter of Romans, which demand further probing. One particular example is the point in Paul's argument where he raises the

---

[162] Exodus 8:15, 32.
[163] Exodus 9:12, cf. 7:13, 22; 8:15, 19, 32; 9:7. The idea of God 'hardening' (Hebrew *chazaq*; חזק (pi'el; the intensive active form)) a person's heart is not to make it intransigent, but to fix a state determined by other factors; in the case of Pharaoh, his own wilful obstinacy: Forster & Marston, 155ff.
[164] Romans 3:30.
[165] Genesis 12:3.

hypothetical objection, "Then why does God still blame us? For who is able to resist his will?" (9:19). Furthermore, he goes on to write about those who are "the objects of his wrath – prepared for destruction", and, on the other hand, those who are "the objects of his mercy, whom he prepared in advance for glory – even us" (9:22-24). He then quotes Hosea 2:23 and 1:10[166] in terms of those who are loved by God and whom he calls "children of the living God", respectively.

With regard to this latter section of Romans, Paul's language *appears* to be soteriological. Whereas, I have been arguing that this whole passage is really about the ways God *manipulates* people and events in order to accomplish his purposes in salvation history, that is the history of Israel in preparation for the coming of their Messiah, Paul seems to slip into what appears to be very explicit language, ostensibly about the salvation and eternal destiny of those he has called God's children. The question therefore arises – Can those whom God has called his children or his people *not* necessarily be among those who will inhabit the eternal glory of his heavenly presence? In other words, can they be excluded from the Elect despite being called his children? The precise texts which cause problems here are the quotations from Hosea, and it is therefore worth thinking about how Paul would have understood Hosea's words. The danger is that we read Paul, and these Old Testament passages through him, with post-Reformation eyes, and it may be that some peeling away of 20 centuries of interpretative gloss may shed a better light on what Paul was really saying and how he used these Hebrew scriptures.

Hosea lived in the mid-8th century BC, working for about 38 years in Israel, the northern kingdom, between the reigns of Uzziah (792-740 BC) and Hezekiah (729-686 BC), kings of Judah, the southern kingdom.[167] His message, although primarily directed towards the northern kingdom, focused on the post-exilic reunification of the whole of Israel,

---

[166] The first of Paul's quotations, Hosea 2:23 (2:25 in MT and LXX) differs considerably from the LXX text, while Hosea 1:10 (2:1 in MT and LXX) is quoted directly from the LXX. See Cranfield (1975), 499.

[167] The fact that Hosea's prophetic activity is dated by the reigns of Judahite kings suggests that the book was completed in the south after the fall of Samaria in 722 BC.

south and north, although the phrase, "in that day"[168] is thought to indicate an eschatological rather than a historical perspective, no matter whether immediate or even more distant. It would be nigh impossible for Hosea to have foreseen the formation of a new Israel in the kind of detail which Paul, or indeed we, may now see - a people which would be brought into being by faith in the crucified and glorified Messiah. Even given the reality of divine prophetic revelation, I suggest that Hosea's vision would not have extended beyond the covenant context of salvation within the Promised Land. What he then would have understood by "my people", "my loved one" and "children of the living God", a phrase unique to Hosea, must, I suggest, have been within the limitations of that terrestrial covenant context, even though with hindsight we may perceive in his words a foretaste of what was to be accomplished through Christ.

Paul, steeped as he was in the text of the Hebrew Scriptures, although, when writing, normally quoting from the Septuagint, would, we may be reasonably certain, have understood those distinctly Hebrew idioms in their Old Covenant context. I would suggest therefore that to spring on us two Old Testament texts, which appear to speak of the blessings of the New Covenant, would be out of place, even in the context of Romans 9, where the argument isn't about salvation in an ultimate sense, but about God's dealings with people in order to bring about his purposes on earth in bringing forth the Saviour through the processes of Israel's history. Perhaps Paul saw a prophetic foretelling of the salvation in Christ in Hosea's words as he re-evaluated them in the light of his understanding of Jesus' redemptive work, but since he does not draw special attention to that in line with that possibility, I suggest that his aim was simply to cite Hosea to illustrate God's willingness to bring back into covenant relationship those who had spurned his grace through covenant disobedience.

A further issue which Romans 9 throws up relates to verses 22 and 23 where Paul speaks of objects of destruction and objects "prepared in advance for glory". Two points need to be made. Firstly, a point

---

[168] Hosea 2:16, 21.

already made, that all of this is found in one of Paul's 'What if?' sections where his argument is hypothetical and should not therefore necessarily be read as though it were a piece of dogma. Secondly, there is no mention that either of these two classes of people, the damned and the saved, is seen as attaining those respective soteriological categories by any choice which God had made about them. Rather, I believe we must consistently say that they find themselves in their respective classes by the exercise of their individual free choice.[169] All Paul says in verse 24 of those "prepared in advance for glory" is that they are called from either the Jews or the Gentiles, and even the Jews must respond to God's call.

Furthermore, although I have had to work quite hard to maintain my previous conclusions as I have worked through this passage, I discover when I get to verse 30 that Paul has all along been speaking about those to whom the gospel has been offered undeservedly – Romans 9:30-32:

> What then shall we say? That the Gentiles, who did not pursue righteousness, have obtained it, a righteousness that is by faith; but the people of Israel, who pursued the law as the way of righteousness, have not attained their goal. Why not? Because they pursued it not by faith but as if it were by works.

The issue in Paul's mind throughout the Roman letter was about the exercise of saving faith, and never about whom God may or may not have chosen to be eternally saved.

This exercise of re-examining our understanding of these passages demonstrates very clearly, once again, that it is essential to bear in mind the wider context of scripture when trying to interpret the minutiae of difficult texts. If we isolate some of these verses in Romans 9 from the broader context of Paul's argument, we may easily be swayed one way or the other. I would still contend therefore that, even though Paul may *seem* to be speaking about eternal salvation, the context of the passage and its place in the overall argument of the Romans letter shows that he is actually writing about the ways God favours individuals and even

---

[169] Klein, 278, notes that if the verb *katartidzō* (καταρτίζω: 'destruction') was in the middle voice with a reflexive use it would mean that these vessels had prepared themselves for destruction; cf. Matthew 21:16: "you have prepared praise for yourself" (NET).

nations in order to bring about his purposes on earth. Whether those individuals and groups of people will eventually find themselves in God's kingdom with us remains to be seen – one of the many surprises we shall all experience when we assemble before the Throne of the Lamb, but clearly a matter of huge importance to Paul as he pleads with his own kindred to accept their Messiah.

g. 1 Corinthians 1:27-28 and James 2:5: People Chosen by God

> But God chose the foolish things of the world to shame the wise; God chose the weak things of the world to shame the strong. He chose the lowly things of this world and the despised things—and the things that are not—to nullify the things that are. (1 Corinthians 1:27-28)

> Listen, my dear brothers and sisters: has not God chosen those who are poor in the eyes of the world to be rich in faith and to inherit the kingdom he promised those who love him? (James 2:5)

We encountered the Corinthians text when considering Louis Berkhof's claim that God chooses individuals.[170] Neither text envisages individuals, however: both refer to *categories* or *types* of people among those whom God has chosen. Furthermore, in neither case is their election to salvation; rather, in Corinthians, it is to demonstrate how God's wisdom can be displayed through the lives of uneducated or underprivileged believers – the kind of people we may not have expected God to choose perhaps, and in James, that a richness of faith may be seen in those who lack material wealth. It is simply a demonstration of the topsy-turvy values system of the Kingdom of God compared with the world's values. Once again, it must be stressed that in both cases the 'foolish' and the 'poor' are categories of people – and that God does not choose groups of people except in ways we have already considered. It is also my consistent contention, of course, that neither does he choose individuals for salvation.

---

[170] Chapter 3, 66 n10.

h. 1 Peter 2:8: Destined for Disobedience?

> They stumble because they disobey the message—which is also what they were destined for. (1 Peter 2:8b)

Many Reformed writers see this text as supporting the idea of reprobation; that God had predestined some to disobey so that they would stumble and fall.[171] In other words, just as God had foreordained that certain individuals should respond in faith to the gospel, so others had been ordained to disbelief and rebellion. Grudem says,

> those who are rejecting Christ and disobeying God's word were also *destined* by God to such action.[172]

Although the natural way to read this text from the Reformed point of view is to see it as referring to reprobation, it is sometimes pointed out that such stumbling does not necessarily signify eternal loss, but that the disobedient may nonetheless repent and be saved; e.g., Grudem,

> This text leaves open the possibility of repentance and saving faith in Christ for the unbelievers it talks about.... it does stop short of saying that their eternal condemnation is already ordained.[173]

Others disagree with the notion that unbelievers were foreordained to disobey, however, saying that it is the *fate* of those who disobey which has been foreordained, "the appointed portion of those who reject Christ",[174] a view which accords with my own. For example, Henry Ironside says,

> Do not misunderstand; they were not appointed or predestined to be disobedient. God does not so deal with any man. The supralapsarian theologians dishonour His name while imagining they are defending His right when they so teach. But when men are determined to go on in the path of disobedience, God gives them up to strong delusion, thus appointing them to stumble.[175]

Not unlike the debate about whether it is faith or salvation through faith

---

[171] E.g., L. Berkhof, 118; Grudem (1988), 106ff.
[172] Grudem (1988), 106ff. (his italics).
[173] Ibid., 108.
[174] G. J. Polkinghorne in Howley *et al*, 1635.
[175] Ironside, 29, quoting 2 Thessalonians 2:11.

OTHER PROBLEMATICAL ELECTION TEXTS

which is God's gift,[176] the argument focuses on the phrase at the end of verse 8: "which is also what they were destined for"[177] and whether the "which" refers to their disobedience or their stumbling because of disobedience. There seems to be no obvious solution, but in line with what I have been arguing throughout, it seems better to say that what was foreordained was the stumbling caused by disobedience rather than the disobedience itself.[178]

i. Revelation 17:8: Names Written in the Book of Life

> The inhabitants of the earth whose names have not been written in the book of life from the creation of the world will be astonished when they see the beast, because it once was, now is not, and yet will come. (Revelation 17:8b)

Five times in the book of Revelation reference is made to those whose names either have or have not been written in "the book of life", also called "the Lamb's book of life".[179] Beale describes this as "a metaphor referring ... to believers, whose salvific life has been secured."[180] If that definition is to be accepted, I suggest that these references ought not to be particularly noteworthy for our present context since, at a first glance, they apparently refer to the inscription of a person's name in the book of life, pictorial language for God's memory perhaps, at the point of their new birth through faith in Christ. A problem arises, however, with Revelation 17:8 where it is said that the names of some inhabitants of the earth were *not* written in the book of life – not a problematic concept in and of itself, but when linked with the phrase, "*from the creation of the world*", strongly suggests that Reformed predestinatory teaching is biblical.[181] Jack Cottrell writes,

---

[176] Ephesians 2:8f.: see Chapter 5, 154, 'Saving Grace'.
[177] Greek: *eis ho kai etethēsan* (εἰς ὃ καὶ ἐτέθησαν).
[178] See also Klein's discussion of 1 Peter 2:8: Klein, 222ff. He relies heavily on Charles Bigg, *Epistles of St. Peter and St. Jude*, International Critical Commentary (Edinburgh: T. & T. Clark, 1902).
[179] Revelation 13:8; 21:27: "Lamb's book of life"; 3:5; 17:8; 20:15: "book of life".
[180] Beale, 866.
[181] "From the creation of the world" also occurs in Revelation 13:8; "all whose names have not been written in the Lamb's book of life, the Lamb who was *slain from the creation of the world.*" This poses an obvious chronological problem, which *might* be

343

> This is a negative statement; but it would be meaningless to say that some persons' names have *not* been written in the book of life since the beginning unless there are others whose names *have* been written there from the beginning.[182]

Cottrell's comment raises two issues. Firstly, coming as he does from the Arminian side of the fence, he argues that the explanation for names being written in God's register of the Elect, so to speak, is that God foresaw that some would receive Christ as Saviour and that he knew them by name. The second issue, arising from his discussion following that point, is that Revelation 3:5 strongly suggests that it is possible for a person to lose their salvation. Furthermore, to the Church at Sardis, the Lord Jesus through John says,

> The one who is victorious will, like them, be dressed in white. I will never blot out the name of that person from the book of life, but will acknowledge that name before my Father and his angels.

To say that names will not be blotted out of the book of life suggests that the opposite is a possibility - that names once inscribed can be removed. At face value, then, this text denies Perseverance, the view espoused by contemporary Arminians, but, it has to be said, not necessarily by Arminius himself.[183] Cottrell explains it by analogy with the Parable of the Sower in Matthew 13, where "the seeds falling on rocky ground ... quickly fall away" and "the seed falling among the thorns refers to someone who hears the word, but the worries of this life and the deceitfulness of wealth choke the word, making it unfruitful."[184]

Returning, for a moment, to the concept of names being written in the book of life *from the foundation of the world*, we need first to note that this seems to be an apparent exception to what the New Testament teaches generally about Election.[185] It is difficult to find commentary on the phrase because either side of the Arminian-Calvinism divide,

---

resolved in the footnote offered by the NIV: "Or *written from the creation of the world in the book of life belonging to the Lamb who was slain*", which brings it into agreement with 17:8.

[182] In Pinnock & Wagner, 77 (his italics).
[183] See Chapters 2, 35, and 4, 70, 'Perseverance'.
[184] Matthew 13:20-22.
[185] The other major exception being Mark 13:20; see section a. above, 282.

predestination of individuals to salvation is accepted although understood differently. The Reformed view explains it in terms of the divine eternal decree, while Arminians say it is based on divine foreknowledge. Aune, for example, simply accepts this as a "predestinarian view", linking the phrase with Ephesians 1:4: "For he chose us in him before the creation of the world".[186] On the other hand, Klein, espousing an Arminian view, comments at greater length:

> The best solution recognises the entire concept of a "book" as metaphorical and discourages any pressing of its details. On one hand, this book points to God's eternal foreknowledge: he knows its precise contents. He has always known who would be his people.... This, I think, explains the meaning of "from the creation of the world." But the need for human response cannot be ignored in the possibility of erasure and the inherent warnings surrounding Revelation 3:5.... Any "erasure" is a divine response to human faithlessness.[187]

In true Arminian fashion, Klein continues, "Only those who remain faithful to Christ have their names permanently engraved on the register."[188] However, in a footnote he says that it would be "pressing the details of this image" to assume that this erasure implies loss of the salvation they once possessed, and that the metaphor of the *book* pictures those finally saved and should not be allegorised. He cites John Walvoord and Paige Patterson, who, "resort to unnecessary contortions" in order to avoid the suggestion that salvation may be lost, an outcome that, even as an Arminian, he seems to wish to avoid:[189]

> The metaphor of the "book" stationed in heaven conveys permanence.... Yet this image does not convey predestination or election, unless we allow that what God has predestined may not occur (that is, a name may be erased and salvation forfeited).[190]

I am uncertain how persuasive Klein's view is here, and I think I detect

---

[186] Aune, 940.
[187] Klein, 126.
[188] Ibid., 127.
[189] Ibid., n111; citing John F. Walvoord, *The Revelation of Jesus Christ* (Chicago: Moody, 1966), 82; and Paige Patterson, *Revelation* (Nashville, TN: B. & H., 2012), 124.
[190] Ibid., 127.

a hint of desperation in his reasoning. I could go along with the view that those named in the book of life are those whom God knew would receive Christ as Saviour, but I am left with the problem of how once entered in the book, a name can then be erased. I tend to be drawn to the solution offered by Patterson that the potential loss of salvation, as implied in Revelation 3:5, should be regarded as a promise, not a threat – the potential of erasure being purely hypothetical, rather than actual.[191]

The problem with Revelation 17:8 is not unlike that posed by Mark 13:20 with which I opened this chapter. What must be recognised is that, when taken at face value, both seem to support the Reformed view of Particular Election. On the other hand, however, both are rare examples which seem to stand opposed to the general tenor of the New Testament, which I maintain does not teach Particular Election. I suggest then that this itself would be a strong argument for not placing too much reliance on them for support of a predestinarian view, and that they should be parked until fresh light can be shed on them.

One aspect of this problem seems to have been overlooked, however. Clearly, the writer of the Revelation was steeped in the Hebrew Scriptures, so it is worth delving into the Old Testament for similar expressions which might shed light on what he might have had in mind when he wrote of the 'book of life' or 'book of the living', an expression (*sepher chayyim*: סֵפֶר חַיִּים) which occurs only in Psalms 69:28:

> May they be blotted out of the book of life
> And not be listed with the righteous.

The word 'book' represents the Hebrew word *sepher* (סֵפֶר), which occurs 185 times in the Hebrew Bible and carries the basic meaning of 'a writing' or something 'written'. Johnston comments that there are a few "intriguing Old Testament references to heavenly books"[192] some of which appear to have a sense similar to those found in Revelation; some are records of the names of God's people, while others record

---

[191] Ibid., 127 n111.
[192] Johnston, 214.

events.[193] The 'book of life' also appears in some extra-biblical Jewish sources:[194] some references concern the erasure of names of wrongdoers,[195] others refer to deeds;[196] some texts record sins[197] and the Rabbinic Pirqe Aboth warns about "all thy deeds written in a book"[198] Apart from the Revelation references already noted, the New Testament elsewhere mentions those "whose names are written in heaven" or "in the book of life".[199]

Johnston cautions that, although intertestamental and New Testament writers understood 'the book of life' as referring to the postmortem fate of those named, that interpretation is often wrongly read back into the Old Testament. Thus, the few Old Testament references might be construed as glimpses of future hope, as in some of the Psalms,[200] but, we cannot be certain that Moses envisaged a personal afterlife, so, all those texts ought to be interpreted otherwise. Since in the Old Testament, life in its full sense meant life lived under God's blessing, to be blotted out of the book of life probably simply meant to die prematurely.[201]

---

[193] Exodus 32:32f.: "blot me out of the book you have written" (words of Moses) and "Whoever has sinned against me I will blot out of my book" (words of God); Psalms 69:28: "May they be blotted out of the book of life"; Isaiah 4:3 also refers to "those who are recorded among the living in Jerusalem" (although *sepher* is not used), and Malachi 3:16 refers to "A scroll of remembrance ... concerning those who feared the LORD and honoured his name." Other books seem to record events: Psalms 40:7: "it is written about me in the scroll"; Psalms 56:8: "list my tears on your scroll"; Psalms 139:16: "all the days ordained for me were written in your book". And in the context of the heavenly court, Daniel 7:10: "The court was seated, and the books were opened"; Daniel 12:1: "everyone whose name is found written in the book", and Daniel 12:4: "the scroll", which presumably refers to the "book" of 12:1.

[194] Johnston, 214f.

[195] E.g., 1 Enoch 108:3: "the names [of wrongdoers] will be erased from the books of the holy ones", and Jubilees 30:20, 22; 36:10 notes that names are recorded in or erased from 'the heavenly tablets', 'the book of life', and the variously described book of destruction.

[196] 1 Enoch 47:3: "the books of the living were opened", conflating the different 'books' of Daniel, and 90:20: "all the sealed books [were] opened".

[197] Jubilees 39:6; 2 Baruch 24:1; 2 Esdras (Ezra) 6:20 [This third reference from Johnston, 215, does not check out, but 1 Esdras 2:18f. and 2 Esdras 4:15 refer to Persian records of Jerusalem being a rebellious city.].

[198] Pirqe Aboth 2:1; Zahavy, 325. Pirqe Aboth or mAboth (*Chapters of the Fathers*) is one of the 63 treatises of the Mishna, a collection of rabbinical sayings ranging from the 3rd century BC to the 3rd century AD.

[199] Luke 10:20; Philippians 4:3; Hebrews 12:23.

[200] Psalms 16:10f.; 49:15; 73:24, etc.

[201] Cf. H. Wildberger, *Isaiah 1-12* (Minneapolis, MN: Augsburg, 1991), 169.

Thus following Moses' request to be blotted out of God's book, God says, "when the time comes for me to punish, I will punish them [the people] for their sin", and the psalmist who wanted his enemies' names erased also wanted them ruined, banished and condemned.[202] Similarly, Isaiah's record for life in Jerusalem[203] applied to life on earth, not to a later life, and when God said of those recorded in Malachi's book of remembrance, "They shall be mine", it is "on the day when I act" that "I will spare them".[204] This latter reference suggests preservation through judgment rather than life after death, and even the book of names in Daniel's final vision,[205] although mentioned just before resurrection, concerns "your people—everyone whose name is found written in the book—will be delivered" - in other words, those who will survive the unprecedented 'anguish' and remain alive on earth. Likewise, the 'books' of events or deeds mentioned in several psalms need imply no more than God's loving concern and provision for his people.[206]

Thus, contrary to the way most authorities have construed the meaning of the book of life, or the Lamb's book of life, in Revelation, the contexts of at least some of these occurrences suggest, not that the heavenly books are records of the Elect in a New Testament sense, but that they are more akin to the scroll of Revelation 5, which seems to contain God's overview or plan of history in time which John is commissioned to reveal to the Church.[207] Admittedly, Daniel 12:1 appears to fit with the way most expositors understand the Revelation references because it suggests that those inscribed in the book from heaven - "the Book of Truth" possibly,[208] will be delivered from the time of distress of which

---

[202] Exodus 32:34; Psalms 69:22-28.
[203] Isaiah 4:3.
[204] Malachi 3:17.
[205] Daniel 12:1.
[206] Johnston, 215.
[207] The form, content and significance of the scroll (*biblion*: βιβλίον) are debated at length by New Testament authorities. See, for example, Aune, 341-6, Beale, 339-48, etc. George R. Beasley-Murray, *The Book of Revelation*, New Century Bible Commentaries (Grand Rapids, MI/London: Eerdmans & Marshall, Morgan & Scott, 1978²), 120, says, "Few features of the Revelation have been so widely discussed as the nature of the scroll". The wealth of scholarly opinion probably arises owing to insufficient understanding of the nature of apocalyptic.
[208] Daniel 10:21.

OTHER PROBLEMATICAL ELECTION TEXTS

Daniel's angel speaks, but as we have seen, that may not refer to life after death.

Although the most common word for 'book' is *sepher*, there is a less common word, *ketab* (כְּתָב), which occurs 17 times and is found only in books of the Hebrew Scriptures which emanate from the later period of the exile.[209] Most of these references relate to royal edicts, letters and family records, but not to divinely inspired scripture. *Ketab* covers much the same semantic range as *sepher*, but in one instance, Daniel 10:21, the sense is like that of Revelation – "the Book of Truth". In view of the author of Revelation's obvious dependency on the book of Daniel,[210] it will be worth examining the four Daniel texts in more detail together with those in Psalms and Exodus.[211]

Notwithstanding Johnston's warning (above) about reflecting later understanding back into the Old Testament, it does seem that in Hebrew thought, there is a clear sense that God has a 'book', but rather than being a register of the redeemed, it is a 'book' more akin to the scroll of Revelation 5:1. The first instance in Exodus 32:32 tells of Moses' pleading with God to forgive Israel for their sin of idolatry in worshiping the golden calf which was fabricated by Aaron in the face of Moses' delay in descending Mount Sinai, and he asks of God, "blot me out of the book you have written." Whereupon "The LORD replies to Moses, 'Whoever has sinned against me I will blot out of my book'". Psalms 69:28 is similar, but Psalms 139:16 refers to "all the days ordained" for David (according to the psalm's title) which had been "written in your book". This seems therefore to accord with the idea of a book which had been written from the foundation of the earth, but it being a kind of divine plan or decree of what will be, specifically for God's people, rather than simply a record of the redeemed. Moses' request to be blotted out from God's book would suggest then that what he had in mind was that he should take no significant place in God's purposes, and that

---

[209] Esther (9x), Chronicles (3x), Ezra-Nehemiah (3x), Ezekiel (1x) and Daniel (1x).
[210] Sweet, 17ff.: "Daniel, which from both the literary and the theological point of view is indispensable for understanding Revelation."; Beale, 77: "Roughly more than half the references are from the Psalms, Isaiah, Ezekiel, and Daniel, and in proportion to its length Daniel yields the most."
[211] Daniel 7:10; 10:21 (*ketab*); 12:1, 4; Exodus 32:32; Psalms 69:28; 139:16.

he should be allowed to die (assuming the above suggestion to be correct).

When we come to Daniel, this sense is continued, especially in 12:1 and in verse 4, where Daniel is instructed to "roll up and seal the words of the scroll (*sepher*) until the time of the end". If this scroll is the same document as the book of verse 1, then the sense that it is more a plan of history than a register is reinforced, and that sense is confirmed earlier in Daniel 10:21 as the angel tells Daniel that he was about to reveal the contents of the Book of Truth.

My suggestion, then, is that the way John thinks of the book of life possibly contains both elements, i.e., that of mapping out the history of God's people as well as recording the results of a Kingdom census, so that, although the reference to "before the foundation of the world" of Revelation 17:8 remains a problem from an Election point of view, it does fit the Hebrew frame of reference, particularly that found in the book of Daniel. That, of course raises another problem for me in that this book would then appear to be God's determinant decree for the world, or perhaps specifically for the people of God, if that makes any real difference, and I would have to agree with Klein when he suggests that God's will may be more flexible than many Reformed theologians would accept.[212]

*****

A few comments are called for as I draw this chapter to a close. I have already admitted that some of these texts challenge my own convictions at times and may cause me to re-examine them. I think that is a consequence of the prevailing climate of Reformed interpretation in evangelical literature and not least in biblical translation. Some effort is therefore required to distance oneself from that very subtle, though pervasive influence. I feel that it accounts not only for my own intellectual wobbles, but also for the blinkeredness of many who hold to a Reformed view but deny a Calvinistic hegemony – just not being able to see how influential that view really is in the wider Church.

---

[212] Klein, 126.

My handling of some of the foregoing texts will not satisfy all, including myself to some extent, I have to admit. As I have said already, my aim has not been to conclusively demolish the Reformed view on these matters; more to cast serious doubt on their validity, and there are instances where I have left loose ends which I have not been able to explain even to my own satisfaction. However, I would resort not to mystery; rather to the sentiment expressed in the famous words of John Robinson (1576-1625) as he addressed the Pilgrims, members of his own congregation, prior to their departure from Delfthaven in the Netherlands, bound for Plymouth in the *Speedwell* and thence to the New World in the *Mayflower* in 1620:

> I am very confident the Lord hath more truth and light yet to break forth out of His Holy Word.[213]

---

[213] Source: <https://www.newtestamentpattern.net/christian-articles/sundry-thoughts/the-words-of-john-robinson_mayflower/> (accessed December 2022) and other Church histories, e.g., Tomkins' chapter 30, *'Twixt cup and lip*. Robinson's words are immortalised in George Rawson's hymn, *We limit not the truth of God*, and are apposite even for today given the context in which they were spoken, a sermon, which, according to Tomkins, quoting Edward Winslow, one of the founders of the Massachusetts colony: Howard Chaplin ed., *Hypocrisie Unmasked* (Massachusetts, MA: Applewood, 1916), 97, lasted "a good part of the day":
"I charge you before God ... that you follow me no further than you have seen me follow the Lord Jesus Christ. If God reveals anything to you by any other instrument of His, be as ready to receive it as you were to receive any truth by my ministry, for I am verily persuaded the Lord hath more truth yet to break forth out of His Holy Word. For my part, I cannot sufficiently bewail the condition of those reformed churches which...will go, at present, no further than the instruments of their reformation. The Lutherans cannot be drawn to go beyond what Luther saw; whatever part of His will our God had revealed to Calvin, they will rather die than embrace it; and the Calvinists, you see, stick fast where they were left by that great man of God, who yet saw not all things. This is a misery much to be lamented."
The exact words of Robinson's sermon cannot be established because they were recalled many years afterwards by Winslow and others – hence the differences between the two extracts given above.

Chapter 11

WHOM THEN HAS GOD REALLY CHOSEN?

Before summing up, and by way of tying up a few loose ends, it may be worthwhile gathering up a number of allusions to individuals and peoples from each Testament who are said to have been chosen by God, and to identify the purposes for which they were chosen.

a. Election of People in the Old Testament

There are approximately 111[1] instances in the Old Testament where God is said to have chosen individuals or groups of people. Table 3 below shows that the most common Hebrew noun or adjective is *bachir* (בָּחִיר) which is always translated in the Septuagint (LXX) by *eklektos* (ἐκλεκτός), and the most common verb is *bachar* (בָּחַר), mostly translated by *eklegō* (ἐκλέγω). Sometimes, when the verb is found in its passive participle form in the Masoretic Text (MT), it is not reflected in the Septuagint, but is translated by adjectives,[2] and in five instances in Jeremiah the corresponding verses are missing from the Hebrew. The Greek version of Jeremiah shows considerable differences in the arrangement of material compared with the Hebrew.

Occasionally, words other than *eklektos*, *bachir* or *bachar* are used to denote choice. For example, where other Greek verbs translate *bachar* and where Hebrew verbs other than *bachar* are used. With a couple of possible exceptions, those Hebrew and Greek verbs can be translated with the English 'choose', but the differences between them have to do with ideas of preference, taking out, removing or separating, and so on, all of which, broadly speaking, really mean to choose.

---

[1] The exact number depends on the choice of vocabulary and the method of search.
[2] The exception is 1 Samuel 20:30 where the participle is active.

Table 3: Choosing People in the Old Testament:

Hebrew MT		Greek LXX		No	Objects of choice
bachir	בָּחִיר	eklektos	ἐκλεκτός	13[3]	Chosen one(s), Saul, Moses.
bachar	בָּחַר	eklegō	ἐκλέγω	52[4]	Aaron, Israel/Jacob, kings, priests, Abraham, God(s), 'my Servant', Ephraim, Judah.
"	"	proaireō	προαιρέω	1[5]	Israel.
"	"	epilegō	ἐπιλέγω	4[6]	Priests, soldiers.
"	"	hairetidzō	αἱρετίζω	8[7]	Solomon, priests, Israel, Zerubbabel.
"	"	haireō	αἱρέω	1[8]	God.
"	"	exaireō	ἐξαιρέω	1[9]	'I have tested you.'
"	"	Verses not in LXX		3[10]	Kingdoms, a chosen one.
"	"	Verb not in LXX		17[11]	Soldiers, chariots.
yāda'	יָדַע	oida	οἶδα	1[12]	Abraham.
"	"	ginōskō	γινώσκω	1[13]	Israel.

---

[3] 2 Samuel [2 Regnorum] 21:6; 1 Chronicles 16:13; Psalms 89[88]:3; 105[104]:6, 43; 106[105]:5, 23; Isaiah 42:1; 43:20; 45:4; 65:9, 15, 22[23]. These account for all 13 occurrences of *bachir* in the Old Testament. Septuagintal references which differ from the Masoretic text are indicated in square brackets.

[4] Genesis 6:2; Exodus 17:9; 18:25; Numbers 16:5, 7; 17:5[20 MT]; Deuteronomy 4:37; 7:7; 10:15; 14:2; 17:15; 18:5; Joshua 24:15 (Codex B); 24:22; Judges 5:8 (Codex B); 10:14; 1 Samuel [1 Regnorum] 2:28; 8:18; 10:24; 12:13; 13:2; 16:8, 9, 10; 17:8 (translates *barach*); 2 Samuel [2 Regnorum] 6:21; 16:18; 1 Kings [3 Regnorum] 3:8; 8:16; 11:34; 1 Chronicles 15:2; 19:10; 28:4, 5; 2 Chronicles 6:5, 6 (twice in MT, but once in LXX); Nehemiah 9:7 [2 Esdras 19:7]; Psalms 33[32 LXX]:12; 65:4[65:5 MT; 64:5 LXX]; 78[77 LXX]:67, 68, 70; 105[104 LXX]:26; 135[134 LXX]:4; Isaiah 14:1; 41:8, 9; 43:10; 44:1, 2; 49:7. Apart from the 35 occurrences of *bachar* which are translated differently in the LXX, the remaining 84 instances in the Old Testament relate chiefly to the choice of places (mainly Jerusalem) or to personal decisions.

[5] Deuteronomy 7:6.

[6] Deuteronomy 21:5; Joshua 8:3; 2 Samuel [2 Regnorum] 10:9; 17:1.

[7] Judges 5:8 (Codex A); 1 Chronicles 28:4, 6, 10; 29:1; 2 Chronicles 29:11; Ezekiel 20:5; Haggai 2:23.

[8] Joshua 24:15 (Codex A: B has *eklegomai*).

[9] Isaiah 48:10.

[10] Jeremiah 33:24; 49:19; 50:44.

[11] Participles are reflected in the LXX by adjectives: ἐκλεκτός (x6): Exodus 14:7; Judges 20:16, 34; 1 Samuel [1 Regnorum] 24:2[3 LXX]; 26:2; Psalms 89:19[20 MT; 88:20 LXX]; μέτοχός (x1): 1 Samuel [1 Regnorum] 20:30; νεανίας (x6): 2 Samuel [2 Regnorum] 6:1; 10:9; 1 Kings [3 Regnorum] 12:21; 1 Chronicles 19:10; 2 Chronicles 11:1; δυνατός (x4): 2 Chronicles 13:3 (x2), 17; 25:5; not translated (1): Judges 20:15.

[12] Genesis 18:19.

[13] Amos 3:2.

THE PREDESTINATION PROBLEM

yakach	יָדַע	ginōskō	γινώσκω	1[14]	Rebekah.
qara	קָרָא	anakaleō	ἀνακαλέω	2[15]	Bezalel.
ra'iti	רָאִיתִי	horaō	ὁράω	3[16]	A son of Jesse, 'what I have seen/found out'.
ahab	אָהֵב	poieō	ποιέω	1[17]	'Chosen ally' (Cyrus).
laqach	לָקַח	Verses not in LXX		2[18]	'I will choose you', a son of David.

The Greek verbs *oida* (οἶδα) and *ginōskō* (γινώσκω) are used once and twice, respectively, to translate either *yāda'* (יָדַע) or *yakach* (יָקַח) in connection with the choosing of Abraham, Israel and Rebekah.[19] These Greek verbs are about knowing, whether personally or knowing about. Although notably few in frequency, not to say very rare – there are only three, they are nevertheless sometimes cited by certain Reformed advocates to reinforce the alleged link between divine election and personal intimate knowledge.[20]

The two instances of *anakaleō* (ἀνακαλέω), both of which relate to the choosing of Bezalel, who supervised the art and craft work in the fabrication of the tabernacle, have the additional nuance of one being called out by name, while the three cases where *horaō* (ὁράω) translates the Hebrew *ra'iti* (רָאִיתִי: root *ra'ach*: רָאָה), all from 1 Samuel, have the basic idea of seeing or finding out.

In the one place in the Septuagint where *poieō* (ποιέω) is used to translate the Hebrew *ahab* (אָהֵב) in Isaiah 48:14, NETS translates the phrase, "Because I love you",[21] while the NIV, translated directly from the Hebrew, has "the LORD's *chosen ally*" – hence its inclusion in this discussion, although the divine name, 'the LORD', is absent from the Septuagint. According to the Brown-Driver-Briggs Lexicon (*BDB*), the

---

[14] Genesis 24:44.
[15] Exodus 31:2; 35:30.
[16] 1 Samuel [1 Regnorum] 16:1, 18; 19:3.
[17] Isaiah 48:14.
[18] Jeremiah 3:14; 33:26.
[19] Genesis 18:19; Amos 3:2; Genesis 24:44 respectively.
[20] See Chapter 8c, 219, 'Foreknowledge'.
[21] Greek: ἀγαπων σε ἐποιησα.

354

Hebrew here has to do with divine love towards people, while the Greek verb basically means 'to do' or 'to make', and so has a wide range of nuances. Alec Motyer suggests that an alternative phrase, "The-LORD-loves-him", might be "a theophoric name" (i.e., bearing the name of God) for the Persian king Cyrus, who, in the context of Isaiah 48 will indeed perform God's purposes against Babylon,[22] and hence is his 'chosen ally'.

The final Hebrew verb in the table, *laqach* (לָקַח), occurs twice in the Hebrew text of Jeremiah but is not reflected in the Septuagint. The Hebrew usually carries the meaning of 'to take' or 'to get', in the sense of transporting or taking someone to another place.[23] Thus, in Jeremiah 3:14, "I will choose you", is about choosing and moving Israel in exile from one place to another – to Zion in particular, while the idea of relocation is absent from Jeremiah 33:26 where God says he will not choose (perhaps 'take') one of David's sons to rule.

In most instances in the Old Testament, and enumerated above, the objects of divine choice were selected to perform specific tasks, whether as priests, kings or leaders of one kind or another. The exceptions are those who were chosen in accordance with what might be termed 'God's purposes in election' – Abraham, Israel, Judah, Ephraim, the Chosen One, etc., although, of course, God's choice of them also served his purposes in contributing towards the bringing of salvation to the world. The nation of Israel was chosen through her descent from the patriarchs, and clearly, these individuals and tribes were not chosen so that they might receive eternal life, but rather for the two-fold purpose of, firstly, bringing the knowledge of godliness to the nations, a task in which they signally failed under the Old Covenant,[24] and secondly, to bring forth through the historical process the One who would make the necessary atonement to restore people of all nations to relationship with their Creator and thus receive eternal life.

We can include the Chosen One in this group because it was through

---

[22] Motyer, 380.
[23] E.g., 2 Kings 18:32; Isaiah 36:17, etc.
[24] E.g., Genesis 12:2f.; 18:18; 22:18; Psalms 9:11; 18:49; 22:27; 45:17; 98:2; Isaiah 11:10; 12:4; 42:6; 49:6; 60:3; 66:18-21, etc.

him alone that the purposes of God's election of the patriarchs and their progeny were brought to fulfilment. What was needed was a sacrifice for sin, and as the old hymn puts it so succinctly, "There was no other good enough to pay the price of sin".[25] Indeed, that whole process of distilling out from the bundle of Israelite humanity the one perfect Servant of God who could be that guilt offering[26] served, among other things, to demonstrate the unworthiness of all other individuals for the task of universal redemption. With the blessed hindsight afforded to us by the New Covenant we can clearly see that the Lord Jesus was the Christ, the chosen and anointed Son of God, who would perform that work of atonement, and through and in whom alone we, as individuals, would become part of his chosenness as we commit ourselves to his grace in his sacrifice for us.

b. Election of People in the New Testament

Turning from the Old to the New Testament, there remain a number of examples of those who were chosen for service of one kind or another.

The Twelve were chosen so that they might be with Jesus for their training as apostles, the designation of purpose for the primary responsibility of bearing lasting fruit which would have its ultimate reproductive purpose in the spread of the Good News of the Kingdom and the inclusion into the Elect of "persons from every tribe and language and people and nation".[27] Several times in John's Gospel, Jesus refers to those he had chosen – the Twelve whom he had appointed to be separate from the world and bear lasting fruit[28] – not chosen for eternal life, although that would inevitably follow for most of them through their faith in Jesus, but that they should emulate Jesus in his earthly ministry, serving for the Church as models of what converted lives should look like. It is worth reiterating that John 15:16 - "You did not choose me, but I chose you", is sometimes used to impress upon believers that by

---

[25] *There is a green hill far away*, Cecil F. Alexander (1818-95).
[26] Isaiah 53:10.
[27] Luke 6:13; Mark 3:14; Revelation 5:9.
[28] John 6:70; 13:18; 15:16, 19; Acts 1:2. See Chapter 10b(ii), 296, on the long-running debate on the purpose for which Jesus chose the apostles; also Shank (*Elect*), 40.

implication Christ had chosen them too, i.e., all subsequent believers in Jesus, for salvation, but his choosing of the apostles was for their training and ultimate ministry, and need not have immediate implications of divine choice for anyone else. That said, of course, Jesus expects all of his disciples to bear witness and produce lasting fruit.

Others in the pages of the New Testament were also said to have been chosen – Matthias to replace Judas Iscariot; the Seven for diaconal or servant service, among whom Stephen was to take the lead; Paul as Christ's "chosen instrument"; witnesses of Jesus' resurrection; Judas Barsabbas and Silas to accompany Paul to Antioch; Paul chosen to know God's will (words spoken by Ananias); Rufus; the foolish, weak and lowly things of the world who would shame the wise; Titus, chosen to accompany Paul; 'elect angels'; high priests and the poor.[29] All were chosen to fulfil some specific function, with the possible exception of the 'elect angels' – a somewhat obscure reference to angels who possibly had not fallen,[30] although Mounce suggests that they may have some elevated function in the heavenly sphere, perhaps participating in the final judgment.[31]

*****

In summary, we have considered how the vocabulary of Election and choice is used theologically as well as in more mundane ways in scripture – the choosing of people for particular tasks or the making up of one's mind about a course of action or preference, and so on. But no matter how one looks at it, H. H. Rowley's conclusion is persuasive:

> Whom God chooses, He chooses for service ... Election is for service.[32]

It's not a new idea, but it has been largely ignored, not only by the

---

[29] Acts 1:21, 24; 6:3 (verb *episkeptomai*: ἐπισκέπτομαι); 6:5; 9:15; 10:41 (verb *procheirotoneō*: προχειροτονέω); 15:22, 40; 22:14 (verb procheiridzomai: προχειρίζομαι); Romans 16:13; 1 Corinthians 1:27f.; 2 Corinthians 8:19 (verb *cheirotoneō*: χειροτονέω); 1 Timothy 5:21; Hebrews 5:1 (verb *lambanō*: λαμβάνω); James 2:5.
[30] Calvin, *Institutes*, 3.23.4: Beveridge, 3:229.
[31] Mounce, 316, cites 1 Corinthians 4:9; 1 Timothy 3:16; Revelation 2:1.
[32] H. H. Rowley, *The Biblical Doctrine of Election* (London: Lutterworth, 1952), 42, 111; quoted by Fisk, 44.

Reformed lobby but by all who cling to the idea of a Particular Election, whether by eternal decree or through foreknowledge. Klein's *The New Chosen People* and Wright's *Paul and the Faithfulness of God* are therefore welcome correctives which it is to be hoped will be more widely read than were former writers who ploughed in the same furrow but whose efforts have gone largely unheeded. Tom Wright, in identifying the governing principle for Paul's understanding of Election, which in a second-Temple context, he asserts, was thoroughly grounded in the Old Testament, says,

> The word 'election' as applied to Israel, usually carries a further connotation: not simply the divine choice of this people, but more specifically the divine choice of this people *for a particular purpose*.[33]

Bringing that thought into the New Testament, Forster and Marston say,

> What did the New Testament writers mean to convey by the word *eklektos*? ... the main idea in the New Testament seems to be one of responsibility and a task to perform.[34]

From Roger Olson too:

> "Election in biblical thought is never a selection, a taking of this and a rejection of that out of multiple realities." Rather, "election is a call to service, a summons to be a co-laborer with God in the actualization of God's elective purpose and goal." That elective purpose and goal revolves around Jesus Christ as God's mission in the world to save it.[35]

These writers speak of a task to perform. We should ask therefore, what is the task or purpose for which *we* are elect? I have consistently tried to maintain the link between a New Testament understanding of Election with the revelation to Abraham that God's call on him was for the blessing of all peoples.[36] That purpose is clear, in the main, when Old Testament saints are under consideration, but in line with these quotes

---

[33] N. T. Wright (2013), 775 (his italics).
[34] Forster & Marston, 118.
[35] Olson (2011), 125; quoting James Daane, *The Freedom of God: A Study of Election and Pulpit* (Grand Rapids, MI: Eerdmans, 1973), 150, 109.
[36] Genesis 12:3.

from Rowley, Wright, Forster & Marston and Olson, our election is not only to bear God's name; to receive adoption and salvation, but carries with it the awesome privilege and responsibility of continuing in our own generation the purpose for which Abraham and Israel were chosen in theirs. It is precisely so that we can bless those around us as we make known the saving grace of God in the gospel. And so, I quote once more from one of my favourite Reformed writers, the late F. F. Bruce:

> Christ selected twelve men to be apostles (Luke 6:13); He selected Saul of Tarsus to be a "chosen vessel" (Acts 9:15); but His selection of these men for a special purpose implies no disparagement of others who were not so selected. God selected Israel from among the nations (Acts 13:17)—to the great benefit of the other nations, not to their disadvantage. When the election of the people of God in this age is in question, it is not so much their "election to salvation" as their election to holiness that is emphasized. This is so, for example, in Eph. 1:4 and 1 Pet. 1:1f.; and similarly, in Rom. 8:29, the purpose for which God foreordained those whom He foreknew was that they should be "conformed to the image of his Son." In none of these places is there any suggestion of "election to damnation" as a correlative. We should beware of generalizing from such particular references as those in Rom. 9:22 ("vessels of wrath made for destruction") and 1 Pet. 2:8 ("they stumble because they disobey the word, as they were destined to do").[37] The general analogy of Biblical teaching on this subject indicates that some are chosen or selected by God—not in order that others, apart from them, may be left in perdition, but in order that others, through them, may be blessed.[38]

---

[37] See Chapter 10f, 332, and 10h, 342, on these two references respectively.
[38] Bruce (1972), 196f.

Chapter 12

CONCLUSION

I have set out my case for the conviction that God doesn't choose individuals for salvation, and that neither does he reject others so that they are consigned to reprobation and a lost eternity. In reviewing the historic debate between Calvinism and Arminianism, I have come to the conclusion that it is a question which cannot satisfactorily be resolved either by resort to the complex logic of Calvinism and the Arminian response to it, nor to the feelings of individuals who believe either that they had no choice in the matter or, on the other hand, feel strongly that the choice for Jesus was theirs alone, even though individuals on either side of that particular fence may claim to have the inner witness of the Holy Spirit supporting their convictions. The only way the historic debate can be satisfactorily resolved is by a rigorous re-examination of the biblical data, and attempting to do so having set aside the predestinatory control beliefs or premature intuitions which have skewed the western Church's understanding of Election at least since Augustine.

However, too often even the attempt to re-evaluate scripture has been marred by what might be called a 'proof-text' approach; in other words, taking verses of scripture, irrespective of their context, to fashion a case for or against a particular point of view. Mostly, that will not have been deliberate, but it is relatively easy to assume that a particular text has a wider application because it appears to contains a universal truth, for example, although in reality its content applies only to its immediate context. Thus, throughout the foregoing discussion, I have tried as consistently as I can to pay due regard to the contexts of the numerous biblical texts which I and others have cited. In some cases that has created further problems; mainly because issues of date, authorship, the purpose of writing, the relationships between the different biblical authors and their work, and a whole host of other considerations, remain unsolved or debatable. The basic problem with the proof-text approach is that, although we may agree that the Holy Spirit inspired all of Holy

Writ, so that a basic agreement between the biblical authors can be assumed, the different human writers, nonetheless, had differences of purpose, audience, and perhaps even understanding of the theology of what they wrote.

It seems to me that the key to a correct understanding of Election is the question of what is to be understood by divine sovereignty. It has to be faced head-on because its solution either validates or negates any other consideration, and that without exception. The idea that everything, comprehensively, is foreordained by God pulls the rug out from under any other aspect of the subject of Election, but, no matter how much the Reformed response may insist that I am still responsible for my actions, it is complete nonsense to insist that I can be held culpable by a just and loving God for actions which I had no choice in bringing about. In saying that, I open myself to the accusation of being unable to appreciate the hidden purposes of God, of course, and I have to admit that there may be some truth in that. However, I find myself completely unable to accept the proposition that God would want a universe populated, even in very small part, by apparently rational beings - a universe which is nothing more than some kind of vast mechanical toy; a toy which at creation he wound up and set in motion until all had been played out, but without any of its components, you and me in particular, the apparently rational parts, having any volitional role in any of it.

We might envisage creation as a huge vastly complex computer-controlled model railway layout where the designer gains complete satisfaction in seeing the whole set-up working perfectly with all the complex shunting of waggons into sidings and journey schedules perfectly synchronised and on time. But it would be totally impersonal. On that basis, the whole purpose of creation, fall and redemption would be a desperately pointless game which could afford absolutely no satisfaction to anyone, least of all to its Creator and Redeemer because it was devoid of relationships, the components being unable to react or respond to the grand designer, and he unable to reciprocate in kind. Reformed doctrine would very quickly condemn any suggestion of deism, but that seems to me to be precisely where that idea leads. My earlier conclusion that God could not possibly delight in the worship, or semblance of worship, of creatures who could do no other than accede to the divine whim, seems to me to clinch the argument – admittedly, not an argument based on scripture in the sense that I could cite supporting Bible passages or proof texts, but nonetheless based on the kind of God I have got to know through scripture and personal experience, albeit far from perfectly, it has to be said, but a God whom scripture and experience demonstrate to be gracious, loving, kind, and above all just.

Foundational to the Christian understanding of our God is that he made us like himself in his own image and likeness. If I am truly made in his image, even though that image be distorted, there must remain some aspects of his character, one of which will be that innate ability to value and respond to the love of others when it is freely given, and to distinguish from that and dismiss as totally worthless a feigned devotion demanded by the object of that devotion, which is ultimately loveless.

Apart from the question of whether God's sovereignty implies that nothing I think or say or do is of my own volition, but is predetermined, it seems to me that *the* remaining key element in this whole debate is the extent to which we can rely on our innate capacity to reason and understand. We need therefore to dismiss out of hand that kind of corruption of what it is to be made in God's image, and the contingent Calvinistic error of underplaying the efficacy of human reason seriously needs to be questioned. I have attempted to show that that road can lead only to intellectual suicide.[1] I therefore reject the notion that human intellect is incapable of encompassing the question of God's sovereignty as set against human freedom of choice, and I regard the so-called compromise positions set forth by advocates of the Reformed tradition who cannot stomach a double-predestinatory stance, and which I have briefly outlined, to be in effect admissions of just that incapability. A consequence of the Reformed hegemony to which I have continually referred seems to have been a loss of confidence on the part of Christians in the power and efficacy of human rationality. While I more or less agree with the concept of Total Depravity when understood in a certain way, I do not accept that our powers of logical analysis were fundamentally flawed in the Fall, although I do accept

---

[1] See Chapter 7, 196.

that our ability to reason lucidly will often be impaired by the delusions of sinful decisions we may have made, the ravages of ageing, mental illness, or even in more critical cases, of demonisation. Not only do we need to clear away the obscuring layers of Calvinistic dogma from the pages of Holy Scripture therefore, some of which has been allowed to accumulate due to the conservatism of Bible translators, but we also need to regain confidence in our God-given innate ability to be rational.

Since all we have in terms of hard data concerning God's sovereignty and the human response is the Bible, I maintain that only by taking the Bible seriously and striving for an accurate rendering and exegesis of the relevant biblical passages can we hope to unravel the complexities of the historic debate, and that is what I have tried to do.

I have alluded several times to what I regard as a Reformed hegemony in Christian literature and biblical translation. My contention is that our understanding of scripture has been seriously skewed by a long history of Augustinian assumptions which have been adopted by much of the Church, and which, because of the convincing-sounding rhetoric of Calvinism, have become the general orthodoxy of the western Church to this day. That Reformed skewing (if that's not too weak an expression) has unfortunately found its way into most of our modern Bible translations. There, the ordinary everyday meaning of what we may regard as Election vocabulary has been accorded a technical or soteriological nuance in many places in the New Testament so that the Reformed case is reinforced by what can only be regarded as mistranslations.

A case in point, is the precise meaning of the word 'elect' or 'chosen'. In the course of my analysis of the election vocabulary, I have come to the conclusion that these terms can bear a wider, less predestinatory-specific meaning, and I have attempted throughout that analysis to find alternative meanings wherever Reformed writers have adopted interpretations which reinforce their particular view. With respect to my section on *eklektos* (208ff.), it was apparent that when applied to Rufus,[2] for example, *eklektos* does not carry soteriological meaning,

---

[2] Romans 16:13.

but rather the sense that he was special in some way. Of the 22 or 23 occurrences of *eklektos* in the New Testament, that single example alone might suggest a broader range of meaning of the word, but there does also seem to be a degree of interchangeability of election vocabulary, especially between *eklektos* and *agapētos* as seen when the various Gospel sayings concerning Jesus at his baptism and transfiguration are compared. That view is reinforced by the way the passive participle of the Hebrew *bachar* is translated in the Septuagint. Normally, the Greek *eklegō* translates the Hebrew *bachar*, but there is a handful of cases (I counted 17) in the Septuagint where *eklegō* is not used and where the meaning is either akin to the application of *eklektos* to Rufus, or has to do with youth, military prowess or some other aspect of being 'choice'.[3]

That broader understanding of the meanings of some of this vocabulary has an impact, of course, on our understanding of passages where the Christ is said to be chosen. We do not therefore need to explain away how his chosenness does not carry soteriological meaning, but, by the same token, we do not either have to insist that the 'chosen' vocabulary must carry soteriological import when applied to other people.

If the Bible could be translated without those narrow assumptions, I believe that a very different story could emerge, and scripture might be read and heard with a new clarity which has evaded lay and academic theologians alike for many centuries. I would therefore urge thinking Christians to free themselves from the categories of theological thought which have brought us to this seeming impasse and to carefully read scripture again, taking due note of Reformed influences and the resultant poor conclusions which the Church historically has drawn pretty well throughout the whole of its existence in the West.

I believe that the evidence I have reviewed supports the notion that none of the New Testament passages which refer to elect *individuals* has their salvation directly in view. On the other hand, when due allowance has been made for translators' interpretative proclivities, all references to 'the Elect', apart from those about Christ, perhaps,[4] are to be

---

[3] See Table 3, 353 and n11.
[4] See discussion on the corporate Christ: Chapter 9, 252, 'What does 'in Christ' mean?',

regarded as envisaging the *community* of the Elect whose salvation is very much in view. I strongly suggest that this contrast between singular and plural, or collective singular usage, itself should alert us to the absence of any hint of divine choice of individuals for either salvation or reprobation.

Emphasis upon the individual, as distinct from the community is a relatively modern phenomenon. A bane of modern Christianity is its tendency towards individualism, whether in terms of personal choice, especially with respect to independence from the authority of church leadership, devotional exercise or Christian service and many other aspects of church life today, including the divisive exercise of personal preferences over the components of worship services – styles of music, Bible versions, gender of the leader, etc. – the list is endless. The culture of ancient West Asia in Bible times, as well as today in large measure, knew little of any of that, and both family and church depended upon the cohesion of their extended communities. It should not seem strange therefore for scripture to prefer to place emphasis upon classes or communities of people rather than upon individuals. While we must not disregard the biblical emphasis upon the individual nature of the response called for by the gospel, a truth which needs to be maintained and stressed, the tenor of the New Testament writings, most of which were directed towards communities of God's people, in line with the spirit of their time and culture, was about the community of the Elect as opposed to individual elect persons, which is where the emphasis of Reformed teaching tends to lie.

Having said that, and in view of a growing understanding of the concept of corporate solidarity,[5] it seems to me that the question emerges as to how the Magisterial Reformers understood Augustine, and whether in consequence *our* understanding of his teachings needs to be re-assessed. I think it likely that Augustine, still under the influence of the kind of corporate solidarity mentality which prevailed until the Renaissance, and which still to a large extent prevails in more eastern cultures

---

and 268 n83, on the meaning of 'Christ' as an honorific, also C. F. D. Moule (1977), 47-89.
[5] See Chapter 9b, 265, 'Unitary Election'.

today, may have been misunderstood by Calvin and his like, who forced upon his theology a strictness and specificity with regard to the individual that his original work possibly cannot bear.

The key concept which unifies all of the biblical teaching on Election is that Jesus Christ is *the* Elect One, *the* Chosen One of God. It is an exclusive divine choice: no other individual has been, nor ever will be chosen. An individual can only be elect in Christ, therefore. The status of Christ in his divine chosenness is imparted to the individual through their becoming incorporated into him by faith; becoming part of Christ, and as such, becoming a partaker in everything that Christ has and will have, even to the ultimate eschatological glory of being seated with him in the heavenly realms.[6] Although Walter Elwell reaches a conclusion different from mine, he rightly draws attention to the fact that in Paul's writings, the closely related ideas of Election and Predestination are "part of the very fabric of his thinking" and are "buried deeply within highly complex theological arguments", although they are never developed as themes.[7] If only Paul had expanded on those themes more fully the Church might have been saved a lot of trouble over the centuries! However, the little expression 'in Christ' or 'in him' is peculiarly characteristic of Paul's theological expression and it seems to encapsulate the case I have been pursuing. For Paul, nothing that God plans nor does is apart from Christ, "the elect one par excellence"; indeed, the *only* elect one. The one goal of the divine plan is to "sum up all things in Christ", with the ultimate end being "the praise of God's glorious grace".[8]

Only if Paul's terminology is given its due weight, that our election is 'in Christ', in the sense that we are transferred into Christ as we exercise saving faith, can we hope to make sense of the New Testament doctrine of Election. In order to be faithful to scripture it is not necessary to perform impossible logical or semantic gymnastics, as have many interpreters on both sides of the Election debate, nor indeed to resort to the unfortunate expedient of explaining away or side-lining divinely

---

[6] Ephesians 2:6.
[7] Elwell in Hawthorne & Martin, 225.
[8] Ibid., 228; Ephesians 1:5, 10f.

inspired scripture. Our God-given attribute of free will is not violated because the choice of accepting the gospel is, indeed, in the gift of the individual, and is his or her choice alone. Indeed, I would insist that it is not saving faith that is God's gift to us, but it is the freedom to exercise that faith. Neither is God's sovereignty imperilled. He has set in motion and upholds a universe, governed by the physical laws he established in creation and where apparently random events do occur, with which both he and we may interact and even influence dynamically. Within that scenario he has gifted every human being the ability and the right to exercise freedom of will, especially with respect to the choice which must be made as whether to learn to love him or not. Rather than being a denial of his sovereignty, I suggest that it is actually the proof of his majesty, his wisdom and awesome power that such a universe does not spin out of control. God is sufficiently great to encompass all of the randomness and the consequences of human choices which make up the bundle of life on earth, and despite all of that, he is still able to bring about his divine purposes throughout history. To me, that magnifies our God; a far better conclusion than attempting to apply limitations on what he may or may not decree or know, an impudence which must surely risk divine censure not unlike that against Job and his so-called comforters as they attempted to second-guess his purposes.[9] Although, on the whole, I am not in favour of invoking mystery whenever problems arise in our understanding, we would still be forced to respond as Job did when we have attempted to speak of such things:

> Surely I spoke of things I did not understand,
> Things too wonderful for me to know.[10]

In a chapter entitled 'Calvinism and Problematic Readings of New Testament Texts Or, Why I am not a Calvinist', Glen Shellrude lists seven observations which summarise his Arminian position.[11] I summarise them by way of drawing to a close the case I have been trying to make:

1. There is a lack of historical and contextual evidence which would

---

[9] Job 38:2; 42:3a.
[10] Job 42:3b.
[11] Shellrude in Pinnock & Wagner, 43ff. I am not hereby advocating Arminianism, but Shellrude's points do agree with my position.

permit us to interpret the New Testament within a framework of theological determinism.

2. Theological determinism conflicts with the natural, intuitive reading of many scriptural texts. A good hypothesis is one that accounts for the largest amount of data with the fewest number of exceptions. If we read the New Testament within the framework which theological determinism creates, we do not find *occasional* tensions which may require a somewhat counterintuitive interpretation of scattered texts. Rather, the challenges are huge. A Calvinist reading requires counterintuitive and unhistorical interpretations of thousands of biblical texts.

3. On a Calvinist reading of scripture, the motivational effectiveness of many scriptural statements is dependent on the reader being deceived. God's people are motivated to faithful service and discipleship with the promise of future blessing when, according to a Reformed reading, God has already determined their precise experience of blessing and rebuke for each person. Believers are promised that God will enable them to resist temptation when in reality he has already determined that in many situations they will give in to temptation and sin. The warnings against apostasy motivate believers to persevere in their faith when in reality apostasy is a theoretical impossibility for Calvinism. God assures his people that he will enable them to be renewed in their thinking while simultaneously ordaining that they embrace a wide range of erroneous ideas. The promise is made that the Spirit will enable obedience when in reality God only intends that believers have a very limited experience of obedience.

4. One needs to account for the chasm between what God says about his moral will for humanity and the way he actually choreographs human experience. God is opposed to evil and is the champion of goodness and truth, but he writes a script for human history in which evil and carnage are the dominant realities. In order to account for this, Calvinists must distinguish between God's "revealed will" ("preceptive will") and his "secret/hidden or ordaining will" ("decretive will"). The result is a view of God which represents him as

having two distinct wills which are deeply conflicted and contradictory.

5. Calvinists use language and concepts in ways unparalleled in human experience. They typically affirm that God loves each and every person (although some dissent on that point) while simultaneously ordaining that many of those he "loves" will have no opportunity to avoid the horror of eternal separation. Likewise, Calvinism affirms that God is pure holiness while simultaneously ordaining and rendering certain all the sins and evils of human experience. Edwin Palmer acknowledges the absurdity of what Calvinism affirms: "He [the Calvinist] realizes that what he advocates is ridiculous ... The Calvinist freely admits that his position is illogical, ridiculous, nonsensical and foolish."[12] However, he argues that the scriptural evidence requires one to embrace this intrinsically absurd view of God. If God has created us with a rational and moral discernment, which to some extent mirrors his own, then the cluster of logical and moral absurdities inherent in the Calvinist system suggests that there is a problem with the theology itself. The appropriate response is not to celebrate absurdity, or as is more commonly done, to appeal to mystery, but rather to rethink the theology in light of the totality of the scriptural evidence.

6. The Calvinist's view of God is contradicted by God's self-revelation in scripture. God reveals an uncompromising opposition to sin and evil, but Calvinism argues that he has decreed every expression of sin and evil in human experience. However, on Calvinist assumptions, God intentionally chose to write a script with all the evil and carnage which we observe. It is impossible to reconcile this with God's self-revelation as one characterised by love, mercy, holiness and an uncompromising opposition to sin and evil. A theistic world view constructed on the assumption that God has created men and women with genuine libertarian freedom provides a much more plausible account of reality in that the explanation for a great deal of what is wrong with the world can be traced to the sinful abuse of

---

[12] Edwin Palmer, *The Five Points of Calvinism* (Grand Rapids, MI: Baker, 1972), 106.

the gift of our libertarian freedom. That being the case, an affirmation of libertarian freedom may not explain everything and certainly leaves plenty of room for mystery.

7. Theological determinism in effect denies the scriptural affirmation that God desires to be in relationship with the people he created. If one day we are able to actualise the science fiction notion of creating artificial intelligence which replicates human behaviour, it is difficult to imagine that people would find joy in relationships with those who are following their programming 100 per cent of the time. It is also impossible to imagine that the God who created men and women for a relationship with him would find joy in relationships with those who were simply following their divine programming at every point.

God desires that *all* should be saved and come to a knowledge of the truth,[13] and by 'all' I understand Paul to have meant every human person who has ever lived or who will ever live. My response and yours is simply to say 'Yes' to Jesus or, with C. S. Lewis, to stop resisting the divine wooing of grace. The essence of repentance is to 'turn again', and with open heart receive him, for we have nothing of ourselves to offer which may earn or contribute to our salvation. Only by his gift of the Holy Spirit can we come to him and begin to grow into his likeness. It is only through his power in us, as in willing obedience we permit his inner working, that we can respond fully to the divine election which is exclusively Christ's, but which he offers to share with us. Only by our willing submission will the process of salvation be enabled and

---

[13] 1 Timothy 2:4. Calvin had particular difficulty with this verse: "the Apostle simply means that there is no people and no rank in the world that is excluded from salvation ... the present discourse relates to classes of men, and not to individual persons; for his sole object is to include in this number princes and foreign nations": *Commentary on 1 Timothy*, quoted by Shank (*Elect*), 94. Likewise, Augustine: "He wills the salvation of all the elect, among whom men of every race and type are represented": Kelly, 369. See also Mounce, 84ff., who shows that the context of this verse argues against Calvin and Augustine's non-specific view. Likewise, Robert Picirilli in Pinnock & Wagner, 55, points out that the occurrence of the word "all" in the similar context of 1 Timothy 4:10: "we have put our hope in the living God, who is the Saviour of *all* people, and especially of those who believe", supports a universal understanding of 1 Timothy 2:4 and 6, and demonstrates how, in providing atonement for all in a universal sense, God's salvation becomes effective only for those who believe.

continue until the day when we shall see him and be like him; when we shall finally and fully share his election and inheritance, and the adoption and calling to which we have been predestined will be complete.

Finally, I hope I have achieved my stated aim of exposing a biblical doctrine of Election without the Reformed overlay that has accumulated at least since the time of Augustine and the Arminian response to it. Not all will be convinced – it is very hard to free oneself from presuppositions (prejudices perhaps) – control beliefs, which have always, it seems, been accepted as orthodoxy, especially as it appears that proof texts do not seem to help to untangle the web of complexity that we have made of it all – but my prayer is that what has gone before will commend itself to serious consideration and perhaps serve to free some from what might even be regarded as an idolatry which lies at the heart of Calvinism.

At the conclusion of each chapter of his *Systematic Theology*, Wayne Grudem poses a number of questions for reflection and discussion. He seems to adopt an even-handed and eirenic stance throughout his tome, continually acknowledging objections that might be raised against what he is saying. So, following his section on 'Election and Reprobation', he imagines that an Arminian and a Calvinist try to accommodate the other's point of view and that they ask each other, "Is there anything that Calvinists and Arminians could do to bring about greater understanding and less division on the question?"[14] Rather like Charles Simeon, in his exchange with the elderly John Wesley,[15] Grudem seems to stand on firm ground in seeking reconciliation, but I wonder how possible it really is to find such a rapprochement. I suppose that both could resolve never again to speak about Predestination: after all, almost all else that they believed was held in common – give or take. It might also be possible to urge the other to set aside their control beliefs and look at scripture afresh, as I have been advocating. But I fear there may still be ground which divides them because: again, as I have been saying, between the thoroughgoing Calvinist and the Arminian there is the problem of what one does with the question of divine determinism. It

---

[14] Grudem (2007), 687.
[15] See Chapter 7, 194 and n8.

seems to me that it is that question alone which determines what kind of God one believes in, whether the seemingly harsh, inflexible God of Calvinism or the loving and accommodating God of (I would say) scripture. I believe that is the issue which causes the predominance of what is often called 'moderate Calvinism', the Reformed stance that denies Double Predestination and rejects the harshness of hyper-Calvinism. It seems to me that many of a Reformed mindset cannot really accept the God they say they believe in, and if I were one of them, I would want to find a solution too. That is what this book has been all about.

Thus, as I type these closing words, I am acutely aware that many, perhaps the majority of Christians I know, have an ambiguous theology of Election. Most of the churches I know which have a Reformed stance espouse a single predestinatory view, and that is true of many other believers who do not necessarily belong to an overtly Reformed congregation. I say this without any sense of judgmentalism or condemnation, but I suggest that stance is, as I have tried to show, untenable, on both logical and scriptural bases. My hope therefore, as I offer this contribution to what has become a debate between deeply entrenched positions, is that brothers and sisters in Christ will take at least some of what I am suggesting and begin to experience a new freedom in Christ as they see our gracious Father God in a whole new light – the light of one who is Love and who acts wholly and only from a motivation of love for the whole of his creation and especially for his human creatures.

EPILOGUE

One of the worship songs we sometimes sing in church claims that God chooses individuals – *The Same Love* by Paul Baloche and Michael Rossback, the opening lines of which run,

> You choose the humble and raise them high;
> You choose the weak and make them strong.

Despite the scriptural context on which these words are based,[1] there is no mention in the song's lyrics of any purpose or role for which the humble and weak were being chosen, so one can only assume, as the song stands without any explanatory context, that the authors meant that those categories of humanity, and by implication, their individual members, were being chosen for salvation – in other words, a Reformed nuance. A quick check through the song books from which most of my church's repertoire comes revealed at least 30 songs which explicitly expressed similar sentiments – "God has chosen me", etc. Other songs did refer to being chosen in Christ or of the Church being chosen, however – the distinction being singular and plural objects of divine choice respectively. Furthermore, in the period of worship following that song on that particular day, the leader reminded the congregation that God had chosen each one of them – reinforcing what the song seemed to imply. However, another song that same Sunday morning provided the needed corrective – Stuart Townend's beautiful *How deep the Father's love for us*, which includes the lines,

> As wounds which mar the Chosen One
> Bring many sons to glory.

Of the 30-odd songs identified as expressing the idea that God chooses individuals, a few could be construed as being ambiguous, admittedly, but I have no idea whether the authors of the majority had in mind that we were chosen 'in Christ' or whether they believed that God had handpicked individuals to be his own and with whom he would share his

---

[1] 1 Corinthians 1:27f. where Paul does state the purpose for which the humble and weak were chosen.

glory. As those songs stand, without that kind of explanatory context, to my way of thinking they express an unbiblical error, an error which I feel can draw sincere believers into a false understanding of their faith which, as I have tried to demonstrate, represents a kind of god that I do not find in scripture – at least, not the kind of god which scripture portrays as the God and Father of our Lord Jesus Christ. Many false gods are encountered in the pages of the Bible, of course, and I suggest that this is yet another; one of the kinds of idol which the Apostle John warns against perhaps.[2]

Christ is *the* Chosen One, as Stuart Townend's song correctly affirms, and I believe he, Christ, alone has been divinely chosen. I wonder if others in our congregation that day sensed any contradiction between those two songs. I suspect not – certainly, the worship leader didn't (and I did ask him). We shouldn't derive our theology from songs and hymns, of course, but songs and hymns are profoundly influential in shaping the way we express faith and therefore our understanding of God. Indeed, notable hymn-writers from the past deliberately composed what have become some of the great hymns of the Church's heritage in order to teach the truth of scripture; Charles Wesley and Isaac Watts being among the very greatest, not to mention many of the hymns of Cecil Frances Alexander who often wrote to teach children the creeds. It is therefore profoundly important, I suggest, that contemporary Christian songwriters, as well as preachers and worship leaders, express themselves clearly, unambiguously and above all biblically.

An example of unambiguous theology in song was experienced by my wife at a recent wedding she attended. The congregation sang Dustin Kensrue's *Grace Alone*, which contains the lines,

> And in love before you laid the world's foundation
> You predestined to adopt me as your own.

Evidently, the New Calvinism is alive and well.

I suspect that I shall have to bear with such ambiguities and confusion of language for the rest of my days, but I shall always glory in the fact

---

[2] 1 John 5:21.

that I have been incorporated into the Chosen One, the Lord Jesus Christ, and that I became part of him through the exercise of my own free choice, having been divinely invited through the gospel to respond to his love and grace. What's more, now that I am 'in Christ', as the Apostle Paul would characteristically put it, I look forward to my resurrection and adoption and to participate in all that God has always predestined for his Elect – the body of those upon whom he has placed his name – not those who have been individually selected for preferential treatment, but those who by faith have placed their trust in Jesus.

I rest my case. But let me underline the one issue above others which has motivated me to commit these thoughts to writing. William G. MacDonald has wisely said,

> When doing theology, one always must ask the supreme question concerning God, *"What is his name?"* (Exod. 3:14). His true identity is ultimately the issue in every doctrine. What kind of God has manifested himself in history, culminating in the infallible revelation in Christ? What does a particular doctrine like election teach and imply about the nature of God? God's character is on the line in every doctrine and especially in the doctrine of election. Whom he chooses, how he chooses, and whether his criterion for choice is arcane or announced tell us much about God, even if we had no other doctrines to compare.[3]

If God did choose you and me beforehand, but at the same time invites us to respond as though we were completely free to do so, then is he the God of integrity and justice in whom you believe? I don't, and I hope you don't either!

---

[3] W. G. MacDonald in Pinnock, 208 (his italics).

APPENDIX 1

Election Vocabulary in the NIV (2011) New Testament

This Table 4 includes only words to which the NIV translation affords a sense of choosing:

Reference	Text	Greek Key Word	
hairetidzō: αἱρετίζω: verb: to choose			
Mat 12:18	my servant whom I have *chosen*	ᾑρέτισα	*hēretisa*

haireō: αἱρέω: verb: to choose			
Phil 1:22	what shall I *choose*?	αἱρήσομαι	*hairēsomai*
2 Thess 2:13	God *chose* you	εἵλατο	*heilato*
Heb 11:25	He *chose* to be ill-treated	ἑλόμενος	*helomenos*

boulomai: βούλομαι: verb: to deliberately purpose			
Jas 1:18	He *chose* to give us birth	βουληθεὶς	*boulētheis*
1 Pet 4:3	what pagans *choose* to do	βούλημα	*boulēma*

eklegomai: ἐκλέγομαι: verb: to choose, select			
Mark 13:20	whom he has *chosen*	ἐξελέξατο	*exelexato*
Luke 6:13	and *chose* twelve of them	ἐκλεξάμενος	*eklexamenos*
Luke 9:35	my Son, whom I have *chosen*	ἐκλελεγμένος	*eklelegmenos*
Luke 10:42	Mary has *chosen* what is better	ἐξελέξατο	*exelexato*
Luke 14:7	guests *picked* the places of honour	ἐξελέγοντο	*exelegonto*
John 6:70	Have I not *chosen* you, the Twelve	ἐξελεξάμην	*exelexamēn*
John 13:18	I know those I have *chosen*	ἐξελεξάμην	*exelexamēn*
John 15:16	You did not *choose* me	ἐξελέξασθε	*exelexasthe*
John 15:16	but I *chose* you	ἐξελεξάμην	*exelexamēn*
John 15:19	I have *chosen* you out of the world	ἐξελεξάμην	*exelexamēn*
Acts 1:2	the apostles he had *chosen*	ἐξελέξατο	*exelexato*
Acts 1:21	necessary to *choose* one of the men	-	(verb implied)
Acts 1:24	which of these two you have *chosen*	ἐξελέξω	*exelexō*

ELECTION VOCABULARY IN THE NIV (2011) NEW TESTAMENT

Acts 6:5	They *chose* Stephen	ἐξελέξατο	exelexato
Acts 13:17	God ... *chose* our ancestors	ἐξελέξατο	exelexato
Acts 15:7	God made a *choice* among you	ἐξελέξατο	exelexato
Acts 15:22	decided to *choose* some of their own	ἐκλεξαμένους	eklexamenous
Acts 15:22	They *chose* Judas	-	(verb implied)
Acts 15:25	we all agreed to *choose* some men	ἐκλεξαμένους	eklexamenous
1 Cor 1:27	God *chose* the foolish things	ἐξελέξατο	exelexato
1 Cor 1:27	God *chose* the weak things	ἐξελέξατο	exelexato
1 Cor 1:28	God *chose* the lowly things	ἐξελέξατο	exelexato
Eph 1:4	he *chose* us in him	ἐξελέξατο	exelexato
Jas 2:5	has not God *chosen* those	ἐξελέξατο	exelexato

eklektos: ἐκλεκτός: participle: chosen/elect (one/ones)			
Mat 20:16 (KJV)	many be called, but few *chosen*	ἐκλεκτοί	eklektoi
Mat 22:14	many are invited, but few are *chosen*	ἐκλεκτοί	eklektoi
Mat 24:22	for the sake of the *elect*	ἐκλεκτοὺς	eklektous
Mat 24:24	to deceive ... the *elect*	ἐκλεκτούς	eklektous
Mat 24:31	they will gather his *elect*	ἐκλεκτοὺς	eklektous
Mark 13:20	for the sake of the *elect*	ἐκλεκτοὺς	eklektous
Mark 13:22	to deceive ... the *elect*	ἐκλεκτούς	eklektous
Mark 13:27	and gather his *elect*	ἐκλεκτοὺς	eklektous
Luke 18:7	justice for his *chosen* ones	ἐκλεκτῶν	eklektōn
Luke 23:35	God's Messiah, the *Chosen* One	ἐκλεκτός	eklektos
John 1:34	God's *Chosen* One	ἐκλεκτός	eklektos
Rom 8:33	those whom God has *chosen*	ἐκλεκτῶν	eklektōn
Rom 16:13	Rufus, *chosen* in the Lord	ἐκλεκτὸν	eklekton
Col 3:12	God's *chosen* people	ἐκλεκτοὶ	eklektoi
1 Tim 5:21	the *elect* angels	ἐκλεκτῶν	eklektōn
2 Tim 2:10	the sake of the *elect*	ἐκλεκτούς	eklektous
Titus 1:1	the faith of God's *elect*	ἐκλεκτῶν	eklektōn
1 Pet 1:1	To God's *elect*	ἐκλεκτοῖς	eklektois
1 Pet 1:2	*chosen* according to	-	(verb assumed)
1 Pet 2:4	but *chosen* by God	ἐκλεκτὸν	eklekton
1 Pet 2:6	a *chosen* and precious cornerstone	ἐκλεκτὸν	eklekton
1 Pet 2:9	you are a *chosen* people	ἐκλεκτόν	eklekton
1 Pet 5:13	*chosen* together with you	συνεκλεκτὴ	suneklektē
2 John 1	The lady *chosen* by God	ἐκλεκτῇ	eklektē

THE PREDESTINATION PROBLEM

| 2 John 13 | your sister ... *chosen* by God | ἐκλεκτῆς | *eklektēs* |
| Rev 17:14 | *chosen* and faithful followers | ἐκλεκτοὶ | *eklektoi* |

eklogē: ἐκλογή: noun/adjective: free choice			
Acts 9:15	This man is my *chosen* instrument	ἐκλογῆς	*eklogēs*
Rom 9:11	God's purpose in *election*	ἐκλογὴν	*eklogēn*
Rom 11:5	a remnant *chosen* by grace	ἐκλογὴν	*eklogēn*
Rom 11:7	The *elect* among them did	ἐκλογὴ	*eklogē*
Rom 11:28	as far as *election* is concerned	ἐκλογὴν	*eklogēn*
1 Thess 1:4	he has *chosen* you	ἐκλογὴν	*eklogēn*
2 Pet 1:10	your calling and *election*	ἐκλογὴν	*eklogēn*

epilegō: ἐπιλέγω: verb: to call, name, select			
John 5:2	which in Aramaic is *called* Bethesda	ἐπιλεγομένη	*epilegomenē*
Acts 15:40	Paul *chose* Silas	ἐπιλεξάμενος	*epilexamenos*

episkeptomai: ἐπισκέπτομαι: verb: to pick out, choose			
Acts 6:3	*choose* seven men from among you	ἐπισκέψασθε	*episkepsasthe*

thelō: θέλω: verb: to wish, want			
Mat 27:15	a prisoner *chosen* by the crowd	ἤθελον	*ēthelon*
John 5:35	you *chose* for a time to enjoy his light	ἠθελήσατε	*ēthelēsate*
Rom 9:22	*choosing* to show his wrath	θέλων	*thelōn*
2 Cor 12:6	if I should *choose* to boast	θελήσω	*thelēsō*
Col 1:27	God has *chosen* to make known	ἠθέλησεν	*ēthelēsen*

klēroō: κληρόω: verb: to appoint, choose by lot[1]			
Eph 1:11	In him we were also *chosen*	ἐκληρώθημεν	*eklērōthēmen*

lambanō: λαμβάνω: verb: to take out of			
Heb 5:1	Every high priest is *selected*	λαμβανόμενος	*lambanomenos*

proginōskō: προγινώσκω: verb: to foreknow			
1 Pet 1:20	He was *chosen* before the creation	προεγνωσμένου	*proegnōsmenou*

---

[1] See Chapter 8a(iv), 213, *klēroō*.

ELECTION VOCABULARY IN THE NIV (2011) NEW TESTAMENT

procheiridzomai: προχειρίζομαι: verb: to appoint

Acts 22:14	God of our ancestors has *chosen* you	προεχειρίσατο	*proecheirisato*

procheirotoneō: προχειροτονέω: verb: to elect/appoint

Acts 10:41	whom God had already *chosen*	προκεχειροτονημένοις	*prokecheirotonēmenois*

stratologeō: στρατολογέω: verb: to assemble an army/enlist soldiers

2 Tim 2:4 (KJV)	who hath *chosen* him to be a soldier	στρατολογήσαντι	*stratologēsanti*

cheirotoneō: χειροτονέω: verb: to appoint

2 Cor 8:19	he was *chosen* by the churches	χειροτονηθείς	*cheirotonētheis*

There are four additional places where the NIV translates the Greek in such a way as to imply the involvement of one of the verbs of choosing:

(a) Luke 1:9: 'he was chosen by lot', referring to Zechariah's temple service. There is actually no verb of choosing, the phrase being, 'his lot was (*elache tou*: ἔλαχε τοῦ) ... to go into the temple ...', a genitive of purpose.

(b) John 2:10: 'the choice wine'. Again, there is no verb; the phrase being, *ton kalon oinon*: (τὸν καλὸν οἶνον).

(c) Romans 8:20: 'the creation was subjected to frustration, not by its own choice' – an adverbial phrase which represents *ouch hekousa* (οὐχ ἑκοῦσα), 'unwillingly', and qualifies the verb 'was subjected' (*hupetagē*: ὑπετάγη).

(d) 1 Peter 1:1 & 2: is a long sentence with no verb in the Greek text. The NIV's 'have been chosen' in verse 2 has been supplied for the sake of clarity. The sense of chosenness derives from the plural dative adjective *eklektois* (ἐκλεκτοῖς) in verse 1.[2]

---

[2] See Chapter 8c, 219, 'Foreknowledge'.

APPENDIX 2

Relationships Between *Beloved, Pleasing, Chosen* and *Only*

In Chapters 8 (211) and 10 (284) I suggested that there may be degrees of interchangeability or synonymity between elements of the New Testament's vocabulary to do with choosing. Using Howard Marshall's observations about links between the sayings at Jesus' baptism and his transfiguration as a starting point,[1] a closer examination of those sayings might shed a little more light.

The nine sayings listed in Table 5 (below) fall into three main groups: (1) the witness of the voice from heaven at Jesus' baptism and John the Baptist's testimony to Jesus' identity, (2) the witness of the voice from the cloud at the Transfiguration scene, and (3) where Matthew, in his characteristic way, links the identity of the Messiah with Old Testament prophecy, here with Isaiah's Chosen Servant from Isaiah 42:1-4. John the Baptist's saying is included in the first category because it is associated with Jesus' baptism and presumably springs from the Apostle John's memory of the words spoken over Jesus at his baptism.

Some of these Greek texts may have suffered from editing or 'correcting', presumably during the copying of manuscripts, but from Table 5 (below), where the most important variants are listed, it is clear that the baptismal sayings in the Synoptic Gospels bear a remarkable similarity to each other. Mark and Luke have, "my Son, whom I love; with *you* I am well pleased", although Matthew has "with *him* I am well pleased". The Transfiguration sayings are more variable, however, although Matthew's is identical to his baptismal saying. Only Luke omits the "I love" element, having instead "chosen", and there are good scholarly reasons for retaining that reading despite the existence of a known

---

[1] I. H. Marshall (1990), 127.

variant which has "I love". Marshall[2] suggests that the verb *eklegō* (ἐκλέγω) is probably a translation variant for *agapētos* (ἀγαπητός), both of which reflect the Hebrew *bachir* (בָּחִיר) from Isaiah 42:1, a passage which is usually assumed to have influenced the baptismal saying. It seems that Luke may have assimilated his choice of vocabulary to the Septuagint which has "my chosen" (*ho eklektos mou*: ὁ ἐκλεκτός μου).

Table 5: Gospel sayings about Jesus as *Beloved, Pleasing, Chosen* and *Only*: NA26[3] readings and significant variants:

	Beloved ἀγαπητός	Pleased εὐδόκησα	Chosen ἐκλεκτός	Only μονογενής
Jesus' Baptism:				
Matthew 3:17: My Son, whom I love; with him I am well pleased. ὁ υἱός μου ὁ ἀγαπητός, ἐν ᾧ εὐδόκησα	X	X		
Mark 1:11: My Son, whom I love; with you I am well pleased. ὁ υἱός μου ὁ ἀγαπητός, ἐν σοὶ εὐδόκησα	X	X		
Luke 3:22: My Son, whom I love; with you I am well pleased. ὁ υἱός μου ὁ ἀγαπητός, ἐν σοὶ εὐδόκησα (or ηὐδόκησα)	X	X		
John 1:34: John the Baptist's testimony about Jesus: God's Chosen One.[4] ὁ υἱός τοῦ θεοῦ ὁ ἐκλεκτός τοῦ θεοῦ (as NIV) ὁ ἐκλεκτὸς υἱός τοῦ θεοῦ ὁ μονογενὴς υἱός τοῦ θεοῦ			X X	X

---

[2] I. H. Marshall (1978), 388.
[3] Evidence for textual variants is also drawn from Kurt Aland, *et al.*, *The Greek New Testament* (United Bible Societies, 2nd ed. 1968).
[4] Although the 2011 edition of the NIV and NET do not follow the NA26 reading, both Barrett (1978), 178, and Carson (1991), 152, favour the ἐκλεκτός τοῦ θεοῦ variant, which is attested in papyrus P[5], although not P[66] or P[75], which are generally regarded as being of greater importance. The occurrence of ἐκλεκτός υἱός, a secondary conflate reading, may bear witness to the existence of an otherwise unknown ἐκλεκτὸς reading. Barrett reasons that it would be easier to understand ἐκλεκτὸς being changed to υἱός rather than the reverse. John does not use ἐκλεκτός elsewhere in his Gospel, however, and the μονογενὴς υἱός variant is found only in texts of John's Gospel.

THE PREDESTINATION PROBLEM

The Transfiguration:

Matthew 17:5:
My Son, whom I love; with him I am well pleased.
ὁ υἱός μου ὁ ἀγαπητός, ἐν ᾧ εὐδόκησα   X   X

Mark 9:7:
My Son, whom I love.
ὁ υἱός μου ὁ ἀγαπητός   X
ὁ υἱός μου ὁ ἀγαπητός ὃν ἐξελεξάμην   X   X

Luke 9:35:
My Son, whom I have chosen.
ὁ υἱός μου ὁ ἐκλελεγμένος[5]   X
ὁ υἱός μου ὁ ἀγαπητός   X
ὁ υἱός μου ὁ ἀγαπητός ἐν ᾧ (ἡ) εὐδόκησα   X   X
ὁ υἱός μου ὁ ἐκλεκτός   X

2 Peter 1:17:
My Son, whom I love; with him I am well pleased.
ὁ υἱός μου ὁ ἀγαπητός μου οὗτός ἐστιν εἰς ὃν ἐγὼ   X   X
εὐδόκησα[6]

Matthew 12:18:
Matthew identifies Jesus with Isaiah's Servant in Isaiah 42:1:
My servant whom I have chosen, the one I love, in whom I delight.
ὁ παῖς [7] μου ὃν ᾑρέτισα, ὁ ἀγαπητός μου εἰς ὃν   X   X   X
εὐδόκησεν

The fact that Luke's text is the most variable of the synoptics might suggest that his copyists were aware of the other Gospels but perhaps felt the need to bring Luke into line, perhaps unconsciously, but with a variety of different results. Unless they were consciously trying to correct Luke's text, what strikes me in particular is whether his copyists felt that switching vocabulary made any significant difference to its meaning. Peter's words, which clearly relate to the Transfiguration, although not from one of the Gospels, are more expansive, and show some variations in word order, but they are closest to Matthew's.

---

[5] I. H. Marshall (1978), 388, says, "There can be little doubt that ὁ ἐκλελεγμένος is the harder text" and should therefore be given preference. The participle is unusual, so "a change to ὁ ἐκλεκτός is understandable."

[6] Variations of this verse exist, but all contain the ἀγαπητός and εὐδόκησα elements.

[7] Matthew uses παῖς rather than υἱός, which can mean 'child' or 'boy', but in context must mean 'servant'.

Apart from Matthew 12:18, which is Matthew's own testimony to the identity of Jesus as Messiah, only John and Luke employ the idea of chosenness. Both of these texts have a number of variants, which suggests a propensity for their copyists to harmonise the Gospel witnesses, but, as we have seen, the scholarly consensus, reflected in the 2011 edition of the NIV and NET, opts for the "chosen" variants of John 1:34[8] and Luke 9:35. As has already been suggested, this might call into question the notion that these two vocabulary options differ significantly in meaning in first century and biblical usage. That conclusion might have significance for the whole doctrine of Election if it can be shown that to be among the chosen ones (election to salvation is never of individuals) is not so much to be a member of a *chosen* segment of humanity, but rather to be among a *cherished* community. It should be noted from Table 6 (below) that the third phrase, "the one I love", for which Matthew uses *ho agapētos mou* (ὁ ἀγαπητός μου), is paralleled in the Septuagint of Isaiah 42:1 by *ho eklektos mou* (ὁ ἐκλεκτός μου). Thus, although Matthew mirrors the pattern of the quotation from Isaiah, he seems to deliberately substitute the vocabulary of belovedness for the Hebrew and septuagintal vocabulary of chosenness, again reinforcing the suggestion of a close affinity between the two concepts.

Although all three elements; *beloved, pleased* and *chosen* are present in Matthew's saying, the verb for choosing is not *eklegomai* (ἐκλέγομαι) as in the other texts, but is the *hapax legomenon, hairetidzō* (αἱρετίζω), which is not present in the Septuagint of Isaiah 42:1. There the noun *eklektos* is employed instead,[9] describing the Servant as "my chosen one", and reflecting the Hebrew noun *bachir*. Matthew can hardly be said to be quoting the Isaiah text, even from the Septuagint, even though he appears to claim to do so. If it is not a reflection of an otherwise unknown text, it seems more likely, therefore, to be his own rendering of the Hebrew.

---

[8] Although not in Tyndale House' recent *Greek New Testament* (Jonkind *et al.*, 2017), which has ὁ υἱός τοῦ θεοῦ.

[9] Morris, 310 n45, observes that *hairetidzō* does not occur in the LXX of Isaiah 42:1, but neither does *eridzō* (ἐρίζω): 'to quarrel' (Matthew 12:19) nor *tuphomai* (τυφόμαι): 'smouldering' (Matthew 12:20), and all three verbs are New Testament *hapax legomena*.

Table 6: Comparison of the Greek and Hebrew variants of Matthew 12:18 and Isaiah 42:1:

Matthew 12:18 (NIV): Here is my servant whom I have chosen, the one I love, in whom I delight;	**Greek NA26:** ἰδοὺ ὁ παῖς μου ὃν ᾑρέτισα, ὁ ἀγαπητός μου εἰς ὃν εὐδόκησεν ἡ ψυχή μου
Isaiah 42:1 (NIV): Here is my servant, whom I uphold, my chosen one in whom I delight;	**Hebrew MT:** הֵן עַבְדִּי אֶתְמָךְ־בּוֹ בְּחִירִי רָצְתָה נַפְשִׁי
Isaiah 42:1 (LXX NETS): Iacob is my servant; I will lay hold of him; Israel is my chosen; my soul has accepted him;	**Greek LXX (Swete):** Ἰακὼβ ὁ παῖς μου, ἀντιλήμψομαι αὐτοῦ Ἰσραὴλ ὁ ἐκλεκτός μου, προσεδέξατο αὐτὸν ἡ ψυχή μου

The idea of chosenness on its own is meaningless unless the goal of that chosenness is specified, of course, but for chosenness to imply something about the relationship which it creates means a great deal more. I suggest therefore that the two ideas, *agapētos* and *eklektos* may have significant semantic overlap - as Carson recognises, "love and election are closely connected".[10]

I have already suggested that it would be difficult to differentiate the meaning of *hairetidzō* from *eklegomai*, particularly since Matthew, when referencing Isaiah 42:1, chooses to use the former in place of *eklektos*, the noun which relates to *eklegomai*, and thus creates somewhat of an enigma by doing so. The question it raises is whether this unique occurrence of *hairetidzō* in the New Testament suggests any semantic difference between the two verbs which might need to be examined – specifically, whether *hairetidzō* implies anything special about the chosenness of Jesus.

Gundry addresses a similar question: he speculates,

> Ὂν ᾑρέτισα [*hon hēretisa*: "whom I have chosen"] in Mt presents

---

[10] Carson (1995), 286. Gundry, 112, discussing Matthew's use of *hairetidzō*, also draws attention to the double 'signification' of *bachar*: 'choice and love'.

several possibilities. The evangelist may have understood תמך [*tamak*: "uphold"] in the sense of "taking hold of to acquire, to bring or *adopt* to oneself." … Or αἱρετίζειν [*hairetidzein*] may anticipate the thought of ἐκλεκτός [*eklektos*] in the next phrase of the LXX. Or parallel influence from Hag 2:23, where σε ᾑρέτισα [*se hēretisa*] (LXX) renders בך בחרתי [*bka bacharti*: "I have chosen you"], may enter. Yet again, Mt's Hebrew text may have read or he himself may have brought in בחרתי בו [*bacharti bo*: "whom I have chosen"] from Is 44:2 (cf. 41:8, 9: בחרתיך [*bachartika*: "whom I have chosen"; "I have chosen you"]; in both passages the LXX has ὃν ἐξελεξάμην [*hon exelexamēn* (aorist): "whom I have chosen"]. Since this provides a reason for Mt's aorist, against the future of the LXX and the imperfects of the MT and the Targum in Is 42:1, and since αἱρετίζειν [*hairetidzein*] is usual in the LXX for בחר [*bachar*],[11] the last view is preferable, with the added consideration that Mt brings in בחרתי בו [*bacharti bo*] … in anticipation of בחירי [*bachiri*] - to make room for ὁ ἀγαπητός μου [*ho agapētos mou*: "in whom I delight"; lit. "my beloved"] from the voice at Jesus' baptism and transfiguration…. Thereby Mt has brought into focus the double signification of בחר [*bachar*], choice and love. Again, the parallel passages Is 44:2; 41:8, 9 contain the ἀγαπητός [*agapētos*]-motif[12] and may have suggested or encouraged the insertion from the baptismal and transfiguration narratives.[13]

A recently published lexicon by J. P. Louw and E. A. Nida, which groups vocabulary in semantic domains, i.e., words with similar contexts, makes no suggestion that *hairetidzo* has the nuance of adoption, as Gundry suggests. Under their domain of 'To choose', they link *eklegomai, haireomai* and *lambanō* (*lambanō* usually means 'to take' or 'receive' in a very general sense), with the definition, "to make a choice of one or more possible alternatives - 'to choose, to select, to prefer'". They add the comment,

> In a number of languages the choice of terms or expressions for 'choosing' or 'selecting' often depends upon either (1) what is

---

[11] Not so: in the LXX *bachar* is translated by *hairetidzō* only 13 times as compared with *eklegomai* 115 times.
[12] The beloved one in Isaiah 41:8 is Abraham.
[13] Gundry, 112. (Interpolations in square brackets with NIV renderings and the italicisation of "*adopt*" are mine.)

385

chosen or selected or (2) the purpose for such a choice, for example, personal pleasure, rational evaluation, or outright prejudice.[14]

They do differentiate between *haireomai* and *eklegomai* in other contexts, however: "to choose or select for the purpose of showing special favor to or concern for — 'to choose, to select'" and "to make a special choice based upon significant preference, often implying a strongly favorable attitude toward what is chosen—'to choose, choice'", respectively.[15] Thayer makes only the distinction that *eklegō* generally has the sense of choosing for oneself. Vine also affirms that *eklegō* in the middle voice means "to choose for oneself, not necessarily implying the rejection of what is not chosen, but choosing with the subsidiary ideas of kindness or favour or love". On the other hand, according to Vine, *hairetidzō*

> signifies to take, with the implication that what is taken is eligible or suitable; hence, to choose, by reason of this suitability, Matt. 12:18, of God's delight in Christ as His "chosen".[16]

BAGD defines *hairetidzō* as 'to choose', perhaps with the specific sense of 'to adopt', citing 1 Chronicles 28:6 and Malachi 3:17 in the Septuagint,[17] while *eklegomai* also means 'to choose', or 'select', but with an indication of that from which the selection is made, or to choose something for oneself, or with an indication of the purpose for which the choice is made, etc. It is uncertain whether *BAGD*'s definition of *hairetidzō* in the sense of adoption as a special sense of choosing really holds up, however. In the two verses cited, 1 Chronicles 28:6 and

---

[14] Louw & Nida, 30.86.
[15] Ibid., 30.91f., citing for *hairetidzō* Matthew 12:18, and for *eklegomai* Luke 9:35 and Acts 13:17.
[16] Vine, 1:189.
[17] W. C. Allen, 131, says, "αἱρετίζειν is a late word common in the LXX [28 times in 27 verses in all books]. It is used as = equivalent to "adopt" in 1 Ch 28⁶ ...; Mal 3¹⁷ ...; Georg Kaibel, *Epigrammata*, 252.... The aorist here and in εὐδόκησεν may simply be due to imitation of the Hebrew tenses, but in the mind of the Christian translator probably imply the eternal pre-temporal act of God in the election of the Messiah." Inscription 252 from Kaibel, 97, from Panticapaeum, an ancient Greek settlement at the farthest eastern extent of Crimea (ancient Taurica) is probably from the first century BC. Allen probably assumed the Gospel of Matthew to have originally been written in Hebrew, making it the first of the synoptics, to have been later translated into Koinē Greek – hence the reference to a translator. For discussion of this point, see Morris, 12-15.

Malachi 3:17, the first might support the idea of adoption where *hairetidzō* translates *bachar*:

> Solomon your son is the one who will build my house and my courts, for I have *chosen* him to be my son, and I will be his father.

But in the preceding verse (28:5), however, *bachar* is translated by *eklegomai* to mean 'one chosen among others':

> Of all my sons ... he has *chosen* my son Solomon to sit on the throne of the kingdom of the LORD over Israel.

On the other hand, in Malachi 3:17, *hairetidzō* occurs twice, each occurrence translating the Hebrew *chamal* (חָמַל), meaning 'to spare' or 'have pity upon':

> 'On the day when I act,' says the LORD Almighty, 'they will be my treasured possession. I will *spare* them, just as a father has compassion and *spares* his son who serves him.

The seven other septuagintal occurrences, where *hairetidzō* represents verbs other than *bachar*, have meanings as follows:

- Genesis 30:20: *zabal* (זָבַל: to exalt, honour): "My husband will *treat me with honour*, because I have borne him six sons."
- Numbers 14:8: *chaphets* (חָפֵץ: to delight in, take pleasure in, desire): "If the LORD *is pleased* with us, he will lead us into that land."
- 1 Samuel 25:35: *nasa'* (נָשָׂא: to lift, bear up, carry, take): "I have heard your words and *granted* your request."
- Psalms 132:13-14 [LXX 131:13-14]: *'avah* (אָוָה: to desire, incline, covet, wait longingly, wish, sigh, want, be greedy, prefer): "For the LORD has chosen (*exelexato*: ἐξελέξατο = *bachar*) Zion, he has *desired* it for his dwelling" and "Here I will sit enthroned, for I have *desired* it."
- Malachi 3:17: *chamal* (חָמַל: to spare, pity, have compassion on): "I will *spare* them, just as a father has compassion and *spares* his son who serves him."

These non-*bachar* examples thus seem to suggest a sense of favour rather than adoption.

As already noted, *eklegomai* occurs only 22 times in the New

Testament and is therefore a relatively uncommon verb.[18] Likewise, in the canonical books of the Septuagint it occurs 122 times in 118 verses[19] of which 116 translate the Hebrew *bachar*,[20] while *hairetidzō* occurs 21 times in 20 verses of which 13 translate *bachar*.[21] There seems to be no significant difference between the usage of either verb in these texts, suggesting that they may be near-synonyms,[22] although *eklegomai* is clearly much more common. The principal usage of *eklegomai* describes the choice of people – priests, kings, soldiers, etc., and the place where God will or has placed his name (i.e., Jerusalem), especially in a number of texts from Deuteronomy. Setting aside those instances where *eklegomai* translates verbs other than *bachar*, there are a few references to the choice of wives, territory, smooth stones, the choice of abstract concepts like life or death, or choosing whom to serve, and so on. There may be a detectable nuance of choosing or selecting from different options, although there are exceptions – for example, God chooses 'this place' (the temple, which was already *in situ* in context) or 'once again' chooses Israel.[23] Likewise, *hairetidzō* refers to choices of Judah and Jerusalem, Solomon, Zerubbabel, ways or precepts, new gods or leaders, etc.

The lexical sources do not therefore seem to provide a clear distinction between the two verbs. Etymologically, *eklegomai* comprises *ek* – 'out of' and *legō* – 'to say', or 'speak', hence the general sense of making a choice. However, words related to *hairetidzō* tend to nuance a sense of choosing with self-opinionated distinction. Thus, *hairetikos*

---

[18] See Chapter 8a(i), 202, *eklegomai*.
[19] These statistics will vary according to which version of the Septuagint is used. I have disregarded non-canonical books because there are no Hebrew equivalents.
[20] The remaining occurrences translate *barar* (בָּרַר) (x2), *laqach* (לָקַח) (x1), *qabal* (קָבַל) (x1), *qabats* (קָבַץ) (x1) and *toor* (תּוּר) (x1).
[21] The remaining occurrences translate *'avah* (אָוָה) (x2), *chamal* (חָמַל) (x2), *chaphets* (חָפֵץ) (x1), *nasa'* (נָשָׂא) (x1), and *zabal* (זָבַל) (x1) respectively. One instance, Hosea 4:18, has no Hebrew equivalent.
[22] Neither verb is listed in Stewart Custer, *A Treasury of New Testament Synonyms* (Greenville, SC: Bob Jones University Press, 1975), nor George Ricker Berry, *A Dictionary of New Testament Greek Synonyms* (Grand Rapids, MI: Zondervan, 1979). See also 1 Chronicles 4-10 LXX where *eklegomai* occurs twice and *hairetidzō* three times with apparently indistinguishable meanings within the space of seven verses.
[23] 2 Chronicles 7:16; Isaiah 14:1.

388

(αἱρετίκός), found in Titus 3:10, means 'one who causes division', hence the English word 'heretic'. Etymology is a hazardous area, however, because the original meanings of words gradually change with time and place. It seems to me then, that the meanings of *eklegomai* and *hairetidzō*, which were presumably distinct when they were originally coined, have probably converged over time so that they have become virtually synonymous and therefore interchangeable. This conclusion is supported from a few of the ways where convergence can be seen in some septuagintal texts. For example, in 1 Chronicles 28:4 and Psalms 132[131 LXX]:13, both verbs occur in close proximity:

> Yet the LORD, the God of Israel, chose (*exelexato*: ἐξελέξατο) me from my whole family to be king over Israel for ever. He chose (*hēiretiken*: ἡρέτικεν) Judah as leader, and from the tribe of Judah he chose (no corresponding verb in LXX) my family, and from my father's sons he was pleased to make me king over all Israel.

Here in 1 Chronicles, both verbs translate the Hebrew *bachar*, while in the Psalm *eklegomai* translates *bachar*, and *hairetidzō* translates *'avah*, which the NIV translates 'desired':

> For the LORD has chosen (*exelexato*: ἐξελέξατο) Zion, he has desired (*hēiretisato*: ἡρετίσατο) it for his dwelling.

Likewise, 1 Chronicles 28:6 has "I have chosen (*hēiretika*: ἡρέτικα) him [Solomon] to be my son", while the preceding verse (28:5) has "he has chosen (*exelexato*: ἐξελέξατο) Solomon."

Table 7 (below) shows the distribution of these verbs throughout almost two millennia of secular and religious Greek literature and demonstrates distinct changes in their usage.

Apart from the Septuagint, only three source texts were found for *hairetidzō* – the New Testament (Matthew 12:18), the Apostolic Fathers (2 Clement 14:1) and *Vita Barlaam et Joasaph* by Euthymius the Athonite (10th century AD: often attributed to John of Damascus – 8th century AD). Although the allocation of authors to particular centuries is fairly approximate, these data do show a complete absence of *hairetidzō* before the second century BC, and an almost complete absence

Table 7: Verbs of Choosing in Greek Literature:[24]

Authors (Number of texts)[25]	Total Texts	*haireō*	*hairetidzō*	*eklegō*
9th Century BC				
Homer (3).	3	641		
8th Century BC				
Hesiod (3) & Lycurgus (1).	4	30		
6th Century BC				
Aristides (2).	2	219		11
5th Century BC				
Aeschylus, Andocides, Antiphon, Apollodorus, Aristophanes, Bacchylides, Euripides, Herodotus, Hippocrates, Lysias, Pindar, Plato, Sophocles, Thucydides & Xenophon.	67	1453		58
4th Century BC				
Aeneas Tacticus (1), Aeschines (1), Aristotle (9), Demosthenes (8), Dinarchus (1), Hyperides (1), Isaeus (1), Isocrates (2) & Theophrastus (1).	25	567		28
3rd Century BC				
Apollonius Rhodius (1), Callimachus (1), Demetrius of Phaleron (1), Polybius (1) & Theocritus (1).	5	259		15
2nd Century BC				
Septuagint (OT & Apocrypha: Swete).	1	9	28	137
1st Century BC				
Bion of Phlossa (1), Diodorus Siculus (3) & Dionysius of Halicarnassus (9).	13	548		38
1st Century AD				
Apostolic Fathers (Lake) & NT.	2	5	2	37
2nd Century AD				
Achilles Tatius (1), Aelian (3), Appian (2), Aretaeus (1), Arrian (5), Athenaeus (2), Epictetus (1), Galen (1), Harpocration (2), Longinus (1), Longus (1), Lucian (35), Marcus Aurelius (1), Pausanias (1) & Philostratus (6).	62	1316		67
3rd Century AD				
Cassius Dio Cocceianus (1), Chariton (1), Clement of Alexandria (3), Diogenes Laertius (1), Philostratus the Lemnian (1) & Xenophon of Ephesus (1).	8	458		29

---

[24] Source data: <www.perseus.tufts.edu> supplemented by the LXX (Swete) and the *Apostolic Fathers* (Kirsopp Lake).

[25] Some texts listed are collected works or symposia.

4th Century AD Basil of Caesarea (1), Eusebius of Caesarea (1) & the Emperor Julian (13).	16	118		21
6th Century AD Moschus (3) & Procopius (2).	5	260		2
10th Century AD Euthymius the Athonite (1).	1	6	1	10
Overall Totals	**289**	**6988**	**32**	**497**

after the first century AD. What is more, the verb seems to appear only in Judeo-Christian texts; obviously, a significant observation, although nonetheless puzzling. It is also significant that the predominant verb is *haireō*, while *eklegō* is far less frequent than might be expected from the perspective of our knowledge of the New Testament.

There is a clear difference between first-century Christian and non-Christian texts, therefore. The ratio of *haireō* to *eklegō* in the New Testament and Apostolic Fathers together is about 1 to 7, with many more occurrences of *eklegō*, whereas other first-century sources demonstrate the opposite – about 27 to 1 with *eklegō* in the minority. This might be explained by the Christian texts having a greater emphasis on the Elect – i.e., the Church, a bias that can also be seen in the greater number of nouns and adjectives based on the *eklektos* root in the Christian texts. The same bias is also seen in the Septuagint, where the proportion of *eklegō* to *haireō* is even greater – about 15 to 1.

On the basis of such evidence, it seems virtually impossible to differentiate between the meanings of *eklegō* and *hairetidzō*, or even *haireō* in the New Testament. Why Matthew should have chosen to use *hairetidzō*, then, remains an enigma, unless, perhaps he wished to import a sense of antiquity as he quoted or paraphrased the eighth-century BC prophet by using what he possibly considered to be an almost obsolete religious word in a way that some today might still prefer to quote the antiquated terminology of the King James Version.

APPENDIX 3

John Piper's *Five Points*: A Critique[1]

Between 1980 and 2013, John Piper exercised a godly and influential ministry, particularly at Bethlehem Baptist Church in Minneapolis, Minnesota. His written output is prodigious: Wikipedia (as of May 2020) lists 75 titles published between 1980 – *Love Your Enemies*, to the present, 2020 - *Coronavirus and Christ*.[2] Although his books are widely read and are significantly influential, my own reading of Piper has been quite selective, so I cannot claim to have a comprehensive overview. I have found much that I have read to have been extremely helpful, but a number of negative characteristics have emerged. In Chapter 2, I reflected Roger Olson's view that Piper's books were "unusually reader-friendly and scholarly", but I now have to confess that I have not found that to be particularly true, possibly because I am at odds with his Reformed theology anyway, but also because he seems to habitually set up novel ideas like "Christian hedonism", "future grace", "the God-centeredness of God", etc., and then takes up what seems like an inordinate amount of space seeking to justify his terminology. It also seems to me that he is afflicted with the old malaise of making syllogistic fallacies, where conclusions drawn are based on logically (often) binary terms but fail to take into account other possible alternatives or exegetical conclusions.

My purpose in writing this book was not primarily to critique the five points of Calvinism (TULIP) because my concerns were fixed on the Reformed take on Election. However, in one way or another it has been necessary to comment on each point in a variety of contexts. I thought therefore, seeing that Piper's writings are so widely read, that it might be helpful to work through his own version of TULIP and see how my conclusions relate to his. His *Five Points: Towards a Deeper*

---

[1] Piper's biblical quotes are from the *English Standard Version* (ESV), 2007. All italics in quotes from Piper are his own.
[2] This text was drafted in the midst of the March 2020 COVID-19 lockdown in the UK.

Experience of God's Grace, is, as his subtitle indicates, a plea to his readership to move towards a deeper experience of God's grace [3] through delving more deeply into the five points of Calvinism. To each he devotes a chapter, although not in the usual TULIP order.

a. Total Depravity (Chapter 3)[4]

Normally regarded as the first of the Five Points of Calvinism, Total Depravity is one I do accept – more or less, provided that it can be adequately explained. It is the foundation of the Reformed understanding of the doctrine of salvation, so it is a pity that Piper chooses to explain it with questionable biblical support.

His main contention is that since humankind is separated from God and the Holy Spirit is not therefore present to motivate and empower our behaviour, nothing we do, no matter how laudable in human terms – whether they be major works of charity or small kindnesses – can be regarded as other than sinful. He is clear that Total Depravity does not imply that an unregenerate person does as much evil as he or she can, but even "if he is restrained from performing more evil acts by motives that are not owing to his glad submission to God, then even his 'virtue' is evil in the sight of God". He supports this conclusion with Romans 14:23: "Whatever does not proceed from faith is sin",[5] which he says is "a radical indictment of all natural 'virtue' that does not flow from a heart humbly relying on God's grace".[6]

Debate over the interpretation of Romans 14:23 goes back at least as far as Chrysostom (AD 347-407) and has played an important part in theological controversy ever since. Sanday and Headlam quote Chrysostom's verdict:

> When a person does not feel sure, nor believe that a thing is clean, how can he do else than sin? Now all these things have been spoken

---

[3] Piper (2013), 9.
[4] Ibid., 17-23.
[5] Greek: πᾶν δὲ ὃ οὐκ ἐκ πίστεως ἁμαρτία ἐστίν. He might have done better to have used Romans 3:23 with an explanation of 'sin' and what it means to 'fall short of the glory of God'.
[6] Ibid., 17f.

by Paul of the object in hand, not of everything.[7]

This is "hardly to be doubted", says Cranfield; "A statement of universal application would be inapposite here. It would break the continuity between v. 23a and 15.1".[8] However, in his *Contra Julianum*, Augustine employed this Romans text to teach that works done by believers before justification and those done by unbelievers can only be sinful – thus, the heathen are unable to do good works.[9] Likewise, Piper cites Thomas Schreiner who claims that "this verse is introduced precisely because it stands as a sweeping maxim with profound biblical warrant: Acting without faith is sinning".[10] Both Piper and Schreiner rely heavily on the biblical truth that acting in faith glorifies God and is the way we should operate in every detail of life, but they assume the antithesis to be correct too: "Not relying on God in any action or thought takes power and glory to ourselves. That is sin, even if the external deed itself accords with God's will."

In Romans 14, Paul had been discussing the vexed questions concerning appropriate diet and the observance of 'holy' days. These were matters over which so-called 'weaker brothers' might be stumbled because they felt obligated to scrupulously avoid non-kosher foods, especially if they had been offered to idols,[11] and also to continue to keep the Jewish festivals and sabbaths, but for 'stronger brothers' they were matters of indifference. The question therefore arises as to whether verse 23b should be seen as applying specifically to these matters, as Chrysostom seems to imply, or whether Paul was applying a universal

---

[7] Sanday & Headlam, 394.
[8] Cranfield (1975), 729. Some authorities see a break after verse 23 in any case, as some manuscripts have the doxology of Romans 11:33ff. interposed at that point: see Longenecker (2011), 19ff.
[9] Sanday & Headlam, 394; Augustine, *Contra Julianum* 4.32; Aquinas, *Summa* 1.2, qu. 19, art. 5.
[10] Piper (2013), 17 n1; Thomas R. Schreiner, *Romans*, Baker Exegetical Commentary on the New Testament, Vol. 6 (Grand Rapids, MI: Baker, 1998), 739. Schreiner cites 1 Peter 4:11; 1 Corinthians 15:10; Galatians 2:20 to make the point that not relying on God's grace and power robs him of glory, but these verses actually teach that God is glorified when we act in his strength and by his grace: they do not say that to do otherwise is sin, and particularly not the actions of unbelievers who are not being addressed by Paul in any case.
[11] Also 1 Corinthians 8.

principle which also included non-Christians within its scope.

Cranfield challenges Augustine's interpretation by asking that very question - whether Romans 14:23b is a general statement or is limited to the immediate context of the 'weak' and the 'strong', but he also asks in what sense Paul used the word 'faith' (*pistis*) and also what he meant by 'is sin' (*hamartia estin*).[12] He concludes that however 'faith' may be construed it must conform with the rest of chapter 14,[13] although I don't see why it necessarily should. With regard to the matter of sinfulness, Cranfield claims that Paul uses the word 'sin' (*hamartia*) here rather differently from the way he normally uses it. Here, he says, it is used in a relative way - to characterise the conduct of the Christian who acts in spite of the fact that he has not received the inner freedom to do so, as opposed to one who does have the inner freedom to do whatever he wills. Thus, Romans 14:23b would seem to say that the action of the strong Christian, who has the necessary inner freedom, is not sin provided he is not thereby hurting a weaker brother or sister. Cranfield concludes his analysis with the observation that none of our actions, even those which can truly be described as 'from faith', is ever entirely free from sin; in other words, "everything which is not done with a clear conscience is sin."[14]

It seems to me, however, that in Romans 14:23 Paul does bring a general principle to bear on the matter, but I suggest it should not apply universally to include unbelievers. Its relevance is only to those being discussed in the immediate context. Those who were not acting in faith were Christians who *could* have acted in faith, but who nevertheless *did not*. That would rule out unbelievers for whom faith in a Christian sense would not be an option in any case since they lived in unbelief. I suggest then, that the Bible does not teach what Piper claims, and he would have done better not to have attempted to go down the proof-text route, but rather use other biblical evidence to establish the validity of

---

[12] Cranfield (1975), 728f.; see also Chapter 6, 168-70, where Paul's usage of *hamartia* is briefly discussed; Longenecker (2016), 373f.
[13] Cf. Romans 14:1, 22 and 23a; also that *pisteuein* in 14:2 denotes the confidence that one's Christian faith permits one to do a particular thing, and all in agreement with the thematic importance of *pistis/pisteuein* throughout the chapter.
[14] Sanday & Headlam, 394.

Total Depravity.

The issue is bound up with the oft-raised question regarding the fate of those who have never heard the gospel, or, as I would prefer, those who have never received an *adequate* account of the gospel.[15] A key passage in this respect is Romans 2:6-16:

> God 'will repay each person according to what they have done.' To those who by persistence in doing good seek glory, honour and immortality, he will give eternal life. But for those who are self-seeking and who reject the truth and follow evil, there will be wrath and anger. There will be trouble and distress for every human being who does evil: first for the Jew, then for the Gentile; but glory, honour and peace for everyone who does good: first for the Jew, then for the Gentile. For God does not show favouritism.
>
> All who sin apart from the law will also perish apart from the law, and all who sin under the law will be judged by the law. For it is not those who hear the law who are righteous in God's sight, but it is those who obey the law who will be declared righteous. (Indeed, when Gentiles, who do not have the law, do by nature things required by the law, they are a law for themselves, even though they do not have the law. They show that the requirements of the law are written on their hearts, their consciences also bearing witness, and their thoughts sometimes accusing them and at other times even defending them.) This will take place on the day when God judges people's secrets through Jesus Christ, as my gospel declares.

The issue, so far as God is concerned, is not to do with obedience to a particular prescribed set of rules - in this case, the Law of Moses, but rather with the manner in which people conduct their lives. Paul makes the point that merely having the Law makes no difference to one's (i.e., a Jew's) ultimate and eternal destiny. Complete obedience can never be achieved, and so can never be the grounds of our acceptance with God, in any case. Romans 2:6 says that God will judge us according to

---

[15] Many have been offended by the efforts of well-meaning Christians to evangelise them. Their offence and rejection may have had nothing to do with the content of the message, but rather with the conduct or manner of the messenger. Thus, they have rejected an inadequate account. See also the statement from Vatican II: *Lumen Gentium* II, 16: <http://www.vatican.va/archive/hist_councils/ii_vatican_council/documents/vat-ii_const_19641121_lumen-gentium_en.html>.

what we have done,[16] and that irrespectively of whether we have a set of rules to measure up to. So, what about those who have no idea of what God requires? Certainly, our salvation cannot be earned, and it is our relationship with God through faith in Christ that determines our salvation, but is God the kind of god who unfairly condemns those who never had that chance in life? The strict Reformed response will be a 'yes', of course.

The world is full of people who have no intention of serving the true God, let alone seeking him out, but Paul does open the door of opportunity to "those who by persistence in doing good seek glory, honour and immortality". The phrase, "they are a law for themselves" (2:14), for some, tends to have negative connotations. In other words, those words might be construed as referring to people who do not care about goodness or morality, but live as they please without regard to others, let alone God. But what Paul is really saying is that it is as though these people instinctively or intuitively know the Law - "the requirements of the law are written on their hearts" (2:15); because they seek to live according to high ideals – the Golden Rule, if you will. Such folk may, indeed, be rare, but the one who reads our secret intentions knows what is in their hearts and minds, and I would suggest that they would gladly have embraced the Saviour if only they had heard of him. Thus, even unbelievers are able to please God although they may do so in ignorance of the gospel and of the possibility of the empowering Holy Spirit.[17] It is those who reject the truth who will be condemned (2:8), but if they do not know the truth, God behaves justly towards them and their true hearts will be revealed on judgment day (2:16). That strongly suggests to me that the 'good' deeds of the ignorant pagan cannot by any stretch be regarded as sinful. They and their deeds are acceptable to God. Jesus taught the same gospel, as John bears witness:

> For God so loved the world that he gave his one and only Son, that

---

[16] Alluding to Psalms 62:12 and/or Proverbs 24:12; also Revelation 20:12.
[17] Some scholars claim that Paul here refers to Christian Gentiles, e.g., Barclay, 80; Cranfield (1975), 155f., following Augustine and Ambrosiaster, but others, e.g., Longenecker (2016), 273ff., see the absence of the article with "Gentiles" (*ethnē*, 2:14) as indicating Gentiles in a "generic, non-specific sense", which fits better the logical flow of Paul's argument.

whoever believes in him shall not perish but have eternal life. For God did not send his Son into the world to condemn the world, but to save the world through him. Whoever believes in him is not condemned, but whoever does not believe stands condemned already because they have not believed in the name of God's one and only Son. This is the verdict: light has come into the world, but people loved darkness instead of light because their deeds were evil. Everyone who does evil hates the light, and will not come into the light for fear that their deeds will be exposed. But *whoever lives by the truth comes into the light*, so that it may be seen plainly that what they have done has been done in the sight of God.[18]

The 'verdict' (3:19) has nothing to do with our deeds, so it is immaterial whether they are sinful or not: it has everything to do with whom we choose to follow. Inevitably, some will never receive a clear invitation, but they could still be those who seek to "live by the truth",[19] in other words, those who act faithfully and honourably, even though the truth is hidden from them or is obscured by false beliefs. They will come "into the light" because God has seen what they have done.

There is some debate about the meaning of that last phrase of verse 21 of the John 3 passage – "what they have done has been done in the sight of God" (NIV), however. The expression is literally, "done in God" or "done through God" (*en theō estin eirgasmena*), which Carson, citing Westcott construes as "in union with Him, and therefore by His power".[20] A Reformed understanding of such phraseology would therefore be about the activity and empowering of the Holy Spirit in a person's life prior to their confession of Christ, and thus be evidence of their election. A survey of a range of Bible versions doesn't help, and it seems that one can choose between different translations according to one's control beliefs. However, the context of the passage is that of light coming into the world and of individuals coming to the light so

---

[18] John 3:16-21.
[19] A Semiticism according to Carson (1991), 207. 'Semiticism' is the correct spelling of the word: Moule (1959), 171, although 'semitism' is commonly found. A helpful article on semiticisms is David A. Black, 'New Testament Semitisms', *The Bible Translator* 39/2 (London: Sage Publications, April 1988), 215-23.
[20] Carson (1991), 208; B. F. Westcott, *The Gospel According to St John: The Greek Text With Introduction and Notes* (John Murray, 1908), 1.124.

that their deeds may be exposed. I suggest then that "done in God" or "done through God" is best seen as having the perfect, absolutely revealing light of God shone on our deeds, so that their true worth can be plainly seen by all – not least by God himself, and with nothing hidden. Thus, a predestinatory understanding of the passage should be rejected,[21] and I suggest that the NIV does come close to being a good translation.

Piper goes on to claim that the totality of human 'depravity' can be seen in four different ways:

- Our rebellion against God is total,
- In his total rebellion everything man does is sin,
- Man's inability to submit to God and do good is total, and
- Our rebellion is totally deserving of eternal punishment.

i. Our rebellion against God is total[22]

One of the problems I find with John Piper's writing is that he often overstates his case, and consequently draws incorrect conclusions. The bases for his conclusion that "Our rebellion against God is total" include an absence of delight in the holiness of God and there being no glad submission to God's sovereign authority. "There is no delight", he says, "apart from the grace of God", and I have to agree. He reminds us that people can be very religious and philanthropic, but still be in rebellion against God. Indeed, "religion is one of the chief ways that man conceals his unwillingness to forsake self-reliance and bank all his hopes on the unmerited mercy of God". And he quotes a string of Old Testament texts[23] which underline the premise that "None is righteous, no, not one; no one understands; no one seeks for God.... There is no fear of God before their eyes".

Piper does accept that "Men do seek God", however, but he wants to qualify that statement: "But they do not seek him for who he is". His emphasis is on whether individuals *genuinely* seek God. He discounts

---

[21] Although, see Barrett (1978), 218f.
[22] Piper (2013), 18ff.
[23] From Romans 3:9-11, 18.

those who seek him out of desperate need – a mistake, I would suggest:[24] "Apart from conversion, no one comes to the light of God". And that raises yet another issue. Although I am in broad agreement, I do find Piper's way of expressing himself confusing: it is because he uses standard soteriological terminology in what I regard as a non-standard way. For instance, in his *Desiring God*, he describes *conversion* thus:

> This meditation on the nature and origin of conversion clarifies two things. One is the sense in which *conversion is a condition for salvation*. Continuous confusion is caused at this point by failing to define salvation precisely. If salvation refers to new birth, conversion is not a condition of it. *New birth comes first and enables the repentance and faith of conversion.* Before new birth we are dead, and dead men don't meet conditions. *Regeneration is totally unconditional.* It is owing solely to the free grace of God. "It depends not on human will or exertion, but on God, who has mercy" (Romans 9:16).[25]

Furthermore, in a footnote, he quotes Samuel Hopkins: "In conversion man is active, and it wholly consists in his act; but in regeneration the Spirit of God is the only active cause."[26]

Contrary to what Piper says in an example of overstatement, I would say that 'dead men'[27] *can* meet conditions because, despite being fallen (depraved) God has left within us the capacity to answer the gospel call. But there are three terms here that I find puzzling: namely, *conversion*, *salvation* and *regeneration*. I have already commented on the latter, *regeneration* or *new birth*,[28] but, whereas Reformed writers distinguish between *salvation*, or being saved, and *conversion*, I understand the two terms to be virtual synonyms, or at least to overlap in meaning. In Reformed thinking, there is a precise sequence of events which constitutes the process from rebirth to glorification based on the *Golden Chain* of Romans 8:29-30.[29] Given that they believe an individual has been

---

[24] See Chapter 5, 154, 'Saving Grace', on the nature of saving faith.
[25] Piper (2011), 67 (my italics).
[26] Ibid., 75; Samuel Hopkins, "Regeneration and Conversion" in Edward Hindson ed., *Introduction to Puritan Theology* (Grand Rapids, MI: Baker, 1976), 180.
[27] Note the dependency of understanding death in the most extreme way.
[28] See Chapter 5, 143, 'Prevenient Grace'.
[29] See Chapter 8d, 238, 'Calling', and 10e, 324, on Romans 8:29-30.

divinely chosen, the next part of the process is the divine unconditional gift of *regeneration* which awakens the individual to respond to this *effectual* or *prevenient* grace. It is this response of repentance and faith that constitutes *conversion* in Reformed thinking. So, what Piper claims with regard to a person coming to the "light of God" is that no human choice is involved. The process is entirely of grace and is determined by God's election of that person to salvation. For me, and I suspect the majority of Christians, *conversion* is not merely my response to the gospel appeal, but relates to the whole process of change or transformation I will go through from the moment I trust Christ until I see him face to face, a process I would also call *regeneration*, or more correctly, *sanctification*. Likewise, *salvation* can describe the whole business of being part of the New Covenant, although, strictly speaking, it refers to my rescue from eternal loss and my translation from darkness to the kingdom of light – "For he has *rescued* us from the dominion of darkness and brought us into the kingdom of the Son he loves".[30]

ii. In his total rebellion everything man does is sin[31]

I have commented on this aspect of depravity and Piper's misuse of Romans 14:23 already, but some of what he also says under this heading calls for additional comment. For example,

> Thus man does many things which he can do only because he is created in the image of God and which in the service of God would be praised. But in the service of man's self-justifying rebellion, these very things are sinful. We may praise them as echoes of God's excellence, but we will weep that they are prostituted for God-ignoring purposes.

Examples abound of selfless service by unbelievers, so not all 'good deeds' can justifiably be regarded as rebellious or 'self-justifying' – more overstatement. There is, I believe, a true altruism even in fallen humankind which is evidence of God's image having not been completely obliterated. Piper does accept that there are many who do

---

[30] Colossians 1:13.
[31] Piper (2013), 20f.

greater and lesser works of love and kindness, but he constantly asserts that these are done in order to gain God's approval. That is patently untrue. The only way he can press his point is by differentiating between good works which are recognised and accepted by God and those which are not. I find no such differentiation and I don't believe God does either.

Furthermore, in citing Paul's confession in Romans 7:18: "I know that nothing good dwells in me, that is, in my flesh", Piper recognises Paul's admission that in his fallen natural state apart from God nothing good can be achieved. It is only through the working of the Holy Spirit in him that good is achieved. However, the second half of the self-same verse offers a corrective: "For I have the desire to do what is good, but I cannot carry it out". Piper claims, "apart from the work of God's Spirit all we think and feel and do is not good",[32] but Paul is able to think good thoughts even in the 'flesh'. Piper's argument is very difficult to counter simply because it contains some truth. The problem is that the truth is emphasised beyond what I believe Paul meant to say, and so it becomes distorted and misleading.

Thus, I would deny Piper's claim that "such outward conformity to the revealed will of God is not righteousness in relation to God". There can be no doubt that thoughts and actions performed in conscious rebellion towards God must be regarded as sinful, but that is a very different thing from claiming that *all* the thoughts and actions of unbelievers are acts of *rebellion*.

iii. Man's inability to submit to God and do good is total[33]

Piper quotes Romans 8:7-8:

> The mind that is set on the flesh is hostile to God, for it does not submit to God's law; indeed, it cannot. Those who are in the flesh cannot please God.

---

[32] Romans 15:18.
[33] Piper (2013), 21f.

The question arises as to the identity of those "who are in the flesh". Piper seems to portray humanity as sharply divided between, on the one hand, those whose minds are set on the flesh – non-Christians, and, on the other hand, those whose minds are set on the Spirit – believers in Jesus - which is good so far as it goes. The problem with that kind of binary analysis is that Paul places himself in both camps, and it is part and parcel of his (and our) spiritual warfare as to which of his two 'minds' gains the ascendency at any particular moment in time. In Romans 7:18, he had referred to his 'flesh', but in Romans 8:9, his readers, and by implication he himself, are those indwelt by the Spirit. Indeed, in the very same verse, he provides a definition of what a true Christian is, albeit framed negatively: "if anyone does not have the Spirit of Christ, they do not belong to Christ".

It is true that scripture portrays humankind as being dead towards God.[34] In other words, in our unregenerate state, we are incapable of any spiritual life with God even though we have physical life for the time being. Being dead towards God is portrayed for us in the story of Eden in the opening chapters of Genesis where Adam and Eve are expelled from the heavenly security of the Garden of Eden. The most significant aspect of that expulsion was their inability to then return to the Tree of Life, the symbol of the presence and life of God.[35] That ejection portrayed their spiritual death, therefore. The Bible defines death as being separated from God. But I maintain that our first parents were still capable of making moral judgments and had the ability to *aspire* after glory, honour and immortality,[36] the difference being that they no longer had access to the grace and friendship of God, the means by which they could *achieve* glory, honour and immortality. They had lost their way to eternal life – which is what the Tree of Life stood for, and they were totally unable to remedy the plight in which they found themselves. That is the state in which the whole of humanity finds itself from birth (perhaps even from conception) – as Paul puts it in the context of his day, "separate from Christ, excluded from citizenship in

---

[34] Piper cites Ephesians 2:1; 4:18.
[35] Genesis 3:22-4.
[36] Romans 2:6

Israel and foreigners to the covenants of the promise, without hope and without God in the world".[37] They were "darkened in their understanding and separated from the life of God because of the ignorance that is in them due to the hardening of their hearts".[38] Furthermore, their inability to find a path back into God's holy presence is reinforced for us by the intervention of angelic beings:

> After he drove the man out, he placed on the east side of the Garden of Eden cherubim and a flaming sword flashing back and forth to guard the way to the tree of life.[39]

And the whole story of scripture from that point on describes for us how God created and opened up for us the way back to the Tree of Life, beautifully depicted in John's vision of the Tree of Life growing along the banks of "the river of the water of life" in the New Jerusalem.[40] What is more, once permanently outside the 'Kingdom', so to speak, we remain prey to the wiles of the 'serpent' who had led our first parents astray in the first place. Again, as Paul puts it,

> The god of this age has blinded the minds of unbelievers, so that they cannot see the light of the gospel that displays the glory of Christ, who is the image of God.[41]

This is the plight of all humankind: that is our depravity. We are born blind and are prey to Satan; we are at enmity with God, and totally unable to remedy that situation. However, as we have seen, scripture speaks of ignorance and the hardness of our hearts rather than our wilful disobedience and rebellion against God's will. That situation escalates as we listen to the 'enemy' and as we allow that original sin of self-exaltation and determination to dominate our thinking and actions.

I am persuaded that from Augustine on, the Church, at least in the West has been preoccupied with the question of sin – hence much of what John Piper and others of a Reformed persuasion have to say. Thus, Original Sin, at least in terms of things we do wrong, is not the primary

---

[37] Ephesians 2:12, referring in context to Gentiles, of course.
[38] Ephesians 4:18.
[39] Genesis 3:24.
[40] Revelation 22:1f.; also, Ezekiel 47:12.
[41] 2 Corinthians 4:4.

issue: our depravity issues from our rejection of God's perfect way for us and the placing of our own wilfulness before his will – as one has famously sung, "I did it my way".[42] The preoccupation with sin has led the Church down many blind alleys, not least the idea that the purpose of the baptising of infants, according to Augustine, was to deal with their original sin.[43] I would suggest that sin, which is best defined as that which displeases God, is simply the inevitable biproduct of our alienation from God.[44] As a depraved race, it is not so much the things we do wrong or the ways in which we transgress God's commandments that is significant, but it is the place where we stand in relation to a holy God whose "eyes are too pure to look on evil".[45] It is our separation that will prove eternally fatal if we do not turn to him in repentance and faith - not the detail of our wrongdoings, those sins which Christ suffered and died to cover so that we might be forgiven. It is our sins that have separated us[46] from God, but it is *separation* itself which is of most crucial importance.

iv. Our rebellion is totally deserving of eternal punishment[47]

> Ephesians 2:3 goes on to say that in our deadness we were "children of wrath." That is, we were under God's wrath because of the corruption of our hearts that made us as good as dead before God.

I suggest that, although I agree, and am assured that scripture teaches a

---

[42] 'My Way'; lyrics by Paul Anka, sung by Frank Sinatra and others.
[43] Augustine's thinking on original sin evidently sprang from his theology of baptism, and not the other way round. By the fourth century, it seems that infant baptism was universally practised in the catholic church and was therefore a given for Augustine. That caused him to ask why children should be baptised if they were sinless at birth: Kurt Aland, *Did the Early Church Baptize Infants?*, G. R. Beasley-Murray tr. (London: SCM, 1963), 107. He rationalised that "the practice of baptizing infants with exorcisms and a solemn renunciation of the Devil was ... proof positive that even they were infected with sin": Kelly, 363; e.g., Augustine, *Marriage and Concupiscence*, 1:22. He concluded that since baptism brings regeneration, it must remove guilt. That guilt must be the guilt of Adam's sin, and since infants have no sin of their own, it must therefore be original sin: *Marriage and Concupiscence*, 1:24.
[44] See Chapter 6, 169f., on Talbert's and Johnson's view of sin.
[45] Habakkuk 1:13.
[46] Isaiah 59:2, spoken, of course, to God's Old Covenant people.
[47] Piper (2013), 22.

lost eternity for those who reject Christ, I do have a quibble with Piper's emphasis. Again, it is the context we must examine:

> As for you, you were dead in your transgressions and sins, in which you used to live when you followed the ways of this world and of the ruler of the kingdom of the air, the spirit who is now at work in those who are disobedient. All of us also lived among them at one time, gratifying the cravings of our flesh and following its desires and thoughts. Like the rest, we were by nature deserving of wrath.[48]

It is our 'nature' that is "deserving of wrath" or "anger" – God's anger, and we transgress because we are by nature dead towards God. Whether we believe that that nature has in some way been inherited from Adam, or whether we think that the Eden story is recapitulated in each and every individual's life, we, nonetheless, individually rebel against God's command whether received through conscience or precept – either way, the entire human race is dead towards God and deserves that death be our eternal state. The "gratifying [of the] the cravings of our flesh and following its desires and thoughts" describes life in our fallen state, but it is our deadness which seals our fate unless the sentence of death is commuted or quashed as another bears the death sentence for us.

The biblical concept of life and death is all about relationships. I am alive towards God if I am in filial relationship with him through faith in Christ. As already noted, the issue of sin is not therefore strictly relevant: whatever we do, whether regenerate or not, is the direct outworking of that relationship or lack of it. We are not judged according to our works, so far as our eternal destiny is concerned,[49] but whether we have received Jesus:

> Whoever believes in him is not condemned, but whoever does not believe stands condemned already because they have not believed in the name of God's one and only Son.[50]

Piper says,

---

[48] Ephesians 2:1-3.
[49] Not forgetting Romans 14:10 and 2 Corinthians 5:10.
[50] John 3:18; also, Romans 8:1.

The reality of hell is God's clear indictment of the infiniteness of our guilt. If our corruption were not deserving of an eternal punishment, God would be unjust to threaten us with a punishment so severe as eternal torment.

This statement brings to mind the medieval fascination with the tortures of hell which were seen as fitting punishments for sins perpetrated. The Bible does, of course, depict hell as the ultimate torment. Jesus spoke of Gehenna as the place of eternal fire and torment for unbelievers, the place where "the worms that eat them do not die, and the fire is not quenched", and John describes hell as the second death, "the fiery lake of burning sulphur" to which "the cowardly, the unbelieving, the vile, the murderers, the sexually immoral, those who practise magic arts, the idolaters and all liars ... will be consigned".[51] But, although John characterises those who will be consigned to that fiery end by listing their sins, they nevertheless stand in the immediate context in contrast to those he describes in relational terms: "I will be their God and they will be my children".[52] We are probably accustomed to hearing evangelistic preachers explain that no matter how good or bad a person may be, their eternal destiny is determined by their relationship with God, and, as we have seen, that truly is the criterion of whether or not they are condemned. To place the blameworthiness of unbelievers on their behaviour therefore seems to me to miss the point, and could reinforce the folk-religion idea that the bad go to hell and the good go to heaven. Writing of those who deserve hell because of their blameworthiness, Piper cites one of the strongest statements about eternal condemnation in the whole of the New Testament – 2 Thessalonians 1:6-9, but the heart of the matter is found in the eighth verse: "He will punish those who do not know God and do not obey the gospel of our Lord Jesus". The context is of those who have afflicted the Thessalonian believers and whom God in his justice will pay back with "everlasting destruction" and "shut out from the presence of the Lord and from the glory of his might", but the crux of the judgment focuses on their obedience or otherwise to the gospel, not on what they have done. These people do not know God, and once the judgment is executed, they will henceforth

---

[51] Mark 9:48; Revelation 21:8.
[52] Revelation 21:7.

never again have the opportunity to know him.

That said, I would never seek to minimise the importance of sin. Sin is the factor that separates us from God – it is "my will, not yours", to parody Jesus' words of submission to God in Gethsemane,[53] and sin is the problem that Jesus solved and overcame in his sacrificial death which was for the "sins of the whole world".[54] But it is our separation and alienation from God that is decisive, and those who are good, bad or indifferent, morally speaking, will find themselves in hell only if they have refused to *obey* the gospel. How much more terrible it will be for those who in life have striven after goodness but have nonetheless rejected the saving grace of our God?

The Reformed doctrine of Total Depravity is difficult on a number of counts.[55] The terminology is misleading and should probably be abandoned. I would suggest too that the legalistic way some writers seek to explain it misses the point. Depravity is a way of describing our fallen condition without God - without access to the Tree of Life, one might say, so the related term, 'inability', comes closer to the nub of the problem. Life after Eden is described in scripture as life characterised by alienation where every possible relationship – between man and man, man and woman, between humanity and the world of nature, between humanity and the "ancient serpent" – has become distorted and dysfunctional.[56] Scripture never entirely takes away from us that basic divine image in which we were made, but, once separated from God, it is our own ego that lies at the centre of our existence. Consequently, our wills are degraded so that we cannot reliably differentiate between what is good and bad; our choices are distorted because our desires centre on ourselves rather than on God, so we choose to act in ways which are displeasing to him – we sin. And as we venture ever further away from the gate of Eden, the more our alienation and independence of spirit are confirmed and hardened, and our mindsets become more godless. The antediluvian accounts of human pre-history in Genesis 4 to 6 amply

---

[53] Matthew 26:39, etc.
[54] 1 John 2:2.
[55] See Chapter 5, 130.
[56] Genesis 3:14-19.

bear out that process. We may desire a way back to God, but apart from his intervention, we are helpless, and it is not until we hear the gospel of our Lord Jesus Christ that we begin to see the remedy. But the remedy can only be attained if we receive what God offers us through Christ. And the crucial issue is whether or not to surrender our precious, fiercely guarded self-sufficiency, and humbly receive God's grace. We saw in a previous section that many believe in a *prevenient* or *effectual* grace.[57] Given that scripture teaches no such thing, but that these are conclusions drawn from a misunderstanding of the human dilemma of how to receive forgiveness and saving grace, my own conclusion is that our ability to respond to God's overtures in the gospel is nothing more nor less than part of what survives of his image in us, that capacity left in us to respond to love and grace whether it be within relationships human or divine.

b. Irresistible Grace (Chapter 4)[58]

Piper acknowledges that many intuitively know that God's grace was decisive in their conversion, and he claims that few would want to take any credit. I agree. But, he asks, "Do we resist grace?" in answer to which he says,

> The doctrine of irresistible grace does not mean that every influence of the Holy Spirit cannot be resisted. It means that the Holy Spirit, whenever he chooses, can overcome all resistance and make his influence irresistible.

Citing apparent contradictions to this assertion from scripture,[59] however, he claims that this resistance doesn't contradict God's sovereignty, rather, "God allows it, and overcomes it whenever he chooses".[60] So far as God's purposes in creation and redemption are

---

[57] Chapter 5, 143, 'Prevenient Grace'.
[58] Piper (2013), 25-36.
[59] Piper cites Acts 7:51: "You stiff-necked people, uncircumcised in heart and ears, you always resist the Holy Spirit"; Ephesians 4:30 and 1 Thessalonians 5:19: the possibility of grieving or quenching the Holy Spirit; Matthew 21:33-43: the parable of the wicked tenants, and Romans 10:21 (quoting Isaiah 65:2), which summarises the whole history of Israel as the protracted story of human resistance to God's commands and promises.
[60] Citing Daniel 4:35; Psalms 115:3; Job 42:2.

concerned, there can be no dispute, but if we accept that God, in his love and grace towards us, permits us to make choices which he honours – and specifically our choice with respect to the gospel, we have the problem of figuring out how our responsibility relates to his determinism.

With regard to how "irresistible grace refers to the sovereign work of God to overcome the rebellion of our heart and bring us to faith in Christ so that we can be saved" is concerned, Piper, citing Paul's argument in Romans 9 about the rights the potter has over his clay, which I claim has nothing to do with election to salvation anyway,[61] affirms,

> If the doctrine of total depravity ... is true, there can be no salvation without the reality of irresistible grace.[62] If we are dead in our sins, and unable to submit to God because of our rebellious nature, then we will never believe in Christ unless God overcomes our rebellion.

Countering the objection that we may use our freedom to resist or accept the drawing of the Holy Spirit,[63] Piper responds,

> that is not what the Bible teaches. Except for the continual exertion of saving grace, we will always use our freedom to resist God. That is what it means to be "unable to submit to God." "The mind that is set on the flesh is hostile to God, for it does not submit to God's law; indeed, it *cannot*. Those who are in the flesh *cannot* please God" (Rom. 8:7-8).

Yet another example of over-emphasising a text beyond what can be seen in experience and thereby missing the point, I suggest. He equates submitting to God with pleasing God. The two are not the same, although to submit to God will inevitably please him. In the first place, Paul is addressing the church – believers in Jesus who have the Holy Spirit, and he appeals to them:

> Therefore, brothers and sisters, we have an obligation—but it is not to the flesh, to live according to it. For if you live according to the flesh, you will die; but if by the Spirit you put to death the misdeeds

---

[61] See Chapter 10f., 332, on Romans 9 to 11.
[62] Note the dependency of Irresistible Grace on the veracity of Total Depravity.
[63] John 6:44; see Chapter 10b(i), 290.

of the body, you will live.[64]

Rather than taking a universal truth which applies to all, believers and unbelievers alike, Paul is suggesting the possibility that a believer, one who has the Spirit, might live according to the flesh. Piper cannot therefore use this verse to justify the claim he is making. Furthermore, such a person, a believer nonetheless, is resisting God's will and consequently cannot please God. It is a serious mistake to assume that now we are born again and filled with the Holy Spirit we cannot live according to the flesh and in so doing displease God. Indeed, it is a mark of our sanctification that we find out what pleases the Lord, bearing in mind that our behaviour as believers has a bearing on our heavenly rewards.[65] If we humbly submit to God, Piper claims that it is because God has already given us "a new, humble nature". Everything, he claims, depends on the mistaken Reformed view that God's sovereignty overrides that part of his image which remains in us and that affords us the ability to recognise our need and curtail our resistance to his advances of grace - not an ability to please God as though we could earn salvation, though, because that would be patently untrue.

Piper goes on to expound his understanding of the idea of the Father drawing people to Jesus in John's Gospel, which I discussed earlier.[66] I suggested there that the texts he cites have to do with Perseverance rather than with Irresistible Grace. He also alludes to the saying of John 11:50-52 where he assumes that Caiaphas referred to Gentiles, whom God had predestined to salvation, when he prophesied that in his death Jesus would "gather into one the children of God who are scattered abroad". The natural sense of his words, however, would suggest that it was not the Elect from every tribe and tongue and nation that were in view, but the Jews of the diaspora, as opposed to the Jews who at that time lived as a nation in The Land.[67]

He goes on to discuss the scope of Jesus' death, citing a number of texts which contain the word 'all' (*pas*: πᾶς), or which he construes as

---

[64] Romans 8:12f.
[65] 2 Corinthians 5:9; Ephesians 5:10.
[66] John 6:44; 12:32. See Chapter 10b(i), 290.
[67] Carson (1991), 422.

implying universality.[68] I agree that the scope of Jesus' atoning sacrifice extends to all peoples – Jews and Gentiles alike, but I do not accept that these verses focus only on all of those God has chosen, in other words, just the Elect.[69] However, he makes an interesting point relating to the failure of Judas Iscariot to be 'drawn'. Quoting John 6:64-65,

> "There are some of you who do not believe." (For Jesus knew from the beginning who those were who did not believe, and who it was who would betray him.) And he said, "This is why I told you that no one can come to me unless it is granted him by the Father."

Piper claims that Judas was not drawn and did not follow Jesus to the end because it had not been granted ("enabled" (NIV): *mē hē dedomenon*)[70] to him by the Father. However, I maintain that the reason Judas was not drawn, irresistibly or otherwise, was that he refused to be drawn. He exercised his own determinative will in the face of all the privileges he had received through being part of the apostleship. Again, Piper overstates his claim:

> And the reason any of us has come to Jesus is not that we are smarter, or wiser, or more virtuous than Judas, but that the Father overcame our resistance and drew us to Christ.

I say 'overstates' because Piper appears to suggest that the claim that human free will is involved in allowing us to be drawn by the Father implies a superior moral or ethical claim on the part of the repentant sinner. That is patently untrue, and I would say that it was an unjustified and unworthy sleight against those who don't accept Piper's logic.

Since, God's grace is irresistible, so, according to Piper, is repentance: indeed, it is part of that grace. We have already noted the confusion caused by the way terms like 'salvation', the 'new birth', 'regeneration', and so on, are redefined in Reformed writings. 'Repentance' is another. According to 2 Timothy 2:24-25, Piper claims that repentance is a gift of God:

> The Lord's servant must not be quarrelsome but kind to everyone,

---

[68] John 6:37; 10:15; 11:50-2; 12:32; 18:37.
[69] See Chapter 10b(i), 290.
[70] The verb is *didōmi* (δίδωμι), to 'give' or 'grant', a common New Testament word.

able to teach, patiently enduring evil, correcting his opponents with gentleness. *God may perhaps grant them repentance* leading to a knowledge of the truth.[71]

However, examination of this context shows that Paul is not writing about the repentant sinner turning to God for salvation, but rather is dealing with disorder in the church and the need to put things right. This is the only scripture Piper uses to establish his point, which itself raises the question as to whether it will bear the weight. In my judgment, it doesn't – it is merely a text drawn out of its context to create a pretext, but that pretext is the logical conclusion to be drawn from his take on Total Depravity.

Likewise, another consequence of his Reformed view of depravity brings him to the conclusion that God never foists his grace upon us:

> irresistible grace never implies that God forces us to repent or believe or follow Jesus against our will. That would even be a contradiction in terms because believing and repenting and following are always willing, or they are hypocrisy. Irresistible grace does not drag the unwilling into the kingdom, it makes the unwilling willing. It does not work with constraint from the outside, like hooks and chains; it works with power from the inside, like new thirst and hunger and compelling desire.[72]

But how does God do that? "God uses the ministry of the word to accomplish his supernatural changes in the heart. These changes bring about repentance and faith."

He also tries to explain the twin ideas of what scripture means when it speaks of our being called. He quotes 1 Corinthians 1:23-24:

> We preach Christ crucified, a stumbling block to Jews and folly to Gentiles, but to those who are called, both Jews and Greeks, Christ the power of God and the wisdom of God.

He sees two kinds of "call" in this text; the *general* call of the gospel, which is implied, and the explicitly named call, the *effectual call* of

---

[71] His italics.
[72] Note the repetitive nature of Piper's argument – an unfortunate characteristic of much of his writing which really belongs in the pulpit.

THE PREDESTINATION PROBLEM

God. The first offers salvation impartially and indiscriminately to all and often falls on unreceptive ears and is thus 'folly' to the hearer, but the second is a call which the hearers cannot regard as foolishness, but is rather the wisdom and power of God. Piper likens this second *effectual* calling to Jesus' calling of Lazarus from death to life.[73] It has power in itself which overcomes spiritual blindness and allows the hearer to receive it as wisdom and power. It is irresistible and grants a new willingness and eagerness to embrace it so that the hearer can be said to be acting freely and not under coercion. Piper cites the example of Lydia whose heart God opened to respond as she listened to Paul on the bank of one of the local rivers of Philippi.[74] The fallacy here is to assume that Lydia was at least neutral to the voice of God, and that her heart was not already inclined towards the truth. That assumption is uncalled for: the fact that she was a faithful Jewess who desired to be among her coreligionists who had gathered to pray, and that in the face of the absence of any men, strongly suggests to me that God didn't have to work too hard to win her over – she was already inclined to receive divine truth.[75]

How the change between the *general* call and the *effectual* call comes about is described as the miracle of God shining the light of the knowledge of his glory in the face of Jesus Christ.[76] "In other words, God causes the glory—the self-authenticating truth and beauty of Christ to be seen and savored in our hearts". And "from that moment on our will toward Christ is fundamentally altered". This is what Piper regards as the "new birth", and he goes on to elaborate the sequence of the successive aspects of the new convert's experience – "being born of God comes first and believing follows". "Believing in Jesus is ... the evidence that we 'have been born of God.'"

We noted earlier that the verb 'to call' does bear at least two distinct senses in the New Testament; firstly, in the sense of the gospel invitation as Piper describes, but secondly, not as a kind of reinforced gospel

---

[73] John 11:43.
[74] Acts 16:14.
[75] See also Chapter 10c, 315, on Acts 13:48 and discussion of *tassō*.
[76] 2 Corinthians 4:4-6.

call which the hearer cannot resist, but rather as a way of describing God's Elect. In several places in his letters, Paul writes of 'the called', describing those who have already responded to the gospel call and have been included in Christ: they are saints, and that sense of calling comes very close to the sense of being elect.[77]

There is so much here that is true, of course. The problem with Piper's exposition of the implications of Total Depravity has less to do with the truth of the matter, and more to do with the ways he uses scripture to illustrate his point – often out of context and repetitiously.

c. Limited Atonement (Chapter 5)[78]

This is by far the longest chapter of *Five Points*: and understandably so because it is the aspect of TULIP doctrine that creates the most problems.

First of all, Piper writes a statement of the meaning of the atonement. Quoting Romans 3:25-26, he emphasises that the work of Christ on the Cross was necessary to vindicate God as he offered a means of forgiveness for those who trust in Jesus. Sinners cannot just be acquitted: the consequences (punishment) of their sins needed to be dealt with in a just and effective way: they cannot just be ignored by God. But, says Piper, "What did Christ actually achieve on the cross for those for whom he died?"

> If you say that he died for every human being *in the same way*, then you have to define the *nature* of the atonement very differently than you would if you believed that Christ, *in some particular way*, died for those who actually do believe. In the first case, you would believe that the death of Christ did not *decisively secure* the salvation of anyone; it only made all men savable so that something else would be decisive in saving them, namely their choice. In that case, the death of Christ did not actually remove the sentence of death and did not actually guarantee new life for anyone. Rather it only created possibilities of salvation which could be actualized by people who provide the decisive cause, namely their faith. In this

---

[77] Romans 1:6f.; 8:28; 1 Corinthians 1:2, 24. See Chapter 8d, 238, 'Calling'.
[78] Piper (2013), 37-52.

understanding of the atonement, faith and repentance are not blood-bought gifts of God for particular sinners, but are rather the acts of some sinners that make the blood work for them.

I hope you can see just how distorted is this appraisal of what happens to be my own position. Once again, in agreement with most other Reformed writers, Piper sees the idea that there can be a freewill human response to the appeal of the gospel as some sort of meretricious work which makes "the blood work for them". He then goes on to emphasise that "none of these acts of irresistible grace is deserved", referring to the new birth, the effectual call and the gift of repentance. But God, he says, "did not secure them for all in the same way. Otherwise all would be born again, and all would be effectually called, and all would receive the gift of repentance". He argues that if Christ died for all people in the same way, then "we must have regenerated ourselves without the blood-bought miracle of Christ, and we must have come to faith and repentance ourselves without the blood-bought gifts of faith and repentance". If that were so then "all men would be brought to faith, but they aren't".

The argument becomes quite convoluted because he claims that "it is those who deny that the atoning death of Christ accomplishes what we most desperately need—namely, salvation from the condition of deadness and hardness and blindness under the wrath of God", who limit the atonement. "They limit the power and effectiveness of the atonement so that they can say that it was accomplished even for those who die in unbelief and are condemned." In other words, people like me would "limit the atonement to a *possibility* or an *opportunity* for salvation" because we could then escape from our deadness and rebellion and obtain faith by an effectual means not provided by the cross". I would say no such thing, of course, although I do believe that the atonement provides the possibility for salvation for everyone – none excepted.

Piper does allow that "Christ died to save all *in some sense*", however, citing 1 Timothy 4:10: God is "the Saviour of all people, and especially of those who believe". He claims that the natural way to read this text is to see that God's intention was to save those he had chosen "in *a more particular sense*". This understanding is in direct conflict with 1

Timothy 2:4 where, having taught that prayer should be offered for "all people" (*pantōn anthrōpōn*: πάντων ἀνθρώπων), Paul says that it pleases "God our Saviour, who wants all people (*pantas anthrōpous*: πάντας ἀνθρώπους) to be saved and to come to a knowledge of the truth". We saw earlier that John Calvin had problems with this verse: he wanted to make it mean that "no people and no rank in the world is excluded from salvation", but the context simply won't bear that kind of limitation.[79] Exactly the same expression is used in 1 Timothy 4:10 - *pantōn anthrōpōn*. If it is true that God wants all people to be saved, then it is incorrect to suggest that the atonement is limited only to those chosen by God. Nonetheless, Piper claims that "God's intention is different for each". God sent Jesus for everyone in the sense that his sacrifice provides the basis of the offer of salvation, which is for all, but only those who trust Christ will be saved. And who are they? They are God's Elect, so the gospel does not merely offer the possibility of salvation for them, but proclaims the guarantee of a person receiving Christ "and in him the infinite achievement that he accomplished for his people by his death and resurrection".

The purchase of the faith of the Elect is based on the biblical concept of the New Covenant, says Piper. He resorts to those wonderful passages in Jeremiah and Ezekiel where God promises Israel a New Covenant where,

> I will put my law within them, and I will write it on their hearts. And ... I will forgive their iniquity, and I will remember their sin no more.

> And I will put the fear of me in their hearts, that they may not turn from me. I will rejoice in doing them good.[80]

His point is that it is God who takes the initiative in the conversion of Israel through a covenant that will succeed where the Old Covenant failed because it depended the efforts of unregenerate hearts of stone. Likewise, Ezekiel speaks of a heart of flesh and God's Spirit which he will give to Israel so that they will walk in his statutes and obey his

---

[79] Calvin, *Commentary on 1 Timothy*; quoted by Shank (*Elect*), 94. Mounce, 84ff., shows that the context argues against Calvin's non-specific view.
[80] Jeremiah 31:33f.; 32:40f.

rules.[81] Moses too had spoken of God circumcising their hearts.[82] So, when we come to the New Testament, we find that Jesus is the mediator of this new covenant that he secured by his own blood: Jesus' blood is the blood of the covenant. The purpose of his death was to establish that covenant. This is illustrated for us in the Gospel accounts of the Last Supper where Jesus said, "This cup is the new covenant in my blood".[83] And Piper rightly says, "I take this to mean that the promises of the new covenant are purchased by the blood of Christ." He is the guarantor and mediator of the New Covenant.[84]

However, from all of this, Piper concludes that "not all the promises of the new covenant depend on the condition of faith". Indeed, he asserts that one of those promises is the gift of faith itself. He continues at some length in similar vein, and with some special pleading, to show that Jesus' atoning death was not for all people, but only for his own. He follows a succession of headings: 'Jesus Lays Down His Life for the Sheep';[85] 'Jesus Died to Gather the Children of God';[86] 'A Ransom for Many',[87] and 'Christ Gave Himself for the Church'.[88] He acknowledges that 1 John 2:2: "He is the propitiation for our sins, and not for ours only but also for the sins of the whole world", needs some explanation. Unfortunately, he links with it the prophecy of Caiaphas in John 11:51-52, which I have already mentioned (above, 411), so he construes "the whole world" as parallel with "the children of God who are scattered abroad" to mean that the propitiation applies to people selected "from every tongue and tribe and people and nation". If "the whole world" means everyone without exception, "Does this mean that Christ died with the intention to appease the wrath of God for every person in the world?" he asks. His answer is "No"; but my answer is, "Yes, that's exactly what it means!"

---

[81] Ezekiel 11:19; 36:26f.
[82] Deuteronomy 30:6.
[83] 1 Corinthians 11:25; Luke 22:20.
[84] Hebrews 7:22; 9:15.
[85] John 10:15.
[86] John 11:50-2.
[87] Mark 10:45.
[88] Ephesians 5:25-7.

I argued earlier that, although sin is the issue so far as our alienation from God is concerned, it is not the damning factor. What condemns us to eternal separation (hell) is our refusal to obey the gospel – our rejection of Christ, our sin-bearer – however we may wish to express it. When Christ died on the Cross of Calvary, he bore the sins of the whole world just as the scape goat bore away the sins of Israel each year on the Day of Atonement.[89] For Israel, the sacrifice of the one goat and the banishment of a second, by which atonement was procured, was a rite which had to be repeated annually. The sacrifice of the Lamb of God for sins, on the other hand, was the once-for-all sacrifice of God himself which procured atonement for the whole human race – those who lived before and after the Cross. I find this an aspect of soteriology that is often not readily grasped. It is the basis of Reformed thinking to think that a death offered for my sin will not have any effect if I don't respond in faith to Christ, so that would be a death wasted, and that cannot be. I sometimes feel too that it is a matter of numbers. We saw earlier that Calvin was prone to quantify grace, as though it was a commodity that had to be spread thinly over humanity. But there is no limit on grace because it is God's nature, not something he distributes and which might run short.[90] One feels that there may be a sense here that God's grace may not be sufficient to cover the sins of the whole human race from the dawn of time to the *parousia*, but it *is* sufficient, and when John says that Christ is the propitiation for the whole world, that is exactly what I believe he means. Those who will be saved are not those drawn from a class of people (sinners) whom God has arbitrarily selected, but they are those who, in the exercise of their capacity for self-determination, have chosen to obey the gospel. It has nothing to do with merit or the capacity to please God: it is all of grace – the grace of God which invites us to use that aspect of the divine image which still resides in each one of us to say 'Yes' to God – although, perhaps it might be better to put it, as I have already suggested, as ceasing to say 'No', and allowing Jesus to rescue us as helpless victims.

---

[89] John 1:29; Leviticus 16:9f.
[90] See Chapter 6, 179, 'The Grace of God'.

Piper concludes his chapter on Limited Atonement by appealing to what he terms, "The Precious Logic of Romans 8:32":

> He who did not spare his own Son but gave him up for us all, how will he not also with him graciously give us all things?[91]

He argues that God did not give his Son for the whole of humanity, otherwise all would be saved, the logic being that had he done so, then all would have received the "all things" to which Paul refers. He asks, "Who are the 'us' in this verse?" and answers by referring to the preceding verses:

> *Those* whom he foreknew he also predestined to be conformed to the image of his Son, in order that he might be the firstborn among *many brothers*. And *those* whom he predestined he also called, and *those* whom he called he also justified, and *those* whom he justified he also glorified.[92]

So far, so good, and undoubtedly the "us" of verse 32 must refer to the Elect. But does this passage from Romans 8 say that God gave up his Son only for the Elect? The blessings of the "all things" which God has graciously given us are certainly withheld from unbelievers, but Piper is quite wrong to insist that the giving of his Son is not also for the whole of humanity. However, he admits that

> Therefore, the design of God in giving the Son is not only a general offer to the whole world, but a rock solid securing of infinite riches for his people.

I suggest that the giving of his Son was for the whole of humanity and by that God offered the possibility of redemption to all without exception. Thus, where I believe Piper and his Reformed friends go wrong is to distinguish between a *general* call in the gospel and an *effectual* call which applies only to his chosen ones.

---

[91] See Chapter 10e, 324.
[92] Romans 8:29f.

d. Unconditional Election (Chapter 6)[93]

Piper opens his chapter on Unconditional Election with the following claim:

> If all of us are so depraved that we cannot come to God without being born again by the irresistible grace of God, and if this particular grace is purchased by Christ on the cross, then it is clear that the salvation of any of us is owing to God's election. He chose those to whom he would show such irresistible grace, and for whom he would purchase it.

It should therefore be clear that the issue at hand is that of free will or human determinism, and whether or not we have a choice about our response to the gospel invitation. This is perhaps the key question in the whole of the debate on Election and it has been discussed at some length already.[94]

Piper says that God's choosing of whom to save is unconditional because there is no condition we must meet before God chooses to save us. We are dead in trespasses and sins, so there is no condition we *can* meet. To that, however, he adds the caveat that our final salvation is not unconditional because we must still meet the condition of faith. Faith, he says, is not a condition for election, but it is a condition for receiving salvation. The way he puts it is that

> God chose us before the foundation of the world ... he purchases our redemption at the cross, and then gives us spiritual life through irresistible grace, and brings us to faith.

He then discusses a series of texts which to his mind proves that election is prior to faith. The first, Acts 13:48, I have discussed already,[95] where the issue of Gentiles being "appointed to eternal life" hinges on the interpretation of the verb *tassō* which is usually translated 'appointed'. But it is an unusual word in the New Testament, and of the seven occurrences, only here is it construed as suggesting a prior choosing. It is one of those interpretations that depends heavily on its context

---

[93] Piper (2013), 53-61.
[94] See Chapter 6, 161.
[95] See Chapter 10c, 315.

THE PREDESTINATION PROBLEM

rather than on lexical considerations, so it is an unsafe text to be used to support predestination to eternal life.

The second text is John 10:26, "You do not believe because you are not among my sheep". Although I have not discussed this particular verse, I have made reference to the identities of those whom Jesus referred to as his sheep.[96] My conclusion was that Jesus' sheep are those who already belong to him through having placed their trust in him. The critical issue is Jesus' claim in John 10:14 that "I *know* my sheep and my sheep *know* me". In both places where Jesus 'knows' his sheep and where they 'know' him, the verb is *ginōskō*. The same is true in the verse following: "just as the Father *knows* me and I *know* the Father". The Reformed tendency to interpret *ginōskō* as indicating divine foreknowledge, and hence divine choice, cannot therefore stand in the context of this 'Good Shepherd' chapter of John's Gospel because we would have to conclude that Jesus' sheep foreknew him as he foreknew them. And that cannot be.

Piper then turns his attention to Romans 9, which is a key passage in much Reformed writing to establish the principle of unconditionality. He says, "Romans 9 is so foundational for the doctrine of unconditional election that I devoted an entire book to verses 1-23".[97] I too devoted some space to the context of the chapter,[98] and I would refer readers to that passage in this book. Piper actually engages with those who hold my own view:

> I know that some interpreters say that Romans 9 has nothing to do with the election of *individuals* to their *eternal* destinies, but only deals with corporate peoples in their historical roles.

He says he thinks it is a mistake "mainly because it simply does not come to terms with the problem Paul is addressing in the chapter". The issues are complex and controversial, and the context and place that the three chapters, Romans 9 to 11, occupy in Paul's letter need to be carefully considered. So, without delving further into how Romans 9

---

[96] See Chapter 10b(iv), 313.
[97] John Piper, *The Justification of God: An Exegetical and Theological Study of Romans 9:1-23* (Grand Rapids, MI: Baker Academic, 1993).
[98] See Chapter 10f, 332.

should be interpreted, I simply refer readers to my discussion in this book.

Piper then turns his attention to Ephesians 1:3-6, which he claims "is another powerful statement of the unconditionality of our election and predestination to sonship":

> Blessed be the God and Father of our Lord Jesus Christ, who has blessed us in Christ with every spiritual blessing in the heavenly places, even as he chose us in him before the foundation of the world, that we should be holy and blameless before him. In love he predestined us for adoption as sons through Jesus Christ, according to the purpose of his will, to the praise of his glorious grace.

And, again, he engages with what is my own conviction:[99]

> Some interpreters argue that this election before the foundation of the world was only an election of Christ, but not an election of which individuals would actually be in Christ. This simply amounts to saying that there is no unconditional election of individuals to salvation. Christ is put forward as the chosen one of God, and the salvation of individuals is dependent on their own initiative to overcome their depravity and be united to Christ by faith. God does not choose them, and therefore God cannot effectually convert them. He can only initiate conviction, but finally must wait to see who will provide the decisive impulse to quicken themselves from the dead and choose him.

I agree with most of this statement, although I would object to the assumption that individuals must "overcome their depravity and be united to Christ by faith" – faith of their own generating is his assumption. That, of course, is not how it is, and I would again refer readers to my prior discussion of Ephesians 1.[100] It is also worth pointing out that he makes the common error amongst Reformed exegetes of confusing Predestination with Election. However, I do agree with his assertion that:

> the wording of verse 5 suggests the election of people to be in Christ, and not just the election of Christ. Literally, it says, "Having predestined us unto sonship through Jesus Christ." *We* are the ones

---

[99] Although, my understanding is based on 1 Peter 1:21, not Ephesians 1:4, where it is our election in Christ that is in view.

[100] See Chapter 9, 248.

predestined, not Christ.

Apart from that last sentence which excepts Christ, predestination in this context, and when correctly understood, is about God's intentions for those who are already his own, the Elect – not for the generality of humanity and his selection of sinners to sonship. Paul was addressing the people of God whom, once they were 'in Christ', could look forward to the spiritual blessings in Christ in the "heavenly realms". God did not predestine anyone from the generality of humanity to do or be anything: he predestined you and me, or better, we entered into his longstanding intentions for believers, once we were believers in Jesus, to those blessings which would eventually bring us to conformity with the image of his beloved Son, Jesus. It is the predestination of those in Christ that Paul wants to underline.

And then, Piper comes to what he regards as "perhaps the most important text", Romans 8:28-33:

> We know that for those who love God all things work together for good, for those who are called according to his purpose. For those whom he foreknew he also predestined to be conformed to the image of his Son, in order that he might be the firstborn among many brothers. And those whom he predestined he also called, and those whom he called he also justified, and those whom he justified he also glorified. What then shall we say to these things? If God is for us, who can be against us? He who did not spare his own Son but gave him up for us all, how will he not also with him graciously give us all things? Who shall bring any charge against God's elect? It is God who justifies.

This time, however, he engages with a view I do not hold, but which is characteristically held by Arminians, that God's predestination is based on his foreknowledge of the faith individuals will have. It is the twin issues, then, of Foreknowledge and Calling, with which we now have to deal.

As before, I have dealt with the issue of Foreknowledge, but Calling is an area which is less familiar to many who engage in the debate.[101] Put

---

[101] See Chapter 8c, 219, 'Foreknowledge' and 8d, 238, 'Calling'.

briefly, Paul often refers to believers as those who are called rather than to those who have simply heard the gospel appeal. The so-called *Golden Chain* of Romans 8:29-30 should not therefore be interpreted as a sequence in which those God calls refers to those whom God calls effectually. Rather, it is those who love God and on whom he has placed his name.[102]

There is no further need to try to unravel the complex logic of Piper's attempt to justify his Reformed stance. I believe I have dealt with all of that in earlier chapters. From the outset, I have made it my aim to clear away the rubbish of errant theology, which can be traced at least as far back to the fourth century to Augustine and his disputation with Pelagius, and seek to allow scripture to speak with a clarity that is seldom heard when it is obfuscated by control beliefs which presume a prior understanding and which so often condition our interpretations.

e. Perseverance of the Saints (Chapter 7)[103]

The Perseverance of the Saints is the fifth tenet of TULIP-Calvinism, and, although it was one of the points on which the early seventeenth-century Remonstrants and the Counter-Remonstrants disagreed, Arminius himself remained ambivalent, and, I would say, with some justification.[104] Perhaps the major reason why there are those who are crystal clear in their minds about Perseverance, as are the Calvinists both of today and of a bygone age, is because it follows on logically from the first four points of Calvinism, and especially the first. If God chose me unconditionally before the foundation of the world, and brought me to faith, despite the fact that I could not produce faith by my own efforts, then nothing can separate me from the love of Christ, to use the wording, perhaps inappropriately, of Paul's statement of faith at the end of Romans 8. I shall persevere to the end: nothing can stop that happening, and I can never be lost.

However, Piper adds that the doctrine of the Perseverance of the Saints

---

[102] Romans 8:28; Klein, 254.
[103] Piper (2013), 63-76.
[104] See Chapter 4, 70, 'Perseverance'.

means more than that. It means "that the saints will and must persevere *in faith and the obedience which comes from faith*". Election, he says, is unconditional, but glorification is not, and there are many warnings in scripture that those who do not hold fast to Christ can be lost in the end. He summarises his understanding of perseverance under eight heads:

i. Our faith must endure to the end if we are to be saved

Even though "the gospel is God's instrument in the preservation of faith as well as the begetting of faith", there is still the "fight of faith to be fought". The conviction that I am saved does not mean that there is no more struggling, but "by God's sovereign grace [we] will win". Thus, there is the possibility of a falling away. Piper cites 1 Corinthians 15:1-2 to show the necessity of perseverance: "*if you hold fast to the word I preached to you—unless you believed in vain.*" Likewise, the Parable of the Sower portrays "rocky ground" which represents those with no root of faith and who fall away in the face of "tribulation or persecution", and thorny ground where the word of God is choked and the soil is "unfruitful".[105] Thus, says Piper, there is such a thing as "believing in vain" - in other words, it is not real faith. I suggest, however, that Piper displays some confusion here. He defines faith in a quite narrow way - only genuine faith, faith that includes "a love for his glory and a hatred for our sin", will persevere. I would say, however, that it is not possible to fall away from faith that is not genuine because it is not real faith at all.

My previous discussion tried to deal with some of the texts which issue warnings about the possibility, at least in theory, of a believer falling away from grace.[106] But Piper wants to distinguish between, on the one hand, the struggle believers have, and through which they persevere in God's grace, and on the other hand, the possibility of renouncing Christ "with such hardness of heart that we can never return" – like the

---

[105] Matthew 13:20-22.
[106] 1 Corinthians 15:1-2; Colossians 1:21-23; 2 Timothy 2:11-12; Revelation 2:7, 10.

example of Esau, cited by Hebrews 12:15-17, who was unable to repent.[107] The New Testament recognises that backsliding and waywardness is a two-way street, and repentance and return are always possible,[108] so, the Christian life will entail "struggles or serious measures of unbelief". But "The fight will be fought and will not be finally lost".

ii. Obedience, evidencing inner renewal from God, is necessary for final salvation

Piper says that God does not demand perfection. I would prefer to say that God doesn't *expect* perfection, although he calls his people to be perfect as he is perfect,[109] and, as Piper says, he does *demand* [110]"that we be morally changed and walk in newness of life".[111] The scriptural emphasis is on keeping a right balance. Thus,

> The perseverance of the saints is not the guarantee of perfection, but rather that God will keep us fighting the fight of faith so that we hate our sin and never make any lasting peace with it.

Although, generally speaking, I agree with Piper's teaching under this head, I am not convinced that this material teaches that obedience is necessary for final salvation despite the fact that it provides evidence of regeneration (in the way I use that word, that is).

iii. God's elect cannot be lost

The proposition is that "God will so work in us that those whom he has chosen for eternal salvation will be enabled by him to persevere in faith to the end and fulfill, by the power of the Holy Spirit, the requirements for a new kind of life." Piper relies on texts such as the *Golden Chain* of Romans 8:29-30, saying, "There are no dropouts in this sequence" -

---

[107] Genesis 25:34.
[108] James 5:20; 1 John 1:8f.; 5:16f.
[109] Matthew 5:48.
[110] 'Demands' is too strong a word: I suggest that God *lovingly* calls his people to sanctification as they permit the Holy Spirit to do his work within us.
[111] Philippians 3:12; 1 John 1:8-10; Matthew 6:12. Piper claims that the following texts teach that God demands holiness: Hebrews 12:14; Romans 8:13; Galatians 5:19-21; 1 John 2:3-6; John 8:31.

likewise, the words of Jesus in John 10:27-30:

> My sheep hear my voice, and I know them, and they follow me. I give them eternal life, and they will never perish, and no one will snatch them out of my hand. My Father, who has given them to me, is greater than all, and no one is able to snatch them out of the Father's hand. I and the Father are one.

This, of course, begs the basic question of Election, which is the whole thesis of my book.

iv. There is a falling away of some believers, but if it persists, it shows that their faith was not genuine and they were not born of God

Piper quotes 1 John 2:19:

> They went out from us, but they were not of us; for if they had been of us, they would have continued with us. But they went out, that it might become plain that they all are not of us.

He sees this as evidence that some who were once believers in Jesus might fall away just as we have seen in the Parable of the Sower. The problem I have with this assertion, however, is that such 'faith' could not have been genuine – "they were not born of God". As I have already said, faith that is not genuine is not faith, so they cannot fall away from a grace they have never known. As such, Piper's point says nothing significant about perseverance.

v. God justifies us completely through the first genuine act of saving faith, but this is the sort of faith that perseveres and bears fruit in the "obedience of faith"

The point Piper makes, and rightly so, is that we have been justified by faith:[112] we have been declared righteous through a faith which produces obedience and perseveres to the end. But here again, unfortunately, he puts the cart before the horse: "Faith is not the ground of our

---

[112] Romans 5:1; Philippians 3:9.

acceptance but the means or the instrument of union with Christ who alone is the ground of our acceptance with God." But he gets back on track with, "The role of the obedience in our justification is to give evidence that our faith is authentic", although I would put it slightly differently – authentic faith produces obedience, so, although our obedience shows that faith is genuine, that is not its primary role or function: obedience is that to which we are called so that "the righteous requirement of the law might be fully met in us, who do not live according to the flesh but according to the Spirit".[113] Obedience is that end to which God calls us.

vi. God works to cause his elect to persevere

Piper cites a series of texts which he claims demonstrate the New Covenant aspect of our election which was promised to Jeremiah.[114] A closer examination of all of these texts, however, shows that in the main, they are aspirational – prayers for the writers' audiences that they will persevere, rather than dogmatic assertions that they will. I do not believe that the process of sanctification this side of the *parousia* is outside of our control. We can either co-operate with or grieve the Holy Spirit, and, as with a point Piper made earlier, but which I did not comment on, our rewards in heaven will be related to our performance so far as our obedience in reliance on the Holy Spirit is concerned. As Paul puts it, the way we build on the foundation which was laid by the apostolic teaching of Christ will be subjected to the judgment of God's fire: only if our building has been with worthwhile materials will it survive, even though our lives will be saved in any case.[115]

God is faithful, as Piper asserts – there can be no doubt about that truth, and he will never leave us,[116] but I am not persuaded that he has proved his point. My obedience is not the measure of my perseverance: what will guarantee my perseverance is my ongoing trust in Christ and my

---

[113] Romans 8:4.
[114] Jeremiah 32:40; 1 Peter 1:5; Jude 24f.; 1 Thessalonians 5:23f.; Philippians 1:6; 1 Corinthians 1:8f.; Hebrews 13:20f. See above, (c), 415, 'Limited Atonement'.
[115] 1 Corinthians 3:11-15.
[116] Hebrews 13:5.

reliance on the sanctifying work of the Holy Spirit. I would venture to put that even differently: it is the *assurance* of my perseverance and eventual salvation that is gained through my ongoing trust in Christ and reliance on the sanctifying work of the Holy Spirit. I do not believe my salvation can ever be rescinded – once saved, always saved! As I asserted earlier in my discussion of Perseverance, the situation is more complex than mere proof-texting can resolve, and I do take comfort in the fact that someone even of the stature of Arminius was honest enough to submit the whole issue of Perseverance to further study and consideration.

vii. Therefore we should be zealous to confirm our calling and election

By quoting 2 Peter 1:10-11,

> Therefore, brothers, be all the more diligent to confirm your calling and election, for if you practice these qualities you will never fall. For in this way there will be richly provided for you an entrance into the eternal kingdom of our Lord and Savior Jesus Christ.

Piper misses the point somewhat. It is not our election, in other words, the idea that God has chosen us, that we are enjoined by Peter to confirm, either to ourselves or to others, but rather the reality of the position in Christ that God has placed us among his Elect. If we truly belong to the category of humanity that the Bible calls 'The Elect', then it must show somehow, and that's what we must work at – to show we truly are elect. This is a difficult distinction to make. Peter is not asking us to prove that God has chosen us – on my accounting, that couldn't be true in any case, but God, having placed us in Christ calls us to work out our election in the obedience of faith. Paul's exhortation to "continue to work out your salvation with fear and trembling"[117] says something very similar. There remains the possibility, of course, that 'election' (*eklogē*) does not refer to divine Election, but rather to the choice made by those to whom Peter addresses his letter – 'your calling and

---

[117] Philippians 2:12.

your choice', perhaps.[118] But whose ever choice it was, the genuineness of it will be manifested by growing in the virtues listed in the preceding verses:

> For this very reason, make every effort to add to your faith goodness; and to goodness, knowledge; and to knowledge, self-control; and to self-control, perseverance; and to perseverance, godliness; and to godliness, mutual affection; and to mutual affection, love.[119]

viii. Perseverance is a community project

Finally, Piper makes the crucial point that we are not meant to fight alone in the fight of faith and the confirmation of our calling and election. He quotes 2 Timothy 2:10, "I endure everything for the sake of the elect, that they also may obtain the salvation that is in Christ Jesus with eternal glory", to show that Paul saw his endurance as an important part of his ministry in encouraging his spiritual children to also persevere. He says that it is wrong to assume that "Salvation is certain for God's elect". I suggest that that is a very misleading thing to say,[120] but what he wants to emphasise is that we need to press on in partnership with other believers. It is an empowering thing that God has ordained for each of us. "The elect will certainly be saved in the end with eternal glory", but God is not indifferent to the ministry of the word, and I would include all other kinds of ministry too, in getting them there. Bearing in mind what I have written about the situation reflected in Hebrews,[121] Piper invokes Hebrews 3:12-13 as demonstrating that truth:

> Take care, brothers, lest there be in any of you an evil, unbelieving heart, leading you to fall away from the living God. But exhort one another every day, as long as it is called 'today,' that none of you may be hardened by the deceitfulness of sin.

---

[118] See Chapter 8a(ii), 204, *eklogē*. Although Davids, 187, shows that 'calling' and 'election here form a synonymous word-pair "with no real difference between them" - in which case, the election is divine. He also draws attention to the interplay of 'called' and 'chose' in 1 Corinthians 1:26-31 and 1 Peter 2:9.
[119] 2 Peter 1:5-7.
[120] See Chapter 4, 82 n58, for a note on 2 Timothy 2:10.
[121] See Chapter 4, 70, 'Perseverance'.

He says,

> This is one of the highest tributes that could possibly be paid to the church. God ordains the body of Christ as the means of his infallible keeping of the elect.

I would quibble with his use of the word "infallible", but he is right to elevate the importance of belonging to a church fellowship in order that we may grow in grace, and so that we may also help others to grow, and so reduce the impact of an unbelieving world that might cause us not to persevere.

Conclusion

In this critique of John Piper's *Five Points*, I have devoted significantly more space to the first Point of Calvinism – Total Depravity, because the remaining four points depend upon it and logically proceed from it. The key issue of our depravity is our inability to regain access to the Tree of Life, to use the Eden portrayal of our original dilemma. The only means whereby we may be saved, then, depends entirely on God's initiative. That principle is widely acknowledged by all evangelical authorities, including both Reformed and Arminian, although their respective understandings of how God's grace is implemented obviously differ. The two aspects of it all, between which, apparently, there is a tension in scripture[122] and throughout the vast literature, are divine determination and human free will.

However, if we accept the principle of Total Depravity, we acknowledge that of ourselves we can do nothing,[123] and the question remains about the dynamic of God's enabling so that we can do something, even though it is simply to accede to the divine command to obey the gospel through trusting Christ. Again, either side of the debate proposes slightly different solutions, but, broadly speaking, both affirm divine election of individuals. That being the case, it is God who chooses – the logical outcome of Total Depravity is therefore a deprivation of any means of choice I might have concerning the gospel. Thus,

---

[122] See Chapter 6, 161.
[123] John 15:5.

Unconditional Election naturally follows because, if the choice is God's prerogative, then there can be no conditions attached to that choice of you or me. Likewise, the Atonement must also be Limited because the sacrifice of Christ at Calvary can only then apply to the Elect. Furthermore, God's grace is irresistible because his will cannot be gainsaid: his determinism with respect to his choice which makes a person elect cannot be thwarted. Many Reformed writers would extend that divine determinism to every minute aspect of all creation – which is where, of course, they run into problems, and have to find ways to work round the problem of the origin of evil. Finally, if all of this is true, the believer has eternal security and perseveres despite everything simply because he or she has been chosen by God.

Total Depravity is therefore the lynch pin of the whole edifice of Five-Point Calvinism, and for all the reasons I have considered, I believe the Reformed exposition of it, including John Piper's, must be heartily rejected.

BIBLIOGRAPHY

This list comprises publications which I have personally consulted: other works may be found in footnotes.

Allen, Willoughby C., *A Critical and Exegetical Commentary on the Gospel According to S. Matthew*, The International Critical Commentary (Edinburgh: T. & T. Clark, 1907³).
Arminius, Jacobus, *The Works of James Arminius DD* in 3 vols. (cited as *Works*):
 Vol. I, James Nichols, tr. (London: Longman, Hurst, Rees, Orme, Brown & Green, 1825);
 Vol. II, James Nichols, tr. (London: Longman, Rees, Orme, Brown & Green, 1828);
 Vol. III, William Nichols, tr. (London: Thomas Baker, 1875).
Aune, David E., *Revelation 17-22*, WBC 52c (Dallas, TX: Nelson, 1998).
Balz, Horst & Gerhard Schneider, eds., *Exegetical Dictionary of the New Testament*, 3 vols. (Edinburgh: T. & T. Clark, 1990).
Bangs, Carl, *Arminius: A Study in the Dutch Reformation* (Nashville, TN: Abingdon Press, 1971).
Barclay, John M. G., *Paul and the Power of Grace* (Grand Rapids, MI: Eerdmans, 2020).
Barr, James, *The Semantics of Biblical Language* (London: SCM, 1983²).
Barrett, C. K., *The Gospel According to St John* (Cambridge: SPCK, 1978²).
_____ *The Second Epistle to the Corinthians*, BNTC (Peabody, MA: Hendrickson, 1973).
Barth, Karl, *Church Dogmatics II/2* (Edinburgh: T. & T. Clark, 1957).
Basinger, David & Randall Basinger, eds., *Predestination and Free Will: Four Views of Divine Sovereignty and Human Freedom*, Spectrum Multiview Books (Downers Grove, IL: InterVarsity Press, 1986).
Bauer, W., W. F. Arndt, F. W. Gingrich, *A Greek-English Lexicon of the New Testament and other Early Christian Literature* (Chicago & London: University of Chicago Press, 1979²) (cited as *BAGD*).
Beale, G. K., *The Book of Revelation*, NIGTC (Grand Rapids, MI: Eerdmans/Cambridge: Paternoster, 1999).

BIBLIOGRAPHY

Berkhof, Hendrikus, *Christian Faith: An Introduction to the Study of the Faith* (Grand Rapids, MI: Eerdmans, 1979).

Berkhof, Louis, *Systematic Theology* (Oxford: Banner of Truth, 1958).

Berkouwer, G. C., *Man: The Image of God* (Grand Rapids, MI: Eerdmans, 1962).

Bettenson, Henry, *Documents of the Christian Church* (Oxford/New York: Oxford University Press, 1963²).

Boice, James Montgomery, *Foundations of the Christian Faith* (Downers Grove, IL/Leicester: InterVarsity, 1986).

Bratt, John H., ed., *The Heritage of John Calvin* (Grand Rapids, MI: Eerdmans, 1973).

Brown, Colin ed., *The New International Dictionary of New Testament Theology*, 4 vols. (Carlisle: Paternoster, 1986²) (cited as *NIDNTT*).

Brown, Francis, S. R. Driver & Charles A. Briggs, *The Brown-Driver-Briggs Hebrew and English Lexicon* (Peabody, MA: Hendrickson, 1906) (cited as *BDB*).

Bruce, F. F., *1 & 2 Thessalonians*, WBC 45 (Waco, TX: Word Books, 1982).

_____ *Answers to Questions* (Exeter: The Paternoster Press, 1972).

_____ *The Acts of the Apostles: The Greek Text with Introduction and Commentary* (London: Tyndale, 1952²).

_____ *The Epistle of Paul to the Romans*, TNTC (London: Tyndale, 1963).

_____ *The Epistle to the Galatians: A Commentary on the Greek Text*, NIGTC (Exeter: The Paternoster Press/Grand Rapids, MI: Eerdmans, 1982).

_____ *The Epistle to the Hebrews: Revised Edition*, NICNT (Grand Rapids, MI: Eerdmans, 1990).

Byrne, Brendan, *Sons of God – Seed of Abraham: A Study of the Idea of Sonship of God of all Christians in Paul against a Jewish Background*, Analecta Biblica 83 (Rome: Biblical Institute Press, 1979).

Calvin, John, *Institutes of the Christian Religion*, Henry Beveridge tr. (Grand Rapids, MI: Eerdmans, One volume edition, 1989) (cited as *Institutes*).

Carson, D. A., *Divine Sovereignty and Human Responsibility: Biblical Perspectives in Tension* (Eugene, OR: Wipf & Stock, 2002) (previously published by Baker Books, 1994).

_____ *Exegetical Fallacies* (Grand Rapids, MI: Baker Book House, 1984).

_____ *Matthew Chapters 1 Through 12*, EBCNIV (Grand Rapids, MI: Zondervan, 1995).

_____ *The Gospel According to John* (Leicester: IVP/Grand Rapids, MI: Eerdmans, 1991).
Carson, D.A. & John D. Woodbridge, eds., *Hermeneutics, Authority and Canon* (Carlisle: Paternoster/Grand Rapids, MI: Baker, 1995).
Chadwick, Owen, *The Reformation*, PHC vol. 3 (London: Penguin, 1972).
Charles, R. H., ed., *The Apocrypha and Pseudepigrapha of the Old Testament*, Vol 2 (Oxford: Clarendon Press, 1913) (Kindle Edition).
_____ tr., *The Book of Enoch (I Enoch)* (London: SPCK, 1917).
Charlesworth, James H., ed., *The Old Testament Pseudepigrapha*, 2 vols. (Peabody, MA: Hendrickson, 1983)
Cochrane, A. C., *Reformed Confessions of the Sixteenth Century* (London: SCM, 1966).
Cranfield, C. E. B., *A Critical and Exegetical Commentary on The Epistle to the Romans*, ICC, 2 vols. (Edinburgh: T. & T. Clark, 1975).
_____ *The Gospel According to Saint Mark* (Cambridge: Cambridge University Press, 1977).
Cundall, Arthur E. & Leon Morris, *Judges and Ruth*, TOTC (Leicester & Downers Grove, IL: Inter-Varsity Press, 1968).
Daniell, David, Introduction to *The New Testament: A Facsimile of the 1526 Edition Translated by William Tyndale* (London: The British Library/Peabody, MA: Hendrickson, 2008).
Davids, Peter H., *The Letters of 2 Peter and Jude* (Grand Rapids, MI: Eerdmans/Nottingham: Apollos, 2006).
Donfried, Karl P., ed., *The Romans Debate: Revised and Expanded Edition* (Edinburgh: T. & T. Clark, 1991).
Douglas, J. D., ed., *The New International Dictionary of the Christian Church* (Exeter: Paternoster, 1974).
_____ *The Illustrated Bible Dictionary*, 3 vols. (Leicester: IVP, 1980).
Edwards, David L. with John R. W. Stott, *Essentials: A Liberal-Evangelical Dialogue* (London: Hodder & Stoughton, 1988).
Ellingworth, Paul, *The Epistle to the Hebrews: A Commentary on the Greek Text*, NIGTC (Grand Rapids, MI: Eerdmans & Carlisle: Paternoster, 1993).
Erickson, Millard J., *Christian Theology* (Basingstoke: Marshall Pickering, 1983).
Ferguson, Sinclair B. & David F. Wright eds., *New Dictionary of Theology* (Leicester/Downers Grove, IL: IVP, 1988).
Fisk, Samuel, *Divine Sovereignty and Human Freedom* (Neptune, NJ: Loizeaux Brothers, 1973).

BIBLIOGRAPHY

Forster, Roger T. & V. Paul Marston, *God's Strategy in Human History* (Bungay, Suffolk: Highland, 1989) (previously published by Send the Light in 1973).

Gæbelein, Frank E., ed., *The Expositor's Bible Commentary Vol. I: Introductory Articles* (Grand Rapids, MI: Regency, 1979).

George, Timothy, *Theology of the Reformers* (Leicester: Apollos, 1988).

Green, E. Michael B., *The Second Epistle General of Peter and the General Epistle of Jude: An Introduction and Commentary*, TNTC (London: Inter-Varity Press, 1968).

Grudem, Wayne, *1 Peter*, TNTC (Grand Rapids, MI/Cambridge: Eerdmans, 1988).

_____ *Systematic Theology: An Introduction to Biblical Doctrine* (Nottingham: Inter-Varsity Press, 2007^2).

Gundry, Robert Horton, *The Use of the Old Testament in St. Matthew's Gospel with Special Reference to the Messianic Hope* (Leiden: E. J. Brill, 1967).

Guthrie, Donald, *The Pastoral Epistles: An Introduction and Commentary*, TNTC (London: Tyndale Press, 1957).

_____ *The Letter to the Hebrews: An Introduction and Commentary*, TNTC 15 (Leicester: Inter-Varsity Press & Grand Rapids, MI: Eerdmens, 1983).

Harrison, A. W., *The Beginnings of Arminianism to the Synod of Dort* (London: London University Press, 1926).

Hawthorne, Gerald F. & Ralph P. Martin, eds., *Dictionary of Paul and His Letters* (Leicester: IVP, 1993).

Hewitt, Thomas, *The Epistle to the Hebrews: An Introduction and Commentary*, TNTC (London: Tyndale Press, 1960).

Hinnells, John R. ed., *A Handbook of Living Religions* (London: Penguin Books, 1984).

Holmes, Michael W., ed., J. B. Lightfoot & J. R. Harmer, *The Apostolic Fathers: Second Edition* (Leicester: Apollos, 1989).

Horton, Michael, *For Calvinism* (Grand Rapids, MI: Zondervan, 2011).

Howley, G. C. D., F. F. Bruce & H. L. Ellison, eds., *A Bible Commentary for Today* (London/Glasgow: Pickering & Inglis, 1979).

Ironside, H. A., *Expository Notes on the Epistles of James and Peter* (Neptune, NJ: Loizeaux Brothers, 1947).

Jobes, Karen H. & Moisés Silva, *Invitation to the Septuagint* (Grand Rapids, MI: Baker & Carlisle: Paternoster, 2000).

Johnston, Philip S., *Shades of Sheol: Death and Afterlife in the Old Testament* (Downers Grove, IL: Inter Varsity Press, 2002).

Johnston, Philip S. & Peter Walker, eds., *The Land of Promise: Biblical, Theological and Contemporary Perspectives* (Downers Grove, IL: InterVarsity Press, 2000).
Jonkind, Dirk, Peter J. Williams, et al., *The Greek New Testament* (Wheaton, IL: Crossway & Cambridge: Cambridge University Press, 2017).
Kaibel, Georg, *Epigrammata graeca* (Berolini, 1878: republished by Hildesheim: Georg Olms Verlagsbuchhandlung, 1965).
Kelly, J. N. D., *Early Christian Doctrines* (A & C Black, 1977).
Kittel, Gerhard & G. Friedrich, eds., *Theological Dictionary of the New Testament*, G. W. Bromiley tr. (Grand Rapids, MI: Eerdmans, 1964-76) (cited as *TDNT*).
Kittel, Rudolph, et al., *Biblia Hebraica* (Stuttgart: Württembergische Bibelanstalt, 1951^7).
Klein, William W., *The New Chosen People: A Corporate View of Election* (Eugene, OR: Wifp & Stock, 2015).
Kümmel, W. G., *The Theology of the New Testament*, John E. Steely tr. (London: SCM, 1973).
Lane, Tony, *The Lion Concise Book of Christian Thought* (Tring: Lion, 1984).
Lewis, C. S., *Mere Christianity* (London & Glasgow: Fontana Books, 1955) (previously published 1952).
_____ *Surprised by Joy: The Shape of My Early Life*, (London: HarperCollins, 1959) (previously published 1955).
_____ *The Great Divorce: A Dream* (Glasgow: Collins Fontana, 1972) (previously published 1946).
_____ *The Problem of Pain* (London & Glasgow: Collins Fontana, 1957) (previously published 1940).
_____ *The Screwtape Letters* (London & Glasgow: Collins Fontana, 1955) (previously published 1942).
Lewis, Peter, Roy Clements & Greg Haslam, *Chosen for Good* (Eastbourne: Kingsway, 1986).
Lindars, Barnabas, *The Theology of the Letter to the Hebrews* (Cambridge: Cambridge University Press, 1991).
Longenecker, Richard N., *Introducing Romans: Critical Issues in Paul's Most Famous Letter* (Grand Rapids, MI/Cambridge UK: Eerdmans, 2011).
_____ *The Epistle to the Romans: A Commentary on the Greek Text*, NIGTC (Grand Rapids, MI: Eerdmans, 2016).
Louw, Johannes P. & Eugene A. Nida, *Greek-English Lexicon of the New Testament Based on Semantic Domains* (New York: United Bible Societies, 1989^2).

Luther, Martin & Henry Cole, tr., *The Collected Works of Martin Luther: Theological Writings, Sermons & Hymns: The Ninety-five Theses, The Bondage of the Will, The Catechism* (e-artnow, Kindle Edition, 1823).

Maclear, G. F., *The Gospel According to St Mark*, CBSC (Cambridge: Cambridge University Press, 1902).

Marshall, Alfred, *The R.S.V. Interlinear Greek-English New Testament* (London: Bagster, 1972).

Marshall, I. Howard, *Jesus the Saviour: Studies in New Testament Theology* (London: SPCK, 1990).

_____ *Kept by the Power of God: Revised Edition* (Carlisle: Paternoster Press, 1995).

_____ *The Acts of the Apostles*, TNTC (Leicester: IVP/Grand Rapids, MI: Eerdmans, 1980).

_____ *The Gospel of Luke*, NIGTC (Exeter: Paternoster/Grand Rapids, MI: Eerdmans, 1978).

McGrath, Alister E., *Inventing the Universe* (London: Hodder & Stoughton, 2015).

_____ *Reformation Thought: An Introduction* (Chichester: Wiley-Blackwell, 2012^4).

Metzger, Bruce M., *A Textual Commentary on the Greek New Testament: Second Edition* (Stuttgart: Deutsche Bibelgesellschaft, 1994).

Moo, Douglas J., *James: An Introduction and Commentary*, TNTC 16 (Nottingham: Inter-Varsity Press England & Downers Grove, IL: Inter-Varsity Press USA, 2009).

Morris, Leon, *The Gospel According to Matthew* (Grand Rapids, MI: Eerdmans & Leicester: Inter-Varity Press, 1992).

Motyer, Alec, *The Prophecy of Isaiah* (Leicester: IVP, 1993).

Moule, C. F. D., *An Idiom Book of New Testament Greek* (Cambridge: Cambridge University Press, 1959^2).

_____ *The Origin of Christology* (Cambridge: Cambridge University Press, 1977).

Moule, Handley C. G., *Charles Simeon*, First IVF Edition (London: Inter-Varsity Fellowship, 1948) (First published 1892).

Mounce, William D., *Pastoral Epistles*: WBC 46 (Dallas, TX: Nelson, 2000).

Moynahan, Brian, *If God Spare My Life: William Tyndale, the English Bible and Sir Thomas More – A Story of Martyrdom and Betrayal* (London: Little, Brown, 2002).

Neill, Stephen & Tom Wright, *The Interpretation of the New Testament 1861-1986* (Oxford: Oxford University Press, 1988^2).

O'Brien, Peter T., *The Letter to the Ephesians* (Grand Rapids, MI: Eerdmans/Leicester: Apollos, 1999).
O'Connell, Robert H., *Concentricity and Continuity: The Literary Structure of Isaiah*, JSOTSup 188 (Sheffield Academic Press, 1994).
OED Compact: *The Compact Edition of the Oxford English Dictionary* (Oxford: Oxford University Press, 1971).
OED Concise: *The Concise Oxford English Dictionary* (Oxford: Oxford University Press, 2009[11]).
Olson, Roger E., *Against Calvinism* (Grand Rapids, MI: Zondervan, 2011).
_____ *Arminian Theology: Myths and Realities* (Downers Grove, IL: IVP Academic, 2006).
Packer, James I., *Evangelism and the Sovereignty of God* (Nottingham: IVP, 2010²).
Pawson J. David, *Unlocking the Bible* (London: Collins, 2003).
Pelikan, Jaroslav, *The Christian Tradition: A History of the Development of Doctrine: I The Emergence of the Catholic Tradition (100-600)* (Chicago, IL & London: University of Chicago Press, 1971).
Pinnock, Clark H., ed., *The Grace of God, The Will of Man: A Case for Arminianism* (Grand Rapids, MI: Zondervan, 1989).
Pinnock, Clark H, & John D. Wagner, eds., *Grace for All: The Arminian Dynamics of Salvation* (Eugene, OR: Wifp & Stock, 2015).
Piper, John S., *Desiring God: Meditations of a Christian Hedonist*, Revised Edition (Colorado Springs, CO: Multnomah Books, 2011).
_____ *Five Points: Towards a Deeper Experience of God's Grace* (Fearn, Ross-shire: Christian Focus, 2013).
Rowland, Christopher, *Christian Origins: An Account of the Setting and Character of the most Important Messianic Sect of Judaism* (London: SPCK, 1985).
Sanday, William & Arthur C. Headlam, *A Critical and Exegetical Commentary on The Epistle to the Romans*, ICC (Edinburgh: T. & T. Clark, 1902⁵).
Scott, James M., *Adoption as Sons of God: An Exegetical Investigation into the Background of ΥΙΟΘΕΣΙΑ in the Pauline Corpus* (Wissenschaftliche Untersuchungen zum Neuen Testament, Reihe 2; 48) (Tübingen: J. C. B. Mohr (Paul Siebeck), 1992).
Sell, Alan P. F., *The Great Debate: Calvinism, Arminianism and Salvation* (Worthing: H. E. Walter Ltd, 1982).
Shank, Robert L., *Life in the Son: A Study of the Doctrine of Perseverance* (Bloomington, MN: Bethany House Publishers, 1989²).

_____ *Elect in the Son: A Study of the Doctrine of Election* (Minneapolis, MN: Bethany House Publishers, 1989).

Silva, Moisés, *Biblical Words and Their Meaning: An Introduction to Lexical Semantics*, Revised and Expanded Edition (Grand Rapids, MI: Zondervan, 1994).

Simeon, Charles, *Horae Homileticae Commentary Volume 1: A Discourses Digested Into One Continued Series, And Forming A Commentary Upon Every Book Of The Old And New Testament* (Harrington, DE: Delmarva Publications, 2014; Kindle Edition (21 Volumes in 7), www.DelmarvaPublications.com).

Smalley, S., *John: Evangelist and Interpreter* (Exeter: The Paternoster Press, 1983²).

Smith, Kym, *The Amazing Structure of the Gospel of John* (Sherwood Publications, 2005/2019⁴).

Staniforth, Maxwell & A. Louth, *Early Christian Writings* (London: Penguin, 1987).

Stott, John R. W., *The Epistles of John: An Introduction and Commentary*, TNTC (London: The Tyndale Press, 1964).

_____ *The Message of 1 Timothy & Titus*, BST (Leicester: IVP, 1996).

_____ *The Message of Ephesians*, BST (Leicester: IVP, 1979).

_____ *The Message of Romans*, BST (Leicester: IVP, 1994).

Stuart, Douglas, *Hosea-Jonah*, WBC 31 (Waco, TX: Word Books, 1987).

Sweet, John, *Revelation*, TPINTC (London: SCM Press & Philadelphia, PA: Trinity Press International, 1990).

Swete, Henry Barclay, *The Old Testament in Greek According to the Septuagint* (Cambridge: Cambridge University Press, 1909).

Tasker, R. V. G., *The General Epistle of James: An Introduction and Commentary*, TNTC (London: The Tyndale Press, 1957).

Taylor, Bernard A., *Analytical Lexicon to the Septuagint: Expanded Edition* (Peabody, MA: Hendrickson/Stuttgart, Deutsche Bibelgesellschaft, 2009).

Thayer, Joseph H., *A Greek-English Lexicon of the New Testament* (Grand Rapids, MI: Baker Book House, 1977).

Thuesen, Peter J., *Predestination: The American Career of a Contentious Doctrine* (Oxford: Oxford University Press, 2009).

Tomkins, Stephen, *The Journey to the Mayflower: God's Outlaws and the Invention of Freedom* (London: Hodder & Stoughton, 2020 (Kindle Edition)).

Turner, George Allen, *The New and Living Way: A Fresh Exposition of the Epistle to the Hebrews* (Minneapolis, MN: Bethany Fellowship, 1975).

Vermes, G., *The Dead Sea Scrolls in English* (London: Penguin, 1987^3).

Vine, W. E., *An Expository Dictionary of New Testament Words* (London: Oliphants Ltd., 1940).

Walton, John H., *The Lost World of Adam and Eve* (Downers Grove, IL: IVP Academic, 2015).

Walton, John H. & D. Brent Sandy, *The Lost World of Scripture* (Downers Grove, IL: IVP Academic, 2013).

Walton, John H. & Jonathan Harvey Walton, *The Lost World of the Israelite Conquest* (Downers Grove, IL: IVP Academic, 2017).

Wanamaker, Charles A., *The Epistles to the Thessalonians: A Commentary on the Greek Text*, NIGTC (Grand Rapids, MI & Cambridge: Eerdmans, 1990).

Ward, Keith, *Sharing in the Divine Nature: A Personal Metaphysics* (Eugene, OR: Cascade Books, 2002).

Wendel, François, *Calvin, The Origins and Development of His Religious Thought*, Philip Mairet tr. (London: Collins/Fontana, 1963).

Westcott, B. F., *The Epistle to the Hebrews: The Greek Text with Notes and Essays* (London: Macmillan, 1889).

_____ *The Epistles of St. John* (Cambridge & London: Macmillan & Co., 1892^3).

Westminster Confession of Faith, 1646
 (e.g., www.reformed.org/documents/wcf_with_proofs).

Westminster Shorter Catechism, 1647
 (e.g., www.reformed.org/documents/WSC_frames.html).

Wilson, Derek, *The Mayflower Pilgrims: Sifting Fact from Fable* (London: SPCK, 2020).

Wright, N. T., *The Resurrection of the Son of God*, COQG vol. 3 (Minneapolis: Fortress Press, 2003).

_____ *Paul and the Faithfulness of God*, COQG vol. 4 (2 vols.) (London: SPCK, 2013).

Yarbrough, Robert W., *1-3 John*, BECNT (Grand Rapids, MI: Baker Academic, 2008).

Zahavy, Tzvee, ed. & Herbert Danby, *The Mishnah in English* (Teaneck, NJ: Amazon, 2022).

INDEX OF SCRIPTURES AND OTHER ANCIENT TEXTS

A: OLD TESTAMENT	
Genesis	
1:26	130
1:27	190
2:16f.	130
2:17	285
2:22f.	190
3:5	222
3:8	130
3:14-19	408
3:22-4	403
3:24	131,404
4-6	408
4:1	222
6:2	353
10:32	130
12:2f.	355
12:3	258,302f., 337,358
12:7	80,268
13:15	80
13:15f.	268
15:5	268
15:18	268
15:18-20	80
17:7-10	268
17:13	285
18:18	258,355
18:19	69,353f.
21:12	258
22:2	267

Genesis contd.	
22:8	270
22:12	267
22:15-18	270
22:16	267
22:17f.	268
22:18	355
24:44	354
25:29-34	108,112
25:34	427
28:20-2	122
30:20	387
34	121
35:1-15	122
45:5	176
49:5	121
49:7	121
50:19f.	176
Exodus	
3:14	375
7:13	337
7:22	337
8:15	337
8:19	337
8:32	337
9:7	337
9:12	337
10:1	176
10:20	176
12:29f.	119
13:1f.	119
13:2	120

Exodus contd.	
14:7	353
17:9	353
18:25	353
19:5	214,336
19:6	121
22:29f.	120
23:16-19	216
31:2	354
32:26-9	120
32:32	349
32:32f.	347
32:34	348
34:22-6	216
35:30	354
Leviticus	
2:12	216
16:9f.	419
23:17	216
Numbers	
3:13	120
3:40	119
3:42-51	119
6:27	240
8:17	120
14:8	387
16:5	353
16:7	353
17:5	353
18:12	216
21:9	294
22-24	93

Numbers contd.		1 Samuel contd.		2 Kings contd.	
22:8f.	93	10:24	353	22-23	43
Deuteronomy		12:13	353	**1 Chronicles**	
1:33	204	13:2	353	4-10	388
4:37	353	16:1	354	7:40	287
4:40	79	16:8-10	353	9:22	287
5:16	79	16:18	354	13:3	80
5:33	79	17	258	15:2	353
7:6	353	17:8	204,353	16:13	353
7:6f.	216	19:1	216	16:41	204,287
7:7	353	19:3	354	19:10	353
10:15	216,353	20:30	352,353	21:11	204
14:2	353	24:2	353	25:8	296
17:15	353	25:35	387	28:4	353,389
18:5	353	26:2	353	28:4f.	353
21:5	353	**2 Samuel**		28:5	353,387,389
24:1	74	6:1	353	28:6	353,386,389
24:3	74	6:21	353	28:10	353
26:17f.	216	7:14	267	29:1	353
27-28	115	10:9	353	**2 Chronicles**	
30:6	418	15:15	216	6:5f.	353
30:19	48	16:10f.	176	7:16	388
32:9	214,336	16:18	353	11:1	353
Joshua		17:1	353	13:3	353
8:3	353	19:44	258	13:17	353
22:22	74	20:1	258	25:5	353
24:15	203,216,353	21:6	353	29:11	353
24:22	353	22:26f.	286	29:29	74
Judges		22:27	287	**Ezra**	
5:8	203,353	**1 Kings**		4:15	347
10:14	353	3:8	353	6:20	347
20:1	237	8:16	353	**Nehemiah**	
20:15	353	11:34	353	5:18	287
20:16	353	12:16	258	9:7	353
20:34	353	12:21	353	**Job**	
1 Samuel		19:18	205	33:3	287
2:28	353	**2 Kings**		34:4	216
8:18	353	18:32	355	38:2	230,367

INDEX OF SCRIPTURES AND OTHER ANCIENT TEXTS

Job contd.		Psalms contd.		Isaiah contd.	
42:2	409	106:5	353	42:1-4	380
42:3	367	106:23	353	42:1-17	271
Psalms		108:6	267	42:6	355
1:6	69	115:3	409	42:19	271
9:11	355	116:15	329	43-48	271
16:10f.	347	127:2	267	43:6	267
17:27	287	132:13	389	43:10	272,353
18:25f.	286	132:13f.	387	43:20	353
18:26	287	135:4	353	44:1f.	272,353
18:49	355	139:16	347,349	44:2	385
22:27	355	**Proverbs**		44:21	272
23:6	145	8:19	212	44:26	271
31:5	85	24:12	397	45:4	272,353
33:12	353	24:47	204	46:10	237
34:8	104	**Ecclesiastes**		48	355
40:7	347	3:11	237	48:10	353
45 title	267	3:18	287	48:14	354
45:17	355	12:12	xiv	48:20	272
49:15	347	**Song of Songs**		49	271
56:8	347	6:10	212	49:2	287
59:10	145	**Isaiah**		49:3-7	272
60:5	267	4:3	347f.	49:5f.	271
62:12	397	5:1	267	49:6	355
65:4	353	10:5-7	176	49:7	353
69:22-8	348	11:9	303	50:1	74
69:28	346f.,349	11:10	355	50:10	272
73:24	347	12:4	355	52:11	287
78:67f.	353	14:1	353,388	52:13	272
78:70	353	28:16	266	53:6	190
84:1	267	36:17	355	53:10	272,356
89:3	353	38:17	216	53:11	272
89:19	353	41:1-42:19	271	54:17	271f.
91	328	41:8	385	55:1	69,190
98:2	355	41:8f.	270,353,385	55:7	190
105:6	284,353	42:1	211,214, 265f.,270, 353,381-5	56:6	272
105:26	353			59:2	405
105:43	284,353			60:3	355

445

THE PREDESTINATION PROBLEM

Isaiah contd.		Ezekiel contd.		Habakkuk contd.	
63:17	272	20:5	353	1:13	405
65:2	409	20:27	106	2:14	303
65:8-15	272	20:38	287	**Zechariah**	
65:9	353	22:4	106	12:10	267
65:9f.	284	33:7-9	321	**Haggai**	
65:15	272,353	33:11	13,69	2:7	212
65:22	353	33:13-19	114f.	2:23	353,385
66:14	272	36:26f.	418	**Malachi**	
66:18-21	355	37	257	3:16	347
Jeremiah		47:12	404	3:17	348,386f.
1:5	222	**Daniel**			
2:19	74	4:35	409	**B: NEW**	
3:6-8	238	7:10	347,349	**TESTAMENT**	
3:8	74	9:20ff.	2	**Matthew**	
3:14	354f.	10:21	348-50	2:7	239
3:19	212	11:35	204,287	2:15	239
4:3	xiii	12:1	347-50	2:23	239
4:11	287	12:4	347,349f.	3:17	381
6:26	267	12:10	287	4:21	239
8:3	216	**Hosea**		5:3	158
28:11	287	1:10	338	5:9	242
31:31-4	115	2:16	339	5:28	81
31:33f.	417	2:21	339	5:31	74
32:40	429	2:23	338	5:48	427
32:40f.	417	4:18	388	6:12	427
33:24	353	10:12	xiii	6:13	72
33:26	354f.	**Joel**		6:14f.	77
49:19	353	2:16	204	7	105
50:44	353	2:32	241,320	7:16	97
Ezekiel		**Amos**		7:20	97
11:19	418	3:2	69,222,353f.	7:21-3	101
11:19f.	115	8:10	267	7:22f.	105
12:3	238	9:12	240	7:23	69
14:13	106	**Zephaniah**		8:9	318
15:1-8	78	3:9	287	9:1	104
15:8	106	**Habakkuk**		10:1	240
18:24	106	1:5	320	10:25	240

INDEX OF SCRIPTURES AND OTHER ANCIENT TEXTS

Matthew contd.		Matthew contd.		Mark contd.	
10:32	72	24:21	294	12:23	283
10:32f.	99	24:22	81,208,283,	13:19	283,294
10:33	83		377	13:20	81,202f.,208,
11:25-30	193,289	24:24	72,81f.,208,		266,282-8,
11:27	193		283f.,377		344,346,376f.
11:28	69,190,193	24:31	208,283,377	13:22	81,95,208,28
12:18	211,214,	24:45	129		3,377
	265f.,376,	25:31-46	101	13:23	82
	382-4,386,	25:32f.	279	13:27	81,208,283,3
	389	26:39	174,408		77
12:19	383	26:69-75	84,234	14:36	164
12:20	383	27:15	378	14:66ff.	234
13:3-8	100	27:34	103	14:68	283
13:18-23	100	28:16	318	15:44	240
13:20-2	344,426	28:19f.	4	**Luke**	
16:18	71	**Mark**		1:2	294
16:23	303	1:9	211	1:9	379
16:28	104	1:11	211,381	1:28	180
17:5	211,382	1:13	283	1:32	239
17:20	157	1:20	239	2:7	119
18:2ff.	158	1:45	283	2:46f.	298
18:21	77	3:14	356	3:22	381
18:21-35	77	3:26	283	5:32	239
18:35	77	4:8	283	6:13	202,356,359,
19:7	74	4:33f.	283		376
19:8	294	4:41	285	7:8	318
20:13-15	67	5:23	283	7:12	266
20:16	208f.,282,377	6:25	283	7:30	60
20:28	190	7:21	283	8:6f.	138
21:16	340	8:15	283	8:11-15	76
21:33-43	409	8:33	303	8:12	76
22:3	239	9:7	211,382	8:13	74,76,95,138
22:14	66,208f.,242,	9:48	407	8:15	76
	282,377	10:4	74	8:42	266
23:13-15	315	10:30	329	9:23	83
24:10-12	95	10:45	418	9:27	104
24:19	283	11:17	239		

447

Luke contd.		John contd.		John contd.	
9:35	202,211,	1:9f.	305	4:35	104
	265f.,273,	1:10	305f.	4:42	305
	376,382,383,	1:12	30	5	292
	386	1:13	96	5:2	217,378
9:38	266	1:14	266	5:24	97
10:20	316,347	1:14-18	311-3	5:30	305
10:21f.	276,289	1:16	310f.	5:35	378
10:42	202,376	1:16f.	311	5:39f.	292
12:8-10	99	1:18	266	5:42	131
12:9	83	1:29	190,305,419	6	289,292,
12:10	95	1:34	266f.,377,		295,314
12:42-6	76		381,383	6:14	305
12:46	77	1:42	239	6:25-59	289
13:23f.	128	1:46	297	6:35	295,305
14:7	202,376	2:1-11	311	6:37	46,67,290-6,
14:26	114	2:2	239		308,412
15:3-7	124	2:10	379	6:37-40	78
15:11-24	4	3	301	6:39	80,290,
15:11-32	124	3:3	96		308-13
17:6	157	3:5	96	6:40	290,294f.
18:7	81,208,283,	3:6	96	6:44	67,132,144,
	377	3:7	96,301		290-6,410f.
18:7f.	81	3;8	96	6:45	293,295
18:16f.	158	3:11	301	6:51	295f.,305
19:13	239	3:13	104	6:51-56	289
22	194	3:14f.	294	6:53-6	114
22:15	285	3:16	3,69,190,	6:54	290
22:20	418		266f.,305	6:64	294
22:22	193	3:16-21	397f.	6:64f.	412
22:34	193	3:17	305	6:65	67,290-6
22:54ff.	234	3:18	153,266,	6:70	202f.,
23:35	208,266,		305f.,406		296-308,356,
	279,377	3:19	153,305,398		376
23:46	85	3:21	398	8:12	305
John		3:31f.	104	8:16	305
1:1-13	312	3:36	153	8:23	305
1:9	103	4:32	104	8:25	294

INDEX OF SCRIPTURES AND OTHER ANCIENT TEXTS

John contd.		John contd.		John contd.	
8:26	305	12:47	305	17:11	xiii
8:27	309	12:48	305	17:12	307,310
8:31	427	13-17	299	17:13	305
8:52	104	13:1	305	17:18	305
9:5	305	13:1-20	189	17:21	xiii,306
9:39	305	13:7	309	17:23	306
10	118,124,170, 313f.	13:10	299	17:24	80,305, 308-13
10:1-6	315	13:17	299	17:25	306
10:1-18	313-5	13:18	202, 296-308,356, 376	18:9	80,308-13
10:4	314			18:15-18	234
10:6	309	14:17	306	18:20	305f.
10:7	315	14:30	306	18:25-27	234
10:7-10	315	15	138,299	18:36	305
10:8	314	15:1-6	78,117	18:37	305,412
10:12	314	15:1-8	302	20:9	309
10:14	96,124,314, 422	15:1-17	302	20:31	125
		15:5	432	21:15-19	84
10:15	314,412,418	15:16	67,202f., 296-308, 311,327,356, 376	21:21f.	128
10:16	314			21:25	305
10:26	282,422			**Acts**	
10:27-30	96,118, 124,427			1:2	202,356,376
		15:18f.	307	1:12	239
10:28	78	15:19	170,202, 296-308, 356,376	1:21	357,376
10:36	305			1:21-6	299
11:9	305			1:23	240
11:23f.	257	15:27	294	1:24	202,357,376
11:43	414	16:4	294	1:25	307
11:50-2	411f.	16:11	305f.	2:7	297
11:51f.	418	16:28	305	2:10	333
12:16	309f.	16:33	305,329	2:21	240f.,320
12:19	306	17:5	305	2:23	151,176, 220f.,282
12:25	114,305	17:6	46,80,170, 308-13		
12:31	305f.			2:37	3
12:32	291,411f.	17:9	80,171, 308-13	2:38f.	241
12:39	282			2:39	241-3
12:46	305	17:9f.	314	3:19ff.	3

449

Acts contd.		Acts contd.		Romans contd.	
4:27f.	151,176	16:10	240	3:2f.	258
4:28	217f.,220f.	16:14	282,319,414	3:3	83
5	91	17:26	130	3:4	58
5:1-11	138	17:30	159	3:9-11	399
6:3	357,378	17:30f.	69	3:11	282
6:5	202f.,357,377	18:1f.	334	3:18	399
6:7	159	18:6	321	3:21	258
7:51	409	18:10	xii,319,322-4	3:22f.	335
7:59	85,240	18:27	206	3:23	153,393
8	105	20:26f.	321	3:24	258
8:13	105	20:29f.	95	3:25f.	415
8:14	3	20:35	300	3:30	337
8:23	105	21:21	74	4:17	242
9:3-6	5	22:10	318	5:1	428
9:15	204,357, 359,378	22:14	357,379	5:12	153,275
		24:15	89	5:12-21	275
10:18	240	25:11	240	5:18	190
10:34f.	323	26:4	294	5:21	179
10:41	357,379	26:5	219	6:5	89
10:43	3	28:19	240	6:11	255
13:2	240	28:23	318	7:5	55
13:17	202,359, 377,386	**Romans**		7:18	55,131,402f.
		1-15	334	7:21ff.	168
13:39	3	1:1	246	7:23	131
13:40f.	320	1:5	180	7:25	55
13:46	320	1:6	244	8	96,218,244, 325,329,420
13:48	46,67,171, 315-22, 414,421	1:6f.	123,243,415		
		1:7	243	8:1	255,406
		2:6	396,403	8:3	55
14:22	329	2:6-16	396	8:4	429
15:2	318	2:8	397	8:7	131
15:7	202f.,377	2:14	397	8:7f.	402,410
15:17	240,242	2:15	397	8:9	403
15:22	202f.,357,377	2:16	397	8:12f.	411
15:25	202f.,377	3	259	8:13	427
15:40	217,357,378	3:1-23	132	8:15	30,210,326f.
16:6-17:9	216	3:1-26	258f.	8:15-17	123

INDEX OF SCRIPTURES AND OTHER ANCIENT TEXTS

Romans contd.		Romans contd.		Romans contd.	
8:16	123	9:1-23	422	11:5	66,204f.,207,
8:17	90,328,330	9:3	335		378
8:18-39	328f.	9:4	30,310,319,	11:6	205
8:19	325		326f.	11:7	204,226,378
8:20	379	9:4f.	332	11:11	73,226
8:21	168	9:6-8	335	11:17	319
8:23	30,325-7	9:7	242	11:17-24	275
8:23f.	329	9:8	337	11:22	73,90,98f.,
8:24	223,326	9:11	204,336,378		138
8:28	123,223,	9:13	225	11:23	72
	243f.,325,	9:14-21	336	11:25f.	337
	328,415,425	9:16	32,400	11:26	226,337
8:28ff.	244	9:17f.	337	11:28	204,378
8:28-33	424	9:19	338	11:29	124,243
8:29	30,68f.,119,	9:19ff.	332	11:32	335
	122,217-21,	9:21	67	11:33ff.	394
	223f.,230,	9:22	359,378	12:3	180
	257,263,	9:22f.	225,339	13:1	318
	325,329,359	9:22-4	338	14	394f.
8:29f.	90,144,217,	9:22-9	336	14:1	395
	242-4,263,	9:24	243,340	14:2	395
	324-32,400,	9:24-6	245	14:4	73
	420,424,427	9:25f.	242	14:10	75,406
8:30	218,243,	9:30	336	14:22	395
	324f.,330f.	9:30-2	340	14:23	131,169,
8:31-9	330	9:31f.	336		393-5,401
8:32	420	9:32	336	15:1	394
8:33	208f.,377	10	336	15:15	180
8:35-9	96	10:1	337	15:18	402
8:36	330	10:13	240	16	208,334
8:38f.	118	10:16	337	16:7	255
9	55,67,171,	10:21	337,409	16:13	208f.,211f.,
	337,339f.,	11	205,335		357,363,377
	410,422	11:1	335,337	16:22	223
9-11	224,247,263,	11:2	219-21,224-6,	**1 Corinthians**	
	272,332-41,		230	1:1	246
	410,422	11:4	205		

451

1 Corinthians contd.		1 Corinthians contd.		2 Corinthians contd.	
1:2	123,240,243,	10	87	5:14f.	190
	415	10:1-10	87	5:17	116,166,255
1:8	98	10:12	73	6:18	267
1:8f.	429	10:13	87	7:15	159
1:9	246	10:27	242	8:19	357,379
1:23f.	413	11:25	418	12:6	378
1:24	123,243f.,415	11:29	42	12:19	88
1:26	243	11:29-32	91	13:5	88
1:26-31	431	11:30	91	13:5-7	87f.
1:27	377	11:30-2	95	**Galatians**	
1:27f.	66,202,341,	12:6	173	1:22	255
	357,373	13:8	73	2:9	180
1:28	377	14:33	196	2:11ff.	269
2:7	217f.	15	89	2:15-4:11	259
2:16	6	15:1f.	426	2:19f.	259
3:10	180	15:2	98	2:20	394
3:10-15	75	15:9	242	3	259
3:10-17	87	15:10	394	3:8	302
3:11-15	429	15:20	257	3:14	302
3:14f.	74	15:22	255,258	3:16	259,268
4:6	168	15:23	257	3:16-20	73,80,259,
4:9	357	15:28	195		267,335
5:3-5	95	15:49	325	3:26-9	259
6:9	75	16:7	184	3:27-9	269
6:14	89	16:15	318	3:29	275
7:7	87	**2 Corinthians**		4:5	30,210,326
7:17-24	246	1:21	260	4:6f.	123,259
7:18-24	243	3:6	117	4:7	267
7:20	243	3:7-9	312	4:9	222
7:22	243	3:18	325	4:26	208
8	394	4:3f.	132	5:1	114,166
8:3	222	4:4	404	5:4	95
9:16	4	4:4-6	414	5:19-21	427
9:22	321	5:7	129	5:21	75
9:24-27	86	5:9	411	5:22f.	107
9:25	87	5:10	75,406	6:8	95
9:27	87	5:11-6:2	270		

INDEX OF SCRIPTURES AND OTHER ANCIENT TEXTS

Ephesians	
1	31,218,262, 264,423
1:1	46
1:3	252,264f.
1:3-6	13,423
1:3-7	263
1:3-12	263
1:4	29,66,171, 202,213, 248,252f., 263,265, 281,345,359, 377,423
1:4f.	67,282
1:5	30,210,217f., 252,263, 325f.,366,423
1:6	253
1:7	252,263
1:9	248,263
1:9f.	190,263
1:10	262
1:10f.	366
1:11	46,139,173, 176,213,217, 252,282,336, 378
1:11f.	218
1:11-14	213
1:12	213,218,263
1:13	97,213,252, 260-4
1:14	213
1:18	103
2:1	403
2:1-3	132,406
2:3	405

Ephesians contd.	
2:5	118
2:6	366
2:8f.	154,343
2:10	117
2:11ff.	214
2:12	404
3:18	6
4:4	243
4:7-11	262
4:18	131,403f.
4:30	409
5:5	75
5:10	411
5:24-32	208
5:25-7	418

Philippians	
1:1	255
1:6	98,429
1:15-18	58
1:22	215,376
1:23	89
1:24f.	90
1:29	155
2:7	181
2:10f.	190
2:12	98,430
2:24	90
3:2-11	259
3:7	259
3:7-11	89
3:8f.	89,255
3:9	89,428
3:10f.	82,88-90
3:11	89
3:12	427
3:18f.	95
4:1	86

Philippians contd.	
4:3	316,347

Colossians	
1:13	401
1:15	119,122,257
1:18	119,122,257
1:20	190
1:21-3	426
1:22f.	98f.
1:26f.	171
1:27	xvii,378
2:13	118
3:1-4	96
3:3f.	118
3:4	97
3:5	96
3:10	325
3:12	208,377
4:16	252

1 Thessalonians	
1:1	255
1:4	66f.,204,206, 378
1:5ff.	207
2:14	255
2:19	86
4:13-5:11	110
5:19	409
5:23f.	98,429

2 Thessalonians	
1:1	255
1:6-9	407
1:8	159
2:3	74
2:11	342
2:13	202,215f., 282,294,376

THE PREDESTINATION PROBLEM

1 Timothy	
1:8	312
1:15	82
1:19f.	95
2:3f.	69
2:4	142,190,370, 417
2:6	190,370
3:1	82
3:16	357
4:1	74,95
4:2	137
4:8	129
4:9f.	82
4:10	86,190,370, 416f.
5:21	208,357,377
6:4	xvii,57
6:10	95
6:12	86
6:19	86
6:20	85

2 Timothy	
1:9	248
1:12	82,84-8,95
1:14	85
2:4	379
2:10	82,208,377, 431
2:11f.	426
2:11-13	82
2:12	82-4,99
2:14	xvii,57,85
2:19	97,222
2:24f.	412
2:26	95
3:2-4	131
4:6	90

2 Timothy contd.	
4:7f.	86
4:8	86
4:10	95

Titus	
1:1	208,377
1:15	131
2:11	143
3:5-8	82
3:10	389

Hebrews	
1:6	119,257
2:1	73
2:1-4	107
2:9	104,190
3:1	102,104,107
3:6	102,107
3:12	74,107,131
3:12f.	431
3:14	99,102,107
4:11	73,107
4:14	107
5:1	212,357,378
6	72,111,114
6:1-8	108
6:3	184
6:4	102,103-5
6:4f.	111
6:4-6	102,107f., 111,138
6:4-8	72,100f.
6:5	103,105
6:6	73f.,106,108
6:7f.	111
6:9-12	111
7:22	418
9:9	110
9:11	106

Hebrews contd.	
9:12	110
9:13f.	32
9:14	110
9:15	123,243,418
9:26	110
9:28	279
10	72,114
10:2	110
10:10	110
10:23	107
10:24	107
10:26	111
10:26-9	138
10:26-31	72,101, 107
10:27	110
10:31	124
10:32	103
10:32-6	107
10:34	103
11:6	156
11:17	266
11:25	215,376
12:3	107
12:5-8	107
12:5-10	107
12:7	27
12:7ff.	329
12:14	427
12:14-17	108
12:15-17	427
12:17	112
12:22f.	119
12:23	122,347
12:25f.	108
13:1-6	107
13:5	98,429

INDEX OF SCRIPTURES AND OTHER ANCIENT TEXTS

Hebrews contd.		1 Peter contd.		1 John contd.	
13:9	108	4:11	394	2:29	96
13:15f.	107	4:17	159	3:1	69
13:18	107	4:19	85	3:8	294
13:20f.	429	5:4	86	3:9	72,76,96,
James		5:13	208f.,377		115f.,122,125
1:12	86	**2 Peter**		3:10-24	126
1:18	96,166,376	1:1-11	94	3:14	107
1:21	91	1:3f.	113	4:7	96
2:5	75,202,341,	1:4	73	4:7f.	107
	357,377	1:5-7	431	4:9	266
2:7	240	1:10	67,204,243,	4:14	190
4:15	184		378	5:1	96,145
5:14	239f.	1:10f.	94,430	5:4	96
5:19f.	91f.	1:17	211,382	5:13	124f.
5:20	427	2:1	93f.,113	5:16	95
1 Peter		2:2	93	5:18	96
1:1	227,377	2:10	55	5:16f.	427
1:1f.	46,68,208,	2:12	93	5:21	374
	227,282,359,	2:15	93	**2 John**	
	379	2:17	93	1	208,377
1:1-3	13	2:18ff.	95	1-3	208
1:2	67,209,220f.,	2:20	93f.,113	5	294
	226-9,377	2:20-2	101,112	5f.	208
1:3	96,118	3:9	3,46,69,190	13	208,378
1:5	429	3:14	94	**Jude**	
1:20	219,221,229,	3:17	94,219f.	1	243f.
	329,378	3:18	94	4	93
1:21	423	**1 John**		7	92
1:23	96,107,116	1:1	294	9	92
2:3	104,106	1:8	181	21	98
2:4	208f.,266,377	1:8f.	427	22f.	92,95
2:4-6	273	1:8-10	427	24	98
2:6	208,266,377	2:2	58,190,408,	24f.	429
2:8	342f.,359		418	**Revelation**	
2:9	208,245,377,	2:3-6	427	1:5	119,122,257
	431	2:13	294	2-3	99
4:3	376	2:19	99,428	2:1	357

455

THE PREDESTINATION PROBLEM

Revelation contd.		1 Maccabees		Jubilees contd.	
2:5	73	2:19	74	39:6	347
2:7	426	**1 Enoch**		**Wisdom**	
2:10	86,426	38:2	278	6:9	106
3	138	39:6f.	278	12:2	106
3:2	95	40:5	278		
3:5	343-6	43:6	278	**D. RABBINIC**	
3:10	98	46:1ff.	278	**Pirqe Aboth**	
3:11	86	45:3ff.	278	**(mAboth)**	
4:2	195	46:3	278	2:1	347
5	348	47:3	347		
5:1	349	48:2ff.	278	**E. QUMRAN**	
5:6	195	48:6	278	1QapGen II	278
5:9	356	49:2ff.	278	4Q534	277
13:8	282,316,343	51:2	279	4QMessAr	277
14:4	215	51:3	278	4QNoahAr	277
17:8	119,316, 343-50	52:6ff.	278		
		53:6	278	**F. CHRISTIAN WRITERS**	
17:14	123,208, 243-5,378	55:4	278		
		61:5ff.	278		
20:5f.	89	62:1ff.	278	**PATRISTIC**	
20:10	306	62:5ff.	278	**1 Clement**	
20:12	397	69:26ff.	278	29:1	280
20:15	306,343	71:17	278	30:1	280
21:6	237	90:20	347	32:4	280
21:7	407	108:3	347	46:4	280
21:8	407	**1 Esdras**		46:6	280
21:9f.	208	2:18f.	347	50:7	280
21:27	343	**2 Esdras**		64	280
22:1f.	404	6:20	347	65:2	280
22:13	237	4:15	347	**2 Clement**	
22:20	129	**Jubilees**		14:1	389
		30:18f.	121	**Ignatian Ephesians**	
C. APOCRYPHA & PSEUDEPIGRAPHA		30:20	347	1	280
		30:22	347		
2 Baruch		31:12-17	122	**AUGUSTINE**	
24:1	347	32:1-9	122	**Against Julian**	
		36:10	347	4.32	394

Confessions
10.29.40 140

Enchiridion on Faith, Hope and Love
32 145

Gift of Perseverance
20.53 140

Marriage and Concupiscence
1:22 405
1:24 405

On Nature and Grace
35 145

On the Predestination of the Saints
34 253

JUSTIN MARTYR
First Apology
61:12f. 103
65:1 103

SUBJECT INDEX

Adoption, xvii,30f.,62,75,123,187, 218f.,225,252,262,310,319,325-7, 329-32,359,375,385-7,423
Aemilius, Theodorus, 16
Ambrosiaster, 397
Apostolic Fathers, 204,277,280f., 389-91
Aquinas, Thomas, 47,173,233,394; Thomism, Thomist, 233,235
Arminius, Jacobus, 2,11,14-23,25-37, 39f.,56f.,68,71f.,95,109,114f.,122, 129,139,142-4,192,199,235f.,249-51, 253f.,264,344,430
 Declaration of Sentiments, 26f.,35
 Dissertation on Romans Seven, 17
 Divine Decrees (Arminius'), 26-8,30
 Examination of Gomarus' Theses, 29
 Examination of Perkins' Pamphlet, 20,32,71
 On the Free Will of Man and its Powers, 33
Arminianism – Five Points (of the Remonstrance), 11,24,51
Augustine, Aurelius (of Hippo), xiii,7, 10,26, 36,55,73,139-42,144f.,167,186, 190f., 199,235,253,273f.,317,360,365, 370f., 394f.,397,404f.,425;
 Confessions, 140
 Contra Julianum, 394
 Enchiridion, 145
 Marriage and Concupiscence, 405
 On Free Choice of the Will, 140
 On Nature and Grace, 145
 On the Gift of Perseverance, 140
 The Predestination of the Saints, 253

Belgic Confession, 19f.,22,24f.,36,253f.
Bernard of Clairvaux, 33
Bertius, Petrus, 17f.
Beza, Theodore, 17-19,22f.,29,38f.,41, 141
Bible Versions;
 Authorised (King James, KJV), 45f., 116,128,196,200,202,208f.,261, 310, 316f.,377,379
 Bishop's Bible, 45

Geneva Bible, 45f.,116,207
Great Bible, 45f.
Luther's Bible, 46
Matthew, Thomas (John Rogers) Bible, 45
Tyndale New Testament, 45f.,116, 210f.
Vulgate, 180,317,322
Book of Common Prayer, 44f.,50,146
Brès, Guido de, 19
Bucer, Martin, 68,145f.
Bunyan, John, 46

Calvin, John, 3,7,12-15,17,19,22f.,26-8, 32-40,45f.,52f.,55,58,61,65,76,103, 141,146,167,173f.,180f.,186,196,199, 223,249,251-3,273f.,351,357,366,370, 417,419;
 Commentaries, 3,19,417
 Concerning the Eternal Predestination of God, 180f.,253
 Institutes of the Christian Religion, 26-8,65,174,181,196,223,253,257
Calling, xiv,67,84,90,102,104,107, 123f.,143f.,201,238-47,298,300,302, 304,306,324f.,331f.,371,378,400,415, 424,430f.
Carey, William, 40
Carlos (Charles) V of Spain, 43
Cassian, John (see also Semi-Pelagianism), 142
Chrysostom, John, 393f.
Claudius (Emperor), 334
Clement of Alexandria, 390
Clement of Rome, 280f.
Clement VII (Pope), 42
Control Belief/Premature Intuition, 182,184f.,187,360,371,398,425
Coornhert, Dirck, 18
Cornelisz, Arent, 18
Corporate identity/solidarity/ personality, 257,271-5,365
Counter Reformation, 137
Coverdale, Miles, 43,45
Cranmer, Thomas, 42-4
Cromwell, Oliver, 46

SUBJECT INDEX

Cromwell, Thomas, 45

Darby, John Nelson, 2
Dead Sea Scrolls/Qumran, 81,164, 277-9
Decretum horribile, 27,65
Determinism, Divine, Predeterminism, xv,3,7,14,29,52,133,137f.,164-6, 175-8,180-91,194,231,233,237f.,320, 368, 370f.,410,421,433
Diognetus, Epistle of Mathetes to, 215
Dispensationalism/Dispensationalist, 2,71,75,289
Divine Decrees, 8,13,18,21,24,26-9,37, 47,64f.,68,148-51,175,182-4,202,223, 230,234,248-50,263 276,281,317, 330f.,337,345,349f.,358,367;
Infralapsarianism, 13,47f.,66,249
Sublapsarianism, 13,18,24,249
Supralapsarianism, 24,66,249
Donteklok, Reynier, 18
Dort, Synod of, 11,14-17,19-21,23-42,44,47,253f.;
Canons of, 11,19f.,23-40,253

Edward VI, 42,44
Effectual Grace: see Prevenient Grace.
Egbertsz, Sebastian, 19
Election, 64-7
Elizabeth I, 44f.
Enoch Similitudes; 1 Enoch, 81,277-80, 347
Ephesians, Authorship, 154,252,255f., 262
Erasmus, Desiderius of Rotterdam, 134-6,180
Erastus, Thomas/Erastianism, 16
Euthymius (also John of Damascus), 389,391;
Vita Barlaam et Joasaph, 389

Felipe (Philip) II of Spain, 19
Firstborn, 90,119-22,223,243,257,420, 424
Firstfruits, 215f.,257
Five Points of Calvinism (TULIP), xv, 10-12,14,23,46,51,54,62,66f.,70f., 105,115,131,150, 369,392-433;
Irresistible Grace, 3,5,11,24,34,47,59, 69,146,148,152,157,243,245,291, 295,409-16,421,433

Limited Atonement, 11,32,38,47,195, 296,415-20,429,433
Perseverance of the Saints, xiv,xvii, 1f.,11,24,31,35-7,44,64,70-129, 138,154,284,295,331,333,344, 411,425-32
Total Depravity, xi,3,11,23f.,33f.,47, 50,131f.,137,149,159,166,173, 197f.,362,393-410,413,415,423, 432f.
Unconditional Election, 11,29,47,49, 55,67f.,149f.,175,180,182,190, 195,248,421-6,433
Foreknowledge, 28-31,51,64f.,67-70, 134,151f.,179,182,201,219-38,243f., 248f.,294,314,322,324f.,329,345,354, 358,378f.,422,424
Forcordination, xi,64f.,134,151f.,173, 178,201,219-21,226,246,316,318f., 321f.,330,342f.,359,361
Foxe, John; *Book of Martyrs*, 43
Free Will, Human Freedom, xi,3-8,14, 17,24,32-4,50,52,59f.,100,114,130, 132-40,142-4,147f.,153,155-7,159f., 161,164-9,171-3,175-8,181-4,186-8, 190-3,195f.,206,230-9,288,293,340, 362,367,369f.,372,375,378,395,410, 412,421,432
Frederick III Prince Elector, 20

George III, 48
Golden Chain(e): Romans 8:30, 18,90, 144,324,330f.,400,425,427
Gomarus, Franciscus, 17,21,23,29,34
Graham, Billy, 1

Heidelberg (Palatinate) Catechism, 19f., 22,36,50,253
Henry VIII, 42f.
Human Freedom: see Free Will

Inability, 5,132,146f.,159,166,173,197, 399,402-5,408
Irresistible Grace: see Five Points of Calvinism.

James I, 45f.
Jerome, 140,297
Jubilees, Book of, 121f.,347
Junius, Franciscus, 19,21
Justin Martyr, 103

Knox, John, 1,45f.

Lambeth Articles, 44
Latimer, Hugh, 43
Leo X (Pope), 42
Limited Atonement: see Five Points of Calvinism.
Lucaris, Cyril (17th century Patriarch of Constantinople), 10
Luther, Martin, 14f.,27,43,46,52,58, 61,68,132,134-6,196,351
Lydius, Martinus, 18

Marcion, 252
Mary (Mother of Jesus), 180,202f.,376
Mary Tudor, 44f.
Martyr, Peter, 44
Matthew, Thomas (=John Rogers), 45
Milton, John, 46
Molina, Luis de, 232f.,235-7;
Molinism (Middle Knowledge), 68, 179,223,232-7

Nero (Emperor), 334
New (Moderate) Calvinism ('Young, Restless, Reformed'), 12

Olevianus, Kaspar, 20
Open Theism/Theology, 49,51f.,68, 179,187,237f.
Origen, Adamantius, 68
Orthodox Theology, 10

Pelagius, Marius Victorinus, 1,139-42, 425;
Pelagianism, 1,19,33,63f.,135f., 139-44,147,154,157,159,235
Semi-Pelagianism (see also John Cassian), 19,64,141-3,147,154, 159
Perkins, William, 17,20,32,34f.,71-3, 98,109,115,122,144,324,330;
A Golden Chaine, 18,90,144,243,324, 330f.,400,425,427
De praedestinationis modo et ordine, (Perkins' Pamphlet), 18,20,32,71, 324
Perseverance of the Saints: see Five Points of Calvinism.
Pilgrim Fathers, 45,351
Plancius, Petrus, 21

Predestination, x,xv,xvii,4,10-12,16-18, 23-31,36f.,42,44,47-51,55,58,61,63-6, 68f.,84,90,127,134,137,139,141, 149-52,163f.,170,179,193f.,199,201, 205,217-9,221-3,232f.,235,238,243-5, 248,252,263f.,291,309,313,315,319f., 324f.,329-32,342,345,366,371f.,374f., 411,420,422-4;
Double, 12f.,26,41,48,65f.,149f.,362, 372
Single, 12,26,41,48,51,65f.,149-54, 175,192,372
Premature Intuition: see Control Belief.
Preterition, 152
Prevenient (Effectual) Grace/Calling, 34f.,47,135,143-8,154,235f.,244,246, 291-3,331,400f., 409,413f.,416,420

Qumran: see Dead Sea Scrolls.

Ramus, Petrus; Ramism, 17f.
Reformation, xi,xii,11,14f.,23,42f.,207,223,233, 338;
English, 42f.
Magisterial, xii,11,14f.,23
Radical (Anabaptist), 16,20
Regeneration (meaning), 144-6,293, 330f.,400f.,412
Remonstrance, Remonstrants, 15,18, 23-36,253;
Articles (*The Remonstrance*), 2,11,18, 23-36,71,253
Renaissance, 17,273f.,365
Robinson, John (Pastor to the *Mayflower* Pilgrims from Holland), 351
Rogers, John (=Thomas Matthew), 45

St. John of the Cross, 126
Septuagint (LXX), xiv,74,106,164, 202-4,211f.,214-7,242,247,258,267, 285-7,311,326,338f.,352-5,364,381, 383-91
Seymour, Edward, 43
Shakespeare, William, 46
Simeon, Charles, 56,194f.,371
Sinatra, Frank, 405
Socinianism, 238
Spurgeon, Charles H., 40,192-6,251, 293
Suarez, Francisco, 334

SUBJECT INDEX

Suetonius, Gaius Suetonius Tranquillus, 321
Syllogism, 22f.,392

Taffin, Jean, 21
Talmid(im), 296-8
Ten Articles (Lutheran), 43
Thirty-Nine Articles of Religion, 44,46, 49f.
Total Depravity: see Five Points of Calvinism.
TULIP: see Five Points of Calvinism
Tyndale, William, 43,45f.,116,210f.

Uitenbogaert, Johannes, 17
Unconditional Election: see Five Points of Calvinism.
Ursinus, Zacharius, 20

Valla, Lorenzo, 180

Warham,William, 43
Wesley, Charles, 374
Wesley, John, 40,58-61,90,143,194,371
Westminster Confession of Faith, 46f., 50,141,150,185
Westminster Shorter Catechism, 65
Whitgift, John (Elizabeth I's Archbishop of Canterbury), 44f.
Winslow, Edward, 351

Zwingli, Huldrych, 14

PEOPLE INDEX

Abasciano, Brian J., 245
Abrahams, Israel, 301
Ackley, Alfred H., 127
Aland, Kurt, 381,405
Alexander, Cecil Frances, 356,374
Alford, Henry, 316-8
Allen, J. A., 256
Allen, Willoughby, C., 386
Allis, Oswald T., 2
Anka, Paul, 405
Araraki, Robert, 10
Aune, David A., 345, 348

Badger, Anthony, 75
Bakhuizen van den Brink J. N., 25,254
Baloche, Paul, 373
Balz, Horst, 209,217, 336
Bangs, Carl, 14-23,25, 27-30,32f.,35f.,71, 73,249,254
Barclay, John M. G., 180,239,397
Barnhart, B., 313
Barr, James, 200f.,247
Barrett, C. K., 116f., 170,244,266,278, 291,304,381,399
Barth, Karl, 29,250f.
Barth, Marcus, 264
Basinger, David, 60, 134,137f.,177,182, 231f.,237f.
Basinger, Randall, 60, 134,137f.,177,182, 231f.
Beale, G. K., 343,348f.
Beasley-Murray, George R., 348,405
Beegle, D. M., 3
Behm, J., 104

Bell, G. K. A., 276
Berkhof, Hendrikus, 181,251
Berkhof, Louis, 27,37, 65f.,69,131,148, 152f.,173,175f.,197, 202,220-4,226,230, 341f.
Berkouwer, G. C., 166-8,171,248,254
Berry, George Ricker, 388
Bettenson, Henry, 11, 24,32,34f.
Beveridge, Henry, 27f., 65,174,196,223,253, 357
Bigg, Charles, 343
Billings, Tod, 12f.
Birdsall, J. N., 92
Bivin, David N., 296f.
Boccaccini, Gabriele, 278f.
Boettner, Loraine, 54 ,66 148,153
Boice, James Montgomery, 54,190
Boyd, Gregory, 238
Bratt, John H., 15f.,19, 21f.,25,27,36, 254
Breward, Ian, 20
Broad (Professor), 191
Brown, Raymond E., 334
Bruce, F. F., 103,105, 209,215,218f.,247, 264,316,326,359
Buchannan, Colin, 20
Bultmann, Rudolph, 220f.,293
Burckhardt, Jacob, 273
Burkeman, Oliver, 133
Byrne, Brendan, 79, 268,326

Caird, G. B., 262

Capon, Robert F., 189
Caroll, Lewis, 157
Carson, D. A., 77f., 148,159,161-6,170-2, 178,182,195,200,217, 288,291f.,295,299, 301-3,307-9,311, 313-5,381,384,398, 411
Chadwick, Owen, 21, 23,65
Chaplin, Howard, 351
Charles, R. H., 122,278
Charlesworth, J. H., 122,278f.
Clark, Gordon, 52
Clements, Roy, 5,63, 67,149,153,157, 159
Clines, David J. A., 267
Cochrane, A. C., 25, 254
Coenen, Lothar, 202, 212,241-3,247
Colwell, John E., 141, 153
Cottrell, Jack W., 175, 182-4,343f.
Cox, Brian E., 132
Cox, William E., 2
Craig, William, 232, 234f.
Cranfield, C. E. B., 255,283,326,338, 394f.,397
Cross, Frank L., 142
Cundall, Arthur E., 237
Custer, Stewart, 388

Daane, James, 358
Daniell, David, 210f.
Davids, Peter H., 113, 431
Davies, W. D., 255
Deissmann, D. Adolf, 254,276

PEOPLE INDEX

Delling, Gerard, 321
Dodd, C. H., 255
Dods, Marcus, 145
Donfried, Karl P., 333f.
Douglas, J. D., 15f.,20, 22-4,172,202
Dunn, James D. G., 244

Edwards, David L., 56, 140
Edwards, Jonathan, 53f.,174f.,178
Eissfeldt, Otto, 272f.
Ellingworth, Paul, 103f.,106
Elliott, Mark W., 139
Ellis, P. F., 313
Elwell, Walter A., 221, 326,366
Erickson, Millard J., 10,13,64f.,68,143, 146-9
Estep, R., 65,194

Feinberg, John, 137-9, 165,182,232
Ferguson, Sinclair B., 22,50,55,141
Fergusson, David A. S., 139
Finney, Charles, 53
Fisk, Samuel, 184, 192f.,282,316-8,357
Fitzmyer, Joseph A., 278,334
Forlines, F. Leroy, 55
Forster, Roger T., 7, 212,226,253,316, 337,358f.
Frame, John, 182f.
Fretheim, Thomas, 187
Fridrichsen, A., 264
Fullerton, W. Y., 194

Gæbelein, Frank E., 278
Geisler, Norman, 232
George, Timothy, 132
Gerstner, John, 52
Godet, Frédéric L., 304
Godfrey, W. Robert, 50f.,55

Goold, William H., 102
Green, E. Michael B., 92f.
Greenwold, Doug, 296-8
Grudem, Wayne, 12, 53,227f.,330f.,342, 371
Gumbel, Nicky, 193, 196,289
Gundry, Robert Horton, 384f.
Guthrie, Donald, 83, 103f.
Guy, Fritz, 188-91

Hansen, Collin, 53f.
Harrison, A. W., 11,18, 24
Harrison, E. F., 148
Hasker, William, 237f.
Haslam, Greg, 97f.
Hawthorne, Gerald F., 202,221,326,366
Headlam, Arthur C., 393-5
Helm, Paul, 176f.
Hewitt, Thomas, 104, 108
Hindson, Edward, 400
Hinnells, John R., 18
Hodge, A. A., 171
Holbrook, C. A., 175
Holmes, Michael W., 280f.
Hopkins, Samuel, 400
Horton, Michael, 12, 50,54,142,149,154, 173f.,223,238
Howley, G. Cecil D., 267,342

Ironside, Henry A., 342

Jellema, Dirk, 15,20
Jeremias, J., 83
Jobes, Karen H., xiv, 201,285
Johnson, L. T., 169,405
Johnston, Philip, S., 3, 346-8
Jonkind, Dirk, 383

Kaibel, Georg, 386
Keathley, Kenneth, 223,232
Kelly, J. N. D., 145, 228,370,405
Kensrue, Dustin, 374
Keyser, L. S., 316f.
Kilby, Karen, 139
Kittel, Gerhard, 167
Kittel, Rudolph, 204
Klein, Günter, 334
Klein, William G., 52, 55,146,181,184,208, 221f.,238-42,244-6, 264f.,272-5,277-9, 291-4,299,314,320f., 340,343,345,350, 358,425
Kümmel, W. G., 332

LaHaye, Tim, 2
Lake, Kirsopp, 280,390
Lane, Tony, 10,25,253
Leith, John H., 11
Letham, R. W. A., 22
Lewis, C. S., 4f.,7f.,52, 59f.,157,197,199, 370
Lewis, Peter, 5,26,40, 52,55,63,65,67-70, 98,149-53,155-8, 165,193
Liddell, H. G., 316
Lindars, Barnabas, 109-13
Linder, R. D., 24
Lindsay, Hal, 2
Livingstone, Elizabeth A., 142
Lloyd-Jones, D. Martyn, 40
Lohmeyer, E., 89
Longenecker, Richard N., 169f.,256,333f., 395
Los, F. J., 19,21
Louth, L., 280f.
Louw, Johannes P., 212,385f.

MacArthur, John F., 54
MacDonald, William G., 185,316,320, 375

463

Maclaren, Alexander, 78,317
Maclear, G. F., 283
Malina, Bruce J., 273f.
Marshall, Alfred, 81, 323
Marshall, I. Howard, 67,70,73f.,76,79-95, 102-6,108f.,127f., 158,202, 211f.,266, 284,319,322,380-2
Marston, V. Paul, 7, 212,226,253,316, 337,358f.
Martin, Ralph P., 202, 221,326,366
Martinez, F. G., 277
McCall, T. H., 165
McFarland, Ian A., 139
McGrath, Alister, 15-17,22,26f.,43, 136f.,141,145f.,180, 273f.
McKim, Donald, 12f.
McLeod, Donald, 152
Meier, J. P., 334
Metzger, Bruce M., 278,283
Meyer, F. B., 318f.
Meyer, H. A. W., 221
Miethe, Terry, 191
Milik, J. T., 279
Minear, P. S., 333
Mitton, C. L., 264
Mlakuzhyil, George, 312
Moo, Douglas, 91
Morris, Leon, 77,237, 383,386
Motyer, Alec, 355
Moule, C. F. D., 106, 254-6,261,365,398
Moule, C. G. Handley, 194
Mounce, William D., 83-5,357,370,417
Moynahan, Brian, 45
Murray, John, 68f.

Neill, Stephen, 301
Nida, Eugene A., 212, 385f.
Nordholt, Gerhard, 202
Novenson, M., 268

O'Brien, Peter T., 155, 213,219,252, 262f.
O'Connell, Robert H., 271
Oesterley, W. O. E., 278
Olson, Roger E., 11-13,41,53-5,64,66, 68,71,143f.,175, 177f.,181,192,196, 358f.,392
Osborne, Grant R., 263f.,283f.
Owen, John, 102-5

Packer, James I., 2, 157,172,202
Paine, Thomas, 48
Palmer, Edwin, 369
Patterson, Paige, 345f.
Pawson, David, 333-5
Pelikan, Jaroslav, 142
Picirilli, Robert E., 144,370
Pinnock, Clark H., 13, 36,51-3,55f.,59-61, 134,146,166,171,175, 177,181f., 184-8, 190f.,223,232,234-8, 264,283,316,320, 344,367,370,375
Pinson, J. Matthew, 36, 166,232,236,238
Piper, John, xiv,xv,12, 54,62,131,144-6, 293,392-433
Polkinghorne, G. J., 342
Preisker, H., 94

Rawlinson, A. E. J., 276
Rawson, George, 351
Raymond, Miner, 184
Reasoner, Vic, 55,146
Reichenbach, Bruce, 138,231
Reid, J. K. S., 264
Reid, W. S., 22f.
Rice, Richard, 237
Richardson, Alan, 165, 246,273
Ridderbos, H., 264

Robinson, John Armitage, 155,213, 264
Rossback, Michael, 373
Rowland, Christopher, 278
Rowley, H. H., 80, 357,359

Safrai, Shmuel, 297
Samuel, David N., 102, 104f.
Sanday, William, 393-5
Sanders, E. P., 256
Sanders, John E., 184-8,191,237f.
Sandy, D. Brent, 301
Schlier, H., 167
Schmidt, Karl, 240
Schneider, Gerard, 209, 217,336
Schreiner, Thomas R., 394
Schrenk, G., 81
Schweitzer, Albert, 256
Scofield, Cyrus I., 2
Scott, James M., 326
Scott, Robert, 316
Sell, Alan P. F., 26
Shank, Robert L., 38f., 76-8,96f.,117,124, 180f.,248,250f.,253f., 303f.,317f.,323,356, 370,417
Shellrude, Glen, 367
Shenk, R. A., 171
Silva, Moisés, xiv,201, 285
Simeon, Charles, 56, 194f.
Sizer, Stephen R., 3
Smalley, S., 301
Smith, E. C., 107
Smith, Kym, 302,312
Snodgrass, K., 264
Sproul, R. C., 12f.,54, 177
Spurgeon, Charles H., 40,192-6,251, 293
Staniforth, Maxwell, 280f.

PEOPLE INDEX

Stendhal, K., 264
Stott, John R. W., xi, 56,72,99,140,155, 214
Suter, David W., 279
Sweet, John, 349
Swete, Henry Barclay, 202,204,212, 286, 384,390

Talbert, Charles H., 169,405
Tasker, R. V. G., 91
Thayer, Joseph H., 74, 226,229,386
Thiessen, H. C., 143
Thompson, Samuel M., 191
Thuesen, Peter, 10f., 18,27,42-5,47-9,53, 139-42,233,235-7, 324,331
Tigchelaar, E. J. C., 277
Tomkins, Stephen, 45, 351
Toon, P., 16
Tozer, A. W., 184
Turner, George Allen, 107f.
Torrance, Iain R., 139
Townend, Stuart, 373f.
Tyacke, Nicholas, 44

Vance, Laurence, 13
Vermes, G., 277f.
Vine, W. E., 317,327, 386

Wagner, John D., 36, 55,146,166,181,223, 232,236,238,264,283, 344,367, 370
Walker, Peter, 3
Walls, Jerry, 59,61
Walton, Jonathan Harvey, 274
Walton, John H., 130, 274,301
Walvoord, John F., 345
Wanamaker, Charles A., 215
Ward, Keith, 185,187
Watts, Isaac, 34
Wendel, François, 27, 68
Wesley, Charles, 374
Wesley, John, 40, 58-61,90,143,194, 371
Westcott, B. F., 102f., 116,264,398
Whitaker, R. A., 312
White, Peter, 44
Whittle, Daniel W., 95
Wiefel, Wolfgang, 333f.

Wilson, Derek, 15,17, 45f.
Windisch, H., 94
Wintermute, O. S., 122
Woodbridge, John D., 182
Wordsworth, Christopher, 318
Wright, David F., 22, 50,55,141,153
Wright, N. Thomas (Tom), 109, 154, 179f.,252, 256-61, 267-70,274-6,358f.

Yarbrough, Robert W., 73
Yuille, Stephen, 238

Printed in Great Britain
by Amazon